k_i	After-tax cost of debt
k_o	Overall cost of capital
n	Number of periods
NPV	Net present value
P/E	Price/earnings ratio
P_t	Market price at time t
PI	Profitability index
PV	Present value
r	Interest rate or return
R_j	Expected return on security j
R_k	Required return on project k
R_m	Expected return on market portfolio
ROA	Return on assets
ROI	Return on investment
S	Stock value
SEC	Securities and Exchange Commission
Σ	Summation sign
SD	Standard deviation
σ	Standard deviation
σ^2	Variance
t	Time period
TV	Terminal or future value
WC	Working capital

Fundamentals of
Financial Management

Seventh Edition

Fundamentals of Financial Management

JAMES C. VAN HORNE

Stanford University

PRENTICE HALL, Englewood Cliffs, New Jersey 07632

Library of Congress Cataloging-in-Publication Data

VAN HORNE, JAMES C.
    Fundamentals of financial management   /   James C. Van Horne.—7th ed.

        p.   cm.
    Includes bibliographies and index.
    ISBN 0-13-339649-5
    1. Corporations—Finance.   I. Title.
HG4011.V36 1989
658.1′5—dc 19   88-19694
                                                          CIP

Editorial/production supervision: Nancy DeWolfe
Interior design: Maureen Eide
Cover design: Maureen Eide
Cover photo: © Charles Blecker, 1988
Manufacturing buyer: Ed O'Dougherty

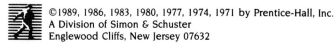 ©1989, 1986, 1983, 1980, 1977, 1974, 1971 by Prentice-Hall, Inc.
A Division of Simon & Schuster
Englewood Cliffs, New Jersey 07632

Printed in the United States of America

10 9 8 7 6 5 4 3 2 1

ISBN 0-13-339649-5   01

Prentice-Hall International (UK) Limited, *London*
Prentice-Hall of Australia Pty. Limited, *Sydney*
Prentice-Hall Canada Inc., *Toronto*
Prentice-Hall Hispanoamericana, S.A., *Mexico*
Prentice-Hall of India Private Limited, *New Delhi*
Prentice-Hall of Japan, Inc., *Tokyo*
Simon & Schuster Asia Pte. Ltd., *Singapore*
Editora Prentice-Hall do Brasil, Ltda., *Rio de Janeiro*

To Mimi, Drew, Stuart, and Stephen

Contents

PART III
TOOLS OF FINANCIAL ANALYSIS AND PLANNING

CHAPTER 6

Financial Analysis   112

CHAPTER 7

Funds Analysis and Financial Planning   153

PART IV
WORKING CAPITAL MANAGEMENT

CHAPTER 8

Current Asset and Liability Structure Decisions   190

CHAPTER 9

Cash and Marketable Securities   208

CHAPTER 10

Accounts Receivable and Inventories   236

CHAPTER 11

Spontaneous Financing   265

CHAPTER 12

Short-term Borrowings   277

PART V
INVESTMENT IN CAPITAL ASSETS

CHAPTER 13

Capital Budgeting   302

CHAPTER 14

Risk and Capital Budgeting   338

CHAPTER 15

Required Returns on Capital Investments   371

PART VI
CAPITAL STRUCTURE AND DIVIDEND POLICIES

CHAPTER 16

Leveraging the Firm   408

CHAPTER 17

Conceptual Aspects of Capital Structure   431

CHAPTER 18

Dividend Policy and Retained Earnings   458

xiv

PART VIII
SPECIAL AREAS OF FINANCIAL MANAGEMENT

CHAPTER 25

International Financial Management   656

CHAPTER 26

Finance for the Smaller Company and Start-up   688

CHAPTER 27

Failure and Reorganization   699

Preface

Just as financial managers seek a good return on their firm's investments, those who are about to study this introductory course in financial management will want a satisfactory return on the investment of their time. With a good yield as its objective, the book offers a basic understanding of

1. What business finance is
2. Allocation of funds within a business enterprise
3. Raising funds
4. Application of certain theoretical concepts to financial problems

Most of the concepts are expressed verbally, but elementary algebra is sometimes brought in for clearer understanding.

Structuring financial decisions continues to be the principal subject of the seventh edition. Unless financial managers focus on what is relevant, they will be hopelessly entwined in conflicting considerations, many of them trivial. In the pages that follow, readers should find a lucid framework for approaching financial decisions. Theory will be explored not for its own sake, but for the help it can give in sorting out the important from the unimportant and in reaching better decisions.

Finance is rapidly changing, in both theory and practice. Tax law changes, financial signaling effects from corporate actions, the market for corporate control, restructurings, changing inflation, interest rates and exchange rates, continual financial innovation in a deregulated marketplace, new valuation techniques, new ways to shift risk, increased sophistication in spreadsheet programming and other computer applications, and a host of other things all have occurred since the last edition. This changing financial landscape has required extensive changes in this edition.

A major change is the availability of computer applications for those who wish to pursue them. A separate booklet, *Financial Management Computer Applications*, by Stuart B. Van Horne and myself, contains programs that are useful to analytical and valuation issues found in this book. Many self-correction exercises are found in the supplement. In addition, certain chapter-end problems in this book lend themselves to the spreadsheet programs contained in the supplement's disk. These are indicated by disk symbols in the margin. Other substantive changes involving this edition include the following.

Chapter 2 has been completely revised to conform to the new tax laws on corporate income, depreciation, and personal income. In addition, the master limited partnership is explained.

The securitization of assets and its relation to financial intermediation is explored in the financial environment chapter.

Compounding of interest is better explained in Chapter 5. There is an extensive new section on dividend discount models, including their reconciliation with price/earnings ratio valuation techniques. Finally, the efficient markets hypothesis is evaluated. The appendix has been reworked with respect to the effect of personal taxes on required returns.

Concerning cash budgeting, assumptions regarding the receivable collection period are analyzed and ways presented for incorporating them into a spreadsheet programming format.

In Chapter 7, sustainable growth modeling is presented for the first time. This powerful planning tool is investigated under steady-state assumptions and under changing assumptions as to financial ratios, operating ratios, and sales growth.

The treatment of capital budgeting is revised to set up the relevant cash flows under the new tax laws.

The creation of value through industry attractiveness and through competitive advantage is brought out in the treatment of required rates of return for corporations. In Chapter 15 there is also expanded discussion of the risk-free rate, the market return, and divisional required returns via proxy companies and leverage.

Chapter 17, on capital structure, has been revised to make clearer certain theoretical concepts and to take up incentive issues, tax shield uncertainty, and financial signaling. The personal tax effect is revised to be consistent with current tax laws.

Similarly, Chapter 18, on dividend policy, has been revised so that it is consistent with current tax laws. There is a new emphasis on financial signaling as well.

The issuance of securities chapter, Chapter 19, contains a new section on signaling effects, particularly as they have to do with the type of security being offered.

Chapter 20 probes the economic foundation of the leasing industry. In addition, lease versus borrow analyses incorporate the current tax laws.

Junk bonds are examined in Chapter 21, as are floating rate notes. The treatment of pension fund liability has been expanded to consider a number of new issues.

Chapter 23 contains an entirely new section on exchangeable bonds.

Chapter 24 has been completely rewritten with mostly new material on corporate restructuring. The emphasis throughout is on value creation, the sources of such value, and empirical evidence concerning mergers and other forms of restructuring.

Initial public offerings of stock are considered in Chapter 26 on financing the small business.

In addition to these more substantive changes, the book has been updated throughout, and new questions, self-correction problems, and regular problems written. It is hoped that these changes make the book highly relevant and current.

Ancillary Materials

A number of materials are available to supplement the text. For the professor, there is a comprehensive *Instructor's Manual,* which contains suggestions for organizing the course, answers to questions, and solutions to problems. Also available are transparency masters of most of the figures in the text. Finally, there is a test item file of extensive questions and problems, both in hard copy and on computer disk. These materials can be obtained from Prentice Hall.

For the student, the text itself contains several self-correction problems at the end of most of the chapters, as well as extensive references to original literature sources. Also available is *Financial Management Computer Applications,* by Stuart B. Van Horne and myself. This booklet and disk previously described, uses Lotus 1-2-3 and TWIN by Prentice Hall. Finally, there is an excellent *Study Guide to Fundamentals of Financial Management* to help the student master financial decision making. This guide contains a number of helpful suggestions on how to approach the materials, alternative expressions of it, and numerous questions and exercises.

To the extent the book and these ancillary materials serve as a conduit to the exciting world of finance from which you come away enthused, we have succeeded.

JAMES C. VAN HORNE
Palo Alto, California

CHAPTER 1

The Role
of Financial
Management

At any moment in time, a business firm can be viewed as a pool of funds fed by a variety of sources: investors in the company's stock, creditors who lend it money, and past earnings retained in the business. Funds provided from these sources are committed to a number of uses: fixed assets used in production of a good or service, inventories used to facilitate production and sales, accounts receivable owed by customers, and cash and marketable securities used for transactions and liquidity purposes. At a given moment, the pool of funds of the firm is static; over time, it changes, and these changes are known as funds flows. In an ongoing business, funds flow continually throughout the enterprise. The term *financial management* connotes that these flows are directed according to some plan; it is with managing the flow of funds within the firm that this book deals.

In recent years, the role of the financial manager has expanded to involve the totality of the enterprise. Put another way, financial managers are now involved in general management, where before they primarily raised funds and managed the firm's cash position. The combination of increased competition among firms, technological improvements that require considerable capital, variable inflation and interest rates, tax law changes, economic uncertainty worldwide, some speculative excesses, and ethical concerns over the financial markets has had an enormous influence in pushing the financial manager into a general management role. Moreover, these factors require considerable flexibility in order to cope with ever-present change. The "old way of doing things" simply is not good enough in a world where old ways quickly become obsolete. Competition requires continual adaptation to changing conditions.

If you become a financial manager, your ability to adapt to change, efficiently plan the proper amount of funds to employ in the firm, oversee the allocation of these funds, and raise funds will affect the success of your firm and the overall economy as well. To the extent that funds are misallocated, the growth of the economy will be slowed. In an era of unfilled economic wants and scarcity, this may work to the detriment of society. Efficient allocation of resources in an economy is vital to optimal growth in that economy; it also is vital in ensuring that individuals obtain the highest level of want satisfaction possible. Through effectively raising and allocating funds, the financial manager contributes to the fortunes of the firm and to the vitality and growth of the economy as a whole.

THE GOAL OF THE FIRM

Efficient management of the flow of funds within the firm implies the existence of some objective or goal, because judgment as to whether or not a financial decision is efficient must be made in the light of some standard. Although various objectives are possible, we assume in this book that the goal of the firm is to maximize the wealth of its present owners.

Ownership in a corporation is evidenced by shares of common stock. Each share indicates that its holder owns 1/nth of the company involved, where n is the total number of shares outstanding.[1] For our purposes, shareholder wealth is

---

[1] For a discussion of the characteristics of common stock, see Chapter 22.

represented by the market price per share of the firm's stock. While the market price may not be a perfect measure of wealth for all stockholders, it is the best measure available. When a public market does not exist for the stock, an opportunity price must be used. By analyzing similar companies whose stock is traded publicly, one can approximate the market value of the company involved.

Profit Maximization Versus Value Creation

Frequently, maximization of profits is regarded as the proper objective of the firm, but it is not as inclusive a goal as that of maximizing shareholder wealth. For one thing, total profits are not as important as earnings per share. Even maximization of earnings per share is not a fully appropriate objective, partly because it does not specify the timing or duration of expected returns. Is the investment project that will produce a $100,000 return 5 years from now more valuable than the project that will produce annual returns of $15,000 in each of the next 5 years? An answer to this question depends on the time value of money to the firm and to investors at the margin. Few existing stockholders would think favorably of a project that promised its first return in 100 years, no matter how large this return. We must take into account the time pattern of returns in our analysis.

Another shortcoming of the objective of maximizing earnings per share is that it does not consider the risk of the prospective earnings stream. Some investment projects are far more risky than others. As a result, the prospective stream of earnings per share would be more risky if these projects were undertaken. In addition, a company will be more or less risky depending on the amount of debt in relation to equity in its capital structure. This financial risk also contributes to the overall risk to the investor. Two companies may have the same expected earnings per share, but if the earnings stream of one is subject to considerably more risk than the earnings stream of the other, the market price per share of its stock may be less.

Finally, this objective does not allow for the effect of dividend policy on the market price of the stock. If the objective were only to maximize earnings per share, the firm would never pay a dividend. At the very least, it could always improve earnings per share by retaining earnings and investing them in marketable securities. To the extent that the payment of dividends can affect the value of the stock, the maximization of earnings per share will not be a satisfactory objective by itself.

For the reasons just given, an objective of maximizing earnings per share may not be the same as maximizing market price per share. The market price of a firm's stock represents the focal judgment of all market participants as to the value of the particular firm. It takes into account present and prospective future earnings per share; the timing, duration, and risk of these earnings; the dividend policy of the firm; and other factors that bear upon the market price of the stock. The market price serves as a performance index or report card of the firm's progress; it indicates how well management is doing in behalf of its stockholders. Management is under continuous review. Stockholders who are dissatisfied with management's performance may sell their stock and invest in another company.

This action, if taken by other dissatisfied stockholders, will put downward pressure on market price per share.

Social Responsibility

Maximizing shareholder wealth does not imply that management should ignore social responsibility such as protecting the consumer, paying fair wages to employees, maintaining fair hiring practices and safe working conditions, supporting education, and becoming involved in environmental issues such as clean air and water. Many people feel that a firm has no choice but to act in socially responsible ways; they argue that shareholder wealth and, perhaps, the corporation's very existence depend on its being socially responsible. Because the criteria for social responsibility are not clearly defined, however, it is difficult to formulate a consistent objective. When society, acting through Congress and other representative bodies, establishes the rules governing the trade-off between social goals and economic efficiency, the task for the corporation is clearer. The company can be viewed as producing both private and social goods, and the maximization of shareholder wealth remains a viable corporate objective.

FUNCTION OF THE FINANCIAL MANAGER

As suggested earlier, the financial manager is concerned with (1) efficient allocation of funds within the enterprise and (2) raising funds on as favorable terms as possible. These functions are pursued with the objective of maximizing shareholder wealth. By and large, this book is organized according to these two functions. Embodied in the first is consideration of the total amount of funds to employ in the enterprise.

The Underpinnings

Before proceeding to examine the allocation and raising of funds, we take up certain background material and tools of analysis. In the next chapter, we examine the legal setting for financial management as it relates in particular to organizational form and taxes. The function of financial markets and institutions as well as interest rates is also pertinent background. These topics are discussed in Chapter 3. In particular, our focus is on how business firms interact with financial markets. Certain concepts involving the time value of money and valuation are taken up in Chapters 4 and 5, and an understanding here is essential to sound financial decisions. Indeed, the foundation for maximizing shareholder wealth is valuation. As a result, we take up the basics of the time value of money and valuation early on.

In order to raise funds efficiently and to allocate them, financial managers must plan carefully. For one thing, they must project future cash flows and then assess the likely effect of these flows on the financial condition of the firm. On the basis of these projections, they plan for adequate liquidity to pay bills and other obligations as they come due. These obligations may make it necessary to raise additional funds. In order to control performance, the financial manager needs to establish certain norms. These norms are then used to compare actual performance with planned performance. Because financial analysis, planning, and control underlie a good deal of the discussion in this book, we examine these topics in Chapters 6 and 7.

Allocation of Funds

The financial manager oversees the allocation of **funds** among alternative uses. This allocation must be made in accordance with the underlying objective of the firm: to maximize shareholder wealth. In Part IV, we examine cash, marketable securities, accounts receivable, and inventories. We shall explore ways of efficiently managing these current assets in order to maximize profitability relative to the amount of funds tied up in the assets. Determining a proper level of liquidity is very much a part of this management. The optimal level of a current asset depends on the profitability and flexibility associated with that level in relation to the cost involved in maintaining it. In the past, the management of working capital dominated the role of financial managers. Although this traditional function continues to be vital, their role has expanded to involve longer-term assets and liabilities.

Funds. Either cash or working capital of the firm.

In Part V, under capital investment, we consider the allocation of funds among fixed assets. Capital budgeting involves allocating capital to investment proposals whose benefits will be realized in the future. When a proposal embodies a current asset component, the latter is treated as part of the capital budgeting decision and not as a separate working capital decision. Because the expected future benefits from an investment proposal are uncertain, risk necessarily is involved. Changes in the business-risk complexion of the firm can have a significant influence on its value in the marketplace. Because of this important effect, attention is devoted to the problem of measuring risk for a capital investment project. Capital is apportioned according to an acceptance criterion. The return required to the project must be in accord with the objective of maximizing shareholder wealth.

In Part VIII, we see mergers and acquisitions from the standpoint of the firm's allocation of funds. Many of the concepts applicable to capital budgeting are applicable here. Also explored is corporate restructuring more broadly defined. This topic involves not only the allocation of funds but financing as well. Growth of a company can be internal, external, or both, and domestic or international in flavor. Since the multinational firm has come into such prominence, it is particularly germane that we study growth through international operations. Nor do we overlook financial management of a smaller company and the things that make such management different from that in a large one. Finally, in this part, we take up failures and reorganizations, which involve a decision to liquidate a company or to rehabilitate it, often by changing it capital structure. This decision should be based on the same economic considerations that govern the allocation of capital.

In summary, the allocation of funds within the firm determines the total amount of assets of the firm, the composition of these assets, and the business-risk complexion of the firm. All of these factors greatly influence its value.

Raising Funds

The second facet of financial management is the acquisition of funds. A wide variety of sources is available. Each has certain characteristics as to cost, maturity, availability, the encumbrance of assets, and other terms imposed by the supplier of capital. On the basis of these factors, the financial manager must determine the best mix of financing for the firm. Its implications for shareholder wealth must be considered when this decision is made.

In Part VI, we take up the appropriate capital structure of a firm. We look at the concept of leverage from a number of different angles in an effort to understand financial risk and how this risk is interrelated with operating risk. In addition, we analyze retained earnings as a source of funds. Because this source represents dividends forgone by stockholders, dividend policy very much impinges on financing policy, and vice versa. In Part IV, we examine the various sources of short-term financing; in Part VII, the sources of long-term financing. Both parts reveal the features, concepts, and problems associated with alternative methods of financing.

Financial management, then, involves the allocation of funds within the firm and the acquisition of funds. The two are interrelated in that a decision to invest in a particular asset necessitates the financing of that asset, whereas the cost of financing affects the decision to invest. The focus of this book is on the allocation and acquisition of funds; together, these activities determine the value of the firm to its shareholders. Mastering the concepts involved is the key to understanding the role of financial management.

QUESTIONS

1. If all companies were to have an objective of maximizing shareholder wealth, would people overall tend to be better or worse off?
2. Contrast the objective of maximizing earnings and that of maximizing wealth.
3. Why is the focal point of financial management the funds flows of the firm?
4. Is the goal of zero profits for some finite period (3 to 5 years, for example) ever consistent with the maximization of wealth objective? Explain.
5. Explain why judging the efficiency of any financial decision requires the existence of a goal.
6. What are the two major functions of the financial manager? How are they related?
7. Should the managers of a company own sizable amounts of stock in the company? What are the pros and the cons?

8. During the last two decades, a number of environment, pollution, hiring, and other regulations have been imposed on businesses. In view of these changes, is maximization of shareholder wealth any longer a realistic objective?

9. As an investor, are not some managers paid too much? Do their rewards come at your expense?

10. How does the notion of risk and reward govern the behavior of financial managers?

SELECTED REFERENCES

BARNEA, AMIR, ROBERT A. HAUGEN, and LEMMA W. SENBET, "Management of Corporate Risk," in *Advances in Financial Planning and Forecasting*. New York: JAI Press, 1985.

CORNELL, BRADFORD, and ALAN C. SHAPIRO, "Corporate Stakeholders and Corporate Finance," *Financial Management*, 16 (Spring 1987), 5–14.

DONALDSON, GORDON, "Financial Goals: Management vs. Stockholders," *Harvard Business Review*, 41 (May–June 1963), 116–29.

FAMA, EUGENE F., "Agency Problems and the Theory of the Firm," *Journal of Political Economy*, 88 (April 1980), 288–307.

FINDLEY, M. CHAPMAN, III, and G. A. WHITMORE, "Beyond Shareholder Wealth Maximization," *Financial Management*, 3 (Winter 1974), 25–35.

FRUHAN, WILLIAM E. JR., *Financial Strategy*. Homewood, Ill.: Richard D. Irwin, 1979.

JENSEN, MICHAEL C., and WILLIAM H. MECKLING, "Theory of the Firm: Managerial Behavior, Agency Costs and Ownership Structure," *Journal of Financial Economics*, 3 (October 1976), 305–60.

JENSEN, MICHAEL C., and CLIFFORD W. SMITH, JR., "Stockholder, Manager, and Creditor Interests: Applications of Agency Theory," pp. 93–132, in *Recent Advances in Corporate Finance*, ed. Edward I. Altman and Marti G. Subrahmanyam.

RAPPAPORT, ALFRED, *Creating Shareholder Value*. New York: Free Press, 1986.

SEITZ, NEIL, "Shareholder Goals, Firm Goals and Firm Financing Decisions," *Financial Management*, 11 (Autumn 1982), 20–26.

TREYNOR, JACK L., "The Financial Objective in the Widely Held Corporation," *Financial Analysts Journal*, 37 (March/April 1981), 68–71.

CHAPTER 2

The Legal and Tax Environment

To understand the role of financial managers, we must be familiar with the legal setting in which they operate. When we look at one aspect of the setting, the basic form of business organization, we shall discover advantages and disadvantages of the various forms. Delving into another aspect, the tax environment, we shall not try to become experts, but we do hope to gain a basic understanding of the tax implications of various financial decisions to be considered in this book.

FORM OF ORGANIZATION

In the United States there are three basic forms of business organization: the sole proprietorship, the partnership, and the corporation. The sole proprietorship outnumbers the other two, but the corporation is largest in sales, assets, profits, and contribution to national income. As this section unfolds, we shall see several important advantages to the corporate form.

The Sole Proprietorship

The sole proprietorship is the oldest form of business organization. As the title suggests, a single person owns the business, holds title to all its assets, and is personally responsible for all of its liabilities. Because of its simplicity, a sole proprietorship can be established with few complications. Simplicity is its greatest virtue; its principal shortcoming is the proprietor's legal responsibility for all obligations the organization incurs. If the organization is sued, the proprietor as an individual is sued and has unlimited liability, which means that his or her personal property as well as the assets of the business may be seized to settle claims. Obviously, this liability places the individual in a risk-prone position.

Another problem with a sole proprietorship is the difficulty in raising capital. In general, this form of organization is not as attractive to creditors as are other forms of organizations. Moreover, the proprietorship has certain tax disadvantages. Fringe benefits, such as medical coverage and group insurance, are not regarded by the Internal Revenue Service as expenses of the firm and therefore are not deductible for tax purposes. A corporation often deducts these benefits. The proprietor must pay for them from income left over after paying taxes. In addition to these drawbacks, the proprietorship form makes the transfer of ownership more difficult than does the corporate form. In estate planning, no portion of the enterprise can be transferred to members of the family during the proprietor's lifetime. For these reasons, this form of organization does not afford the flexibility that other forms do.

The Partnership

A partnership is similar to a proprietorship in all aspects except that there is more than one owner. In a *general partnership* all partners have unlimited liability; they are jointly liable for the liabilities of the partnership. Because an individual partner can bind the partnership with obligations, general partners should be selected with care. In most cases there is a formal arrangement, or partnership agreement; this sets forth the powers of an individual partner, the distribution of profits, the amounts of capital to be invested by the partners, procedures for admitting new partners, and procedures for reconstituting the partnership in case of the death or withdrawal of a partner. Legally, the partnership is terminated if one of the partners dies or withdraws. In such cases, settlements invariably are "sticky," and reconstitution of the partnership is a difficult matter. For these reasons, many people view the partnership as an unattractive form of business organization.

The decision-making process of a partnership is often cumbersome. Unless the agreement specifies otherwise, important decisions must be made by majority vote. In most cases, group decisions are difficult, to say the least. On less weighty matters, individual partners may transact business for the firm but must be careful to keep the other partners informed. The powers of an individual partner will vary according to the formal or informal agreement among partners. Some partnerships specify a hierarchy of two or more layers of partners. This hierarchy determines the magnitude of decision an individual partner can make and the degree to which a partner can commit the firm.

In a number of states, *limited partnerships* are permitted. A limited partner contributes capital and has liability confined to that amount of capital. There must, however, be at least one general partner in the partnership, whose liability is unlimited. Limited partners do not participate in the operation of the business; this is left to the general partners. The limited partners are strictly investors, and they share in the profits or losses of the partnership according to the terms of the partnership agreement. This type of arrangement is frequently used in financing real estate ventures.

Finally, a *master limited partnership* (MLP) is yet another type of organizational form. The MLP has many of the advantages of a corporation, but it avoids the double taxation of earnings distributed to the owners. Like the stockholders in a corporation, the owners of a MLP do not have personal liability for the decisions of the enterprise. To date, most master limited partnerships have involved companies engaged in the processing of natural resources.[1]

The Corporation

Because of the importance of the corporate form in the United States, the focus of this book is on corporations. A corporation is an "impersonal" entity created by law; it can own assets and incur liabilities. In the famous *Dartmouth College* decision in 1819, Justice Marshall concluded that

> a corporation is an artificial being, invisible, intangible, and existing only in contemplation of the law. Being a mere creature of law, it possesses only those properties which the charter of its creation confers upon it, either expressly or as incidental to its very existence.[2]

[1] See J. Markham Collins and Roger P. Bey, "The Master Limited Partnership: An Alternative to the Corporation," *Financial Management*, 15 (Winter 1986), 5–14.

[2] *The Trustees of Dartmouth College v. Woodward*, 4 Wheaton 636 (1819).

The principal feature of this form is that the corporation exists separately and apart from its owners. An owner's liability is limited to his or her investment. Limited liability represents an important advantage over the proprietorship and the general partnership. Capital can be raised in the corporation's name without exposing the owners to unlimited liability. Therefore, personal assets cannot be seized in the settlement of claims. Ownership itself is evidenced by shares of stock, with each stockholder owning that proportion of the enterprise represented by his shares in relation to the total number of shares outstanding. These shares are transferable, representing another important advantage of the corporate form. Moreover, the corporation can continue even though individual owners may die or wish to sell their stock.

A corporation is incorporated in a specific state. To establish a corporation, the owners must file an application with the secretary of state or some other state official. This application includes the location of the company, the purpose of the business, the names of the owners and directors, the names of the management, the number of shares of stock authorized, the paid-in capital, and the length of the corporation's life, which in most cases is perpetual. Upon approval by the appropriate state official, a *charter* is issued to establish the corporation as a legal entity and spell out the conditions under which it can exist.

Because of the advantages associated with limited liability, transferability of ownership, and the ability of the corporation to raise capital apart from its owners, the corporate form of business organization has grown enormously during the last century. With the large demands for capital that accompany an advanced economy, the proprietorship and partnership have proven unsatisfactory, and the corporation has emerged as the most important organizational form. A possible disadvantage of the corporation is the tax treatment, which we take up shortly. Even here, the disadvantage exists only under certain circumstances. Minor disadvantages include the length of time required to incorporate and the red tape involved, as well as the incorporation fee that must be paid to the state. Thus, a corporation is more difficult to establish than either a proprietorship or a partnership. For a moderate-sized organization, however, this is not a serious problem.

CORPORATE INCOME TAXES

Few business decisions are not affected either directly or indirectly by taxes. Through their taxing power, federal, state, and local governments have a profound influence on the behavior of business organizations and that of their owners. What might be an optimal business decision in the absence of taxes may prove to be a very inferior one with taxes. In this section we trace some of the essentials of taxation. This basic understanding is used in later chapters when we consider specific financial decisions. We begin with the corporate income tax; then we consider personal income taxes. We must be mindful that tax laws frequently change. The last major alteration that affected almost everything was the Tax Reform Act of 1986. All discussion is based on tax laws in effect in mid-1988.

A corporation's taxable income is found by deducting all expenses, including depreciation and interest. There is a three-step graduated tax rate structure, the steps being

TAXABLE INCOME	TAX RATE
Not over $50,000	15%
$50,000 to $75,000	25%
Over $75,000	34%

For larger companies, the effective tax rate is a flat 34 percent; the benefit of graduated rates is fully phased out for corporations with more that $335,000 in taxable income. The small company, however, does benefit from the graduated rate schedule.

While no company likes to pay taxes and will take advantage of all the law allows, the Internal Revenue Service has a fallback. That is the alternative minimum tax (AMT) for companies that have tax deductions of a preference type. Examples include the difference between accelerated depreciation and straight line and intangible drilling costs. The law is complicated, but the gist of it is that a tax rate of 20 percent applies to companies that are profitable but have preference tax deductions that otherwise reduce sharply or even eliminate taxes. More will be said about this when we come to lease financing.

Corporations of any significant size are required to make quarterly tax payments on essentially a current basis. More specifically, they are required to pay 25 percent of their estimated taxes in any given year on April 15, June 15, September 15, and December 15 of that year. When actual income differs from that which has been estimated, adjustments are made. A company that is on a calendar-year basis of accounting must make final settlement by April 15 of the subsequent year.

Depreciation

Depreciation. The annual charge made to earnings to recover the cost of an asset. Deductible for tax purposes.

Because **depreciation** charges are deductible as an expense, they affect the amount of tax to be paid. The greater these charges, the lower the tax, all other things remaining constant. There are three methods for depreciating a capital asset: straight-line, declining-balance, and sum-of-the-years'-digits methods. The last two are forms of *accelerated* depreciation. Under the **accelerated cost recovery system** (ACRS) for depreciation, it is necessary to start with the recovery period of the asset. Machinery, equipment, and real estate fall into defined classes, depending on their nature.

A general description of the classes follows. The reader should refer to the tax code for more detail.

■ *3-Year Class.* Includes property with a midpoint life of 4 years or less. The midpoint life of various types of assets is determined by the Treasury Department under the asset depreciation range (ADR) system.

- *5-Year Class.* Includes property with an ADR midpoint life of 4 to 10 years. Included in this class are most machinery, automobiles, light trucks, most technological and semiconductor equipment, switching equipment, small power production facilities, and research and experimental equipment.
- *7-Year Class.* Includes property with an ADR midpoint life of 10 to 16 years and railroad track and single-purpose agriculture structures.
- *10-Year Class.* Includes property with an ADR midpoint life of 16 to 20 years.
- *15-Year Class.* Includes property with a midpoint life of 20 to 25 years and telephone distribution plants.
- *20-Year Class.* Includes property with an ADR midpoint life of 25 years or more, other than real property described below.
- *$27\frac{1}{2}$-Year Class.* Includes residential rental property.
- *$31\frac{1}{2}$-Year Class.* Other real estate.

The property category in which an asset falls determines its depreciable life for tax purposes.

To illustrate the various methods of depreciation, consider first straight-line depreciation. If an asset costing $15,000 falls in the 5-year property class, the annual depreciation charges using straight-line depreciation would be $15,000/5, or $3,000. The declining-balance method of depreciation must specify some multiple. Let us assume initially that this multiple is 2. With the double-declining-balance method, depreciation charges in any year are

$$2(BV/n) \tag{2-1}$$

where BV is the undepreciated book value of the asset at the start of the year, and n is the depreciable life of the asset. For a $15,000 asset, with a 5-year life, depreciation charges in the first year would be

$$2(\$15,000/5) = \$6,000$$

Depreciation charges in the second year are based on an undepreciated book value of $9,000; we arrive at the $9,000 by subtracting the first year's depreciation charges, $6,000, from the asset's original book value. Depreciation charges in the second year would therefore be

$$2(\$9,000/5) = \$3,600$$

In the third year they would be

$$2(\$5,400/5) = \$2,160$$

and so on.

Accelerated Cost Recovery System.   For the 3-year, 5-year, 7-year, and 10-year property classes, the method of depreciation is the 200 percent declining-balance method. This method switches to straight line in the year that provides the quickest write-off. Moreover, a half-year convention is used in the first year and in the year following the last year. For the 15-year and 20-year property classes, 150 percent declining-balance depreciation is used with subsequent switching to straight line. Finally, for the $27\frac{1}{2}$- and $31\frac{1}{2}$-year classes, straight-line depreciation is used throughout.

To illustrate for the 5-year property class, assume an asset costing $10,000 is acquired at the start of the year. The formula for the declining-balance method is $m(1/n)$, where m is the multiplier and n is the number of years in the property class. For our example, $2(1/5) = 40$ percent. However, in the first year a one-half-year convention is employed so first-year depreciation is 20 percent, or $2,000. At the end of the third year, it is favorable to switch to straight-line depreciation. Thus, the depreciation schedule is as follows:

YEAR	DEPRECIATION	DEPRECIATION CHARGE	BALANCE
0			$10,000
1	.2 of $10,000	$2,000	8,000
2	.4 of $8,000	3,200	4,800
3	.4 of $4,800	1,920	2,880
4	$2,880/2.5 years	1,152	1,728
5	$2,880/2.5 years	1,152	576
6	$2,880 × .20	576	0

At the beginning of the fourth year, the balance remaining is divided by the remaining life to get straight-line depreciation. The remaining life is $2\frac{1}{2}$ years, owing to the half-year convention in the sixth year. Finally, in the sixth year the remaining balance is $576, or one-fifth of the balance at the end of the third year.

Instead of making such calculations, the Treasury publishes depreciation percentages of original cost for each property class. For the first four property categories, they are

RECOVERY YEAR	3-YEAR	5-YEAR	7-YEAR	10-YEAR
1	33.33%	20.00%	14.29%	10.00%
2	44.44	32.00	24.29	18.00
3	14.82	19.20	17.49	14.40
4	7.41	11.52	12.49	11.52
5		11.52	8.93	9.22
6		5.76	8.93	7.37
7			8.92	6.56
8			4.46	6.55
9				6.55
10				6.55
11				3.28

These percentages correspond to the principles taken up in our previous calculations, and they should be used for determining depreciation.

Interest Expense

Interest charges on debt issued by a corporation are treated as an expense and are deductible for tax purposes. This treatment contrasts with that for common and preferred stock dividends, which are not deductible for tax purposes. If a company is profitable and pays taxes, the use of debt in its financing mix results in a significant tax advantage relative to the use of preferred or common stock. If the marginal tax rate were 34 percent, the firm would need to earn approximately $1.52 before taxes for every $1 paid out in dividends—$1/(1 − tax rate)—versus only $1 for the payment of $1 of interest. Thus, we see the tax advantages associated with using debt.

Dividend Income

A corporation may own stock in another company. If it receives a **dividend** on this stock, 80 percent of the dividend is tax exempt. The remaining 20 percent is taxed at the corporate income tax rate. A firm that receives $10,000 in dividend income pays taxes on only $2,000 of this income. At a tax rate of 34 percent, taxes would amount to $680 as opposed to $3,400 if the entire dividend income were treated as taxable income.

Carryback and Carryforward

If a corporation sustains a net operating loss, this loss may be carried back 3 years and forward 15 years to offset taxable income in those years. The loss must be applied first to the earliest preceding year. If a firm sustained an operating loss of $200,000 in 1989, it would first carry this loss back to 1986. If the company had net profits of $200,000 in that year and paid taxes of $72,750, it would recompute its taxes for 1986 to show zero profit for tax purposes. Consequently, the company would be eligible for a tax refund of $72,750. If the 1989 operating loss was greater than operating profits in 1986, the residual would be carried back to 1987 and taxes recomputed for that year. If part of the loss was not used in that year, it would be carried back to 1988. However, if the net operating loss was greater than net operating income in all three years, the residual would be carried forward in sequence to future profits in 1990 to 2004. Profits in each of these years would be reduced for tax purposes by the amount of the unused loss carryforward. This feature of the tax law is designed to avoid penalizing the company with sharply fluctuating net operating income.

Capital Gains and Losses

When a capital asset is sold, a **capital gain** or loss is incurred. Often in our tax laws there has been a differential taxation of capital gains and operating income, with the capital gain being treated more favorably. Under the 1986 Tax Reform Act, however, capital gains are taxed at ordinary income tax rates for both corporations and for individuals. In the case of corporations, this rate is 34 percent.

Capital gain. The sales price of an asset less its cost.

PERSONAL INCOME TAXES

The subject of personal taxes is extremely comprehensive, but here our main concern is with the personal taxes of individuals owning stock in corporations. Any income reported by a sole proprietorship or a partnership becomes income of the owners, and it is taxed at the personal rate. For individuals, there are two tax brackets, 15 percent and 28 percent. The rate structure depends on whether you file a joint return or a single return or if you are classified as a head of household. For these classifications

TAX RATE	JOINT	HEAD OF HOUSEHOLD	SINGLE
15%	Up to $29,750	Up to $25,288	Up to $17,850
28%	Over $29,750	Over $25,288	Over $17,850

Thus, the joint return is treated more favorably, as a greater portion of taxable income is subject to the 15 percent rate.

In addition, there is a standard deduction, which enables very low income people to pay no taxes. For a joint return, this deduction is $5,000, whereas for heads of households and single individuals it is $4,400 and $3,000, respectively. If Sylvia Collins had income of $65,000 after deductions and personal exemptions, and she were filing a joint return, her taxable income would be $60,000. On this amount, she would pay 15 percent on $29,750, or $4,462.50, and 28 percent on $60,000 minus $29,750, or $8,470. Thus her taxes would be $12,932.50.

However, if taxable income exceeds a certain level ($71,900 for joint returns), the benefit of the 15 percent rate is phased out. On any income above this level, a 5 percent additional tax is imposed until the benefit of the lower tax bracket is eliminated.

Interest, Dividends, and Capital Gains

For the individual, interest received on corporate and Treasury securities is fully taxable at the federal level. (Interest on Treasury securities is not taxable at the state level.) However, interest received on a municipal security is exempt from federal taxation. For interest and dividends as well as capital gains, such income is subject to the ordinary income tax rate.

Stock Options

Executives of corporations often are given stock options as a performance incentive. An option is a contract that gives the holder the right to buy common stock in the company at some specified price and during some stated period of time.

For example, Feldstein Focal Company may give its president, Mark Bender, a 3-year option to purchase 10,000 shares of stock at $23 per share, which is the current market price. The exercise price of this incentive stock option must be at least 100 percent of the fair market value of the stock on the day that it is granted. If the stock rises in price, Mark Bender stands to gain; if it drops in price, he does not lose, because presumably he will not exercise his option. (His job may be in jeopardy, however!) At the end of three years, the stock is worth $51 per share. Bender exercises his option and buys 10,000 shares for $23 per share. If he then elects to sell some of this stock, the difference between the selling price and the exercise price ($51 − $23) is a capital gain, which is taxed as ordinary income.

Subchapter S

Subchapter S of the Internal Revenue Code allows the owners of small corporations—those having 35 or fewer stockholders—to use the corporate organization form but to be taxed as though the firm were a partnership. Thus, the owners are able to avail themselves of the legal advantages extended to corporations, but they are able to avoid any tax disadvantage that might result. They simply declare any corporate profits as personal income on a pro rata basis and pay the appropriate tax on this income. This treatment eliminates the double taxation normally associated with dividend income—that is, the corporation paying dividends from after-tax income, and shareholders paying taxes on the dividend income they receive. In addition, stockholders may deduct any operating losses on a pro rata basis against their personal income.

SUMMARY

Of the three basic forms of business organization—the sole proprietorship, the partnership, and the corporation—the corporation has become most prominent because it offers a number of advantages. We observed these advantages together with aspects of the other two forms of business organization.

The tax environment has a profound influence on business decisions. Certain basic features of the tax law apply to corporations, and these were explored. Depreciation, interest expense, intercorporate dividends, the carryback–carryforward provision, and capital gains all affect the amount of taxes paid by the corporation.

Personal taxes affect debt holders and stockholders of a corporation through the interest, dividends, and capital gains they receive from their investment. Taxes affect employees and executives through their compensation and stock options. This chapter serves only as an introduction to the issue; relevant taxes and the implication of these taxes will be discussed throughout the book when we consider specific financial decisions.

QUESTIONS

1. What is the principal advantage of the corporate form of business organization? Discuss the importance of this advantage to the owner of a small family restaurant. Discuss the importance of this advantage to a wealthy entrepreneur who owns several businesses.

2. How does being a limited partner in a business enterprise differ from being a stockholder, assuming the same percentage of ownership?

3. What are some of the disadvantages of a sole proprietorship? of a partnership?

4. What kind of corporation benefits from the graduated income tax?

5. In general, what are the principles on which the accelerated cost recovery system (ACRS) is based?

6. Interest on Treasury securities is not taxable at the state level, whereas interest on municipal securities is not taxable at the federal level. What is the reason for this feature?

7. Are individual tax rates progressive or regressive in the sense of increasing (or decreasing) with income levels?

8. If capital gains were to be taxed at a lower rate than ordinary income, as has been the case in the past, what types of investments would be favored?

9. The method of depreciation does not alter the total amount of deductions from income during the life of an asset. What does it alter and why is that important?

10. If the owners of a new corporation number less than 35, does Subchapter S make sense for tax purposes?

11. Tax laws have become extremely complex. In addition, there is little theoretical or moral justification for a substantial number of tax incentives (loopholes). Why and how are these incentives created? In your opinion, is there any indication that these incentives will be eliminated?

12. What is the purpose of the carryback and the carryforward provisions in the tax laws?

SELF-CORRECTION PROBLEMS

1. John Henry has a small house-cleaning business that presently is a sole proprietorship. The business has nine employees, annual sales of $480,000, current (and total) liabilities of $90,000, and total assets of $263,000. Including the business, Henry has a personal net worth of $467,000 and nonbusiness liabilities of $42,000, represented by a mortgage on his home. He would like to give one of his employees, Tori Kobayashi, an equity interest in the business. Henry is considering either the partnership form or the corporate form, where Kobayashi would be given some stock. Kobayashi has a personal net worth of $36,000.

   a. What is the extent of Henry's exposure under the sole proprietorship in the case of a large lawsuit (say, $600,000)?

   b. What is his exposure under a partnership form? Do the partners share the risk?

   c. What is his exposure under the corporate form?

2. Bernstein Tractor Company has just invested in new equipment costing $16,000. The equipment falls in the 5-year property class for cost recovery (depreciation) purposes. What depreciation charges can it claim on the asset?

3. Mabel Harare has taxable income of $38,000 arising from her salary after standard deduction and exemption. In addition, she has a portfolio of stocks and taxable bonds. Last year she received $2,100 in dividends and $1,200 in interest. Finally, she sold stock and realized a capital gain of $6,500. What personal taxes does she pay if she files a single return where the tax rate is 15 percent up to $17,850 in taxable income and 28 percent on amounts over that?

PROBLEMS

1. Zaharias-Liras Wholesalers, a partnership, owes $418,000 to various shipping companies. Armand Zaharias has a personal net worth of $1,346,000, including a $140,000 equity interest in the partnership. Nick Liras has a personal net worth of $893,000, including the same equity interest in the business as his partner. The partners have kept only a moderate equity base of $280,000 in the business, with earnings being taken out as partner withdrawals. They wish to limit their risk exposure and are considering the corporate form.

   a. What is their liability now for the business? What would it be under the corporate form?

   b. Will creditors be more or less willing to extend credit with a change in organization form?

2. In Problem 1, suppose that business profits average $200,000 and that the two partners share equally in them. Zaharias and Liras have other taxable incomes of $30,000 and $20,000, respectively. These other taxable incomes are after all deductions and exemptions have been taken.

   a. If both Zaharias and Liras file joint returns, what personal taxes does each pay now?

   b. What total taxes (corporate and personal) will be paid if the business were a corporation and all the above-mentioned profits were paid out to the two people in the salaries?

   c. What total taxes would be paid if one-half of the above-mentioned profits were paid in salaries and the other half in dividends? Is there a special provision under the Internal Revenue Service code that might ameliorate the problem?

3. The Burleigh Milling Company is going to purchase a new piece of testing equipment for $28,000 and a new machine for $53,000. The equipment falls in the 3-year property class and the machine is in the 5-year class. What annual depreciation will the company be able to take on the two assets?

4. Tripex Consolidated Industries owns $1.5 million in 12 percent bonds of Solow Electronics Company. It also owns 100,000 shares of preferred stock of Solow. In the year just past, Solow paid the stipulated interest on its bonds and dividends of $3 per share on its preferred stock. The marginal tax rate of Tripex is 34 percent. What taxes must Tripex pay on this interest and dividend income?

5. The Castle Cork Company was founded in 1984 and had the following taxable income through 1988:

1984	1985	1986	1987	1988
$0	$35,000	$68,000	−$120,000	$52,000

Compute the corporate income tax or tax refund in each year, assuming the graduated tax rates discussed in the chapter.

SOLUTIONS TO SELF-CORRECTION PROBLEMS

1. a. Henry is responsible for all liabilities, book as well as contingent. If the lawsuit were lost, he could lose all his net assets, as represented by a net worth of $467,000. Without the lawsuit, he still is responsible for $90,000 in liabilities if for some reason the business is unable to pay them.

   b. He still could lose all his net assets because Kobayashi's net worth is insufficient to make a major dent in the lawsuit: $600,000 − $36,000 = $564,000. As the two partners have substantially different net worths, they do not share equally in the risk. Henry has much more to lose.

   c. Under the corporate form, he could lose the business, but that is all. The net worth of the business is $263,000 − $90,000 = $173,000, and this represents Henry's personal financial stake in it. The remainder of his net worth, $467,000 − $173,000 = $294,000, would be protected under the corporate form.

2. Depreciation charges for the equipment:

YEAR	PERCENT	AMOUNT
1	20.00%	$3,200.00
2	32.00	5,120.00
3	19.20	3,072.00
4	11.52	1,843.20
5	11.52	1,843.20
6	5.76	921.60

3. Taxable income from:

Salary	$38,000
Dividends	2,100
Interest	1,200
Capital gains	6,500
Total	$47,800

Personal taxes paid:

15% of $17,850	$2,677.50
28% of $47,800 − $17,850	8,386.00
Total	$11,063.50

CHAPTER 3

The Financial Environment

In varying degrees, all business firms operate within the financial system. When a product or service is sold, the seller receives either cash or a financial asset in the form of an account receivable. In addition, the firm invests idle funds in marketable securities, and here it has direct contact with the financial markets. More important, most firms use financial markets to finance their investment in assets. In the final analysis, the market prices of a company's securities are the test of whether it is a success or a failure. While business firms compete with each other in the product markets, they must continually interface with the financial markets. The financial system consists of a number of institutions and markets serving business firms, individuals, and governments. Because of the importance of this environment to the financial manager as well as to the individual as a consumer of financial services, this chapter is devoted to exploring the financial system and the ever-changing environment in which capital is raised.

THE PURPOSE OF FINANCIAL MARKETS

Financial assets exist in an economy because the savings of various individuals, corporations, and governments during a period of time differ from their investment in real assets. By real assets, we mean things such as houses, buildings, equipment, inventories, and durable goods. If savings equaled investment in real assets for all economic units in an economy over all periods of time, there would be no external financing, no financial assets, and no money and capital markets. Each economic unit would be self-sufficient; current expenditures and investment in real assets would be paid for out of current income. A financial asset is created only when the investment of an economic unit in real assets exceeds its savings, and it finances this excess by borrowing or issuing equity securities. Of course, another economic unit must be willing to lend. This interaction of borrowers with lenders determines interest rates. In the economy as a whole, savings-surplus economic units (those whose savings exceed their investment in real assets) provide funds to savings-deficit units (those whose investment in real assets exceeds their savings). This exchange of funds is evidenced by pieces of paper representing a financial asset to the holder and a financial liability to the issuer.

Efficiency of Financial Markets

The purpose of financial markets in an economy is to allocate savings efficiently to ultimate users. If those economic units that saved were the same as those that engaged in capital formation, an economy could prosper without financial markets. In modern economies, however, the economic units most responsible for capital formation—nonfinancial corporations—use more than their total savings for investing in real assets. Households, on the other hand, have total savings in excess of total investment. The more diverse the patterns of desired savings and investment among economic units, the greater the need for efficient financial markets to channel savings to ultimate users. The ultimate investor in real assets and the ultimate saver should be brought together at the least possible cost and inconvenience.

Efficient financial markets are absolutely essential to ensure adequate capital formation and economic growth in an economy. If there were no financial assets other than money, each economic unit could invest only to the extent that it saved. Without financial assets, then, an economic unit would be greatly constrained in its investment behavior. If the amounts required for investment in a real asset were large in relation to current savings, an economic unit simply would have to postpone investment until it had accumulated sufficient savings in the form of paper money. Because of the absence of financing, economic units that lacked sufficient savings would have to postpone or abandon many worthwhile investment opportunities.

In such a system, savings in the economy would not be channeled to the most promising investment opportunities, and capital would be less than optimally allocated. Economic units that lacked promising investment opportunities would have no alternative but to accumulate money. Likewise, economic units with very promising opportunities might not be able to accumulate sufficient savings rapidly enough to undertake the projects. Consequently, inferior investments might be undertaken by some economic units, while very promising opportunities would be postponed or abandoned by others. It is not difficult to see the value of being able to issue financial assets. Even with this ability, there are still degrees of efficiency with which savings are channeled to investment opportunities.

The more developed the financial markets of a country, the greater the efficiency. A number of institutions have evolved to improve this efficiency. One is the loan broker, whose purpose is to find savers and to bring them together with economic units needing funds. Because brokers are specialists, continually in the business of matching the need for funds with the supply, usually they are able to do it more efficiently and at a lower cost than are individual economic units themselves. Another institution that enhances the efficiency of the flow of savings is the secondary market, where existing securities can be bought or sold. With a viable secondary market, a purchaser of a financial instrument achieves marketability. If it needs to sell the security in the future, it will be able to do so. Thus, the existence of a strong secondary market enhances the primary market in which funds flow from ultimate savers to ultimate users. Investment bankers also enhance funds flows, and we study their role later in the chapter.

Financial Intermediaries

Up to now, we have considered only the direct flow of savings from savers to users of funds. If there are financial intermediaries in an economy, the flow can be indirect. Financial intermediaries include institutions such as commercial banks, savings banks, savings and loan associations, life insurance companies, and pension and profit-sharing funds. These intermediaries come between ultimate borrowers and lenders by transforming direct claims into indirect ones. They purchase primary securities and, in turn, issue their own securities. The primary security that a savings and loan association purchases is a mortgage; the indirect claim issued is a savings account or a certificate of deposit. A life insurance company, on the other hand, purchases corporate bonds, among other things, and issues life insurance policies.

Financial intermediaries transform funds in a way that makes them more attractive. A variety of services and economies are provided. Economies of scale are possible and may be passed on to the borrower and lender in the form of lower cost of operations. In a related matter, a financial intermediary is able to develop information on the borrower in a more efficient manner than is the individual. A financial intermediary also is able to pool savings to purchase primary securities of varying sizes. Individual savers who would have difficulty investing in a $60,000 mortgage can put funds in a savings and loan association and indirectly invest in that mortgage. Diversification of risk is another service— something not always possible for the individual saver. Also, financial intermediaries are able to transform the maturity of a primary security into indirect securities of different maturities. As a result, the maturities may be more attractive to the ultimate lender than they would be if the loan were direct. Finally, the financial intermediary provides often needed expertise in investing in primary securities.

Thus, financial intermediaries tailor the denomination and type of indirect securities they issue to the desires of savers. Their purpose, of course, is to make a profit by purchasing primary securities yielding more than their expenses and the return they must pay on the indirect securities issued. In so doing, they channel funds from the ultimate lender to the ultimate borrower at a lower cost and/or with less inconvenience than would be possible if the ultimate lender directly purchased primary securities. Otherwise, they have no reason to exist.

Disintermediation and Securitization

We usually think of financial intermediation making the markets more efficient by lowering the cost and/or inconvenience to consumers of financial services. However, this is not always the case. Sometimes the intermediation process becomes cumbersome and must be undone. Securitization bypasses part of the process by taking an illiquid asset and transforming it into a security.

In securitization, assets such as mortgages are pooled together and securities are issued against the pool. In the case of mortgage pass-through securities, the investor has a direct claim on a portion of the mortgage pool. That is to say, interest and principal payments on the mortgages are passed directly along to the investor. Other securities involve bonds backed by the pool of assets. While securitization of assets was originally confined to residential mortgages, in the mid- to late 1980s it spread to auto loans, credit card receivables, commercial mortgages, and lease contracts. In addition, attempts have been made to securitize trade credit and commercial loans. The reason for the spread of securitization is that the total transaction costs of credit often are less with securitization than they are when a depository institution intermediates between borrowers and savers. The forces of competition work to lower costs, and this is yet another dimension of the unfolding deregulation of the financial services industry.

The securitization movement has implications for the financial manager in financing the corporation, so the movement requires careful monitoring. Whenever it is cheaper to finance directly in the securities markets than through a financial intermediary, the financial manager is compelled to consider it.

FUNDS FLOWS IN THE ECONOMY

With financial intermediaries, we have four main sectors in the economy: households, nonfinancial business firms, governments, and financial institutions. These four sectors form a matrix of claims against one another, as we see in Fig. 3-1, which shows a hypothetical balance sheet for each sector. Households are the ultimate owners of all business enterprises, be they nonfinancial corporations or private financial institutions. The distinct role of financial intermedi-

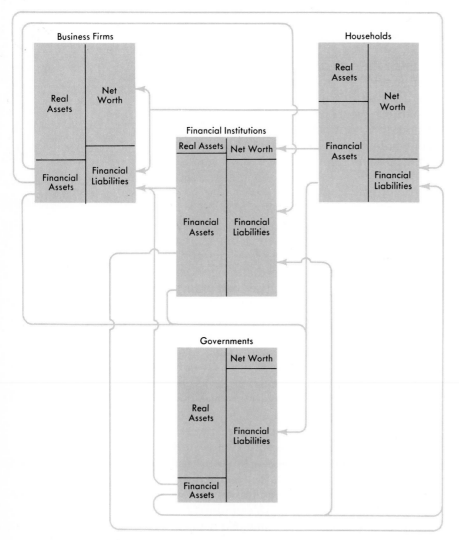

FIGURE 3-1
Relationship of claims

aries is revealed in the nature of their assets, which are primarily financial; they hold a relatively small amount of real assets. On the right-hand side of their balance sheet, financial liabilities predominate. Financial institutions, then, are engaged in transforming direct claims into indirect ones that have a wider appeal.

Flow-of-Funds Matrix

We can study the flow of savings between sectors through the use of flow-of-funds data published by the Federal Reserve Bank. This system of social accounting provides an interlocking picture of funds flows in the economy.[1] Essentially, a source-and-use statement is prepared for each sector. The starting point is a balance sheet at the beginning of the period as well as one at the end. These balance sheets are similar to those in Fig. 3-1, but with financial assets categorized as *money* and as *other financial assets*—that is, paper claims—which are useful classifications. The flows are simply the changes in balance sheet figures between the two moments in time. When source-and-use statements are combined, we obtain a matrix for the entire economy. Table 3-1 is a hypothetical matrix for a closed economy consisting of four sectors. Total uses of funds equals total sources for each sector; that is, the investment in real assets plus changes in financial assets must equal savings plus changes in financial liabilities.

We see also that business firms in aggregate invested in real assets to a greater extent than they saved. The difference was financed by issuing financial liabilities in excess of the increase in financial assets held. The existence of this large savings-deficit sector implies the existence of one or more savings-surplus sectors. When we analyze the matrix, we see that households were a savings-surplus sector and primarily responsible for financing the business firms sector on a net basis. In addition, financial institutions were a savings-surplus sector, although the excess of savings over investment for this sector was small. This sector acts almost entirely as an intermediary, increasing its holdings of financial assets by issuing financial liabilities. Finally, governments, the fourth category,

[1] See James C. Van Horne, *Financial Market Rates and Flows,* 2nd ed. (Englewood Cliffs, N.J.: Prentice-Hall, 1984), chap. 2, for a further analysis of this system.

TABLE 3-1
Matrix of flow of funds of entire economy, 19xx

	HOUSEHOLDS		BUSINESS FIRMS		FINANCIAL INSTITUTIONS		GOVERNMENTS		ALL SECTORS	
	U	S	U	S	U	S	U	S	U	S
Net worth (savings)		101		77		4		−3		179
Real assets (investment)	82		96		1				179	
Money	2		2			5	1		5	5
Other financial assets	37		18		60		17		132	
Financial liabilities		20		39		52		21		132
	121	121	116	116	61	61	18	18	316	316

were a savings-deficit sector. Although governments make substantial expenditures for real assets, those expenditures, unfortunately, are not officially recorded. The budget deficit for governments is financed by an increase in financial liabilities in excess of the increase in financial assets. Because the financial institutions sector contains commercial banks and the monetary authorities, it "provides" money to other sectors in the economy. The $5 source of money for this sector represents an increase in demand deposits and currency held by the public and governments as claims against commercial banks and the monetary authorities.

In the "All Sectors" column, we see that total uses equal total sources. More important, total savings for all sectors in the economy equal the total increase in real assets. Likewise, the total change in financial assets equals the total change in financial liabilities. Thus, financial assets and financial liabilities cancel out in the economy as a whole. In other words, there is no such thing as saving through financial assets for the economy as a whole. The financial asset held by one economic unit is the financial liability of another. However, individual economic units can save through financial assets, and this is the process we wish to study. The fact that financial assets wash out when they are totaled for all economic units in the economy is a recognized identity. The important interaction is the one between issuers of financial claims and potential holders of those claims.

Funds Flows for Business Firms

We know from our previous discussion that business firms are a savings-deficit sector. When they invest more in real assets than they can pay for with their savings, they turn chiefly to households and financial institutions for funds. Households represent a direct flow; financial institutions, an indirect one. Of course, business firms finance each other through accounts receivable and other arrangements, but these funds flows wash out when we consider business firms in the aggregate. To take a single year, 1986, for example, corporations invested approximately $337 billion in plant and equipment. Far and away, this was the major use of funds; others were small in comparison. Total uses of funds in that year were about $403 billion. Of the total sources of funds, internal sources—composed of retained earnings and depreciation allowances—were dominant, accounting for about three-quarters of the total. Some of the more important external sources (on a net basis) were bank loans, $65 billion, and corporate bonds, $92 billion. External debt financing was used in part to retire stock, $81 billion, in the wake of the many mergers and corporate restructurings in that year. The relationship between various external sources of funds varies with the economic cycle.

FINANCIAL INSTITUTIONS

Among the number of institutions involved in the financial system, only a handful invest heavily in the securities of business firms. In what follows, we concentrate on those institutions involved in buying and selling corporate securities.

Deposit Institutions

Commercial banks are the most important source of funds for business firms in the aggregate. Banks acquire demand and time deposits from individuals, companies, and governments and, in turn, make loans and investments. Among the loans made to business firms are seasonal and other short-term loans, intermediate-term loans of up to 5 years, and mortgage loans. There are around 13,000 commercial banks in the nation, and their assets total around $3 trillion, a staggering sum indeed. Besides performing a banking function, commercial banks affect business firms through their trust departments, which invest in corporate bonds and stocks. They also make mortgage loans available to companies and manage pension funds.

Other deposit institutions include *savings and loan associations, mutual savings banks,* and *credit unions.* These institutions are primarily involved with individuals, acquiring their savings and making home loans as well as consumer loans.

Insurance Companies

Insurance companies are in the business of collecting periodic premiums from those they insure in return for providing a payout should some event, usually adverse, occur. With the funds received in premium payments, insurance companies build reserves, which, together with a portion of their capital, are invested in financial assets. Insurance companies are of two types: (1) property and casualty and (2) life. Together both have around $1.5 trillion in assets.

Property and casualty companies insure against fires, thefts, car accidents, and similar unpleasantness. As these companies pay taxes at the full corporate income tax rate, they invest heavily in municipal bonds, which offer tax-exempt interest income. To a lesser extent they invest also in corporate bonds and stocks.

Life insurance companies insure against the loss of life. Because the mortality of a large group of individuals is highly predictable, these companies are able to invest in long-term securities. Also, the income of these institutions is partially exempt from taxes, owing to the buildup of reserves over time. They seek therefore taxable investments with yields higher than those of tax-exempt municipal bonds. As a result, life insurance companies invest heavily in corporate bonds, which represent the largest single financial asset they hold. Next in importance comes mortgages, some of which are granted to business firms.

Other Financial Intermediaries

Pension funds and other *retirement funds* are established to provide income to individuals when they retire. During the employees' working lives, they usually contribute to the fund, as does the employer. The fund invests these contributions and either pays out the cumulative amount periodically to the retired worker or arranges an annuity. In the accumulation phase, monies paid into a fund are not taxed; only when the benefits are paid out in retirement are taxes paid by the recipient. Commercial banks, through their trust departments, and insurance companies offer pension funds, as do the federal government, local governments, and certain other noninsurance organizations. Because of the long-term nature of their liabilities, pension funds are able to invest in longer-term securities. As a result, they invest heavily in corporate bonds and stocks. In fact, pension funds are the largest single institutional investor in corporate stocks. Although individuals hold the largest amount of corporate stock, on a net basis they have liquidated stock in recent years. Pension and retirement funds have been important net purchasers. In total, such funds have approximately $1.5 trillion in assets.

Mutual investment funds also invest heavily in corporate stocks and bonds. These funds accept monies contributed by individuals and invest them in specific types of financial assets. The mutual fund is connected with a management company to which the fund pays a fee, frequently 0.5 percent per annum, for professional investment management. Each individual owns a specified percentage of the mutual fund, which depends on that person's original investment. Individuals can sell their shares at any time, as the mutual fund is required to redeem them. While many mutual funds invest only in common stocks, others specialize in corporate bonds, money market instruments, including commercial paper issued by corporations, or municipal securities. Various stock funds have different investment philosophies, ranging from income and safety to a highly aggressive pursuit of growth. In all cases, the individual obtains a diversified portfolio managed by professionals. Unfortunately, there is no evidence that such management results in consistently superior performance.

Finance companies are private corporations established to make consumer installment loans, personal loans, and secured loans to business enterprises. These companies raise capital through stock issues as well as through borrowings, some of which is long term but most of which comes from commercial banks. In turn, the finance company makes loans. As discussed in Chapter 12, finance companies sometimes play an influential financing role for smaller, emerging companies.

Financial Brokers

Certain financial institutions perform a necessary brokerage function. When brokers bring together parties who need funds with those who have savings, they are not performing a direct lending function but rather are matching the demand and supply of funds.

Investment banker. A financial institution that underwrites and distributes securities.

Investment bankers are involved in the sale of corporate stocks and bonds. When a company decides to raise funds, an investment banker often will buy the issue and then turn around and sell it to investors. Because investment bankers are continually in the business of matching users of funds with suppliers, they can sell issues more efficiently than can the issuing companies. For this service the investment banker receives a fee in the form of the difference between the amount received from the sale of the securities to the public and the amount paid to the company. Much more will be said about the role of investment bankers in Chapter 21, when we consider long-term finnancing.

Mortgage bankers are involved in acquiring and placing mortgages. These mortgages come either directly from individuals and businesses or, more typically, through builders and real estate agents. In turn, the mortgage banker locates institutional and other investors for the mortgages. Although mortgage bankers function as brokers and have no funds of their own committed, they typically service **mortgages** for investors. This involves receiving payments and following through on loan delinquencies. For this service they receive fees.

Mortgage. The pledge of real property to secure a loan.

Security Exchanges and Markets

Various security exchanges and markets facilitate the smooth functioning of the financial system. The purchase and sale of existing financial assets occur in the *secondary market*. Transactions in this market do not increase the total amount of financial assets outstanding, but the presence of viable secondary markets increases the liquidity of financial assets and therefore enhances the primary or direct market for securities. In this regard, *organized exchanges* such as the New York Stock Exchange, the American Stock Exchange, and the New York Bond Exchange provide a means by which buy and sell orders can be efficiently matched. In this matching, the forces of supply and demand determine price.

In addition, the over-the-counter market (OTC) serves as a secondary market for stocks and bonds not listed on an exchange. It is composed of brokers and dealers who stand ready to buy and sell securities at quoted prices. Most corporate bonds, and a growing number of stocks, are traded OTC as opposed to on an organized exchange. The OTC market has become highly mechanized, with market participants linked together by a telecommunications network. They do not come together in a single place as they would on an organized exchange. The National Association of Securities Dealers Automated Quotation Service (NASDAQ) maintains this network, and price quotations are instantaneous. Whereas once it was considered a matter of prestige, as well as necessity in many cases, for a company to list its shares on a major exchange, the electronic age has changed that. Many companies now prefer to have their shares traded OTC, despite the fact that they qualify for listing, because they feel that they get as good, or sometimes better, execution of buy and sell orders.

While there are a number of other financial institutions, we have looked only at those having an interface with business firms. As the book unfolds, we will become better acquainted with many of the ones discussed. Our purpose here was only to introduce you briefly to them; a lasting relationship will come later.

ALLOCATION OF FUNDS AND INTEREST RATES

The allocation of funds in an economy occurs primarily on the basis of price, expressed in terms of expected return. Economic units in need of funds must outbid others for their use. Although the allocation process is affected by capital rationing, government restrictions, and institutional constraints, expected returns are the primary mechanism whereby supply and demand are brought into balance for a particular financial instrument across financial markets. If risk is held constant, economic units willing to pay the highest expected return are the ones entitled to the use of funds. If rationality prevails, the economic units bidding the highest prices will have the most promising investment opportunities. As a result, savings will tend to be allocated to the most efficient uses.

It is important to recognize that the equilibration process by which savings are allocated in an economy occurs not only on the basis of expected return but on the basis of risk as well. Different financial instruments have different degrees of risk. In order for them to compete for funds, these instruments must provide different expected returns, or yields. If all financial instruments had exactly the same risk characteristics, they would provide the same expected return in market equilibrium. Because of differences in default risk, marketability, maturity, coupon rate, and taxability, however, different instruments pose different degrees of risk and provide different effective returns to the investor. (A fifth factor, callability, is considered in detail in Chapter 21.)

Default Risk

Default. The failure to meet the terms of a contract, such as the failure to make a payment on a loan.

When we speak of **default** risk, we mean the danger that the borrower may not meet payments due on principal or interest. Investors demand a risk premium to invest in other than default-free securities. The greater the possibility that the borrower will default in his obligation, the greater the default risk and the premium demanded by the marketplace, Treasury securities usually are regarded as default free, and other securities are judged in relation to them. The greater the default risk of a security issuer, then, the greater the expected return or yield of the security, all other things the same.[2]

For the typical investor, default risk is not judged directly but rather in terms of quality ratings assigned by Moody's Investor Service or Standard & Poor's. These investment agencies assign and publish letter grades for the use of investors. In their ratings, the agencies attempt to rank issues according to the probability of default. Analyzing an issue, an agency weighs a number of factors, including the cash-flow ability of the issuer to service debt, the amount and composition of existing debt, and the stability of cash flows. The highest-grade securities, judged to have negligible default risk, are rated triple A. The ratings used by the two agencies are shown in Table 3-2.

Marketability

Marketability of a security relates to the owner's ability to convert it into cash. There are two dimensions: the price realized and the amount of time required to sell the asset. The two are interrelated in that it is often possible to sell an asset in a short period of time if enough price concession is given. For financial instruments, marketability is judged in relation to the ability to sell a significant volume of securities in a short period of time without significant price conces-

---

[2] For an extended discussion of the influence of default risk on yields as well as a review of the various empirical studies, see Van Horne, *Financial Market Rates and Flows*, chap. 8.

TABLE 3-2
Ratings by investment agencies

	MOODY'S		STANDARD & POOR'S
Aaa	Best quality	AAA	Highest grade
Aa	High quality	AA	High grade
A	Higher medium grade	A	Upper medium grade
Baa	Lower medium grade	BBB	Medium grade
Ba	Possess speculative elements	BB	Lower medium grade
B	Generally lack characteristics of desirable investment	B	Speculative
Caa	Poor standing; may be in default	CCC-CC	Outright speculation
Ca	Speculative in a high degree; often in default	C	Reserved for income bonds
C	Lowest grade	DDD-D	In default, with rating indicating relative salvage value

sion. The more marketable the security, the greater the ability to execute a large transaction near the quoted price. In general, the lower the marketability of a security, the greater the yield necessary to attract investors. Thus, the yield differential between different securities of the same maturity is caused not only by differences in default risk but also by differences in marketability.

Maturity

The relationship between yield and maturity can be studied graphically by plotting yield and maturity for securities differing only in the length of time to maturity. In practice, this means holding constant the degree of default risk. An example of the yield-maturity relationship for default-free Treasury securities on two separate dates is shown in Fig. 3-2. Maturity is plotted on the horizontal axis and yield on the vertical; their relationship is described by a yield curve fitted to the observations.

Generally, when interest rates are expected to rise, the yield curve is upward-sloping, whereas it is humped and downward-sloping when they are expected to fall significantly. However, the yield differential between short- and long-term securities is greater for the steepest upward-sloping yield curve than the negative difference is for the steepest downward-sloping yield curve. In other words, there is a tendency toward positive-sloped yield curves. Most economists attribute this tendency to the presence of risk for those who invest in long-term securities vis-à-vis short-term securities. In general, the longer the maturity, the greater the risk of fluctuation in the market value of the security. Consequently, investors need to be offered a risk premium to induce them to invest in long-term securities. Only when interest rates are expected to fall significantly are they willing to invest in long-term securities yielding less than short- and intermediate-term securities.[3]

[3] For a much deeper discussion of this concept as well as that of the level of the coupon rate on bond price volatility, see Van Horne, *Financial Market Rates and Flows*, chaps. 5 and 6.

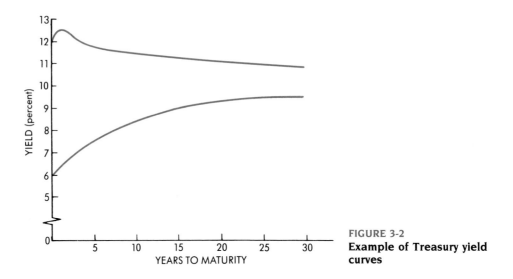

FIGURE 3-2
Example of Treasury yield curves

Coupon Rate

In addition to maturity, price fluctuations also depend on the magnitude of the coupon payment. For a given fixed-income security, the lower the coupon rate the greater the price change for a given shift in interest rates. The reason is that a low coupon or a zero coupon issue has a longer duration. The investor receives less in near-term interest payments, and more of his or her total return is embraced in the final payment of principal at maturity. Expressed differently, investors realize their return sooner with high coupon bonds than they do with low coupon ones.

Taxability

Another factor affecting observed differences in market yields is the differential impact of taxes. The most important tax, and the only one we shall consider, is the income tax. The interest income on all but one category of securities is taxable to taxable investors. Interest income from state and local government securities is tax exempt; as a result, they sell in the market at lower yields to maturity than Treasury and corporate securities of the same maturity. For corporations located in states with income taxes, interest income on Treasury securities is exempt from state income taxes. As a result, such instruments may hold an advantage over the debt instruments of corporations or of banks where the interest income is fully taxable at the state level. Under present tax law, capital gains arising from the sale of a security at a profit are taxed at the full corporate tax rate.

Inflation

In addition to these factors, which affect the yield of one security relative to that of another, inflation expectations have a substantial influence on interest rates overall. It generally is agreed that the nominal rate of interest on a security embodies a premium for inflation. The higher the expected inflation, the higher the nominal yield on the security; and the lower the expected inflation, the lower the nominal yield. Many years ago Irving Fisher expressed the nominal rate of interest on a bond as the sum of the real rate of interest and the rate of price change expected to occur over the life of the instrument.[4] If the annual real rate of interest in the economy were 4 percent for prime risks, and inflation of 6 percent per annum were expected over the next 10 years, this would imply a yield of 10 percent for 10-year, high grade bonds. This states merely that lenders require a nominal rate of interest high enough to earn the real rate of interest.

It is important to differentiate between expected inflation and unexpected inflation. If inflation over the life of a security is exactly that which was anticipated when the terms of the loan were set, neither the borrower nor the lender gains (or loses) with respect to inflation. In other words, the terms of the loan reflect expected inflation, and the debt obligation is paid in keeping with the inflation that actually occurs. If part of the inflation that occurs is unanticipated, there is a redistributional effect from lender to borrower, or vice versa. With an unanticipated increase in inflation, the lender suffers by receiving a real rate of return lower than that anticipated at the time the terms of the loan were set.

To illustrate: The nominal rate of interest on a 10-year loan is 10 percent, of which 4 percent is the expected real rate and 6 percent is a premium for expected inflation. Over the 10 years, inflation of 8 percent per annum actually occurs. As a result, the borrower's real interest cost is 2 percent instead of 4 percent. The lender loses, of course, because its real return is less than it anticipated at the time the loan contract was made. With an unanticipated decrease in inflation, the borrower loses in having to repay the loan in more "expensive" dollars than originally anticipated, whereas the lender gains.

Unanticipated increases in inflation result in a transfer of real wealth from net creditors to net debtors, whereas the opposite occurs with unanticipated decreases. A *net creditor* is defined as one whose financial assets exceed its financial liabilities; for the *net debtor*, the opposite holds. Whether a given company gains or loses with respect to inflation depends upon whether there is an unanticipated increase or decrease in inflation and whether the firm is a net debtor or a net creditor. In the aggregate, nonfinancial corporations have been consistent net debtors. Individually, companies can be net debtors or net creditors, and this can vary over time.

The relationship between the nominal rate of interest and expected inflation is far from simple, as implied by the Fisher effect of one-to-one. If the nominal rate rose and fell exactly in keeping with the rate of inflation, generalizations would be easy. We simply would subtract the inflation rate from the

---

[4] *Appreciation and Interest* (New York: Macmillan, 1896). Actually, Fisher expressed the nominal rate as $R+\alpha+R\alpha$, where R is the real rate, α is the expected rate of inflation, and $R\alpha$ is the product of the two. Like others, we ignore the product term, as it has not been found to be important.

nominal rate of interest to give us the real rate of interest. However, the real rate has not been stable in recent years. Whereas it was very low in the 1970s, it has been significant in the 1980s (around 5 percent on average). This historically high real rate has puzzled followers of financial markets, as did the negligible real interest rate in the 1970s. While we would believe there still is a positive relationship between inflation and interest rates, it is not stable and consistent over time.

What is clear is that the real cost of borrowing was high in the early 1980s. In the history of interest rates in the United States, such high real rates of interest had never persisted for such a long period of time. It is difficult to imagine strong capital expenditures and sustained economic growth in the face of high real rates of interest.

Behavior of Yields on Corporate Securities

Because of differences in default risk, marketability, maturity, and taxability, as well as because of changes in inflation expectations over time, the costs of funds to business firms vary. In Fig. 3-3 the yields on Aaa corporate bonds, Baa corporate bonds, and prime grade commercial paper are shown for the 1968–1987 period. Because of the difference in default risk, Baa bonds provide higher yield than do Aaa bonds. Moreover, this differential tends to widen during recessionary periods as investors become more risk averse. This phenomenon is particularly evident in the 1974–1975 and the 1981–1982 periods. The difference in yield between Aaa bonds and prime, short-term commercial paper issued by corporations is due primarily to differences in maturity. As reflected in the figure, short-term interest rates, as typified by the commercial paper rate, fluctuate more than do long-term rates. This fluctuation is attributable to expectations of the future course of interest rates affecting short- and long-term rates in different ways. The maturity of a short-term instrument, by definition, is near. At maturity, the investor receives the face value of the instrument, assuming there is no default. Accordingly, short-term investors are less uncertain about fluctuations in the market value of their instruments than are holders of long-term securities.

The salient point in all of this discussion is that short-term rates reflect immediate supply and demand pressures in financial markets; long-term rates are much more influenced by long-run expectations. As a result, the two sets of rates can behave differently on occasion. Over the long run, however, short and long rates tend to move in the same direction, as shown in the figure. Differences in marketability and taxability are not observable in the figure. Aaa corporate bonds are more liquid as a class than are Baa corporate bonds, and more liquid than commercial paper, because the latter is not traded in a secondary market. The interest income on all three securities is subject to taxation, so they are not different in this regard.

During the time span shown in the figure, the secular trend in interest rates was generally upward in the 1970s. Each cyclical peak in interest rates exceeded the previous interest rate peak. Most people attributed this behavior to increasing inflation expectations. In the 1980s, there was a downward trend in interest rates, which occurred once the previous inflation psychology was broken.

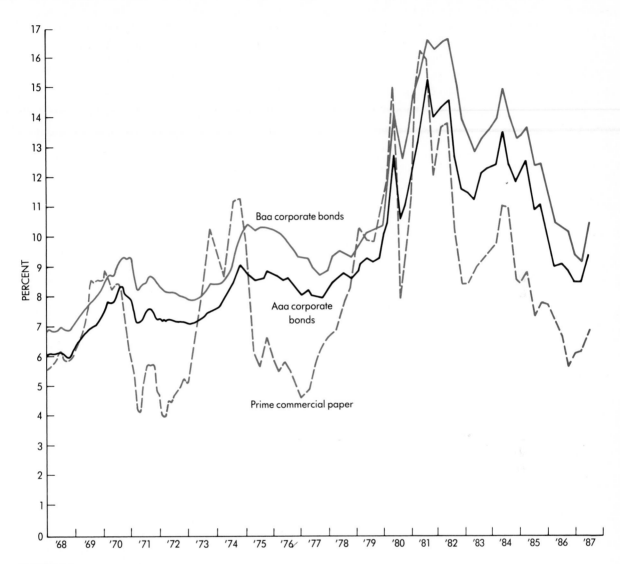

FIGURE 3-3
**Yields for Aaa corporate bonds, Baa corporate bonds,
and prime grade commercial paper, 1968–1987**

MONEY AND CAPITAL MARKETS

Different financial markets are classified according to the final maturity of the instrument involved. **Money markets** usually are regarded as including financial assets that are short term, that are highly marketable, and that have a low degree of risk. These instruments are traded in highly impersonal markets, where funds move on the basis of price and risk alone. Thus, a short-term loan negotiated between a company and a bank is not considered a money market instrument. *Cap-*

Money market. The market where short-term, safe instruments are traded. Money flows on the basis of small differences in return and risk.

ital markets include instruments with longer terms to maturity and often less liquidity. The maturity boundary that divides the money and capital markets is rather arbitrary, ranging from 1 to 5 years, depending on who is doing the classifying.

Highly sophisticated, the *money market* is composed of commercial banks as well as a number of security dealers. It is a national market, but the focus of activity is New York City. Interest rates on money market instruments are extremely sensitive to ever-changing supply and demand conditions. New information is quickly acted upon and transmitted to price. Funds transfers between buyers and sellers usually are electronic, allowing prompt settlements on transactions.

The existence of an efficient money market serves the liquidity needs of the nation. Large amounts of securities can be exchanged quickly with little concession from the previous traded price. Given this liquidity, financial institutions as well as corporations and individuals are better able to manage and plan their overall portfolios of assets. Examples of money market instruments include *Treasury bills, commercial paper, bankers' acceptances,* and *negotiable certificates of deposit.* These instruments are examined in some detail in Chapter 9, when we consider the marketable security position of the busines firm. Our purpose here is to place these instruments in perspective with respect to financial markets overall.

The *capital markets,* comprising a handful of distinctly different instruments, tend to be more varied than the money market. The market for *Treasury notes and bonds* is highly organized; dealers are strong, and the securities possess considerable marketability. The U.S. Treasury is the largest single borrower in the world and is engaged in continuous borrowing and refinancing. Because Treasury securities are free of default risk and are highly marketable, they command the lowest yield of all securities providing taxable income. The *mortgage market* has somewhat less liquidity than does that for Treasury securities. While mortgages used to be primarily local, more and more we are seeing individual residential mortgages being packaged together and sold as a security. A distinctly different capital market is the *municipal security market.* Because the interest income on a municipal bond is exempt from taxation, municipals are mainly of interest to individuals in high tax brackets and to corporations paying taxes at the full corporate tax rate. For this reason, the market for this security is segmented, and yields sometimes behave differently from those of other securities. Municipal securities have varying degrees of default risk, depending on the issuer.

Finally, the markets for *corporate bonds* and *corporate stock* are different from other capital markets. The income of corporate bonds is fully taxable, so their appeal is not to the same people who invest in municipal bonds. In general, corporate bonds are not nearly so marketable as Treasury bonds and somewhat less marketable than municipal bonds. Common stocks are evidence of ownership in a corporation, and their price behavior is substantially different from that of bonds. This behavior will be discussed in depth in Chapter 5, when we consider the valuation of corporate bonds and stocks. It is clear from our brief examination of the capital markets, however, that its instruments are much more varied than are those of the money market.

FINANCIAL INNOVATIONS AND THE CHANGING FINANCIAL ENVIRONMENT

The last 15 years have been characterized by tremendous financial innovation, first in the United States and then in Europe and the developed countries of the Far East. The listing of developments is awesome; it includes zero coupon bonds, money market preferred stock, securitization of assets, options and futures markets, interest rate swaps, interest cap loans, multicurrency loans and hedges, point-of-sale terminal transactions, and many more. These innovations encompass new or improved products as well as processes. Financial innovations do not just happen. There are reasons for their occurrence, both conceptual and environmental.

Making Markets More Efficient and/or Complete

The principal force behind any financial innovation is the profit motive. In an economic sense, a new financial product or process will be profitable only if it makes the market more *efficient* and/or *complete*. Recall from the discussion earlier in the chapter that the purpose of financial markets is to channel savings in our society to the most efficient uses. However, the intermediation process is not costless. Cost is represented by the spread between what the ultimate saver receives for funds and what the ultimate borrower pays, holding risk constant, as well as by the inconvenience to one or both parties. A financial innovation may make the market more efficient in the sense of reducing the spread, as defined, or of lowering inconvenience costs. If such occurs, the overall cost of intermediation is reduced by definition.

Market completeness is different in concept. A complete market exists when every possible demand by investors is satisfied with a distinct marketable security. With an incomplete market there is, by definition, an unfilled desire for a particular type of security on the part of an investor clientele. If the market is incomplete, it pays the firm or financial institution to exploit the opportunity by tailoring security offerings to the unsatisfied desires of investors. By so doing, a lower financing cost will be achieved. An example of satisfying an unfilled investor demand is the issuance of zero coupon bonds beginning in the early 1980s. (See Chapter 21 for details.) As long as the market remains incomplete, a firm or financial institution should continue to tailor the securities it issues to the market.

Causes of Financial Innovations

In steady state, of course, we would not expect to be able to make the market more efficient and/or complete. Presumably all opportunities for profitable exploitation would be exhausted, and no further gains would be possible. As a result, there would be no financial innovations. Indeed, an unchanging world would be marked by a lack of new financial products and/or processes. The environment simply must change for there to be exploitable opportunities with respect to inefficiencies and/or incompleteness. There are a number of causes for change, and we consider them in turn.

Volatile Inflation Rates and Interest Rates.   During the last dozen years, there has been considerable variability in inflation and in interest rates, both nominal and real. In this environment, new financial products are designed to reduce such risk. Put another way, a changing inflation and interest rate setting creates demand for different types of financial instruments. New deposit and investment accounts, floating rate loans, and loans with caps (ceilings on the maximum rate of interest paid) are examples of responses to these stimuli.

Regulatory Changes.   A second, and very important, factor prompting financial innovation is regulatory change. Beginning in the 1970s and accelerating rapidly, we have had a deregulation of the financial services industry. The boundaries that previously separated the functions of various financial institutions were broken, and the competitive arena changed dramatically. As constraints were reduced, the distinction among commercial banks, savings and loan associations, investments banks, insurance companies, mortgage bankers, large retailers, and certain financial conglomerates, such as American Express, was blurred. Institutions invaded the previously inviolable turf of others. In the mid-1980s deregulation of financial markets began to occur in Britain, France, Germany, Japan, the Netherlands, Switzerland, and some other countries. With deregulation, the market equilibration process undergoes constant perturbation.

Tax Changes.   Changes in the tax laws also lead to financial innovations. Where once major changes occurred infrequently, they are much more frequent now, with major tax legislation occurring most every year. When changes impact the after-tax returns on financial instruments, new financial products, and sometimes processes, emerge in response to the tax law change.

Technological Advances.   The computer age has brought with it a continual broadening of applications to the financial services industry and a lowering in costs per transaction. As with other industries, technology has had a profound influence. Electronic funds transfer, automatic teller machines, point-of-sale terminals, personal computers permitting in-home financial transactions, and telecommunications all have changed dramatically the way in which financial products and processes are provided and the way in which they are priced. Structurally, costs have been lowered through automation, and technology has reduced the need for bricks and mortar on the part of financial institutions. Oftentimes the accuacy and speed of a transaction are improved, which increases customer satisfaction, whether that customer is a depositor, a corporate borrower, an investor, or a corporate issuer of stock.

Economic Activity.   Finally, changes in the business cycle can prompt financial innovation. In a period of economic prosperity, there is greater incentive to offer new financial products and processes than there is in a recession. In the former period, financial institutions are eager to try new ideas in their ongoing quest for growth. In a steep recession, such as the one that occurred in 1981 and 1982, the emphasis tends to shift to risk reduction. During these times, there is an increasing preference for liquidity. While certain types of financial innovations are possible with this focus, more will occur in a period of economic prosperity, all other things being the same.

Implications for the Corporation

Thus, the impetuses for financial innovation are multifold: the level and volatility of inflation and interest rates, regulatory changes, tax changes, technological advances, and the level of economic activity. There are others, such as international developments, but we have focused on the major ones. Perhaps the overriding consideration presently is the continual adjustment to financial deregulation. Like any other industry that undergoes deregulation, such as the airline industry, aftershocks occur for many years. Expressed differently, it takes a long time before anything approaching a stable equilibrium appears.

While this chapter introduces the topic of financial innovation, we do not stop here. Indeed, we merely set the stage for many of the remaining chapters of the book. Later we learn about specific financial innovations. The fact that the environment in which capital is raised is rapidly changing requires the financial manager to remain ever vigilant. Not only do financial innovations change the cost, features, and access to certain types of financing, but they affect cash and marketable security management as well. The ability to shift risk through financial markets has expanded enormously as a result of financial innovation—options, futures, currency, and swap markets. For the most part, financial deregulation has helped the corporation, particularly the large corporation.

SUMMARY

Financial assets exist in an economy because an economic unit's investment in real assets frequently differs from its savings. An excess of investment over savings is financed by issuing a financial liability; a surplus of savings over investment in real assets is held in the form of financial assets. The purpose of financial markets is the efficient allocation of savings to ultimate users of funds.

A number of factors make financial markets efficient. Among the most important is the presence of financial intermediaries. A financial intermediary transforms the direct claim of an ultimate borrower into an indirect claim, which is sold to ultimate lenders. Intermediaries channel savings from ultimate savers to ultimate borrowers at a lower cost and with less inconvenience than is possible on a direct basis.

We can study the flow of savings from ultimate savers to ultimate borrowers through flow-of-funds data. We saw that for the economy as a whole, investment in real assets must equal savings. This is not true for individual economic units, which can have considerable divergence between savings and investment for a particular period. In considerable measure, business firms support investment in real assets through internal financing, or savings. But since business is a savings-deficit sector, it makes use of external financing as well—chiefly bond issues, stock issues, mortgage debt, and bank loans.

The greatest portion of funds received does not come directly from individuals but usually from commercial banks, life insurance companies, finance companies, pension funds, and mutual funds. In addition to these financial institutions, investment bankers and mortgage bankers are among the brokers who are valuable to a business firm. Finally, the secondary market is enhanced by the presence of strong security exchanges and an over-the-counter market.

The allocation of savings in an economy occurs primarily on the basis of expected return and risk. In turn, the overall risk of a security depends on the likelihood of default, its marketability, its maturity, the coupon rate, and certain tax considerations. In addition, expected inflation and unanticipated inflation have a major effect on all yields. Different financial instruments provide different yields over time because of variation in these factors.

Financial markets are classified into money or capital markets, depending upon their liquidity. Money markets include short-term, highly marketable financial assets with little risk. Capital markets are characterized by longer terms to maturity and much more variation among instruments with respect to marketability and default risk.

Financial innovation, where new products and processes are introduced, occurs because of the profit motive. By making financial markets more efficient and/or complete, financial innovations reward the initiator while at the same time they benefit other market participants through reduced costs and inconvenience together with greater variety of financial instruments. There are a number of causes of financial innovation: volatile inflation rates and interest rates, regulatory changes, tax changes, technological advances, and the business cycle. The financial services industry has undergone deregulation and the adjustment process is ongoing. As a result, the financial manager must keep abreast of the ever-changing environment in which capital is raised. The ideas developed in this chapter will be drawn upon in subsequent chapters.

QUESTIONS

1. What is the purpose of financial markets? How can this purpose be accomplished efficiently?
2. Discuss the functions of financial intermediaries.
3. A number of factors give rise to different interest rates or yields being observed for different types of debt instruments. What are these factors?
4. What is meant by making the financial markets more efficient? more complete?
5. What is the purpose of stock market exchanges such as the New York Stock Exchange?
6. In general, what would be the likely effect of the following occurrences on the money and capital markets?

a. The savings rate of individuals in the country declines.

b. Individuals increase their savings at savings and loan associations and decrease their savings at banks.

c. The government taxes capital gains at the ordinary income tax rate.

d. Unanticipated inflation of substantial magnitude occurs, and price levels are rising rapidly.

e. Savings institutions and lenders increase the transaction charge for savings and for making loans.

7. What are the causes for innovation in our financial markets that bring about new financial products and processes?

8. Can you name an innovation in financial instrument, institution, or practice? What is the characteristic of a financial innovation? Whom do they benefit?

9. Pick a financial intermediary with which you are familiar and explain its economic role. Does it make the financial markets more efficient?

10. What is the distinction between the money markets and the capital markets? Is the distinction real or artificial?

11. How do transaction costs affect the flow of funds and the efficiency of financial markets?

12. What are the major sources of external financing for business firms?

13. In addition to financial intermediaries, what other institutions and arrangements facilitate the flow of funds to and from business firms?

SELF-CORRECTION PROBLEMS

1. Wallopalooza Financial, Inc., believes that it can intermediate successfully in the mortgage market. Presently, borrowers pay 12 percent on adjustable rate mortgages. The deposit rate necessary to attract funds to lend is 8 percent, also adjustable with market conditions. Wallopalooza's administrative expenses, including information costs, are $2 million per annum on a base business of $100 million in loans.

    a. What interest rates on mortgage loans and on deposits would you recommend to obtain business?

    b. If $100 million in loans and an equal amount of deposits are attracted, what would be Wallopalooza's annual before-tax profit on the new business? (Assume that interest rates do not change.)

    c. In a market equilibration process, what would likely happen?

2. Suppose that 91-day Treasury bills currently yield 9 percent to maturity and that 25-year Treasury bonds yield $10\frac{1}{4}$ percent. Lopez Pharmaceutical Company recently has issued long-term, 25-year bonds that yield 12 percent to maturity.

    a. If the yield on Treasury bills is taken to be the short-term, risk-free rate, what premium in yield is required for the default risk and lower marketability associated with the Lopez bonds?

b. What premium in yield above the short-term, risk-free rate is attributable to maturity?

PROBLEMS

1. Loquat Foods Company is able to borrow at an interest rate of 12 percent for one year. For the year, market participants expect 7 percent inflation.

   a. What approximate real rate of return does the lender expect? What is the inflation premium embodied in the nominal interest rate?

   b. If inflation proves to be 4 percent for the year, does the lender suffer? Does the borrower suffer? Why?

   c. If inflation proves to be 10 percent, who gains and who loses?

2. For 19xx, suppose that the following changes in the balance sheets of business firms, households, and governments in the aggregate occur (in billions):

	BUSINESS FIRMS	HOUSEHOLDS	GOVERNMENTS
Net worth (savings)	$220	$380	−$50
Real assets	275	280	
Money	5	10	2
Other financial assets	75	215	70
Financial liabilities	135	125	122

   a. Which sectors are savings-deficit sectors? savings-surplus sectors? why?

   b. From which sector do the savings-deficit sectors finance their deficits? How is it done?

3. In Problem 2, suppose that the economy is composed of the three sectors described, along with a financial institutions sector. For the year, the change in balance sheet for *all sectors* is as follows:

	CHANGE
Net worth (savings)	$565
Real assets	565
Money	0 net ($17 use, $17 source)
Other financial assets	560
Financial liabilities	560

   a. Using a flow-of-funds matrix, derive the sources and uses of funds for the financial institutions sector on the basis of the information presented in these two problems.

   b. What are the characteristics of the financial institutions sector?

4. Companies X and Y have the following balance sheets at the latest year end (in thousands):

	COMPANY X	COMPANY Y
Cash	$ 1,000	$ 500
Receivables	7,000	2,000
Inventories	2,000	4,000
Net fixed assets	2,000	5,500
Total	$12,000	$12,000
Current liabilities	$ 2,000	$ 3,000
Long-term debt	1,000	5,000
Net worth	9,000	4,000
Total	$12,000	$12,000

a. Are the companies net monetary creditors or debtors?

b. If the rate of inflation should increase unexpectedly from 8 percent presently to 10 percent, who gains and who loses?

c. If inflation unexpectedly drops from 8 percent to 6 percent, what happens?

5. Lexalt Systems, Inc., has observed that computer-aided access to corporate bond price quotations and other information could be improved. Beare, Kelly and Zlotney, an investment banking firm, is particularly interested in an application proposed by Lexalt, as it wishes to introduce a new financial product—options on convertible bonds. To develop the necessary secondary market, information availability to market participants is critical. Beare, Kelly and Zlotney feel that the computer application and new financial product must be treated as a package, and the two parties have agreed to a joint venture. In words, what are the requisites for this innovation to succeed?

6. From a recent Monday *Wall Street Journal*, collect yield information on yields for a long-term Treasury bond, a public utility bond (probably AA in quality), municipal bonds as described by the municipal bond index, Treasury bills, and commercial paper. (This information appears at the back of the paper under the Bond Market section, the Money Market Rates section, and the Treasury Issues section.) What reasons can you give for the differences in yield on these various instruments?

SOLUTIONS TO SELF-CORRECTION PROBLEMS

1. a. At $2 million in expenses per $100 million in loans, administrative costs come to 2 percent. As a result, the deposit rate must be no more than 10 percent and the mortgage rate no less than 10 percent. Suppose that Wallopalooza wished to increase the deposit rate and lower the mortgage rate by equal amounts while earning a before-tax return

spread of 1 percent. It would then offer a deposit rate of $8\frac{1}{2}$ percent and a mortgage rate of $11\frac{1}{2}$ percent. Of course, other answers are possible, depending on your profit assumptions.

b.   1 percent of $100 million in loans equals $1 million.

c.   The intermediation spread is reduced from 4 percent to 3 percent by the entry of Wallopalooza. As both the depositor and the borrower gain, Wallopalooza will attract a lot of new business. In competitive markets, other financial institutions will respond to this price-cutting by offering the same or perhaps even lower mortgage rates and the same or higher deposit rates. As a result, Wallopalooza's gains will be checked, particularly if other institutions engage in a price war. However, consumers of financial services are well served with lower borrowing rates and higher deposit rates.

2.   a.   The premium attributable to default risk and lower marketability is $12\% - 10\frac{1}{4}\% = 1\frac{3}{4}\%$.

b.   The premium attributable to maturity is $10\frac{1}{4}\% - 9\% = 1\frac{1}{4}\%$. In this case, default risk is held constant and marketability for the most part also is held constant.

SELECTED REFERENCES

BENSTON, GEORGE, ed., *Financial Services: The Changing Institutions and Government Policy.* Englewood Cliffs, N.J.: Prentice-Hall, 1983.

CAMPBELL, TIM S., *Money and Capital Markets.* Glenview, Ill.: Scott, Foresman, 1988.

DOUGALL, HERBERT E., and JACK E. GAUMNITZ, *Capital Markets and Institutions,* 5th ed., Englewood Cliffs, N.J.: Prentice-Hall, 1985.

KAUFMAN, GEORGE G., *The U.S. Financial System: Money, Markets, and Institutions,* 3rd ed. Englewood Cliffs, N.J.: Prentice-Hall, 1987.

KIDWELL, DAVIS S., and RICHARD L. PETERSON. *Financial Institutions, Markets, and Money,* 2nd ed. Chicago: Dryden Press, 1984.

ROSE, PETER S., *Money and Capital Markets.* Plano, Tex.: Business Publications, 1986.

VAN HORNE, JAMES C., *Financial Market Rates and Flows,* 2nd ed. Englewood Cliffs, N.J.: Prentice-Hall, 1984.

_____, "Of Financial Innovations and Excesses," *Journal of Finance,* 40 (July 1985).

CHAPTER 4

Compound Interest and Present Value

Because finance is concerned with decisions involving monetary variables, and because the price of money is the interest rate, most financial decisions involve interest rate considerations. This chapter deals with the mathematics of compound interest and present value. In Chapter 1, we learned that the objective of management should be to maximize shareholder wealth and that this depended in part on the timing of cash flows. Hence, one important application of the concepts of this chapter is the valuation of a stream of cash flows. Indeed, much of the development of the book depends on notions taken up here. Although discussion obviously is mathematical in orientation, we focus on only a handful of formulas so that we may easily grasp the essentials. The examples frequently involve numbers that must be raised to the nth power, an operation that is easy with a calculator.

COMPOUND INTEREST AND TERMINAL VALUES

Compound interest. Interest earned on reinvested interest payments.

The notion of compound interest is central to understanding the mathematics of finance. The term itself merely implies that interest paid on a loan or an investment is added to the principal. As a result, interest is earned on interest. This concept can be used to solve a class of problems illustrated in the following examples.

To begin with, consider a person who has $100 in a savings account. If the interest rate is 8 percent compounded annually, how much will the $100 be worth at the end of a year? Setting up the problem, we solve for the terminal value (also known as **future value**) of the account at the end of the year (TV_1)

Future value. The value in the future of $1 invested today. Also known as terminal value.

$$TV_1 = \$100(1 + .08) = \$108$$

For a deposit of 2 years, the $100 initial deposit will become $108 at the end of the first year at 8 percent interest. Going to the end of the second year, $108 becomes $116.64, as $8 in interest is earned on the initial $100 and $.64 is earned on the $8 in interest paid at the end of the first year. In other words, interest is earned on previously earned interest, hence the name *compound interest*. Therefore, the terminal value at the end of the second year is $100 times 1.08 squared, or times 1.1664. Thus

$$TV_2 = \$100(1.08)^2 = \$116.64$$

At the end of 3 years the depositor would have

$$TV_3 = \$100(1.08)^3 = \$125.97$$

Looked at in a different way, $100 grows to $108 at the end of the first year if the interest rate is 8 percent, and when we multiply this amount by 1.08 we obtain $116.64 at the end of the second year. Multiplying $116.64 by 1.08, we obtain $125.97 at the end of the third year.

Similarly, at the end of n years the terminal value of a deposit is

$$TV_n = X_0(1 + r)^n \tag{4-1}$$

where X_0 = amount of savings at the beginning

   r = interest rate.

A calculator makes the equation very simple to use. Table 4-1, showing the terminal values for our example problem at the end of years 1 through 10, illustrates the concept of interest being earned on interest.

Equation (4-1) is our fundamental formula for calculating terminal values. Obviously, the greater the interest rate r, and the greater the number of periods n, the greater the terminal value. In Fig. 4-1 we graph the growth in terminal value for a $100 initial deposit with interest rates of 5, 10, and 15 percent. As can be seen, the greater the interest rate, the steeper the growth curve by which terminal value increases. Also, the greater the number of years during which compound interest can be earned, obviously the greater the terminal value.

Although our concern has been with interest rates, the concept involved applied to compound growth of any sort. Suppose that the earnings of a firm are $100,000, but we expect them to grow at a 10 percent compound rate. At the end of years 1 through 5 they will be as follows:

YEAR	GROWTH FACTOR	EXPECTED EARNINGS
1	(1.10)	$110,000
2	$(1.10)^2$	121,000
3	$(1.10)^3$	133,100
4	$(1.10)^4$	146,410
5	$(1.10)^5$	161,051

Similarly, we can determine the level at the end of so many years for other problems involving compound growth. The principle is particularly important when we consider certain valuation models for common stock, as we shall do in the next chapter.

TABLE 4-1
**Illustration of compound interest
with $100 initial deposit and 8 percent interest**

PERIOD	BEGINNING VALUE	INTEREST EARNED DURING PERIOD (8 PERCENT OF BEGINNING VALUE)	TERMINAL VALUE
1	$100.00	$ 8.00	$108.00
2	108.00	8.64	116.64
3	116.64	9.33	125.97
4	125.97	10.08	136.05
5	136.05	10.88	146.93
6	146.93	11.76	158.69
7	158.69	12.69	171.38
8	171.38	13.71	185.09
9	185.09	14.81	199.90
10	199.90	15.99	215.89

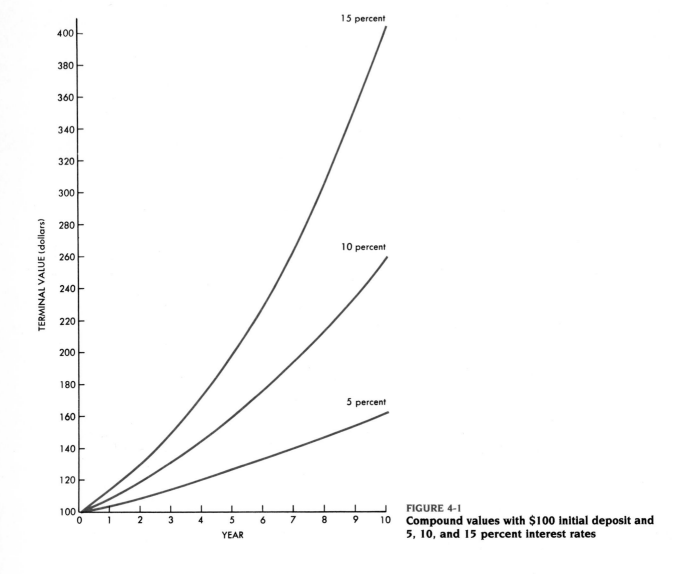

FIGURE 4-1
Compound values with $100 initial deposit and 5, 10, and 15 percent interest rates

Tables of Terminal Values

Using Eq. (4-1), we can derive tables of terminal values (also known as future values). Table 4-2 is an example showing interest rates of 1 to 15 percent. In the 8% column, we note that the terminal value shown for $1 invested at this compound rate corresponds to our calculations for $100 in Table 4-1. Notice, too, that in rows tabulating two or more years, the proportional increase in terminal value becomes greater as the interest rate rises. This heightened growth is impressive when we look a century ahead. A dollar deposited today will be worth only $2.70 if the interest rate is 1 percent, but it will fatten to $1,174,313 if the interest rate is 15 percent. Behold (or let your heirs behold) the wonders of compound interest.

TABLE 4-2
Terminal value of \$1 at the end of _n_ years

YEAR	1%	2%	3%	4%	5%	6%	7%	8%	9%	10%	12%	15%
1	1.0100	1.0200	1.0300	1.0400	1.0500	1.0600	1.0700	1.0800	1.0900	1.1000	1.1200	1.1500
2	1.0201	1.0404	1.0609	1.0816	1.1025	1.1236	1.1449	1.1664	1.1881	1.2100	1.2544	1.3225
3	1.0303	1.0612	1.0927	1.1249	1.1576	1.1910	1.2250	1.2597	1.2950	1.3310	1.4049	1.5209
4	1.0406	1.0824	1.1255	1.1699	1.2155	1.2625	1.3108	1.3605	1.4116	1.4641	1.5735	1.7490
5	1.0510	1.1041	1.1593	1.2167	1.2763	1.3382	1.4026	1.4693	1.5386	1.6105	1.7623	2.0114
6	1.0615	1.1262	1.1941	1.2653	1.3401	1.4185	1.5077	1.5869	1.6771	1.7716	1.9738	2.3131
7	1.0721	1.1487	1.2299	1.3159	1.4071	1.5036	1.6058	1.7138	1.8280	1.9487	2.2107	2.6600
8	1.0829	1.1771	1.2668	1.3686	1.4775	1.5938	1.7182	1.8509	1.9926	2.1436	2.4760	3.0590
9	1.0937	1.1951	1.3048	1.4233	1.5513	1.6895	1.8385	1.9990	2.1719	2.3579	2.7731	3.5179
10	1.1046	1.2190	1.3439	1.4802	1.6289	1.7908	1.9672	2.1589	2.3674	2.5937	3.1058	4.0456
11	1.1157	1.2434	1.3842	1.5395	1.7103	1.8983	2.1049	2.3316	2.5804	2.8531	3.4785	4.6524
12	1.1268	1.2682	1.4258	1.6010	1.7959	2.0122	2.2522	2.5182	2.8127	3.1384	3.8960	5.3503
13	1.1381	1.2936	1.4685	1.6651	1.8856	2.1329	2.4098	2.7196	3.0658	3.4523	4.3635	6.1528
14	1.1495	1.3195	1.5126	1.7317	1.9799	2.2609	2.5785	2.9372	3.3417	3.7975	4.8871	7.0757
15	1.1610	1.3459	1.5580	1.8009	2.0789	2.3966	2.7590	3.1772	3.6425	4.1772	5.4736	8.1371
20	1.2202	1.4859	1.8061	2.1911	2.6533	3.2071	3.8697	4.6610	5.6044	6.7275	9.6463	16.3665
25	1.2824	1.6406	2.0938	2.6658	3.3864	4.2919	5.4274	6.8485	8.6231	10.8347	17.0001	32.9190
50	1.6446	2.6916	4.3839	7.1067	11.4674	18.4201	29.4570	46.9016	74.3575	117.3907	289.0022	1,083.6574
100	2.7048	7.2446	19.2186	50.5049	131.5010	339.3014	867.7149	2,199.7569	5,529.0304	13,780.5890	83,522.2657	1,174,313.4510

51

In 1790 John Jacob Astor bought approximately an acre of land on the east side of Manhattan Island for $58. Astor, who was considered a shrewd investor, made many such purchases. How much would his descendants have in 1990 if, instead of buying the land, Astor had invested the $58 at 6 percent compound interest? In Table 4-2 we see that $1 compounded at an interest rate of 6 percent is worth $339.30 in 100 years. Therefore, the value of $1 in 200 years is simply

$$\$1 \times 339.30 \times 339.30 = \$115,124.49.$$

As the land was purchased for $58, we have a value of

$$\$58 \times 115,124.49 = \$6,677,220.42$$

in 1990 at a compound interest rate of 6 percent. This translates into a value of about $153 a square foot.

Compound Value With Uniform Payments or Receipts

Consider now a situation in which an individual makes an initial deposit but adds to it a given amount at the end of each period. Continuing with our earlier example, suppose the initial deposit is $100 and the compound annual interest rate 8 percent, but the individual adds to it $50 per year. At the end of 1 year the terminal value will be

$$TV_1 = \$100(1.08) + \$50 = \$158$$

At the end of 2 years it would be

$$TV_2 = \$158(1.08) + \$50 = \$220.64$$

Although we could calculate the terminal value at the end of any period in this step-by-step manner, a more general formula is available for solution of the problem. It is

$$TV_n = \left(X_0 + \frac{x}{r}\right)(1 + r)^n - \frac{x}{r} \tag{4-2}$$

where x is the increment added each period. For the example just given, the terminal value at the end of 2 years would be

$$TV_2 = \left(\$100 + \frac{\$50}{.08}\right)(1.08)^2 - \frac{\$50}{.08}$$

$$= (\$100 + \$625)(1.1664) - \$625$$

$$= \$220.64$$

which, of course, is the same as calculated before. The terminal value at the end of 5 years would be

$$TV_5 = (\$100 + \$625)(1.08)^5 - \$625$$

$$= \$440.26$$

The formula in Eq. (4-2) is complicated, but it has widespread applicability. With the use of a calculator and with care to detail, one should have no difficulty. Remember that there is such a formula, but do not memorize it.

Annuity Contracts

An **annuity** can be defined as a series of uniform receipts occurring over a specified number of years, which result from an initial deposit. Figure 4-2 shows the cash-flow sequence for an annuity. An initial deposit is followed by a series of equal withdrawals over a given period of time. In our illustration we have as-

Annuity. A series of equal payments for a specified period of time.

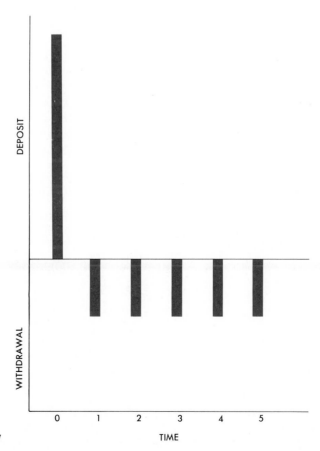

FIGURE 4-2
Cash flow of an annuity

sumed 5 years. Total withdrawals over the 5 years exceed the initial deposit because of the presence of compound interest.

Let us imagine that you inherit $10,000 and wish to have a steady income over the next 10 years. A life insurance company sells annuities that will pay you, or your beneficiary if you should die, a fixed dollar amount annually for 10 years. The insurance company calculates the amount of distribution on the basis of a 5 percent return. What is the annual amount it will pay? Referring to Eq. (4-2), the terminal value at the end of 10 years would be zero, as everything would be paid out. We know also that X_0 is $10,000, r is .05, and n is 10. Therefore, we must solve for x, which we know will be negative, as it is a withdrawal. Setting the problem up in this manner, we have

$$0 = \left(\$10,000 - \frac{x}{.05}\right)(1.05)^{10} + \frac{x}{.05}$$

$$= (\$10,000 - 20x)(1.628894) + 20x$$

$$32.57788x - 20x = 16,288.94$$

$$12.57788x = 16,288.94$$

$$x = \$1,295.05$$

Thus, you are able to obtain $1,295.05 per year for 10 years with an annuity.

Reversing our earlier problem, we also are able to determine the amount of initial deposit or balance that is necessary to afford a person a withdrawal of a certain amount over so many years. You may want to be able to withdraw $5,000 per year over the next 10 years. If a savings institution pays 8 percent per annum, how much will you need to deposit for this to happen? In this case, x in Eq. (4-2) is −$5,000. At the end of 10 years there will be no terminal value, so $TV_n = 0$. With an interest rate of 8 percent, we have

$$0 = \left(X_0 - \frac{\$5,000}{.08}\right)(1.08)^{10} + \frac{\$5,000}{.08}$$

where we wish to solve for X_0. We have

$$0 = (X_0 - \$62,500)(2.1589) + \$62,500$$

$$2.1589X_0 = \$72,431$$

$$X_0 = \$33,550$$

Therefore, $33,550 must be deposited initially in order for the annuity to pay $5,000 at the end of each of the next 10 years.

Compounding More Than Once a Year

Up to now, we have assumed that interest was paid annually. It is easiest to work with this assumption. Now we consider the relationship between terminal value and interest rates for different periods of compounding. To begin, suppose that interest were paid semiannually. If one then deposited $100 in a savings account at 8 percent, the terminal value at the end of 6 months would be

$$TV_{1/2} = \$100\left(1 + \frac{.08}{2}\right) = \$104.00$$

In other words, at the end of one-half year one would receive 4 percent in interest, not 8 percent. At the end of a year the terminal value of the deposit would be

$$TV_1 = \$100\left(1 + \frac{.08}{2}\right)^2 = \$108.16$$

This amount compares with $108.00 if interest were paid only once a year. The $.16 difference is attributable to the fact that during the second 6 months, interest is earned on the $4.00 in interest paid at the end of the first 6 months. The more times during a year that interest is paid, the greater the terminal value at the end of a given year.

The general formula for solving for the terminal value at the end of year n where interest is paid m times a year is

$$TV_n = X_0\left(1 + \frac{r}{m}\right)^{mn} \tag{4-3}$$

To illustrate, suppose that in our previous example interest were paid quarterly and that we wished again to know the terminal value at the end of 1 year. It would be

$$TV_1 = \$100\left(1 + \frac{.08}{4}\right)^4 = \$108.24$$

which, of course, is higher than it would have been with semiannual or annual compounding.

The terminal value at the end of 3 years for the example with quarterly interest payments is

$$TV_3 = \$100\left(1 + \frac{.08}{4}\right)^{12} = \$126.82$$

compared to a terminal value with semiannual compounding of

$$TV_3 = \$100\left(1 + \frac{.08}{2}\right)^6 = \$126.53$$

and with annual compounding of

$$TV_3 = \$100\left(1 + \frac{.08}{1}\right)^3 = \$125.97$$

Thus, the more frequently each year interest is paid, the greater the terminal value. In the appendix to this chapter we show how to determine terminal value when interest is compounded continuously. As m in Eq. (4-3) increases, terminal value increases at a decreasing rate until ultimately it approaches that achieved with continuous compounding. With continuous compounding, for example, the terminal value for our example problem is $127.12.

In summary, then, the terminal value of $100 at the end of 3 years with an 8 percent interest rate under various compounding intervals is as follows:[1]

COMPOUNDING	TERMINAL VALUE
Annual	$125.97
Semiannual	126.53
Quarterly	126.82
Monthly	127.02
Continuous	127.12

We see that as the compounding interval shortens, terminal value increases but at a decreasing rate. The limit is continuous compounding. In order to attract deposits by paying a higher effective interest rate, many financial institutions have shortened their compounding period. In fact, certain institutions compound continuously.

To Double Your Money!

Several rules of thumb apply to compound interest and doubling your money over a particular period of time. One is the rule of 72: Divide 72 by the interest rate to find the number of years it will take you to double your money. If the interest rate on time deposits is 4 percent and you deposit $1 now, it will take roughly 18 years to double your money. If the interest rate is 6 percent, the number of years becomes 12; if 8 percent, 9 years. Referring to Table 4-2, we see that for annual compounding, $1 at a 6 percent rate is worth $2.01 in 12 years, and at an 8 percent rate it is worth $2.00 in 9 years. Therefore, the rule of 72 seems to give reasonable answers.

Indeed, for most interest rates one encounters, the rule of 72 gives a good approximation of the number of years required to double your money, but the answer is not exact. At 2 percent interest, the rule tells us our money will double in 36 years. In fact, our money will double in 35 years. At 24 percent interest, the rule tells us that we will double our money in 3 years. In fact, it will take a bit longer—3.2 years with annual compounding. Also, when interest is paid more than once a year, it will take somewhat less time to double our money than with annual compounding. With quarterly compounding it will take 11.6 years to double our money if the interest rate is 6 percent as opposed to 11.9 years with annual compounding. (The rule of 72 tells us 12 years.)

[1] With monthly compounding, m in Eq. (4-3) is 12, and mn is 36.

Another rule of thumb is the 7–10 rule. This rule tells us that our money will double in 10 years at 7 percent interest and in 7 years at 10 percent interest. Turning to Table 4-2, we see that with annual compounding, $1 is worth $1.97 at the end of 10 years at an interest rate of 7 percent, whereas it is worth $1.95 at the end of 7 years at an interest rate of 10 percent. However, with quarterly compounding, $1 at the end of 10 years at 7 percent interest is worth

$$TV_{10} = \$1\left(1 + \frac{.07}{4}\right)^{40} = \$2.002$$

and $1 at the end of 7 years at 10 percent interest is worth

$$TV_7 = \$1\left(1 + \frac{.10}{4}\right)^{28} = \$1.996$$

Therefore, the rule of 7–10 gives accurate results if the compounding interval is quarterly, but only approximate results if it is annual.

Both of these rules of thumb are useful to remember. They allow you to make certain compound interest approximations in your head. Not only can you estimate the number of years it will require to double your money at a given interest rate, but also the interest rate required in order to double your money in a given number of years.

PRESENT VALUES

Having considered compound interest, we now are ready to take up **present values.** In any economy in which capital has value, a dollar today is worth more than a dollar to be received 1 year, 2 years, or 3 years from now. Therefore, we need a means for standardizing differences in timing of cash flows so that the time value of money is properly recognized. Calculating the present value of future cash flows allows us to isolate differences in the timing of these cash flows.

Present value. The discounted value of future cash flow(s).

Perhaps you will be given an opportunity to receive, with complete certainty, $1,000 at the end of each of the next 2 years. If your opportunity cost of funds is 8 percent per annum, what is this proposal worth to you today? We might begin by asking, What amount today would grow to be $1,000 at the end of 1 year at 8 percent interest? In calculating the terminal value in the preceding section, we multipled the initial deposit by (1 + r), where r is the rate of interest, to obtain the terminal value. In this case, we are given the terminal value as well as the required interest rate and must solve for the appropriate beginning value. Consequently, we divide the terminal value by the required rate of interest—an operation known as *discounting*. For our example, the present value of $1,000 to be received at the end of 1 year is

$$PV = \frac{\$1,000}{(1.08)} = \$925.93$$

Similarly, the present value of $1,000 to be received at the end of 2 years is

$$PV = \frac{\$1,000}{(1.08)^2} = \$857.34$$

Thus, $1,000 received 2 years from now has a lower present value than $1,000 received 1 year from now. That is the whole idea of the time value of money. Overall, then, the opportunity is worth $925.93 + $857.34 = $1,783.27 to us today.

In solving present-value problems, it is useful to express the interest factor separate from the amount to be received in the future. For example, our problem involving $1,000 to be received at the end of 2 years can be expressed as

$$PV = \$1,000 \left[\frac{1}{(1.08)^2} \right] = \$857.34$$

Discount rate.   The rate of interest used to determine the present value of future cash flow(s).

In this way we are able to isolate the interest factor, and this isolation facilitates present-value calculations. In such calculations, the interest rate is known as the **discount rate**. The general formula for finding the present value of X_n to be received at the end of year n where k is the discount rate is

$$PV = X_n \left[\frac{1}{(1 + k)^n} \right] \tag{4-4}$$

Note that Eq. (4-4) for discounting is simply the reciprocal of the formula for finding the terminal value, Eq. (4-1), of x dollars so many years hence.

Figure 4-3 illustrates the present value of $100 received from 1 through 10 years in the future with discount rates of 5, 10, and 15 percent. This graph shows that the present value of $100 decreases by a decreasing rate the farther in the future it is to be received. The greater the interest rate, of course, the lower the present value but also the more pronounced the curve. At a 15 percent discount rate, $100 to be received 10 years hence is worth only $24.72 today.

For an annuity involving a series of uniform receipts for a specified number of periods, the present value of the stream is

$$PV = \sum_{t=1}^{m} \frac{X}{(1 + k)^t} \tag{4-5}$$

where m is the number of periods over which receipts of X occur at the end of each period and Σ denotes the sum of discounted receipts at the end of period 1 through period m. If $1,000 were expected at the end of each of the next 2 years and the discount rate were 8 percent, we would have

$$PV = \frac{\$1,000}{(1.08)} + \frac{\$1,000}{(1.08)^2} = \$925.93 + \$857.34 = \$1,783.27$$

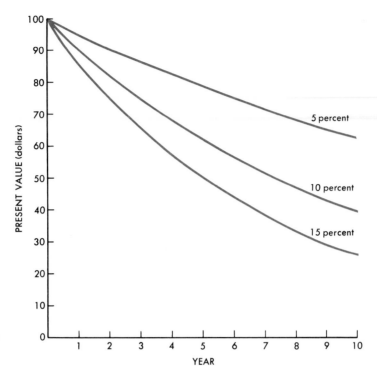

FIGURE 4-3
Present values with
$100 cash flow and 5,
10, and 15 percent
discount rates

Construction of Present-Value Tables

Fortunately, one does not have to calculate present values by hand using Eq. (4-4). Present-value tables allow us easily to determine the present value of $1 received so many years from now at such and such a rate. To illustrate the construction of such a table, we make a few calculations using a discount rate of 10 percent. Suppose we wish to know the present value of $1 to be received 1 year from today. The formula is

$$PV = \frac{1}{(1 + .10)} = .90909$$

Similarly, if we wish to know the present value of $1 received 2 years from today, the formula is

$$PV = \frac{1}{(1 + .10)^2} = \frac{1}{1.21} = .82645$$

A present-value table relieves us of making these calculations every time we have a problem to solve; it is shown in Table A in the appendix at the end of the book. We see in the table that for a 10 percent discount rate, the discount factors for 1 and 2 years in the future are .90909 and .82645, respectively—just as we calculated by hand.

If we had an uneven series of cash flows—$1 one year hence, $3 two years hence, and $2 three years from now—the present value of this series, using a 10 percent discount rate, would be

PV of $1 to be received at the end of 1 year $1(.90909) = $0.90909

PV of $3 to be received at the end of 2 years $3(.82645) = 2.47935

PV of $2 to be received at the end of 3 years $2(.75131) = 1.50262

Present value of series = $4.89106

With a present-value table, we are able to calculate the present value for any series of future cash flows in the above manner.

The procedure can be simplified for a series if the cash flows in each future period are the same, that is, for an annuity. Suppose that in a series of future cash flows, $1 is to be received at the end of each of the next 3 years. The calculation of the present value of this stream, using the procedure just given, is

PV of $1 to be received in 1 year = $0.90909

PV of $1 to be received in 2 years = 0.82645

PV of $1 to be received in 3 years = 0.75131

Present value of series = $2.48685

Discount factor. The present value of $1 received so many periods in the future.

With an even series of future cash flows, it is unnecessary to go through these calculations. The **discount factor,** 2.48685, can be applied directly. Simply multiply $1 by 2.48685 to obtain $2.48685.

Present-value tables for even series of cash flows allow us to look up the appropriate compound discount factor (see Table B in the appendix at the end of the book). We note that the discount factor for an even series of cash flows for 3 years, using a 10 percent discount rate, is 2.4868, as we calculated. Thus, for an even series of cash flows, we simply multiply the appropriate discount factor times the cash flow.

Use of Tables

Using the present-value Tables A and B in the appendix to this book, we are able to calculate the present value of various future streams of cash flows. If we trace across any of the rows in Tables A and B, we see that the higher the discount rate, the lower the discount factor. It is not a linear relationship, because the discount factor decreases less and less as the discount rate increases. Therefore, the present value of an amount of money to be received in the future decreases at a decreasing rate as the discount rate increases. The relationship is illustrated in Fig. 4-3. At a zero rate of discount, the present value of $1 to be received in the future is $1. In other words, there is no time value of money. As the discount rate increases, however, the present value declines but at a decreasing rate. As the discount rate approaches infinity, the present value of the future $1 approaches zero.

As an additional illustration of the use of these tables, suppose that we wished to determine the present value of $500 to be received at the end of 1 year, $400 to be received at the end of 2 years, $300 to be received at the end of 3 years, and $200 to be received at the end of years 4 through 10, all at a discount rate of 12 percent. Here we have an uneven series for the first 3 years and an even series, or annuity, for years 4 through 10. Consequently, we use Table A for the first series and Table B for the second. For the first series, the present value is

PV of $500 at the end of 1 year—$500(.89286) = $446.43

PV of $400 at the end of 2 years—$400(.79719) =   318.88

PV of $300 at the end of 3 years—$300(.71178) =   213.53

$978.84

For the second series, the annuity begins not at time 0, but at the beginning of the fourth year. Referring to Table B, we calculate the present value of an annuity of 10 years and subtract from it the present value of an annuity of 3 years to obtain the present value of an annuity from years 4 through 10.

PV of $200 for 10 years—$200(5.6502) = $1,130.04

PV of $200 for 3 years—$200(2.4018) =   480.36

$ 649.68

Thus, the present value of the whole series is

PV of uneven series = $978.84

PV of annuity =   649.68

$1,628.52

A wide variety of present-value problems could be illustrated. To appreciate this variety, be sure to do the problems at the end of this chapter.

With most calculators it is possible to solve for present and terminal values, either directly or indirectly. The more sophisticated calculators have built-in functions, so one can solve directly. Otherwise one must make calculations for each cash flow and store them in memory. In addition to calculators, computer-based spreadsheet programs have present- and terminal-value functions built into them that allow solution of the number inputted. There still are occasions when it is easier to use the tables, however, and that is the reason for our attention to them here.

Present Value When Interest Is Compounded
More Than Once a Year

When interest is compounded more than once a year, the formula for calculating present values must be revised along the same lines as for the calculation of terminal value. Instead of dividing the future cash flow by $(1 + k)^n$ as we do when annual compounding is involved, we determine the present value by

$$PV = \frac{x_n}{\left(1 + \dfrac{k}{m}\right)^{mn}} \qquad (4\text{-}6)$$

where, as before, x_n is the cash flow at the end of year n, m is the number of times a year interest is compounded, and k is the discount rate. The present value of $100 to be received at the end of year 3, the discount rate being 10 percent compounded quarterly, is

$$PV = \frac{\$100}{\left(1 + \dfrac{.10}{4}\right)^{(4)(3)}} = \$74.36$$

On the other hand, if the discount rate is compounded only annually, we have

$$PV = \frac{\$100}{(1.10)^3} = \$75.13$$

Thus, the fewer times a year the discount rate is compounded, the greater the present value. This relationship is just the opposite of that for terminal values. In the appendix to this chapter, we show how to calculate present values when interest is compounded continuously. To illustrate the relationship between present value and the number of times a year the discount rate is compounded, consider again our example involving $100 to be received at the end of 3 years with a discount rate of 10 percent. The following present values result from various compounding intervals.[2]

COMPOUNDING	PRESENT VALUE
Annual	$75.13
Semiannual	74.62
Quarterly	74.36
Monthly	74.17
Continuous	74.08

We see that present value decreases but at a decreasing rate as the compounding interval shortens, the limit being continuous compounding.

While it is important to understand discounting where interest is compounded more than once a year, all of the present-value calculations in this book will involve annual compounding. However, the reader should be able to adjust any of the discount calculations undertaken for compounding more than once a year.

---

[2] For semiannual compounding, m is 2 in Eq. (4-6) and mn is 6. With monthly compounding, m is 12 and mn is 36.

Solving for the Number of Periods

In the preceding section we solved for the present value, given the interest rate, number of periods, and cash flows. In this section we wish to solve for the number of periods given the other three variables. To illustrate such a problem, suppose that for $10,000 you can acquire an asset that will generate cash inflows of $2,000 at the end of each year until it becomes obsolete, after which no more cash flows are generated and the asset has no salvage value. If the opportunity cost of funds is 18 percent, how long must the asset last to be a worthwhile investment? In this case, we have an annuity producing $2,000 a year. Setting up the problem, we have

$$\$10,000 = \frac{\$2,000}{(1.18)} + \frac{\$2,000}{(1.18)^2} + \cdots + \frac{\$2,000}{(1.18)^n}$$

We must determine that value of n where the cumulative sum on the right-hand side of the equation equals $10,000. To do so, we first divide the amount of the investment, $10,000, by the annual cash flow, $2,000, and obtain 5.0. When we go to Table B in the appendix at the back of the book, we find that for 18 percent the discount factor is 5.0081 for 14 years, whereas it is 4.9095 for 13 years. Therefore, the asset must last nearly 14 years if it is to be a worthwhile investment.

AMORTIZING A LOAN

Certain loans require the repayment of both interest and principal in a series of equal installments. Examples include mortgage loans, automobile loans, and some business loans. A bank may make you an $80,000 loan at 15 percent interest to be repaid in 10 equal annual installments. From the bank's standpoint, the cash-flow stream represents an annuity with a cash outflow at time 0, followed by a series of even annual cash inflows. The amount of annual payment may be calculated by solving the following equation for x:

$$\$80,000 = \sum_{t=1}^{10} \frac{x}{(1.15)^t} \tag{4-7}$$

Looking under the 15 percent column in Table B in the appendix at the back of the book, we see that the discount factor for an even stream of cash flows for 10 years is 5.0188. Therefore, we have

$$\$80,000 = 5.0188x$$

$$x = \$15,940$$

Thus, $15,940 is the annual payment necessary to pay off the loan in 10 years and return the lender 15 percent. In Table 4-3, the loan **amortization** schedule is shown. The interest payment is based on the amount owed at the beginning of the year. In the first year, it is 15 percent of $80,000, or $12,000. The principal

Amortization. The installment repayment schedule on a loan necessary to pay it off eventually.

TABLE 4-3
Loan amortization schedule (rounded to nearest dollar)

END OF YEAR	PAYMENT	INTEREST	PRINCIPAL REPAYMENT	REMAINING PRINCIPAL AMOUNT OWING
1	$15,940	$12,000	$ 3940	$76,060
2	15,940	11,409	4,531	71,529
3	15,940	10,729	5,211	66,318
4	15,940	9,948	5,992	60,326
5	15,940	9,049	6,891	53,435
6	15,940	8,015	7.925	45,510
7	15,940	6,826	9,114	36,396
8	15,940	5,459	10,481	25,915
9	15,940	3,887	12,053	13,862
10	15,941	2,079	13,862	0

payment in the first year is $15,940 − $12,000, or $3,940. Therefore, the balance owing at the end of the year is $80,000 − $3,940 = $76,060, and this becomes the base on which the interest payment in the second year is calculated: $76,060 × 0.15 = $11,409. And so the process goes through successive iterations through year 10. Note that in the early years, the payment is composed largely of interest, whereas at the end it is mainly **principal.** This relationship reflects the decline in interest as the principal amount is paid down. Similar to present-value tables, mortgage payment tables allow one to look up the amount of payment required.

Principal.   The amount of money that must be repaid on a loan, exclusive of interest payments. The par value of a bond at issuance.

SUMMARY

Mastering the concept of compound interest and growth is fundamental to understanding much of what goes on in financial management. In an economy where capital has value, interest rates are positive, and these rates must be embodied in any analysis involving future payments or receipts. In this chapter we considered the determination of terminal, or compound, values, as well as the determination of present values.

The terminal value, or future value, at the end of year n for an initial deposit of X_0 that grows at a compound annual rate r is

$$TV = X_0(1 + r)^n$$

This basic formula may be modified to take account of payment of interest more than once a year by

$$TV = X_0\left(1 + \frac{r}{m}\right)^{mn}$$

The greater the number of times a year interest is paid, the greater the terminal value.

We may also determine the terminal value when there are uniform payments or receipts over n years. Where receipts are involved, the situation is known as an *annuity*. Rules of thumb can be used to approximate the time required for one to double one's money, given a particular compound rate of interest.

The second major concept we considered was the determination of the present value of a future cash flow. It can be expressed as

$$PV = \frac{x_n}{(1 + k)^n}$$

where x_n is a cash flow at the end of year n and k is the discount rate or interest rate required. As in the previous case, this formula may be modified for compounding more than once a year. We proceeded to show how present-value tables are constructed and used. Also, we considered how to solve for n, given the other three variables in the present-value equation. Finally, we showed how a loan may be amortized with equal installment payments and how to solve for the correct annual payment. Many of the concepts presented in this chapter will be used throughout the book, so a mastery of them is important.

APPENDIX
Continuous Compounding

In practice, interest sometimes is compounded continuously. Certain valuation models in finance also employ continuous compounding. Therefore, it is useful to consider how it works. Recall from the chapter that the general formula for solving for the terminal value at the end of year n is

$$TV_n = X_0\left(1 + \frac{r}{m}\right)^{mn} \qquad (4A\text{-}1)$$

where X_0 = the initial deposit
$\quad r$ = the interest rate
$\quad m$ = number of times a year interest is paid.

If interest were compounded daily on the basis of a 365-day year, the terminal value of an X_0 initial deposit at the end of n years would be

$$TV_n = X_0\left(1 + \frac{r}{365}\right)^{365n}$$

As m approaches infinity, the term $(1 + r/m)^{mn}$ approaches e^{rn}, where e is approximately 2.71828 and is defined as

$$e = \lim_{m \to \infty} \left(1 + \frac{1}{m} \right)^m \tag{4A-2}$$

where ∞ is the sign for infinity. To see that e approaches 2.71828 as m increases, simply increase m in Eq. (4A-2) from, say, 5 to 10 to 20 and solve for e. The terminal value at the end of n years of an initial deposit of X_0 where interest is compounded continuously at a rate of r is

$$TV_n = X_0 e^{rn} \tag{4A-3}$$

For our earlier example problem, the terminal value at the end of 3 years would be

$$TV_3 = \$100(2.71828)^{(.08)(3)} = \$127.12$$

This compares with a terminal value with annual compounding of

$$TV_3 = \$100(1.08)^3 = \$125.97$$

Continuous compounding results in the maximum possible terminal value at the end of n periods for a given rate of interest.

When interest is compounded continuously, the present value of a cash flow at the end of year n is

$$PV = \frac{X_n}{e^{rn}} \tag{4A-4}$$

The present value of \$1,000 to be received at the end of 10 years with a discount rate of 20 percent compounded continuously is

$$PV = \frac{\$1,000}{2.71828^{(.20)(10)}} = \$135.34$$

We see then that present-value calculations involving continuous compounding are merely the reciprocal of terminal-value calculations. While continuous compounding results in the maximum possible terminal value, it results in the minimum possible present value.

QUESTIONS

1. What is compound interest? Why is it important?
2. What kinds of personal financial decisions have you made that involve compound interest?
3. In calculating the terminal value, we multiply by 1 plus the interest rate to the nth power, whereas to calculate the present value we divide by this

amount. If the initial deposit and cash flow were $100, would the present value be the reciprocal of the terminal value?

4. What is an annuity? Is it worth more or less than a lump sum received now equal to the sum of the annuity payments?

5. What type of compounding would you prefer in your savings account? Why?

6. Contrast the calculation of terminal value with the calculation of present value. What is the difference?

7. What is the advantage of present-value tables over hand calculations?

8. If you were to receive a sum of money 5 years hence but wished to sell your contract for its present value, which type of compounding would you prefer? Why?

9. In order to solve for the number of periods in a present-value situation, what do you need to know?

10. The 7–10 rule of thumb suggests that an amount will double in 7 years at a 10 percent compound annual rate or double in 10 years at a 7 percent annual rate. Is this a useful rule and is it an accurate one?

11. Does present value decrease at a linear rate, at an increasing rate, or at a decreasing rate with the discount rate? Why?

12. Does present value decrease at a linear rate, at an increasing rate, or at a decreasing rate with the length of time in the future the payment is to be received? Why?

13. Toby Belch (of Shakespearean fame) is 35 years old and is presently experiencing the good things in life. As a result, he anticipates he will increase his weight at a rate of 3 percent a year. Presently he weighs 200 pounds. What will he look like at age 60?

SELF-CORRECTION PROBLEMS

1. The following cash-flow streams need to be analyzed:

CASH-FLOW STREAM	YEAR				
	1	2	3	4	5
1	$100	$200	$200	$300	$ 300
2	600	—	—	—	—
3	—	—	—	—	1,200
4	200	—	500	—	300

a. Calculate the total terminal value of each stream at the end of year 5 with an interest rate of 10 percent.

b. Compute the present value of each stream if the discount rate is 14 percent.

2. Sally Ronk is considering two different savings plans. The first plan would have her deposit $500 every 6 months, and she would receive interest at a 7 percent annual rate, compounded semiannually. Under the second plan she would deposit $1,000 every year with a rate of interest of $7\frac{1}{2}$ percent, compounded annually. The initial deposit with plan 1 would be made 6 months hence and with plan 2 one year hence.

   a. What is the terminal value of the first plan at the end of 10 years?
   b. What is the terminal value of the second plan at the end of 10 years?
   c. Which plan should Ronk use, assuming that her only concern is with the value of her savings at the end of 10 years?
   d. Would your answer change if the rate of interest on the second plan were 7 percent?

3. On a contract you have a choice of receiving $25,000 six years from now or $50,000 twelve years hence. What is the implied discount rate that equates these two amounts?

4. Toby Markovich wishes to purchase an annuity contract that will pay him $7,000 a year for the rest of his life. Sierra Nevada Life Insurance Company figures that his life expectancy is 21 years, based on its actuary tables. The company imputes an interest rate of 6 percent in its annuity contracts.

   a. How much will Markovich have to pay for the annuity?
   b. How much would he have to pay if the interest rate were 8 percent?

5. You borrow $10,000 at 14 percent for 4 years. The loan is repayable in four equal installments at year ends.

   a. What is the annual payment that will completely amortize the loan over 4 years? (You may wish to round to the nearest dollar.)
   b. Of each payment, what is the amount of interest? the amount of principal?

PROBLEMS

1. The following are exercises in terminal values:

   a. At the end of 3 years, how much is an initial deposit of $100 worth, assuming an annual interest rate of (i) 10 percent? (ii) 100 percent? (iii) 0 percent?
   b. At the end of 5 years, how much is an initial $500 deposit plus annual $100 payments worth, assuming an annual interest rate of (i) 10 percent? (ii) 5 percent? (iii) 0 percent?
   c. At the end of 3 years, how much is an initial $100 deposit worth, assuming a quarterly compounded interest rate of (i) 10 percent? (ii) 100 percent?
   d. Why does your answer to part c differ from that to part a?
   e. At the end of 10 years, how much is a $100 initial deposit worth, assuming an interest rate of 10 percent compounded (i) annually? (ii) semiannually? (iii) quarterly? (iv) continuously? (See the appendix.)

2. The following are exercises in present values:

   a. $100 at the end of 3 years is worth how much today, assuming a discount rate of (i) 10 percent? (ii) 100 percent? (iii) 0 percent?

   b. What is the aggregate present value of $500 received at the end of each of the next 3 years, assuming a discount rate of (i) 4 percent? (ii) 25 percent?

   c. $100 is received at the end of 1 year, $500 at the end of 2 years, and $1,000 at the end of 3 years. What is the aggregate present value of these receipts, assuming a discount rate of (i) 4 percent? (ii) 25 percent?

   d. $1,000 is to be received at the end of 1 year, $500 at the end of 2 years, and $100 at the end of 3 years. What is the aggregate present value of these receipts assuming a discount rate of (i) 4 percent? (ii) 25 percent?

   e. Compare your solutions in 2c with those in 2d and explain the reason for the differences.

3. Joe Hernandez has inherited $25,000 and wishes to purchase an annuity that will provide him with a steady income over the next 12 years. He has heard that the local savings and loan association is currently paying 6 percent on an annual basis. If he were to deposit his funds here, how much would he be able to withdraw annually (to the nearest dollar)?

4. You need to have $50,000 at the end of 10 years. To accumulate this sum, you have decided to save a certain amount at the end of each of the next 10 years and deposit it in the bank. The bank pays 8 percent interest compounded annually for long-term deposits. How much will you have to save each year (to the nearest dollar)?

5. Joel Dunway wishes to borrow $10,000 for 3 years. A group of individuals agrees to lend him this amount if he contracts to pay them $18,000 at the end of the 3 years. What is the implicit annual interest rate to the nearest percentage?

6. You have been offered a note with 4 years to maturity, which will pay $3,000 at the end of each of the 4 years. The price of the note to you is $10,200. What is the implicit interest rate you will receive to the nearest percentage?

7. Sales of the P. J. Cramer Company were $500,000, and they are expected to grow at a compound rate of 20 percent for the next 6 years. What will be the sales at the end of each of the next 6 years?

8. The H & L Bark Company is considering the purchase of a scraping machine that is expected to provide cash flows as follows:

YEAR	1	2	3	4	5	6	7	8	9	10
Cash flow	$1,200	$2,000	$2,400	$1,900	$1,600	$1,400	$1,400	$1,400	$1,400	$1,400

If the appropriate discount rate is 14 percent, what is the present value of this cash-flow stream?

9. Suppose you were to receive $1,000 at the end of 10 years. If your opportunity rate is 10 percent, what is the present value of this amount if interest is compounded annually? compounded quarterly? compounded continuously? (See the appendix.)

10. In connection with the Bicentennial, the U.S. Treasury once contemplated offering a savings bond for $1,000, which would be worth $1 million in 100 years. Would such a large increase in value be possible if the interest rate were only around 7 percent?

11. Patricia Van Auken is a prospective buyer of an apartment building on leased land. At the end of 20 years, the land and the building revert to the lessor with no terminal value to the buyer. Annual rentals on the building are expected to be $126,000, while maintenance and other cash expenses are expected to average $60,000 per year. If Van Auken's opportunity cost of funds is 13 percent, what is the maximum price she should pay for the building?

12. Selyn Cohen is 63 years old and recently retired. He wishes to provide retirement income for himself and is considering an annuity contract with Monument Life Insurance Company. Such a contract pays him an equal amount each year he lives. For this cash-flow stream, he must put up so much money at the beginning. According to actuary tables, his life expectancy is 15 years, and that is the duration on which the insurance company bases its calculations regardless of how long he actually lives.

    a. If Monument Life uses an interest rate of 5 percent in its calculations, what must Cohen pay at the outset for an annuity providing him $10,000 per year? (Assume that annual payments are at the end of each of the 15 years.)

    b. What would be the purchase price if the interest rate were 10 percent?

    c. If Cohen had $30,000 to put into an annuity, how much would he receive each year if the insurance company used a 5 percent interest rate in its calculations? a 10 percent rate?

13. The Happy Hang Glide Company is purchasing a building and has obtained a $190,000 mortgage loan for 20 years. The loan bears an interest rate of 17 percent and calls for equal annual installment payments at the end of each of the 20 years. What is the amount of the annual payment?

14. Establish loan amortization schedules for the following loans to the nearest cent (see Table 4-3 for an example):

    a. A 36-month loan of $8,000 with equal installment payments at the end of each month. The interest rate is 1 percent per month.

    b. A 25-year mortgage loan of $184,000 with equal installment payments at the end of each year. The interest rate is 10 percent per annum.

15. You have borrowed $14,300 at an interest rate of 15 percent. You feel you will be able to make annual payments of $3,000 per year on your loan. (Payments include both principal and interest.) How long will it be before the loan is entirely paid off (to the nearest year)?

16. Barquez Mines, Inc., is considering investing in Peru. It makes a bid to the government to participate in the development of a mine, the profits of which will be realized at the end of 5 years. The mine is expected to pro-

duce $5 million in cash to Barquez at that time. Other than the bid at the outset, no other cash flows will occur, as the government will reimburse the company for all costs. If Barquez requires a return of 20 percent, what is the maximum bid it should make for the participation right if interest is compounded (a) annually? (b) semiannually? (c) quarterly? (d) continuously?

SOLUTIONS TO SELF-CORRECTION PROBLEMS

1. a. Terminal value of each cash flow and total future value of the stream:

CASH-FLOW STREAM	YEAR					TOTAL TERMINAL VALUE
	1	2	3	4	5	
1	$146.41	$266.20	$242	$330	$ 300	$1,284.61
2	878.46	—	—	—	—	878.46
3	—	—	—	—	1,200	1,200.00
4	292.82	—	605	—	300	1,197.82

  b. Present value of each cash flow and total present value of the stream:

CASH-FLOW STREAM	YEAR					TOTAL PRESENT VALUE
	1	2	3	4	5	
1	$ 87.72	$153.89	$134.99	$177.62	$155.81	$710.03
2	526.31	—	—	—	—	526.31
3	—	—	—	—	623.24	623.24
4	175.44	—	337.49	—	155.81	668.74

2. a. TV plan 1 $= \dfrac{(\$500)}{.035}(1.035)^{20} - \dfrac{\$500}{.035} = \$14{,}139.82$

  b. TV plan 2 $= \dfrac{(\$1{,}000)}{.075}(1.075)^{10} - \dfrac{\$1{,}000}{.075} = \$14{,}147.08$

  c. Plan 2 would be preferred by a slight margin.

  d. TV plan 2 $= \dfrac{(\$1{,}000)}{.07}(1.07)^{10} - \dfrac{\$1{,}000}{.07} = \$13{,}816.44$

   Plan 1 now would be preferred.

3. $50,000/$25,000 = 2.0 or a doubling in 6 years. The reciprocal of this is .50. In Table A in the appendix at the back of the book the discount factor for 12 percent is .50663 and that for 13 percent is .48032. Interpolating, we have

$$12\% + \left(\frac{.50663 - .50000}{.50663 - .48032}\right) = 12.25\%$$

as the interest rate implied in the contract in going from the end of year 6 to the end of year 12.

4. Solving for x, we have

$$x = \sum_{t=1}^{21} \frac{\$7{,}000}{(1.06)^t} = \$7{,}000(11.7640) = \$82{,}348$$

$$x = \sum_{t=1}^{21} \frac{\$7{,}000}{(1.08)^t} = \$7{,}000(10.0168) = \$70{,}118$$

5. a.

$$\$10{,}000 = \sum_{t=1}^{4} \frac{x}{(1.14)^t}$$

$$\$10{,}000 = 2.9137x$$

$$x = \frac{\$10{,}000}{2.9137} = \$3{,}432$$

b.

END OF YEAR	INSTALLMENT	PRINCIPAL AMOUNT AT YEAR END	ANNUAL INTEREST	PRINCIPAL PAYMENT
0	—	$10,000	—	—
1	$3,432	7,968	$1,400	$2,032
2	3,432	5,652	1,116	2,316
3	3,432	3,011	791	2,641
4	3,432	0	421	3,011

SELECTED REFERENCES

CISSELL, ROBERT, HELEN CISSELL, and DAVID C. FLASPOHLER, *Mathematics of Finance*, 6th ed. Dallas: Houghton Mifflin, 1982.

JOHNSON, RAMON, *Financial Valuation and Analysis*. Dubuque, Iowa: Kendall/Hunt, 1981.

KEMENY, JOHN G., ARTHUR SCHLEIFER, JR., J. LAURIE SNELL, and GERALD L. THOMPSON, *Finite Mathematics with Business Applications*, 2nd ed. Englewood Cliffs, N.J.: Prentice-Hall, 1972.

VICHAS, ROBERT P., *Handbook of Financial Mathematics, Formulas, and Tables*. Englewood Cliffs, N.J.: Prentice-Hall, 1979.

CHAPTER 5

The Valuation of Securities

In the last chapter we investigated the wonders of compound interest as well as the time value of money. We now are able to apply these concepts to the valuation of different securities. By *valuation* we mean the process by which the market price of a security is determined. In particular, we are concerned with the valuation of bonds, preferred stocks, and common stocks, though the principles discussed apply to other financial instruments as well. These principles will underlie much of the later development of the book. Because the major decisions of a company are all related in their effect on valuation, we must understand how investors value the financial instruments of a company.

VALUATION IN GENERAL

A key factor in the valuation of any financial instrument is an implied positive relationship between risk and expected return. It has been shown that investors overall dislike risk. As a result, they must be offered additional expected return for taking greater risk. Assume for purposes of illustration that you are among investors who concentrate on some common holding period—say, one year. The return from holding a security is simply the change in market price, plus any cash payments received from the company, divided by the beginning price. You might buy a security for $100 that paid $7 in cash to you and was worth $106 one year hence. The return would be ($7 + $6)/$100 = 13 percent. Assume further that you are concerned with what we shall call *unavoidable risk*, the risk that cannot be avoided by diversification of the securities you hold. In other words, if you invest in a number of securities, some of the individual security risks cancel out. What is left over we call the unavoidable risk. Much more will be said about this later in the chapter; for now, our purpose is to illustrate a simple but fundamental concept.

   If investors overall are averse to risk, there exists a relationship between the return they expect from holding a security and its unavoidable risk. This relationship, known as the **security market line**, is illustrated in Fig. 5-1. The expected 1-year return is shown on the vertical axis, and unavoidable risk is on the

Security market line. The market equilibrium linear trade-off between expected return and systematic risk.

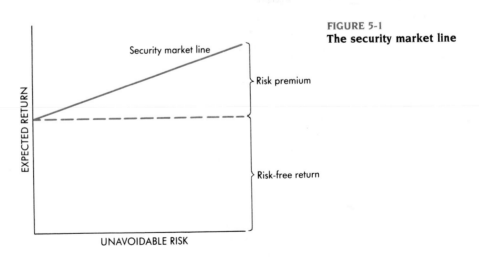

FIGURE 5-1
The security market line

horizontal. At zero risk, the security market line has an intercept on the vertical axis at a positive expected rate of return. As no risk is involved, this rate is known as the *risk-free rate*. As risk increases, the required rate of return increases in the manner depicted. Thus, there is a positive relationship between risk and expected return, which, as we shall see, governs the valuation of marketable securities.[1]

The slope of the security market line tells us the degree to which investors are risk averse. The steeper the slope, the more averse they are to risk. If investors were not at all averse to risk, the security market line would be horizontal. In other words, they would require the same expected return on Treasury securities as they would on the securities of the most speculative of companies. As this equality of expected returns is not the case, we shall assume that the line has a positive slope.

Changes in Security Market Line

We must be alert to the fact that the security market line depicts the trade-off between expected return and unavoidable risk at a particular moment. This line can change over time with changes in interest rates and investor psychology. For one thing, the risk-free rate is expressed in nominal terms; that is, it is not adjusted for inflation. As we discussed in Chapter 3, the nominal rate of interest can be thought of as composed of the real rate of interest plus a premium for inflation. Suppose for purposes of illustration that the nominal risk-free rate is 4 percent. Now if there were an unanticipated burst in inflation, the nominal rate might increase to 7 percent. As a result, the security market line would shift upward. This shift might be depicted by the graph in the upper panel of Fig. 5-2. Note that the line shifts upward by a given amount throughout.

In the lower panel of the figure we show a hypothetical change in investor psychology from pessimism regarding the economy to optimism. Note here that the slope of the security market line decreases, as opposed to a shift throughout. The same expected return as before is required for a risk-free security. However, lower returns are required for all risky securities; the greater the unavoidable risk, the lower the return required relative to the pessimistic period. Thus, we must allow for the fact that the relationship between risk and expected return is not necessarily stable. The degree of risk aversion of the market can and does change over time. With these general valuation concepts in mind, we are able to explore in more detail the valuation of specific types of securities.

FIXED-INCOME SECURITIES

A fixed-income security is one that pays a stated amount of money to the investor each period until it is retired by the issuing company. Before we can understand the valuation of such securities, certain terms must be discussed. For

---

[1] The concepts underlying the security market line will be explored in more depth in the latter part of this chapter when we take up the valuation of common stocks.

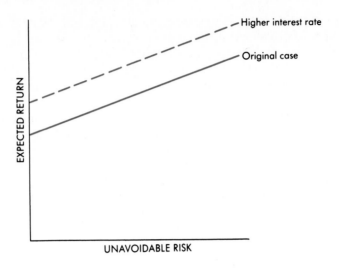

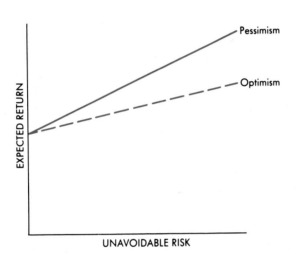

FIGURE 5-2
Security market line with changes in interest rates and investor psychology

Face value. The stated value of an asset, such as the face value of a bond being $1,000.

Coupon rate. The stated rate of interest on an instrument; the annual interest payment divided by the instrument's face value.

one thing, the instrument has a stated **face value**. This value is almost always $1,000 per bond and usually $50 or $100 per share of preferred stock. The bond also has a stated *maturity*, which is the time when the company must pay the holder the face value of the instrument. Preferred stock, on the other hand, has no stated maturity; like common stock, it is perpetual. Finally, the **coupon rate of interest** is stated, and it is paid each year. If the coupon rate is 12 percent on a $1,000 face value bond, the company pays the holder $120 each year until the bond matures. Remember that the terms of a fixed-income security are established at the time it is originally issued and cannot be changed.

Bond Valuation

Bond. A long-term debt instrument.

The terms of a **bond** call for the payment of a stated amount of interest over a given number of years, at the conclusion of which the face value of the instrument must be paid. The value of the instrument can be viewed as simply the present value of this cash-flow stream. The valuation equation for a bond that pays interest at the end of the year and has a face value of $1,000 is

$$P = \frac{C}{(1 + k)} + \frac{C}{(1 + k)^2} + \cdots + \frac{C}{(1 + k)^n} + \frac{\$1,000}{(1 + k)^n} \qquad (5\text{-}1)$$

where P is the present value of the payment stream, C is the annual interest payment as given by the coupon rate, n is the number of years to final maturity, and k is the required rate of return, given its risk. The latter is also known as the *yield to maturity*.

We may wish to determine the market price necessary for a bond with a 12 percent coupon and 10 years to maturity to provide a return of 14 percent. The coupon rate corresponds to interest payments of $120 a year. Therefore

$$P = \frac{\$120}{(1.14)} + \frac{\$120}{(1.14)^2} + \cdots + \frac{\$120}{(1.14)^{10}} + \frac{\$1,000}{(1.14)^{10}}$$

Referring to Table B in the appendix at the back of the book, we find that the present-value discount factor for 10 years of annual payments at a 14 percent discount rate is 5.2161. From Table A in the appendix to this book, we find under the 14 percent column that the discount factor for a single payment 10 years in the future is .26974. Therefore, the value, P, of the bond is

PERIOD	PAYMENT	DISCOUNT FACTOR	PRESENT VALUE
1–10	$ 120	5.2161	$625.93
10	1,000	.26974	269.74
		Value of bond =	$895.67

Expressed differently, the value of the bond is simply the sum of the present value of the stream of future interest payments plus the present value of the final payment at maturity.

If, instead of 12 percent, the bond provided only a 10 percent return, the valuation equation would become

$$P = \frac{\$120}{(1.10)} + \frac{\$120}{(1.10)^2} + \cdots + \frac{\$120}{(1.10)^{10}} + \frac{\$1,000}{(1.10)^{10}}$$

Looking up the appropriate discount factors in Tables A and B in the appendix at the back of the book, we find the following:

PERIOD	PAYMENT	DISCOUNT FACTOR	PRESENT VALUE
1–10	$ 120	6.1446	$ 737.35
10	1,000	.38554	385.54
		Value of bond =	$1,122.89

In this case, the value of the bond is in excess of its $1,000 face value, whereas before it was less than its face value.

Behavior of Bond Values.   On the basis of these examples, a number of observations can be made concerning the valuation of bonds.

Discount bond.   A bond whose market value is less than its face value.

Premium bond.   A bond whose market value is greater than its face value.

1. When the required rate of return is more than the stated coupon rate, the value of the bond will be *less* than its face value. Such a bond is said to be selling at a **discount.**
2. When the required rate of return is less than the stated coupon rate, the value of the bond will be *greater* than its face value. Such a bond is said to be selling at a **premium.**
3. When the required rate of return equals the stated coupon rate, the value of the bond will be equal to its face value.
4. If interest rates rise so that the required rate of return increases, the bond will decline in value. If interest rates fall, it will increase in value.

A further relationship, not apparent from the previous examples, needs to be illustrated separately.

5. For a given change in required return, the value of a bond will change by a greater amount, the longer its maturity.[2]

To illustrate, consider a 5-year bond with annual interest payments of $120 a year and a required rate of return of 14 percent. Its valuation is

$$P = \frac{\$120}{(1.14)} + \frac{\$120}{(1.14)^2} + \cdots + \frac{\$120}{(1.14)^5} + \frac{\$1,000}{(1.14)^5} = \$931.34$$

which is determined in the same manner as illustrated before. Suppose now that interest rates fall so that the required rate of return is 10 percent. The value of the bond now is

$$P = \frac{\$120}{(1.10)} + \frac{\$120}{(1.10)^2} + \cdots + \frac{\$120}{(1.10)^5} + \frac{\$1,000}{(1.10)^5} = \$1,075.82$$

The increase in value for the bond is $1,075.82 − $931.34 = $144.48. Yet this illustration is exactly the same as our earlier one except for a maturity of 10 years instead of 5. In the former example, the bond increased in value from $895.67 to $1,122.89. The absolute increase was $227.22. Thus, the change in value accompanying a decline in the required rate of return is greater for a 10-year bond than for a 5-year bond.

Similarly, one is able to take other maturities and demonstrate that, in general, the longer the maturity, the greater the price fluctuation associated with a given change in yield. One can think of the face value of $1,000 serving as an an-

---

[2] For bonds selling at a discount with very long maturities, it is possible for prices to change by a lesser amount, the longer the maturity. This occurrence is unusual, so we shall not discuss it further. The interested reader may look into Michael H. Hopewell and George G. Kaufman, "Bond Price Volatility and Term to Maturity," *American Economic Review*, 63 (September 1973), 749–53.

chor. The closer it is to being realized, the less important are interest payments in determining the market price, and the less important is a change in required return on the market price of the security. In general, then, the longer the maturity of a bond, the greater the risk of price change to the investor when changes occur in the overall level of interest rates.

One last relationship also needs to be illustrated separately, and it is related to the maturity question.

6. For a given change in required return, the value of a bond will change by more proportionally, the lower its coupon rate.

Going back to our previous example for a 10-year maturity and a 12 percent coupon rate, recall that the price increased by $227.22 when the required return went from 14 percent to 10 percent. This translates into a percentage increase of $227.22/$895.67 = 25.4%. Now consider what happens if the coupon rate is 4 percent. The valuation of a 10-year, 4 percent coupon bond with a required rate of return of 14 percent is

$$P = \frac{\$40}{(1.14)} + \frac{\$40}{(1.14)^2} + \cdots + \frac{\$40}{(1.14)^{10}} + \frac{\$1,000}{(1.14)^{10}} = \$478.39$$

Notice how sizable the discount needs to be when the coupon rate is low. If, as before, the required rate of return falls to 10 percent, the value of the bond becomes

$$P = \frac{\$40}{(1.10)} + \frac{\$40}{(1.10)^2} + \cdots + \frac{\$40}{(1.10)^{10}} + \frac{\$1,000}{(1.10)^{10}} = \$631.33$$

The increase in value is $631.33 - $478.39 = $152.94. Percentagewise, this translates into an increase of $152.94/$478.39 = 32.0%.

This percentage is higher than the 25.4 percent increase that occurred for the 12 percent coupon bond. With low coupons, the total income stream (interest and principal payments) is farther to realization than it is with high coupons. The farther in the future the income stream, the greater the present value effect of a change in required return.[3] Thus, the lower the coupon rate and the longer the maturity of a bond, the greater its volatility with changing interest rates in the capital markets.

Semiannual Compounding of Interest. Most bonds pay interest twice a year as opposed to annually. As a result, it is necessary to modify Eq. (5-1) as follows:

$$P = \frac{C/2}{\left(1 + \dfrac{k}{2}\right)} + \frac{C/2}{\left(1 + \dfrac{k}{2}\right)^2} + \cdots + \frac{C/2}{\left(1 + \dfrac{k}{2}\right)^{2n}} + \frac{\$1,000}{\left(1 + \dfrac{k}{2}\right)^{2n}} \tag{5-2}$$

[3] The interested reader is referred to James C. Van Horne, *Financial Market Rates and Flows*, 2nd ed. (Englewood Cliffs, N.J.: Prentice-Hall, 1984), chaps. 5 and 6.

where P is the present market price of the bond, C is the annual coupon payment, n is the number of years to maturity, and k is the required return or yield to maturity. Because of semiannual compounding, the annual coupon rate is divided by two, and the total periods to maturity is found by multiplying the years to maturity by two.

To illustrate, if the 10 percent coupon bonds of UB Corporation have 12 years to maturity and the current market price is $960 per bond, Eq. (5-2) becomes

$$\$960 = \frac{\$50}{\left(1 + \dfrac{r}{2}\right)} + \frac{\$50}{\left(1 + \dfrac{r}{2}\right)^2} + \cdots + \frac{\$1,050}{\left(1 + \dfrac{r}{2}\right)^{24}}$$

When we solve for r, we find the yield to maturity of the bond to be 10.60 percent.

If interest on a bond is paid quarterly or monthly, Eq. (5-2) can be modified in keeping with our discussion in the previous chapter; however, most bonds issued today have semiannual interest payments. Rather than having to solve for value by hand, we can turn to bond value tables. Given the maturity, coupon rate, and yield, we can look up the market price. Similarly, given any three of these four factors, we can look up the fourth. Also, some specialized calculators are programmed to compute bond values and yields, given the inputs mentioned. You will want to turn to these tools when working with bonds.

Perpetual Bonds and Preferred Stock

Perpetuity. An investment that promises a fixed cash payment forever.

It is possible to have a security that is a **perpetuity**. The British consol, a bond issued in the early nineteenth century with no maturity date, carries the obligation of the British government to pay a fixed coupon perpetually. If an investment promises a fixed annual payment of C forever, its present value is

$$P = \frac{C}{k} \tag{5-3}$$

Here k is the yield required on a perpetual investment. Suppose we could buy a security that paid $50 a year forever. If the appropriate yield, k, were 12 percent, the market value of the security would be

$$P = \frac{\$50}{.12} = \$416.67$$

Preferred stock. Stock that promises a fixed divident but at the discretion of the board of directors. Claim on assets after all debt holders, but before common stockholders.

Preferred stock is a fixed-income security in the sense that it specifies a fixed dividend to be paid at regular intervals. The features of this financial instrument are discussed in Chapter 23. While virtually all preferred stock issues have a call feature and many are eventually retired, they have no maturity as such. Therefore, they can be treated as perpetuities when it comes to valuation. Thus, we have

$$P = \frac{D}{k} \qquad\qquad (5\text{-}4)$$

where P is the market price, D is the stated dividend per share, and k is the appropriate discount rate. If Hi-Lo Corporation had a 9 percent, $100 par value preferred stock issue outstanding where the appropriate yield was 14 percent, its value per share would be

$$P = \frac{\$9}{.14} = \$64.29$$

Appropriate Return for a Fixed-Income Security

As has been illustrated in several instances, the valuation of a fixed-income security simply involves capitalizing interest payments or preferred stock dividends, using an appropriate discount rate. This rate can be thought to be composed of the risk-free rate plus a premium for risk. Thus

$$k = i + \theta \qquad\qquad (5\text{-}5)$$

where i = risk-free rate
$\quad\theta$ = risk premium.

If the security involved were a Treasury bill, there would be no risk of default, and we would expect θ to approximate zero.[4] Fixed-income securities of corporations obviously possess greater default risk than do Treasury bills. Therefore, there must exist a risk premium. The risk involved varies according to the company. Moreover, the financial instruments of an individual company possess more or less risk, depending on their maturity, whether they are secured, and so forth. All of this is in keeping with our discussion in Chapter 3 of the reasons that different interest rates prevail in the financial markets.

If we assume that investors overall are concerned with unavoidable risk, as described in the opening section of this chapter, the appropriate discount rate can be approximated by use of the security market line. Given the degree of risk, one traces up to the security market line in Fig. 5-1, then over to the vertical axis to obtain the appropriate required rate of return. Similar securities, such as 30-year bonds issued by electric utilities and rated Aa, will cluster at approximately the same degree of risk and, accordingly, require about the same rate of return. The risk associated with 5-year bonds of General Electric, however, will be considerably less than that associated with, say, the preferred stock of a new company in the electronics industry.

Our discussion of risk has been general, but it is possible to measure un-

---

[4] Even with Treasury bills, there are fluctuations in market price caused by changes in interest rates. Moreover, there is uncertainty about the return available upon reinvestment at maturity if one's holding period is longer than the maturity of the instrument. Nonetheless, Treasury bills are thought to represent a good proxy for the risk-free rate.

avoidable risk and, as a result, approximate the required rate of return. As the work in this regard has been concerned primarily with the valuation of common stocks, we have deferred its illustration to the subsequent section. In closing, it is appropriate to stress that the same concepts that apply to the valuation of fixed-income securities apply also to the valuation of common stocks.

VALUATION OF COMMON STOCKS

The theory surrounding the valuation of common stocks has undergone profound change during the last two decades. It is a subject of considerable controversy, and no one method for valuation is universally accepted. Still, in recent years there has emerged growing acceptance of the idea that individual common stocks should be analyzed as a part of a total portfolio of common stocks the investor might hold. In other words, investors are not so concerned with whether a particular stock goes up or down as they are with what happens to the overall value of their portfolios. We shall explore the valuation of common stocks in a portfolio context later in this section. First, however, we need to take up what is meant by the return to the common stock investor.

Dividends and Capital Gains

If an investor's holding period were 1 year, most of us would agree that the return on investment in a common stock would be the sum of cash dividends received plus the selling price, all over the purchase price, minus one. More formally, the one-period return is

$$r = \frac{\text{Dividends} + \text{Ending Price}}{\text{Beginning price}} - 1 \tag{5-6}$$

On your next birthday, someone may give you a share of DSS Corporation worth $50 a share. The company is expected to pay a $2 dividend at the end of the year, and its market price after the payment of the dividend is expected to be $55 a share. Your expected return will be

$$k = \frac{\$2 + \$55}{\$50} - 1 = 14 \text{ percent}$$

Solving for the Return.   Another way to solve for the expected return is to set the problem up as follows:

$$\$50 = \frac{\$2}{(1 + k)} + \frac{\$55}{(1 + k)}$$

In this formulation, we are interested in solving for the rate of return, k, which will equate the present value of the dividend and the terminal value at the end of year 1 with the beginning value. We want to determine the discount factor that, when multiplied by $2 plus $55, will equal the beginning value of $50. If we start with a discount rate of 14 percent, we find in Table A in the appendix at the back of the book that the discount factor for 1 year is .87719. Therefore, the present value of the amounts to be received at the end of the year is .87719 × $55 = $50, or the exact value of the stock at the beginning of the year. Therefore, the expected return is 14 percent.

Now suppose that, instead of holding the security 1 year you intend to hold it 2 years and sell it at the end of that time. Moreover, you expect the company to pay a $3 dividend at the end of year 2 and the market price of the stock to be $60 after this dividend is paid. Your expected return can be found by solving the following equation for k:

$$\$50 = \frac{\$2}{(1 + k)} + \frac{\$3}{(1 + k)^2} + \frac{\$60}{(1 + k)^2}$$

Here solving for k is more difficult. Suppose we start with two discount rates, 14 and 15 percent, because we have a "feel" from the numbers that the return will be somewhat higher than the 14 percent calculated before. Using these discount rates and Table A, we find

YEAR	DISCOUNT RATE	DISCOUNT FACTOR	CASH FLOW	PRESENT VALUE
1	14%	.87719	$ 2	$ 1.754
2	14	.76947	63	48.477
			Total	$50.231
1	15%	.86957	$ 2	$ 1.739
2	15	.75614	63	47.637
			Total	$49.376

As the beginning value of $50 lies between these two total present-value figures, we know that the expected return falls between 11 and 12 percent. To approximate the actual rate, we interpolate as follows:

	DISCOUNT RATE	PRESENT VALUE
	14%	$50.231
	15	49.376
Difference	1%	.855

$$\frac{\$.231}{\$.855} = .27 \qquad 14\% + .27\% = 14.27\%$$

Thus, the rate of return necessary to equate the present value of the expected dividends and terminal value with the beginning value is approximately 14.27 percent. With trial and error then, we can solve for the expected return on a particular investment. With practice, a person can come surprisingly close in selecting the discount rates from which to begin. Fortunately, computer programs and even special calculators exist for solving for the rate of return, and these eliminate the need for the calculations just illustrated.

Multiple-Year Holding Period Returns.   For general purposes, the return formula for a 2-year holding period can be expressed as

$$P_0 = \sum_{t=1}^{2} \frac{D_t}{(1 + k)^t} + \frac{P_2}{(1 + k)^2} \tag{5-7}$$

where P_0 is the market price at time 0; D_t is the expected dividend at the end of period t; Σ denotes the sum of discounted dividends at the end of periods 1 and 2; and P_2 is the expected terminal value at the end of period 2.

If an investor's holding period were 10 years, the expected rate of return would be determined by solving the following equation for k:

$$P_0 = \sum_{t=1}^{10} \frac{D_t}{(1 + k)^t} + \frac{P_{10}}{(1 + k)^{10}} \tag{5-8}$$

The investor might be a perpetual trust fund, and the trustee expects to hold the stock forever. In this case, the expected return would consist entirely of cash dividends and perhaps a liquidating dividend. Thus, the expected rate of return would be determined by solving the following equation for k:

$$P_0 = \sum_{t=1}^{\infty} \frac{D_t}{(1 + k)^t} \tag{5-9}$$

where ∞ is the sign for infinity.

Are Dividends the Foundation?

It is clear that the intended holding period of different investors will vary greatly. Some will hold stock only a few days; others might expect to hold it forever. Investors with holding periods shorter than infinity expect to be able to sell the stock in the future at a price higher than they paid for it. This assumes, of course, that at that time there will be investors willing to buy it. In turn, these investors will base their judgments of what the stock is worth on expectations of future dividends and future terminal value beyond that point. That terminal value will depend on the willingness of other investors at that time to buy the stock. The price they are willing to pay will depend on their expectations of dividends and terminal value. And so the process goes through successive investors.

Note that the total cash return to all successive investors in a stock is the sum of distributions by the company, whether they be regular cash dividends, liquidating dividends, or share repurchases. (See Chapter 18 for a discussion of share repurchase as part of an overall dividend decision.) Thus, cash distributions are all that stockholders as a whole receive from their investment; they are all the company pays out. Consequently, the foundation for the valuation of common stock must be dividends. These are construed broadly to mean any cash distribution to shareholders, including share repurchases.

The logical question to be raised at this time is, Why do the stocks of companies that pay no dividends have positive, often quite high values? The answer is that investors expect to sell the stock in the future at a price higher than they paid for it. Instead of a dividend income plus terminal value, they rely only on the terminal value. In turn, terminal value will depend on the expectations of the marketplace at the end of the horizon period. The ultimate expectation is that the firm eventually will pay dividends, either regular or liquidating ones, and that future investors will receive a cash return on their investment. In the interim investors are content with the expectation that they will be able to sell the stock at a subsequent time, because there will be a market for it. In the meantime, the company is reinvesting earnings and, everyone hopes, enhancing its future earning power and ultimate dividends.

DIVIDEND DISCOUNT MODELS

We saw in Eq. (5-9) that the expected return on investment is the rate of discount that equates the present value of the stream of expected future dividends with the current market price of the stock. Dividend discount models are designed to compute this implied stock return under specific assumptions as to the expected growth pattern of future dividends. Merrill Lynch, First Boston, and a number of other investment banks routinely publish such calculations for a large number of stocks, based on their particular model and security analysts' estimates of future earnings and dividend payout ratios. In what follows we examine such models, beginning with the simplest one.

Perpetual Growth Model

If dividends of a company are expected to grow at a constant rate, the calculation of the implied return is an easy matter. If this constant rate is g, Eq. (5-9) becomes

$$P_0 = \frac{D_0(1 + g)}{(1 + k)} + \frac{D_0(1 + g)^2}{(1 + k)^2} + \cdots + \frac{D_0(1 + g)^\infty}{(1 + k)^\infty} \qquad (5\text{-}10)$$

where D_0 is the present dividend per share. Thus, the dividend expected in period n is equal to the most recent dividend times the compound growth factor, $(1 + g)^n$.

Assuming that k is greater than g, Eq. (5-10) can be expressed as[5]

$$P_0 = \frac{D_1}{k - g} \tag{5-11}$$

Rearranging, the expected return becomes

$$k = \frac{D_1}{P_0} + g \tag{5-12}$$

The critical assumption in this valuation model is that dividends per share are expected to grow perpetually at a compound rate of g. For many companies, this assumption may be a fair approximation of reality. To illustrate the use of Eq. (5-12), suppose that A & G Company's dividend per share at $t = 1$ was expected to be $4, that it was expected to grow at a 6 percent rate forever, and that the appropriate discount rate was 14 percent. The market price would be

$$P_0 = \frac{\$4}{.14 - .06} = \$50$$

For companies in the mature stage of their life cycle, the perpetual growth assumption is not unreasonable.

Conversion to a Price/Earnings Ratio.   If we use the perpetual growth model, we can easily go from dividend valuation, Eq. (5-11), to price/earnings ratio valuation. Suppose a company retained a constant portion of its earnings each year, call it b. The dividend payout ratio (dividends per share divided by earnings per share) also would be constant.

$$1 - b = \frac{D_1}{E_1} \tag{5-13}$$

---

[5] If we multiply both sides of Eq. (5-10) by $(1 + k)/(1 + g)$ and subtract Eq. (5-10) from the product, we obtain

$$\frac{P_0(1 + k)}{(1 + g)} - P_0 = D_0 - \frac{D_0(1 + g)^\infty}{(1 + k)^\infty}$$

Because k is greater than g, the second term on the right side will be zero. Consequently

$$P_0\left[\frac{1 + k}{1 + g} - 1\right] = D_0$$

$$P_0\left[\frac{(1 + k) - (1 + g)}{1 + g}\right] = D_0$$

$$P_0[k - g] = D_0(1 + g)$$

$$P_0 = \frac{D_1}{k - g}$$

where E_1 is earnings per share in period 1. Equation (5-11) can be expressed as

$$P_0 = \frac{(1 - b)E_1}{r - g} \qquad (5\text{-}14)$$

Rearranging, this becomes

$$\frac{P_0}{E_1} = \frac{(1 - b)}{r - g} \qquad (5\text{-}15)$$

where P_0/E_1 is the price/earnings ratio based on expected earnings in period 1. In our earlier example, suppose A & G Company had a retention rate of 40 percent. Therefore

$$\frac{P_0}{E_1} = \frac{(1 - .40)}{.13 - .07} = 10 \text{ times}$$

Growth Phases

When the pattern of expected growth is such that a perpetual growth model is not appropriate, modifications of Eq. (5-10) can be used. A number of valuation models are based on the premise that the growth rate will taper off eventually. The transition might be from a present above-normal growth rate to one that is considered normal. If dividends per share were expected to grow at a 10 percent compound rate for 5 years and thereafter at a 6 percent rate, Eq. (5-10) would become

$$P_0 = \sum_{t=1}^{5} \frac{D_0(1.10)^t}{(1 + k)^t} + \sum_{t=6}^{\infty} \frac{D_5(1.06)^{t-5}}{(1 + k)^t} \qquad (5\text{-}16)$$

Note that the growth in dividends in the second phase uses the expected dividend in period 5 as its foundation. Therefore, the growth-term exponent is $t - 5$, which means that in period 6 it is 1, in period 7 it is 2, and so forth. If the current dividend, D_0, were \$2 per share and the required rate of return, k, were 14 percent, we would solve for P_0 in the following manner:

END OF YEAR	DIVIDEND		PRESENT VALUE OF DIVIDEND AT 14 PERCENT
1	$2(1.10) = \$2.20$	×	$.87719 = \$1.93$
2	$2(1.10)^2 = 2.42$	×	$.76947 = 1.86$
3	$2(1.10)^3 = 2.66$	×	$.67497 = 1.80$
4	$2(1.10)^4 = 2.93$	×	$.59208 = 1.73$
5	$2(1.10)^5 = 3.22$	×	$.51937 = \underline{1.67}$

Present value of dividends: first five years $= \$8.99$

Dividend at the end of year 6 $= \$3.22 (1.06) = \$3.41$

Market value at the end of year 5 $= \dfrac{D_6}{k - g} = \dfrac{\$3.41}{.14 - .06} = \$42.63$

Present value of \$42.63 at the end of year 5 $= \$42.63 \times .51937 = \$22.14$

$P_0 = \$8.99 + \$22.14 = \$31.13$

The transition from an above-normal to a normal rate of growth could be specified as more gradual than the rate just calculated. We might expect dividends to grow at a 10 percent rate for 5 years, followed by an 8 percent rate for the next 5 years and a 6 percent growth rate thereafter. The more growth segments that are added, the more closely the growth in dividends will approach a curvilinear function. But even Microsoft cannot grow at an above-normal rate forever. Typically, companies tend to grow at a very high rate initially, after which their growth opportunities slow down to a rate that is normal for companies in general. If maturity is reached, the growth rate may stop altogether.

For any stream of expected future dividends, we can solve for the rate of discount that equates the present value of this stream with the current share price. While this is tedious when there is multiphased growth, the calculations can be streamlined. If enough computations are involved, it is worthwhile to program a computer algorithm. The rate of discount for which we solve is, by definition, the expected return on investment in the stock. However, we must be mindful that the accuracy of this estimate depends on the precision with which we are able to forecast expected future dividends.

Price/Earnings Horizon Value

For the growth-phase example, a perpetual dividend growth assumption was invoked to obtain a terminal value at the end of some horizon—5 years. This terminal value also can be determined by assuming a price/earnings ratio at the horizon and multiplying earnings per share by it. To illustrate, we disaggregate dividends into earnings per share and the dividend payout ratio. Suppose that earnings per share for a company were expected to grow at a 25 percent rate the first 4 years, 15 percent the next 4, and 8 percent thereafter. Moreover, the dividend payout ratio is expected to increase with the transition from the initial growth phase to the eventual mature phase of the company.

As a result, we might have the following for the three phases:

PHASE	EPS GROWTH	DIVIDEND PAYOUT RATIO
1–4 years	25%	20%
5–8 years	15%	26%, 32%, 38%, 44%
Year 9 and beyond	8%	50%

Suppose that the price/earnings ratio at the end of year 8 were expected to be 10 times. Suppose further that this ratio is based on expected earnings per share in year 9. If present earnings per share (at time 0) are $3, the expected cash flows to the investor are as shown in Table 5-1. In the table we see that the terminal value at the end of year 8 is determined by multiplying expected earnings per share in year 9 by the price/earnings ratio of 10 to obtain $138.30.

To determine the implied expected return to the investor, we solve for the rate of discount that equates the cash-flow stream shown in the last column with

TABLE 5-1
Expected dividend and terminal-value cash flows for example

TIME	EARNINGS PER SHARE	DIVIDEND PAYOUT	DIVIDEND PER SHARE	CASH FLOW TO INVESTOR
1	$ 3.75	.20	$0.75	$0.75
2	4.69	.20	0.94	0.94
3	5.86	.20	1.17	1.17
4	7.32	.20	1.46	1.46
5	8.42	.26	2.19	2.19
6	9.69	.32	3.10	3.10
7	11.14	.38	4.23	4.23
8	12.81	.44	5.64	5.64
	Year 9 EPS = $12.81 (1.08) = $13.83			
	$P_8 = \$13.83 \times 10 \ P/E = \$138.30$			
8 Terminal value				138.30

the market price per share at time 0. If this price were $52, the implied return would be 15.59 percent when we solve for the internal rate of return. If we knew the required rate of return and wished to determine the present value of the cash-flow stream, we would simply present each value of the cash flows in the table and sum them. If the required return were 17 percent, the present value would be $47.45 per share. With these examples, we illustrate the mechanics by which dividend discount models may be used to determine either the expected return or the present value for a stock.

REQUIRED RATE OF RETURN ON A STOCK

We have seen that the expected return on a stock is the rate of discount that equates the present value of the stream of expected future dividends (and terminal value) with the market price of the stock. Conversely, the market price of a stock might be thought to be the stream of expected future dividends (and terminal value) discounted to their present value using the required rate of return. Frequently, the terms *required* and *expected* are used interchangeably. The two rates of return are the same in market equilibrium, but they are not the same when disequilibrium prevails. To appreciate the distinction and to understand the equilibrating process, we explore in detail the required rate of return for a stock.

Risk and Return in a Portfolio Context

Picking up our previous discussion of the security market line, we now want to consider how this line is derived and how the required rate of return is determined for a common stock. We do this in the context of Sharpe's capital-asset pricing model, which was developed in the 1960s. Like any model, this one is a simplification of reality. Nevertheless, it allows us to draw certain implications about the required rate of return for a stock, assuming the market for stocks overall is in equilibrium. As we shall see, the value of an individual security depends on its risk in relation to the risk of other securities available for investment. Because a complete and mathematically rigorous presentation of the model is beyond the scope of an introductory book, we shall concentrate on the general aspects of the model and its important implications.[6] Certain corners have been cut in the interest of simplicity.

As with any model, there are assumptions to be made. First, we assume that capital markets are efficient in that investors are well informed, transaction costs are low, there are negligible restrictions on investment, and no investor is large enough to affect the market price of a stock. We assume also that investors are in general agreement about the likely performance of individual securities and that their expectations are based on a common holding period, say, 1 year. There are two types of investment opportunities with which we will be concerned. The first is a risk-free security whose return over the holding period is known with certainty. Frequently, the rate on Treasury securities is used as a surrogate for the risk-free rate. The second is the market **portfolio** of common stocks. It is represented by all available stocks, weighted according to their market values outstanding. As the market portfolio is a somewhat unwieldy thing with which to work, most people use a surrogate such as Standard & Poor's 500-stock index, a broad-gauged index reflecting performance of 500 New York Stock Exchange stocks.

Earlier we discussed the idea of *unavoidable risk*; it was defined as risk that cannot be avoided by efficient diversification. Because one cannot hold a more diversified portfolio than the market portfolio, it represents the limit to attainable diversification. Thus, the risk associated with the market portfolio is unavoidable, or "systematic." Put another way, the only risk remaining after efficient diversification is systematic in the sense that it affects all securities. In essence, this is the risk of market swings caused by things such as changes in the economy or the political situation. It affects all stocks, no matter how efficiently one is diversified.

The Characteristic Line

Now we are in a position to compare the expected return for an individual stock with the expected return for the market portfolio. In our comparison, it is useful to deal with returns in excess of the risk-free rate. The *excess return* is simply the expected return less the risk-free return. Figure 5-3 shows an example of a comparison of expected excess returns for a specific stock with those for the market portfolio. The colored line is known as the **characteristic line**; it depicts the expected relationship between excess returns for the stock and excess returns for the market portfolio. This expected relationship may be based on past experience, in which case actual excess returns for the stock and for the market

Portfolio. The combination of two or more securities or assets.

Characteristic line. A line that describes the relationship between the variation of returns on a stock and the variation of returns on the market portfolio. Ths slope of this line is beta.

[6] See William F. Sharpe, *Investments*, 3rd ed. (Englewood Cliffs, N.J.: Prentice-Hall, 1985), for a more complete discussion of the model.

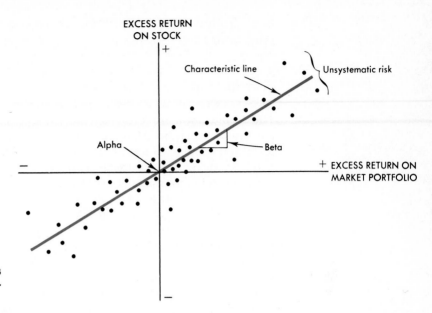

FIGURE 5-3
Relationship between excess returns for stock and excess returns for market portfolio

portfolio would be plotted on the graph and a line would be drawn best characterizing the historical relationship. Such a situation is illustrated by the scatter diagram shown in the figure. Each point represents the excess return of the stock and that of the S&P 500-stock index for a given month in the past, 60 in total. The monthly return for both is the ending price minus the beginning price plus any dividend that was paid, all over the beginning price. From these returns the monthly risk-free rate is subtracted to obtain excess returns.

We see that when returns on the market portfolio are high, returns on the stock tend to be high as well. Instead of using historical return relationships, one might obtain future return estimates from security analysts who follow the stock. As this approach usually is restricted to investment organizations with a number of security analysts, we illustrate the relationship assuming the use of historical data.

In the figure, three measures are important. The first, known as the *alpha*, is simply the intercept of the characteristic line on the vertical axis. If the excess return for the market portfolio were expected to be zero, the alpha would be the expected excess return for the stock. In theory, the alpha for an individual stock should be zero.[7] Using past data to approximate the characteristic line, however, we might observe alphas that differ from zero if the market were in disequilibrium, if there were market imperfections, or if there were statistical problems

---

[7] If the alpha of a stock were above zero, market participants would recognize the opportunity for an expected return greater than that required for the systematic risk involved. They would buy the stock, and this buying pressure would raise the price of the stock and lower its expected return. As a result, the characteristic line would decline throughout. Such buying would continue until the stock provided the same expected return as other stocks with that systematic risk. At this point, the vertical intercept of the characteristic line would be zero. If the alpha of a stock is negative, market participants will sell it, and these sales will cause the market price to decline. With this decline, the stock's expected return will rise, as will the characteristic line until it passes through zero.

in measurement. We assume for now, however, that the alpha for a particular stock is zero.

Betas and Systematic Risk

Beta. A coefficient measuring the average responsiveness of a stock's return with that of the market. Systematic risk.

The second measure with which we are concerned, and the most important for our purposes, is the **beta**. The beta is simply the slope of the characteristic line. If the slope is one, it means that excess returns for the stock vary proportionally with excess returns for the market portfolio. In other words, the stock has the same unavoidable risk as the market as a whole. If the market goes up and provides an excess return of 5 percent for a month, we would expect on average for the stock's excess return to be 5 percent as well. A slope steeper than one means that the stock's excess return varies more than proportionally with the excess return of the market portfolio. Put another way, it has more unavoidable risk than the market as a whole. This type of stock is often called an "aggressive" investment. A slope of less than one means that the stock has less unavoidable or **systematic risk** than the market as a whole. This type of stock is often called a "defensive" investment. Examples of the three types of relationships are shown in Fig. 5-4.

Systematic risk. The risk of a stock that is associated with movements in the overall market that cannot be diversified away. This risk is measured by the security's beta.

The greater the slope of the characteristic line for a stock, as depicted by its beta, the greater its systematic risk. This means that for both upward and downward movements in market excess returns, movements in excess returns for the individual stock are greater or less depending on its beta. Thus, the beta is a

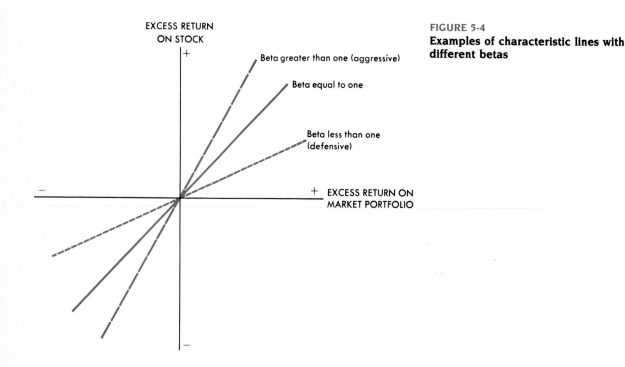

EXCESS RETURN
ON STOCK

Beta greater than one (aggressive)

Beta equal to one

Beta less than one
(defensive)

EXCESS RETURN ON
MARKET PORTFOLIO

FIGURE 5-4

Examples of characteristic lines with different betas

measure of a stock's systematic or unavoidable risk. This risk cannot be diversified away by investing in more stocks, as it depends on such things as changes in the economy and in the political atmosphere, which affect all stocks. In summary, the beta of a stock represents its contribution to the risk of a highly diversified portfolio of stocks.

Unsystematic Risk

The last of the three measures with which we are concerned is the **unsystematic risk** or **residual risk**, of a stock. This risk is described by the dispersion of the estimates involved in predicting a stock's characteristic line. In Fig. 5-3 it is represented by the relative vertical distance of the dots from the solid line. If all of the points in the scatter diagram were plotted along the characteristic line, there would be no unsystematic risk. All risk would be market related. If the points are widely scattered around the characteristic line, this occurrence implies that a good deal of the total risk of the stock is company related. The greater the dispersion of the points in the figure, the greater the unsystematic risk of the stock. By diversification of stocks in one's portfolio, however, we can reduce unsystematic risk. It has been shown that unsystematic risk is reduced at a decreasing rate toward zero as more stocks are added to the portfolio. Thus, a substantial proportion of the unsystematic risk of a stock can be eliminated with a relatively moderate amount of diversification, say, 15 or 20 stocks. For the well-diversified portfolio, unsystematic risk approaches zero. Conceptually, this can be illustrated as in Fig. 5-5. As the number of randomly selected securities held in the portfolio increases, the total risk of the portfolio is reduced in keeping with the reduction in unsystematic risk. However, this reduction is at a decreasing rate, as seen in the figure.

Residual risk. The risk of a stock unique to the company involved. This risk may be diversified away. Known also as unsystematic risk.

FIGURE 5-5
Total, unsystematic, and systematic risk

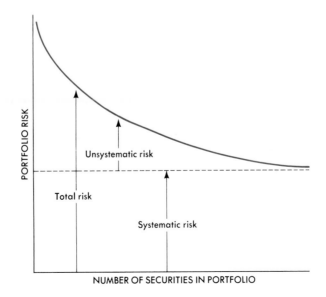

Thus, the total risk involved in holding a stock is composed of two parts:

$$\text{Total risk} = \text{Systematic risk} + \text{Unsystematic risk} \qquad (5\text{-}17)$$
$$\text{(nondiversifiable)} \qquad \text{(diversifiable)}$$

The first part is due to the overall market risk—changes in the economy, tax reform by the Congress, a change in the world energy situation—risks that affect securities overall and consequently cannot be diversified away. In other words, even the investor who holds a well-diversified portfolio will be exposed to this type of risk. The second risk component, however, is unique to a particular company, being independent of economic, political, and other factors that affect securities in a systematic manner. A wildcat strike may affect only one company; a new competitor may produce essentially the same product; a technological breakthrough can make obsolete an existing product.

For the typical stock, unsystematic risk acounts for around 70 percent of the total risk or variance of the stock. Expressed differently, systematic risk explains only about 30 percent of the total variability of an individual stock. The proportion of total risk explained by movements of the market is represented by the R-square statistic for the regression of excess returns for a stock against excess returns for the market portfolio. (R-square measures the proportion of the total variance of the dependent variable that is explained by the independent variable; it is simply the **correlation coefficient** squared.) The proportion of total risk unique to the stock is 1 minus R-square.

The proportion of systematic to total risk depends on the particular stock. The excess-return relationship depicted in Fig. 5-3 is an example of relatively little unsystematic risk; the observations are tightly clustered around the characteristic line. Contrast this with a more typical situation, such as that shown in panel (a) of Fig. 5-6. Here the observations are scattered rather widely around the

Correlation coefficient. A measure that describes how closely two variables move together over time.

FIGURE 5-6
Relationships between excess returns

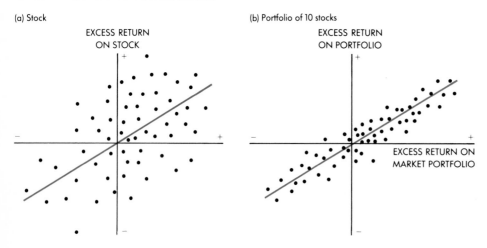

(a) Stock

(b) Portfolio of 10 stocks

characteristic line, indicating a good deal of unsystematic risk. However, this variability can be reduced through diversification. Suppose you diversify by investing in 10 stocks whose weighted average beta is the same as the slope of the characteristic line in panel (a). The result might be that shown in panel (b). We see that with reasonable diversification, the scatter of excess return observations about the characteristic line is reduced considerably. It is not eliminated, because it would take more stocks to do that. However, the scatter is much less than it is for the individual security, and this is the essence of diversification.

Measuring the Required Rate of Return

If we assume that financial markets are efficient and that investors as a whole are efficiently diversified, unsystematic risk is a minor matter. The major risk associated with a stock becomes its unavoidable or systematic risk. The greater the beta of a stock, the greater the risk of that stock, and the greater the return required. If we assume that unsystematic risk is diversified away, the required rate of return for stock j is

$$\bar{R}_j = i + (\bar{R}_m - i)\beta_j \tag{5-18}$$

where i is the risk-free rate, $\bar{R}_m$ is the expected return for the market portfolio, and β_j is the beta coefficient for stock j as defined earlier.

Put another way, the required rate of return for a stock is equal to the return required by the market for a riskless investment plus a risk premium. In turn, the risk premium is a function of (1) the expected market return less the risk-free rate, which represents the risk premium required for the typical stock in the market; and (2) the beta coefficient. Suppose that the expected return on Treasury securities is 10 percent, the expected return on the market portfolio is 15 percent, and the beta of Pro-Fli Corporation is 1.3. The beta indicates that Pro-Fli has more systematic risk than the typical stock. Given this information and using Eq. (5-18), we find that the required return on Pro-Fli's stock would be

$$\bar{R}_j = .10 + (.15 - .10)1.3 = 16.5\%$$

What this tells us is that on average the market expects Pro-Fli to show a 16.5 percent annual return. Because Pro-Fli has more systematic risk, this return is higher than that expected of the typical stock in the marketplace. For the typical stock, the expected return would be

$$\bar{R}_j = .10 + (.15 - .10)1.0 = 15.0\%$$

Suppose now that we are interested in a defensive stock whose beta coefficient is only .7. Its expected return is

$$\bar{R}_j = .10 + (.15 - .10).7 = 13.5\%$$

Obtaining Information for the Model.   If the past is thought to be a good surrogate for the future, one can use past data on excess returns for the stock and for the market to calculate the beta. Several services provide betas on companies whose stocks are actively traded; these betas usually are based on weekly or monthly returns for the past three to five years. Services providing beta information include the Value Line Investment Survey; Merrill Lynch, Pierce, Fenner, and Smith; and First Boston Corporation. The obvious advantage is that one can obtain the historical beta for a stock without having to calculate it oneself. An example of betas for a sample of companies is shown in Table 5-2. The betas of most stocks range from .7 to 1.4, though some are lower and some are higher, as shown in the table. If one feels the past systematic risk of a stock is likely to prevail in the future, the historical beta can be used as a proxy for the expected beta coefficient.

TABLE 5-2
Betas for selected stocks (June 1987)

STOCK	BETA
American Standard	1.15
Bristol Myers	1.00
Control Data Corporation	1.30
Dow Chemical	1.15
Eastman Kodak	0.80
Exxon	0.85
General Electric	1.05
Georgia-Pacific (forest products)	1.40
Hewlett-Packard	1.30
International Business Machines	1.05
Iowa-Illinois Gas & Electric	0.60
McDonnell-Douglas	1.00
Pillsbury Company	0.90
Sizzler (restaurants)	1.50
Washington Post	0.90
Wrigley Company (chewing gum)	0.80

In addition to the beta, the numbers used for the market return and for the risk-free rate must be the best possible estimates of the future. The past may or may not be a good proxy. If the past was represented by a period of relative economic stability but in the future considerable inflation is expected, averages of past market returns and past risk-free rates would be biased, low estimates of the future. In this case, it would be a mistake to use historical average returns in the calculation of the required return for a security. In another situation, realized market returns in the recent past might be very high and not expected to continue. As a result, the use of the historical past would result in too high an estimate of the future market return.

In situations of this sort, direct estimates of the risk-free rate and of the market return must be made. The risk-free rate is easy; one simply looks up the current rate of return on an appropriate Treasury security. The market return is more difficult, but even here forecasts are available. These forecasts might be consensus estimates of security analysts, economists, and others who regularly predict such returns. Over the last 30 years or so, the annual return on the market portfolio, as represented by the Standard & Poor's Composite Index, has been around 11 percent. Estimates in recent years of the return on common stocks overall have been in the 12 to 18 percent range.

Use of the Risk Premium.   The excess return of the market portfolio (over the risk-free rate) is known as the market risk premium. It is represented by $(\bar{R}_m - i)$ in Eq. (5-18). The expected excess return for the Standard & Poor's 500-market index has ranged from 3 to 7 percent. Instead of estimating the market portfolio return directly, one might simply add a risk premium to the prevailing risk-free rate. To illustrate, suppose the current rate of interest on Treasuries is 10 percent. Moreover, suppose we feel that we are in a period of uncertainty, and there is considerable risk aversion in the market. Therefore, we estimate the risk premium to be in the upper part of the range, namely, 6 percent. Therefore, our estimated market return is $\bar{R}_m = .10 + .06 = 16$ percent. If, on the other hand, we feel that there is substantially less risk aversion in the market, we might use a risk premium of 4 percent, in which case the estimated market return is 14 percent.

The important thing is that the expected market return on common stocks and the risk-free rate employed in Eq. (5-18) be current market estimates. Blind adherence to historical rates of return may result in faulty estimates of these data inputs to the capital-asset pricing model.

EQUILIBRIUM RETURNS AND STOCK PRICES

The capital-asset pricing model provides us a means by which to estimate the required rate of return on a security. This return then can be used as the discount rate in a dividend-capitalization model. You will recall that the market price per share of a stock can be expressed as the present value of the stream of expected future dividends.

$$P_0 = \sum_{t=1}^{\infty} \frac{D_t}{(1 + k)^t} \qquad (5\text{-}19)$$

where D_t is the expected dividend in period t, k is the required rate of return for the stock, and Σ is the sum of the present value of future dividends going from period 1 to infinity.

Suppose that we wished to determine the value of the stock of Pro-Fli Corporation and that the perpetual dividend growth model was appropriate. This model is

$$P_0 = \frac{D_1}{k - g} \qquad (5\text{-}20)$$

where g is the expected future growth rate in dividends per share. Suppose that Pro-Fli's expected dividend in period 1 is $2 per share and that the expected annual growth rate in dividends per share is 10 percent. In previous computations, we determine that the required rate of return for Pro-Fli was 16.5 percent. On the basis of these expectations, the value of the stock is

$$P_0 = \frac{\$2.00}{.165 - .100} = \$30.77$$

This represents the *equilibrium price* of the stock based on investor expectations about the company, about the market as a whole, and about the return available on a riskless asset.

These expectations can change; and when they do, the value of the stock changes. Suppose that inflation in the economy has abated and we enter a period of relatively stable growth. As a result, interest rates decline, and investor risk aversion lessens. Moreover, suppose that Pro-Fli develops a new product line that has much less systematic risk than its existing product lines. However, the growth rate of the company also declines somewhat. The variables before and after these changes are

	ORIGINAL	NEW
Risk-free rate	.10	.08
Market return	.15	.12
Pro-Fli beta	1.30	1.10
Pro-Fli growth rate	.10	.09

The required rate of return for Pro-Fli's stock becomes

$$\overline{R}_j = .08 + (.12 - .08)1.10 = 12.4\%$$

Using this rate as k, the new value of the stock is

$$P_0 = \frac{\$2.00}{.124 - .09} = \$58.82$$

Thus, the combination of these events causes the value of the stock to go from $30.77 to $58.82, per share, almost doubling. Thus, the equilibrium price of a stock can change very quickly as expectations in the marketplace change.

Market-Determined Relationship

From these examples, we see that the greater the systematic or unavoidable risk of a stock, as denoted by its beta, the higher the return that is expected. Given the assumptions of the model, there exists a linear and positive relationship between the beta of a particular stock and its required rate of return. This relationship is known as the security market line, and it was illustrated for securities in general in Fig. 5-1. The work to date on devising return measures for combinations of fixed-income securities and common stocks leaves something to be desired. As a result, it is difficult in practice to derive satisfactory beta information for fixed-income securities and common stocks. In contrast, when the market portfolio is restricted to common stocks, beta information is well developed and readily available. For this reason, most of the work on the capital-asset pricing model has involved common stocks. The concept of the relationship between unavoidable risk and the required return is important, however, for both fixed-income securities and common stocks.

Returns in Disequilibrium Situations.   We said earlier that in market equilibrium the required rate of return on a stock equals its expected return. What happens when this is not so? Suppose that in Fig. 5-7 the security market line is drawn on the basis of what investors as a whole know to be the appropriate relationship between the required rate of return and systematic or unavoidable risk. For some reason, two stocks—call them X and Y—are improperly priced. Stock X is underpriced relative to the security market line, while stock Y is overpriced.

As a result, stock X provides a higher expected return than the security market line for the systematic risk involved, while stock Y provides a lower expected return. Investors seeing the opportunity for superior returns by investing in stock X should rush to buy it. This action would drive the price up and the expected return down. How long would this continue? It would continue until the market price was driven up and the expected return down to the point at which the expected return was on the security market line. In the case of stock

FIGURE 5-7
Equilibrating process in cases of market disequilibrium

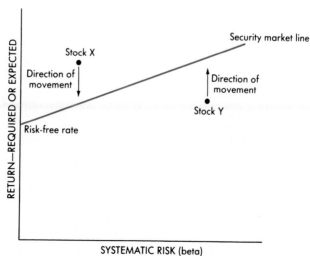

Y, investors holding this stock would sell it, recognizing that they could obtain a higher return for the same amount of systematic risk with other stocks. This selling pressure would drive Y's market price down and its expected return up until the expected return was on the security market line.

When the expected returns for these two stocks were both on the security market line, market equilibrium would again prevail. As a result, the expected returns for the two stocks would equal their required returns. Available evidence suggests that disequilibrium stituations in stock prices do not long persist and that stock prices adjust rapidly to new information. With the vast amount of evidence indicating market efficiency, the security market concept becomes a useful means for determining the expected and required rate of return for a stock. This rate then can be used as the discount rate in the valuation procedures described earlier.

Some Qualifications

Capital-asset pricing model. A model of market equilibrium, where a security's expected return is the risk-free rate plus a premium based on the risk of the security in a portfolio context.

In this book, we use the **capital-asset pricing model** (CAPM) to look at the valuation implications of various financial decisions. The model has been found to have considerable predictive power. Perhaps best of all, it is easy to get your hands around and to apply. Still it is not perfect, as if anything were! Such imperfections as taxes, bankruptcy costs, restrictions on investors, inflations, differing borrowing and lending rates, measurement problems involving the market index as well as other difficulties have led to refinements in the model. Some of these refinements are explored in subsequent chapters when we apply the model in a world with market imperfections.

Furthermore, in the appendix to this chapter we investigate the effect of taxes. In addition to taxes, the CAPM has been extended to include other variables explaining returns: inflation, liquidity, size, seasonal, and industry effects. When factors other than beta are added to the model, a better data fit generally is obtained. Expressed differently, variables additional to beta have been found to explain successfully some of a security's total return not explained by beta. However, beta still remains the dominant determinant of security returns. The basic concepts of the original CAPM have stood the test of time.

Arbitrage pricing theory. A theory of market equilibrium where the price of an asset depends on multiple factors.

Perhaps the most important challenge to the CAPM comes from the **arbitrage pricing theory** (APT). Originally developed by Stephen A. Ross, this theory is based on the idea that in competitive financial markets investors will seek risk-adjusted returns consistent with each other.[8] When disequilibrium prevails, they are said to buy and sell different securities in the pursuit of arbitrage profits. Arbitrage simply means finding two things that are essentially the same and buying the cheaper and selling, or selling short, the more expensive. When such profit opportunities have been eliminated, security prices are said to be in

---

[8] Stephen A. Ross, "The Arbitrage Theory of Capital Asset Pricing," *Journal of Economic Theory*, 13 (December 1976), 341–60; See also Richard Roll and Stephen A. Ross, "The Arbitrage Pricing Approach to Strategic Portfolio Planning," *Financial Analysts Journal*, 40 (May–June 1984), 14–26.

equilibrium. Rather than basing their decisions on a single factor, such as beta in the CAPM, the arbitrage pricing theory suggests that investors base their decisions on multiple factors. The arbitrage pricing theory does not tell us why the factors are relevant, only that there is a relationship between returns and the factors. In other words, the APT does not try to explain underlying causes of security returns, as does the CAPM. For our purposes, a disadvantage of the APT is that to date there has been little applicability of the model to corporate finance.

The problems mentioned in this section do not negate the importance of the capital-asset pricing model. However, we must recognize that the model does not permit a precise measurement of the market equilibration process or of the required return for a particular stock. However, it does provide us with reasonable concepts concerning risk and return as well as a way in which to approximate the required return for a stock. The CAPM has its detractors, but its usefulness to corporate finance cannot be denied.

Efficient Markets Hypothesis

Throughout this chapter we have implicitly considered the efficiency of financial markets. An efficient financial market is said to exist when security prices reflect all available public information about the economy, about financial markets, and about the specific company involved. The implication is that market prices of individual securities adjust very rapidly to new information. As a result, security prices are said to fluctuate randomly about their "intrinsic" values. New information can result in a change in the "intrinsic" value of a security, but subsequent security price movements will follow what is known as a *random walk* (changes in price will not follow any pattern).[9]

Contrary to often quoted passages of Shakespeare and Santayana, history—at least in the stock market—is not repetitious or helpful. This simply means that one cannot use past security prices to predict future prices in such a way as to profit on average. Moreover, close attention to news releases will be for naught. Alas, by the time you are able to take action, security price adjustments already will have occurred, according to the efficient market notion.

On balance, the evidence indicates that the market for stocks, particularly those listed on the New York Stock Exchange, is reasonably efficient. Security prices appear to be a good reflection of available information, and market prices adjust quickly to new information. Market participants seem to be ready to seize on any recurring price pattern; and in doing so, they drive price changes about a security's "intrinsic" value to a random walk. About the only way one can consistently profit is to have insider information, that is, information about a company known to officers and directors but not to the public. If security prices impound all available public information, they tell us a good deal about the future. In efficient markets, one can hope to do no better.

---

[9] For a formalized presentation of this condition, see Eugene F. Fama, "Efficient Capital Markets: A Review of Theory and Empirical Work," *Journal of Finance*, 25 (May 1970) 384–87.

James H. Lorie, Peter Dodd, and Mary T. Hamilton,[10] as well as a number of others, point out that the efficient market theory presents a curious paradox: The hypothesis that stock markets are efficient will be true only if a sufficiently large number of investors disbelieve its efficiency and behave accordingly. In other words, the theory requires that there be a sufficiently large number of market participants who, in their attempts to earn profits, promptly receive and analyze all the information that is publicly available concerning companies whose securities they follow. Should this considerable effort devoted to data accumulation and evaluation cease—that is, if *all* market participants behaved in a manner consistent with the acceptance of the efficient markets theory—financial markets would become markedly less efficient. In this book, we assume that financial markets are reasonably efficient in the information sense described. However, we do not rule out market imperfections that, on occasion, can affect security pricing.

SUMMARY

The valuation of any financial instrument involves a capitalization of its expected income stream by a discount rate appropriate for the risk involved. The important risk to the investor is that which cannot be avoided by diversification. This risk, known as *unavoidable risk*, is systematic in the sense that it affects all securities, although in different degrees. Unsystematic risk is company specific in that it does not depend on general market movements. This risk is avoidable through proper diversification of one's portfolio. If we assume that investors as a whole are efficiently diversified in the securities they hold, the important risk to the investor is the security's systematic risk.

The degree of systematic risk a security possesses can be determined by drawing a *characteristic line*. This line depicts the relationship between expected returns in excess of the risk-free rate for the specific security involved and for the market portfolio. The slope of this line, known as *beta*, is a measure of systematic risk. The greater the beta, the greater the unavoidable risk of the security involved. The relationship between the required rate of return for a security and its beta is known as the *security market line*. It is linear and reflects a positive relationship between the return investors require and systematic risk. Thus, the required return is the risk-free rate plus some premium for systematic risk.

With the security market line concept, one is able to approximate the appropriate discount rate for both fixed-income securities and common stocks. Bonds and preferred stocks represent fixed-income securities in the sense that the cash payment, whether interest or preferred dividend, is established at issuance and is invariant. We illustrated the calculation of the present value of a bond under various assumptions as to maturity, coupon rate, required return,

---

[10] *The Stock Market*, 2nd ed. (Homewood, Ill.: Richard D. Irwin, 1985).

and the number of times a year interest is paid. The price behavior accompanying a change in interest rates was illustrated.

Expected future dividends are the foundation for the valuation of common stocks. The dividend-capitalization model embodies the notion of capital gains. We went on to consider various growth models in which dividends are expected to grow over time either at a constant rate or at different rates. Instead of valuing only dividends, one can value dividends plus a terminal value based on an assumed price/earnings ratio at some horizon. The key to valuation is determining the appropriate discount rate that properly takes account of risk. Several examples demonstrated how to calculate the required rate of return for a stock and obtain the necessary information. Once the discount rate is determined, it can be used in a dividend-capitalization model to determine the value of a stock.

The market equilibrium relationship between systematic risk (beta) and expected return is known as the security market line. With this approach, we are able to estimate required rates of return for individual securities. The original CAPM can be extended to include consideration of variables in addition to beta. In an alternative approach, the arbitrage pricing theory, multiple factors are used to capture risk and to estimate security returns. Market efficiency is described in this context as an absence of arbitrage opportunities. Another definition is that market efficiency exists when security prices reflect all available public information.

APPENDIX
The Effect of Personal Taxes

In the chapter, the required rate of return we calculated for stock j, $\overline{R}_j$, was a before-tax return to the investor. The return realized from holding a stock is composed of two parts: (1) dividends, if any, received during the holding period, and (2) the capital gain or loss that occurs when the stock is sold. If all investors paid either no taxes or the same taxes on dividends and capital gains, the CAPM generalizations made about an individual stock would be unaffected by whether the company paid high or low dividends. In many countries capital gains are taxed at a more favorable rate than dividends. Under the 1986 Tax Act in the United States, dividend income and capital gains are taxed at the same rate at the federal level. However, capital gains income is not recognized until the stock is sold. If held until death, the capital gain is largely unrecognized. Therefore, there are present-value advantages to capital gains versus dividend income. Moreover, certain states tax capital gains at a more favorable rate than dividends.

Suppose we expect Alpha Company to have a 12 percent dividend yield for the year (dividends divided by initial value) and a 3 percent capital gain on initial value, while Baker Company is expected to have a 2 percent dividend yield and a $12\frac{1}{2}$ percent capital gain. The expected before-tax return of Alpha Company, 15 percent, is higher than that of Baker Company, $14\frac{1}{2}$ percent. If an investor is in a 30 percent tax bracket, but the "effective economic" tax on capital gains is 24 percent, the after-tax returns are as follows:

	ALPHA COMPANY			BAKER COMPANY		
	Before Taxes	Tax Effect	After Taxes	Before Taxes	Tax Effect	After Taxes
Dividend yield	12%	(1 − .30)	8.40%	2.0%	(1 − .30)	1.40%
Capital gain	3	(1 − .24)	2.28	12.5	(1 − .24)	9.50
Expected return	15%		10.68%	14.5%		10.90%

We see that despite the lower expected return before taxes, the expected after-tax return is higher for Baker Company, owing to a greater portion of the return being realized in capital gains. On the other hand, a tax-exempt investor, such as a pension fund, would prefer Alpha Company, with its higher before-tax expected return, all other things being the same.

The implication is that holding risk-constant, high-dividend stocks may have to provide higher expected returns before taxes than will low-dividend stocks, in order to offset the tax effect. If this were the case, the expected before-tax return on security j would be a function of both the stock's beta and its dividend yield:

$$\bar{R}_j = i + b\beta_j + t(d_j - i) \tag{5A-1}$$

where i = risk-free rate

β_j = the security's beta

b = a coefficient indicating the relative importance of beta

d_j = dividend yield on security j

t = a coefficient indicating the relative importance of the tax effect.

This equation tells us that the greater the dividend yield, d_j, the greater the expected before-tax return that investors require. If t were .1 and the dividend yield were to rise by 1.0 percent, the expected return would have to increase by .1 percent to make the stock attractive to investors. Put another way, the market trade-off would be $1.00 of dividends for $.90 of capital gains.

If there is a systematic bias in the market in favor of capital gains, the expected return on a stock would depend on both its beta and its dividend yield. Instead of the two-dimensional (expected return–beta) security market line in Fig. 5-1, we would need a three-dimensional surface of the sort shown in Fig. 5-8. In this approach, we see that expected return is on the vertical axis, whereas beta and dividend yield are on the other axes. Looking at expected return and dividend yield, we see that the higher the dividend yield, the higher the expected return. Similarly, the higher the beta, the higher the expected return. Instead of a security market line, we have a security market surface, depicting the three-dimensional relationship among expected return, beta, and dividend yield. Whether the use of such a trade-off surface is appropriate and practical depends on the fundamental existence of a tax effect and its proper measurement.

We must point out that the existence of a tax effect is an open question, empirically as well as theoretically. While a number of studies support the idea of a systematic preference in the market for capital gains over dividends, some studies point to a neutral effect. The evidence here is said to be consistent with a

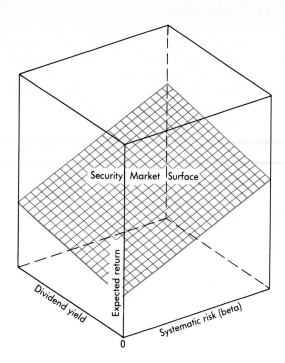

FIGURE 5-8
Three-dimensional security market surface illustrating a tax effect

number of tax-free investors as well as special categories of investors being indifferent between dividend income and capital gains, with tax avoidance schemes designed to neutralize the taxation of dividend income, and with the notion that corporations will alter the supply of dividends to suit demand. When the unsatisfied demand is filled, investors at the margin would be indifferent between dividends and capital gains. We will return to this topic in Chapter 18, when we consider dividend policy of a company in its entirety. For now, it is sufficient to say that the tax trade-off portrayed in Fig. 5-8 is controversial.

QUESTIONS

1. If investors were not risk averse on average, but rather were either risk neutral or even liked risk, would the risk-return concepts presented in this chapter be valid?
2. Why do we treat bonds and preferred stock in the same way when it comes to valuation?
3. Why do bonds with long maturities fluctuate more in value than do bonds with short maturities, given the same change in yield to maturity?
4. A 20-year bond has a coupon rate of 8 percent, and another bond of the same maturity has a coupon rate of 15 percent. If the bonds are alike in all other respects, which will have the greater relative market price decline if interest rates increase sharply? Why?
5. Why are dividends the basis for the valuation of common stock?
6. Suppose controlling stock of IBM Corporation were placed in a perpetual trust with an irrevocable clause that cash or liquidating dividends would

never be paid. Earnings per share continued to grow. What would be the value of the company?

7. Why is the growth rate in earnings and dividends of a company likely to taper off in the future? Could not the growth rate increase as well? If it did, what would be the effect?

8. Define the *characteristic line* and its *alpha* and *beta*.

9. Why is beta a measure of systematic risk? What is its meaning?

10. What is the required rate of return of a stock? How can it be measured?

11. Is the security market line constant over time?

12. What would be the effect of the following changes on the market price of a company's stock, all other things the same?

   a. Investors demand a higher required rate of return for stocks in general.

   b. The covariance between the company's rate of return and that for the market decreases.

   c. The standard deviation of the probability distribution of rates of return for the company's stock increases.

   d. Market expectations of the growth of future earnings of the company are revised downward.

13. Suppose that you are highly risk averse but that you still invest in common stocks. Will the betas of the stocks in which you invest be more or less than 1.0?

14. Using the perpetual growth dividend valuation model, could you have a situation in which a company grows at 30 percent per annum (after subtracting out inflation) forever?

15. If a security is undervalued in terms of the capital-asset pricing model, what will happen if investors come to recognize this undervaluation?

SELF-CORRECTION PROBLEMS

1. Fast and Slow Plaid Company has outstanding an 8 percent, 4-year bond where interest is paid annually.

   a. If the required rate of return is 15 percent, what is the market value of the bond?

   b. What would be its market value if the required return dropped to 12 percent? to 8 percent?

   c. If the coupon rate were 15 percent instead of 8 percent, what would be the market value under part a? If the required return dropped to 8 percent, what would happen to the market price of the bond?

2. Zachery Zorro Company presently pays a dividend of $1.60 per share, and the market price per share is $30. The company expects to increase the dividend at a 20 percent annual rate the first 4 years, at a 13 percent rate the next 4 years, and then grow the dividend at a 7 percent rate thereafter. This phased-growth pattern is in keeping with the expected life cycle of earnings. What is the stock's expected return on investment? *Hint:* This prob-

lem involves trial and error to determine the present values of the dividend stream for two returns. Try 16 percent as one of the returns in order to get started.

3. Sorbond Industries has a beta of 1.45. The risk-free rate is 10 percent and the expected return on the market portfolio is 16 percent. The company presently pays a dividend of $2 a share, and investors expect it to experience a growth in dividends of 10 percent per annum for many years to come.

    a. What is the stock's required rate of return according to the CAPM?

    b. What is the stock's present market price per share, assuming this required return?

    c. What would happen to the required return and to market price per share if the beta were 0.80? (Assume that all else stays the same.)

PROBLEMS

1. Gonzalez Electric Company has outstanding a 10 percent bond issue with a face value of $1,000 per bond and 3 years to maturity. Interest is payable annually. The bonds are privately held by Suresafe Fire Insurance Company. Suresafe wishes to sell the bonds and is negotiating with another party. It estimates that in current market conditions, the bonds should provide a return of 14 percent (yield to maturity). What price per bond should Suresafe be able to realize on the sale?

2. What would be the price per bond in problem 1 if interest payments were semiannual?

3. Superior Cement Company has an 8 percent preferred stock issue outstanding, with each share having a $100 face value. Currently, the yield is 10 percent. What is the market price per share? If interest rates in general should rise so that the required return becomes 12 percent, what will happen to the market price per share?

4. The stock of the Health Corporation is currently selling for $20 a share and is expected to pay a $1 dividend at the end of the year. If you bought the stock now and sold it for $23 after receiving the dividend, what rate of return would you earn?

5. Delphi Products Corporation currently pays a dividend of $2 per share, and this dividend is expected to grow at a 15 percent annual rate for 3 years, then at a 10 percent rate for the next 3 years, after which it is expected to grow at a 5 percent rate forever. What value would you place on the stock if an 18 percent rate of return were required?

6. For Delphi Products Corporation in problem 5, suppose the company were expected to have a price/earnings ratio of 8 times at the end of year 6. Moreover, earnings per share in year 7 are expected to be $7.50. If the present market price per share is $35, what is the expected return on investment? (Assume that terminal value at the end of year 6 is based on year 7 earnings.)

7. Suppose that you were given the following data for past excess quarterly returns for Karochi Corporation and for the market portfolio:

QUARTER	EXCESS RETURNS KAROCHI	EXCESS RETURNS MARKET PORTFOLIO
1	.04	.05
2	.05	.10
3	−.04	−.06
4	−.05	−.10
5	.02	.02
6	.00	−.03
7	.02	.07
8	−.01	−.01
9	−.02	−.08
10	.04	.00
11	.07	.13
12	−.01	.04
13	.01	−.01
14	−.06	−.09
15	−.06	−.14
16	−.02	−.04
17	.07	.15
18	.02	.06
19	.04	.11
20	.03	.05
21	.01	.03
22	−.01	.01
23	−.01	−.03
24	.02	.04

On the basis of this information, graph the relationship between the two sets of excess returns and draw a characteristic line. What is the approximate alpha? The approximate beta? What can you say about the systematic risk of the stock, based on past experience?

8. Assuming that the capital-asset pricing model approach is appropriate, compute the required rate of return for each of the following stocks, given a risk-free rate of .07 and an expected return for the market portfolio of .13:

Stock	A	B	C	D	E
Beta	1.5	1.0	0.6	2.0	1.3

What implications can you draw?

9. North Great Timber Company will pay a dividend of $1.50 a share next year. After this, earnings and dividends are expected to grow at a 9 percent annual rate indefinitely. Investors presently require a rate of return of 13 percent. The company is considering several business strategies and wishes to determine the effect of these strategies on the market price per share of its stock.

  a. Continuing the present strategy will result in the expected growth rate and required rate of return shown.

b. Expanding timber holdings and sales will increase the expected dividend growth rate to 11 percent, but will increase the risk of the company. As a result, the rate of return required by investors will increase to 16 percent.

c. Integrating into retail stores will increase the dividend growth rate to 10 percent and increase the required rate of return to 14 percent.

From the standpoint of market price per share, which strategy is best?

10. On the basis of an analysis of past returns and of inflationary expectations, Marta Gomez feels that the expected return on stocks in general is 15 percent. The risk-free rate on short-term Treasury securities is now 10 percent. Gomez is particularly interested in the return prospects for Kessler Electronics Corporation. Based on monthly data for the past 5 years, she has fitted a characteristic line to the responsiveness of excess returns of the stock to excess returns of Standard & Poor's 500-stock index and has found the slope of the line to be 1.67. If financial markets are believed to be efficient, what return can she expect from investing in Kessler Electronics Corporation?

11. Presently, the risk-free rate is 10 percent and the expected return on the market portfolio is 15 percent. The expected returns for four stocks are listed here, together with their expected betas.

	STOCK	EXPECTED RETURN	EXPECTED BETA
1.	Stillman Zinc Corporation	17.0%	1.3
2.	Union Paint Company	14.5	0.8
3.	National Automobile Company	15.5	1.1
4.	Parker Electronics, Inc.	18.0	1.7

a. On the basis of these expectations, which stocks are overvalued? Which are undervalued?

b. If the risk-free rate were to rise to 12 percent and the expected return on the market portfolio to 16 percent, which stocks would be overvalued? Which would be undervalued? (Assume that the betas stay the same.)

SOLUTIONS TO SELF-CORRECTION PROBLEMS

1. a, b.

END OF YEAR	PAYMENT	DISCOUNT FACTOR, 15%	PRESENT VALUE, 15%	DISCOUNT FACTOR, 12%	PRESENT VALUE, 12%
1–3	$ 80	2.2832	$182.66	2.4018	$192.14
4	1,080	.57175	617.49	.63552	686.36
Market value			$800.15		$878.50

The market value of an 8 percent bond yielding 8 percent is its face value, or $1,000.

c.   The market value would be $1,000 if the required return were 15 percent.

END OF YEAR	PAYMENT	DISCOUNT FACTOR, 8%	PRESENT VALUE, 8%
1–3	$ 150	2.5771	$ 386.57
4	1,150	.73503	845.28
Market value			$1,231.85

Percentagewise, this is a ($1,231.85 − $1,000)/$1,000 = 23.2% increase in value. For the first example, it was a ($1,000 − $800.15)/$800.15 = 25.0%. This illustrates that the lower the coupon rate, the greater the change in value with a change in required return.

2.

YEAR	DIVIDEND	P_8 AT 16%	P_8 AT 17%
1	$1.92		
2	2.30		
3	2.76		
4	3.32		
5	3.75		
6	4.24		
7	4.79		
8	5.41	$64.33*	$57.90†
9	5.79		

PV of 1—8 year dividends and P_8(16%) = $33.46
PV of 1—8 year dividends and P_8(17%) = $29.81

$$IRR = .16 + \frac{3.46}{33.46 - 29.81} = 16.95\%$$

$$*P_8 = \frac{\$5.79}{.16 - .07} = \$64.33$$

$$†P_8 = \frac{\$5.79}{.17 - .07} = \$57.90$$

3.   a. $R_s = 10\% + (16\% - 10\%)1.45 = 18.70\%$

   b.   If we use the perpetual dividend growth model, we would have

$$P_0 = \frac{D_1}{R_s - g} = \frac{\$2(1.10)}{.187 - .10} = \$25.29$$

   c. $R_s = 10\% + (16\% - 10\%).80 = 14.80\%$

$$P_0 = \frac{\$2(1.10)}{.148 - .10} = \$45.83$$

SELECTED REFERENCES

BAUMAN, W. SCOTT, "Investment Returns and Present Values," *Financial Analysts Journal*, 25 (November–December 1969), 107–18.

EVANS, JACK, and STEPHEN H. ARCHER, "Diversification and the Reduction of Dispersion: An Empirical Analysis," *Journal of Finance*, 23 (December 1968), 761–67.

FAMA, EUGENE F., "Components of Investment Performance," *Journal of Finance*, 27 (June 1972), 551–67.

_____, and MERTON H. MILLER, *The Theory of Finance*. New York: Holt, 1972.

FULLER, RUSSELL J., and CHI-CHENG HSIA, "A Simplified Model for Estimating Stock Prices of Growth Firms," *Financial Analysts Journal*, 40 (September–October 1984), 49–56.

HARRINGTON, DIANA R., *Modern Portfolio Theory, the Capital Asset Pricing Model & Arbitrage Pricing Theory: A User's Guide*, 2nd ed. Englewood Cliffs, N.J.: Prentice-Hall, 1987.

HAUGEN, ROBERT A., *Modern Investment Theory*. Englewood Cliffs, N.J.: Prentice-Hall, 1986.

JOHNSON, RAMON, *Financial Valuation and Analysis*. Dubuque, Iowa: Kendall/Hunt, 1981.

LORIE, JAMES H., PETER DODD, and MARY T. HAMILTON, *The Stock Market*, 2nd ed. Homewood, Ill.: Irwin, 1985.

MODIGLIANI, FRANCO, and GERALD A. POGUE, "An Introduction to Risk and Return," *Financial Analysts Journal*, 30 (March–April 1974), 68–80, and (May–June 1974), 69–86.

MULLINS, DAVID W., JR., "Does the Capital Asset Pricing Model Work?" *Harvard Business Review*, 60 (January–February 1982), 105–14.

REILLY, FRANK K., *Investment Analysis and Portfolio Management*, 3rd ed. Hinsdale, Ill.: Dryden, 1988.

ROLL, RICHARD, "Performance Evaluation and Benchmark Errors," *Journal of Portfolio Management*, 6 (Summer 1980), 5–12.

_____, and STEPHEN A. ROSS, "The Arbitrage Pricing Theory Approach to Strategic Portfolio Planning," *Financial Analysts Journal*, 40 (May–June, 1984), 14–26.

ROSENBERG, BARR, "The Capital Asset Pricing Model and the Market Model," *Journal of Portfolio Management*, 7 (Winter 1981), 5–16.

SHARPE, WILLIAM, "Capital Asset Prices: A Theory of Market Equilibrium Under Conditions of Risk," *Journal of Finance*, 19 (September 1964), 425–42.

_____, *Investments*, 3rd ed. Englewood Cliffs, N.J.: Prentice-Hall, 1985.

SIEGEL, JEREMY J., "The Application of the DCF Methodology for Determining the Cost of Equity Capital," *Financial Management*, 14 (Spring 1985), 46–53.

VAN HORNE, JAMES C., *Financial Market Rates and Flows*, 2nd ed. Englewood Cliffs, N.J.: Prentice-Hall, 1984.

CHAPTER 6

Financial Analysis

Financial analysis means different things to different people. Trade creditors are primarily interested in the liquidity of the firm being analyzed. Their claims are short term, and the ability of the firm to pay these claims can best be judged by an analysis of its liquidity. The claims of bondholders, on the other hand, are long term. Accordingly, they are interested in the cash-flow ability of the firm to service debt over a long period of time. The bondholder may evaluate this ability by analyzing the capital structure of the firm, the major sources and uses of funds, the firm's profitability over time, and projections of future profitability. Finally, an investor in a company's common stock is concerned principally with present and expected future earnings as well as with the stability of these earnings about a trend. As a result, the investor usually concentrates on analyzing the profitability of the firm.

The point of view of the analyst may be either external or internal. In the cases just described, it is external, involving suppliers of capital. From an internal standpoint, the firm needs to undertake financial analysis in order to plan and control effectively. To plan for the future, the financial manager must assess the firm's present financial position and evaluate opportunities in relation to their effect on this position. With respect to internal control, the financial manager is particularly concerned with return on investment in the various assets of the company and in the efficiency of asset management. Finally, to bargain effectively for outside funds, the financial manager needs to be attuned to all aspects of financial analysis that outside suppliers of capital use in evaluating the firm. We see, then, that the type of financial analysis varies according to the particular interests of the analyst.

FINANCIAL STATEMENTS

Financial analysis involves the use of financial statements. These statements attempt to do several things. First, they portray the assets and liabilities of a business firm at a moment in time, usually at the end of a year or a quarter. This portrayal is known as the *balance sheet*. On the other hand, an *income statement* portrays the revenues, expenses, taxes, and profits of the firm for a particular period of time, again usually a year or a quarter. While the balance sheet represents a snapshot of the firm's financial position at a moment in time, the income statement depicts its profitability over time. From these statements certain derivative information can be obtained, such as a statement of retained earnings and a source-and-use-of-funds statement. (We consider the latter in the next chapter.)

In analyzing financial statements, many of you will want to use a computer spreadsheet program, such as Lotus 1-2-3. For repetitive analyses, such a program permits changes in assumptions and simulations to be done with ease. Analyzing various scenarios allows richer insight than otherwise would be the case. In fact, financial statements are an ideal application for these powerful programs, and their use by financial statement analysts and companies is quite common. In the supplement, *Financial Management Computer Applications*, programs are provided for analyzing the financial condition and performance of a company.

Balance Sheet Information

Table 6-1 shows the balance sheet of Aldine Manufacturing Company for the fiscal years ending March 31, 1989, and March 31, 1988. The assets are listed in the upper panel according to their relative degree of liquidity. Cash and marketable securities are the most liquid of assets, and they appear first. On the other hand, fixed assets, long-term investment, and goodwill are the least liquid, and they appear last. Accounts receivable represent IOUs from customers, which should convert into cash within a given billing period, usually 30 to 60 days. Inventories, on the other hand, are used in the production of a product. The product first must be sold and a receivable generated before it can go the next step and be converted into cash. Goodwill is not a tangible asset. Rather, it represents the imputed value associated with a brand label, a product line, or the like. Its value, if realized at all, will come from future earnings of the firm.

Net worth. The book value of a company's common stock, paid-in capital, and retained earnings.

Equity. The net worth of a company consisting of common stock, paid-in capital, and retained earnings.

The bottom panel of the table shows the liabilities and **net worth** of the company. These items are ordered according to the nearness with which they are likely to be paid. All current liabilities are payable within 1 year, whereas the long-term debt is payable beyond 1 year. Stockholders' **equity** will be paid only through regular dividends and, perhaps, a final liquidation dividend.

TABLE 6-1
Aldine Manufacturing Company balance sheet (in thousands)

ASSETS	MARCH 31, 1989	MARCH 31, 1988
Cash and marketable securities	$ 177,689	$ 175,042
Accounts receivable	678,279	740,705
Inventories, at lower cost or market	1,328,963	1,234,725
Prepaid expenses	20,756	17,197
Accumulated tax prepayments	35,203	29,165
Current assets	$2,240,890	$2,196,834
Fixed assets at cost	1,596,886	1,538,495
Less: Accumulated depreciation	856,829	791,205
Net fixed assets	$ 740,057	$ 747,290
Investment, long term	65,376	—
Goodwill	205,157	205,624
Total assets	$3,251,480	$3,149,748

LIABILITIES AND NET WORTH	MARCH 31, 1989	MARCH 31, 1988
Bank loans and notes payable	$ 448,508	$ 356,511
Accounts payable	148,427	136,793
Accrued taxes	36,203	127,455
Other accrued liabilities	190,938	164,285
Current liabilities	$ 824,076	$ 785,044
Long-term debt	630,783	626,460
Common stock, $1 par value	420,828	420,824
Paid-in capital	361,158	361,059
Retained earnings	1,014,635	956,361
Total net worth	$1,796,621	$1,738,244
Total liabilites and net worth	$3,251,480	$3,149,748

Stockholders' equity, or *net worth* as it is called, consists of several subcategories. The first, common stock, represents stock purchased by investors and paid into the company in years gone by. As we discuss in Chapter 22, a par value usually is assigned to the stock. In this case the par value is $1 per share, which means that on March 31, 1989, there were 420,828,000 shares of common stock outstanding. The paid-in capital section is the excess of monies paid for the stock above its par value. If the company were to sell an additional share of stock for $6, there would be a $1 increase in the common stock section and a $5 increase in the paid-in capital section. Retained earnings represent a company's cumulative profits after dividends from the time of its inception. In this sense, it is a residual.

We see in the table that total assets equal total liabilities plus net worth. Indeed, that is an accounting identity. Also, it follows that assets minus liabilities equals net worth. For the most part, the liabilities of a firm are known with certainty. Most accounting questions concerning the balance sheet have to do with the numbers attached to the assets. We must remember that the figures are accounting numbers as opposed to estimates of the economic value of the assets. The value of fixed assets is based on their actual costs, not on what they would cost today (the replacement cost). Inventories are valued in the same manner. The receivable figure implies that all of these receivables will be collected. This may or may not be the case. Often it is necessary to go beyond the reported figures in order to analyze properly the financial condition of the firm. Depending on the analysis, the net-worth figure shown on the financial statement, which is a residual, may or may not be a reasonable approximation of the true net worth of the firm.

Income Statement

The income statement in Table 6-2 shows Aldine's revenues and net profits for the two fiscal years. The cost of goods sold represents the cost of actually pro-

TABLE 6-2
Aldine Manufacturing Company statement of earnings (in thousands)

	YEAR ENDED MARCH 31, 1989	YEAR ENDED MARCH 31, 1988
Net sales	$3,992,758	$3,721,241
Cost of goods sold	2,680,298	2,499,965
Gross profit	$1,312,460	$1,221,276
Selling, general, and administrative expenses	801,395	726,959
Depreciation	111,509	113,989
Interest expense	85,274	69,764
Earnings before taxes	$ 314,282	$ 310,564
Income taxes (federal and state)	113,040	112,356
Earnings after taxes	$ 201,242	$ 198,208
Cash dividends	142,968	130,455
Increase in retained earnings	$ 58,274	$ 67,753

ducing the product. Included here are purchases of raw materials and other items, labor costs associated with production, and other production-related expenses. Selling, general, and administrative expenses are shown separately from the costs of goods sold, so that we can analyze them directly. Depreciation was discussed in Chapter 2, but remember that depreciation is based on historical costs, which in a period of inflation do not correspond to economic costs. Therefore, the profit figure may be distorted. The matter of inflation and financial analysis is explored in the appendix to this chapter.

The last three rows of the income statement shown in Table 6-2 represent a simplified statement of retained earnings. Dividends are deducted from earnings after taxes to give the increase in retained earnings. The increase of $58,274 in fiscal year 1989 should agree with the balance sheet figures in Table 6-1. On the two dates, retained earnings were $1,014,635 and $956,361, their difference being $58,274. Therefore, there is agreement. Note that retained earnings represent a residual. They do not imply funds available to the stockholders. Such availability depends on the firm's liquidity. With this background in mind, we are ready to examine financial analysis.

A POSSIBLE FRAMEWORK FOR ANALYSIS

A number of conceptual frameworks might be used in analyzing a firm. Many analysts have a favorite procedure for coming to some generalizations about the firm being analyzed. At the risk of treading on some rather sacred ground, we present a conceptual framework that lends itself to situations in which external financing is contemplated. The factors to be considered are shown in Fig. 6-1.

Taking them in order, our concern in the first case is with the trend and seasonal component of a firm's funds requirements. How much will be required in the future and what is the nature of these needs? Is there a seasonal component to the needs? Analytical tools used to answer these questions include

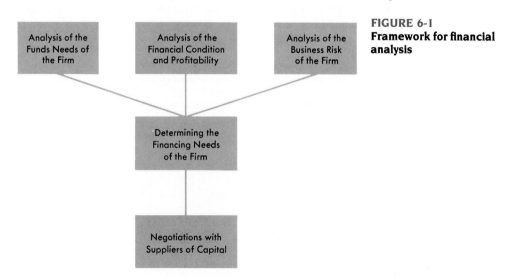

FIGURE 6-1
Framework for financial analysis

source-and-use-of-funds statements and the cash budget, both of which are considered in Chapter 7. The tools used to assess the financial condition and performance of the firm are financial ratios, a topic taken up in this chapter. With these ratios, the skilled analyst dissects the company being analyzed from a number of different angles, in the hope of obtaining valuable insight into its financial condition and profitability. The last factor in the first row of Fig. 6-1, *business risk*, relates to the risk inherent in the operations of the enterprise. Some companies are in highly volatile lines of endeavor, while others are in very stable lines. A machine tool company would fall in the volatile category, an electric utility in the stable. The analyst needs to estimate the degree of business risk of the firm being analyzed.

All three of these factors should be used in determining the financial needs of the firm. Moreover, they should be considered jointly. The greater the funds requirements, of course, the greater the total financing that will be necessary. The nature of the needs for funds influences the type of financing that should be used. If there is a seasonal component to the business, this component lends itself to short-term financing, and bank loans in particular. The basic business risk of the firm also strongly affects the type of financing that should be used. The greater the business risk, the less desirable debt financing usually becomes relative to common stock financing. In other words, equity financing is safer in that there is no contractual obligation to pay interest and principal, as there is with debt. A firm with a high degree of business risk generally is ill advised to take on considerable financial risk as well. The financial condition and performance of the firm also influence the type of financing that should be used. The greater the liquidity, the stronger the overall financial condition and the greater the profitability of the firm, the more risk can be incurred with respect to type of financing. That is, debt financing becomes more attractive with improvements in liquidity, financial condition, and profitability.

The last box in Fig. 6-1 indicates that it is not sufficient simply to determine the best financing plan from the standpoint of the firm and assume that it can be consummated. The plan needs to be sold to outside suppliers of capital. The firm may determine that it needs $1 million in short-term financing, but lenders may not go along with either the amount or the type of financing. In the end, the firm may have to compromise its plan to meet the realities of the marketplace. The interaction of the firm with these suppliers of capital determines the amount, terms, and price of financing. The fact that the firm must negotiate with outside suppliers of capital serves as a feedback mechanism to the other four factors in Fig. 6-1. Analysis cannot be undertaken in isolation from the fact that ultimately an appeal will have to be made to suppliers of capital. Similarly, suppliers of capital must keep an open mind to a company's approach to financing, even if it is different from their own.

Thus, there are a number of facets to financial analysis. Presumably, analysis will be in relation to some structural framework similar to that presented earlier. Otherwise, it is likely to be loose and will not really answer the questions for which it was intended. As we shall see, an integral part of financial analysis is the analysis of financial ratios; that will occupy our attention in the remainder of this chapter.

Use of Financial Ratios

Financial ratio. The ratio of one accounting number to another.

To evaluate a firm's financial condition and performance, the financial analyst needs certain yardsticks. The yardstick frequently used is a **financial ratio**, or index, relating two pieces of financial data to each other. Analysis and interpretation of various ratios should give experienced, skilled analysts a better understanding of the financial condition and performance of the firm than they would obtain from analysis of the financial data alone.

Internal Comparisons.   The analysis of financial ratios involves two types of comparison. First, the analyst can compare a present ratio with past and expected future ratios for the same company. The current ratio (the ratio of current assets to current liabilities) for the present year end could be compared with the current ratio for the previous year end. When financial ratios are arrayed on a spreadsheet over a period of years, the analyst can study the composition of change and determine whether there has been an improvement or a deterioration in the firm's financial condition and performance over time. Financial ratios also can be computed for projected, or pro forma, statements and compared with present and past ratios.

External Comparisons and Sources of Industry Ratios.   The second method of comparison involves comparing the ratios of one firm with those of similar firms or with industry averages at the same point in time. Such a comparison gives insight into the relative financial condition and performance of the firm. Financial ratios for various industries are published by Robert Morris Associates, by Dun & Bradstreet, by Prentice-Hall (*Almanac of Business and Industrial Financial Ratios*), by the Federal Trade Commission and the Securities and Exchange Commission, and by various credit agencies and trade associations.[1] The analyst should avoid using "rules of thumb" indiscriminately for all industries. The criterion that all companies have at least a 2 to 1 current ratio is inappropriate. The analysis must be in relation to the type of business in which the firm is engaged and to the firm itself. The true test of liquidity is whether a company has the ability to pay its bills on time. Many sound companies, including electric utilities, have this ability despite current ratios substantially below 2 to 1. It depends on the nature of the business. Only by comparing the financial ratios of one firm with those of similar firms can one make a realistic judgment.

To the extent possible, accounting data from different companies should be standardized. Apples cannot be compared with oranges. Even with standardized figures, the analyst should use caution in interpreting the comparisons.

---

[1] Robert Morris Associates, an association of bank credit and loan officers, publishes industry averages based on financial statements supplied to banks by borrowers. Eleven ratios are computed annually for over 150 lines of business. In addition, each line of business is divided into 4 size categories. Dun & Bradstreet annually calculates 14 important ratios for over 100 lines of business. *Almanac of Business and Industrial Financial Ratios* (Englewood Cliffs, N.J.: Prentice-Hall, 1989) shows industry averages for some 22 financial ratios. Approximately 170 businesses and industries are listed, covering the complete spectrum. The data for this publication come from U.S. corporate tax filings with the Internal Revenue Service. *The Quarterly Financial Report for Manufacturing Corporations* is published jointly by the Federal Trade Commission and the Securities and Exchange Commission. This publication contains balance sheet and income statement information by industry groupings and by asset-size categories.

Types of Ratios

For our purposes, financial ratios can be grouped into four types: liquidity, debt, profitability, and coverage ratios. No one ratio gives us sufficient information by which to judge the financial condition and performance of the firm. Only when we analyze a group of ratios are we able to make reasonable judgments. We must be sure to take into account any seasonal character of a business. Underlying trends may be assessed only through a comparison of raw figures and ratios at the same time of year. We would not compare a December 31 balance sheet with a May 31 balance sheet but would compare December 31 with December 31.

Although the number of financial ratios that might be computed increases geometrically with the amount of financial data, only the more important ratios are considered in this chapter. Actually, the ratios needed to assess the financial condition and performance of a company are relatively few. Computing un-needed ratios adds not only complexity to the problem but also confusion. To illustrate the ratios taken up in this chapter, we use the balance sheet and income statements of the Aldine Manufacturing Company shown in Tables 6-1 and 6-2.

LIQUIDITY RATIOS

Current Ratio

Liquidity ratios are used to judge a firm's ability to meet short-term obligations. From them, much insight can be obtained into the present cash solvency of the firm and its ability to remain solvent in the event of adversities. One of the most general and most frequently used of these ratios is the **current ratio**:

Current ratio. Current assets divided by current liabilities.

$$\frac{\text{Current assets}}{\text{Current liabilities}}$$

For Aldine, the ratio for 1989 year end is

$$\frac{\$2,240,890}{\$824,076} = 2.72$$

Aldine is engaged in making household electrical appliances. Its current ratio is somewhat above the median ratio for the industry of 2.1. (The median for the industry is taken from Robert Morris Associates, *Statement Studies*.) Although comparisons with industry averages do not always reveal financial strength or weakness, they are meaningful in identifying companies that are out of line. Where a significant deviation occurs, the analyst will want to determine the reasons. Perhaps the industry is overly liquid, and the company being examined is basically sound despite a lower current ratio. In another situation, the company being analyzed may be too liquid, relative to the industry, with the result that it forgoes profitability. Whenever a "red flag" is raised, the analyst must search out the reasons behind it.

Supposedly, the higher the current ratio, the greater the ability of the firm to pay its bills; however, the ratio must be regarded as crude because it does not take into account the **liquidity** of the individual components of the current assets. A firm having current assets composed principally of cash and current receivables is generally regarded as more liquid than a firm whose current assets consist primarily of inventories.[2] Consequently, we must turn to "finer" tools of analysis if we are to evaluate critically the liquidity of the firm.

Liquidity. The assets of the firm that are readily marketable, such as cash and marketable securities. Assets that may be converted to cash quickly and with little price concession.

Acid-Test Ratio

Acid-test, or quick, ratio. Ratio of cash, marketable securities, and receivables to current liabilities.

A somewhat more accurate guide to liquidity is the **quick**, or **acid-test, ratio**:

$$\frac{\text{Current assets} - \text{Inventories}}{\text{Current liabilities}}$$

For Aldine, this ratio is

$$\frac{\$2,240,890 - \$1,328,963}{\$824,076} = 1.11$$

This ratio is the same as the current ratio except that it excludes inventories—presumably the least liquid portion of current assets—from the numerator. The ratio concentrates on cash, marketable securities, and receivables in relation to current obligations and thus provides a more penetrating measure of liquidity than does the current ratio. Aldine's acid-test ratio is slightly above the industry median of 1.1, indicating that it is in line with the industry.

Liquidity of Receivables

When there are suspected imbalances or problems in various components of the current assets, the financial analyst will want to examine these components separately in assessing liquidity. Receivables, for example, may be far from current. To regard all receivables as liquid, when in fact a sizable portion may be past due, overstates the liquidity of the firm being analyzed. Receivables are liquid assets only insofar as they can be collected in a reasonable amount of time. For our analysis of receivables, we have two basic ratios, the first of which is the **average collection period** ratio:

Average collection period. Accounts receivable times days in year divided by annual credit sales.

$$\frac{\text{Receivables} \times \text{Days in year}}{\text{Annual credit sales}}$$

---

[2] We have defined *liquidity* as the ability to realize value in money, the most liquid of assets. Liquidity has two dimensions: (1) the time required to convert the asset into money and (2) the certainty of the realized price. To the extent that the price realized on receivables is as predictable as that realized on inventories, receivables would be a more liquid asset than inventories, owing to the shorter time required to convert the asset into money. If the price realized on receivables is more certain than that on inventories, receivables would be regarded as being even more liquid.

If we assume that all sales for Aldine are credit sales, this ratio is

$$\frac{\$678,279 \times 365}{\$3,992,758} = 62 \text{ days}$$

The average collection period tells us the average number of days receivables are outstanding.

The second ratio is the *receivable turnover ratio:*

$$\frac{\text{Annual credit sales}}{\text{Receivables}}$$

For Aldine, this ratio is

$$\frac{\$3,992,758}{\$678,279} = 5.89$$

These two ratios are inverses of each other. The number of days in the year, 365, divided by the average collection period, 62 days, gives the receivable turnover ratio, 5.89. The number of days in the year divided by the turnover ratio gives the average collection period. Thus, either of these two ratios can be employed.

When credit sales figures for a period are not available, we must resort to total sales figures. The receivable figure used in the calculation ordinarily represents year-end receivables. However, when sales are seasonal or have grown considerably over the year, using the year-end receivable balance may not be appropriate. With seasonality, an average of the monthly closing balances may be the most appropriate figure to use. With growth, the receivable balance at the end of the year will be deceptively high in relation to sales. The result is that the collection period calculated is a biased and high estimate of the time it will take for the receivable balance at year end to be collected. In this case, an average of receivables at the beginning and end of the year might be appropriate if the growth in sales was steady throughout the year. The idea is to relate the relevant receivable position to the credit sales over the year so that apples are compared with apples.

The median industry receivable turnover ratio is 8.1, which tells us that Aldine's receivables are considerably slower in turning over than is typical for the industry (62 days versus 45 days). This finding should cause the analyst concern. One thing to check is the billing terms given on sales. If the average collection period is 62 days and the terms given are 2/10, net 30,[3] a sizable proportion of the receivables are past due beyond the final due date of 30 days. On the other hand, if the terms are net 60, the typical receivable is being collected only two days after the final due date.

Although too high an average collection period is usually bad, a very low average collection period may not necessarily be good. It may be that credit policy is excessively restrictive. The receivables on the book may be of prime qual-

---

[3] The notation means that the supplier gives a 2 percent discount if the receivable invoice is paid within 10 days, and payment is due within 30 days if the discount is not taken.

ity, yet sales may be curtailed unduly—and profits less than they might be—because of this policy. In this situation, credit standards for an acceptable account might be relaxed somewhat.

Aging of Accounts.   Another means by which we can obtain insight into the liquidity of receivables is through an *aging of accounts*. With this method, we categorize the receivables at a moment in time according to the proportions billed in previous months. We might have the following hypothetical aging of accounts receivable at December 31:

Proportion of receivable billed in

DECEMBER	NOVEMBER	OCTOBER	SEPTEMBER	AUGUST AND BEFORE	TOTAL
67%	19%	7%	2%	5%	100%

If the billing terms are 2/10, net 30, this aging tells us that 67 percent of the receivables at December 31 are current, 19 percent are up to 1 month past due, 7 percent are 1 to 2 months past due, and so on. Depending on the conclusions drawn from our analysis of the aging, we may want to examine more closely the credit and collection policies of the company. In the example we might be prompted to investigate the individual receivables that were billed in August and before to determine if any should be charged off. The receivables shown on the books are only as good as the likelihood that they will be collected. An aging of accounts receivable gives us considerably more information than does the calculation of the average collection period, because it pinpoints the trouble spots more specifically.

Duration of Payables

From a creditor's point of view, it is desirable to obtain an *aging of accounts payable* or a *conversion matrix for payables*. These measures, combined with the less exact turnover of payables (annual credit purchases divided by payables), allow us to analyze payables in much the same manner as we analyze receivables. Also, we can compute the average age of a firm's **accounts payable.** The average payable period is

Accounts payable. Amounts owed to suppliers. A short-term liability.

$$\frac{\text{Accounts payable} \times 365}{\text{Purchases}}$$

where accounts payable is the average balance oustanding for the year and the denominator is external purchases during the year.

When information on purchases is not available, one occasionally can use the cost of goods sold in the denominator. A department store chain, for example, typically does no manufacturing. As a result, the cost of goods sold consists primarily of purchases. However, in situations where there is sizable value added, such as with a manufacturer, the use of the cost of goods sold is inappropriate. One must have the amount of purchases if the ratio is to be used. Another caveat has to do with growth. As with receivables, the use of a year-end payable balance will result in a biased and high estimate of the time it will take a company to make payment on its payables if there is strong underlying growth. In this situation, it may be better to use an average of payables at the beginning and end of the year.

The average payable period is valuable in evaluating the probability that a credit applicant will pay on time. If the average age of payables is 48 days, and the terms in the industry are net 30, we know that a portion of the applicant's payables is not being paid on time. A credit check of other suppliers will give insight into the severity of the problem.

Liquidity of Inventories

We may compute the *inventory turnover ratio* as an indicator of the liquidity of inventory:

$$\frac{\text{Cost of goods sold}}{\text{Average inventory}}$$

For Aldine, the ratio is

$$\frac{\$2,680,298}{\$1,281,844} = 2.09$$

The figure for cost of goods sold used in the numerator is for the period being studied—usually 1 year; the average inventory figure used in the denominator typically is an average of beginning and ending inventories for the period. As is true with receivables, however, it may be necessary to compute a more sophisticated average when there is a strong seasonal element. The inventory turnover ratio tells us the rapidity with which the inventory is turned over into receivables through sales. This ratio, like other ratios, must be judged in relation to past and expected future ratios of the firm and in relation to ratios of similar firms, the industry average, or both.

Generally, the higher the inventory turnover, the more efficient the inventory management of a firm. Sometimes, a relatively high inventory turnover ratio may be the result of too low a level of inventory and frequent stockouts. It might also be the result of too many small orders for inventory replacement. Either of these situations may be more costly to the firm than carrying a larger investment in inventory and having a lower turnover ratio. Again, caution is necessary in interpreting the ratio. When the inventory turnover ratio is relatively low, it indicates slow-moving inventory or obsolescence of some of the stock. Obsolescence may necessitate substantial write-downs, which, in turn, would negate the treatment of inventory as a liquid asset. Because the turnover ratio is a somewhat crude measure, we would want to investigate any perceived inefficiency in inventory management. In this regard, it is helpful to compute the turnover of the major categories of inventory to see if there are imbalances, which may indicate excessive investment in specific components of the inventory. Once we have a hint of a problem, we must investigate it more specifically to determine its cause.

Aldine's inventory turnover ratio of 2.09 compares with a median turnover for the industry of 3.3. This unfavorable comparison suggests the company is less efficient in inventory management than is the industry and that Aldine holds excessive stock. A question also arises as to whether the inventory on the books is worth its stated value. If not, the liquidity of the firm is less than the current or quick ratio alone suggests. Once we have a hint of an inventory problem, we must investigate it along the lines of our previous discussion to determine its cause.

Summary of Aldine's Liquidity

Although comparisons of Aldine's current and quick ratios with medians for the industry are favorable, a more detailed examination of receivables and inventory reveals some problems. The turnover ratios for both of these assets are significantly less than the median ratios for the industry. These findings suggest that the two assets are not entirely current, and this factor detracts from the favorable current and quick ratios. A sizable portion of receivables is slow, and there appear to be inefficiencies in inventory management. On the basis of our analysis, we conclude that these assets are not particularly liquid in the sense of turning over into cash in a reasonable period of time.

DEBT RATIOS

Debt ratio. The amount of debt divided by either the amount of equity or the amount of total assets.

Extending our analysis to the long-term liquidity of the firm (i.e., its ability to meet long-term obligations), we may use several **debt ratios**. The *debt-to-net-worth ratio* is computed by simply dividing the total debt of the firm (including current liabilities) by its net worth:

$$\frac{\text{Total debt}}{\text{Net worth}}$$

For Aldine, the ratio is

$$\frac{\$1,454,859}{\$1,796,621} = .81$$

The ratio tells us that for every $1.81 of assets creditors have furnished $.81 of financing, or 45 percent. Theoretically, asset values could shrink by 55 percent before creditors would stand to lose. Whether in practice this is true depends on the book value of assets reasonably reflecting market value. The median debt-to-net-worth ratio for the electrical appliance industry is .8, so Aldine is right in line with the industry. Presumably it would not experience difficulty with creditors because of an excessive debt ratio.

When intangible assets are significant, they frequently are deducted from net worth to obtain the tangible net worth of the firm. Depending on the purpose for which the ratio is used, preferred stock sometimes is included as debt rather than as net worth. Preferred stock represents a prior claim from the standpoint of the investors in common stock; consequently, we might include preferred stock as debt when analyzing a firm. The ratio of debt to equity will vary according to the nature of the business and volatility of cash flows. An electric utility, with very stable cash flows, usually will have a higher debt ratio than will a machine tool company, whose cash flows are far less stable. A comparison of the debt ratio for a given company with those of similar firms gives us a general indication of the creditworthiness and financial risk of the firm.

In addition to the ratio of total debt to equity, we may wish to compute the following ratio, which deals with only the long-term capitalization of the firm:

$$\frac{\text{Long-term debt}}{\text{Total capitalization}}$$

where total capitalization represents all long-term debt and net worth. For Aldine, the ratio is

$$\frac{\$630,783}{\$2,427,404} = .26$$

This measure tells us the relative importance of long-term debt in the capital structure. Again this ratio is in line with the median ratio of .24 for the industry. The debt ratios just computed have been based on book-value figures; it is sometimes useful to calculate these ratios using market values. In summary, debt ratios tell us the relative proportions of capital contribution by creditors and by owners.

Cash Flow to Debt

A measure of the ability of a company to service its debt is the relationship of annual cash flow to the amount of debt outstanding. The cash flow of a company usually is defined as the cash generated from the operations of the company. In the case of a profitable company, it is composed of net income and depreciation. The *cash-flow-to-total-liabilities* ratio is simply

$$\frac{\text{Cash flow}}{\text{Total liabilities}}$$

For Aldine, the ratio is

$$\frac{\$312,751}{\$1,454,859} = .21$$

The cash flow is composed of earnings after taxes of $201,242 and depreciation of $111,509, whereas total debt is composed of $824,076 in current liabilities and $630,783 in long-term debt. This ratio is useful in assessing the creditworthiness of a company seeking short- or intermediate-term debt, such as a bank loan.

Another ratio is the *cash-flow-to-long-term-debt ratio*:

$$\frac{\text{Cash flow}}{\text{Long-term debt}}$$

Here we have the following for Aldine

$$\frac{\$312,751}{\$630,783} = .50$$

This ratio tends to be used in the evaluation of the bonds of a company. The two cash-flow ratios just described have proven useful in predicting the deteriorating financial health of a company. Unfortunately, median ratios for the industry are not available for comparison.

COVERAGE RATIOS

Times interest earned. Annual earnings divided by annual inerest on debt. A coverage ratio.

Coverage ratios are designed to relate the financial charges of a firm to its ability to service them. Bond rating services such as Moody's Investors Service and Standard & Poor's make extensive use of these ratios. One of the most traditional of the coverage ratios is the *interest coverage ratio*, or **times interest earned**, simply the ratio of earnings before interest and taxes for a particular reporting period to the amount of interest charges for the period. We must differentiate which interest charges should be used in the denominator. The *overall coverage method* stresses a company's meeting all fixed interest, regardless of the seniority of the claim. We have the following financial data for a hypothetical company:

Average earnings	$2,000,000
Interest on senior 10% bonds	−400,000
	$1,600,000
Interest on junior 12% bonds	160,000

The overall interest coverage would be $2,000,000/$560,000, or 3.57. This method implies that the creditworthiness of the senior bonds is only as good as the firm's ability to cover all interest charges.

Of the various coverage ratios, the most objectionable is the *prior-deductions method*. Using this method, we deduct interest on the senior bonds from average earnings and then divide the residual by the interest on the junior bonds. We find that the coverage on the junior bonds in our example is 10 times

($1,600,000/$160,000). Thus, the junior bonds give the illusion of being more se-cure than the senior obligations. Clearly, this method is inappropriate.

The *cumulative-deduction method* is, perhaps, the most widely used method of computing interest coverage. Under this method, coverage for the se-nior bonds would be five times. Coverage for the junior bonds is determined by adding the interest charges on both bonds and relating the total to average earn-ings. Thus, the coverage for the junior bonds would be $2,000,000/$560,000 = 3.57 times.

One of the principal shortcomings of an interest coverage ratio is that a firm's ability to service debt is related both to interest and principal payments. Moreover, these payments are not met out of earnings, per se, but out of cash. Hence, a more appropriate coverage ratio relates the cash flow of the firm to the sum of interest and principal payments. *The cash-flow coverage ratio* may be ex-pressed as

$$\frac{\text{EBIT} + \text{Depreciation } [1/(1-t)]}{\text{Interest} + \text{Principal payments } [1/(1-t)]}$$

where EBIT is earnings before interest and taxes, and t is the income tax rate.[4] Because principal payments are made after taxes, it is necessary to gross up this figure by $[1/(1-t)]$ so that it corresponds to interest payments, which are made before taxes. If the tax rate were $33\frac{1}{3}$ percent and annual principal payments $100,000, before-tax earnings of $150,000 would be needed to cover these pay-ments. Similarly, the depreciation charges in the numerator need to be grossed up to put them on a basis equivalent to the principal payments. If there is tax rate uncertainty owing to fluctuating earnings, both of these adjustments would be less.

A broader type of analysis would evaluate the ability of the firm to cover all charges of a fixed nature in relation to its cash flow. In addition to interest and principal payments on debt obligations, we would include preferred stock divi-dends, lease payments, and possibly even certain essential capital expenditures. As we will see in Chapter 17, an analysis of this type is a far more realistic gauge than is a simple interest coverage ratio in determining whether a firm has the ability to meet its long-term obligations.

In assessing the financial risk of a firm, then, the financial analyst should first compute the debt ratios as a rough measure of financial risk. Depending on the payment schedule of the debt and the average interest rate, debt ratios may or may not give an accurate picture of the ability of the firm to meet its financial obligations. Therefore, it is necessary to analyze additionally the cash-flow abil-ity of the firm to service debt. This is done by relating cash flow not only to the amount of debt outstanding but also to the amount of financial charges. In this way, the financial analyst is able to get an accurate idea of the financial risk of the firm. Neither debt ratios nor coverage ratios are sufficient by themselves.

---

[4] I am grateful to Robert J. Angell for suggesting this equation.

PROFITABILITY RATIOS

Profitability ratios are of two types: those showing profitability in relation to sales and those showing profitability in relation to investment. Together, these ratios indicate the firm's efficiency of operation.

Profitability in Relation to Sales

The first ratio we consider is the *gross profit margin:*

$$\frac{\text{Sales less cost of goods sold}}{\text{Sales}}$$

or simply gross profit divided by sales. For Aldine, the gross profit margin is

$$\frac{\$1,312,460}{\$3,992,758} = 32.9 \text{ percent}$$

This ratio tells us the profit of the firm relative to sales after we deduct the cost of producing the goods sold. It indicates the efficiency of operations as well as how products are priced. Aldine's gross profit margin is significantly above the median of 23.8 percent for the industry, indicating that it is relatively more efficient in producing appliances.

A more specific ratio of profitability is the *net profit margin:*

$$\frac{\text{Net profits after taxes}}{\text{Sales}}$$

For Aldine, this ratio is

$$\frac{\$201,242}{\$3,992,758} = 5.04\%$$

The net profit margin tells us the relative efficiency of the firm after taking into account all expenses and income taxes, but not extraordinary charges. Aldine's net profit margin is above the median margin (2.7 percent) for the industry, which indicates that it is more profitable on a relative basis than are most other firms in the industry.

By considering both ratios jointly, we are able to gain considerable insight into the operations of the firm. If the gross profit margin essentially is unchanged over a period of several years, but the net profit margin has declined over the same period, we know that the cause is either higher expenses relative to sales or a higher tax rate. Therefore, we would analyze these factors more specifically to determine the cause of the problem. On the other hand, if the gross profit margin falls, we know that the cost of producing goods relative to sales has increased. This occurrence, in turn, may be due to lower prices or to lower operating efficiency in relation to volume.

Profitability in Relation to Investment

The second group of profitability ratios relates profits to investments. One of these measures is the rate of **return on equity**, or the *ROE*.

$$\frac{\text{Net profits after taxes less preferred stock dividend}}{\text{Net worth less par value of preferred stock}}$$

Return on equity. Average annual earnings divided by equity, usually in bookvalue terms.

For Aldine, the rate of return is

$$\frac{\$201,242}{\$1,796,621} = 11.20\%$$

This ratio tells us the earning power on shareholders' book investment and ·is frequently used in comparing two or more firms in an industry. Aldine's rate of return is somewhat below the median return (10.6 percent) for the industry. Thus, while Aldine has a higher profit margin on its sales than the industry has, it has a lower return on its net worth. This phenomenon suggests that Aldine needs relatively greater assets to produce sales than do most other firms in the industry.

To investigate the problem more directly, we turn to the *return on assets ratio:*

$$\frac{\text{Net profits after taxes}}{\text{Total tangible assets}}$$

For Aldine, the ratio is:

$$\frac{\$201,242}{\$3,046,323} = 6.19\%$$

where goodwill is deducted from total assets to obtain total tangible assets. This ratio compares with a median of 5.2 percent for the industry. Higher profitability per dollar of sales but a slightly lower return on assets tells us that Aldine must employ more assets to generate a dollar of sales than does the industry on the average.

Turnover and Earning Power

The relationship of sales to total assets is known as the *turnover ratio:*

$$\frac{\text{Sales}}{\text{Total tangible assets}}$$

Aldine's turnover for the 1989 fiscal year was

$$\frac{\$3,992,758}{\$3,046,323} = 1.31$$

The median turnover for the industry is 1.66, so it is clear that Aldine employs more assets per dollar of sales than does the industry on average. The turnover ratio tells us the relative efficiency with which a firm utilizes its resources to generate output. Aldine is less efficient than the industry in this regard. For our previous analysis of Aldine's liquidity, we may suspect excessive investments in receivables and inventories.

When we multiply the asset turnover of the firm by the net profit margin, we obtain the return on assets ratio, or *earning power* on total tangible assets:

$$\text{Earning power} = \frac{\text{Sales}}{\text{Total tangible assets}} \times \frac{\text{Net profits after taxes}}{\text{Sales}}$$

$$= \frac{\text{Net profits after taxes}}{\text{Total tangible assets}}$$

For Aldine, we have

$$\frac{\$3,992,758}{\$3,046,323} \times \frac{\$201,242}{\$3,992,758} = 6.19\%$$

Neither the net profit margin nor the turnover ratio by itself provides an adequate measure of operating efficiency. The net profit margin ignores the utilization of assets, whereas the turnover ratio ignores profitability on sales. The return on assets ratio, or earning power, resolves these shortcomings. An improvement in the earning power of the firm will result if there is an increase in turnover on existing assets, an increase in the net profit margin, or both. The interrelation of these ratios is shown in Fig. 6-2. Two firms with different asset

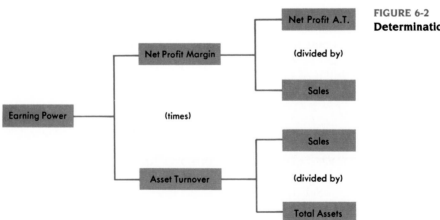

FIGURE 6-2
Determination of earning power

turnovers and net profit margins may have the same earning power. Firm A, with an asset turnover of 4 to 1 and a net profit margin of 3 percent, has the same earning power—12 percent—as Firm B, with an asset turnover of $1\frac{1}{2}$ to 1 and a net profit margin of 8 percent.

With all of the profitability ratios, comparing one company to similar companies is extremely valuable. Only by comparison are we able to judge whether the profitability of a particular company is good or bad, and why. Absolute figures provide some insight, but it is relative performance that is most revealing.

TREND OVER TIME

Up to now, our concern has been with presenting the various financial ratios, explaining their use in analysis, and comparing the ratios computed for our example company with industry averages. As we pointed out earlier, it also is valuable to compare the financial ratios for a given company over time. In this way, the analyst is able to detect any improvement or deterioration in its financial condition and performance.

To illustrate, Table 6-3 shows some of the financial ratios we have studied for Aldine Manufacturing Company over the 1980–1989 period. As can be seen, the current and acid-test ratios tended to fluctuate through 1984 and then increase through 1988, falling off somewhat in 1989. Paralleling this behavior were movements in the average receivable collection period and the inventory turnover ratio. The former increased steadily from 1984 through 1987, after which it declined somewhat while the latter decreased steadily throughout. The trends here tell us that there has been a relative buildup in receivables and inventory. The turnover of both has slowed, which raises questions as to the quality of these assets. When a trend analysis of receivables and inventory is coupled with a comparison to median ratios for the industry, the only conclusion possible is that a problem exists. The analyst would want to investigate the credit policies of Aldine, the company's collection experience, and its bad-debt losses.

TABLE 6-3
**Financial ratios of Aldine Manufacturing Company
for fiscal years 1980–1989**

	1980	1981	1982	1983	1984	1985	1986	1987	1988	1989
Current ratio	2.21	2.09	2.11	2.06	1.98	2.19	2.41	2.37	2.79	2.72
Acid-test ratio	0.94	0.86	0.92	0.90	0.88	0.95	1.01	1.02	1.22	1.11
Average receivable collection period (days)	38	37	45	41	39	46	48	55	72	62
Inventory turnover	3.61	3.34	3.28	3.55	3.40	3.19	2.94	2.68	2.17	2.09
Total debt/net worth	0.95	0.92	0.98	0.97	0.93	0.90	0.87	0.86	0.81	0.81
Gross profit margin	35.8%	32.6%	28.4%	29.7%	30.9%	27.4%	28.9%	30.6%	32.8%	32.9%
Net profit margin	4.63%	4.02%	2.68%	3.07%	3.36%	2.04%	2.67%	3.02%	5.33%	5.04%
Return on assets	8.45%	7.53%	4.82%	5.92%	6.47%	4.23%	4.97%	5.21%	6.29%	6.19%
Turnover ratio	1.42	1.44	1.43	1.48	1.46	1.47	1.42	1.38	1.26	1.31

Moreover, one should investigate inventory management, obsolescence of inventory, and any imbalances that might exist. Thus, despite the overall improvement in current and acid-test ratios, the apparent deterioration in receivables and inventory is a matter of concern and needs to be investigated in depth.

The debt-to-net-worth ratio has declined somewhat since 1982, indicating some improvement in overall condition from the standpoint of creditors, all other things staying the same. The gross profit margin and net profit margin have fluctuated over time. Since 1985, however, both ratios have shown steady improvement, which is encouraging. Similarly, the return on assets has shown steady improvement during this time span, though both it and the net profit margin fell off modestly in 1989. The improvement in return on assets during the 1985–1988 period is particularly striking because the turnover ratio declined. This means that more assets were needed to generate a dollar of sales. From our analysis of liquidity, we know that the primary cause was the large relative increase in receivables and inventory.

We see, then, that the analysis of the trend of financial ratios over time can give the analyst valuable insight into the changes that have occurred in a firm's financial condition and performance. When a trend analysis is combined with comparisons of similar companies and the industry average, the depth of analysis possible is magnified considerably.

COMMON-SIZE AND INDEX ANALYSES

In addition to financial ratio analysis over time, often it is useful to express balance sheet and income statement items as percentages. The percentages can be related to totals, such as total assets or total sales, or to some base year. Called *common-size* and *index* analyses, respectively, these evaluations of trends in financial statement percentages over time afford the analyst insight into the underlying improvement or deterioration in financial condition and performance. While a good portion of this insight is revealed in the analysis of financial ratios, a broader understanding of the trends is possible when the analysis is extended to include the foregoing considerations. To illustrate these two types of analyses, we shall use the balance sheet and income statements of Riker Electronics Company for the 1986 through 1989 fiscal years. These statements are shown in Tables 6-4 and 6-5.

Statement Items as Percents of Totals

In common-size analysis, we express the various components of a balance sheet as percentages of a company's total assets. In addition, this can be done for the income statement, but here items are related to sales. The gross and net profit margins, which we took up earlier, are examples of this type of expression, and it can be extended to all of the items on the income statement. The expression of

TABLE 6-4
Riker Electronics Company balance sheet (in thousands)

ASSETS	1986	1987	1988	1989
Cash	$ 2,507	$ 4,749	$ 11,310	$ 19,648
Accounts receivable	70,360	72,934	85,147	118,415
Inventory	77,380	86,100	91,378	118,563
Other current assets	6,316	5,637	6,082	5,891
Current assets	$156,563	$169,420	$193,917	$262,517
Fixed assets, net	79,187	91,868	94,652	115,461
Other long-term assets	4,695	5,017	5,899	5,491
Total assets	$240,445	$266,305	$294,468	$383,469

LIABILITIES AND NET WORTH	1986	1987	1988	1989
Accounts payable	$ 35,661	$ 31,857	$ 37,460	$ 62,725
Notes payable	20,501	25,623	14,680	17,298
Other current liabilities	11,054	7,330	8,132	15,741
Current liabilities	$ 67,216	$ 64,810	$ 60,272	$ 95,764
Long-term debt	888	979	1,276	1,917
Total liabilities	$ 68,104	$ 65,789	$ 61,548	$ 97,681
Preferred stock	0	0	0	2,088
Common stock	12,650	25,649	26,038	26,450
Paid-in capital	36,134	33,297	45,883	63,049
Retained earnings	123,557	141,570	160,999	194,201
Net worth	$172,341	$200,516	$232,920	$283,700
Total liabilities and net worth	$240,445	$266,305	$294,468	$383,469

TABLE 6-5
Riker Electronics Company income statement (in thousands)

	1986	1987	1988	1989
Sales	$323,780	$347,322	$375,088	$479,077
Cost of goods sold	148,127	161,478	184,507	223,690
Gross profit	$175,653	$185,844	$190,581	255,387
Selling expenses	79,399	98,628	103,975	125,645
General and administrative expenses	43,573	45,667	45,275	61,719
Total expenses	$122,972	$144,295	$149,250	$187,364
Earnings before interest and taxes	52,681	41,549	41,331	68,023
Other income	1,757	4,204	2,963	3,017
Earnings before taxes	$ 54,438	$ 45,753	$ 44,294	$ 71,040
Taxes	28,853	22,650	20,413	32,579
Earnings after taxes	$ 25,585	$ 23,103	$ 23,881	$ 38,461

individual financial statement items as percentage of totals usually offers insights not yielded by a review of the raw figures themselves. In this as well as in index analysis the use of a spreadsheet program, such as Lotus 1-2-3, makes the task much easier.

To illustrate, common-size balance sheet and income statements are shown in Tables 6-6 and 6-7 for Riker Electronics Company for the fiscal years 1986 through 1989. In Table 6-6 we see that over the 4-year span, the percentage of current assets increased and that this was particularly true for cash. In addition, we see that accounts receivable showed a relative increase from 1988 to 1989. On the liability and net worth side of the balance sheet, the debt of the company declined on a relative basis from 1986 to 1989. However, with the large absolute increase in assets that occurred in 1988, the debt ratio increased from 1988 to 1989. This is particularly apparent in accounts payable, which increased substantially in both absolute and relative terms.

The common-size income statement shown in Table 6-7 shows the gross profit margin fluctuating from year to year. When this is combined with selling, general, and administrative expenses, which also fluctuate over time, the end result is a relative profit picture that varies from year to year. While 1989 shows a sharp improvement over 1988 and 1987, it still is not as good as 1986 on a before-tax relative basis.

TABLE 6-6
Riker Electronics Company common-size balance sheet

ASSETS	1986	1987	1988	1989
Cash	1.0%	1.8%	3.8%	5.1%
Accounts receivable	29.3	27.4	28.9	30.9
Inventory	32.2	32.3	31.0	30.9
Other current assets	2.6%	2.1%	2.1%	1.5%
Current assets	65.1%	63.6%	65.9%	68.5%
Fixed assets, net	32.9	34.5	32.1	30.1
Other long-term assets	2.0	1.9	2.0	1.4
Total assets	100.0%	100.0%	100.0%	100.0%

LIABILITIES AND NET WORTH	1986	1987	1988	1989
Accounts payable	14.8%	12.0%	12.7%	16.4%
Notes payable	8.5	9.6	5.0	4.5
Other current liabilities	4.6	2.8	2.8	4.1
Current liabilities	28.0%	24.3%	20.5%	25.0%
Long-term debt	0.4	0.4	0.4	0.5
Total liabilities	28.3%	24.7%	20.9%	25.5%
Preferred stock	0.0	0.0	0.0	0.5
Common stock	5.3	9.6	8.8	6.9
Paid-in capital	15.0	12.5	15.6	16.4
Retained earnings	51.4	53.2	54.7	50.6
Net worth	71.7%	75.3%	79.1%	74.0%
Total liabilities and net worth	100.0%	100.0%	100.0%	100.0%

TABLE 6-7
Riker Electronics Company common-size income statement

	1986	1987	1988	1989
Sales	100.0%	100.0%	100.0%	100.0%
Cost of goods sold	45.7	46.5	49.2	46.7
Gross profit	54.3%	53.5%	50.8%	53.3%
Selling expenses	24.5	28.4	27.7	26.2
General and administrative				
expenses	13.5	13.1	12.1	12.9
Total expenses	38.0%	41.5%	39.8%	39.1%
Earnings before interest				
and taxes	16.3	12.0	11.0	14.2
Other income	0.5	1.2	0.8	0.6
Earnings before taxes	16.8%	13.2%	11.8%	14.8%
Taxes	8.9	6.5	5.4	6.8
Earnings after taxes	7.9%	6.7%	6.4%	8.0%

Statement Items as Indexes Relative to a Base Year

The common-size balance sheet and income statement can be supplemented by the expression of items as trends from a base year. In the case of Riker Electronics Company, the base year is 1986, and all financial statement items are 100.0 for that year. Items for the three subsequent years are expressed as an index relative to that year. If a statement item were $22,500 compared with $15,000 in the base year, the index would be 150. Tables 6-8 and 6-9 show indexed balance sheet and income statements. In Table 6-8 the buildup in cash from the base year is particularly apparent, and this agrees with our previous assessment. Note also the large increase in accounts receivable and inventories from 1988 to 1989. The latter was not apparent in the common-size analysis. To a lesser extent, there was a sizable increase in fixed assets. On the liability side of the balance sheet, we note the large increase in accounts payable as well as in other current liabilities that occurred from 1988 to 1989. This, coupled with retained earnings and the sale of common stock, financed the large increase in assets that occurred between these two points in time.

The indexed income statement in Table 6-9 gives much the same picture as the common-size income statement, namely, fluctuating behavior. The sharp improvement in 1989 profitability is more easily distinguished. Moreover, the indexed statement gives us information on the magnitude of absolute change in profits and expenses. With the common-size statement, we have no information about how total assets or total sales change over time.

In summary, the standardization of balance sheet and income statement items as percentages of totals and as indexes to a base year often gives us insights additional to those obtained from analysis of financial ratios. Common-size and index analyses are much easier when a computer spreadsheet program is employed. The division calculations by rows or by columns can be done quickly and accurately with such a program.

TABLE 6-8
Riker Electronics Company indexed balance sheet

ASSETS	1986	1987	1988	1989
Cash	100.0	189.4	451.1	783.7
Accounts receivable	100.0	103.7	121.0	168.3
Inventory	100.0	111.3	118.1	153.2
Other current assets	100.0	89.2	96.3	93.2
Current assets	100.0	108.2	123.9	167.7
Fixed assets, net	100.0	116.0	119.5	145.8
Other long-term assets	100.0	106.9	125.6	117.0
Total assets	100.0	110.8	122.5	159.5

LIABILITIES AND NET WORTH	1986	1987	1988	1989
Accounts payable	100.0	89.3	105.0	175.9
Notes payable	100.0	125.0	71.6	84.4
Other current liabilities	100.0	66.3	73.6	142.4
Current liabilities	100.0	96.4	89.7	142.5
Long-term debt	100.0	110.2	143.7	215.9
Total liabilities	100.0	96.6	90.4	143.4
Preferred stock	0.0	0.0	0.0	0.0
Common stock	100.0	202.8	205.8	209.1
Paid-in capital	100.0	92.1	127.0	174.5
Retained earnings	100.0	114.6	130.3	157.2
Net worth	100.0	116.3	135.2	165.8
Total liabilities and net worth	100.0	110.8	122.5	159.5

TABLE 6-9
Riker Electronics Company indexed income statement

	1986	1987	1988	1989
Sales	100.0	107.3	115.8	148.0
Cost of goods sold	100.0	109.0	124.6	151.0
Gross profit	100.0	105.8	108.5	145.4
Selling expenses	100.0	124.2	131.0	158.2
General and administrative expenses	100.0	104.8	103.9	141.6
Total expenses	100.0	117.3	121.4	152.4
Earnings before interest and taxes	100.0	78.9	78.5	129.1
Other income	100.0	239.3	168.6	171.7
Earnings before taxes	100.0	84.0	81.4	130.5
Taxes	100.0	78.5	70.7	112.9
Earnings after taxes	100.0	90.3	93.3	150.3

SUMMARY

Financial analysis necessarily involves financial statements. In this regard, the important items on the balance sheet and the income statement were presented, and interrelationships were discussed. In financial analysis, one is concerned with the funds needs of the firm, its financial condition and performance, and its business risk. Upon analysis of these factors, one is able to determine the firm's financing needs and to negotiate with outside suppliers of capital. The framework proposed provides an interlocking means for structuring analysis.

Financial ratios are the tools used to analyze financial condition and performance. These ratios can be divided into four types: liquidity, debt, profitability, and coverage. No one ratio is sufficient in itself for realistic assessment of the financial condition and performance of a firm. With a group of ratios, however, reasonable judgments can be made. The number of ratios needed for this purpose is not particularly large—about a dozen.

Outside creditors and investors extensively employ the ratios taken up in this chapter. These ratios are also helpful for managerial control and for a better understanding of what outside suppliers of capital expect in financial condition and performance. The usefulness of the ratios depends on the ingenuity and experience of the financial analyst who employs them. By themselves, financial ratios are fairly meaningless; they must be analyzed on a comparative basis. A comparison of ratios of the same firm over time uncovers leading clues in evaluating changes and trends in the firm's financial condition and profitability. The principles of trend analysis were illustrated.

Insight can be gained also by common-size and index analyses. In the former, we express the various balance sheet items as a percentage of total assets and the income statement items as a percentage of total sales. In the latter, balance sheet and income statement items are expressed as an index relative to an initial base year. In addition to historical comparisons for the same company, financial ratios may be judged in comparison with those of similar firms in the same line of business and, when appropriate, with an industry average. Much can be gleaned from a thorough analysis of financial ratios about the firm's financial condition and performance.

APPENDIX
Inflation and Financial Analysis

In financial ratio analysis, inflationary forces may mask the results. Part of the financial performance of a company may result from management decisions, but part may be attributable to external factors over which management has little control. In particular, inflation may give rise to holding-period gains that are not attributable to management decisions. The problem with holding-period gains is that they vary with inflation, and this clouds the analysis of the overall results. To the extent the financial analyst wishes to differentiate performance based on conventional accounting data from economic profitability, he will need to adjust the accounting numbers.

The Problem Illustrated

Foster Tool Company, a wholesaler of tools, began business on December 31, 19x1, and had the following balance sheet at that time:

ASSETS		LIABILITIES AND NET WORTH	
Cash	$ 40,000		
Inventory	100,000	Common stock	$240,000
Net fixed assets	100,000		
	$240,000		$240,000

The fixed assets are depreciable over 10 years, and for ease of illustration we assume straight-line depreciation. Inventory is reported on the first-in, first-out (FIFO) basis.[5] Sales occur entirely at the end of the first year of operation, and inflation for that year was 20 percent. For ease of understanding, we assume that inflation occurred at the beginning of 19x2 and that we live in a world of no taxes.

Operations for the first year are reported on an historical cost basis and are as follows:

INCOME STATEMENT		
Sales		$170,000
Cost of goods sold		
Beginning inventory	$100,000	
Purchases	120,000	
Ending inventory	(120,000)	100,000
Depreciation ($100,000/10)		10,000
Selling and administrative expenses		30,000
Net profit		$ 30,000

Note that the company's ending inventory is higher than its beginning inventory by the percentage increase in prices, namely, 20 percent. The balance sheet of the company at December 31, 19x2 would be

ASSETS		LIABILITIES AND NET WORTH	
Cash	$ 60,000		
Inventory	120,000	Common stock	$240,000
Net fixed assets	90,000	Retained earnings	30,000
	$270,000		$270,000

---

[5] This example draws on Lawrence Revsine, *Accounting in an Inflationary Environment* (New York: Laventhol & Horwath, 1977).

If we compute two of the more widely used profitability ratios, we find them to be

$$\text{Net profit margin } (\$30,000/\$170,000) = 17.65\%$$

$$\text{Return on assets } (\$30,000/\$240,000) = 12.50\%$$

In both cases the underlying economic profitability of the company is overstated. For one thing, with the FIFO method, inventories that are sold are assumed to have been purchased at the prices prevailing when the oldest items in the inventory were purchased. With inflation, these prices will be considerably below their replacement costs. In the case of Foster Tool Company, the inventories sold are valued at $100,000 for accounting purposes, whereas their replacement cost at the time they were sold was $120,000. The costing of inventories in this manner tends to understate economic costs and to overstate economic profits. A remedy is to use the last-in, first-out (LIFO) method. With this method, the inventory most recently purchasesd is employed in the cost of goods sold. As a result, the value attached to the inventory approximates the replacement cost.

In addition to inventory valuation on a FIFO basis overstating economic profits, depreciation charges in our example are based on the original cost of the fixed assets, less accumulated depreciation. Again, with inflation, the original cost is less than the current replacement cost of these assets. If these assets increase in value by 20 percent, their replacement vaue is $120,000, and economic depreciation would be $12,000 instead of the $10,000 used for accounting depreciation purposes.

Restating the income statement of Foster Tool Company on a replacement cost basis, we have for 19x2

INCOME STATEMENT	
Sales	$170,000
Cost of goods sold (replacement cost)	120,000
Depreciation ($120,000/10)	12,000
Selling and administrative expenses	30,000
Net profit	$ 8,000

The profitability ratios are as follows when economic profits as opposed to profits on an historical cost basis are used:

$$\text{Net profit margin } (\$8,000/\$170,000) = 4.70\%$$

$$\text{Return on assets } (\$8,000/\$240,000) = 3.33\%$$

We see, then, that the economic performance results are substantially lower than those originally supposed when accounting data were used.

Implications

The example illustrates the problems involved when the analyst tries to compare the financial ratios of a company over time in the face of differing rates of inflation. Historical cost accounting data are distorted from year to year as a result of inflation. Financial ratios, particularly those dealing with profitability, likewise are distorted. Some of the operating results are due to inflation, which is beyond management's control. What may appear to be a significant change in profitability may, upon closer examination, be due to the vagaries of inflation. In most cases the financial analyst must not only recognize the underlying cause of the distortion but make appropriate modifications in assessing the financial performance of the company over time.

Not only a company's financial ratios but also intercompany comparisons may be distorted over time. When historical costs are used, the company with older fixed assets will often show a higher return on investment in an inflationary environment than will a company whose fixed assets were acquired more recently. Not only will the depreciation charges for the former company be less, which, in turn, will result in greater reported profits, but total assets will be lower. This combination of higher profits and lower investment will result in a higher return on investment ratio, all other things staying the same. This difference in return performance may be due entirely to assets being purchased at different times, not to the relative efficiency of management. The danger is that even though the company with older fixed assets is much less efficient in an economic sense, its return on investment, as based on conventional accounting data, may be as good as, if not better than, that of a more efficient producer. As a result, comparisons of return on investment ratios based on historical costs may lead to incorrect conclusions.

For both types of comparisons—intercompany and financial ratios of the same company over time—inflation can lead the financial analyst to derive faulty economic assessments. In periods of rapidly changing inflation, particular caution is necessary, and it is desirable to recompute financial ratios using replacement cost accounting data. This can be done in the manner illustrated. The financial analyst then can differentiate between performance attributable to inflation and performance more directly under management's control. Only in this way can the analyst get a handle on economic return as opposed to accounting return. Oranges must be compared with oranges, and apples with apples, if the inferences derived are to be meaningful.

To assist in these comparisons, the Financial Accounting Standards Board (FASB) requires in Statement No. 33 that large corporations restate certain items in constant dollars. The items restated are inventories and plant and equipment, and the consumer price index is used in the manner illustrated earlier. This FASB requirement causes a corporation to provide both an historical cost financial statement and one that is adjusted for general inflation. Also, such financial data as operating earnings, profits, cash dividends, and share price are required to be presented in a 5-year comparison of historical costs with constant-dollar costs. While not full-blown inflation accounting, these restatements may be useful to the financial statement analyst. However, bear in mind that only large corporations are required to restate such items for inflation.

QUESTIONS

1. What is the purpose of financial statements? What are the major components of a financial statement?
2. Why is the analysis of trends in financial ratios important?
3. Zakor Manufacturing Company has a current ratio of 4 to 1 but is unable to pay its bills. Why?
4. Can a firm generate a 25 percent return on assets and still be technically insolvent? Explain.
5. The traditional definitions of *collection period* and *inventory turnover* are criticized because in both cases balance sheet figures that are a result of the last month of sales are related to annual sales. Why do these definitions present problems? Suggest a solution.
6. Explain why a long-term creditor should be interested in liquidity ratios.
7. Which financial ratios would you be most likely to consult if you were the following? Why?
   a. A banker considering the financing of seasonal inventory
   b. A wealthy equity investor
   c. The manager of a pension fund considering the purchase of bonds
   d. The president of a consumer products firm
8. In trying to judge whether a company has too much debt, what financial ratios would you use and for what purpose?
9. Why might it be possible for a company to make large operating profits, yet still be unable to meet debt payments when due? What financial ratios might be employed to detect such a condition?
10. Does increasing a firm's inventory turnover ratio increase its profitability? Why is this ratio computed using cost of goods sold (rather than sales, as is done by some compilers of financial statistics)?
11. Is it appropriate to insist that a financial ratio, such as the current ratio, exceed a certain absolute standard?
12. Which firm is more profitable? Firm A with a turnover of 10.0 and a net profit margin of 2 percent or Firm B with a turnover of 2.0 and a net profit margin of 10 percent? Provide examples of both types of firms.
13. Why do short-term creditors, such as banks, emphasize balance sheet analysis when considering loan requests? Should they also analyze projected income statements? Why?
14. How can index analysis be used to reinforce the insight gained from a trend analysis of financial ratios?

SELF-CORRECTION PROBLEMS

1. Drummey Cartage Company has current assets of $800,000 and current liabilities of $500,000. What effect would the following transactions have on the current ratio?

a. Two new trucks are purchased for $100,000 in cash.

b. The company borrows $100,000 short term to carry an increase in receivables of the same amount.

c. Additional common stock of $200,000 is sold to invest in the expansion of several terminals.

d. The company increases its accounts payable to pay a cash dividend of $40,000 out of cash.

2. High-Low Plumbing Company sells plumbing fixtures on terms of 2/10, net 30. Its financial statements over the last 3 years follow:

	19x1	19x2	19x3
Cash	$ 30,000	$ 20,000	$ 5,000
Accounts receivable	200,000	260,000	290,000
Inventory	400,000	480,000	600,000
Net fixed assets	800,000	800,000	800,000
	$1,430,000	$1,560,000	$1,695,000
Accounts payable	$ 230,000	$ 300,000	$ 380,000
Accruals	200,000	210,000	225,000
Bank loan, short term	100,000	100,000	140,000
Long-term debt	300,000	300,000	300,000
Common stock	100,000	100,000	100,000
Retained earnings	500,000	550,000	550,000
	$1,430,000	$1,560,000	$1,695,000
Sales	$4,000,000	$4,300,000	$3,800,000
Cost of goods sold	3,200,000	3,600,000	3,300,000
Net profit	300,000 200,000	100,000	

Using the ratios discussed in the chapter, analyze the company's financial condition and performance over the last 3 years. Are there any problems?

3. Using the following information, complete the balance sheet:

Long-term debt to net worth	.5 to 1
Total asset turnover	2.5 times
Average collection period*	18 days
Inventory turnover	9 times
Gross profit margin	10%
Acid-test ratio	1 to 1

*Assume a 360-day year and all sales on credit.

Cash	$ _____	Notes and payables	$100,000
Accounts receivable	_____	Long-term debt	
Inventory	_____	Common stock	$100,000
Plant and equipment	_____	Retained earnings	100,000
Total assets	$ _____	Total liabilities and net worth	$ _____

4. Kedzie Kord Company had the following balance sheets and income statements over the last three years (in thousands):

	19x1	19x2	19x3
Cash	$ 561	$ 387	$ 202
Receivables	1,963	2,870	4,051
Inventories	2,031	2,613	3,287
Current assets	$ 4,555	$ 5,870	$ 7,540
Net fixed assets	2,581	4,430	4,364
Total assets	$ 7,136	$10,300	$11,904
Payables	$ 1,862	$ 2,944	$ 3,613
Accruals	301	516	587
Bank loan	250	900	$ 1,050
Current liabilities	$ 2,413	$ 4,360	$ 5,250
Long-term debt	500	1,000	950
Net worth	4,223	4,940	5,704
Total liabilities and net worth	$ 7,136	$10,300	$11,904
Sales	$11,863	$14,952	$16,349
Cost of goods sold	8,537	11,124	12,016
Selling, general, and administrative expenses	2,349	2,659	2,993
Profit before taxes	$ 977	$ 1,169	$ 1,340
Taxes	390	452	576
Profit after taxes	$ 587	$ 717	$ 764

Using common-size and index analyses, evaluate trends in the company's financial condition and performance.

PROBLEMS

1. The data for various companies in the same industry and of about the same size are as follows:

COMPANY	A	B	C	D	E	F
Sales (in millions)	$10	$20	$8	$5	$12	$17
Total assets (in millions)	8	10	6	2.5	4	8
Net income (in millions)	.7	2	.8	.5	1.5	1

Determine the asset turnover, net profit margin, and earning power for each of the companies.

2. Cordillera Carson Company has the following balance sheet and income statement for 19x2 (in thousands):

BALANCE SHEET	19x2
Cash	$ 400
Accounts receivable	1,300
Inventories ($1,800 for 19x1)	2,100
Current assets	$3,800
Net fixed assets	3,320
Total assets	$7,120
Accounts payable	$ 320
Accruals	260
Short-term loans	1,100
Current liabilities	$1,680
Long-term debt	2,000
Net worth	3,440
Total liabilities and net worth	$7,120

INCOME STATEMENT	
Net sales (all credit)	$12,680
Cost of goods sold*	8,930
Gross profit	$ 3,750
Selling, general, and administrative expenses	2,230
Interest expense	460
Profit before taxes	$ 1,060
Taxes	390
Profit after taxes	$ 670

*Includes depreciation of $480.

On the basis of this information, compute (a) the current ratio, (b) the acid-test ratio, (c) the average collection period, (d) the inventory turnover ratio, (e) the debt-to-net-worth ratio, (f) the long-term-debt-to-total-capitalization ratio, (g) the gross profit margin, (h) the net profit margin, (i) the rate of return on common stock equity, and (j) the ratio of cash flow to long-term debt.

3. Selected financial ratios for RMN Incorporated are as follows:

	19x1	19x2	19x3
Current ratio	4.2	2.6	1.8
Quick ratio	2.1	1.0	0.6
Debt to total assets	23%	33%	47%
Inventory turnover	8.7×	5.4×	3.5×
Average collection period	33	36	49
Fixed-assets turnover	11.6×	10.6×	12.3×
Total assets turnover	3.2×	2.6×	1.9×
Profit margin on sales	3.8%	2.5%	1.4%
Return on total assets	12.1%	6.5%	2.8%
Return on net worth	15.7%	9.7%	5.4%

a. Why did return on assets decline?
b. Was the increase in debt a result of greater current liabilities or of greater long-term debt? Explain.

4. The following information is available on the Vanier Corporation:

BALANCE SHEET DECEMBER 31, 19x6 (IN THOUSANDS)

Cash and marketable securities	$500	Accounts payable	$ 400
Accounts receivable	?	Bank loan	?
Inventories	?	Accruals	200
Current assets	?	Current liabilities	?
		Long-term debt	?
Net fixed assets	?	Common stock and	
		retained earnings	3,750
		Total liabilities and	
Total assets	?	net worth	?

INCOME STATEMENT FOR 19x6 (IN THOUSANDS)

Credit sales	$8,000
Cost of goods sold	?
Gross profit	?
Selling and administrative expenses	?
Interest expense	400
Profit before taxes	?
Taxes (44% rate)	?
Profit after taxes	?

OTHER INFORMATION

Current ratio	3 to 1
Depreciation	$500
Cash flow/long-term debt	0.40
Net profit margin	7%
Total liabilities/net worth	1 to 1
Average collection period	45 days
Inventory turnover ratio	3 to 1

Assuming that sales and production are steady throughout the year and a 360-day year, complete the balance sheet and income statement for Vanier Corporation.

5. A company has total annual sales (all credit) of $400,000 and a gross profit margin of 20 percent. Its current assets are $80,000; current liabilities, $60,000; inventories, $30,000; and cash, $10,000.

a. How much average inventory should be carried if management wants the inventory turnover to be 4?

b. How rapidly (in how many days) must accounts receivable be collected if management wants to have an average of $50,000 invested in receivables? (Assume a 360-day year.)

6. Stella Stores, Inc., has sales of $6 million, an asset turnover ratio of 6 for the year, and net profits of $120,000.

a. What is the company's return on assets or earning power?

b. The company is considering the installation of new point-of-sales cash registers throughout its stores. This equipment is expected to increase efficiency in inventory control, reduce clerical errors, and improve record keeping throughout the system. The new equipment will increase the investment in assets by 20 percent and is expected to increase the net profit margin from 2 to 3 percent. No change in sales is expected. What is the effect of the new equipment on the return on assets ratio or earning power?

7. The long-term-debt section of the balance sheet of the Diters Corporation appears as follows:

$9\frac{1}{4}$% mortgage bonds of 2005	$2,500,000
$12\frac{3}{8}$% second mortgage bonds of 1998	1,500,000
$10\frac{1}{4}$% debentures of 2001	1,000,000
$14\frac{1}{2}$% subordinated debentures of 2008	1,000,000
	$6,000,000

   a. If the average earnings before interest and taxes of the Diters Corporation are $1.5 million, what is the overall interest coverage?

   b. Using the cumulative deduction method, determine the coverage for each issue.

8. Tic Tac Homes has had the following balance sheet statements the past 4 years (in thousands):

	19x1	19x2	19x3	19x4
Cash	$ 214	$ 93	$ 42	$ 38
Receivables	1,213	1,569	1,846	2,562
Inventories	2,102	2,893	3,678	4,261
Net fixed assets	2,219	2,346	2,388	2,692
Total assets	$5,748	$6,901	$7,954	$9,553

	19x1	19x2	19x3	19x4
Accounts payable	$1,131	$1,578	$1,848	$2,968
Notes payable	500	650	750	750
Accruals	656	861	1,289	1,743
Long-term debt	500	800	800	800
Common stock	200	200	200	200
Retained earnings	2,761	2,812	3,067	3,092
Total liabilities and net worth	$5,748	$6,901	$7,954	$9,553

Using index analysis, what are the major problems in the company's financial condition?

9. **U.S. Republic Corporation balance sheet, December 31, 19x3**

ASSETS		LIABILITIES AND STOCKHOLDERS' EQUITY	
Cash	$ 1,000,000	Notes payable, bank	$ 4,000,000
Accounts receivable	5,000,000	Accounts payable	2,000,000
Inventory	7,000,000	Accrued wages and	
		taxes	2,000,000
Fixed assets, net	15,000,000	Long-term debt	12,000,000
Excess over book		Preferred stock	4,000,000
value of assets			
acquired	2,000,000	Common stock	2,000,000
		Retained earnings	4,000,000
		Total liabilities and	
Total assets	$30,000,000	net worth	$30,000,000

U.S. Republic Corporation statement of income and retained earnings, year ended December 31, 19x3

Net sales		
Credit		$16,000,000
Cash		4,000,000
Total		$20,000,000
Cost and expenses		
Cost of goods sold	$12,000,000	
Selling, general, and administrative expenses	2,200,000	
Depreciation	1,400,000	
Interest on long-term debt	1,200,000	$16,800,000
Net income before taxes		$ 3,200,000
Taxes on income		1,200,000
Net income after taxes		$ 2,000,000
Less: Dividends on preferred stock		240,000
Net income available to common		$ 1,760,000
Add: Retained earnings at 1/1/x3		2,600,00
Subtotal		$ 4,360,000
Less: Dividends paid on common		−360,000
Retained earnings 12/31/x3		$ 4,000,000

a. Fill in the 19x3 column in the table that follows.

U.S. Republic Corporation

RATIO	19x1	19x2	19x3	INDUSTRY NORMS
1. Current ratio	250%	200%		225%
2. Acid-test ratio	100%	90%		110%
3. Receivables turnover	5.0×	4.5×		6.0×
4. Inventory turnover	4.0×	3.0×		4.0×
5. Long-term debt/total				
capitalization	35%	40%		33%
6. Gross profit margin	39%	41%		40%
7. Net profit margin	17%	15%		15%

U.S. Republic Corporation (cont.)

RATIO	19x1	19x2	19x3	INDUSTRY NORMS
8. Rate of return on equity	15%	20%		20%
9. Return on tangible assets	15%	12%		10%
10. Tangible-asset turnover	.9×	.8×		1.0×
11. Overall interest coverage	11×	9×		10×
12. Cash flow/long-term debt	0.46	0.39		0.40

   b. Evaluate the position of the company from the table. Cite specific ratio levels and trends as evidence.

   c. Indicate which ratios would be of most interest to you and what your decision would be in each of the following situations:

     (i) U.S. Republic wants to buy $500,000 worth of raw materials from you, with payment due in 90 days.

     (ii) U.S. Republic wants you, a large insurance company, to pay off its note at the bank and assume it on a 10-year maturity basis at a current rate of 14 percent.

     (iii) There are 100,000 shares outstanding, and the stock is selling for $80 a share. The company offers you 50,000 additional shares at this price.

Appendix Problem

10. Using historical costs, Patell Patterns, Inc., had the following income statement (in thousands of dollars) for the year, during which 15 percent inflation occurred:

Sales		$5,000
Cost of goods sold		
Beginning inventory	$ 800	
Purchases	3,200	
Ending inventory	(920)	3,200
Depreciation		500
Selling and admin. expenses		800
Profit before taxes		620
Taxes (40 percent)		248
Profit after taxes		$ 372

At the beginning of the year, the fixed assets of the company amounted to $6 million on an historical cost basis, and they were depreciated on a straight-line basis with an average depreciable life of 12 years. The FIFO method is used for inventories.

   a. Determine the income statement on a replacement cost basis.

   b. What is the difference between the two methods?

SOLUTIONS TO SELF-CORRECTION PROBLEMS

1. Present current ratio = $800/$500 = 1.60.

    a. $700/$500 = 1.40. Current assets decline, and there is no change in current liabilities.

    b. $900/$600 = 1.50. Current assets and current liabilities each increase by the same amount.

    c. $800/$500 = 1.60. Neither current assets nor current liabilities are affected.

    d. $760/$540 = 1.41. Current assets decline and current liabilities increase by the same amount.

2.

	19x1	19x2	19x3
Current ratio	1.19	1.25	1.20
Acid-test ratio	.43	.46	.40
Average collection period	18	22	27
Inventory turnover	NA	8.2	6.1
Total debt/net worth	1.38	1.40	1.61
Long-term debt/total			
capitalization	.33	.32	.32
Gross profit margin	.200	.163	.132
Net profit margin	.075	.047	.026
Asset turnover	2.80	2.76	2.24
Return on assets	.21	.13	.06

The company's profitability has declined steadily over the period. As only $50,000 is added to retained earnings, the company must be paying substantial dividends. Receivables are growing slower, although the average collection period is still very reasonable relative to the terms given. Inventory turnover is slowing as well, indicating a relative buildup in inventories. The increase in receivables and inventories, coupled with the fact that net worth has increased very little, has resulted in the total debt-to-net-worth ratio increasing to what would have to be regarded on an absolute basis as a quite high level.

    The current and acid-test ratios have fluctuated, but the current ratio is not particularly inspiring. The lack of deterioration in these ratios is clouded by the relative buildup in both receivables and inventories, evidencing a deterioration in the liquidity of these two assets. Both the gross profit and net profit margins have declined substantially. The relationship between the two suggests that the company has reduced relative expenses in 19x3 in particular. The buildup in inventories and receivables has resulted in a decline in the asset turnover ratio, and this, coupled with the decline in profitability, has resulted in a sharp decrease in the return on assets ratio.

3. $\dfrac{\text{Long-term debt}}{\text{Net worth}} = .5 = \dfrac{\text{Long-term debt}}{200,000}$ Long-term debt = $100,000

Total liabilities and net worth = $400,000

Total assets = $400,000

$\dfrac{\text{Sales}}{\text{Total assets}} = 2.5 = \dfrac{\text{Sales}}{400,000}$ Sales = $1,000,000

Cost of goods sold = (.9)($1,000,000) = $900,000

$\dfrac{\text{Cost of goods sold}}{\text{Inventory}} = \dfrac{900,000}{\text{Inventory}} = 9$ Inventory = $100,000

$\dfrac{\text{Receivables} \times 360}{1,000,000} = 18 \text{ days}$ Receivables = $50,000

$\dfrac{\text{Cash} + 50,000}{100,000} = 1$ Cash = $50,000

Plant and equipment = $200,000

BALANCE SHEET			
Cash	$ 50,000	Notes and payables	$100,000
Accounts receivable	50,000	Long-term debt	100,000
Inventory	100,000	Common stock	100,000
Plant and equipment	200,000	Retained earnings	100,000
Total	$400,000	Total	$400,000

4.

COMMON-SIZE ANALYSIS	19x1	19x2	19x3
Cash	7.9%	3.8%	1.7%
Receivables	27.5	27.8	34.0
Inventories	28.4	25.4	27.6
Current assets	63.8%	57.0%	63.3%
Net fixed assets	36.2	43.0	36.7
Total assets	100.0%	100.0%	100.0%
Payables	26.1%	28.6%	30.4%
Accruals	4.2	5.0	4.9
Bank loan	3.5	8.7	8.8
Current liabilities	33.8%	42.3%	44.1%
Long-term debt	7.0	9.7	8.0
Net worth	59.2	48.0	47.9
Total liabilities and net worth	100.0%	100.0%	100.0%
Sales	100.0%	100.0%	100.0%
Cost of goods sold	72.0	74.4	73.5
Selling, general, and administrative expenses	19.8	17.8	18.3
Profit before taxes	8.2%	7.8%	8.2%
Taxes	3.3%	3.0	3.5
Profit after taxes	4.9%	4.8%	4.7%

INDEX ANALYSIS	19x1	19x2	19x3
Cash	100.0	69.0	36.0
Receivables	100.0	146.2	206.4
Inventories	100.0	128.7	161.8
Current assets	100.0	128.9	165.5
Net fixed assets	100.0	171.6	169.1
Total assets	100.0	144.3	166.8
Payables	100.0	158.1	194.0
Accruals	100.0	171.4	195.0
Bank loan	100.0	360.0	420.0
Current liabilities	100.0	180.7	217.6
Long-term debt	100.0	200.0	190.0
Net worth	100.0	117.0	135.1
Total liabilities and net worth	100.0	144.3	166.8
Sales	100.0	126.0	137.8
Cost of goods sold	100.0	130.3	140.8
Selling, general, and administrative expenses	100.0	113.2	127.4
Profit before taxes	100.0	119.7	137.2
Taxes	100.0	115.9	147.7
Profit after taxes	100.0	122.2	130.2

The common-size analysis shows that receivables are growing faster than total assets and current assets, while cash declined dramatically as a percentage of both. Net fixed assets surged in 19x2, but then fell back as a percentage of the total to almost the 19x1 percentage. The absolute amounts suggest that the company spent less than its depreciation on fixed assets in 19x3. With respect to financing, net worth has not kept up, so the company has had to use somewhat more debt percentagewise. It appears to be leaning more on the trade as payables increased percentagewise. Bank loans and long-term debt also increased sharply in 19x2, no doubt to finance the bulge in net fixed assets. The bank loan remained about the same in 19x3 as a percentage of total liabilities and net worth, while long-term debt declined as a percentage. Profit after taxes slipped slightly as a percentage of sales over the 3 years. In 19x2, this decline was a result of the cost of goods sold, as expenses and taxes declined as a percentage of sales. In 19x3, cost of goods sold declined as a percentage of sales, but this was more than offset by increases in expenses and taxes as percentages of sales.

Index analysis shows much the same picture. Cash declined faster than total assets and current assets, and receivables increased faster than these two benchmarks. Inventories fluctuated, but were about the same percentagewise to total assets in 19x3 as they were in 19x1. Net fixed assets increased more sharply than total assets in 19x2 and then fell back into line in 19x3. The sharp increase in bank loans in 19x2 and 19x3 and the sharp increase in long-term debt in 19x2 were evident. Net worth increased less than total assets did, so debt increased more percentagewise. With respect to profitability, net profits increased less than sales, for the reasons indicated earlier.

SELECTED REFERENCES

Almanac of Business and Industrial Ratios. Englewood Cliffs, N.J.: Prentice-Hall, 1983.

ALTMAN, EDWARD I., "Financial Ratios, Discriminant Analysis and the Prediction of Corporate Bankruptcy," *Journal of Finance,* 23 (September 1968), 589–609.

———, ROBERT G. HALDEMAN, and P. NARAYNAN, "Zeta Analysis: A New Model to Identify Bankruptcy Risk of Corporations," *Journal of Banking and Finance,* 1 (June 1977).

BACKER, MORTON, and MARTIN L. GOSMAN, "The Use of Financial Ratios in Credit Downgrade Decisions," *Financial Management,* 9 (Spring 1980), 53–56.

BEAVER, WILLIAM H., *Financial Reporting: An Accounting Revolution.* Englewood Cliffs, N.J.: Prentice-Hall, 1981.

CHEN, KUNG H., and THOMAS A. SHIMERDA, "An Empirical Analysis of Useful Financial Ratios," *Financial Management,* 10 (Spring 1981), 51–60.

FORD, JOHN KINGSTON, *A Framework for Financial Analysis.* Englewood Cliffs, N.J.: Prentice-Hall, 1981, chaps. 2 and 3.

FOSTER, GEORGE, *Financial Statement Analysis,* 2nd ed. Englewood Cliffs, N.J.: Prentice-Hall, 1986.

GOMBOLA, MICHAEL J., and J. EDWARD KETZ, "Financial Ratio Patterns in Retail and Manufacturing Organizations," *Financial Management,* 12 (Summer 1983), 45–56.

HARRINGTON, DIANA R., and BRENT D. WILSON, *Corporate Financial Analysis.* Plano, Tex.: Business Publications, 1983, chap. 1.

HELFERT, ERICH A., *Techniques of Financial Analysis,* 7th ed. Homewood, Ill.: Richard D. Irwin, 1987.

HIGGINS, ROBERT C., *Analysis for Financial Management.* Homewood, Ill.: Richard D. Irwin, 1984.

LEWELLEN, W. G., and R. O. EDMISTER, "A General Model for Accounts Receivable Analysis and Control," *Journal of Financial and Quantitative Analysis,* 8 (March 1973), 195–206.

STONE, BERNELL K., "The Payments-Pattern Approach to the Forecasting of Accounts Receivable," *Financial Management,* 5 (Autumn 1976), 65–82.

CHAPTER 7

Funds Analysis and Financial Planning

The second portion of our examination of the tools of financial analysis and planning deals with the analysis of fund flows and financial forecasting. A funds-flow statement is a valuable aid to a financial manager or a creditor in evaluating the uses of funds by a firm and in determining how the firm finances those uses. In addition to studying past flows, the analyst can evaluate future flows by means of a funds statement based on forecasts. Such a statement provides an efficient method for the financial manager to assess the firm's growth and its resulting financial needs, and to determine the best way to finance those needs. In particular, funds statements are very useful in planning intermediate- and long-term financing.

Closely related to a projected funds-flow statement are the cash budget and pro forma statements. The cash budget is indispensable to the financial manager in determining the short-term cash needs of the firm and, accordingly, in planning its short-term financing. When cash budgeting is extended to include a range of possible outcomes, the financial manager can evaluate the business risk and liquidity of the firm and plan a realistic margin of safety. This margin of safety might come from adjusting the firm's liquidity cushion, rearranging the maturity structure of its debt, arranging a line of credit with a bank, or a combination of the three. Cash budgets prepared for a range of possible outcomes are valuable also in appraising the ability of the firm to adjust to unexpected changes in cash flows. The preparation of pro forma balance sheets and income statements enables the financial manager to analyze the effect of various policy decisions on the future financial condition and performance of the firm. We examine each of these tools in turn.

The final method of analysis involves sustainable growth modeling. Here we determine whether the sales growth objectives of the company are consistent with its operating efficiency and with its financial ratios. This powerful tool of analysis allows us to simulate the likely effects of changes in target ratios when we move from a steady state environment. The integration of marketing, operational, and financial objectives permits better management of growth.

As we discussed in the previous chapter, a computer-based spreadsheet program, such as Lotus 1-2-3, is particularly applicable. Cash budgeting, the preparation of pro forma statements, and even sustainable growth modeling are made easier. In the supplementary *Financial Management Computer Applications*, such programs are provided.

BUSINESS FIRM FLOW OF FUNDS

The flow of funds in a firm may be visualized as a continuous process. For every use of funds, there must be an offsetting source. In a broad sense, the assets of a firm represent the net uses of funds; its liabilities and net worth represent net sources. A funds-flow cycle for a typical manufacturing company is illustrated in Fig. 7-1. For the going concern, there is really no starting or stopping point. A finished product is a variety of inputs—raw material, net fixed assets, and labor—ultimately paid for in cash. The product then is sold either for cash or on credit. A credit sale involves a receivable, which, when collected, becomes cash. If the selling price of the product exceeds all costs (including depreciation on as-

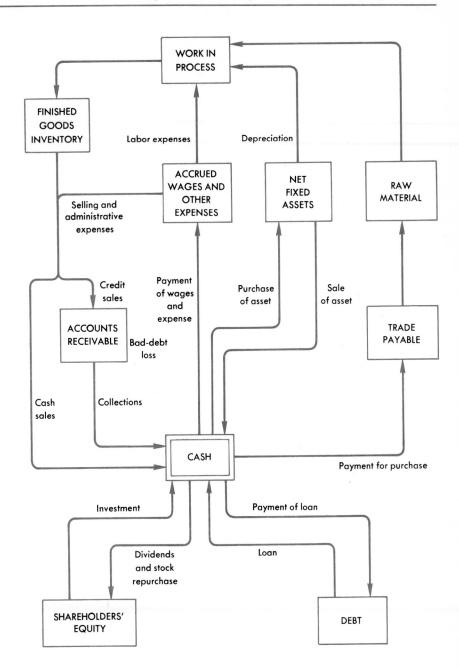

FIGURE 7-1
Funds flow within the firm

sets) for a period of time, there is a profit for the period; if not, there is a loss. The reservoir of cash, the focal point in the figure, fluctuates over time with the production schedule, sales, collection of receivables, capital expenditures, and financing. On the other hand, reservoirs of raw materials, work in process, finished goods inventory, accounts receivable, and trade payables fluctuate with sales, the production schedule, and policies with respect to managing receivables, inventories, and trade payables.

The funds statement is a method by which we study the net funds flow between two points in time. These points conform to beginning and ending financial statement dates for whatever period of examination is relevant—a quarter, a year, or 5 years. We must emphasize that the funds statement portrays net rather than gross changes between two comparable financial statements at different dates. For example, gross changes might be thought to include all changes that occur between the two statement dates, rather than the sum of these changes—the net change as defined. Although an analysis of the gross funds flow of a firm over time would be much more revealing than an analysis of net funds flow, we are usually constrained by the financial information available, namely, balance sheets and income statements that span particular periods of time. Funds may be defined in several different ways, depending on the purpose of the analysis. Although they are often defined as cash, many analysts treat funds as working capital (current assets less current liabilities), a somewhat broader definition. Other definitions are possible, although the two described are the most common by far. Depending on the analyst's objective, the definition can be broadened or narrowed. Because a funds-flow analysis on a cash basis serves as a building block for analyses using broader definitions of funds, we begin by defining funds as cash.

Source-and-Use Statements

Basically, one prepares a funds statement on a cash basis by (1) classifying net balance sheet changes that occur between two points in time: changes that increase cash and changes that decrease cash; (2) classifying, from the income statement and the surplus statement, the factors that increase cash and the factors that decrease cash; and (3) consolidating this information in a source-and-use-of-funds statement form. In the first of these steps, we simply place one balance sheet beside the other and compute the changes in the various accounts.
Sources of funds that increase cash are

1. A net decrease in any asset other than cash or fixed assets
2. A gross decrease in fixed assets
3. A net increase in any liability
4. Proceeds from the sale of preferred or common stock
5. Funds provided by operations

Funds provided by operations usually are not expressed directly on the income statement. To determine them, one must add back depreciation to net income after taxes. For the Aldine Manufacturing Company, our example in the preceding chapter (Tables 6-1 and 6-2), we have (in thousands)

Net income after taxes	$201,242
Add noncash expenses: depreciation	111,509
Funds provided by operations	$312,751

Thus, the net income of Aldine understates funds provided by operations by $111,509. Depreciation is not a source of funds, for funds are generated only from operations. If operating losses before depreciation are sustained, funds are not provided regardless of the magnitude of depreciation charges.

Uses of funds include

1. A net increase in any asset other than cash or fixed assets
2. A gross increase in fixed assets
3. A net decrease in any liability
4. A retirement or purchase of stock
5. Cash dividends

To avoid double counting, we compute gross additions to fixed assets in the following manner:

$$\frac{\text{Gross additions}}{\text{Fixed assets}} = NFA_1 + DPR_1 - NFA_0 \tag{7-1}$$

where NFA_1 = net fixed assets at the ending financial statement date, NFA_0 = net fixed assets at the beginning statement date, and DPR_1 = depreciation during the intervening period. As depreciation is part of the funds provided by operations, a source of funds, we must use gross changes in fixed assets as opposed to net changes in fixed assets.

Once all source and uses are computed, they may be arranged in statement form so that we can analyze them better. Table 7-1 shows a source-and-use-of-funds statement for the Aldine Manufacturing Company for the fiscal year ended March 31, 1989. The balance sheet and income statement for this corporation on which the funds statement is based are shown in Tables 6-1 and 6-2 in Chapter

TABLE 7-1
Aldine Manufacturing Company sources and uses of funds
March 31, 1988, to March 31, 1989 (in thousands)

SOURCES		USES	
Funds provided by operations			
Net profit	$201,242	Dividends	$142,968
Depreciation	111,509	Additions to fixed assets	104,276
		Increase, inventories	94,238
Decrease, accounts receivable	62,426	Increase, prepaid expenses	3,559
Decrease, other assets	467	Increase, tax prepayments	6,038
Increase, bank loans	91,997	Increase, investments	65,376
Increase, accounts payable	11,634		
Increase, other accruals	26,653	Decrease, accrued taxes	91,252
Increase, long-term debt	4,323		
Increase, common stock and			
paid-in capital	103	Increase, cash position	2,647
	$510,354		$510,354

6. When we subtract the total uses of funds in Table 7-1 from the total sources, the difference should equal the actual change in cash between the two statement dates. If it does not, then the analyst must search for the cause of the discrepancy. Frequently, discrepancies will be due to surplus adjustments, and the analyst should be alert to this possibility.

In Table 7-1 we see that the principal uses of funds for the 1989 fiscal year were additions to fixed assets, increases in inventories and in investments, and a sizable decrease in taxes payable. These uses were financed primarily by funds provided by operations in excess of dividends; a decrease in accounts receivable; and increases in bank loans, payables, and accruals. As sources exceeded slightly the uses of funds, the cash balance rose by $2,647,000. In a source-and-use-of-funds analysis, it is useful to place cash dividends opposite net profits, and additions to fixed assets opposite depreciation. Doing this allows the analyst to evaluate easily both the amount of dividend payout and the net increase in fixed assets.

Funds as Working Capital

Working capital.
Current assets minus
current liabilities.

Financial analysts also frequently prepare a source-and-use-of-working-capital statement. This statement is very similar to the source-and-use-of-funds statement, but the residual is net **working capital** instead of cash. A statement of the source and use of working capital for the Aldine Manufacturing Company for the year ended March 31, 1989, is shown in Table 7-2. We see that the only difference between this statement and a funds statement on a cash basis is the omission of changes in the various components of current assets and current liabilities. This statement is analyzed much the same as the source-and-use-of-funds statement is. Bankers frequently use a source-and-use-of-working-capital statement, for they often require a borrower to maintain some sort of minimum working capital. Other lenders and management use it for internal control.

Implications of Technique

The analysis of cash and working capital funds statements gives us a rich insight into the financial operations of a firm—an insight that will be especially valuable to you as a financial manager analyzing past and future expansion plans of the firm and their impact on liquidity. You can detect imbalances in the uses of funds and undertake appropriate actions. An analysis spanning the past several years might reveal a growth in inventories out of proportion with the growth of other assets and with sales. Upon analysis, you might find that the problem was due to inefficiencies in inventory management. Thus, a funds statement alerts you to problems that you can analyze in detail and take proper actions to correct. When a company has a number of divisions, individual funds statements may prove useful. These statements enable top management to appraise the performance of divisions in relation to the funds committed to them.

Another use of funds statements is in the evaluation of the firm's financing. An analysis of the major sources of funds in the past reveals what portion of the firm's growth was financed internally and what portion externally. In evaluating

TABLE 7-2
Aldine Manufacturing Company sources and uses of working capital
March 31, 1988, to March 31, 1989 (in thousands)

SOURCES		USES	
Funds provided by operations			
Net profit	$201,242	Dividends	$142,968
Depreciation	111,509	Additions to fixed assets	104,276
Decrease, other assets	467	Increase, investments	65,376
Increase, long-term debt	4,323	Increase, working capital	5,024
Increase, common stock and			
paid-in capital	103		
	$317,644		$317,644

the firm's financing, you will wish to evaluate the ratio of dividends to earnings relative to the firm's total need for funds. Funds statements are useful also in judging whether the firm has expanded at too fast a rate and whether financing is strained. You can determine if trade credit has increased out of proportion to increases in current assets and to sales. If trade credit has increased at a significantly faster rate, you would wish to evaluate the consequences of increased slowness in trade payments on the credit standing of the firm and its ability to finance in the future. It is also revealing to analyze the mix of short- and long-term financing in relation to the funds needs of the firm. If these needs are primarily for fixed assets and permanent increases in working capital, you might be disturbed if a significant portion of total financing came from short-term sources.

An analysis of a funds statement for the future will be extremely valuable to you as a financial manager planning the intermediate- and long-term financing of your firm. It reveals the firm's total prospective need for funds, the expected timing of these needs, and their nature; that is, whether the increased investment is primarily for inventories, fixed assets, and so forth. Given this information, along with the expected changes in trade payables and the various accruals, you can arrange your firm's financing more effectively. In addition, you can determine the expected closing cash position of the firm simply by adjusting the beginning cash balance for the change in cash reflected on the projected source-and-use statement. In essence, the projected change in cash is a residual. Alternatively, you can forecast future cash positions of the firm through a cash budget, where direct estimates of future cash flows are made.

CASH-FLOW FORECASTING

A **cash budget** is arrived at through a projection of future cash receipts and cash disbursements of the firm over various intervals of time. It reveals the timing and amount of expected cash inflows and outflows over the period studied. With this information, the financial manager is better able to determine the future cash needs of the firm, plan for the financing of these needs, and exercise control over the cash and liquidity of the firm.

Cash budgeting. A forecast of the future cash flows of the firm arising from collections and disbursements, usually on a monthly basis.

Cash budgets may be made for almost any period of time. For near-term forecasts, monthly periods probably are most frequently used because they take into account seasonal variations in cash flows. When cash flows are extremely volatile but predictable, budgets at more frequent intervals may be necessary for determining peak cash requirements. By the same token, when cash flows are relatively stable, budgeting at quarterly or even longer intervals may be justified. Generally, the farther in the future the period for which one is trying to predict cash flows, the more uncertain the forecast. The expense of preparing monthly cash budgets usually is warranted only for predictions concerning the near future. As we shall see, the cash budget is only as useful as the accuracy of the forecasts that are relied on in its preparation.

The Forecast of Sales

The key to the accuracy of most cash budgets is the forecast of sales. This forecast can be based on an internal analysis, an external one, or both. With an internal approach, sales representatives are asked to project sales for the forthcoming period. The product sales managers screen these estimates and consolidate them into sales estimates for product lines. The estimates for the various product lines are then combined into an overall sales estimate for the firm. The basic problem with an internal approach is that it can be too myopic. Often, significant trends in the economy and in the industry are overlooked.

For this reason, many companies use an external analysis as well. With an external approach, economic analysts make forecasts of the economy and of industry sales for several years to come. They may use regression analysis to estimate the association between industry sales and the economy in general. After these basic predictions of business conditions and industry sales, the next step is to estimate market share by individual products, prices that are likely to prevail, and the expected reception of new products. Usually, these estimates are made in conjunction with marketing managers, even though the ultimate responsibility should lie with the economic forecasting department. From this information, an external forecast of sales can be prepared.

When the internal forecast of sales differs from the external one, as it is likely to do, a compromise must be reached. Past experience will show which of the two forecasts is more accurate. In general, the external forecast should serve as a foundation for the final sales forecast, often modified by the internal forecast. For example, the firm might expect several large orders from customers, and these orders might not show up in the external forecast. A final sales forecast based on both internal and external analyses is usually more accurate than is either an internal or an external forecast by itself. The final sales forecast should be based on prospective demand, not modified initially by internal constraints such as physical capacity. The decision to remove these constraints will depend on the forecast. The value of accurate sales forecasts cannot be overestimated, for most of the other forecasts, in some measure, are based on expected sales.

*Collections and
Other Cash Receipts*

The sales forecast out of the way, the next job is to determine the cash receipts from these sales. For cash sales, cash is received at the time of the sale; for credit sales, the receipts do not come until later. How much later depends on the billing terms given, the type of customer, and the credit and collection policies of the firm. Continental Sheetmetal Company offers terms of net 30, meaning that payment is due within 30 days after the invoice date. Assume also that in the company's experience, 90 percent of receivables are collected, on the average, 1 month from the date of the sale, and 10 percent are collected 2 months from the date of the sale, with no bad-debt losses. Moreover, on the average, 10 percent of total sales are cash sales.

If the sales forecasts are those shown in the first line of Table 7-3, we can compute a schedule of the expected sales receipts based on the foregoing assumptions. This schedule appears in Table 7-3. For January, we see that total sales are estimated to be $250,000, of which $25,000 are cash sales. Of the $225,000 in credit sales, 90 percent, or $202,500, is expected to be collected in February, and 10 percent, or $22,500, is expected to be collected in March. Similarly, sales in other months are estimated according to the same percentages. The firm should be ready to change its assumptions with respect to collections when there is an underlying shift in the payment habits of its customers. If there is a slowdown in the economy, certain customers are likely to become slower in their trade payments. The firm must take account of this change if its cash budget is to be realistic.

From this example, it is easy to see the effect of a variation in sales on the magnitude and timing of cash receipts, all other things held constant. For most firms, there is a degree of correlation between sales and collection experience. In times of recession and sales decline, the average collection period is likely to lengthen; bad-debt losses are likely to increase. Thus, the collection experience of a firm may reinforce a decline in sales, magnifying the downward impact on total sales receipts.

TABLE 7-3
Schedule of sales receipts (in thousands)

	NOV.	DEC.	JAN.	FEB.	MAR.	APR.	MAY	JUNE
Total sales	$300.0	$350.0	$250.0	$200.0	$250.0	$300.0	$350.0	$380.0
Credit sales	270.0	315.0	225.0	180.0	225.0	270.0	315.0	342.0
Collections, 1 month		243.0	283.5	202.5	162.0	202.5	243.0	283.5
Collections, 2 months			27.0	31.5	22.5	18.0	22.5	27.0
Total collections			$310.5	$234.0	$184.5	$220.5	$265.5	$310.5
Cash sales			25.0	20.0	25.0	30.0	35.0	38.0
Total sales receipts			$355.5	$254.0	$209.5	$250.5	$300.5	$348.5

Cash receipts may arise from the sale of assets, as well as from sales of the product. If Continental intends to sell $40,000 in fixed assets in February, total cash receipts that month would be $294,000. For the most part, the sale of assets is planned in advance and easily predicted for purposes of cash budgeting. In addition, cash receipts may arise from interest and dividend income.

Receivable Collection Period.   Digressing for the moment, consider now how other collection forecasts might be set up for cash budgeting purposes. In our example, we assumed 90 percent of credit sales in 1 month was collected 1 month later and that 10 percent was collected 2 months later. If credit sales are steady throughout the month and each month has 30 days, this corresponds to an average collection period of 33 days (the weighted average of 30 and 60 days). If the average collection period were 30 days, all credit sales would be collected 1 month later. That is, the $315,000 in December credit sales would be collected in January, and so forth. If the average collection period were 60 days, of course, collections would be lagged 2 months so that the $315,000 in December would be collected in February.

If the average collection period were 45 days, however, one-half of December credit sales, or $157,500, would be collected in January and the other half in February. The assumption is that credit sales billed in the first half of December will be collected in the last half of January, and sales billed in the last half of December will be collected in the first half of February. Other months will reflect this lag structure as well. If the average collection period were 40 days, implied is that two-thirds of December sales, or $210,000, will be collected in January and that one-third, or $105,000, will be collected in February. The weighted average of $(2/3 \times 30 \text{ days}) + (1/3 \times 60 \text{ days})$ equals 40 days.

By similar reasoning, an average collection period of 50 days means that one-third of December credit sales, or $105,000, will be collected in January and two-thirds, or $210,000, will be collected in February. Similarly, the 30-day month can be divided into fifths, sixths, tenths, fifteenths, and thirtieths to come to grips with other average collection periods. The situation for tenths was illustrated in our example. Finally, if the average collection period were 37 days, the implication is that 23/30 of December credit sales, or $241,500, will be collected in January and 7/30, or $73,500, will be collected in February. These are enough examples to illustrate the effect of a change in average collection period assumptions on collections. With a computer-based spreadsheet program, it is an easy matter to set up lagged collections for credit sales. Now, back to our example.

Cash Disbursements

Next comes a forecast of cash disbursements. Given the sales forecast, management may choose either to gear production closely to sales or to produce at a relatively constant rate over time. When production is geared to sales, inventory carrying costs generally are lower, but total production costs are higher than they are when work continues steadily. If sales fluctuate, finished goods inventories build up during certain periods and require storage. Because storage is uneven throughout the year, inventory carrying costs are generally higher than they would be if production were geared to sales. On the other hand, steady production typically is more efficient. Which alternative is best will depend on the cost of carrying inventory when production is geared to sales compared to the savings available if production is steady. The final production schedule embodies decisions with respect to inventory management, a topic taken up in Chapter 11.

Production Outlays.   Once a production schedule has been established, estimates can be made of the needs in materials, labor, and additional fixed assets. As with receivables, there is a lag between the time a purchase is made and the time of actual cash payment. If suppliers give average billing terms of net 30, and the firm's policy is to pay its bills at the end of this period, there is approximately a 1-month lag between a purchase and the payment. If the production program of Continental Sheetmetal calls for the manufacture of goods in the month preceding forecasted sales, we might have a schedule of expenses like that in Table 7-4. As we see, there is a 1-month lag between the time of purchase and the payment for the purchase. As with the collection of receivables, payment for purchases can be lagged for other average payable periods. The setup is the same as illustrated for collections, and the lagged structure is facilitated using a computer-based spreadsheet program.

Wages are assumed to increase with the amount of production. Generally, wages are more stable over time than are purchases. When production dips slightly, workers are usually not laid off. When production picks up, labor becomes more efficient with relatively little increase in total wages. Only after a certain point is overtime work required or new workers have to be hired to meet the increased production schedule. Included in other expenses are general, administrative, and selling expenses; property taxes; interest expenses; power, light, and heat expenses; maintenance expenses; and indirect labor and material expenses. These expenses tend to be reasonably predictable over the short run.

Other Disbursements.   In addition to cash expenses, we must take into account capital expenditures, dividends, federal income taxes, and any other cash outflows. Because capital expenditures are planned in advance, they usually are predictable for the short-term cash budget. As the forecast becomes more distant, however, prediction of these expenditures becomes less certain. Dividend payments for most companies are stable and are paid on specific dates. Estimation of federal income taxes must be based on projected profits for the period under review. Other cash outlays might consist of the repurchase of stock or

TABLE 7-4
Schedule of expenses (in thousands)

	DEC.	JAN.	FEB.	MAR.	APR.	MAY	JUNE
Purchases	$100	$ 80	$100	$120	$140	$150	$150
Cash payment for purchases		100	80	100	120	140	150
Wages paid		80	80	90	90	95	100
Other expenses		50	50	50	50	50	50
Total cash expenses		$230	$210	$240	$260	$285	$300

payment of long-term debt. These outlays are combined with total cash expenses to obtain the schedule of total cash disbursements shown in Table 7-5.

Net Cash Flow and Cash Balance

Once we are satisfied that we have taken into account all foreseeable cash inflows and outflows, we combine the cash receipts and cash disbursements schedules to obtain the net cash inflow or outflow for each month. The net cash flow may then be added to beginning cash in January, which is assumed to be $100,000, and the projected cash position computed month by month for the period under review. This final schedule is shown in Table 7-6.

The cash budget shown indicates that the firm is expected to have a cash deficit in April and May. Its deficit is caused by a decline in collections through March, capital expenditures totaling $200,000 in February and March, and a cash dividend of $20,000 in March. With the increase in collections in May and June, the cash balance without financing rises to $13,500 in June. The cash budget indicates that peak cash requirements occur in April. If the firm has a policy of maintaining a minimum cash balance of $75,000 and of borrowing from its bank to maintain this minimum, it will need to borrow an additional $66,000 in March. Additional borrowings will peak at $105,500 in April, after which they will decline to $61,500 in June, if all goes according to prediction.

Alternative means of meeting the cash deficit are available. The firm may

TABLE 7-5
Schedule of cash disbursements (in thousands)

	JAN	FEB.	MAR.	APR.	MAY	JUNE
Total cash expenses	$230	$210	$240	$260	$285	$300
Capital expenditures		150	50			
Dividend payments			20			20
Income taxes	30			30		
Total cash disbursements	$260	$360	$310	$290	$285	$320

TABLE 7-6
Net cash flow and cash balance (in thousands)

	JAN.	FEB.	MAR.	APR.	MAY	JUNE
Total cash receipts	$335.5	$294.0*	$ 209.5	$250.5	$300.5	$348.5
Total cash disbursements	260.0	360.0	310.0	290.0	285.0	320.0
Net cash flow	$ 75.5	$(66.0)	$(100.5)	$(39.5)	$ 15.5	$ 28.5
Beginning cash without financing	100.0	175.5	109.5	9.0	(30.5)	(15.0)
Ending cash without financing	175.5	109.5	9.0	(30.5)	(15.0)	13.5

*Includes receipts of $254,000 and cash sale of assets of $40,000.

be able to delay its capital expenditures or its payments for purchases. Indeed, one of the principal purposes of a cash budget is to determine the timing and magnitude of prospective financing needs so that the most appropriate method of financing can be arranged. A decision to obtain long-term financing should be based on long-range funds requirements and on considerations apart from a cash forecast. In addition to helping the financial manager plan for short-term financing, the cash budget is valuable in managing the firm's cash position. On the basis of a cash budget, the manager can plan to invest excess funds in marketable securities. The result is an efficient transfer of funds from cash to marketable securities and back.

RANGE OF CASH-FLOW ESTIMATES

Often there is a tendency to place considerable faith in the cash budget simply because it is expressed in figures. We stress again that a cash budget represents merely an *estimate* of future cash flows. Depending on the care devoted to preparing the budget and the volatility of cash flows resulting from the nature of the business, actual cash flows will deviate more or less widely from those that were expected. In the face of uncertainty, we must provide information about the range of possible outcomes. Analyzing cash flows under only one set of assumptions, as is the case with conventional cash budgeting, results in a faulty perspective of the future.

Deviations From
Expected Cash Flows

To take into account deviations from expected cash flows, it is desirable to work out additional cash budgets. We might want to base one cash forecast on the assumption of a maximum probable decline in business and another on the assumption of the maximum probable increase in business. By bringing possible events into the open for discussion, management is better able to plan for contingencies. Not only will such discussion sharpen its perspective on the probability of occurrence of a particular event, but it will give management a better understanding of the magnitude of its impact on the firm's cash flows.[1] Given the preparation of a cash budget based on expected cash flows, it is often a simple matter to trace through a change in one or a series of figures in order to take into account a large number of possibilities. Examples of a change in assumptions include a decline in sales or an increase in the average collection period. For each set of assumptions and resulting cash budget, a probability of occurrence should be attached.

A spreadsheet program may be used to calculate cash budgets under varying assumptions. With such a program, the analyst can type in a change, such as an increase in the average collection period, and the computer will recompute

---

[1] See Gordon Donaldson, "Strategy for Financial Emergencies," *Harvard Business Review*, 47 (November–December 1969), 69.

and display a new cash budget in seconds. A cash budget format for such simulations is found in the supplement, *Financial Management Computer Applications*.

The final product might be a series of distributions of end-of-the-month cash without financing. Figure 7-2 shows relative frequency distributions for the months of January through June. Bar graphs are used. The most likely values of ending cash are depicted by the highest bar; these conform with the values shown in Table 7-6. We note that while several of the distributions are reasonably symmetrical, others are skewed. In particular, the distributions for March and April are skewed to the left. As a result, the need for cash during these months might be considerably greater than that depicted in Table 7-6. It is clear that the type of information portrayed in Fig. 7-2 better enables management to plan for contingencies than does information giving only single-point estimates of monthly cash flows.

Use of Probabilistic Information

The expected cash position plus the distribution of possible outcomes gives us a considerable amount of information. We can see the additional funds required or the funds released under various possible outcomes. This information enables us to determine more accurately the minimum cash balance, maturity structure of debt, and borrowing power necessary to give the firm a margin of safety.

We also can analyze the ability of the firm to adjust to deviations from the

FIGURE 7-2
Distributions of ending cash

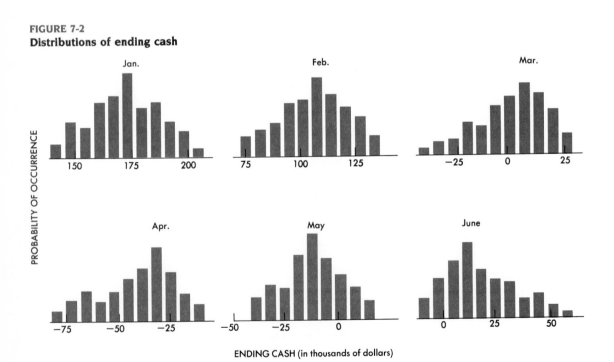

ENDING CASH (in thousands of dollars)

expected outcomes. If sales should fall off, how flexible are our expenses? What can be cut? By how much? How quickly? How much effort should be devoted to the collection of receivables? If there is an unexpected increase in business, what additional purchases will be required, and when? Can labor be expanded? Can the present plant handle the additional demand? How much in funds will be needed to finance the buildup? Answers to these questions provide valuable insight into the efficiency and flexibility of the firm under a variety of conditions.[2]

From the standpoint of internal planning, it is far better to allow for a range of possible outcomes than to rely solely on the expected outcome. This allowance is particularly necessary for firms whose business is relatively unstable in character. If the firm bases its plans on expected cash flows only, it is likely to be caught flat-footed if there is a significant deviation from the expected outcome, and it will have difficulty making an adjustment. An unforeseen deficit in cash may be difficult to finance on short notice. Therefore, it is essential for the firm to be honest with itself and attempt to minimize the costs associated with deviations from expected outcomes. It may do this by taking the steps necessary to ensure accuracy and by preparing additional cash budgets to take into account the range of possible outcomes. When significant deviations from expected outcomes occur, the cash budget should be revised in keeping with new information.

FORECASTING FINANCIAL STATEMENTS

In addition to projecting the cash flow of a firm over time, it is often useful to prepare a projected, or **pro forma,** balance sheet and income statement for selected future dates. A cash budget gives us information only as to the prospective future cash positions of the firm, whereas pro forma statements embody forecasts of all assets and liabilities as well as of income statement items. Much of the information that goes into the preparation of the cash budget can be used to derive a pro forma statement. In practice, the pro forma income statement usually precedes the cash budget. In this way the financial manager is able to use the tax estimates derived therefrom in the cash budget.

Pro forma. Projected future financial statements.

Pro Forma Income Statement

The pro forma income statement is a projection of income for a period of time in the future. As was true with our cash budget, the sales forecast is the key to

---

[2] Donaldson (ibid., pp. 71–79) develops a framework for evaluating the resources available to meet adverse financial contingencies. These resources include surplus cash, unused lines of credit, negotiated bank loans, long-term debt, new equity, the reduction of planned outflows, and the liquidation of certain assets. Once these resources have been determined, together with the time necessary to put them to use, a strategy of response can be formulated. This strategy lays out the sequence in which resources will be brought into play to deal with an unanticipated event.

scheduling production and estimating production costs. The analyst may wish to evaluate each component of the cost of goods sold. A detailed analysis of purchases, production wages, and overhead costs is likely to produce the most accurate forecasts. Often, however, costs of goods sold are estimated on the basis of past ratios of costs of goods sold to sales.

Selling, general, and administrative expenses are estimated next. Because these expenses usually are budgeted in advance, estimates of them are fairly accurate. Typically, these expenses are not overly sensitive to changes in sales in the very short run, particularly to reductions in sales. Next, we estimate other income and expenses as well as interest expenses to obtain net income before taxes. Income taxes are then computed—based on the applicable tax rate—and deducted, to arrive at estimated net income after taxes. All of these estimates are then combined into an income statement.

To illustrate for Continental Sheetmetal Company, suppose that projected sales for January through June in Table 7-3 are $1,730,000, as reflected in our cash budget in Table 7-3. In the cash budget, the cost of goods sold is not depicted directly. However, we know that purchases fall into this category. For financial statement purposes, the purchases associated with January through June sales are those for December through May, because production occurs in the month preceding forecasted sales. Purchases are shown in Table 7-4, and they total $690,000 for December through May. Wages also are a cost of goods sold, and here, too, the relevant period for financial statement purposes is December through May. For this period, wages totaling $505,000 are expected to be paid. (See Table 7-4.) We stated earlier that depreciation of $110,000 was expected for the January–June period. Other expenses (selling, general, and administrative) are expected to be $50,000 a month and are also shown in Table 7-4. For the 6-month period they total $300,000. Finally, let us assume a federal plus state income tax rate of 48 percent. Given this information, we can derive a pro forma income statement for the January–June period (in thousands):

Sales		$1,730
Cost of goods sold		
Purchases	$690	
Wages	505	
Depreciation	110	$1,305
Gross profit		425
Selling, general, and adminstrative expenses		300
Profit before taxes		125
Taxes		60
Profit after taxes		$ 65

The pro forma income statement need not be based on a cash budget. Instead, one can make direct estimates of all of the items. By first estimating a sales level, one can multiply historical ratios of cost of goods sold and various expense items by the level in order to derive the statement. Where historical ratios no longer are appropriate, new estimates should be employed.

Pro Forma Balance Sheet

To illustrate the preparation of a pro forma balance sheet, suppose that we wish to prepare one for Continental Sheetmetal for June 30 and that the company has the following balance sheet the previous December 31:

ASSETS (IN THOUSANDS)		LIABILITIES (IN THOUSANDS)	
Cash	$ 100	Bank borrowings	$ 50
Receivables	342	Accounts payable	200
Inventory	350	Accrued wages and expenses	250
		Accrued income taxes	70
Current assets	$ 792	Current liabilities	$ 570
Net fixed assets	800	Net worth	1,022
Total assets	$1,592	Total liabilities and net worth	$1,592

Receivables at June 30 can be estimated by adding to the receivable balance at December 31 the total projected credit sales from January through June, less total projected credit collections for the period. On the basis of the information in the cash budget, receivables at June 30 would be $342,000 + $31,500, or $373,500.

Forecasting Assets.   If a cash budget is not available, the receivable balance may be estimated on the basis of a turnover ratio. This ratio, which depicts the relationship between cash sales and receivables, should be based on past experience. To obtain the estimated level of receivables, projected sales simply are divided by the turnover ratio. If the sales forecast and turnover ratio are realistic, the method will produce a reasonable approximation of the receivable balance. The estimated investment in inventories at June 30 may be based on the production schedule, which, in turn, is based on the sales forecast. This schedule should show expected purchases, the expected use of inventory in production, and the expected level of finished goods. On the basis of this information, together with the beginning inventory level, a pro forma estimate of inventory can be made.

Rather than use the production schedule, estimates of future inventory can be based upon a turnover ratio of cost of goods sold to inventory. This ratio is applied in the same manner as for receivables, except that we solve for the ending inventory position, which emanates from the average. We have

$$\frac{\text{Cost of goods sold}}{(\text{Beginning} + \text{Ending inventory})/2} = \frac{\text{Turnover}}{\text{ratio}}$$

Given an assumed turnover ratio and assumed cost of goods sold figure, and knowing the beginning inventory, we rearrange the equation to solve for the unknown.

$$\frac{\text{Ending}}{\text{inventory}} = \frac{2\,(\text{CofGS})}{\text{Turnover ratio}} - \text{Beginning inventory}$$

If the estimated inventory turnover ratio in our example were 3.4 for the 6 months and the estimated cost of goods sold were $1,309,000, we would have

$$\frac{\text{Ending}}{\text{inventory}} = \frac{2(1,309,000)}{3.4} - 350,000 = \$420,000$$

Thus, $420,000 would be our estimate of inventory on June 30, a figure that represents a moderate increase over the inventory level of December 31, in keeping with the buildup in sales.

Future net fixed assets are estimated by adding planned expenditures to existing net fixed assets and subtracting from this sum depreciation for the period, plus any sale of fixed assets at book value. From the cash budget, we note that capital expenditures are estimated at $200,000 over the period and that $40,000 in fixed assets will be sold at what we assume to be their depreciated book values. If depreciation for the period is expected to be $110,000, the expected net addition to fixed assets would be $50,000 ($200,000 − $40,000 − $110,000), and projected net fixed assets at June 30 would be $850,000. Because capital expenditures are planned in advance, fixed assets generally are fairly easy to forecast.

Forecasting Liabilities and Net Worth.   Turning now to the liabilities, accounts payable are estimated by adding total projected purchases for January through June, less total projected cash payments for purchases for the period, to the December 31 balance. Our estimate of accounts payable, therefore, is $200,000 + $50,000, or $250,000. The calculation of accrued wages and expenses is based on the production schedule and the historical relationship between these accruals and production. We assume the estimate of accrued wages and expenses to be $240,000. Accrued income taxes are estimated by adding to the current balance taxes on forecasted income for the 6-month period, less the actual payment of taxes. If income taxes for the period are forecast at $60,000, as shown in the pro forma income statement, and the firm is scheduled to make $60,000 in actual payments, estimated accrued income taxes at June 30 would be $70,000.

Net worth at June 30 would be the net worth at December 31 plus profits after taxes for the period, less the amount of cash dividends paid. If profits after taxes are estimated at $65,000 in the pro forma income statement, net worth at June 30 would be $1,022,000 plus $65,000 minus dividends of $40,000, or $1,047,000. Two items remain: cash and bank loans. We see from the cash budget that estimated cash at June 30 would be $13,500 without additional financing. If the firm has the policy of maintaining a minimum cash balance of $75,000 and borrowing from its bank to maintain this balance, cash at June 30 would be $75,000, and bank borrowings would increase by $61,500 to $111,500. In general, cash and notes payable serve as balancing factors in the preparation of pro forma balance sheets, whereby assets and liabilities plus net worth are brought into balance.

Once we have estimated all the components of the pro forma balance sheet, they are combined into a balance sheet format. The pro forma balance sheet at June 30 is

ASSETS (in thousands)		LIABILITIES (in thousands)	
Cash	$ 75.0	Bank borrowings	$ 111.5
Receivables	373.5	Accounts payable	250.0
Inventory	420.0	Accrued wages and expenses	240.0
		Accrued income taxes	70.0
Current assets	$ 868.5	Current liabilities	$ 671.5
Net fixed assets	850.0	Net worth	1,047.0
Total assets	$1,718.5	Total liabilities and net worth	$1,718.5

Use of Ratios and Implications

As before, the cash budget method is but one way to prepare a pro forma statement; one can also make direct estimates of all of the items on the balance sheet by projecting financial ratios into the future and then making estimates on the basis of these ratios. Receivables, inventories, accounts payable, and accrued wages and expenses frequently are based on historical relationships to sales and production when a cash budget is not available. For example, if the average collection period is 45 days, turnover would be eight times a year. If receivables were $500,000 but the firm were predicting a $2 million increase in sales for the coming year, it would take approximately $2 million/8 = $250,000 in additional receivables to support the added sales. Thus, the level of receivables 1 year hence might be forecast at $750,000.

Pro forma statements allow us to study the composition of expected future balance sheets and income statements. Financial ratios may be computed for analysis of the statements; these ratios and the raw figures may be compared with those for present and past balance sheets. Using this information, the financial manager can analyze the direction of change in the financial condition and performance of the firm over the past, the present, and the future. If the firm is accustomed to making accurate estimates, the preparation of a cash budget, pro forma statements, or both literally forces it to plan ahead and to coordinate policy in the various areas of operation. Continual revision of these forecasts keeps the firm alert to changing conditions in its environment and in its internal operations. Again, it is useful to prepare more than one set of pro forma statements in order to take into account the range of possible outcomes.

SUSTAINABLE GROWTH MODELING

The management of growth requires careful balancing of the sales objectives of the firm with its operating efficiency and financial resources. Many a company overreaches itself financially at the altar of growth; the bankruptcy courts are filled with such cases. The trick is to determine what sales growth rate is consistent with the realities of the company and of the financial marketplace. In this regard, sustainable growth modeling is a powerful planning tool and has found enthusiastic use in companies like Hewlett-Packard. In the way of definition, the *sustainable growth rate (SGR)* is the maximum annual percentage increase in sales that can be achieved based on target operating, debt, and dividend-payout ratios. If actual growth exceeds the SGR, something must give, and frequently it is the debt ratio. By modeling the process of growth, we are able to make intelligent trade-offs.

A Steady State Model

To illustrate the calculation of a sustainable growth rate, we begin with a steady state model where the future is exactly like the past with respect to balance sheet and performance ratios. Assumed also is that the firm engages in no external equity financing; the equity account builds only through earnings retention. Both of these assumptions will be relaxed when we consider sustainable growth modeling under changing assumptions.

Variables Employed.   In a steady state environment, the variables necessary to determine the sustainable growth rate are

A/S = the total assets-to-sales ratio
NP/S = the net profit margin (net profits divided by sales)
b = the retention rate of earnings ($1 - b$ is the dividend payout ratio)
D/Eq = the debt-to-equity ratio
S_0 = the most recent annual sales (beginning sales)
ΔS = the absolute change in sales from the most recent annual sales.

The first four variables are target variables. The total assets-to-sales ratio is a measure of operating efficiency, the reciprocal of the traditional assets turnover ratio. The lower the ratio the more efficient the utilization of assets. In turn, this ratio is a composite of (1) receivable management, as depicted by the average collection period; (2) inventory management, as indicated by the inventory turnover ratio; (3) fixed-assets management, as reflected by the throughput of product through the plant; and (4) liquidity management, as suggested by the proportion of and return on liquid assets. For purposes of illustration, we assume liquid assets are kept at moderate levels.[3]

The net profit margin is a relative measure of operating efficiency, after taking account of all expenses and income taxes. While both the assets-to-sales ratio and the net profit margin are affected by the external product markets, they largely capture internal management efficiency. The earnings retention rate and the debt ratio should be determined in keeping with dividend and capital structure theory and practice. They are influenced importantly by the external financial markets. Our purpose is not to touch on how they are established, as that is done elsewhere in this book, but to incorporate them in the planning model presented.

Sustainable Growth Rate.   With thes variables we can derive the sustainable growth rate (SGR). The idea is that an increase in assets (a use of funds)

---

[3] If this is not the case, it may be better to use the operating assets-to-sales ratio.

must equal the increase in liabilities and net worth (a source of funds). The increase in assets can be expressed as $\Delta S(A/S)$, the change in sales times the total assets-to-sales ratio. The increase in net worth (through retained earnings) is $b(NP/S)(S_0 + \Delta S)$, or the retention rate times the net profit margin times total sales. Finally, the increase in total debt is simply the net worth increase multiplied by the target debt-to-equity ratio, or $[b(NP/S)(S_0 + \Delta S)]D/Eq$. Putting these things together, we have[4]

$$\Delta S\left(\frac{A}{S}\right) = b\left(\frac{NP}{S}\right)(S_0 + \Delta S) + \left[b\left(\frac{NP}{S}\right)(S_0 + \Delta S)\right]\frac{D}{Eq} \qquad (7\text{-}2)$$

| Assets increase | Retained earnings increase | Increase in debt |

By rearrangement, this equation can be expressed as[5]

$$\frac{\Delta S}{S} \quad \text{or SGR} \quad = \frac{b\left(\dfrac{NP}{S}\right)\left(1 + \dfrac{D}{Eq}\right)}{\left(\dfrac{A}{S}\right) - \left[b\left(\dfrac{NP}{S}\right)\left(1 + \dfrac{D}{Eq}\right)\right]} \qquad (7\text{-}3)$$

This is the maximum rate of growth in sales that is consistent with the target ratios. Whether or not this growth rate can be achieved, of course, depends on the external product markets and on the firm's marketing efforts. A particular growth rate may be feasible financially, but the product demand may simply not be there. Implicit in the formulations presented is that depreciation charges are sufficient to maintain the value of operating assets. A final caveat has to do with interest on new borrowings. The implicit assumption is that all interest expenses are incorporated in the target net profit margin.

An Illustration. Suppose a company were characterized by the data shown in Table 7-7. If this were the case, the sustainable growth rate would be

[4] This is the same formulation as in Robert C. Higgins, *Analysis for Financial Management* (Homewood, Ill.: Richard D. Irwin, 1984), chap. 5. See his book for application and further illustration.

[5] Equation (7-2) can be expressed as

$$\Delta S\left(\frac{A}{S}\right) = b\left(\frac{NP}{S}\right)(S_0 + \Delta S)\left(1 + \frac{D}{Eq}\right)$$

$$\Delta S\left(\frac{A}{S}\right) = b\left(\frac{NP}{S}\right)\left(1 + \frac{D}{Eq}\right)S_0 + b\left(\frac{NP}{S}\right)\left(1 + \frac{D}{Eq}\right)\Delta S$$

$$\Delta S\left(\frac{A}{S}\right) - b\left(\frac{NP}{S}\right)\left(1 + \frac{D}{Eq}\right)\Delta S = b\left(\frac{NP}{S}\right)\left(1 + \frac{D}{Eq}\right)S_0$$

$$\Delta S\left[\left(\frac{A}{S}\right) - b\left(\frac{NP}{S}\right)\left(1 + \frac{D}{Eq}\right)\right] = b\left(\frac{NP}{S}\right)\left(1 + \frac{D}{Eq}\right)S_0$$

$$\frac{\Delta S}{S_0} = \frac{b\left(\dfrac{NP}{S}\right)\left(1 + \dfrac{D}{Eq}\right)}{\left(\dfrac{A}{S}\right) - \left[b\left(\dfrac{NP}{S}\right)\left(1 + \dfrac{D}{Eq}\right)\right]}$$

TABLE 7-7
Initial inputs and variables used to illustrate sustainable growth rates

SYMBOL	INITIAL INPUT AND/OR VARIABLE	
Eq_0	Beginning equity capital (in millions)	$100
$Debt_0$	Beginning debt (in millions)	$ 80
$Sales_0$	Sales the previous year (in millions)	$300
b	Target earnings retention rate	.70
NP/S	Target net profit margin	.04
D/Eq	Target debt-to-equity ratio	.80
A/S	Target assets-to-sales ratio	.60

$$SGR = \frac{.70(.04)(1.8)}{.60 - [.70(.04)(1.80)]} = 9.17\%$$

Thus, 9.17 percent is the sales growth rate consistent with the steady state variables shown in Table 7-7. It can be demonstrated that initial equity increases by 9.17 percent to $109.17 and that debt grows by 9.17 percent to $87.34, as everything increases in stable equilibrium. If the actual growth rate is other than 9.17 percent, however, one or more of the variables must change. In other words, operating efficiency, leverage, or earnings retention must change or there must be the sale or repurchase of stock.

Modeling Under Changing Assumptions

To see what happens when we move from steady state and variables change from year to year, we must model sustainable growth in a different way. In effect, the growth in equity base and the growth in sales are unbalanced over time. More specifically, we must bring in beginning sales, S_0, and beginning equity capital, Eq_0, as foundations on which to build. Additionally, we express dividend policy in terms of the absolute amount of dividends a company wishes to pay. Finally, we allow for the sale of common stock in a given year, though this can be specified as zero.

With these variables, the sustainable growth rate in sales for the next year, SGR in decimal form, becomes

$$SGR = \frac{(Eq_0 + New\ Eq - Div)\left(1 + \frac{D}{Eq}\right)\left(\frac{S}{A}\right)}{1 - \left[\left(\frac{NP}{S}\right)\left(1 + \frac{D}{Eq}\right)\left(\frac{S}{A}\right)\right]} \left[\frac{1}{S_0}\right] - 1 \qquad (7\text{-}4)$$

where New Eq is the amount of new equity capital raised, Div is the absolute amount of annual dividend, and S/A is the sales-to-total-assets ratio. The latter is simply the reciprocal of the assets-to-sales ratio that we used before. Intuitively, the numerator in the first bracket in Eq. (7-4) represents the sales that could occur on the basis of existing capital plus any change occasioned by common stock sales or dividends. The equity base is expanded by the debt employed and then multiplied by the sales-to-assets ratio. The denominator in the first bracket is one minus the target earning power of the company, $(NP/S)(S/A)$, magnified by the proportion of debt employed. When the numerator is divided by the denominator, we obtain the new level of sales that can be achieved. In the last bracket we divided this new level by beginning sales to determine the change in sales that is sustainable for the next year.

To illustrate, suppose that the target dividend were $3.93 million, no new equity issuance was planned, and that the other variables in Table 7-7 held. The sustainable growth rate, using Eq. (7-4), is

$$SGR = \left[\frac{(100 - 3.93)(1.80)(1.6667)}{1 - [(.04)(1.80)(1.6667)]} \right] \left[\frac{1}{300} \right] - 1 = 9.17\%$$

This is exactly the same as computed with the steady state model because a dividend of $3.93 million corresponds to an earnings retention rate of .70. Note also that an assets-to-sales ratio of .60 is the same as a sales-to-assets ratio of 1.6667.

Suppose now that the target assets-to-sales ratio is .55 (a sales-to-assets ratio of 1.8182) instead of .60. Moreover, the target net profit margin also is better, .05 instead of .04. Finally, the target debt-to-equity ratio is moved up from .80 to 1.00. Assuming a dividend of $4 million, the sustainable growth rate for next year becomes

$$SGR = \left[\frac{(100 - 4)(2.00)(1.8182)}{1 - [(.05)(2.00)(1.8182)]} \right] \left[\frac{1}{300} \right] - 1 = 42.22\%$$

This substantial increase in SGR is due to improved operating efficiency, which generates more retained earnings, and a higher debt ratio. It is important to recognize that the sales growth rate possible is for 1 year only. Even if operating efficiency continues on an improved basis, the debt ratio would have to increase continually in order to generate a SGR of 42.22 percent. The change in debt ratio affects all assets, not just the growth component.

To illustrate, suppose the debt-to-equity ratio were to remain at 1.00 and the other ratios also stayed the same. At the end of the year, we would be building from higher equity and sales bases:

$$S_1 = \$300(1.4222) = \$426.66$$

$$E_1 = \$300(1.4222).05 - \$4 + 100 = \$117.333$$

The sustainable growth rate for year 2 becomes

$$SGR_2 = \left[\frac{(117.333 - 4)(2.00)(1.8182)}{1 - [(.05)(2.00)(1.8182)]} \right] \left[\frac{1}{426.66} \right] - 1 = 18.06\%$$

Thus, the model produces the sustainable growth rate year by year in a changing environment. Just because a high SGR is possible one year does not mean that this growth rate is sustainable in the future. In fact, it will not be sustainable unless further variable changes in the same direction occur. In this sense it represents a one-shot occurrence.

Let us return to our earlier example, which produced a 9.17 percent SGR under the assumptions of

$$NP/S = .04 \qquad S/A = 1.6667 \qquad D/Eq = .80 \qquad Div = \$3.93$$

If the company were to raise $10 million in new equity capital, we would have

$$SGR = \left[\frac{(100 + 10 - 3.93)(1.80)(1.6667)}{1 - [(.04)(1.80)(1.6667)]} \right]\left[\frac{1}{300} \right] - 1 = 20.54\%$$

This SGR is higher than earlier because of the new equity infusion, which, again, may be one-shot occurrence. In summary, sustainable growth modeling year by year is considerably different than steady state modeling.

Solving for Other Variables

With any five of the six variables, together with beginning equity and beginning sales, it is possible to solve for the sixth. For example, suppose that we wished to determine the *assets-to-sales ratio* consistent with a growth in sales of 25 percent next year and the following other target variables:

$$NP/S = .05 \qquad D/Eq = .50 \qquad Div = \$4 \qquad New\ Eq = \$10$$

The relevant formula is

$$\frac{S}{A} = \frac{(1 + SGR)S_0}{\left[1 + \dfrac{D}{E}\right]\left[Eq_0 + New\ Eq - Div + \left(\dfrac{NP}{S}\right)(1 + SGR)S_0\right]} \qquad (7\text{-}5)$$

and solving for our example, we have

$$\frac{S}{A} = \frac{(1.25)300}{[1.50][100 + 10 - 4 + (.05)(1.25)300]} = 2.00$$

$$\frac{A}{S} = 1/2.00 = .50$$

This suggests that the company will need to have an assets-to-sales ratio of .50 if it is to grow at a 25 percent rate next year. This assumes a 5 percent net profit margin and the sale of $10 million in new equity capital.

If a sales growth rate of 25 percent is again desired but a sales-to-assets ratio of 1.70 is all that is likely (assets-to-sales ratio of .5882), we might be interested in the *debt-to-equity ratio* consistent with this and the other variables. The relevant formula is

$$\frac{D}{Eq} = \frac{(1 + SGR)S_0}{\left[Eq_0 + New\ Eq - Div + \left(\frac{NP}{S}\right)(1 + SGR)S_0\right]\left[\frac{S}{A}\right]} - 1 \qquad (7\text{-}6)$$

For our example

$$\frac{D}{Eq} = \frac{(1.25)300}{[(100 + 10 - 4 + (.05)(1.25)300][1.70]} - 1 = .7682$$

If the sales-to-assets ratio were 1.70 instead of 2.00, an increase in debt ratio from .50 to .7682 would be necessary to sustain a growth in sales of 25 percent next year. Thus, the sales-to-assets ratio and the debt-to-equity ratio have a powerful effect on the results.

Finally, suppose the company wished to grow at 20 percent in sales, raise no new equity capital, and had other target variables of

$$S/A = 1.90 \qquad D/Eq = .60 \qquad Div = \$4$$

It now wishes to determine the net profit margin it would need to achieve in order to make this happen. The formula is

$$\frac{NP}{S} = 1 \Big/ \left(1 + \frac{D}{Eq}\right)\left(\frac{S}{A}\right) - (Eq_0 + New\ Eq - Div)/(1 + SGR)S_0 \qquad (7\text{-}7)$$

which, for our example, becomes

$$\frac{NP}{S} = 1/(1.60)(1.90) - (100 - 4)/(1.20)300 = .0623$$

To achieve a 20 percent growth in sales in the face of no new equity financing, the net profit margin needs to be 6.23 percent.

By simulation, then, one is able to gain insight into the sensitivity of certain variables in the overall growth picture. With an algorithm for solving for the variables, these simulations can be made with ease. In Table 7-8, we present certain simulations, where the missing variables for which we solve are shown in the boxes.

Implications

To grow in a stable, balanced way, the equity base must grow proportionally with sales. When this is not the case, one or more of the financial ratios must change in order for the divergence in the two growth rates to be accommodated.

TABLE 7-8
Simulations using sustainable growth modeling

VARIABLE	1	2	3	4	5	6	7	8	9	10	11	12	13
A/S	.60	.60	.55	.50	.65	.70	.50	.4292	.5263	.60	.5882	.60	.60
NP/S	.04	.04	.05	.05	.035	.03	.05	.04	.0623	.0538	.05	.04	.04
D/E	.80	.80	1.00	.50	.80	.80	.50	.50	.60	1.00	.7682	1.0272	1.1659
Div	4.00	4.00	4.00	4.00	4.00	4.00	4.00	4.00	4.00	4.00	4.00	4.00	4.00
New Eq	0	10.00	0	0	5.00	0	10.00	10.00	0	0	10.00	0	0
SGR	.0909	.2046	.4222	.1294	.0325	−.1083	.25	.30	.20	.30	.25	.25	.35

Beginning sales = $300; beginning equity = $100.

By putting things into a sustainable growth model, we are able to check·the consistency of various growth plans. Often in corporate planning the company wants a number of good things: high sales growth, manufacturing flexibility, moderate use of debt, and high dividends. However, these things may be inconsistent with one another.

Sustainable growth modeling enables one to check for such inconsistency. By simulation, we can better understand the sensitivity of certain factors to the growth objectives of the firm, and vice versa. In this way, more informed and wiser marketing, finance, and manufacturing decisions can be reached. Sustainable growth modeling provides an integrative tool for helping the decision-making process. With the current emphasis in corporations on return on assets and on asset management, such modeling can play an integral part.

SUMMARY

Continuing our examination of the analytical tools of the financial manager, we looked at source-and-use-of-funds statements, the cash budget, pro forma statements, and sustainable growth modeling. The source-and-use-of-funds statement gives the financial analyst considerable insight into the uses of funds and how these uses are financed over a specific period of time. Funds-flow analysis is valuable in analyzing the commitments of funds to assets and in planning the firm's intermediate- and long-term financing. The flow of funds studied, however, represents net rather than gross transactions between two points in time.

A cash budget is a forecast of a firm's future cash receipts and cash disbursements. This forecast is particularly useful to the financial manager in determining the probable cash balances of the firm over the near future and in planning for the financing of prospective cash needs. In addition to analyzing expected cash flows, the financial manager should take into account possible deviations from the expected outcome. An analysis of the range of possible outcomes enables management to assess better the efficiency and flexibility of the firm and to determine the appropriate margin of safety.

Next we considered the preparation of pro forma income statements and balance sheets. These statements offer financial managers insight into the prospective future financial condition and performance of their firms, giving them yet another tool for financial planning and control.

Finally, we took up sustainable growth modeling and learned that it is a powerful tool in checking the consistency among sales growth goals, operating efficiency, and financial objectives. Two variations of the model exist: steady state, where the equity base and sales grow in concert, and unbalanced growth, where the ratios and growth change from year to year. With the latter, the sustainable growth rate is determined year by year. Given a desired growth in sales, through simulation one is able to determine the operating and financial variables necessary to achieve it.

QUESTIONS

1. Contrast the source-and-use-of-funds statements with a cash budget as planning tools.
2. In constructing a cash budget, which variable is most important in order to arrive at accurate projections? Explain.
3. Discuss the benefits that can be derived by the firm from cash budgeting.
4. Explain why a decrease in cash constitutes a source of funds while an increase in cash is a use of funds in the source-and-use statement.
5. Explain why selling inventory to credit customers is considered as a source of funds when in fact no funds were generated.
6. Why do most audited financial reports to the stockholders include a source-and-use-of-funds statement in addition to the balance sheet and income statement?
7. Is depreciation a source of funds? Under what conditions might the "source" dry up?
8. Why do bankers closely analyze the source-and-use-of-funds statement in considering credit applications?
9. Which of the following are sources of funds and which are uses of funds?
   a. Sale of land
   b. Quarterly dividend payment
   c. Lease payment
   d. Decrease in raw materials inventory
   e. Increase in depreciation charges
   f. Sale of government bonds
10. What are the major points of difference between a cash budget and the source-and-use-of-funds statement?
11. On what items should the financial manager concentrate to improve the accuracy of the cash budget? Explain your reasoning.
12. Is the cash budget a better measure of liquidity than traditional measures such as the current ratio and quick ratio?
13. Why is the sales forecast so important in preparing the cash budget?
14. What is the principal purpose of pro forma statements? Being a projection of the future, how do they differ from the cash budget?

15. What are the two principal ways by which one can prepare pro forma financial statements?

16. What is a sustainable growth rate for a company? Of what value is sustainable growth modeling?

17. Explain the differences between steady state sustainable growth modeling and year-by-year modeling.

18. List the variables used in sustainable growth modeling. Which variables usually have the most effect on the growth rate in sales?

SELF-CORRECTION PROBLEMS

1. Serap-Jones, Inc., had the following financial statements for 19x1 and 19x2. Prepare a source-and-use-of-funds statement and evaluate your findings.

ASSETS	19x1	19x2
Cash	$ 53,000	$ 31,000
Marketable securities	87,000	0
Accounts receivable	346,000	528,000
Inventories	432,000	683,000
Current assets	$ 918,000	$1,242,000
Net fixed assets	1,113,000	1,398,000
Total	$2,031,000	$2,640,000

LIABILITIES AND EQUITY	19x1	19x2
Accounts payable	$ 413,000	$ 627,000
Accruals	226,000	314,000
Bank borrowings	100,000	235,000
Current liabilities	$ 739,000	$1,176,000
Common stock	100,000	100,000
Retained earnings	1,192,000	1,364,000
Total	$2,031,000	$2,640,000

Note: Depreciation was $189,000 for 19x2 and no dividends were paid.

2. At December 31, the balance sheet of Rodriguez Malting Company was the following (in thousands):

Cash	$ 50	Accounts payable	$ 360
Accounts receivable	530	Bank loan	400
Inventories	545	Accruals	212
Current assets	$1,125	Current liabilities	$ 972
Net fixed assets	1,836	Long-term debt	450
		Common stock	100
		Retained earnings	1,439
		Total liabilities	
Total assets	$2,961	and net worth	$2,961

The company has received a large order and anticipates the need to go to its bank in order to increase its borrowings. As a result, it needs to forecast its cash requirements for January, February, and March.

Typically, the company collects 20 percent of its sales in the month of sale, 70 percent the subsequent month, and 10 percent in the second month after the sale. All sales are credit sales.

Purchases of raw materials to produce malt are made in the month prior to the sale and amount to 60 percent of sales in the subsequent month. Payments for these purchases occur in the month after the purchase. Labor costs, including overtime, are expected to be $150,000 in January, $200,000 in February, and $160,000 in March. Selling, administrative, tax, and other cash expenses are expected to be $100,000 per month for January through March. Actual sales in November and December and projected sales for January through April are as follows (in thousands):

November	$500	February	$1,000
December	600	March	650
January	600	April	750

On the basis of this information,

a. Prepare a cash budget for the months of January, February, and March.

b. Determine the amount of additional bank borrowings necessary to maintain a cash balance of $50,000 at all times.

c. Prepare a pro forma balance sheet for March 31. (It should be noted that the company maintains a safety stock of inventory.)

3. Downeast Nautical Company expects sales of $2.4 million next year and the same amount the following year. Sales are spread evenly throughout the year. On the basis of the following information, prepare a pro forma balance sheet and income statement for year end:

- Cash: Minimum of 4 percent of annual sales.
- Accounts receivable: 60-day average collection period based on annual sales.
- Inventories: Turnover of eight times a year.
- Net fixed assets: $500,000 now. Capital expenditures equal to depreciation.
- Accounts payable: 1 month's purchases.
- Accruals: 3 percent of sales.
- Bank borrowings: $50,000 now. Can borrow up to $250,000.
- Long-term debt: $300,000 now, payable $75,000 at year end.
- Common stock: $100,000. No additions planned.
- Retained earnings: $500,000 now.
- Net profit margin: 8 percent of sales.
- Dividends: None.
- Cost of goods sold: 60 percent of sales.

■ Purchases: 50 percent of cost of goods sold.

■ Income taxes: 50 percent of before-tax profits.

4. Zippo Industries has equity capital of $12 million, total debt of $8 million, and sales last year of $30 million.

a. It has a target assets-to-sales ratio of .6667, a target net profit margin of .04, a target debt-to-equity ratio of .6667, and a target earnings retention rate of .75. In steady state, what is its sustainable growth rate?

b. Suppose now the company has established for next year a target assets-to-sales ratio of .62, a target net profit margin of .05, and a target debt-to-equity ratio of .80. It wishes to pay an annual dividend of $0.3 million and raise $1 million in equity capital next year. What is its sustainable growth rate for next year? Why does it differ from that in part a?

PROBLEMS

1. Galow Fish Canning Company reports the following changes from the previous year end. Categorize these items as either a source of funds or a use of funds.

ITEM		ITEM	
Cash	−$ 100	Accounts payable	$300
Accounts receivable	700	Accruals	− 100
Inventory	− 300	Long-term debt	− 200
Gross fixed assets	900	Net profit	600
Depreciation	1,000	Dividends	400

2. **Kohn Corporation comparative balance sheets at December 31 (in millions)**

ASSETS	19x1	19x2	LIABILITIES AND NET WORTH	19x1	19x2
Cash	$ 5	$ 3	Notes payable	$ 20	$ 0
Accounts receivable	15	22	Accounts payable	5	8
Inventories	12	15	Accrued wages	2	2
Fixed assets, net	50	55	Accrued taxes	3	5
Other assets	8	5	Long-term debt	0	15
			Common stock	20	26
			Retained earnings	40	44
			Total liabilities		
Total assets	$ 90	$100	and net worth	$ 90	$100

Kohn Corporation statement of income and retained earnings, year ended December 31, 19x2 (in millions)

Net sales		$48
Expenses		
Cost of goods sold	$25	
Selling, general, and administrative expenses	5	
Depreciation	5	
Interest	2	37
Net income before taxes		$11
Less: Taxes		4
Net income		$ 7
Add: Retained earnings at 12/31/x1		40
Subtotal		$47
Less: Dividends		3
Retained earnings at 12/31/x2		$44

a. Prepare a source-and-use-of-funds statement on a cash basis for 19x2 for the Kohn Corporation.

b. Prepare a source-and-use-of-working-capital statement for 19x2 for the Kohn Corporation.

3. Financial statements for the Sennet Corporation follow.

Sennet Corporation balance sheet at December 31 (in millions)

Total current assets	19x1	19x2	Total current liabilities	19x1	19x2
Cash	$ 4	$ 5	Accounts payable	$ 8	$10
Accounts receivable	7	10	Notes payable	5	5
Inventory	12	15	Accrued wages	2	3
Total current assets	$23	$30	Accrued taxes	3	2
Net plant	40	40	Total current liabilities	$18	$20
			Long-term debt	20	20
			Common stock	10	10
			Retained earnings	15	20
Total	$63	$70		$63	$70

Sennet Corporation income statement 19x2 (in millions)

Sales		$95
Cost of goods sold	$50	
Selling, general, and administrative expenses	15	
Depreciation	3	
Interest	2	70
Net income before taxes		$25
Taxes		10
Net income		$15

a. Prepare a source-and-use-of-funds statement for Sennet.
b. Prepare a source-and-use-of-working-capital statement.

4. Prepare a cash budget for the Ace Manufacturing Company, indicating receipts and disbursements for May, June, and July. The firm wishes to maintain at all times a minimum cash balance of $20,000. Determine whether or not borrowing will be necessary during the period, and if it is, when and for how much. As of April 30, the firm had a balance of $20,000 in cash.

ACTUAL SALES		FORECASTED SALES	
January	$50,000	May	$ 70,000
February	50,000	June	80,000
March	60,000	July	100,000
April	60,000	August	100,000

■ Accounts receivable: 50 percent of total sales are for cash. The remaining 50 percent will be collected equally during the following 2 months (the firm incurs a negligible bad-debt loss).
■ Cost of goods manufactured: 70 percent of sales. 90 percent of this cost is paid during the first month after incurrence; the remaining 10 percent is paid the following month.
■ Selling, general, and administrative expenses: $10,000 per month plus 10 percent of sales. All of these expenses are paid during the month of incurrence.
■ Interest payments: A semiannual interest payment on $150,000 of bonds outstanding (12 percent coupon) is paid during July. An annual $50,000 sinking-fund payment is also made at that time.
■ Dividends: A $10,000 dividend payment will be declared and made in July.
■ Capital expenditures: $40,000 will be invested in plant and equipment in June.
■ Taxes: Income tax payments of $1,000 will be made in July.

5. Given the information that follows, prepare a cash budget for the Central City Department Store for the first 6 months of 19x2.
a. All prices and costs remain constant.
b. Sales are 75 percent for credit and 25 percent for cash.
c. With respect to credit sales, 60 percent are collected in the month after the sale, 30 percent in the second month, and 10 percent in the third. Bad-debt losses are insignificant.
d. Sales, actual and estimated, are

October 19x1	$300,000	March 19x2	$200,000
November 19x1	350,000	April 19x2	300,000
December 19x1	400,000	May 19x2	250,000
January 19x2	150,000	June 19x2	200,000
February 19x2	200,000	July 19x2	300,000

e. Payments for purchases of merchandise are 80 percent of the following month's anticipated sales.

f. Wages and salaries are

January	$30,000	March	$50,000	May	$40,000
February	40,000	April	50,000	June	35,000

g. Rent is $2,000 a month.

h. Interest of $7,500 is due on the last day of each calendar quarter.

i. A tax prepayment of $50,000 for 19x2 income is due in April.

j. A capital investment of $30,000 is planned in June, to be paid for then.

k. The company has a cash balance of $100,000 at December 31, 19x1, which is the minimum desired level for cash. Funds can be borrowed in multiples of $5,000. (Ignore interest on such borrowings.)

6. Use the cash budget worked out in Problem 5 and the following additional information to prepare a pro forma income statement for the first half of 19x2 for the Central City Department Store. (Note that the store maintains a safety stock of inventory.)

a. Inventory at 12/31/x1 was $200,000.

b. Depreciation is taken on a straight-line basis on $250,000 of assets with an average remaining life of 10 years and no salvage value.

c. The tax rate is 50 percent.

7. Given the following information and that contained in Problem 5 and 6, construct a pro forma balance sheet as of June 30, 19x2, for the Central City Department Store. (Assume that accounts payable stay the same as at December 31, 19x1.)

**Central City Department Store balance sheet
at December 31, 19x1**

ASSETS		LIABILITIES AND EQUITY	
Cash	$100,000	Accounts payable	$130,000
Accounts receivable	427,500	Bonds	500,000
Inventory	200,000		
		Common stock and	
Fixed assets, net	250,000	retained earnings	347,500
	$977,500		$977,500

8. Liz Clairsorn Industries has $40 million in net worth and sales of $150 million last year.

a. Its target ratios are assets to sales, .40; net profit margin, .07; debt to equity, .50; and earnings retention, .60. If these ratios correspond to steady state, what is its sustainable growth rate?

b. What would be the sustainable growth rate next year if the company moved from steady state and had the following targets? Assets-to-sales ratio, .42; net profit margin, .06; debt-to-equity ratio, .45; dividend of $5 million; and no new equity financing.

9. Hildebrand Hydronics Corporation wishes to achieve a 35 percent increase in sales next year. Sales last year were $30 million and the company has equity capital of $12 million. It intends to raise $0.5 million in new equity by sale of stock to officers. No dividend is planned. Tentatively, the company has set the following target ratios: assets to sales, .67; net profit margin, .08; and debt to equity, .60. The company has determined that these ratios are not sufficient to produce a growth in sales of 35 percent.

a. Holding the other two target ratios constant, what assets-to-sales ratio would be necessary to attain the 35 percent sales increase?

b. Holding the other two ratios constant, what net profit margin would be necessary?

c. Holding the other two ratios constant, what debt-to-equity ratio would be necessary?

SOLUTIONS TO SELF-CORRECTION PROBLEMS

1.   **Source-and-use-of funds statement for Serap-Jones, Inc. (in thousands)**

SOURCES		USES	
Funds provided by operations		Addition to fixed assets	$474
Net profit	$172		
Depreciation	189	Increase,	
	$361	accounts receivable	182
Decrease, marketable securities	87	Increase, inventories	251
Increase, accounts payable	214		
Increase, accruals	88		
Increase, bank borrowings	135		
Decrease, cash	22		
	$907		$907

The company has had substantial capital expenditures and increases in current assets. This growth has far outstripped the growth in retained earnings. To finance this growth, the company has reduced its marketable securities to zero, has leaned heavily on the trade, and has increased its accruals and bank borrowings. All of this is short-term financing of mostly long-term buildups in assets.

2. a.

Cash budget (in thousands)

	NOV.	DEC.	JAN.	FEB.	MAR.	APR.
Sales	$500	$600	$600	$1,000	$650	$750
Collections, current month sales			120	200	130	
Collections, previous month's sales			420	420	700	
Collections, previous 2 months' sales			50	60	60	
Total cash receipts			$590	$680	$860	
Purchases		$360	$600	$390	$450	
Payment for purchases			360	600	390	
Labor costs			150	200	160	
Other expenses			100	100	100	
Total cash disbursements			$610	$900	$650	
Receipts less disbursements			$(20)	$(220)	$240	

b.

Additional borrowings	$ 20	$220	($240)
Cumulative borrowings	420	640	400

The amount of financing peaks in February owing to the need to pay for purchases made the previous month and higher labor costs. In March, substantial collections are made on the prior month's billings, causing a large net cash inflow sufficient to pay off the additional borrowings.

c.   **Pro forma balance sheet, March 31 (in thousands)**

Cash	$ 50	Accounts payable	$ 450
Accounts receivable	620	Bank loan	400
Inventories	635	Accruals	212
Current assets	$1,305	Current liabilities	$1,062
Net fixed assets	1,836	Long-term debt	450
		Common stock	100
		Retained earnings	1,529
Total assets	$3,141	Total liabilities and net worth	$3,141

- Accounts receivable = sales in March times .8 plus sales in February times .1.
- Inventories = $545 plus (total purchases January through March minus total sales January through March times .6).

- Accounts payable = purchases in March.
- Retained earnings = $1,439 plus sales, minus payment for purchases, minus labor costs, and minus other expenses, all for January through March.

3.

Pro forma income statement (in thousands)

Sales	$2,400
Cost of goods sold	1,440
Gross profit	$ 960
Expenses	576
Profit before taxes	$ 384
Taxes	192
Profit after taxes	$ 192

Pro forma balance sheet (in thousands)

Cash	$ 96	Accounts payable[1]	$ 60	
Accounts receivable[2]	400	Accruals	72	
Inventories[3]	180	Bank borrowings[4]	27	
Current assets	$ 676	Current liabilities	$ 159	
Net fixed assets	500	Long-term debt	225	
		Common stock	100	
		Retained earnings[5]	692	
Total assets	$1,176	Total liabilities and net worth	$1,176	

[1] (Cost of goods sold × .5)/12 = ($2.4 million × .6 × .5)/12 = $60,000.
[2] Sales/(360/60) = $2.4 million/6 = $400,000.
[3] Cost of goods sold/8 = ($2.4 million × .6)/8 = $180,000.
[4] Total assets minus accounts payable, accruals, long-term debt, common stock, and retained earnings = $27,000.
[5] Retained earnings now plus net profits = $692,000.

4. a. $$SGR = \frac{.75(.04)(1.6667)}{.6667 - [.75(.04)(1.6667)]} = 8.11\%$$

b. $$SGR = \left[\frac{(12 + 1 - 0.3)(1.80)(1.6129)}{1 - [(.05)(1.80)(1.6129)]}\right]\left[\frac{1}{30}\right] - 1 = 43.77\%$$

The company has moved from steady state with higher target operating efficiency, a higher debt ratio, and the sale of common stock. All of these things permit a high rate of growth in sales next year. Unless further changes in these directions occur, the SGR will decline.

SELECTED REFERENCES

CHAMBERS, JOHN C., SATINDER K. MULLICK, and DONALD D. SMITH, "How to Choose the Right Forecasting Technique," *Harvard Business Review*, 49 (July–August 1971), 45–74.

DONALDSON, GORDON, "Strategy for Financial Emergencies," *Harvard Business Review*, 47 (November–December 1969), 67–79.

HELFERT, ERICH A., *Techniques of Financial Analysis*, 5th ed. Homewood, Ill.: Richard D. Irwin, 1982, chaps. 1 and 3.

HIGGINS, ROBERT C., "How Much Growth Can a Firm Afford?" *Financial Management*, 6 (Fall 1977), 7–16.

_____, "Sustainable Growth under Inflation," *Financial Management*, 10 (Autumn 1981), 36–40.

_____, *Analysis for Financial Management*. Homewood, Ill.: Richard D. Irwin, 1984.

HILL, NED C., "Planning and Control Techniques," chap. 1, in *Handbook of Corporate Finance*, ed. Edward I. Altman. New York: Wiley, 1986.

PAPPAS, JAMES L., and GEORGE P. HUBER, "Probabilistic Short-Term Financial Planning," *Financial Management*, 2 (Autumn 1973), 36–44.

PARKER, GEORGE G. C., "Financial Forecasting," chap. 2, in *Handbook of Corporate Finance*, ed. Edward I. Altman. New York: John Wiley, 1986.

VAN HORNE, JAMES C., "Sustainable Growth Modeling," *Journal of Corporate Finance*, forthcoming.

CHAPTER 8

Current Asset and Liability Structure Decisions

INTRODUCTION

Current assets, by accounting definition, are assets normally converted into cash within one year. Working capital management usually is considered to involve the administration of these assets—namely, cash and marketable securities, receivables, and inventories—and the administration of current liabilities. Administration of *fixed assets* (assets normally not converted into cash within the year), on the other hand, is usually considered to fall within the realm of capital budgeting, which we take up in Part V. By and large, investment in current assets is more divisible than investment in fixed assets, a fact that has implications for flexibility in financing. Differences in divisibility as well as in durability of economic life are the essential features that distinguish current from fixed assets.

Significance of Working Capital Management

Why is the management of working capital, which is taken up in this and the subsequent four chapters, important? For several reasons. For one thing, the current assets of a typical manufacturing company account for over half of its total assets. For a distribution company, they account for even more. Even a public utility with little in the way of inventories has a sizable investment in accounts receivable. If a company is to operate efficiently, receivables and inventories must be tightly monitored and controlled. For the fast-growing company, this is particularly important because the investment in such assets can quickly mushroom out of control.

For the smaller company, current liabilities are the principal source of external financing. These firms simply do not have access to the longer-term capital markets, other than to a mortgage on a building. The fast-growing, but larger, company also makes use of current liability financing. For these reasons, the financial manager and his or her staff devote a considerable portion of their time to working capital matters. The management of cash, marketable securities, accounts receivable, accounts payable, accruals, and other means of short-term financing usually is the direct responsibility of the financial manager; only inventories are not. Moreover, these responsibilities require day-by-day supervision. Unlike dividend and capital structure decisions, you cannot study the issue, reach a decision, and set the matter aside for many months to come. For working capital matters, the decision process is continuous. Thus, working capital management is important simply because of the proportion of time that must be devoted to it. More fundamental is the effect that working capital decisions have on the company's overall risk-return complexion.

Profitability and Risk

Determining the appropriate levels of current assets and current liabilities, which determine the level of working capital, involves fundamental decisions on the firm's liquidity and the maturity composition of its debt. In turn, these decisions are influenced by a trade-off between profitability and risk. In a broad sense, the appropriate decision variable to examine on the asset side of the balance sheet is the maturity composition, or liquidity, of the firm's assets, that is, the turnover of these assets into cash. Decisions that affect the asset liquidity of the firm include the management of cash and marketable securities, credit policy and procedures, inventory management and control, and the administration of fixed assets. For purposes of illustration, we hold constant the last three factors; the efficiency in managing them is taken up elsewhere in the book.[1] We assume also that the cash and marketable securities held by the firm (hereafter called liquid assets) yield a return lower than the return on investment in other assets.

For current assets, then, the lower the proportion of liquid assets to total assets, the greater the firm's return on total investment. Profitability with respect to the level of current liabilities relates to differences in costs between various methods of financing and to the use of financing during periods when it is not needed. To the extent that the explicit costs of short-term financing are less than those of intermediate- and long-term financing, the greater the proportion of short-term debt to total debt, the higher the profitability of the firm.

Although short-term interest rates sometimes exceed long-term rates, generally they are less. Even when they are higher, the situation is likely to be only temporary. Over an extended period of time we would expect to pay more in interest cost with long-term debt than we would with short-term borrowings, which are continually rolled over at maturity. Moreover, the use of short-term debt as opposed to longer-term debt is likely to result in higher profits because debt will be paid off during periods when it is not needed.

These profitability assumptions suggest a low proportion of current assets to total assets and a high proportion of current liabilities to total liabilities. This strategy, of course, will result in a low level of working capital or, conceivably, even negative working capital. Offsetting the profitability of this strategy is the risk to the firm. For our purposes, risk is the probability of technical insolvency. In a legal sense, insolvency occurs whenever the assets of a firm are less than its liabilities—negative net worth. Technical insolvency, on the other hand, occurs whenever a firm is unable to meet its cash obligations.[2] In this chapter, we study the trade-off between risk and profitability as it relates to the financing of current assets.

THE MATURITY STRUCTURE OF FINANCING

The way in which the assets of a company are financed involves a trade-off between risk and profitability. For purposes of analysis, we assume that the company has an established policy of payment for purchases, labor, taxes, and other expenses. Thus, the amounts of accounts payable and accruals included in cur-

---

[1] See Chapter 10 and Part V.

[2] James E. Walter, "Determination of Technical Solvency," *Journal of Business*, 30 (January 1957), 30–43.

rent liabilities are not active decision variables.[3] These current liabilities are regarded as spontaneous financing, and they are the topic of Chapter 11. They finance a portion of the current assets of the firm and tend to fluctuate with the production schedule and, in the case of taxes, with profits. As the underlying investment in current assets grows, accounts payable and accruals also tend to grow, in part financing the buildup in assets. Our concern is with how assets not supported by spontaneous financing are handled. This residual financing requirement pertains to the net investment in assets after spontaneous financing is deducted.

Hedging Approach

If the firm adopts a hedging approach to financing, each asset would be offset with a financing instrument of the same approximate maturity. Short-term or seasonal variations would be financed with short-term debt; the permanent component of current assets would be financed with long-term debt or equity. The situation is illustrated in Fig. 8-1. If total funds requirements behave in the manner shown, only the short-term fluctuations shown at the top of the figure would be financed with short-term debt. To finance short-term requirements with long-term debt would necessitate the payment of interest for the use of funds during times when they were not needed. This occurrence can be illustrated by drawing a straight line across the seasonal humps in Fig. 8-1 to represent the total amount of long-term debt and equity. It is apparent that financing would be employed in periods of seasonal lull when it was not needed. With a hedging approach to financing, the borrowing and payment schedule for short-term financing would be arranged to correspond to the expected swings in current assets, less spontaneous financing. (Note again that some of the current assets are financed by payables and accruals, but that we deduct such spontaneous financing to arrive at the upper line in the figure.) Fixed assets and the permanent component of current assets would be financed with long-term debt, equity, and the permanent component of current liabilities.

A hedging approach to financing suggests that apart from current installments on long-term debt, a firm would show no current borrowings at the seasonal troughs in Fig 8-1. Short-term borrowings would be paid off with surplus cash. As the firm moved into a period of seasonal funds needs, it would borrow on a short-term basis, again paying the borrowings off as surplus cash was generated. In this way, financing would be employed only when it was needed. Permanent funds requirements would be financed with long-term debt and equity. In a growth situation, permanent financing would be increased in keeping with increases in permanent funds requirements. In other words, the financing of the firm would follow a self-liquidating principle.

[3] Delaying the payment of accounts payable can be a decision variable for financing purposes. However, there are limits to the extent to which a firm can "stretch" its payables. For simplicity, we assume in this analysis that the firm has a definite policy for paying bills, such as taking advantage of all cash discounts and paying all other bills at the end of the credit period. See Chapter 11 for a discussion of trade credit as a means of financing.

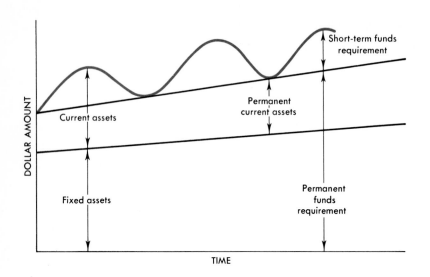

FIGURE 8-1
Funds requirement; hedging financing policy

Short- Versus Long-Term Financing

Although an exact synchronization of the schedule of expected future net cash flows and the payment schedule of debt is appropriate under conditions of certainty, it usually is not appropriate under uncertainty. Net cash flows will deviate from expected flows in keeping with the business risk of the firm. As a result, the schedule of maturities of the debt contracts is very significant in assessing the risk-profitability trade-off. The question is: What margin of safety should be built into the maturity schedule to allow for adverse fluctuations in cash flows? This depends on the trade-off between risk and profitability.

The Relative Risks Involved.   In general, the shorter the maturity schedule of a firm's debt obligations, the greater the risk that it will be unable to meet principal and interest payments. On the other hand, the longer the maturity schedule, the less risky the financing of the firm, all other things the same.

Suppose a company borrows on a short-term basis in order to build a new plant. The cash flows from the plant are not sufficient in the short run to pay off the loan. As a result, the company bears the risk that the lender may not renew the loan at maturity. This risk could be reduced by financing the plant on a long-term basis, the expected cash flows being sufficient to retire the debt in an orderly manner. Thus, committing funds to a long-term asset and borrowing short carries the risk that the firm may not be able to renew its borrowings. If the company should fall on hard times, creditors might regard renewal as too risky and demand immediate payment. In turn, this would cause the firm either to retrench or to go into bankruptcy.

In addition to this sort of risk, there also is the uncertainty associated with interest costs. When the firm finances with long-term debt, it knows precisely its interest costs over the time period it needs the funds. If it finances with short-term debt, it is uncertain of interest costs upon refinancing. In a sense, then, the uncertainty of interest costs represents risk to the borrower. We know that short-term interest rates fluctuate far more than long-term interest rates. A firm forced to refinance its short-term debt in a period of rising interest rates may pay an overall interest cost on short-term debt that is higher than it would have been on long-term debt. Therefore, the absence of knowledge of future short-term interest costs may represent risk to a company.

The Trade-off with Costs.   Differences in risk between short- and long-term financing must be balanced against differences in interest costs. The longer the maturity schedule of a firm's debt, the more costly the financing is likely to be. For one thing, the expected cost of long-term financing usually is more than that of short-term financing. Figure 8-2 illustrates the typical relationship which prevailed in the 1970s and 1980s between interest rates and maturity for high-grade corporate bonds. The line is known as a *yield curve*, and it tells us the **yield** associated with a given maturity. As shown, the yield curve is upward-sloping, which suggests that long-term borrowings are more costly than short-term borrowings. In periods of high interest rates, the rate on short-term borrowings may exceed that on long-term borrowings; but over a reasonable period of time, the firm typically pays more for long-term borrowings. Expressed differently, the long-run expected cost of short-term borrowings, represented by the present short-term rate and expected future short-term rates when the debt is rolled over, will be lower than the expected cost of long-term debt.

In addition to the higher expected interest costs of long-term borrowings, the firm may pay interest on debt over periods of time when the funds are not needed. Put another way, short-term financing gives the firm flexibility. If there is a probability that the firm's need for funds will decrease, the use of short-term

Yield. Rate of discount that equates the present value of the stream of expected future interest and principal payments with the security's market price.

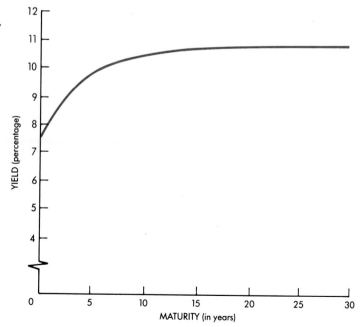

FIGURE 8-2
Typical yield curve for high-grade corporate bonds

debt permits debt to be paid off in keeping with the diminished need for funds. Thus, there is an expected cost inducement to finance funds requirements on a short-term basis.

Consequently, we have a trade-off between risk and profitability. We have seen that in general short-term debt has greater risk than long-term debt, but also less cost. The margin of safety provided by the firm can be thought of as the lag between the firm's expected net cash flow and the contractual payments on its debt. This margin of safety will depend on the risk preferences of management. In turn, its decision on the maturity composition of the firm's debt will determine the portion of current assets financed by current liabilities and the portion financed on a long-term basis.

To allow for a margin of safety, management might decide on the proportions of short-term and long-term financing shown in Fig. 8-3. Here, we see, the firm finances a portion of its expected seasonal funds requirement, less payables and accruals, on a long-term basis. If the expected net cash flows do occur, it will pay interest on debt during seasonal troughs when the funds are not needed. In the extreme, peak requirements might be financed entirely on a long-term basis, as would be the case if we drew the long-term financing line across the seasonal humps at the top of Fig. 8-3. The higher the long-term financing line, the more conservative the financing policy of the firm and the higher the cost. Also, we are mindful of the practical difficulties of smaller firms in particular being able to attract long-term debt financing in sufficient magnitude to cover all funds requirements long term.

In contrast to a conservative financing policy, an aggressive one might look like that shown in Fig. 8-4. Here we see that there is a "negative" margin of safety. The firm has financed part of its permanent current assets with short-term debt. As a result, it must refinance this debt at maturity, and this involves an element of risk. The greater the portion of the permanent funds requirements financed with short-term debt, the more aggressive the financing is said to be.

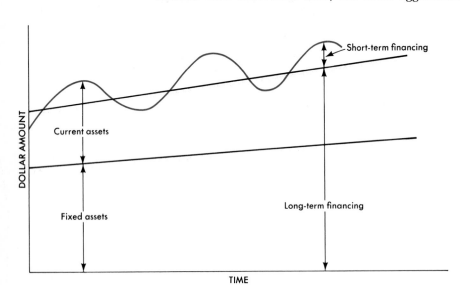

FIGURE 8-3
Funds requirement—conservative financing policy

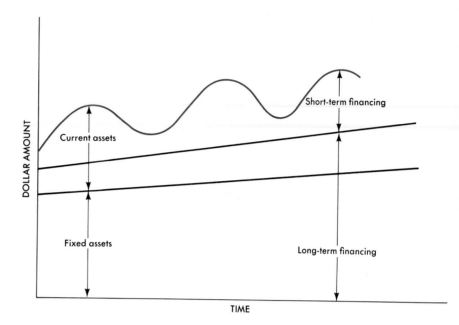

FIGURE 8-4
Funds requirement— aggressive financing policy

Therefore, the expected margin of safety associated with financing policy can be either positive, negative, or zero. Zero would be the case in a hedging policy, illustrated in Fig. 8-1.

As we shall see in the subsequent section, however, the firm also can create a margin of safety by increasing the proportion of liquid assets. Thus, the firm can reduce the risk of cash insolvency either by increasing the maturity schedule of its debt or by decreasing the relative "maturity" of its assets. At the end of the chapter we explore the interdependence of these two facets.

THE AMOUNT OF CURRENT ASSETS

In determining the appropriate level of current assets, management must again consider the trade-off between profitability and risk. To illustrate this trade-off, we hold constant the amount of the firm's fixed assets and vary the amount of current assets. Moreover, we assume that the management of receivables and inventories is efficient and consistent throughout the range of output under consideration. In other words, at every level of output, the investment in receivables and inventories is predetermined.[4] As a result, we are concerned only with the cash and marketable securities portion of the current assets of the firm.[5]

---

[4] The efficiency of management of receivables and inventory is examined in Chapter 10. The quality of these assets, as determined by the efficiency of their management, has a significant bearing on the liquidity of the firm.

[5] The allocation of funds between cash and marketable securities, near cash, is taken up in Chapter 9.

Risk-Profitability Trade-off

Under these assumptions there exists a risk-return trade-off with respect to the relative proportion of current assets held by the firm. In general, the greater the ratio of current assets to total assets, the less risky the company's working capital policy. This makes sense in that the firm will have sufficient cash and cash equivalents to pay its bills the greater the cushion. On the other hand, the lower the ratio, the more aggressive—and risky—the company's working capital policy. At any sales level, the greater the firm's proportion of current assets, the lower its relative profitability. What happens is that the firm has money tied up in idle or near idle current assets. As a result, its profitability is not as high as it would be if the funds were invested in assets providing a higher return.

To illustrate these concepts, suppose that with its existing fixed assets a firm can produce up to 100,000 units of output a year. Production is continuous throughout the period under consideration, in which there is a particular level of output. For each level of output, the firm can have a number of different levels of current assets. We assume initially three current asset alternatives. The relationship between output and current asset level for these alternatives is illustrated in Fig. 8-5. We see from the figure that the greater the output, the greater the need for investment in current assets. However, the relationship is not linear; current assets increase at a decreasing rate with output. This relationship is based on the notion that it takes a greater proportional investment in current assets when only a few units of output are produced than it does later on when the firm can use its current assets more efficiently. Fixed assets are assumed not to vary with output.

Of the three alternatives, alternative A in Fig. 8-5 is the most conservative level of current assets, for the ratio of current assets to fixed assets is greatest at every level of output. The greater the proportion of current to fixed assets, the

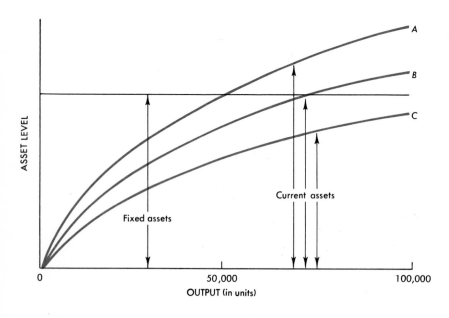

FIGURE 8-5
Current to fixed assets

greater the liquidity of the firm and the lower the risk of technical insolvency, all other things held constant. Alternative C is the most aggressive policy, because the ratio of current assets to fixed assets is lowest at all levels of output. The probability of technical insolvency is greatest under alternative C if net cash flows are less than expected.

Suppose that for the forthcoming year a firm expects sales of $2 million on 80,000 units of output and expects to realize a profit margin before interest and taxes of 10 percent, or $200,000 in total profits. We assume that this figure will not vary with the levels of current assets considered. Fixed assets are $500,000 for the period under review, and management is considering current asset positions of $400,000, $500,000, or $600,000. Given this information, we are able to make the profitability calculations shown in Table 8-1. As evidenced in this table, the greater the proportion of current assets to fixed assets, the lower the rate of return. Alternative A, the most conservative plan, gives the firm the greatest liquidity cushion to meet unexpected needs for funds. It also provides the lowest rate of return of the three alternatives. Alternative C, on the other hand, provides the highest rate of return but has the lowest liquidity and, correspondingly, the greatest risk.

TABLE 8-1
Profitability under alternative current-asset positions

	A	B	C
Sales	$2,000,000	$2,000,000	$2,000,000
Earnings before interest and taxes	200,000	200,000	200,000
Current assets	600,000	500,000	400,000
Fixed assets	500,000	500,000	500,000
Total assets	1,100,000	1,000,000	900,000
Asset turnover (sales/total assets)	1.82:1	2:1	2.22:1
Rate for return (earnings/total assets)	18.2%	20%	22.2%

Some Qualifications

This is a very simple example of the trade-off between risk and profitability. Our assumptions were such that changes in the level of current assets were composed entirely of changes in liquid assets—cash and marketable securities. We should recognize that the generalizations possible become far more complicated when it comes to changes in accounts receivable and inventory. Although receivables do not provide the buffer against running out of cash that cash and marketable securities do, they provide more of a buffer than do inventories or fixed assets. By the same token, the profit forgone by holding receivables generally is less than that for holding cash or marketable securities, but greater than that for holding inventories and fixed assets. Though we may have some idea of the relative ordering of receivables and inventories with respect to risk and profits forgone, the differences are extremely difficult to quantify. In subsequent chapters we deal with the optimal level of each of these assets, taking into consideration both profitability and risk. For now, we continue to restrict our definition of liquid assets to cash and marketable securities.

COMBINING LIABILITY STRUCTURE AND CURRENT ASSET DECISIONS

In the preceding sections we examined two broad facets of working capital management: how to finance current assets and what proportion of liquid assets to maintain. The two facets are interdependent. All other things held constant, a firm with a high proportion of liquid assets is better able to finance its current assets on a short-term basis than is a firm with a low proportion of liquid assets. On the other hand, a firm that finances its current assets entirely with equity will have less need for liquidity than it would if it financed these assets entirely with short-term borrowings. Because of their interdependence, these two facets of working capital management must be considered jointly.

Uncertainty and the Margin of Safety

If the firm knows its future cash flows with certainty, it will be able to arrange its maturity schedule of debt to correspond exactly with its schedule of future net cash flows. As a result, profits will be maximized, for there will be no need to hold low-yielding liquid assets nor to have more long-term financing than is absolutely necessary. When cash flows are subject to uncertainty, however, the situation is changed. As discussed in Chapter 7, cash forecasts can be prepared for a range of possible outcomes, with a probability attached to each. This information enables management to assess the possibility of technical insolvency and to plan accordingly for a margin of safety. The greater the dispersion of the probability distribution of possible net cash flows, the greater the margin of safety that management will wish to provide.

We assume initially that the firm cannot borrow on short notice to meet unexpected cash drains. As a result, it can provide a margin of safety only by (1) increasing the proportion of liquid assets or (2) lengthening the maturity schedule of financing. Both of these actions affect profitability. In the first choice, funds are committed to low-yielding assets; in the second, the firm may pay interest on borrowings over periods of time when the funds are not needed. In addition, long-term debt has a higher expected interest cost than does short-term debt.

Risk and Profitability

A decision on the appropriate margin of safety will be governed by considerations of risk and profitability and by the utility preferences of management with respect to bearing risk. To the extent that the cost of running out of cash is measurable, the optimal margin of safety can be determined by comparing the expected costs of running out of cash with the profits forgone when a particular solution is used to avoid that possibility. The expected cost of a cash stockout is the cost associated with a particular stockout times its probability of occurrence. Suppose that associated with a particular solution there is a 10 percent probability for a cash stockout of $50,000 and a 5 percent probability that the stockout will be $100,000. If the costs of these stockouts are $10,000 and $25,000, respectively, the expected costs will be .10($10,000) = $1,000 and .05($25,000) = $1,250, respectively. The total expected cost of cash stockout for that solution is $2,250.

The optimal solution could be determined by comparing the reduction in the expected cost of cash stockout accompanying a particular solution with the opportunity cost of implementing that solution. The optimal solution is at the point where the marginal opportunity cost equals the marginal decrease in the expected cost of cash stockout. The difficulty with this approach, however, is in estimating the cost of a cash stockout. Costs such as deterioration in a firm's credit standing and the inability to pay certain obligations are intangible and defy precise quantification.

Because of this difficulty, it may be easier for management to consider subjectively the costs associated with various cash stockouts and then simply specify a tolerable level of risk. Suppose we find that there is a 5 percent probability that the cash balance of the firm will be −$300,000 or less during the next several periods. If management is willing to tolerate a 5 percent probability of running out of cash, the firm should increase its liquid assets by $300,000. If it does so, there will be only a 5 percent probability that possible deviations from expected cash flows will result in the firm's running out of cash. The firm may be able to achieve the same results by lengthening its maturity schedule of financing. By refinancing existing debt that matures within 2 years into intermediate-term debt maturing in 5 to 7 years, the firm may be able to reduce the probability of technical insolvency to 5 percent. Likewise, various combinations of liquidity increase and debt lengthening may achieve this result.

Each solution (increasing liquidity, lengthening the maturity structure, or a combination of the two), will cost the firm something in profit-making ability. For a given risk tolerance, management may determine which solution is least costly and then implement that solution. On the other hand, management might determine the least costly solution for various levels of risk. Then management could formulate risk tolerances on the basis of the cost involved in providing a margin of safety. Presumably these tolerances would be in keeping with an objective of maximizing shareholder wealth. The approach, however, has been to provide an information framework specifying risk and profitability that management can use to make informal and rational decisions.

If the firm can borrow in times of emergency, the foregoing analysis needs to be modified. The greater the ability of the firm to borrow, the less it needs to provide for a margin of safety by the means discussed previously. Certain companies can arrange for lines of credit or revolving credits that enable them to borrow on short notice.[6] When a company has access to such credit, it must compare the cost of these arrangements (compensating balances, interest costs, and

---

[6] For a discussion of these methods, see Chapter 12.

use of debt capacity) with the cost of other solutions. There are, of course, limits on how much a firm may borrow on short notice. Consequently, it must provide for some margin of safety on the basis of the considerations discussed in this chapter.

SUMMARY

Working capital management involves deciding upon the amount and composition of current assets and how to finance these assets. These decisions involve trade-offs between risk and profitability. The greater the relative proportion of liquid assets, the less the risk of running out of cash, all other things being equal. Profitability, unfortunately, also will be less. The longer the composite maturity schedule of securities used to finance the firm, the less the risk of cash insolvency, all other things being equal. Again, the profits of the firm are likely to be less. Resolution of the trade-off between risk and profitability with respect to these decisions depends on the risk preferences of management, who, it is hoped, have an eye on the likely impact of a decision on the firm's valuation.

In this chapter we have been concerned with working capital management in a broad sense. We assumed the efficient management of the various components of current assets. The efficiency of credit and collection procedures and inventory control have a significant bearing on the liquidity of the firm. Moreover, we did not differentiate between cash and marketable securities (near cash) or consider the optimal split between these two assets. In the two subsequent chapters we analyze specifically the management of cash and marketable securities, the management of receivables, and the management of inventories. Still later in this part, we consider methods of short- and intermediate-term financing.

QUESTIONS

1. What does working capital management encompass? What fundamental decisions are involved, and what underlying principle or trade-off influences the decision process?

2. The amount of current assets that a firm maintains will be determined by the trade-off between risk and profitability.

   a. Is there a unique combination of risk and profitability for each level of current assets?

   b. Discuss the factors that affect the risk associated with holding current assets.

3. Utilities hold 10 percent of total assets in current assets; retail trade industries hold 60 percent of total assets in current assets. Explain how industry characteristics account for this difference.

4. Some firms finance their permanent working capital with short-term liabilities (commercial paper and short-term notes). Explain the impact of this decision on the profitability and risk parameters of these firms.

5. Suppose that a firm finances its seasonal (temporary) current assets with long-term funds. What is the impact of this decision on the profitability and risk parameters of this firm?

6. Risk associated with the amount of current assets is assumed to decrease with increased levels of current assets. Is this assumption correct for all levels of current assets? Explain.

7. Can you compare the net working capital position with the cash budget to measure the ability of a firm to meet maturing obligations?

8. At times, long-term interest rates are lower than short-term rates, yet the discussion in the chapter suggests that long-term financing is more expensive. If long-term rates are lower, should not the firm finance itself entirely with long-term debt?

9. How does shortening the maturity composition of outstanding debt increase the firm's risk? Why does increasing the liquidity of the firm's assets reduce that risk?

10. Why do firms invest in any current assets at all if the returns on those assets are less than the returns from fixed assets?

11. What are the costs of maintaining too large a net working capital position? too small a net working capital position?

12. How is a margin of safety provided for in working capital management?

SELF-CORRECTION PROBLEMS

1. Doremus Door and Pillar Company presently has total assets of $3.2 million, of which cash and marketable securities are $.2 million. Sales are $10 million annually, and the gross profit margin (before interest charges) is 12 percent. Given the cyclical nature of the business, the company is considering higher levels of liquidity as a buffer against adversity. Specifically, levels of $.5 million and $.8 million are being considered instead of the $.2 million presently held. The new liquidity will be financed with new equity capital.

   a. Determine the asset turnover, return on assets, and the gross profit margin under the three alternative levels of liquidity.

   b. If the new liquidity levels were financed with long-term debt at 15 percent interest, what would be the before-tax interest "cost" of the two new policies?

2. The Ipanema Swim Suit Company must decide between three liability strategies, which differ in maturity structure. For each strategy, the annual interest costs, the annual flotation costs of the issues, and the annual ex-

pected costs of cash stockout (probability weighted) are estimated. On the basis of the information given in the accompanying table, which is the best strategy? Why do the various costs change with changes in strategy?

STRATEGY	MATURITY	SECURED OR UNSECURED	ANNUAL INTEREST COSTS	ALL FLOTATION COSTS	CASH STOCKOUT COSTS
A	$\frac{1}{2}$ short-, $\frac{1}{4}$ medium-, $\frac{1}{4}$ long-term debt	All unsecured	$1,400,000	$300,000	$200,000
B	$\frac{1}{3}$ short-, $\frac{1}{3}$ medium-, $\frac{1}{3}$ long-term debt	Unsecured Secured Unsecured	1,520,000	250,000	150,000
C	$\frac{1}{4}$ short-, $\frac{1}{4}$ medium-, $\frac{1}{2}$ long-term debt	Unsecured Secured Secured	1,600,000	200,000	75,000

PROBLEMS

1. The Anderson Corporation has a sales level of $280,000 with a 10 percent profit margin before interest and taxes. To generate this sales volume, the firm maintains a fixed-asset investment of $100,000. Currently, the firm maintains $50,000 in current assets.

   a. Determine the asset turnover for the firm and compute the rate of return on assets before taxes.

   b. Compute the rate of return on assets at different levels of current assets starting with $10,000 and increasing in $15,000 increments to $100,000.

   c. What implicit assumption is being made about sales in part b? Appraise the significance of this assumption along with the policy to choose the level of current assets that will maximize the return on investments as computed in part b.

2. The Malkiel Corporation has made the 3-year projection of its asset investment given in the following table. It has found that payables and accruals tend to equal one-third of current assets. It currently has $50 million in equity and the remainder of its capitalization in long-term debt. The earnings retained amount to $1 million per quarter.

   a. Graph the time path of total and fixed assets.

DATE	FIXED ASSETS (IN MILLIONS)	CURRENT ASSETS (IN MILLIONS)
3/31/x1 (now)	$50	$21
6/30/x1	51	30
9/30/x1	52	25
12/31/x1	53	21
3/31/x2	54	22
6/30/x2	55	31
9/30/x2	56	26
12/31/x2	57	22
3/31/x3	58	23
6/30/x3	59	32
9/30/x3	60	27
12/31/x3	61	23

b. Devise a financing plan, assuming that your objective is to use a hedging approach.

c. If short-term rates average 10 percent and long-term rates average 12 percent, how much would the firm save if its entire current assets were financed by short-term debt?

3. Mendez Metal Specialties, Inc., has a seasonal pattern to its business. It borrows under a line of credit from Central Bank at 1 percent over prime. Its total asset requirements now (at year end) and estimated requirements for the coming year are (in millions)

	NOW	1ST QUARTER	2ND QUARTER	3RD QUARTER	4TH QUARTER
Amount	$4.5	$4.8	$5.5	$5.9	$5.0

Assume that these requirements are level throughout the quarter. Presently, the company has $4,500,000 in equity capital plus long-term debt plus the permanent component of current liabilities, and this amount will remain constant throughout the year.

The prime rate presently is 11 percent, and the company expects no change in this rate for the next year. Mendez Metal Specialties is also considering issuing intermediate-term debt at an interest rate of $13\frac{1}{2}$ percent. In this regard, three alternative amounts are under consideration: zero, $500,000, and $1 million. All additional funds requirements will be borrowed under the company's bank line of credit.

a. Determine the total dollar borrowing costs for short-and intermediate-term debt under each of the three alternatives for the coming year. (Assume that there are no changes in current liabilities other than borrowings.) Which is lowest?

b. Is there a consideration other than expected cost?

SOLUTIONS TO SELF-CORRECTION PROBLEMS

1. a.

POLICY	EXISTING	2	3
Sales (millions)	$10.0	$10.0	$10.0
EBIT (millions)	1.2	1.2	1.2
Total assets (millions)	3.2	3.5	3.8
Asset turnover	3.125	2.857	2.632
Return on assets	37.5%	34.3%	31.6%
Gross profit margin	20.0%	20.0%	20.0%

The latter is unchanged, as sales and earnings before interest and taxes (EBIT) are the same regardless of the liquidity policy employed.

b.

POLICY	2	3
Additional debt	$300,000	$600,000
Additional interest	45,000	90,000

The "cost" of liquidity would be reduced by the amount that could be earned on the investment of liquidity in marketable securities. A hidden cost is that part of the debt capacity of the firm is used up by virtue of financing the liquidity.

2.   The total estimated annual costs for the three strategies are

	STRATEGY		
	A	B	C
Total Cost	$1,900,000	$1,920,000	$1,875,000

Strategy C, involving the highest portion of long-term debt, is best, despite the higher interest cost. As we see, interest costs increase with the greater use of long-term and medium-term debt. This pattern is consistent with interest rates rising at a decreasing rate with maturity. Flotation costs decrease the longer the average maturity of the debt, which is in keeping with fewer offerings per year. Finally, expected cash stockout costs decline the longer the average maturity. This occurrence is consistent with less uncertainty associated with long-term debt. Also, expected bankruptcy costs decline as more of the debt is made secured and lenders can turn directly to assets for payment in cases of adversity as opposed to settlement through the bankruptcy courts.

SELECTED REFERENCES

EMERY, GARY W., "Optimal Liquidity Policy: A Stochastic Process Approach," *Journal of Financial Research*, 5 (Fall 1982), 273–84.

GILMER, R. H. JR., "The Optimal Level of Liquid Assets: An Empirical Test," *Financial Management*, 14 (Winter 1985), 39–43.

HAWAWINI, GABRIEL, CLAUDE VIALLET, and ASHOK VORA, "Industry Influence on Corporate Working Capital Decisions," *Sloan Management Review*, 27 (Summer 1986), 15–24.

MORRIS, JAMES R., "The Role of Cash Balances in Firm Valuation," *Journal of Financial and Quantitative Analysis*, 18 (December 1983), 533–46.

PETTY, J. WILLIAM, and DAVID F. SCOTT, "The Analysis of Corporate Liquidity," *Journal of Economics and Business*, 32 (Spring–Summer 1980), 206–18.

SATORIS, WILLIAM L., and NED C. HILL, "A Generalized Cash Flow Approach to Short-Term Financial Decisions," *Journal of Finance*, 38 (May 1983), 349–60.

SILVERS, J. B., "Liquidity, Risk and Duration Patterns of Corporate Financing," *Financial Management*, 5 (Autumn 1976), 54–64.

VAN HORNE, JAMES C., "A Risk-Return Analysis of a Firm's Working-Capital Position," *Engineering Economist*, 14 (Winter 1969), 71–89.

WALKER, ERNEST W., "Towards a Theory of Working Capital," *Engineering Economist*, 9 (January–February 1964), 21–35.

CHAPTER 9

Cash and Marketable Securities

We have been occupied with the overall level of liquid and current assets of the firm. By examining the trade-off betweeen profitability and risk, we were able to determine in a general way the proper amount of liquid assets the firm should carry. (*Liquid assets* were defined as cash and marketable securities.) Once the overall level of liquid assets is determined, other questions arise. How much will be carried in cash? How much will be carried in marketable securities? We are going to find out how to answer these questions. We shall also find out how to improve the efficiency of cash management and how to invest excess funds in marketable securities.

THE FUNCTION OF CASH MANAGEMENT

There are three motives for holding cash: the transactions motive, the precautionary motive, and the speculative motive.[1] The transactions motive is the need for cash to meet payments arising in the ordinary course of business—for things such as purchases, labor, taxes, and dividends. The precautionary motive for holding cash has to do with maintaining a cushion or buffer to meet unexpected contingencies. The more predictable the cash flows of the business, the fewer precautionary balances needed. Ready borrowing power to meet emergency cash drains also reduces the need for this type of balance. It is important to point out that not all of the firm's transactions and precautionary balances need to be held in cash; indeed, a portion may be held in marketable securities—near-money assets.

The speculative motive relates to holding cash in order to take advantage of expected changes in security prices. When we expect interest rates to rise and security prices to fall, this motive would suggest that the firm should hold cash until the rise in interest rates ceases. When interest rates are expected to fall, cash may be invested in securities; the firm will benefit by any subsequent fall in interest rates and rise in security prices. For the most part, companies do not hold liquidity for the purpose of taking advantage of expected changes in interest rates. Consequently, we concentrate only on the transactions and precautionary motives of the firm, with these balances held both in cash and in marketable securities.

Cash management involves managing the monies of the firm in order to maximize cash availability and interest income on any idle funds. At one end, the function starts when a customer writes a check to pay the firm on its accounts receivable. The function ends when a supplier, employee, or the government realizes collected funds from the firm on an account payable or accrual. All activities between these two points fall within the realm of cash management. The firm's efforts to get customers to pay their bills at a certain time fall within accounts receivable management. On the other hand, the firm's decision about when to pay its bills involves accounts payable and accrual management.

The treasurer's office of a company usually manages cash. A cash budget, instrumental in the process (see Chapter 7), tells us how much cash we are likely

[1] John Maynard Keynes, *The General Theory of Employment, Interest, and Money* (New York: Harcourt Brace Jovanovich, 1936), pp. 170–74.

to have, when, and for how long. Thus, it serves as a foundation for cash planning and control. In addition to the cash budget, the firm needs systematic information on cash as well as some kind of control system. Usually the information is computer based as opposed to manually based. In either case, it is necessary to obtain frequent reports—preferably daily or even more frequently—on cash balances in each bank account, on the cash disbursed, on the average daily balances, and on the marketable security position of the firm as well as a detailed report on changes in this position. Also, it is useful to have information on major anticipated cash receipts and cash disbursements. All of this information is essential if a firm is to manage its cash in an efficient manner.

ACCELERATING COLLECTIONS

The various collection and disbursement methods by which a firm can improve its cash management efficiency constitute two sides of the same coin. They exercise a joint impact on the overall efficiency of cash management. The general idea is to collect accounts receivable as soon as possible, but pay accounts payable as late as is consistent with maintaining the firm's credit standing with suppliers. Today, most companies of reasonable size use sophisticated techniques to speed up collections and tightly control disbursements. Let us see how they do it.

We consider first the acceleration of collections, which simply means reducing the delay between the time customers pay bills and the time the checks are collected and become usable funds for the firm. A number of methods are designed to speed up this collection process by doing one or all of the following: (1) speed the mailing time of payments from customers to the firm, (2) reduce the time during which payments received by the firm remain uncollected funds, and (3) speed the movement of funds to disbursement banks.

The second item, representing float, has two aspects. The first is the time it takes a company to process checks internally. This interval extends from the moment a check is received to the moment it is deposited with a bank for credit to the company's account. The second aspect of float involves the time consumed in clearing the check through the banking system. A check becomes collected funds when it is presented to the drawee bank and actually paid by that bank. In order to streamline the availability of credit, the Federal Reserve System has established a schedule specifying availability for all checks deposited with it for collection. This schedule is based on the average time required for a check deposited with a particular Federal Reserve Bank to be collected in a particular geographic area of the country. The maximum period for which credit is deferred is 2 days. This means that even if a check is not actually collected through the Federal Reserve System within 2 days, it becomes collected funds because the Federal Reserve carries the float.

Float is important to the financial manager because usually a company cannot make withdrawals on a deposit until the checks in that deposit are collected. As the name of the game is usable funds, the financial manager wants to reduce float as much as possible. In what follows, we examine various ways to speed up the collection process in order to have more usable funds.

Concentration Banking

Concentration banking is a means of accelerating the flow of funds of a firm by establishing strategic collection centers. Instead of a single collection center located at the company headquarters, multiple collection centers are established. The purpose is to shorten the period between the time customers mail in their payments and the time when the company has the use of the funds. Customers in a particular geographic area are instructed to remit their payments to a collection center in that area. Location of the collection centers usually is based on the geographic areas served and the volume of billings in an area. When payments are received, they are deposited in the collection center's local bank. Surplus funds are then wire transferred from these local bank accounts to a concentration bank or banks. A bank of concentration is one with which the company has a major account—usually a disbursement account.

The advantage of a system of decentralized billings and collections over a centralized system is twofold:

> **Concentration banking.** A system where customers make payments to regional centers and surplus funds are channeled to a concentration bank.

1. The time required for mailing is reduced. Because the collection center bills customers in its area, these customers usually receive their bills earlier than if bills were mailed from the head office. In turn, when customers pay their bill, the mailing time to the nearest collection center is shorter than the time required for the typical remittance to go to the head office.
2. The time required to collect checks is reduced, because remittances deposited in the collection center's local bank usually are drawn on banks in that general area.

Profits from the investment of the released funds must be compared with any additional costs of a decentralized system over a centralized one. Also consider any differences between the two systems in total compensating balances. The greater the number of collection centers, the more local bank accounts that must be maintained.

Transferring Funds

In order to accelerate the movement of funds, transfers are necessary between financial institutions. There are three principal methods: (1) wire transfers, (2) depository transfer checks, and (3) electronic transfer checks through automatic clearinghouses. The quickest is the *wire transfer* arrangement. Such transfers may be made through the Federal Reserve Wire System or through a private wire system. The advantage is that funds become immediately available.

Wire transfers differ from a **depository transfer check** (DTC) arrangement for the movement of funds, whereby a preprinted depository check is drawn on the local bank, payable to a concentration bank. Funds are not immediately available, for the check must be collected through the usual channels. A transfer check costs only 50 cents or so for processing compared with about $10 for a wire transfer, but it is not nearly as fast. A variation of the depository transfer check is an *electronic check image*, which is processed through automatic clearinghouses (ACH). The funds become available 1 business day later, as the pro-

> **Depository transfer check.** A means for transferring money from bank to bank by check.

cess is electronic as opposed to physical transportation. As the cost is not particularly large, the electronic DTC has largely replaced the mail-based DTC.

Lock-Box System

Lock box. A method for accelerating the collection of checks. Customers send checks directly to a bank, which processes them immediately and sends a statement of record to the company.

Another means of accelerating the flow of funds is a **lock-box** arrangement. With concentration banking, a collection center receives remittances, processes them, and deposits them in a bank. The purpose of a lock-box arrangement is to eliminate the time between the receipt of remittances by the company and their deposit in the bank. A lock-box arrangement usually is on a regional basis, with the company choosing regional banks according to its billing patterns. Before determining the regions to be used, a feasibility study is made of the availability of checks that would be deposited under alternative plans. If a company divided the country into five sections on the basis of a feasibility study, it might pick New York City for the Northeast, Atlanta for the Southeast, Chicago for the Midwest, Dallas for the Southwest, and San Francisco for the West Coast.

The company rents a local post office box and authorizes its bank in each of these cities to pick up remittances in the box. Customers are billed with instructions to mail their remittance to the lock box. The bank picks up the mail several times a day and deposits the checks in the company's account. The checks are recorded and cleared for collection. The company receives a deposit slip and a list of payments, together with any material in the envelope. This procedure frees the company from handling and depositing the checks.

The main advantage of a lock-box system is that checks are deposited at banks sooner and become collected balances sooner than if they were processed by the company prior to deposit. In other words, the lag between the time checks are received by the company and the time they actually are deposited at the bank is eliminated. The principal disadvantage of a lock-box arrangement is the cost. The bank provides a number of services in addition to the usual clearing of checks and requires compensation for them, usually preferring increased deposits. Because the cost is almost directly proportional to the number of checks deposited, lock-box arrangements usually are not profitable if the average remittance is small.

The appropriate rule for deciding whether or not to use a lock-box system—or, for that matter, concentration banking—is simply to compare the added cost of the more efficient system with the marginal income that can be generated from the released funds. If costs are less than income, the system is profitable; if not, the system is not a profitable undertaking. The degree of profitability depends primarily on the geographic dispersion of customers, the size of the typical remittance, and the earnings rate on the released funds.

Other Procedures

Frequently, firms give special attention to handling large remittances so that they may be deposited in a bank as quickly as possible. This special handling may involve personal pickup of these checks or the use of airmail or special delivery. When a small number of remittances account for a large proportion of total deposits, it may be worthwhile to initiate controls to accelerate the deposit and collection of large checks. Instead of processing all checks for collection through the Federal Reserve System, some commercial banks offer special services that present high-dollar-volume checks directly to the drawee bank. The benefit is a speedup in collection of these checks, and it is passed on to the bank customer in having usable funds more quickly.

Some companies maintain too many bank accounts, thereby creating unecessary pockets of idle funds. A company that has an account in every city where it has either a sales office or a production facility might be able to reduce cash balances considerably if it were to eliminate some of these accounts. The banking activities of a sales office can often be handled from a larger account with little loss in service or availability of funds. Even though small accounts may create a degree of goodwill with bankers, they make little sense in the overall cash management of the firm. By closing such unnecessary accounts, a firm may be able to release funds that it then can put to profitable use.

Traditionally, many companies use the postmark date on the envelope to determine whether a payment qualifies for a discount. This requires considerable manual verification. To eliminate such verification as well as speed up collections, some firms are instigating the time of actual receipt as the benchmark for discount qualification. In so doing, the firm may extend the discount period by a day or two so as not to upset customers with the change. Even with such extensions, collections from discount-paying customers usually accelerate on average.

CONTROL OF DISBURSEMENTS

Effective control of disbursements can also result in a faster turnover of cash. Whereas the underlying objective of collections is maximum acceleration, the objective in disbursements is to slow them down as much as possible. The combination of fast collections and slow disbursements will result in maximum availability of funds.

Maximizing the Float

One way of maximizing cash availability is "paying the float." For disbursements, **float** is the difference between the total dollar amount of checks drawn on a bank account and the amount shown on the bank's books. It is possible, of course, for a company to have a negative balance on its books and a positive bank balance, because checks outstanding have not been collected from the account on which they are drawn. If the size of float can be estimated accurately, bank balances can be reduced and the funds invested to earn a positive return.

Float. Funds tied up in checks that have been written, but have not yet been collected at the drawee bank.

A company with multiple banks should be able to shift funds quickly to banks from which disbursements are made, to prevent excessive balances from building up temporarily in a particular bank. The idea is to have adequate cash at the various banks, but not to let excessive balances build up. This requires daily information on collected balances. Excess funds then are transferred to the disbursement banks, either to pay bills or to invest in marketable securities. Many companies have developed sophisticated computer systems to provide the necessary information and to transfer excess funds automatically. Instead of developing one's own system, a firm can hire outside computer services to provide the described functions.

One procedure for tightly controlling disbursements is to centralize payables into a single account, presumably at the company's headquarters. In this way, disbursements can be made at the precise time they are desired. Needless to say, operating procedures for disbursements should be well established. If cash discounts are taken on accounts payable, procedures should aim toward eliminating or minimizing the loss of discounts due to clerical inefficiencies. The timing of payments is important. For maximum use of cash, payments should be made on the due dates, not before.

A means for delaying disbursements is through the use of drafts. Unlike an ordinary check, the draft is not payable on demand. When it is presented to the issuer's bank for collection, the bank must present it to the issuer for acceptance. The funds then are deposited by the issuing firm to cover payment of the draft. The advantage of the draft arrangement is that it delays the time the firm actually has to have funds on deposit to cover the draft. Consequently, it allows the firm to maintain smaller deposits at its banks. A possible disadvantage of a draft system is that certain suppliers may prefer checks. Also, banks do not like to process drafts because they require special attention, often manual. As a result, banks typically impose a higher service charge to process drafts than they do to process ordinary checks.

When a company has multiple bank accounts located throughout the country, the opportunities for playing the float expand. Taking advantage of inefficiencies in the check-clearing processes of the Federal Reserve System and of certain commercial banks, as well as inefficiencies in the postal system, a firm may maximize the time the checks it writes remain outstanding. Various models have been proposed to maximize disbursement float through the selection of geographically optimal disbursing banks.[2] The idea is to locate disbursing banks and to draw checks on them in a way that will maximize the time a check will remain outstanding. A check payable to a supplier in Arizona might be drawn on a bank in Portland, Maine. The solution depends on the location of, and the amount of billings from, suppliers, on procedural delays in the bank system associated with various supplier location–disbursing bank location combinations, and on the cost of banking services, be it compensating balances or fees.

By maximizing disbursement float, the firm can reduce the amount of cash it holds and employ these funds in more profitable ways. One firm's gain, however is another's loss. Maximizing disbursement float means that suppliers will not have collectible funds as early as would otherwise be the case. To the extent that they look with disfavor on such payment habits, supplier relations may be hurt. If so, this factor must be taken into account in planning disbursements.

[2] See Lawrence J. Gitman, D. Keith Forrester, and John R. Forrester, Jr., "Maximizing Cash Disbursement Float," *Financial Management*, 5 (Summer 1976), 15–24, for such an approach. See also Steven F. Maier and James H. Vander Weide, "What Lockbox and Disbursement Models Really Do," *Journal of Finance*, 38 (May 1983), 361–71.

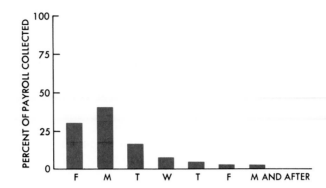

FIGURE 9-1
Percentage of payroll checks collected

Payroll and Dividend Disbursements

Many companies maintain a separate account for payroll disbursements. In order to minimize the balance in this account, one must predict when the payroll checks issued will be presented for payment. If payday falls on a Friday, not all of the checks will be cashed on that day. Consequently, the firm need not have funds on deposit to cover its entire payroll. Even on Monday, some checks will not be presented because of delays in their deposit. Based on its experience, the firm should be able to construct a distribution of when, on the average, checks are presented for collection. An example is shown in Fig. 9-1. With this information, the firm can approximate the funds it needs to have on deposit to cover payroll checks. Similar to the payroll account, a separate account for dividends is one that many firms establish. Here, too, the idea is to predict when such checks will be presented for payment so that the firm can minimize the cash balance in the account.

ELECTRONIC FUNDS TRANSFER

The procedures for accelerating collections and slowing disbursements discussed in the previous two sections are based on a paper transfer system. However, increasingly funds flow electronically for both collections and disbursements. The reasons for this evolution are twofold: changes in financial institution regulation and advances in computer-based information systems as well as in electronic communications. Recent regulatory changes have permitted greater competition among financial institutions. Most institutions have been allowed a much broader menu of accounts and instruments that they may offer. This increased flexibility has affected payments mechanisms as well.

The second aspect of the changing environment is the increased sophistication in computer applications to cash management and in electronic funds transfers. As individuals, we all are aware of plastic cards with magnetic coding that can be used to obtain cash, to transfer funds from one account to another, to pay bills, to borrow, and to do other things. These transactions can occur at a financial institution, at an unattended electronic payments machine that is open 24 hours a day, and at certain retail stores. At stores, one is able to pay for a purchase with such a card, as funds are transferred electronically from the customer to the store. The advantage to retailers is obvious; they are assured that the payments for the purchase are good, and they are immediate. Retailers also can reduce the possibility of bad checks by using guarantee systems that a number of banks offer. With such a system, a customer's check is scanned electronically and verified by the computer that it is good. Because the bank guarantees the checks it verifies, the retailer is not exposed to bad-check losses.

The electronic transfer of funds is illustrated in Fig. 9-2. The supplier, Company Y, sends an invoice to its customer, Company X. On the appropriate payment date, Company X instructs its bank to pay its supplier via a prearranged procedure. The instructions can be transmitted by computer tape, terminal, or some other means. The bank then debits Company X's account and either credits directly or wire transfers the credit to Company Y's bank, along with communicating electronically the supporting information. The latter bank then credits Company Y's account, sending it the supporting information, again electronically. Company Y is then in a position to update its accounts receivable ledgers. In addition to paying bills, electronic funds transfers can be used to deposit payrolls automatically in employee accounts, to pay taxes, and to make dividend and other payments.

Rather than a direct transfer of funds through banks, the transfer can be through an *automatic clearinghouse*. Some of the major networks include *CHIPS*, the Clearing House Interbank System of New York banks involving next-day settlement; *SWIFT*, the Society of Worldwide Interbank Financial Telecommunications consisting of hundreds of banks worldwide, which permits international transfers; and *NACHA*, the National Automated Clearing House Association, which consists of thousands of banks and thrift institutions and is suited to high-volume batch transfers. Continual improvements are occurring in these and other networks. Depending on the task involved, one or more of the transfer networks will be most suitable.

Of course with electronic funds transfer float is eliminated. Unlike paper transfer, there are no uncollected funds, for one party's account is debited the instant another's is credited. For some corporations, the loss of float in disbursements is too great a cost to pay. To be sure, there are benefits. A tighter control over disbursements is possible, owing to the dates of settlement being known with certainty. Also, supplier relations usually improve. However, these benefits may not offset the perceived cost of float reduction.

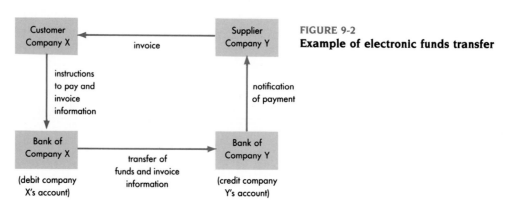

FIGURE 9-2

Example of electronic funds transfer

Because electronic banking is capital intensive, the cost per transaction is reduced as volume increases. Indeed, this has occurred in recent years, and much of the saving is passed along to users of financial services. The customer benefits from the intense competition among financial institutions and large retailers that provide financial services. For the firm, electronic banking means less time in the collection of receivables, more efficient control of cash, and perhaps a reduction in servicing costs.

Thus, the use of electronic funds transfers can result in greater economization of money balances. In turn, the movement toward these techniques depends in part on the level of interest rates in financial markets. The greater the interest rate, of course, the greater the opportunity cost of holding cash and the more attractive electronic banking techniques become, all other things the same. The use of a new cash management technique, however, typically involves significant start-up costs. As a result, once a new method is in place, there is tendency to keep it even if interest rates should decline somewhat thereafter.

Another development is the zero balance account, from which funds are automatically transferred into securities when there are excesses and reversed when there are deficits. Sometimes a deficit is filled by a prearranged overdraft (borrowing) arrangement with the bank. With a zero balance account, as the name implies, funds are not tied up unnecessarily. Activity in the account usually is supported by fees.

CASH BALANCES TO MAINTAIN

Most business firms establish a target level of cash balances to maintain. They do not want to carry excess cash, for interest can be earned on the investment of these funds in marketable securities. The greater the interest rate on investments, of course, the greater the opportunity cost to maintaining idle balances. The optimal level of cash should be the larger of (1) the transactions balances required when cash management is efficient and (2) the compensating balance requirements of commercial banks with which the firm has deposit accounts.

Transactions balances are determined in keeping with considerations taken up earlier in the chapter. Also, we suggested that the higher the interest rate, the greater the opportunity cost of holding cash and the greater the corresponding desire to reduce the firm's holding, all other things the same. A number of cash management models have been developed for determining an optimal split between cash and marketable securities. These models embody the demand for cash, the interest rate on marketable securities, and the cost of transfers between marketable securities and cash. The appendix to this chapter presents two of the more widely used models.

Compensating Balances and Fees

Establishing a minimum level of cash balances depends in part on the compensating balance requirements of banks. These requirements are set on the basis of the profitability of the account. A bank begins by calculating the average collected balance shown on its books over a period of time. This balance often is higher than the cash balance shown on the company's books. From the average collected balance, the bank subtracts the percentage of deposits it is required to maintain as a reserve requirement—around 12 percent. The residual constitutes the earnings base on which income is generated. Total income is determined by multiplying the base times the earnings rate of the bank. This rate fluctuates in keeping with money market conditions.

Once the income from an account is determined, the cost of the account must be computed. Most banks have a schedule of costs on a per item basis for such transactions as transfers and processing checks. The account is analyzed for a typical month, during which all transactions are multiplied by the per item cost and totaled. If the total cost is less than the total income from the account, the account is profitable; if more, it is unprofitable. The minimum average level of cash balances required is the point at which the account is just profitable. Because banks differ in the earnings rate they use as well as in their costs and method of account analysis, the determination of compensating balances varies. The firm, therefore, may be wise to shop around and find the bank that requires the lowest compensating balances for a given level of activity. If a firm has a lending arrangement with a bank, the firm may well be required to maintain balances in excess of those required to compensate the bank for the activity in its account. Because we consider compensation for a lending arrangement in Chapter 11, no discussion of this form of compensation will be undertaken at this time.

In recent years, there has been a marked trend toward paying cash for services rendered by a bank instead of maintaining compensating balances. The advantage to the firm is that it may be able to earn more on funds used for compensating balances than the fee for the services. The higher the interest rate in the money markets, the greater the opportunity cost of compensating balances and the greater the advantage of service charges. It is an easy matter to determine if the firm would be better off with service charges as opposed to maintaining compensating balances. One simply compares the charges with the earnings on the funds released. Where a service offered can better be paid for by a fee, the firm should be alert to take advantage of the situation and to reduce its compensating balances.

INVESTMENT IN MARKETABLE SECURITIES

In general, excess cash above some target level needed for transactions or compensating balances is invested in marketable securities. In this section we explore the types of marketable securities available to a company as near-money investments, allowing for varying yields and for fluctuations in market price. The yield available on a security depends on its maturity and coupon rate, its default risk, its marketability, and perhaps its tax situation if it is selling at a price other than its face value. All of these influences were explored in Chapter 3, when we reviewed the role of interest rates in financial markets. Here we investigate various instruments that, by definition, are highly marketable, typically subject to little default risk, and usually mature in less than a year. After we have discussed the various instruments available for investment, we will conclude with some observations on the overall management of the marketable security portfolio.

Treasury Securities

U.S. Treasury obligations constitute the largest segment of the money markets. The principal securities issued are bills, tax anticipation bills, notes, and bonds. Treasury bills are auctioned weekly by the Treasury with maturities of 91 days and 182 days. In addition, 9-month and 1-year bills are sold every month. All sales by the Treasury are by auction. Smaller investors can enter a "noncompetitive" bid, which is filled at the average price of successful competitive bids. Treasury bills carry no coupon but are sold on a discount basis. Denominations range from $10,000 to $1 million. These securities are popular with some companies as short-term investments, in part because of the large amount outstanding. The market is very active, and the transaction costs involved in the sale of Treasury bills in the secondary market are small.

The original maturity on Treasury notes is 1 to 10 years, whereas the original maturity on Treasury bonds is over 10 years. With the passage of time, of course, a number of these securities have maturities of less than 1 year and serve the needs of short-term investors. Notes and bonds are coupon issues, and there is an active market for them. Overall, Treasury securities are the safest and most marketable investments. Therefore, they provide the lowest yield for a given maturity of the various instruments we consider. While the interest income on these securities is taxed at the federal level, it is exempt from state income taxes.

Repurchase Agreements

In an effort to tap important sources of financing, government security dealers offer repurchase agreements to corporations. The repurchase agreement, or "repo," is the sale of short-term securities by the dealer to the investor whereby the dealer agrees to repurchase the securities at a specified future time. The investor receives a given yield while holding the security. The length of the holding period itself is tailored to the needs of the investor. Thus, repurchase agreements give the investor a great deal of flexibility with respect to maturity. Rates on repurchase agreements are related to the rates on Treasury bills, federal funds, and loans to government security dealers by commercial banks. There is little marketability to the instrument, but the usual maturity is only a few days. Because the instrument involved is a U.S. Treasury security, the default risk depends solely on the reliability and financial condition of the dealer.

Agency Securities

Obligations of various agencies of the federal government are guaranteed by the agency issuing the security but not by the U.S. government as such. Principal agencies issuing securities are the Federal Housing Administration and the Government National Mortgage Association (Ginnie Mae). In addition, there are a number of government-sponsored, quasi-private agencies. Their securities are not guaranteed by the federal government, nor is there any stated "moral" obligation, but there is an implied backing. It would be hard to imagine the federal government allowing them to fail. Major government-sponsored agencies include the Farm Credit System, Federal Home Loan Banks, and the Federal National Mortgage Association (Fannie Mae). Agency issues typically provide a modest yield advantage over Treasury securities of the same maturity, and they have a fairly high degree of marketability. Although interest income on these securities is subject to federal income taxes, issues of the Farm Credit System are not subject to state and local income taxes. Maturities range from several days up to approximately 15 years. About half of the securities outstanding mature in less than a year.

Bankers' Acceptances

Bankers' acceptance. A promissory trade note between two parties that is accepted by a bank, thereby guaranteeing it. A money market instrument.

Bankers' acceptances are drafts that are accepted by banks, and they are used in financing foreign and domestic trade. The creditworthiness of banker's acceptances is judged relative to the bank accepting the draft, not relative to the drawer. Acceptances generally have maturities of less than 6 months and are of very high quality. They are traded in an over-the-counter market dominated by five principal dealers. The rates on bankers' acceptances tend to be slightly higher than rates on Treasury bills of like maturity, and both are sold on a discount basis. Bankers' acceptances can be on domestic banks and on large foreign banks, where the yield tends to be higher.

Commercial Paper

Commercial paper. The unsecured, short-term promissory notes of large companies. A money market instrument.

Commercial paper consists of short-term unsecured promissory notes issued by finance companies and certain industrial concerns. Commercial paper can be sold either directly or through dealers. A number of large sales finance companies have found it profitable, because of the volume, to sell their paper directly to investors, thus bypassing dealers. Among companies selling paper on this basis are the General Electric Credit Corporation, Ford Motor Credit Company, General Motors Acceptance Corporation (GMAC), and Sears, Roebuck Acceptance Corporation. Paper sold through dealers is issued by industrial companies and smaller finance companies. Dealers very carefully screen the creditworthiness of potential issuers. In a sense, dealers stand behind the paper they place with investors.

Rates on commercial paper are somewhat higher than rates on Treasury bills of the same maturity and about the same as the rates available on banker's acceptances. Paper sold directly generally commands a lower yield than does paper sold through dealers. Usually, commercial paper is sold on a discount basis, and maturities generally range from 30 to 270 days. Most paper is held to maturity, for there is essentially no secondary market. Direct sellers of commercial paper will repurchase the paper on request. Arrangements may also be made through dealers for repurchase of paper sold through them. Commercial paper is sold only in fairly large denominations, usually at least $100,000.

Negotiable Certificates of Deposit

A short-term investment that originated in 1961, the **certificate of deposit** (CD) is evidence of the deposit of funds at a commercial bank for a specified period of time and at a specified rate of interest. The most common denomination is $100,000, so its appeal is mostly to large investors. Money market banks quote rates on CDs; these rates are changed periodically in keeping with changes in other money market rates. The maximum rate that banks are allowed to pay, however, is regulated by the Federal Reserve System under Regulation Q. Yields on CDs are greater than those on Treasury bills and repos and about the same as those on bankers' acceptances and commercial paper. Original maturities of CDs generally range from 30 to 360 days. A fair secondary market has developed for the CDs of the large money market banks. Default risk is that of the bank failing, a possibility that is remote in most cases. Like bankers' acceptances, corporations buy domestic CDs as well as CDs of large foreign banks. The latter are known as "Yankee" CDs, and they typically carry a higher expected return.

Certificate of deposit. A time deposit at a bank that earns a stated interest. A money market instrument for large CDs.

Eurodollars

Although most **Eurodollars** are deposited in Europe, the term applies to any dollar deposit in foreign banks or in foreign branches of U.S. banks. There exists a substantial, very active market for the deposit and lending of Eurodollars. This market is a wholesale one in that the amounts involved are at least $100,000 in size. Moreover, the market is free of government regulation, as it is truly international in scope. The rates quoted on deposits vary according to the maturity of the deposit, while the rates on loans depend on maturity and default risk. For a given maturity, the lending rate always exceeds the deposit rate. The bank makes its money on the spread.

Eurodollar. A U.S. dollar deposit in a bank outside the United States.

As a marketable security, the Eurodollar time deposit is like a negotiable certificate of deposit. Most deposits have a maturity of less than a year, and they can be sold in the market prior to maturity. Call money deposits are available, allowing investors to get their money back on demand, and there are 1-day (overnight) deposits. For the large corporation with ready contact with international money centers, the Eurodollar deposit usually is an important investment.

Adjustable Rate and Money Market Preferred Stock

Beginning in 1982, a special type of preferred stock originated, and it found considerable favor in the marketable security portfolios of corporations. As we shall see in Chapter 22, straight preferred stock is a perpetual security, where the dividend can be omitted by the issuer when its financial condition deteriorates. For these reasons, we usually do not think of preferred stock as being suitable for the marketable security portfolio of a corporation. However, the corporate investor gains a considerable tax advantage, in that 80 percent of the preferred stock dividend is exempt from federal taxation. (The full dividend is subject to state income taxes.)

This advantage, together with regulatory changes, prompted the innovation of adjustable rate preferred stock (ARPS). The quarterly dividend rate usually "floats" with movements in Treasury security interest rates. Typically, the benchmark Treasury security is the higher in yield of (1) the 3-month Treasury bill rate, (2) the rate on a 10-year Treasury security, or (3) the rate on a 20-year Treasury security, and the ARPS rate floats at a discount from the appropriate benchmark. Usually there is a ceiling and a floor to the return the investor earns. If the current floating rate were 7 percent, for example, the floor might be 5 percent and the ceiling 10 percent. The ceiling poses a risk to the investor. If interest rates should rise above 10 percent, the security will sell at a discount from its par value. As a result, the security has some of the features of a short-term security, due to the floating rate, but also some of the risks associated with a long-term security, because of the ceiling and the fact that the payment of a preferred dividend is not a legal obligation of the issuer as is the payment of interest on debt. (See Chapter 22.)

To circumvent some of these problems, money market preferred stock (MMP) was introduced in 1985. It is like ARPS in some ways, but instead of a floating rate arrangement an auction is held every 49 days. The new rate is set by the forces of supply and demand in keeping with interest rates in the money market. A typical rate might be .75 times the commercial paper rate, with more creditworthy issuers commanding an even greater discount. As long as enough investors bid at each auction, the effective maturity date is 49 days. As a result, there is little variation in the market price of the instrument over time and this represents a substantial advantage over the ARPS. However, the possibility of default remains. The MMP has largely displaced the ARPS in popularity with corporate investors.

Portfolio Management

The decision to invest excess cash in marketable securities involves not only the amount to invest but also the type of security in which to invest. To some extent, the two decisions are interdependent. Both should be based on an evaluation of expected net cash flows and the uncertainty associated with these cash flows. If future cash-flows patterns are known with reasonable certainty and the yield curve is upward-sloping in the sense of longer-term securities yielding more than shorter-term ones, a company may wish to arrange its portfolio so that securities will mature approximately when the funds will be needed. Such a cash-flow pattern gives the firm a great deal of flexibility in maximizing the average return on the entire portfolio, for it is unlikely that significant amounts of securities will have to be sold unexpectedly.

Suppose that the liquidity position of a firm were expected to fluctuate in the manner shown by the dotted line in Fig. 9-3. Although the figure shows only 4 months, we assume that the dotted line is not expected to decline below

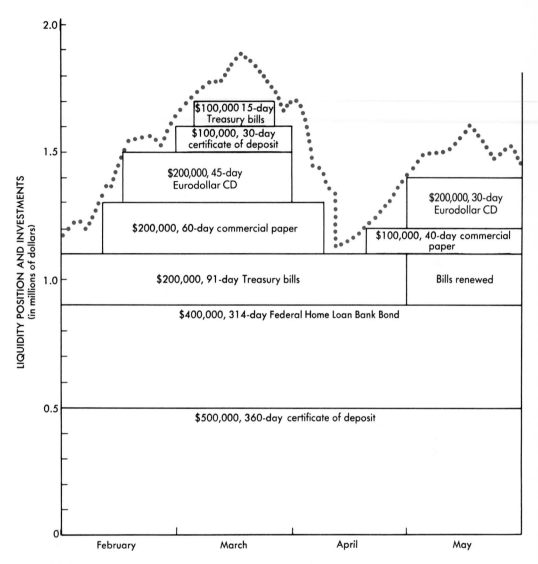

FIGURE 9-3
Investment strategy in relation to projected liquidity position

$900,000 over the next 12 months. Based on these projections, an appropriate investment strategy might be that shown by the horizontal bars in the figure. The bottom portion is represented by a 360-day investment in a certificate of deposit, followed by a Federal Home Loan Bank bond with about 10 months to final maturity. Next the firm has invested in 91-day Treasury bills, and these are expected to be renewed, or rolled over, at maturity. The other investments shown in the figure are designed to match the fluctuating pattern of cash flows shown. Finally, the remaining areas under the dotted line are assumed to be filled as much as possible with repurchase agreements. With repos, maturities of only one or a few days can be tailored to the availability of funds for investment. Overall, then, the firm is able to match the maturities of its investments in marketable securities with its expected cash-flow patterns. In this way it is able to maximize its return on investment insofar as maturity decisions alone will allow.

Again, we have assumed an upward-sloping yield curve. If the yield curve is downward-sloping, the maturity matching strategy just outlined may not be appropriate. The company may wish to invest in securities having maturities shorter than the intended holding period, then to reinvest at maturity. In this way, it can avail itself of the higher initial yield on shorter-term securities, but it does not know what the securities will yield upon reinvestment at maturity. Another key factor is the degree of certainty one has in the cash-flow projections. With a high degree of certainty, the maturity of a marketable security becomes its most important characteristic.[3] If future cash flows are fairly uncertain, the most important characteristics of a security become its marketability and risk with respect to fluctuations in market value. Treasury bills and short-term repos are perhaps best suited for the emergency liquidity needs of the firm. Higher yields can be achieved by investing in longer-term, less marketable securities with greater default risk. Although the firm should always be concerned with marketability, some possibility of loss of principal is tolerable provided the expected return is high enough. In addition to risk and marketability, transaction costs are a factor with uncertain cash flows. If securities must be sold unexpectedly, transaction costs will be incurred, reducing the net return. Thus, the firm faces the familiar trade-off between risk and profitability.

The larger the security portfolio, the more chance there is for specialization and economies of operation. A large enough security portfolio may justify a staff solely responsible for managing it. Such a staff can undertake research, plan diversification, keep abreast of market conditions, and continually analyze and improve the firm's position. When investment is a specialized function in a firm, the number of different securities considered for investment is likely to be diverse. Moreover, continual effort can be devoted to achieving the highest yield possible in keeping with cash needs of the firm. Trading techniques in such a firm tend to be very sophisticated. For companies with smaller security positions, there may be no economic justification for a staff. Indeed, a single individual may handle investments on a part-time basis. For this type of company, the diversity of securities in the portfolio will probably be limited.

SUMMARY

In the management of cash, we should attempt to accelerate collections and slow up disbursements so that a maximum of cash is available. Collections can be accelerated by means of concentration banking, a lock-box system, and certain other procedures. Disbursements should be handled to give maximum transfer

---

[3] This statement assumes that all of the securities considered are of reasonably high quality from the standpoint of default risk. Otherwise they would not fall within the usual definition of a marketable security.

flexibility and the optimum timing of payments, being mindful, however, of supplier relations. Several methods for controlling disbursements were described. Electronic funds transfers are becoming increasingly important, and most corporations use such transfers in one way or another.

The appropriate level of cash to maintain will be the higher of (1) that required for transactions purposes and (2) the compensating balance requirements of commercial banks with which the firm has accounts. Usually the latter dominates; the requirement itself depends on the activity in the firm's accounts. The level of transactions balances desirable depends in part on the opportunity cost of holding cash as typified by the interest rate on marketable securities. In the appendix, we discuss models that allow us to take this as well as other factors into account in determining an optimal level of cash.

Among the numerous marketable securities in which the firm can invest are Treasury securities, government agency securities, bankers' acceptances, commercial paper, repurchase agreements, certificates of deposit, Eurodollar deposits, and adjustable rate and money market preferred stock. In the management of the marketable security portfolio, one tries to match to some degree the maturities of investments with the likely future need for funds.

APPENDIX
Cash Management Models

Given the overall liquidity of the firm (its transactions and precautionary balances), we must determine an optimal split between cash and marketable securities. In turn, this split tells us the average levels of cash and marketable securities to maintain. The optimal level of cash depends on the firm's needs for cash, the predictability of these needs, the interest rate on marketable securities, and the cost of effecting a transfer between marketable securities and cash. A number of formal models have been developed to provide solutions to the cash management problem. This appendix presents two of the more widely used models. The first approaches the problem under the assumption of a high degree of certainty as to the future cash needs of the firm. The second assumes just the opposite—that the future cash needs of the firm are highly uncertain. Let us examine these models.

Inventory Model

Under conditions of certainty, the economic-order-quantity (EOQ) formula used in inventory management may be used to determine the optimal average amount of transactions balances to maintain. This model provides a useful conceptual foundation for the cash management problem.[4] In the model, the carrying cost of

[4] The model was first applied to the problem of cash management by William J. Baumol, "The Transactions Demand for Cash: An Inventory Theoretic Approach," *Quarterly Journal of Economics*, 46 (November 1952), 545–56. It has been further refined and developed by a number of others.

holding cash—namely, the interest forgone on marketable securities—is balanced against the fixed cost of transferring marketable securities to cash, or vice versa. The model is illustrated by the sawtoothed lines in Fig. 9-4.

In the figure, we assume that the firm has a steady demand for cash over some period of time, say, 1 month. The firm obtains cash during this period by selling marketable securities. Suppose that it starts out with C dollars in cash and, when this amount is expended, replenishes it by selling C dollars of marketable securities. Thus, the transfer of funds from securities to cash occurs whenever cash touches zero. If a cushion is desired or if lead times are necessary to effect a transaction, the threshold for initiating a transfer can be higher. The principle is the same regardless of whether or not a cushion is used.

The objective is to specify the value of C that minimizes total cost—that is, the sum of the fixed costs associated with transfers and the opportunity cost of earnings forgone by holding cash balances. These costs can be expressed as

$$b\left(\frac{T}{C}\right) + i\left(\frac{C}{2}\right) \tag{9A-1}$$

where b is the fixed cost of a transaction that is assumed to be independent of the amount transferred, T is the total demand for cash over the period of time involved, and i is the interest rate on marketable securities for the period involved (assumed to be constant). T/C represents the number of transactions during the period, and when it is multiplied by the fixed cost per transaction, we obtain the total fixed cost for the period. $C/2$ represents the average cash balance, and when it is multiplied by the interest rate, we obtain the earnings forgone by virtue of holding cash. The larger the C, the larger the average cash balance, $C/2$, and the smaller the average investment in securities and earnings from these securities. Thus, there is a higher opportunity cost of interest income forgone. However, the larger the C, the fewer the transfers, T/C, that occur, and the lower the transfer costs. The object is to balance these two costs so that total costs are minimized.

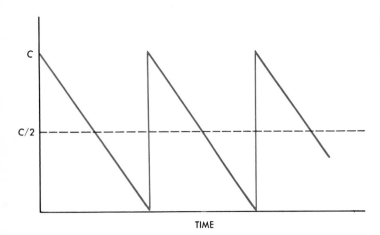

FIGURE 9-4
Inventory model applied to cash management

TIME

The optimal level of C is found to be

$$C^* = \sqrt{\frac{2bT}{i}} \qquad\qquad (9A\text{-}2)$$

Thus, cash will be demanded in relation to the square root of the dollar volume of cash payments. This phenomenon implies that as the level of cash payments increases, the amount of transactions cash the firm needs to hold increases by a lesser percentage. In other words, economies of scale are possible. The implication is that the firm should try to consolidate individual bank accounts into as few as possible in order to realize economies of scale in cash management. We see from Eq. (9A-2) that C^* varies directly with order cost, b, and inversely with the interest rate on marketable securities, i. However, the relationship is dampened by the square-root sign in both cases.

To illustrate the use of the EOQ formula, consider a firm with estimated cash payments of $6 million for a 1-month period, the payments expected to be steady over the period. The fixed cost per transaction is $100, and the interest rate on marketable securities is 6 percent per annum, or .5 percent for the 1-month period. Therefore,

$$C = \sqrt{\frac{2bT}{i}} = \sqrt{\frac{2(100)(6,000,000)}{.005}} = \$489,898$$

Thus, the optimal transaction size is $489,898 and the average cash balance will be $489,898/2 = $244,949. This means that the firm should make $6,000,000/$489,898 = 12 plus transactions of marketable securities to cash during the month.

It is useful now to consider in more detail the two costs involved. The interest rate is fairly straightforward; it simply represents the rate of interest on securities that would be sold to replenish cash. The fixed cost associated with a transaction is more difficult to measure because it consists of both explicit and implied costs. Included are the fixed component of transaction costs, the time it takes the treasurer or other official to place an order with an investment trader, the time consumed in recording the transaction, the secretarial time needed to type the transaction and the purchase order, the time needed to record the transaction on the books, and the time needed to record the safekeeping notification. With a number of transactions, the procedures for placing an order can be streamlined to reduce the average fixed cost per transaction. Nevertheless, these costs do exist and too often are either overlooked or underestimated.

One limitation to the use of the model is that cash payments are seldom completely predictable. For modest degrees of uncertainty, one need only add a cushion so that a transfer from marketable securities to cash is triggered at some level of cash above zero. In general, the EOQ model gives the financial manager a benchmark for judging the optimal cash balance. It does not have to be used as a precise rule to govern behavior. The model merely suggests what would be the optimal balance under a set of assumptions. The actual balance may be more if the assumptions do not entirely hold.

Stochastic Model

In those cases in which the uncertainty of cash payments is large, the EOQ model may not be applicable and other models should be used to determine optimal behavior. If cash balances fluctuate randomly, one can apply control theory to the problem. Assume that the demand for cash is stochastic and unknown in advance. We then can set control limits such that when cash reaches an upper limit, a transfer of cash to marketable securities is consummated, and when it hits a lower limit, a transfer from marketable securities to cash is triggered. As long as the cash balance stays between these limits, no transactions take place.

How the limits are set depends in part on the fixed costs associated with a securities transaction and the opportunity cost of holding cash. As before, we assume that these costs are known and that the fixed cost of selling a marketable security is the same as that for buying it. In essence, we want to satisfy the demand for cash at the lowest possible total cost. Although there are a number of applications of control theory to the problem, we take up a relatively simple one. The Miller-Orr model specifies two control limits—h dollars as an upper bound and zero (z) dollars as lower bound.[5] The model is illustrated in Fig. 9-5. When the cash balance touches the upper bound, $h - z$ dollars of marketable securities are bought and the new balance becomes z dollars. When the cash balance touches zero, z dollars of marketable securities are sold and the new balance again becomes z. As long as the cash balance fluctuates somewhere between the upper and lower control limits, no action is taken. The situation is illustrated in the figure. The minimum bound can be set at some amount higher than zero, and h and z will move up in the figure. We will use zero as the lower bound for purposes of illustration, recognizing that a firm can set the lower bound at some positive amount. This obviously would be necessary if there were delays in transfer.

The solution for the optimal values of h and z depends not only on the fixed and opportunity costs but also upon the degree of likely fluctuation in cash balances. The optimal value of z, the return to point for security transactions, is

[5] See Merton H. Miller and Daniel Orr, "A Model of the Demand for Money by Firms," *Quarterly Journal of Economics,* 80 (August 1966), 413–35.

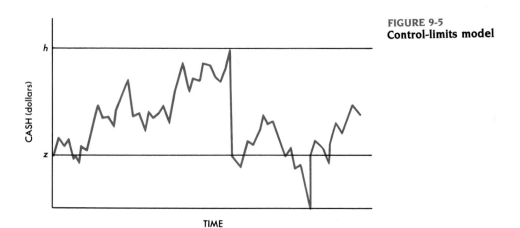

FIGURE 9-5
Control-limits model

$$z = \sqrt[3]{\frac{3b\sigma^2}{4i}} \qquad\qquad (9A\text{-}3)$$

where b = fixed cost associated with a security transaction
σ^2 = variance of daily net cash flows (a measure of the dispersion of these flows)
i = interest rate per day on marketable securities.

The optimal value of h is simply $3z$. With these control limits set, the model minimizes the total costs (fixed and opportunity) of cash management. Again, the critical assumption is that cash flows are random. The average cash balance cannot be determined exactly in advance, but it is approximately $(z + h)/3$. As experience unfolds, however, it can be easily calculated.

We have presented two models for determining an optimal level of cash balances under the self-imposed constraint. The EOQ model assumes that the demand for cash is predictable; the control-limits model assumes that it is random. For most firms, the first model is more applicable than the second, owing to near-term cash flows being relatively predictable. When there is only moderate uncertainty, the EOQ model can be modified to incorporate a cushion. The second model serves primarily as a benchmark for determining cash balances under a rather extreme assumption as to their predictability. The average cash balance generally will be much higher when this model is used as opposed to the EOQ one. Thus, when cash balances of a firm are higher than those dictated by a controls-limit model and the demand for cash is relatively predictable, we know cash is too high.

QUESTIONS

1. Define the function of cash management.
2. Explain the concept of concentration banking.
3. Explain how the lock-box system can improve the efficiency of cash management.
4. Money market instruments are used an an investment vehicle for idle cash. Discuss the primary criterion for asset selection in investing temporary idle cash.
5. Discuss the impact of lock-box banking on corporate cash balances.
6. Explain the application of the economic-order-quantity model to managing cash balances. (See the appendix.)
7. Discuss the primary criterion for assigning priorities to assets that will serve as investment vehicles for a firm's temporary excess liquidity.
8. What are compensating bank balances, and why are they not the same for all depositors?
9. What is float? How might a company play the float in its disbursements?

10. Assuming that the return on real assets of a company exceeds the return on marketable securities, why should a company hold any marketable securities?

11. Under what conditions would it be possible for a company to hold no cash or marketable securities? Are these conditions realistic?

12. What are the three motives for holding cash?

13. Compare and contrast bankers' acceptances and Treasury bills as marketable security investments for the corporation.

14. What are some of the things that can be done with electronic funds transfers from the standpoint of the financial manager?

SELF-CORRECTION PROBLEMS

1. The Zindler Company currently has a centralized billing system. Payments are made by all customers to the central billing location. It requires, on the average, 4 days for customers' mailed payments to reach the central location. An additional $1\frac{1}{2}$ days are required to process payments before a deposit can be made. The firm has a daily average collection of $500,000. The company has recently investigated the possibility of initiating a lock-box system. It has estimated that with such a system customers' mailed payments would reach the receipt location $2\frac{1}{2}$ days sooner. Further, the processing time could be reduced by an additional day because each lock-box bank would pick up mailed deposits twice daily.

   a. Determine the reduction in cash balances that can be achieved through the use of a lock-box system.

   b. Determine the opportunity cost of the present system, assuming a 5 percent return on short-term instruments.

   c. If the annual cost of the lock-box system will be $75,000, should such a system be initiated?

2. Over the next year, El Pedro Steel Company, a California corporation, expects the following returns on continual investment in the following marketable securities:

Treasury bills	8.00%
Commercial paper	8.50%
Money market preferred stock	7.00%

   The company's marginal tax rate for federal income tax purposes is 30 percent (after allowance for the payment of state income taxes), while its marginal, incremental tax rate with respect to California income taxes is 7 percent. On the basis of after-tax returns, which is the most attractive investment? Are there other considerations?

APPENDIX
SELF-CORRECTION PROBLEM

3. The city of Richmond has two tax dates where it receives cash inflows: February 15 and August 15. On each of these dates, it expects to receive $15 million in tax revenue. Cash expenditures are expected to be steady throughout the subsequent 6 months. Presently, the return on investment in marketable securities is 8 percent per annum, and the cost of transfer from securities to cash is $125 each time a transfer occurs.

   a. What is the optimal transfer size using the EOQ model? What is the average cash balance?

   b. What would be your answers if the return on investment were 12 percent per annum and the transfer cost were $75? Why do they differ from those in part a?

PROBLEMS

1. Speedway Owl Company franchises Gas and Go stations in North Carolina and Virginia. All payments by franchisees for gasoline and oil products are by check, which average $420,000 a day. Presently, the overall time between the mailing of the check by the franchisee to Speedway Owl and the time the company has collected or available funds at its bank is 6 days.

   a. How much money is tied up in this interval of time?

   b. To reduce this delay, the company is considering pickups daily from the stations. In all, 3 cars would be needed and 3 additional people hired. This daily pickup would cost $93,000 on an annual basis, and it would reduce the overall delay by 2 days. Currently, the opportunity cost of funds is 9 percent, that being the interest rate on marketable securities. Should the company inaugurate the pickup plan?

   c. Rather than mail checks to its bank, the company could deliver them by messenger service. This procedure would reduce the overall delay by 1 day and cost $10,300 annually. Should the company undertake this plan?

2. The List company, which can earn 7 percent on money market instruments, currently has a lock-box arrangement with a New Orleans bank for its southern customers. The bank handles $3 million a day in return for a compensating balance of $2 million.

   a. The List Company has discovered that it could divide the southern region into a southwestern region (with $1 million a day in collections, which could be handled by a Dallas bank for a $1 million compensating balance) and a southeastern region (with $2 million a day in collections, which could be handled by an Atlanta bank for a $2 million compensating balance). In each case, collections would be $\frac{1}{2}$ day quicker than with the New Orleans arrangement. What would be the annual savings (or cost) of dividing the southern region?

b. In an effort to retain the business, the New Orleans bank has offered to handle the collections strictly on a fee basis (no compensating balance). What would be the maximum fee the New Orleans bank could charge and still retain List's business?

3. The Frazini Food Company has a weekly payroll of $150,000 paid on Friday. On average, its employees cash their checks in the following manner:

DAY CHECK CLEARED ON COMPANY'S ACCOUNT	PERCENTAGE OF CHECKS CASHED
Friday	20%
Monday	40
Tuesday	25
Wednesday	10
Thursday	5

As treasurer of the company, how would you arrange your payroll account? Are there any problems?

4. Sitmore and Dolittle, Inc., has 41 retail clothing outlets scattered throughout the country. Each outlet sends an average of $5,000 daily to the head office in South Bend, Indiana, through checks drawn on local banks. On average, it takes 6 days before the company's South Bend bank collects the checks. Sitmore and Dolittle is considering an electronic funds transfer arrangement that would completely eliminate the float.

a. What amount of funds will be released?

b. What amount will be released on a net basis if each local bank requires an increase in compensating balances of $15,000 to offset the loss of float?

c. Suppose that the company could earn 10 percent interest on the net released funds in part b. If the cost per electronic transfer were $7, and each store averaged 250 transfers per year, would the arrangement proposed be worthwhile? (Assume that the cost of issuing checks on local banks is negligible.)

5. In the *Wall Street Journal* or some other financial paper, determine in the money rate section the rate of interest on Treasury bills, commercial paper, certificates of deposit, and bankers' acceptances. Do the differentials in return have to do with marketability and default risk? If you were a corporate treasurer of a company with considerable business risk, in what security or securities would you invest? How would you arrange the maturities?

Appendix Problems

6. The Schriver Company expects to have $1 million in cash outlays for next year. The firm believes that it will face an opportunity interest rate of 5 per-

cent and will incur a cost of $100 each time it transfers from marketable securities to cash. Cash outlays are expected to be steady over the year. Using the inventory model

a. Determine the optimal transfer size for the Schriver Company.

b. What is the total cost for the use of cash needed for transactions demand?

c. What will be the cash cycle for the firm (velocity)?

d. What will be the average cash balance for the firm?

7. Assume that the Schriver Company (Problem 6) began the year with $1 million in cash.

a. How much would initially be invested in securities?

b. How much would be invested in securities after 231 days?

8. The Verloom Berloop Tulip Bulb Company has experienced a stochastic demand for its product, with the result that cash balances fluctuate randomly. The standard deviation of daily net cash flows, σ, is $1,000. The company wishes to make the transfer of funds from cash to marketable securities and, vice versa, as automatic as possible. It has heard that this can be done by imposing upper- and lower-bound control limits. The current interest rate on marketable securities is 6 percent. The fixed cost associated with each transfer is $100, and transfers are instantaneous.

a. What are the optimal upper- and lower-bound control limits? (Assume a 360-day year.) *Hint:* On a calculator, treat the $1,000 as 1 and solve for the cube root by trial and error. Move the decimal point of the final answer two places to the right.

b. What happens at these control limits?

9. The O. K. Zarter Company employs a control-limits model for managing its cash position and marketable securities transactions. This is done because of the essential random nature of the cash flows. Using the formula, the company has found the optimal value of z, the return to point, to be $312,000. What approximately are the average transaction balances of the company?

SOLUTIONS TO SELF-CORRECTION PROBLEMS

1. a. Total time savings $= 3\frac{1}{2}$ days
   Time savings $\times$ daily average collection $=$ reduction in cash balances achieved.
   $3\frac{1}{2} \times \$500,000 = \$1,750,000$

   b. $5\% \times \$1,750,000 = \$87,500$

   c. Since the opportunity cost of the present system ($87,500) exceeds the cost of the lock-box system ($75,000), the system should be initiated.

2.

SECURITY	FEDERAL TAX	STATE TAX	COMBINED EFFECT	AFTER-TAX EXPECTED RETURN
Treasury bills	.30	0	.30	$(1 - .30)8.00\% = 5.60\%$
Commercial paper	.30	.07	.37	$(1 - .37)8.50\% = 5.36\%$
Money market preferred stock	$(1 - .80).30$ $= .06$	.07	.13	$(1 - .13)7.00\% = 6.09\%$

The money market preferred is the most attractive after taxes, owing to the 80 percent exemption for federal income tax purposes. Commercial paper is less attractive than Treasury bills because of the state income tax from which Treasury bills are exempt. (In states with no income taxes, the after-tax yield on commercial paper would be higher.)

Preferred stock may not be the most attractive investment when risk is taken into account. There is the danger that interest rates will rise above the ceiling and the market value will fall. There also is default risk with respect to dividend payment, whereas the Treasury bill has none.

3. a. $C = \sqrt{\dfrac{2bT}{i}}$

$C = \sqrt{\dfrac{2(\$125)(\$15,000,000)}{.04}} = \$306,186$

Average cash balance $= \dfrac{C}{2} = \dfrac{\$306,186}{2} = \$153,093$

Note that the interest rate for 6 months is approximately 4 percent, or one half the 8 percent annualized rate.

b. $C = \sqrt{\dfrac{2(\$75)(\$15,000,000)}{.06}} = \$193,649$

Average cash balance $= \dfrac{\$193,649}{2} = \$96,825$

The amounts are lower because there is a higher opportunity cost to holding cash and the cost of transferring to cash is less. Consequently, more transactions can take place, all other things being the same.

SELECTED REFERENCES

BATLIN, C. A., and SUSAN HINKO, "Lockbox Management and Value Maximization," *Financial Management*, 10 (Winter 1981), 39–44.

BAUMOL, WILLIAM J., "The Transactions Demand for Cash: An Inventory Theoretic Approach," *Quarterly Journal of Economics*, 46 (November 1952), 545–56.

GALE, BRADLEY T., and BEN BRANCH, "Cash Flow Analysis: More Important Than Ever," *Harvard Business Review*, 59 (July–August 1981), 131–36.

GITMAN, LAWRENCE J., D. KEITH FORRESTER, and JOHN R. FORRESTER, JR., "Maximizing Cash Disbursement Float," *Financial Management*, 5 (Summer 1976), 15–24.

KAMATH, RAVINDRA R., SHAHRIAR KHAKSARI, HEIDI HYLTON MEIER, and JOHN WINKLEPLECTK, "Management of Excess Cash: Practices and Developments," *Financial Management*, 14 (Autumn 1985), 70–77.

MAIER, STEVEN F., and JAMES H. VANDER WEIDE, "What Lockbox and Disbursement Models Really Do," *Journal of Finance*, 38 (May 1983), 361–71.

MILLER, MERTON H., and DANIEL ORR, "The Demand for Money by Firms: Extension of Analytic Results," *Journal of Finance*, 23 (December 1968), 735–59.

NAUSS, ROBERT M., and ROBERT E. MARKLAND, "Solving Lock Box Location Problems," *Financial Management*, 8 (Spring 1979), 21–31.

STONE, BERNELL K., "Design of a Receivable Collection System," *Management Science*, 27 (August 1981), 866–80.

——, "The Design of a Company's Banking System," *Journal of Finance*, 38 (May 1983), 373–85.

——, "Corporate Trade Payments: Hard Lessons in Product Design," *Economic Review of Fed of Atlanta*, 71 (April 1986), 9–21.

——, and NED C. HILL, "Cash Transfer Scheduling for Efficient Cash Concentration," *Financial Management*, 9 (Autumn 1980), 35–43.

VAN HORNE, JAMES C., *Financial Market Rates and Flows*, 2nd ed. Englewood Cliffs, N.J.: Prentice-Hall, 1984.

VANDER WEIDE, JAMES H., *Managing Corporate Liquidity*. New York: John Wiley, 1985, chap. 4.

WRIGHT, F. K., "Minimizing the Costs of Liquidity," *Australian Journal of Management*, 3 (October 1978), 203–24.

CHAPTER 10

Accounts Receivable
and Inventories

In Chapter 8, we saw that the investment of funds in **accounts receivable** involves a trade-off between profitability and risk. The optimum investment is determined by comparing benefits to be derived from a particular level of investment with the costs of maintaining that level. This chapter will reveal the key variables involved in managing **receivables** efficiently, and it will show how they can be varied to obtain the optimal investment. We consider first the credit and collection policies of the firm as a whole and then discuss credit and collection procedures for the individual account. The last part of the chapter investigates techniques for efficiently managing inventories. The cash-flow cycle involves inventories being acquired ahead of sales, whereas receivables are generated at the time of sales and become cash only after a further lapse of time.

Accounts receivable. Amounts owed the firm by customers. A current asset.

CREDIT AND COLLECTION POLICIES

Economic conditions and the firm's credit policies are the chief influences on the level of a firm's accounts receivables. Economic conditions, of course, are largely beyond the control of the financial manager. As with other current assets, however, the manager can vary the level of receivables in keeping with the trade-off between profitability and risk. Lowering quality standards may stimulate demand, which, in turn, should lead to higher profits. But there is a cost to carrying the additional receivables, as well as a greater risk of bad-debt losses. It is this trade-off we wish to examine.

The policy variables we consider include the quality of the trade accounts accepted, the length of the credit period, the cash discount, and the collection program of the firm. Together, these elements largely determine the average collection period and the proportion of bad-debt losses. We analyze each element in turn, holding constant certain of the others, as well as all exogenous variables that affect the average collection period and the percentage of bad-debt losses. In addition, we assume that the evaluation of risk is sufficiently standardized that degrees of risk for different accounts can be compared objectively.

Credit Standards

Credit policy can have a significant influence on sales. If competitors extend credit liberally and we do not, our policy may have a dampening effect on the marketing effort. Credit is one of many factors that influence the demand for a firm's product. Consequently, the degree to which credit can promote demand depends on what other factors are being employed. In theory, the firm should lower its quality standard for accounts accepted as long as the profitability of sales generated exceeds the added costs of the receivables. What are the costs of relaxing credit standards? Some arise from an enlarged credit department, the clerical work involved in checking additional accounts, and servicing the added volume of receivables. We assume that these costs are deducted from the profitability of additional sales to give a net profitability figure for computational purposes. Another cost comes from the increased probability of bad-debt losses.

Credit standard. The minimum quality of creditworthiness of a credit applicant that is acceptable to the firm.

We postpone consideration of this cost to a subsequent section; we assume for now that there are no bad-debt losses.

Finally, there is the opportunity cost of the additional receivables, resulting from (1) increased sales and (2) a slower average collection period. If new customers are attracted by the relaxed credit standards, collecting from these customers is likely to be slower than is collecting from existing customers. In addition, a more liberal extension of credit may cause certain existing customers to be less conscientious about paying their bills on time.

An Example of the Trade-off.   To assess the profitability of a more liberal extension of credit, we must know the profitability of additional sales, the added demand for products arising from the relaxed credit standards, the increased slowness of the average collection period, and the required return on investment. Suppose that a firm's product sells for $10 a unit, of which $8 represents variable costs before taxes, including credit department costs. The firm is operating at less than full capacity, and an increase in sales can be accommodated without any increase in fixed costs. Therefore, the contribution margin of an additional unit of sales is the selling price less variables costs involved in producing the unit, or $10 − $8 = $2.

Presently, annual credit sales are running at a level of $2.4 million, and there is no underlying trend in such sales. The firm may liberalize credit, which will result in an average collection experience of new customers of 2 months. Existing customers are not expected to alter their payment habits. The relaxation in credit standards is expected to produce a 25 percent increase in sales, to $3 million annually. The $600,000 increase represents 60,000 additional units if we assume that the price per unit stays the same. Finally, assume that the firm's opportunity cost of carrying the additional receivables is 20 percent before taxes.

This information reduces our evaluation to a trade-off between the added profitability on the additional sales and the opportunity cost of the increased investment in receivables. The increased investment arises solely from new, slower-paying customers; we have assumed existing customers continue to pay in 1 month. With the additional sales of $600,000 and receivable turnover of six times a year (12 months divided by the average collection period of 2 months), the additional receivables are $600,000/6 = $100,000. For these additional receivables, the firm invests the variable costs tied up in them. For our example, $.80 of every $1.00 in sales represents variable costs. Therefore, the added investment in receivables is .80 × $100,000 = $80,000. With these inputs, we are able to make the calculations shown in Table 10-1. Inasmuch as the profitability on additional sales, $120,000, far exceeds the required return on the additional investment in receivables, $16,000, the firm would be well advised to relax its credit standards. An optimal credit policy would involve extending trade credit more liberally until the marginal profitability on additional sales equals the required return on the additional investment in receivables necessary to generate those sales. However, as we take on poorer credit risks, we also increase the risk of the firm, as depicted by the variance of the expected cash-flow stream. This increase in risk is largely reflected in additional bad-debt losses, a subject we deal with shortly.

TABLE 10-1
Profitability versus required return—credit standard change

Profitability of additional sales	=	$2 × 60,000 units = $120,000
Additional receivables	=	(Additional sales/Receivable turnover) $600,000/6 = $100,000
Investment in additional receivables	=	(Variable costs/Sales price) (Additional receivables) (.80)($100,000) = $80,000
Required return on additional investment	=	.20 × $80,000 = $16,000

Credit Terms

Credit Period.   Credit terms involve both the length of credit period and the discount given. The terms "2/10, net 30" mean that a 2 percent discount is given if the bill is paid before the tenth day after the date of invoice; payment is due by the thirtieth day. The credit period, then, is 30 days. Although the customs of the industry frequently dictate the terms given, the credit period is another means by which a firm may be able to affect product demand, hoping to increase demand by extending the credit period. As before, the trade-off is between the profitability of additional sales and the required return on the additional investment in receivables.

Let us say that the firm in our example increases its credit period from 30 to 60 days. The average collection period for existing customers goes from 1 month to 2 months. The more liberal credit period results in increased sales of $360,000, and these new customers also pay, on average, in 2 months. The total additional receivables are composed of two parts. The first part represents the receivables associated with the increased sales. In our example, there are $360,000 in additional sales. With a receivable turnover of six times a year, the additional receivables associated with the new sales are $360,000/6 = $60,000. For these additional receivables, the investment by the firm is the variable costs tied up in them. For our example, we have ($8/$10)($60,000) = $48,000.

The second part of the total additional receivables represents the slowing in collections associated with original sales. The old receivables are collected in a slower manner resulting in a higher receivable level. With $2.4 million in original sales, the level of receivables with a turnover of 12 times a year is $2,400,000/12 = $200,000. The new level with a turnover of six times a year is $2,400,000/6 = $400,000. Thus, there are $200,000 in additional receivables associated with the original sales. For this addition, the relevant investment using marginal analysis is the full $200,000. In other words, the use of variable costs pertains only to new sales. The incremental $200,000 in receivables on original sales would have been collected earlier had it not been for the change in credit standards. Therefore, the firm must increase its investment in receivables by $200,000.

Based on these inputs, our calculations are shown in Table 10-2. The ap-

TABLE 10-2
Profitability versus required return—
credit period change

Profitability of additional sales	=	$2 × 36,000 units = $72,000
Additional receivables associated with new sales	=	(New sales/Receivable turnover) $360,000/6 = $60,000
Additional investment in receivables associated with new sales	=	(Variable costs/Sales price)(Additional receivables) (.80)($60,000) = $48,000
Present level of receivables	=	(Annual sales/Receivable turnover) $2.4 million/12 = $200,000
New level of receivables associated with original sales	=	$2.4 million/6 = $400,000
Additional investment in receivables associated with original sales	=	$400,000 − $200,000 = $200,000
Total additional investment in receivables	=	$48,000 + $200,000 = $248,000
Carrying cost of additional investment	=	.20 × $248,000 = $49,600

propriate comparison is the profitability of additional sales with the opportunity cost of the additional investment in receivables. Inasmuch as the profitability on additional sales, $72,000, exceeds the required return on the investment in additional receivables, $49,600, the change in credit period from 30 to 60 days is worthwhile. The profitability of the additional sales more than offsets the added investment in receivables, the bulk of which comes from existing customers slowing their payments.

Discount Given.   Varying the discount involves an attempt to speed up the payment of receivables. Here we must determine whether a speedup in collections would more than offset the cost of an increase in the discount. If it would, the present discount policy should be changed. Suppose that the firm has annual credit sales of $3 million and an average collection period of 2 months and that the sales terms are net 45 days, with no discount given. Consequently, the average receivable balance is $500,000. By instigating terms of 2/10, net 45, the average collection period can be reduced to 1 month, as 60 percent of the customers (in dollar volume) take advantage of the 2 percent discount. The opportunity cost of the discount to the firm is .02 × .6 × $3 million, or $36,000 annually. The turnover of receivables has improved to 12 times a year, so that average receivables are reduced from $500,000 to $250,000 (i.e., $3,000,000/ 12 = $250,000).

Thus, the firm realizes $250,000 from accelerated collections. The value of the funds released is their opportunity cost. If we assume a 20 percent rate of return, the opportunity saving is $50,000. In this case the opportunity saving arising from a speedup in collections is greater than the cost of the discount. The firm should adopt a 2 percent discount. If the speedup in collections had not resulted in sufficient opportunity savings to offset the cost of discount, the discount policy would not be changed. It is possible, of course, that discounts other than 2 percent may result in an even greater difference between the opportunity saving and the cost of the discount.

Default Risk

In the foregoing examples we assumed no bad-debt losses. Our concern in this section is not only with the slowness of collection but also with the portion of the receivables defaulting. Different credit standard policies will involve both of these factors. Suppose that we are considering the present credit standard policy (sales of $2,400,000) together with two new ones and that these policies are expected to produce the following results:

	PRESENT POLICY	POLICY A	POLICY B
Demand (sales)	$2,400,000	$3,000,000	$3,300,000
Default losses on incremental sales (percentage)	2	10	18
Average collection period on incremental sales	1 month	2 months	3 months

We assume that after 6 months an account is turned over to a collection agency and that, on average, 2 percent of the original sales of $2.4 million is never received by the firm, 10 percent is never received on the $600,000 in additional sales under policy A, and 18 percent on the $300,000 in additional sales under policy B is never received. Similarly, the 1-month average collection period pertains to the original sales, 2 months to the $600,000 in additional sales under policy A, and 3 months to the $300,000 in additional sales under policy B. These numbers of months correspond to annual receivable turnovers of 12 times, 6 times, and 4 times, respectively.

The incremental profitability calculations associated with these two new credit standard policies are shown in Table 10-3. We would want to adopt policy A but would not want to go as far as policy B in relaxing our credit standards. The marginal benefit is positive in moving from the present policy to policy A but negative in going from policy A to policy B. It is possible, of course, that a relaxation of credit standards that fell on one side or the other of policy A would provide an even greater marginal benefit; the optimal policy is the one that provides the greatest marginal benefit.

Collection Policy and Procedures

The firm determines its overall collection policy by the combination of collection procedures it undertakes. These procedures include things such as letters, phone calls, personal visits, and legal action. One of the principal policy variables is the amount expended on collection procedures. Within a range, the

TABLE 10-3
Profitability versus required return—
bad-debt losses and collection period changes

	POLICY A	POLICY B
1. Additional sales	$600,000	$300,000
2. Profitability of additional sales (20%)	120,000	60,000
3. Additional bad-debt losses (Additional sales × bad-debt percentage)	60,000	54,000
4. Additional receivables (Additional sales/Receivable turnover)	100,000	75,000
5. Investment in additional receivables (.8 × additional receivables)	80,000	60,000
6. Required return on additional investment (20 percent)	16,000	12,000
7. Bad-debt losses plus additional required return	76,000	66,000
8. Incremental profitability (2) − (7)	44,000	(6,000)

greater the relative amount expended, the lower the proportion of bad-debt losses and the shorter the average collection period, all other things being the same.

The relationships are not linear. Initial collection expenditures are likely to cause little reduction in bad-debt losses. Additional expenditures begin to have a significant effect up to a point; then they tend to have little effect in further reducing these losses. The hypothesized relationship between expenditures and bad-debt losses is shown in Fig. 10-1. The relationship between the average collection period and the level of collection expenditure is likely to be similar to that shown in the figure.

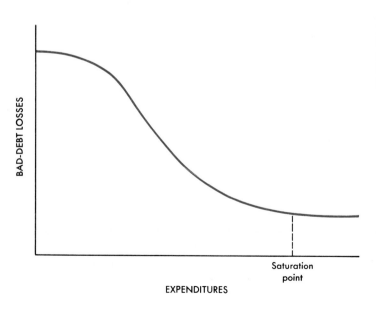

FIGURE 10-1
Relationship between amount of bad-debt losses and collection expenditures

If sales are independent of the collection effort, the appropriate level of collection expenditure again involves a trade-off—this time between the level of expenditure on the one hand and the reduction in the cost of bad-debt losses and reduction in investment in receivables on the other. Calculations are the same as for the discount given and for default losses illustrated earlier. The reader easily can verify the trade-off.

Because a receivable is only as good as the likelihood that it will be paid, a firm cannot afford to wait too long before initiating collection procedures. On the other hand, if it initiates procedures too soon, it may anger reasonably good customers who, for some reason, fail to make payments by the due date. Procedures, whatever they are, should be firmly established. Initially, a letter is usually sent, followed perhaps by additional letters that become ever more serious in tone. Next may come a telephone call from the credit manager and then, perhaps, one from the company's attorney. Some companies have collection personnel who make personal calls on the account.

If all else fails, the account may be turned over to a collection agency. The agency's fees are quite substantial—frequently one-half the amount of the receivable—but such a procedure may be the only feasible alternative, particularly for a small account. Direct legal action is costly, sometimes serves no real purpose, and may only force the account into bankruptcy. When payment cannot be collected, compromise settlements may provide a higher percentage of collection.

Credit and Collection Policies—Summary

We see that the credit and collection policies of a firm involve several decisions: (1) the quality of account accepted, (2) the credit period, (3) the cash discount given, and (4) the level of collection expenditures. In each case, the decision should involve a comparison of possible gains from a change in policy with the cost of the change. Optimal credit and collection policies would be those that resulted in the marginal gains equaling the marginal costs.

To maximize profits arising from credit and collection policies, the firm should vary these policies jointly until it achieves an optimal solution. That solution will determine the best combination of credit standards, credit period, cash discount policy, special terms, and level of collection expenditures. For most policy variables, profits increase at a decreasing rate up to a point and then decrease as the policy is varied from no effort to an extreme effort. Figure 10-2 depicts this relationship with the quality of accounts rejected. When there are no credit standards, when all applicants are accepted, sales are maximized, but they are offset by large bad-debt losses as well as by the opportunity cost of carrying a very large receivable position. The latter is due to a long average collection period. As credit standards are initiated and applicants rejected, revenue from sales declines, but so do the average collection period and bad-debt losses. Because the last two decline initially at a faster rate than do sales, profits increase. As credit standards are tightened increasingly, sales revenue declines at an increasing rate. At the same time, the average collection period and bad-debt losses decrease at a decreasing rate. Fewer and fewer bad credit risks are eliminated. Because of the combination of these influences, total profits of the firm in-

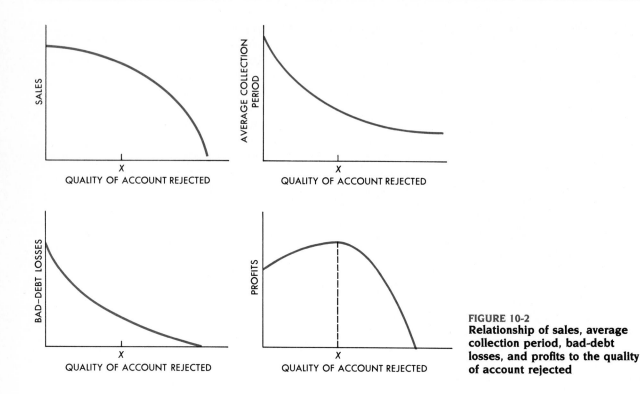

FIGURE 10-2
Relationship of sales, average collection period, bad-debt losses, and profits to the quality of account rejected

crease at a diminishing rate with stricter credit standards up to a point, after which they decline. The optimal policy with respect to credit standards is represented by point X in the figure. In turn, this policy determines the level of accounts receivable held by the firm.

The analysis in the last several sections has purposely been rather general, to provide insight into the chief concepts of credit and collection policies. Obviously, a policy decision should be based on a far more specific evaluation than that contained in the examples. Estimating the increased demand and increased slowness of collections that might accompany a relaxation of credit standards is difficult. Nevertheless, management must make estimates of these relationships if it is to appraise realistically its existing policies.

ANALYZING THE CREDIT APPLICANT

Having established the terms of sale to be offered, the firm must evaluate individual credit applicants and consider the possibilities of a bad debt or slow payment. The credit evaluation procedure involves three related steps: obtaining information on the applicant, analyzing this information to determine the applicant's creditworthiness, and making the credit decision. The credit decision, in turn, establishes whether credit should be extended and what its maximum amount should be.

Sources of Information

A number of sources supply credit information, but for some accounts, especially small ones, the cost of collecting it may outweigh the potential profitability of the account. The firm extending credit may have to be satisfied with a limited amount of information on which to base a decision. In addition to cost, the firm must consider the time it takes to investigate a credit applicant. A shipment to a prospective customer cannot be delayed unnecessarily pending an elaborate credit investigation. Thus, the amount of information collected needs to be considered in relation to the time and expense required. Depending on these considerations, the credit analyst may use one or more of the following sources of information.

Financial Statement.   At the time of the prospective sale, the seller may request a financial statement, one of the most desirable sources of information for credit analysis. Frequently, there is a correlation between a company's refusal to provide a statement and its weak financial position. Audited statements are preferable, and interim statements are helpful, particularly for companies having seasonal patterns of sales.

Credit Ratings and Reports.   In addition to financial statements, credit ratings are available from various mercantile agencies. Dun & Bradstreet is perhaps the best known and most comprehensive of these agencies. It provides credit ratings to subscribers for a vast number of business firms throughout the nation. A key to its individual ratings is shown in Fig. 10-3. As we can see, D&B ratings give the credit analyst an indication of the estimated size of net worth and a credit appraisal for companies of a particular size, ranging from "high" to "limited." D&B also indicates when the information available is insufficient to provide a rating for a given business. In addition to its rating service, D&B provides credit reports containing a brief history of a company and its principal officers, the nature of the business, certain financial information, and a trade check of suppliers—the length of their experience with the company and whether payments are discount, prompt, or past due. The quality of the D&B reports varies with the information available externally and the willingness of the company being checked to cooperate with the D&B reporter.

TRW, Inc., in conjunction with the National Association of Credit Management, has developed a data base on some 7 million businesses. Typically, the information is not as extensive as that of Dun & Bradstreet, but it is of considerable use in credit analysis. TRW information is computer based, so teletype credit reports can be obtained through an automated retrieval system in a matter of minutes.

Bank Checking.   Another source of information for the firm is a credit check through a bank. Many banks have large credit departments that undertake credit checks as a service for their customers. By calling or writing a bank in which the credit applicant has an account, a firm's bank is able to obtain information on the average cash balance carried, loan accommodations, experience, and sometimes financial information. Because banks generally are more willing

New Key to Ratings

ESTIMATED FINANCIAL STRENGTH			COMPOSITE CREDIT APPRAISAL			
			HIGH	GOOD	FAIR	LIMITED
5A	Over	$50,000,000	1	2	3	4
4A	$10,000,000 to	50,000,000	1	2	3	4
3A	1,000,000 to	10,000,000	1	2	3	4
2A	750,000 to	1,000,000	1	2	3	4
1A	500,000 to	750,000	1	2	3	4
BA	300,000 to	500,000	1	2	3	4
BB	200,000 to	300,000	1	2	3	4
CB	125,000 to	200,000	1	2	3	4
CC	75,000 to	125,000	1	2	3	4
DC	50,000 to	75,000	1	2	3	4
DD	35,000 to	50,000	1	2	3	4
EE	20,000 to	35,000	1	2	3	4
FF	10,000 to	20,000	1	2	3	4
GG	5,000 to	10,000	1	2	3	4
HH	Up to	5,000	1	2	3	4

CLASSIFICATION FOR BOTH
ESTIMATED FINANCIAL STRENGTH AND CREDIT APPRAISAL

FINANCIAL STRENGTH BRACKET   EXPLANATION

1 $125,000 and Over

2   20,000 to 125,000

When only the numeral (1 or 2) appears, it is an indication that the estimated financial strength, while not definitely classified, is presumed to be within the range of the ($) figures in the corresponding bracket and that a condition is believed to exist which warrants credit in keeping with that assumption.

NOT CLASSIFIED OR ABSENCE OF RATING

The absence of a rating, expressed by two hyphens (--), is not to be construed as unfavorable but signifies circumstances difficult to classify within condensed rating symbols. It suggests the advisability of obtaining a report for additional information.

FIGURE 10-3
Dun & Bradstreet key to ratings

to share information with other banks than with a direct inquirer, it usually is best for the firm to initiate the credit check through its own bank rather than to inquire directly.

Trade Checking.   Credit information frequently is exchanged among companies selling to the same customer. Through various credit organizations, credit people in a particular area become a closely knit group. A company can ask other suppliers about their experiences with an account.

The Company's Own Experience.   A study of the promptness of past payments, including any seasonal patterns, is very useful. Frequently, the credit department will make written assessments of the quality of the management of a company to whom credit may be extended. These assessments are very important, for they pertain to the first of the famous "three C's" of credit: *character*, *collateral*, and *capacity*. The person who made the sale to a prospective customer frequently can offer useful impressions of management and operations. Caution is necessary in interpreting this information, because a salesperson has a natural bias toward granting credit and making the sale.

Credit Analysis

Having collected credit information, the firm must make a credit analysis of the applicant. In practice, the collection of information and its analysis are closely related. If, on the basis of initial credit information, a large account appears to be relatively risky, the credit analyst will want to obtain further information. Presumably, the expected value of the additional information will exceed the cost of acquiring it. Given the financial statements of an applicant, the credit analyst should undertake a ratio analysis, as described in Chapter 6. The analyst will be particularly interested in the applicant's liquidity and ability to pay bills on time. Such ratios as the quick ratio, receivable and inventory turnovers, the average payable period, debt-to-net-worth ratio, and cash-flow coverage ratio are particularly germane.

In addition to analyzing financial statements, the credit analyst will consider the financial strength of the firm, the character of the company and its management, and various other matters. Then the analyst attempts to determine the ability of the applicant to service trade credit, the probability of an applicant's not paying on time and of a bad-debt loss. On the basis of this information together with information about the profit margin of the product or service being sold, a decision is reached as to whether or not to extend credit.

The amount of information collected should be determined in relation to the expected profit from an order and the cost of investigation. More sophisticated analysis should be undertaken only when there is a chance that a credit decision based on the previous stage of investigation will be changed. If an analysis of a Dun & Bradstreet report resulted in an extremely unfavorable picture of the applicant, an investigation of the applicant's bank and its trade suppliers might have little prospect of changing the reject decision. Therefore, the added cost associated with this stage of investigation would not be worthwhile. With incremental stages of investigation each having a cost, they can be justified only if the information obtained has value in changing a prior decisions.[1] Rather than perform all stages of investigation regardless of the profitability of the order, the firm should undertake investigation in stages and go to a new stage only when the expected net benefits of the additional information exceed the cost of acquiring it.

Although quantitative approaches have been developed to measure ability to service trade credit, the final decision for most companies extending trade credit rests on the credit analyst's judgment in evaluating available information. Numerical evaluations are successful in consumer credit, where various characteristics of an individual are quantitatively rated and a credit decision is made on the basis of the total score. The plastic credit cards many of us hold are often given out on the basis of a credit scoring system in which things such as age, occupation, duration of employment, home ownership, years of residence, telephone, and annual income are taken into acount. Numerical ratings systems also

---

[1] For such an analysis, see Dileep Mehta, "The Formulation of Credit Policy Models," *Management Science*, 15 (October 1968), 30–50.

are being used by companies extending trade credit.[2] With the overall growth of trade credit, a number of companies are finding it worthwhile to use numerical credit-scoring systems to screen out clear accept and reject applicants. Credit analysts, then, can devote their energies to evaluating marginal applicants.

Credit Decision

Once the credit analyst has marshaled the necessary evidence and has analyzed it, a decision must be reached as to the disposition of the account. In an initial sale, the first decision to be made is whether or not to ship the goods and extend credit. If repeat sales are likely, the company will probably want to establish procedures so that it does not have to evaluate the extension of credit each time an order is received. One means for streamlining the procedure is to establish a **line of credit** for an account. A line of credit is a maximum limit on the amount the firm will permit to be owed at any one time. In essence, it represents the maximum risk exposure that the firm will allow itself to undergo for an account. The establishment of a credit line streamlines the procedure for shipping goods, but the line must be reevaluated periodically in order to keep abreast of developments in the account. What was a satisfactory risk exposure today may be more or less than satisfactory a year from today. Despite comprehensive credit procedures, there will always be special cases that must be dealt with individually. Here, too, a firm can streamline the operation by defining responsibilities clearly.

Line of credit. A limit to the amount of credit extended to an account. Purchaser can buy on credit up to that limit.

INVENTORY MANAGEMENT AND CONTROL

Inventories form a link between production and sale of a product. A manufacturing company must maintain a certain amount of inventory during production, the inventory known as goods in process. Although other types of inventory—in-transit, raw materials, and finished goods inventories—are not necessary in the strictest sense, they allow the firm to be flexible. Inventory in transit—that is, inventory between various stages of production or storage—permits efficient production scheduling and utilization of resources. Without this type of inventory, each stage of production would have to wait for the preceding stage to complete a unit. Resultant delays and idle time give the firm an incentive to maintain in-transit inventory.

Raw materials inventory gives the firm flexibility in its purchasing. Without it, the firm must exist on a hand-to-mouth basis, buying raw materials strictly in keeping with its production schedule. Finished goods inventory allows the firm flexibility in its production scheduling and in its marketing. Production does not need to be geared directly to sales. Large inventories allow efficient servicing of customer demands. If a certain product is temporarily out of stock, present as

---

[2] See Robert O. Edmister and Gary G. Schlarbaum, "Credit Policy in Lending Institutions," *Journal of Financial and Quantitative Analysis*, 9 (June 1974), 335–56. For a discussion of the updating of the underlying sample used in a credit-scoring system, see Michael S. Long, "Credit Screening System Selection," *Journal of Financial and Quantitative Analysis* 11 (June 1976), 313–28.

well as future sales to the customer may be lost. Thus, there is an incentive to maintain stocks of all three types of inventory.

The advantages of increased inventories, then, are several. The firm can effect economies of production and purchasing and can fill orders more quickly. In short, the firm is more flexible. The obvious disadvantages are the total cost of holding the inventory, including storage and handling costs, and the required return on capital tied up in inventory. An additional disadvantage is the danger of obsolescence. Because of the benefits, however, the sales manager and production manager are biased toward relatively large inventories. Moreover, the purchasing manager often can achieve quantity discounts with large orders, and there may be a bias here as well. It falls upon the financial manager to dampen the temptation for large inventories. This is done by forcing consideration of the cost of funds necessary to carry inventories as well as perhaps of the handling and storage costs. (The latter costs usually will concern the production manager and purchasing manager as well.)

Like accounts receivable, inventories should be increased as long as the resulting savings exceed the total cost of holding the added inventory. The balance finally reached depends on the estimates of actual savings, the cost of carrying additional inventory, and the efficiency of inventory control. Obviously, this balance requires coordination of the production, marketing, and finance areas of the firm in keeping with an overall objective. Our purpose is to examine various principles of inventory control by which an appropriate balance might be achieved.

Economic Order Quantity

The economic order quantity (EOQ) is an important concept in the purchase of raw materials and in the storage of finished goods and in-transit inventories. In our analysis, we wish to determine the optimal order quantity for a particular item of inventory, given its forecasted usage, ordering cost, and carrying cost. Ordering can mean either the purchase of the item or its production. Assume for the moment that the usage of a particular item of inventory is known with certainty. This usage is stationary or steady throughout the period of time being analyzed. In other words, if usage is 2,600 items for a 6-month period, 100 items are used each week. Moreover, usage is assumed to be independent of the level of inventory.

We assume that ordering costs, O, are constant regardless of the size of the order. In the purchase of raw materials or other items, these costs represent the clerical costs involved in placing an order as well as certain costs of receiving and checking the goods once they arrive. For finished goods inventories, ordering costs involve scheduling a production run. When start-up costs are large—as they are in a machined piece of metal, for example—ordering costs can be quite significant. For in-transit inventories, ordering costs are likely to involve nothing more than record keeping. The total ordering cost for a period is simply the number of orders for that period times the cost per order.

Carrying costs per period, C, represent the cost of inventory storage, handling, and insurance, together with the required rate of return on the investment in inventory. These costs are assumed to be constant per unit of inventory, per unit of time. Thus, the total carrying cost for a period is the average number of units of inventory for the period times the carrying cost per unit. In addition, we assume for now that inventory orders are filled without delay. Because out-of-stock items can be replaced immediately, there is no need to maintain a buffer or safety stock. Although the assumptions made up to now may seem overly restrictive, they are necessary for an initial understanding of the conceptual framework that follows. Subsequently, we shall relax some of them.

If the usage of an inventory item is perfectly steady over a period of time and there is no safety stock, average inventory (in units) can be expressed as

$$\text{Average inventory} = \frac{Q}{2} \qquad (10\text{-}1)$$

where Q is the quantity (in units) ordered and is assumed to be constant for the period. This problem is illustrated in Fig. 10-4. Although the quantity demanded is a step function, we assume for analytical purposes that it can be approximated by a straight line. We see that zero inventory always indicates that further inventory must be ordered.

The carrying cost of inventory is the carrying cost per unit times the average number of units of inventory, or $CQ/2$. The total number of orders for a period of time is simply the total usage (in units) of an item of inventory for that period, S, divided by Q. Consequently, total ordering costs are represented by the ordering cost per order times the number of orders, or SO/Q. Total inventory costs, then, are the carrying costs plus ordering costs, or

$$\frac{CQ}{2} + \frac{SO}{Q} \qquad (10\text{-}2)$$

We see from Eq. (10-2) that the higher the order quantity, Q, the higher the carry-

FIGURE 10-4
Order-quantity example

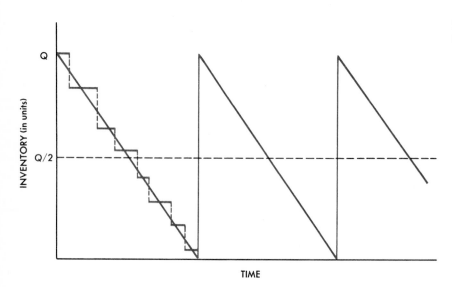

ing costs but the lower the total ordering costs. The lower the order quantity, the lower the carrying costs but the higher the total ordering costs. We are concerned with the trade-off between the economies of increased order size and the added cost of carrying additional inventory.

Optimal Order Quantity.   From Eq. (10-2) we can obtain the optimal order quantity, Q^*:

$$Q^* = \sqrt{\frac{2SO}{C}} \qquad (10\text{-}3)$$

This equation is known as the economic-lot-size formula. To illustrate its use, suppose that usage of an inventory item is 2,000 units during a 100-day period, ordering costs are $100 an order, and carrying costs are $10 per unit per 100 days. The most economic order quantity, then, is

$$Q^* = \sqrt{\frac{2(2,000)(100)}{10}} = 200 \text{ units}$$

With an order quantity of 200 units, the firm would order (2,000/200), or ten times, during the period under consideration or, in other words, every 10 days. We see from Eq. (10-3) that Q^* varies directly with total usage, S, and order cost, O, and inversely with the carrying cost, C. However, the relationship is dampened by the square-root sign in both cases. As usage increases, then, the optimal order size and the average level of inventory increase by a lesser percentage. In other words, economies of scale are possible.

In our example, we have assumed that inventory can be ordered and received without delay. Usually, there is a time lapse between placement of a purchase order and receipt of the inventory, or in the time it takes to manufacture an item after an order is placed. This lead time must be considered. If it is constant and known with certainty, the optimal order quantity is not affected. In this example, the firm would still order 200 units at a time and place 10 orders during the specified time period, or every 10 days. If the lead time for delivery were 3 days, the firm simply would place its order 7 days after delivery of the previous order.

The EOQ function is shown in Fig. 10-5. In the figure, we plot ordering costs, carrying costs, and total costs—the sum of the first two costs. We see that whereas carrying costs vary directly with the size of the order, ordering costs vary inversely with the size of the order. The total cost line declines at first as the fixed costs of ordering are spread over more units. The total cost line begins to rise when the decrease in average ordering cost is more than offset by the additional carrying costs. Point X, then, represents the economic order quantity, which minimizes the total cost of inventory. The EOQ formula taken up in this section is a useful tool for inventory control. In purchasing raw materials or other items of inventory, it tells us the amount to order and the best timing of our orders. For finished goods inventory, it enables us to exercise better control over the timing and size of production runs. In general, the EOQ model gives us a rule for deciding when to replenish inventories and the amount to replenish.

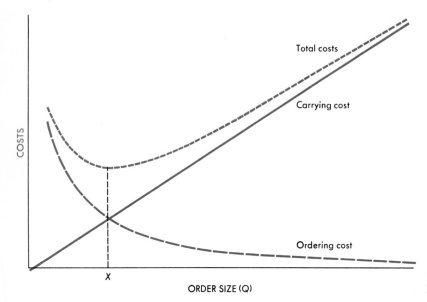

COSTS

Total costs

Carrying cost

Ordering cost

X

ORDER SIZE (Q)

FIGURE 10-5
Economic-order-quantity relationship

SAFETY STOCKS AND OTHER CONSIDERATIONS

In practice, the demand or usage of inventory generally is not known with certainty; usually it fluctuates during a given period of time. Typically, the demand for finished goods inventory is subject to the greatest uncertainty. In general, the usage of raw materials inventory and in-transit inventory, both of which depend on the production scheduling, is more predictable. In addition to demand, the lead time required to receive delivery of inventory once an order is placed usually is subject to some variation. Owing to these fluctuations, it is not feasible usually to allow expected inventory to fall to zero before a new order is anticipated, as the firm could do when usage and lead time were known with certainty. A **safety stock** is necessary.

Safety stock.
Inventories held as a cushion against uncertain demand or usage.

Order Point and Safety Stock

Before discussing safety stocks, we consider at what point inventory will be ordered. Suppose that demand for inventory is known with certainty, but that it takes 5 days before an order is received. In our previous illustration of the economic-order-quantity formula, we found that the EOQ for our example firm was 200 units, resulting in an order being placed every 10 days. If usage is steady, the firm now would need to order 5 days before it ran out of stock, or at 100 units of stock on hand. Thus, the order point is 100 units. When the new order is received 5 days later, the firm will just have exhausted its existing stock. This example of an order point is illustrated in Fig. 10-6.

When we allow for uncertainty in demand for inventory as well as in lead time, a safety stock becomes advisable. The concept here is illustrated in Fig. 10-7. The upper panel of the figure shows what would happen if the firm had a

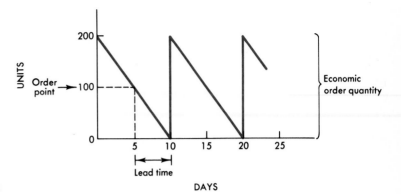

FIGURE 10-6
Order point when lead time is certain

safety stock of 100 units and if expected demand of 200 units every 10 days and lead time of 5 days were to occur. Note that with a safety stock of 100 units, the order point must be set at 200 units of inventory on hand as opposed to the previous 100 units. In other words, the order point determines the amount of safety stock held.

FIGURE 10-7
Safety stock when demand and lead time are uncertain

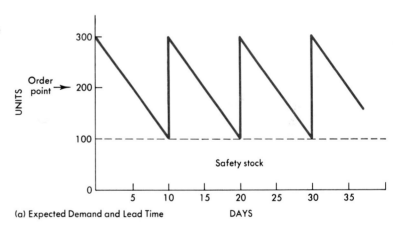

(a) Expected Demand and Lead Time

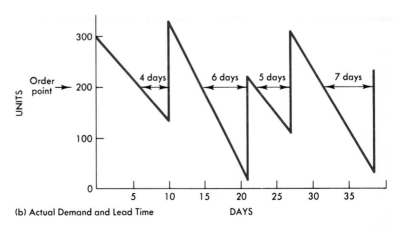

(b) Actual Demand and Lead Time

253

The bottom panel of the figure shows the actual experience for our hypothetical firm. In the first segment of demand, we see that actual usage is somewhat less than expected. (The slope of the line is less than the expected demand line in the upper panel.) At the order point of 200 units of inventory held, an order is placed for 200 units of additional inventory. Instead of taking the expected 5 days for the inventory to be replenished, we see that it takes only 4 days. The second segment of usage is much greater than expected, and, as a result, inventory is rapidly used up. At 200 units of remaining inventory, a 200-unit order again is placed, but here it takes 6 days for the inventory to be received. As a result of both of these factors, heavy inroads are made into the safety stock.

In the third segment of demand, usage is about the same as expected; that is, the slopes of expected and actual usage lines are about the same. Because inventory was so low at the end of the previous segment of usage, an order is placed almost immediately. The lead time turns out to be 5 days. In the last segment of demand, usage is slightly greater than expected. The lead time necessary to receive the order is 7 days, much longer than expected. The combination of these two factors again causes the firm to go into its safety stock. The example illustrates the importance of safety stock in absorbing random fluctuations in usage and in lead times. Without such stock, the firm would have run out of inventory on two occasions.

The Amount of Safety Stock

The proper amount of safety stock to maintain depends on several things. The greater the uncertainty associated with forecasted demand for inventory, the greater the safety stock the firm will wish to carry, all other things being the same. Put another way, the risk of running out of stock is greater, the larger the unforeseen fluctuations in usage. Similarly, the greater the uncertainty of lead time to replenish stock, the greater the risk of running out of stock, and the more safety stock the firm will wish to maintain, all other things being equal. Another factor influencing the safety stock decision is the cost of running out of inventory. The cost of being out of raw materials and in-transit inventories is a delay in production. How much does it cost when production closes down temporarily? Where fixed costs are large, this cost will be quite high, as can be imagined in the case of an aluminum extrusion plant. The cost of running out of finished goods is customer dissatisfaction. Not only will the immediate sale be lost, but future sales will be endangered if customers take their business elsewhere. Although this opportunity cost is difficult to measure, it must be recognized by management and incorporated into the safety stock decision. The greater the costs of running out of stock, of course, the greater the safety stock management will wish to maintain, all other things staying the same.

The final factor is the cost of carrying additional inventory. If it were not for this cost, a firm could maintain whatever safety stock was necessary to avoid all possibility of running out of inventory. The greater the cost of carrying inventory, the more costly it is to maintain a safety stock, all other things being equal.

Determination of the proper amount of safety stock involves balancing the probability and cost of a stockout against the cost of carrying enough safety stock to avoid this possibility. Ultimately, the question reduces to the probability of inventory stockout that management is willing to tolerate. In a typical situation, this probability is reduced at a decreasing rate as more safety stock is added. A firm may be able to reduce the probability of inventory stockout by 20 percent if it adds 100 units of safety stock, but only by an additional 10 percent if it adds another 100 units. There comes a point when it becomes very expensive to reduce further the probability of stockout. Management will not wish to add safety stock beyond the point at which incremental carrying costs exceed the incremental benefits to be derived from avoiding a stockout.

In recent years, the management of inventory has become very sophisticated. In certain industries, the production process lends itself to "just in time" inventory control. As the name implies, the idea is that inventories are acquired and inserted in production at the exact times they are needed. This requires a very accurate production and inventory information system, highly efficient purchasing, very reliable suppliers, and an efficient inventory-handling system. While raw materials inventory and in-transit inventory never can be reduced to zero, the notion of "just in time" is one of extremely tight control so as to minimize inventories. How close a company comes to the ideal depends on the type of production process and the nature of supplier industries, but it is a worthy objective for most companies.

Relation to Financial Management

Although inventory management usually is not the direct operating responsibility of the financial manager, the investment of funds in inventory is a very important aspect of financial management. Consequently, the financial manager must be familiar with ways to control inventories effectively so that capital may be allocated efficiently. The greater the opportunity cost of funds invested in inventory, the lower the optimal level of average inventory and the lower the optimal order quantity, all other things held constant. This statement can be verified by increasing the carrying costs, C, in Eq. (10-3). The EOQ model also can be used by the financial manager in planning for inventory financing.

When demand or usage of inventory is uncertain, the financial manager may try to effect policies that will reduce the average lead time required to receive inventory once an order is placed. The lower the average lead time, the lower the safety stock needed and the lower the total investment in inventory, all other things held constant. The greater the opportunity cost of funds invested in inventory, the greater the incentive to reduce this lead time. The purchasing department may try to find new vendors that promise quicker delivery, or it may pressure existing vendors to deliver faster. The production department may be able to deliver finished goods faster by producing a smaller run. In either case, there is a trade-off between the added cost involved in reducing the lead time and the opportunity cost of funds tied up in inventory. This discussion serves to point out the value of inventory management to the financial manager.

SUMMARY

Credit and collection policies encompass the quality of accounts accepted, the credit period extended, the cash discount given, and the level of collection expenditures. In each case, the credit decision involves a trade-off between the additional profitability and the cost resulting from a change in any of these elements. By liberalizing the quality requirements for accounts, the firm might hope to make more on the additional sales than it spends to carry the additional receivables plus the additional bad-debt losses. To maximize profits arising from credit and collection policies, the firm should vary these policies jointly until an optimal solution is obtained. The firm's credit and collection policies, together with its credit and collection procedures, determine the magnitude and quality of its receivable position.

In evaluating a credit applicant, the credit analyst obtains financial and other information about the applicant, analyzes this information, and reaches a credit decision. If the account is new, the firm must decide whether or not to accept the order. With repeat orders, the firm must usually decide on the maximum credit to extend. This maximum, known as a line of credit, is based on the creditworthiness of the applicant.

The optimal level of inventories should be judged in relation to the flexibility inventories afford. If we hold constant the efficiency of inventory management, the lower the level of inventories, the less the flexibility of the firm. The higher the amount of inventories, the greater the flexibility of the firm. The higher the amount of inventories, the greater the flexibility of the firm. In evaluating the level of inventories, management must balance the benefits of economies of production, purchasing, and increased product demand against the cost of carrying the additional inventory. Of particular concern to the financial manager is the cost of funds invested in inventory.

In this chapter we examined several tools of inventory control. One is the economic order quantity, whereby we determine the optimal size of order to place on the basis of the demand or usage of the inventory, the ordering costs, and the carrying costs. Under conditions of uncertainty, the firm must usually provide for a safety stock, owing to fluctuations in demand for inventory and in lead times. By varying the point at which orders are placed, one varies the safety stock that is held.

QUESTIONS

1. Is it always good policy to reduce the firm's bad-debt losses by "getting rid of the deadbeats"?
2. What are the probable effects on sales and profits of each of the following credit policies?
   a. A high percentage of bad-debt loss but normal receivable turnover and rejection rate
   b. A high percentage of past-due accounts and a low credit rejection rate

c. A low percentage of past-due accounts but high receivable rejection and turnover rates

d. A low percentage of past-due accounts and a low rejection rate but a high turnover rate

3. Is an increase in the collection period necessarily bad? Explain.

4. What are the various sources of information you might use to analyze a credit applicant?

5. What are the principal factors than can be varied in setting credit policy?

6. If credit standards for the quality of account accepted are changed, what things are affected?

7. Why is a saturation point reached in spending money on collections?

8. What is the purpose of establishing a line of credit for an account? What are the benefits of this arrangement?

9. The analysis of inventory policy is analogous to the analysis of credit policy. Propose a measure to analyze inventory policy that is analogous to aging of accounts receivable.

10. What are the principal implications to the financial manager of ordering costs, storage costs, and cost of capital as they relate to inventory?

11. Explain how efficient inventory management affects the liquidity and profitability of the firm.

12. How can the firm reduce its investment in inventories? What costs might the firm incur from a policy of very low inventory investment?

13. Explain how a large seasonal demand complicates inventory management and production scheduling.

14. Do inventories represent an investment in the same sense as fixed assets?

15. Should the required rate of return for investment in inventories of raw materials be the same as that for finished goods?

SELF-CORRECTION PROBLEMS

1. Durham-Feltz Corporation presently gives terms of net 30 days. It has $60 million in sales, and its average collection period is 45 days. To stimulate demand, the company may give terms of net 60 days. If it does instigate these terms, sales are expected to increase by 15 percent. After the change, the average collection period is expected to be 75 days, with no difference in payment habits between old and new customers. Variable costs are $.80 for every $1.00 of sales, and the company's required rate of return on investment in receivables is 20 percent. Should the company extend its credit period? (Assume a 360-day year.)

2. Matlock Gauge Company makes wind and current gauges for pleasure boats. The gauges are sold throughout the Southeast to boat dealers, and the average order size is $50. The company sells to all registered dealers without a credit analysis. Terms are net 45 days, and the average collection pe-

riod is 60 days, which is regarded as satisfactory. Jane Sullivan, vice-president of finance, is now uneasy about the increasing number of bad-debt losses on new orders. With credit ratings from local and regional credit agencies, she feels she would be able to classify new orders into one of three risk categories. Past experience shows the following:

	ORDER CATEGORY		
	---	---	---
	Low Risk	Medium Risk	High Risk
Bad-debt loss (percent)	3%	7%	24%
Percent of category orders to total orders	30%	50%	20%

The cost of producing and shipping the gauges and of carrying the receivables is 78 percent of sales. The cost of obtaining credit rating information and of evaluating it is $4 per order. Surprisingly, there does not appear to be any association between the risk category and the collection period; the average for each of the three risk categories is around 60 days. Based on this information, should the company obtain credit information on new orders instead of selling to all new accounts without credit analysis?

3. Vostick Filter Company is a distributor of air filters to retail stores. It buys its filters from several manufacturers. Filters are ordered in lot sizes of 1,000, and each order costs $40 to place. Demand from retail stores is 20,000 filters per month, and carrying cost is $.10 a filter per month.

   a. What is the optimal order quantity with respect to so many lot sizes?
   b. What would be the optimal order quantity if the carrying cost were $.05 a filter per month?
   c. What would be the optimal order quantity if ordering costs were $10?

4. To reduce production start-up costs, Bodden Truck Company may manufacture longer runs of the same truck. Estimated savings from the increase in efficiency are $260,000 per year. However, inventory turnover will decrease from eight times a year to six times a year. Costs of goods sold are $48 million on an annual basis. If the required rate of return on investment in inventories is 15 percent, should the company instigate the new production plan?

PROBLEMS

1. To increase sales from their present annual $24 million, Jefferson Knu Monroe Company, a wholesaler, may try more liberal credit standards. Currently, the firm has an average collection period of 30 days. It believes that with increasingly liberal credit standards, the following will result:

Credit policy	A	B	C	D
Increase in sales from previous level (in millions)	$2.8	$1.8	$1.2	$.6
Average collection period for incremental sales (days)	45	60	90	144

The prices of its products average $20 per unit, and variable costs average $18 per unit. No bad-debt losses are expected. If the company has a pretax opportunity cost of funds of 30 percent, which credit policy should be pursued? (Assume a 360-day year.)

2. Upon reflection, Jefferson Knu Monroe Company has estimated that the following pattern of bad-debt losses will prevail if it initiates more liberal credit terms:

Credit polity	A	B	C	D
Bad-debt losses on incremental sales	3%	6%	10%	15%

Given the other assumptions in Problem 1, which credit policy should be pursued?

3. Recalculate Problem 2, assuming the following pattern of bad-debt losses:

Credit policy	A	B	C	D
Bad-debt losses on incremental sales	1.5%	3.0%	5.0%	7.5%

Which policy now would be best?

4. The Chickee Corporation has a 12 percent opportunity cost of funds and currently sells on terms of n/10, EOM. (This means that goods shipped before the end of the month must be paid for by the tenth of the following month.) The firm has sales of $10 million a year, which are 80 percent on credit and spread evenly over the year. The average collection period is currently 60 days. If Chickee offered terms of 2/10, net 30, 60 percent of its credit customers would take the discount, and the average collection period would be reduced to 40 days. Should Chickee change its terms from net/10, EOM to 2/10, net 30?

5. Porras Pottery Products, Inc., spends $220,000 per annum on its collection department. The company has $12 million in credit sales, its average collection period is $2\frac{1}{2}$ months, and the percentage of bad-debt losses is 4 percent. The company believes that if it were to double its collection personnel, it could bring down the average collection to 2 months and bad-debt losses to 3 percent. The added cost is $180,000, bringing total expenditures

to $400,000 annually. Is the increased effort worthwhile if the opportunity cost of funds is 20 percent? If it is 10 percent?

6. The Pottsville Manufacturing Corporation is considering extending trade credit to the San Jose Company. Examination of the records of San Jose has produced the following financial statements:

San Jose Company balance sheet (in millions)

ASSETS	19×1	19×2	19×3
Current assets	$ 1.5	$ 1.6	$ 1.6
Cash	1.3	1.8	2.5
Receivables	1.3	2.6	4.0
Inventories (at lower of cost or market)	.4	.5	.4
Total current assets	$ 4.5	$ 6.5	$ 8.5
Fixed assets			
Buildings (net)	2.0	1.9	1.8
Machinery and equipment (net)	7.0	6.5	6.0
Total fixed assets	$ 9.0	$ 8.4	$ 7.8
Other assets	1.0	.8	.6
Total assets	$14.5	$15.7	$16.9

LIABILITIES	19×1	19×2	19×3
Current liabilities			
Notes payable ($8\frac{1}{2}$%)	$ 2.1	$ 3.1	$ 3.8
Trade payables	.2	.4	.9
Other payables	.2	.2	.2
Total	$ 2.5	$ 3.7	$ 4.9
Term loan ($8\frac{1}{2}$%)	4.0	3.0	2.0
Total	$ 6.5	$ 6.7	$ 6.9
Net worth			
Common stock	$ 5.0	$ 5.0	$ 5.0
Preferred stock ($6\frac{1}{2}$%)	1.0	1.0	1.0
Retained earnings	2.0	3.0	4.0
Total liabilities and net worth	$14.5	$15.7	$16.9

San Jose Company income statement (in millions)

	19×1	19×2	19×3
Net credit sales	$15.0	$15.8	$16.2
Cost of goods sold	11.3	12.1	13.0
Gross profit	$ 3.7	$ 3.7	$ 3.2
Operating expenses	1.1	1.2	1.0
Net profit before taxes	$ 2.6	$ 2.5	$ 2.0
Tax	1.3	1.2	1.0
Profit after taxes	$ 1.3	$ 1.3	$ 1.0
Dividends	.3	.3	.0
	$ 1.0	$ 1.0	$ 1.0

The San Jose Company has a Dun & Bradstreet rating of 4A-2. Inquiries into its banking disclosed balances generally in the low millions. Five suppliers to San Jose revealed that the firm takes its discounts from the three creditors offering of 2/10, net 30 terms, though it is about 15 days slow in paying the two firms offering terms of net 30.

Analyze the San Jose Company's application for credit.

7. A college bookstore is attempting to determine the optimal order quantity for a popular book on psychology. The store sells 5,000 copies of this book a year at a retail price of $12.50, and the cost to the store is 20 percent less, which represents the discount from the publisher. The store figures that it costs $1 per year to carry a book in inventory and $100 to prepare an order for new books.

  a. Determine the total costs associated with ordering 1, 2, 5, 10, and 20 times a year.

  b. Determine the economic order quantity.

  c. What implicit assumptions are being made about the annual sales rate?

8. The Hedge Corporation manufactures only one product: planks. The single raw material used in making planks is the dint. For each plank manufactured, 12 dints are required. Assume that the company manufactures 150,000 planks per year, that demand for planks is perfectly steady throughout the year, that it costs $200 each time dints are ordered, and that carrying costs are $8 per dint per year.

  a. Determine the economic order quantity of dints.

  b. What are total inventory costs for Hedge (carrying costs plus ordering costs)?

  c. How many times per year would inventory be ordered?

9. A firm that sells 5,000 gidgets per month is trying to determine how many gidgets to keep in inventory. The financial manager has determined that it costs $200 to place an order. The cost of holding inventory is 4¢ per month per average gidget in inventory. A 5-day lead time is required for delivery of goods ordered. (This lead time is known with certainty.)

  a. Develop the algebraic expression for determining the total cost of holding and ordering inventory.

  b. Plot the holding cost and the ordering cost on a graph where the abscissa represents size of order and the ordinate represents costs.

  c. Determine the EOQ from the graph.

10. Fouchee Scents, Inc., makes various scents for use in the manufacture of food products. Although the company does maintain a safety stock, it has a policy of "lean" inventories, with the result that customers sometimes must be turned away. In an analysis of the situation, the company has estimated the cost of being out of stock associated with various levels of safety stock:

	LEVEL OF SAFETY STOCK (IN GALLONS)	ANNUAL COST OF STOCKOUTS
Present safety stock level	5,000	$26,000
New safety stock level 1	7,500	14,000
New safety stock level 2	10,000	7,000
New safety stock level 3	12,500	3,000
New safety stock level 4	15,000	1,000
New safety stock level 5	17,500	0

Carrying costs are $.65 per gallon per year. What is the best level of safety stock for the company?

SOLUTIONS TO SELF-CORRECTION PROBLEMS

1. Receivables turnover = 360/75 = 4.8 times
   Profitability of additional sales = $9,000,000 × .2
   $$= \$1,800,000$$
   Additional receivables associated with the new sales
   $$= \$9,000,000/4.8$$
   $$= \$1,875,000$$
   Additional investment in receivables associated with the new sales
   $$= \$1,875,000 \times .8$$
   $$= \$1,500,000$$
   New level of receivables associated with the original sales
   $$= \$60,000,000/4.8$$
   $$= \$12,500,000$$
   Old level of receivables associated with the original sales
   $$= \$60,000,000/8$$
   $$= \$7,500,000$$
   Incremental receivable investment, original sales
   $$= \$5,000,000$$
   Total increase in receivable investment
   $$= \$1,500,000 + \$5,000,000 = \$6,500,000$$
   Carrying cost of additional investment = .20 × $6.5 million
   $$= \$1,300,000$$
   As the incremental carrying cost is less than the incremental profitability, the company should lengthen its credit period from 30 to 60 days.

2. As the bad-debt loss ratio for the high-risk category exceeds the profit margin of 22 percent, it would be desirable to reject orders from this risk class if such orders could be identified. However, the cost of credit information, as a percentage of the average order, is $4/$50 = 8%, and this cost is appli-

cable to all new orders. As the high-risk category is one-fifth of sales, the comparison would be 5 × 8% = 40% relative to the bad-debt loss of 24%. Therefore, the company should not undertake credit analysis of new orders.

An example can better illustrate the solution. Suppose that new orders were $100,000. The following would then hold:

| | ORDER CATEGORY | | |
	Low Risk	Medium Risk	High Risk
Total orders	$30,000	$50,000	$20,000
Bad-debt loss	900	3,500	4,800

Number of orders = $100,000/$50 = 2,000
Credit analysis cost = 2,000 × $4 = $8,000
To save $4,800 in bad-debt losses by identifying the high-risk category of new orders, the company must spend $8,000. Therefore, it should not undertake the credit analysis of new orders. This is a case where the size of order is too small to justify credit analysis. After a new order is accepted, the company will gain experience and can reject subsequent orders if its experience is bad.

3. a. $Q^* = \sqrt{\dfrac{2(20)(40)}{100}} = 4$

Carrying costs = $.10 × 1,000 = $100
The optimal order size would be 4,000 filters, which represents five orders a month.

b. $Q^* = \sqrt{\dfrac{2(20)(40)}{50}} = 5.66$

Since the lot size is 1,000 filters, the company would order 6,000 filters each time. The lower the carrying cost, the more important ordering costs become relatively, and the larger the optimal order size.

c. $Q^* = \sqrt{\dfrac{2(20)(10)}{100}} = 2$

The lower the order cost, the more important carrying costs become relatively and the smaller the optimal order size.

4. Inventories after change = $48 million/6 = $8 million
    Present inventories = $48 million/8 = $6 million
    Additional inventories = $2 million
Opportunity cost = $2 million × .15 = $300,000
The opportunity cost is greater than the savings. Therefore, the new production plan should not be undertaken.

SELECTED REFERENCES

BARZMAN, SOL, *Everyday Credit Checking: A Practical Guide*, rev. ed. New York: National Association of Credit Management, 1980.

BRICK, IVAN E., and WILLIAM K. H. FUNG, "The Effect of Taxes on the Trade Credit Decision," *Financial Management*, 13 (Summer 1984), 24–30.

DYL, EDWARD A., "Another Look at the Evaluation of Investment in Acounts Receivable," *Financial Management*, 6 (Winter 1977), 67–70.

HALLOREN, JOHN A., and HOWARD P. LANSER, "The Credit Policy Decision in an Inflationary Environment," *Financial Management*, 10 (Winter 1981), 31–38.

HILL, NED C., and KENNETH D. RIENER, "Determining the Cash Discount in the Firm's Credit Policy," *Financial Management*, 8 (Spring 1979), 68–73.

LEWELLEN, W. G., and R. O. EDMISTER, "A General Model for Accounts Receivable Analysis and Control," *Journal of Financial and Quantitative Analysis*, 8 (March 1973), 195–206.

MAGEE, JOHN F., "Guides to Inventory Policy," I–III, *Harvard Business Review*, 34 (January–February 1956), 49–60; (March–April 1956), 103–16; and (May–June 1956), 57–70.

MEHTA, DILEEP, "The Formulation of Credit Policy Models," *Management Science*, 15 (October 1968), 30–50.

OH, JOHN S., "Opportunity Cost in the Evaluation of Investment in Accounts Receivable," *Financial Management*, 5 (Summer 1976), 32–36.

SACHDEVA, KANWAL S., "Accounts Receivable Decisions in a Capital Budgeting Framework," *Financial Management*, 10 (Winter 1981), 45–49.

SATORIS, WILLIAM L., and NED C. HILL, "A Generalized Cash Flow Approach to Short-Term Financial Decisions," *Journal of Finance*, 38 (May 1983), 349–60.

SNYDER, ARTHUR, "Principles of Inventory Management," *Financial Executive*, 32 (April 1964), 16–19.

TIERNAN, FRANK M., and DENNIS A. TANNER, "How Economic Order Quantity Controls Inventory Expense," *Financial Executive*, 51 (July 1983), 46–52.

WESTON, J. FRED, and PHAM D. TUAN, "Comment on Analysis of Credit Policy Changes," *Financial Management*, 9 (Winter 1980), 59–63.

CHAPTER 11

Spontaneous Financing

Short-term financing can be categorized according to whether or not the source is spontaneous. Accounts payable and accruals are classified as spontaneous because their magnitude is primarily a function of a company's level of operations. As operations expand, these liabilities typically increase and finance in part the buildup in assets. While both accounts payable and accruals behave in this manner, there still remains a degree of discretion on the part of a company as to their exact magnitude. In this chapter we consider these two methods of financing and how such discretion might be used. In the next chapter we examine the other major sources of short-term financing—money market credit and short-term loans, the latter being either from banks or finance companies. Unlike the sources discussed in this chapter, such financing is not spontaneous or automatic. It must be arranged on a formal basis.

TRADE CREDIT FINANCING

Trade debt. Monies owed to suppliers. Accounts payable.

Trade debt is a form of short-term financing common to almost all businesses. In fact, it is the largest source of short-term funds for business firms collectively. In an advanced economy, most buyers are not required to pay for goods upon delivery but are allowed a short deferment period before payment is due. During this period the seller of the goods extends credit to the buyer. Because suppliers generally are more liberal in the extension of credit than are financial institutions, small companies in particular rely on trade credit.

Of the three types of trade credit—open account, notes payable, and trade acceptances—by far the most common type is the open-account arrangement. The seller ships goods to the buyer and sends an invoice that specifies the goods shipped, the price, the total amount due, and the terms of the sale. Open-account credit derives its name from the fact that the buyer does not sign a formal debt instrument evidencing the amount owed the seller. The seller extends credit based on a credit investigation of the buyer (see Chapter 10).

In some situations promissory notes are employed instead of open-account credit. The buyer signs a note that evidences a debt to the seller. The note itself calls for the payment of the obligation at some specified future date. This arrangement is employed when the seller wants the buyer to recognize the debt formally. For example, a seller might request a promissory note from a buyer if the buyer's open account became past due.

A trade acceptance is another arrangement by which the indebtedness of the buyer is formally recognized. Under this arrangement, the seller draws a draft on the buyer, ordering the buyer to pay the draft at some date in the future. The seller will not release the goods until the buyer accepts the time draft.[1] Accepting the draft, the buyer designates a bank at which the draft will be paid when it comes due. At that time, the draft becomes a trade acceptance, and depending on the creditworthiness of the buyer, it may possess some degree of marketability. If the trade acceptance is marketable, the seller of the goods can

---

[1] If the instrument is a sight draft, the buyer is ordered to pay the draft upon presentation. Under this arrangement, trade credit is not extended.

sell it at a discount and receive immediate payment for the goods. At final maturity, the holder of the acceptance presents it to the designated bank for collection.

Terms of Sale

Because the use of promissory notes and trade acceptances is rather limited, the subsequent discussion will be confined to open-account trade credit. The terms of sale make a great deal of difference in this type of credit. These terms, specified in the invoice, may be placed in several broad categories according to the net period within which payment is expected and according to the terms of the cash discount.

COD and CBD—No Extension of Credit. COD terms mean *cash on delivery* of the goods. The only risk the seller undertakes is that the buyer may refuse the shipment. Under such circumstances, the seller will be stuck with the shipping costs. Occasionally a seller might ask for cash before delivery (CBD) to avoid all risk. Under either COD or CBD terms, the seller does not extend credit. CBD terms must be distinguished from progress payments, which are very common in certain industries. With progress payments, the buyer pays the manufacturer at various stages of production before the actual delivery of the finished product. Because large sums of money are tied up in work in progress, aircraft manufacturers request progress payments from airlines in advance of the actual delivery of aircraft.

Net Period—No Cash Discount. When credit is extended, the seller specifies the period of time allowed for payment. The terms "net 30" indicate that the invoice or bill must be paid within 30 days. If the seller bills on a monthly basis, it might require such terms as "net 15 EOM," which means that all goods shipped before the end of the month must be paid for by the fifteenth of the following month.

Net Period with Cash Discount. In addition to extending credit, the seller may offer a cash discount if the bill is paid during the early part of the net period. The terms "2/10, net 30" indicate that the seller offers a 2 percent discount if the bill is paid within 10 days; otherwise, the buyer must pay the full amount within 30 days. Usually, a cash discount is offered as an incentive to the buyer to pay early. In Chapter 10, we discussed the optimal cash discount the seller might offer. A cash discount differs from a trade discount and from a quantity discount. A trade discount is greater for one class of customers (e.g., wholesalers) than for others (e.g., retailers). A quantity discount is offered on large shipments.

Datings. In a seasonal business, sellers frequently use datings to encourage customers to place their orders before a heavy selling period. A manufacturer of lawn mowers may give **seasonal datings** specifying that any shipment to a dealer in the winter or spring does not have to be paid for until summer. Earlier orders benefit the seller, who can gauge the demand more realistically

Seasonal dating. The extension of credit with the period geared to the customer's selling season.

and schedule production more efficiently. Also, the seller does not have to store finished goods inventory. The buyer has the advantage of not having to pay for the goods until the height of the selling period. Under this arrangement, credit is extended for a longer than normal period of time.

Trade Credit as a Means of Financing

We have seen that trade credit is a source of funds because the buyer does not have to pay for goods until after they are delivered. If the firm automatically pays its bills a certain number of days after the date of invoice, trade credit becomes a built-in source of financing that varies with the production cycle. As the firm increases its production and corresponding purchases, accounts payable increase and provide part of the funds needed to finance the increase in production. As production decreases, accounts payable tend to decrease. Under these circumstances, trade credit is not a discretionary source of financing. It is entirely dependent on the purchasing plans of the firm, which, in turn, are dependent on its production cycle. In examining trade credit as a discretionary form of financing, we want to specifically consider situations in which (1) a firm does not take a cash discount but pays on the last day of the net period and (2) a firm pays its bills beyond the net period.

Payment on the Final Due Date

In this section we assume that the firm forgoes a cash discount but does pay its bill on the final due date of the net period. If no cash discount is offered, there is no cost for the use of credit during the net period. By the same token, if a firm takes the discount, there is no cost for the use of trade credit during the discount period. If a cash discount is offered but not taken, however, there is a definite opportunity cost. If the terms of sale are 2/10, net 30, the firm has the use of funds for an additional 20 days if it does not take the cash discount but pays on the final day of the net period. For a $100 invoice, it would have the use of $98 for 20 days. The approximate annual interest cost is[2]

$$\frac{2}{98} \times \frac{360}{20} = 36.7\%$$

Thus, we see that trade credit can be a very expensive form of short-term financing when a cash discount is offered.

The cost of trade credit declines as the net period becomes longer in relation to the discount period. Had the terms in our example been 2/10, net 60, the annual interest cost would have been

$$\frac{2}{98} \times \frac{360}{50} = 14.7\%$$

---

[2] For ease of calculation, 360 rather than 365 is used as the number of days in the year. The simple formula presented does not take account of compound interest.

The relationship between the annual interest cost of trade credit and the number of days between the end of the discount period and the end of the net period is shown in Fig. 11-1. We assume 2/10 discount terms. We see that the cost of trade credit decreases at a decreasing rate as the net period increases. The point is that if a firm does not take a cash discount, its cost of trade credit declines with the length of time it is able to postpone payment.

Stretching Accounts Payable

In the preceding section we assumed that payment was made at the end of the due period; however, a firm may postpone payment beyond this period. We shall call this postponement "stretching" accounts payable or "leaning on the trade." The cost of stretching accounts payable is twofold: the cost of the cash discount forgone and the possible deterioration in credit rating. In Chapter 10 we discussed the rating system of credit agencies such as Dun & Bradstreet. If a firm stretches its payables excessively, so that trade payables are significantly delinquent, its credit rating will suffer. Suppliers will view the firm with apprehension and may insist on rather strict terms of sale if, indeed, they sell at all. In assessing a company, banks and other lenders do not favorably regard excessive slowness. Although it is difficult to measure, there is certainly an opportunity cost to a deterioration in a firm's credit reputation.

FIGURE 11-1
Annual rate of interest on accounts payable with terms of 2/10

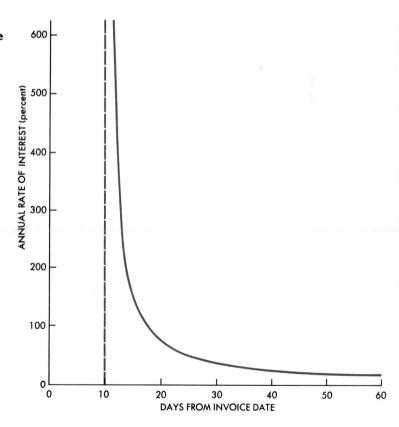

Notwithstanding the possibility of a deteriorating credit rating, it may be possible to postpone certain payables beyond the net period without severe consequences. Suppliers are in business to sell goods, and trade credit may increase sales. A supplier may be willing to go along with stretching payables, particularly if the risk of bad-debt loss is negligible. If the funds requirement of the firm is seasonal, suppliers may not view the stretching of payables in an unfavorable light during periods of peak requirements, provided that the firm is current in the trade during the rest of the year. There may be an indirect charge for this extension of credit, in the form of higher prices, a possibility that the firm should carefully consider in evaluating the cost of stretching accounts payable.

Periodic and reasonable stretching of payables is not necessarily bad, per se. It should be evaluated objectively in relation to its cost and in relation to alternative sources of short-term credit. When a firm does stretch its payables, effort should be made to keep suppliers fully informed of its situation. A large number of suppliers will allow a firm to stretch payables if the firm is honest with the supplier and consistent in its payments. Sometimes a firm with seasonal funds requirements is able to obtain a dating from a supplier. When a firm obtains a dating, it does not stretch its payables; as long as it pays the bill by the final date, no deterioration in its credit rating is likely.

Advantages of Trade Credit

The firm must balance the advantages of trade credit against the cost of forgoing a cash discount, the opportunity cost associated with a possible deterioration in credit reputation if it stretches its payables, and the possible increase in selling price the seller imposes on the buyer. There are several advantages of trade credit as a form of short-term financing. Probably the major advantage is its ready availability. The accounts payable of most firms represent a continuous form of credit. There is no need to arrange financing formally; it is already there. If the firm is now taking cash discounts, additional credit is readily available by not paying existing accounts payable until the end of the net period. There is no need to negotiate with the supplier; the decision is entirely up to the firm. In stretching accounts payable, the firm will find it necessary, after a certain degree of postponement, to negotiate with the supplier.

In most other types of short-term financing, it is necessary to negotiate formally with the lender over the terms of loan. The lender may impose restrictions on the firm and seek a secured position. Restrictions are possible with trade credit, but they are not nearly as likely. With other sources of short-term financing, there may be a lead time between the time the need for funds is recognized and the time the firm is able to borrow them. Trade credit is a more flexible means of financing. The firm does not have to sign a note, pledge collateral, or adhere to a strict payment schedule on the note. A supplier views an occasional delinquent payment with a far less critical eye than does a banker or other lender.

The advantages of using trade credit must be weighed against the cost. As we have seen, the cost may be very high when all factors are considered. Many firms utilize other sources of short-term financing in order to be able to take advantage of cash discounts. The savings in cost over other forms of short-term financing, however, must offset the loss of flexibility and convenience associated with trade credit. For certain firms, there are no alternative sources of short-term credit.

Who Bears the Cost?

We should recognize that trade credit involves a cost for the use of funds over time. In the previous sections, it was implied that there is no explicit cost to trade credit if the buyer pays the invoice during the discount period or, if no cash discount is given, during the net period. Although this supposition is valid from the standpoint of marginal analysis, it overlooks the fact that somebody must bear the cost of trade credit, for the use of funds over time is not free. The burden may fall on the supplier, the buyer, or both parties. The supplier may be able to pass the cost on to the buyer in the form of higher prices.

The supplier of a product for which demand is elastic may be reluctant to increase prices and may end up absorbing most of the cost of trade credit. Under other circumstances the supplier is able to pass the cost on to the buyer. The buyer should determine who is bearing the cost of trade credit. A buyer who is bearing the cost may shop around for a better deal. The buyer should recognize that the cost of trade credit changes over time. In periods of rising interest rates and tight money, suppliers may raise the price of their products to take account of the rising cost of carrying receivables. This rise in price should not be confused with other rises caused by changing supply and demand conditions in the product markets.

ACCRUAL ACCOUNTS

Perhaps even more than accounts payable, **accrual** accounts represent a spontaneous source of financing. The most common accrual accounts are for wages and taxes. For both accounts, the expense is incurred or accrued but not paid. Usually a date is specified when the accrual must be paid. Income taxes are paid quarterly; property taxes are paid semiannually. Wages typically are paid weekly, every other week, bimonthly, or monthly. Like accounts payable, accruals tend to expand with the scope of the operation. As sales increase, labor costs usually increase, and with them, accrued wages increase. As profits increase, accrued taxes increase.

In a sense, accruals represent costless financing. Services are rendered for wages, but employees are not paid and do not expect to be paid until the end or after the end of the pay period. The lapse is established by the company, although unions and competing employers in the labor market influence its length. Similarly, taxes are not expected to be paid until their due date. Thus, accruals represent an interest-free source of financing.

Unfortunately for the company, they do not represent discretionary financing. For taxes, the government is the creditor, and it likes to be paid on

Accruals. Amounts owed but not yet paid for wages, taxes, interest, and dividends. A short-term liability.

time. A company in extreme financial difficulty can postpone a tax payment for a short while but there is a penalty charge. It may also postpone payment of wages—at the expense of employees and morale. Employees may respond with absenteeism or reduced efficiency or seek employment elsewhere. A company must be extremely careful in postponing wages. It must fully inform employees and set a firm date for payment. Such a measure is one of last resort; nevertheless, many a company on the precipice of cash-flow disaster finds itself having to postpone wages as well as all other payments.

Accrued wages are partially discretionary in that a company can change the frequency of wage payments and thereby affect the amount of financing. If the interval of time between the last working day of a pay period and payday stays the same, the less frequent the paydays, the more the financing. Suppose that a company had a weekly payroll of $400,000 with an average amount accrued of $200,000. If the company were to increase its pay period from 1 week to 2 weeks, the payroll at the end of the period would be $800,000. The average amount of accrued wages now would be $400,000 ($800,000 divided by 2). Therefore, the company increases its interest-free financing by $200,000.

The longer the pay period, the greater the amount of accrued wage financing. This linear relationship is illustrated in Fig. 11-2 for $1 in weekly wages. (For a specific situation, we must multiply the amount of accrual shown on the vertical axis by the actual weekly payroll to determine the average amount accrued.) Obviously, it would be desirable from the standpoint of a company to have as long a pay period as possible, but union pressures and competition for labor from other employers limit the feasible range of options. Moreover, an increase in the pay period is usually "one-shot" in that it is not possible to repeat

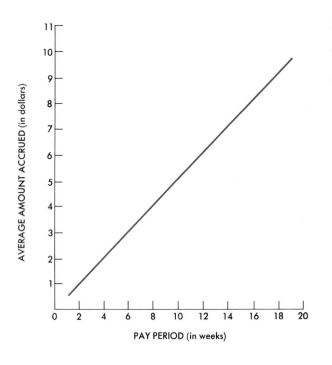

FIGURE 11-2
Relationship between average wages accrued and the length of the pay period for wages of $1 per week

with a subsequent increase. In most companies, the maximum pay period is no more than 1 month. In summary, then, accruals are a discretionary source of financing only within a very narrow range.

SUMMARY

Trade credit can be a significant source of short-term financing for the firm. It is a discretionary source of financing only if a firm does not have a strict policy regarding its promptness in paying bills. When a cash discount is offered but not taken, the cost of trade credit is the cash discount forgone. The longer the period between the end of the discount period and the time the bill is paid, the less the opportunity cost. "Stretching" accounts payable involves postponement of payment beyond the due period. The opportunity cost of stretching payables is the possible deterioration in the firm's credit rating. The firm must balance the costs of trade credit against its advantages and the costs of other short-term credit. The major advantage of trade credit is the flexibility it gives the firm.

Like accounts payable, accruals represent a spontaneous source of financing, albeit offering the firm even less discretion than it has with trade credit financing. The principal accrual items are wages and taxes, and both are expected to be paid on established dates. In the interim, interest-free financing is available to the company, and for an ongoing company, this financing is continuous. A company can increase the amount of its accrued wages by lessening the frequency of paydays within a narrow range. A company in dire financial straits will sometimes postpone tax and wage payments, but the consequences of such postponement can be severe.

QUESTIONS

1. Explain why trade credit is a "spontaneous source of funds."
2. Trade credit is a very costly source of funds when discounts are lost. Explain why many firms rely on this source of funds to finance their temporary working capital.
3. Stretching payables provides "free" funds to the customers for a short period. The supplier, however, can face serious financial problems if all of its customers stretch their accounts. Discuss the nature of the problems the supplier may face and suggest different approaches to cope with stretching.
4. Explain the difference between COD terms and a seasonal dating. Do they represent the extremes with respect to credit terms?
5. Suppose that a firm elected to tighten its trade credit policy from 2/10, net 90 to 2/10, net 30. What effect could the firm expect this change to have on its liquidity?
6. Why do small firms in particular rely heavily on trade credit as a source of funds? Why will suppliers advance credit to firms when banks will not?

7. In what ways can accruals be varied to obtain more interest-free financing?
8. Why is the U.S. government an involuntary creditor with respect to accrued taxes?
9. Why are accruals a more spontaneous source of financing than trade credit?
10. What is to prevent a company from postponing payment on its accruals?
11. If a company has seasonal funds requirements, would you recommend that it increase its pay period to, say, 1 month when it needs funds and to shorten it to, say, 1 week when it has surplus funds?

SELF-CORRECTION PROBLEMS

1. Determine the effective annual cost of capital for the following terms, assuming that discounts are not taken and a year has 360 days.

    a. 1/10, n/30   e. 3/10, n/60
    b. 2/10, n/30   f. 2/10, n/90
    c. 3/10, n/30   g. 3/10, n/90
    d. 10/30, n/60   h. 5/10, n/100

2. The Halow Harp and Chime Company is negotiating a new labor contract. Among other things, the union is demanding that the company pay its workers weekly as opposed to twice a month. The payroll currently is $260,000 per pay day and accrued wages average $130,000. What is the annual cost of the union's demand if the company's opportunity cost of funds is 9 percent?

PROBLEMS

1. The Dud Company purchases raw materials on terms of 2/10, net 30. A review of the company's records by the owner, Mr. Dud, revealed that payments are usually made 15 days after purchases are received. When asked why the firm did not take advantage of its discounts, the bookkeeper, Mr. Grind, replied that it cost only 2 percent for these funds, whereas a bank loan would cost the firm 12 percent.

    a. What mistakes is Grind making?
    b. What is the real cost of not taking advantage of the discount?
    c. If the firm could not borrow from the bank and were forced to resort to the use of trade credit funds, what suggestion might be made to Grind that would reduce the annual interest cost?

2. Determine the annual percentage interest cost for each of the following terms of sale, assuming that the firm does not take the cash discount but pays on the final day of the net period (assume a 360-day year):

a. 1/20, net 30 ($500 invoice)   c. 2/5 net 10 ($100 invoice)

b. 2/30, net 60 ($1,000 invoice)   d. 3/10, net 30 ($250 invoice)

3. Does the dollar size of the invoice affect the percentage annual interest cost of not taking discounts? Illustrate with an example.

4. Recompute Problem 2, assuming a 10-day stretching of the payment date.

5. Under a seasonal dating arrangement, the Green Thumb Retail Garden Center usually pays for its annual $16,000 lawn mower shipment, which it receives the first of May, at the end of July. Lion Mowers, Inc., its supplier, has offered Green Thumb a 10 percent discount if it will take shipment on the first of March under net 30 days terms. It costs Green Thumb $500 per month to store the lawn mowers, and its cost of borrowing is $1\frac{1}{4}$ percent per month. Should Green Thumb accept Lion Mowers' offer? (Assume that the cost of borrowing is the opportunity cost of funds.)

6. On January 1, Faville Car Company, a large car dealer, gave its employees a 10 percent pay increase in view of the substantial profits the prior year. Before the increase, the weekly payroll was $50,000. What is the effect of the change on accruals?

7. El Pedro Chili Company pays its employees weekly, and its payroll is $28,000. It plans to change this procedure so that it pays them every 2 weeks. Presently accrued wages are $14,000.

a. What is the effect of this change on accrued wages?

b. Suppose that the company also increases wages for all employees by 5 percent. Its opportunity cost of funds is 12 percent. Is the company better or worse off with these combined events (procedure change and wage increase)?

SOLUTIONS TO SELF-CORRECTION PROBLEMS

1. a. 1/10, n/30   (1/99)(360/20) = 18.2%

    b. 2/10, n/30   (2/98)(360/20) = 36.7%

    c. 3/10, n/30   (3/97)(360/20) = 55.7%

    d. 10/30, n/60   (10/90)(360/30) = 133.3%

    e. 3/10, n/60   (3/97)(360/50) = 22.3%

    f. 2/10, n/90   (2/98)(360/80) = 9.2%

    g. 3/10, n/90   (3/97)(360/80) = 13.9%

    h. 5/10, n/100   (5/95)(360/90) = 21.1%

2. New average amount of accrued wages = $(\$130,000)\left(\dfrac{1}{52}\right)\left(\dfrac{24}{1}\right) = \$60,000$

Note: Fifty-two is the number of paydays in a year if wages are paid weekly; 24 is the number if wages are paid twice a month.

Decrease in average accrued wages = $130,000 − $60,000 = $70,000

Cost = $70,000 × .09 = $6,300

SELECTED REFERENCES

BROSKY, JOHN J., *The Implicit Cost of Trade Credit and Theory of Optimal Terms of Sale.* New York: Credit Research Foundation, 1969.

HARRINGTON, DIANA R., and BRENT D. WILSON, *Corporate Financial Analysis.* Plano, Tex.: Business Publications, 1983, chap. 2.

CHAPTER 12

Short-term Borrowings

From trade credit and accruals, two of the main spontaneous sources of short-term financing, we turn to methods of external short-term financing in the public or private market. In the public market, various money market instruments are sold to investors either directly by the issuer or indirectly through dealers. Short-term loans are placed privately, the principal sources being commercial banks and finance companies. With both money market credit and short-term loans, financing must be arranged on a formal basis.

MONEY MARKET CREDIT

Large, well-established companies sometimes borrow on a short-term basis through commercial paper and other money market instruments. Commercial paper represents an unsecured short-term negotiable promissory note sold in the money market. Because these notes are unsecured and are a money market instrument, only the more creditworthy companies are able to use commercial paper as a source of short-term financing.

Market for Commercial Paper

The commercial paper market is composed of two parts: the dealer market and the direct-placement market.[1] Industrial firms, utilities, and medium-sized finance companies sell commercial paper through dealers. The dealer organization is composed of a half-dozen major dealers who purchase commercial paper from the issuer and, in turn, sell it to investors. The typical commission a dealer earns is $\frac{1}{8}$ percent, and maturities on dealer-placed paper generally range from 30 to 90 days. The market is a highly organized and sophisticated one; paper is generally sold in denominations of $100,000. Although the dealer market has been characterized in the past by a significant number of issuers who borrowed on a seasonal basis, the trend definitely is toward financing on a revolving or more permanent basis.

A number of large sales finance companies, such as General Motors Acceptance Corporation, bypass the dealer organization in favor of selling their paper directly to investors. These issuers tailor both the maturity and the amount of the note to the needs of investors, mostly large corporations with excess cash. Maturities on directly placed paper can range from as little as a few days up to 9 months. Unlike many industrial issuers, finance companies use the commercial paper market as a permanent source of funds. Both dealer-placed and directly placed paper is rated as to its quality by one or more of the independent rating agencies—Moody's, Standard & Poor's and Fitch's. The top ratings are P-1, A-1, and F-1 for the three agencies, respectively. Only 1 and 2 grade paper find favor in the market.

The principal advantage of commercial paper as a source of short-term financing is that it is generally cheaper than a short-term business loan from a commercial bank. Depending on the interest rate cycle, the rate on commercial

---

[1] For a discussion of commercial paper from the standpoint of a short-term investor, see Chapter 9.

paper is from 1 to 6 percent lower than the prime rate for bank loans to the highest-quality borrower. For most companies, commercial paper is a supplement to bank credit. In fact, commercial paper dealers require borrowers to maintain lines of credit at banks in order to backstop the use of commercial paper. This ensures them that commercial paper borrowings can be paid off. In the aggregate, however, the growth of the commercial paper and other money markets has been at the expense of bank borrowings. The market share of total corporate financing enjoyed by banks has declined over time.

Instead of issuing "stand-alone" paper, some corporations issue what is known as "bank-supported" commercial paper. Here a bank provides a letter of credit guaranteeing the investor that the company's obligation will be paid. The quality of the investment then depends on the creditworthiness of the bank, and the paper is rated as such by the rating agencies. For making available the letter of credit arrangement, the bank charges a commitment fee on the maximum credit it will provide. Usually, the commitment fee is $\frac{1}{8}$ or $\frac{1}{4}$ percent. In addition, the bank frequently charges a usage fee on the amount of funds actually borrowed in the commercial paper market, again usually $\frac{1}{8}$ or $\frac{1}{4}$ percent. For example, suppose that the Second National Bank of Palo Alto issued a letter of credit of $50 million in support of commercial paper borrowings by Insell Corporation. The commitment fee is $\frac{1}{4}$ percent and the usage fee is $\frac{1}{8}$ percent. If commercial paper borrowings averaged $20 million, the annual cost of the letter of credit arrangement would be $\frac{1}{4}\% \times \$50,000,000 = \$125,000$ plus $\frac{1}{8}\% \times \$20,000,000 = \$25,000$, or $150,000 in total. For companies not well known, such as those privately held, as well as for companies that would be rated somewhat less than prime quality if they were to try to issue stand-alone paper, a bank-supported arrangement makes sense. It affords access to the commercial paper market at times when the total cost is less than direct borrowings at the bank.

Bankers' Acceptances

For a company engaged in foreign trade or the domestic storage and shipment of certain marketable goods, bankers' acceptances can be a meaningful source of financing. When an American company wishes to import $100,000 worth of electronic components from a company in Japan, the two companies agree that a 90-day time draft will be used in settlement of the trade. The American company arranges a letter of credit with its bank, whereby the bank agrees to honor drafts drawn on the company as presented through a Japanese bank. The Japanese company ships the goods and at the same time draws a draft ordering the American company to pay in 90 days. It then takes the draft to its Japanese bank. By prearrangement, the draft is sent to the American bank and is accepted by that bank. At that time it becomes a bankers' acceptance. In essence, the bank accepts responsibility for payment, thereby substituting its creditworthiness for that of the drawee, the American company.

If the bank is large and well known—and most banks accepting drafts are—the instrument becomes highly marketable upon acceptance. As a result, the drawer, the Japanese company, does not have to hold the draft until the final due date; it can sell the draft in the market for less than its face value. The discount involved represents the interest payment to the investor. At the end of 90 days the investor presents the acceptance to the accepting bank for payment and receives $100,000. At this time the American company is obligated to have funds on deposit to cover the draft. Thus it has financed its import for a 90-day period. Presumably, the Japanese exporter would have charged a lower price if payment were to be made upon shipment. In this sense the American company is the borrower.

The presence of an active and viable bankers' acceptance market makes possible the financing of foreign trade at interest rates approximating those on commercial paper. Although the principles by which the acceptance is created are the same for foreign and domestic trade, a smaller portion of the total bankers' acceptances outstanding is domestic. In addition to trade, domestic acceptance financing is used in connection with the storage of such things as grain. The bank involved advances funds on the basis of a draft from the company. By accepting the draft, it then can be sold in the bankers' acceptance market. The borrower's interest cost is the rate the investor receives plus fees to the bank and dealer, which frequently aggregate $\frac{7}{8}$ percent. In recent years bankers' acceptances have greatly multiplied as more companies recognize the usefulness of this form of financing.

UNSECURED BANK CREDIT

For expository purposes it is convenient to separate business loans into two categories: unsecured loans and secured loans. Almost without exception, finance companies do not offer unsecured loans, simply because a borrower who deserves unsecured credit can borrow at a lower cost from a commercial bank. Consequently, our discussion of unsecured loans will involve only commercial banks.

Short-term, unsecured bank loans typically are regarded as "self-liquidating" in that the assets purchased with the proceeds generate sufficient cash flows to pay the loan. At one time, banks confined their lending almost exclusively to this type of loan, but they now provide a wide variety of business loans tailored to the specific needs of the borrower. Still, the short-term, self-liquidating loan is a popular source of business financing, particularly in financing seasonal build-ups in accounts receivable and inventories. Unsecured short-term loans may be extended under a line of credit, under a revolving credit agreement, or on a transaction basis. The debt itself is evidenced formally by a promissory note signed by the borrower, showing the time and amount of payment and the interest to be paid.

Line of Credit

Line of credit. A limit to the amount of credit extended to an account. Purchaser can buy on credit up to that limit.

A **line of credit** is an arrangement between a bank and its customer specifying the maximum amount of unsecured credit the bank will permit the firm to owe at any one time. Usually, credit lines are established for a 1-year period and are subject to 1-year renewals. Frequently, lines of credit are set for renewal after the bank receives the audited annual report and has had a chance to review the progress of the borrower. If the borrower's year-end statement date is December 31, a bank may set its line to expire sometime in March. At that time, the bank and the company would meet to discuss the credit needs of the firm for the coming year in light of its past year's performance. The amount of the line is based on the bank's assessment of the creditworthiness and credit needs of the borrower. Depending on changes in these conditions, a line of credit may be adjusted at the renewal date or before, if conditions necessitate a change.

The cash budget, perhaps, gives the best insight into the borrower's short-term credit needs. If maximum or peak borrowing needs over the forthcoming year are estimated at $800,000, a company might seek a line of credit of $1 million to give it a margin of safety. Whether the bank will go along with the request, of course, will depend on its evaluation of the creditworthiness of the firm. If the bank agrees, the firm then may borrow on a short-term basis—usually 90 days—up to the full $1 million line. Because certain banks regard borrowing under lines of credit as seasonal or temporary financing, they may require that the borrower be out of bank debt at some time during the year. Frequently, the borrower will be required to clean up (pay off) bank debt for a period of time during the year. The cleanup period required usually is 1 or 2 months. The cleanup itself is evidence to the bank that the loan is truly seasonal in nature. If the interval during which a profitable firm were out of bank debt decreased from 4 months two years ago to 2 months last year and to no cleanup this year, the trend would suggest the use of bank credit to finance permanent funds requirements.

Despite its many advantages to the borrower, a line of credit does not constitute a legal commitment on the part of the bank to extend credit. The borrower is usually informed of the line by means of a letter indicating that the bank is willing to extend credit up to a certain amount. An example of such a letter is shown in Fig. 12-1. This letter is not a legal obligation of the bank to extend credit. If the creditworthiness of the borrower should deteriorate over the year, the bank might not want to extend credit and would not be required to do so. Under most circumstances, however, a bank feels bound to honor a line of credit.

Revolving Credit Agreement

A **revolving-credit** agreement is a legal commitment by a bank to extend credit up to a maximum amount. While the commitment is in force, the bank must extend credit whenever the borrower wishes to borrow, provided that total borrowings do not exceed the maximum amount specified. If the revolving credit is for $1 million, and $700,000 is already owing, the borrower can borrow an additional $300,000 at any time. For the privilege of having this formal commitment, the borrower usually is required to pay a commitment fee on the unused portion of the revolving credit. If the revolving credit is for $1 million, and borrowing for the year averages $400,000, the borrower will be required to pay a commitment

Revolving credit. A legal commitment to extend credit up to some maximum amount over a stated period of time.

```
┌─────────────────────────────────────────────────────────────┐
│                                                               │
│                    Second National Bank                       │
│                    Palo Alto, California                      │
│                                                               │
│                                                               │
│                                                               │
│                                          March 23, 1989       │
│                                                               │
│         Mr. Joseph A. Ralberg                                 │
│         Vice President & Treasurer                            │
│         Barker Manufacturing Corporation                      │
│         Palo Alto, California                                 │
│                                                               │
│         Dear Mr. Ralberg:                                     │
│                                                               │
│         Based upon our analysis of your year-end audited      │
│         statements, we are pleased to renew your $1 million    │
│         unsecured line of credit for the forthcoming year.    │
│         Borrowings under this line wiil be at a rate of       │
│         one-half percent (½%) over the prime rate.            │
│                                                               │
│         This line is subject to only the understanding that   │
│         your company will maintain its financial position     │
│         and that it will be out of bank debt for at least     │
│         45 days during the fiscal year.                       │
│                                                               │
│                         Yours very truly,                     │
│                                                               │
│                                                               │
│                         John D. Myers                         │
│                         Vice President                        │
│                                                               │
└─────────────────────────────────────────────────────────────┘
```

FIGURE 12-1
Sample letter extending line of credit

fee on the $600,000 unused portion. If the fee is $\frac{1}{2}$ percent, the cost of this privilege will be $3,000 for the year. Revolving credit agreements frequently extend beyond 1 year. Because lending arrangements of more than a year must be regarded as intermediate rather than short-term credit, we shall examine revolving credits more extensively in Chapter 21. The purpose of introducing them at this time is to illustrate the formal nature of the arrangement in contrast to the informality of a line of credit.

Transaction Loans

Borrowing under a line of credit or under a revolving credit arrangement is not appropriate when the firm needs short-term funds for only one purpose. A contractor may borrow from a bank in order to complete a job. When the contractor receives payment for the job, he pays the loan. For this type of loan, a bank evaluates each request by the borrower as a separate transaction. In these evaluations, the cash-flow ability of the borrower to pay the loan is usually of paramount importance.

Interest Rates

Unlike interest rates on impersonal money market instruments such as Treasury bills, bankers' acceptances, and commercial paper, most business loans are determined through personal negotiation between the borrower and the lender. In some measure, banks try to vary the interest rate charged according to the creditworthiness of the borrower; the lower the creditworthiness, the higher the interest rate. Interest rates charged also vary in keeping with money market conditions. One measure that changes with underlying market conditions is the **prime rate**. The prime rate is the rate charged on business loans to financially sound companies. The rate itself is usually set by large money market banks and is relatively uniform throughout the country.

Prime rate.   Interest rate charged by banks to large, creditworthy customers.

Differentials from Prime.   Despite the term *prime rate* implying the price a bank charges its most creditworthy customers, this has not been the recent practice. With banks becoming more competitive for corporate customers and facing extreme competition from the commercial paper market, the well-established, financially sound company often is able to borrow at a rate of interest below prime. The rate charged is based on the bank's marginal cost of funds, as typically reflected by the rate paid on money market certificates of deposit. An interest rate margin is added to the cost of funds, and the sum becomes the rate charged the customer. This rate is changed daily in keeping with changes in money market rates. Generally, the rate paid by the customer is $\frac{1}{4}$ to 1 percent below the prime rate. The differential depends on competitive conditions and on the relative bargaining power of the borrower.

Other borrowers will pay either the prime rate or a rate above prime, the bank's pricing of the loan being relative to the prime rate. A bank might extend a line of credit to a company at a rate $\frac{1}{2}$ percent above prime. If the prime rate is 10 percent, the borrower is charged an interest rate of 10.5 percent. If the prime rate changes to 8 percent, the borrower will pay 8.5 percent. Interest rate differentials among the various customers of a bank supposedly should reflect only differences in creditworthiness.

Other factors, however, influence the differential. Among them are the balances maintained and other business the borrower has with a bank (such as trust business). A good customer who has maintained very attractive balances in the past may be able to obtain a more favorable interest rate than will a firm of equal creditworthiness that has carried rather meager balances. Also, the cost of servicing a loan is a factor determining the differential in rate from prime. Certain collateral loans are costly to administer, and this cost must be passed on to the borrower either in the interest rate charged or in a special fee.

Thus, the interest rate charged on a short-term loan will depend on the prevailing cost of funds to banks, the existing prime rate, the creditworthiness of the borrower, the present and prospective relationships of the borrower with the bank, and sometimes on other considerations. Because of the fixed costs involved in credit investigation and in the processing of a loan, we would expect the interest rate on small loans to be higher than the rate on large loans.

Methods of Computing Interest Rates.   There are three ways in which interest on a loan may be paid: on a collect basis, on a discount basis, and on an add-on basis. When paid on a collect basis, the interest is paid at the maturity of the note; when paid on a discount basis, interest is deducted from the initial loan. On a $10,000 loan at 12 percent interest for 1 year, the effective rate of interest on a collect note is

$$\frac{\$1,200}{\$10,000} = 12.00\%$$

On a discount basis, the effective rate of interest is not 12 percent but

$$\frac{\$1,200}{\$8,800} = 13.64\%$$

When we pay on a discount basis, we have the use of only $8,800 for the year but must pay back $10,000 at the end of that time. Thus, the effective rate of interest is higher on a discount note than on a collect note. We should point out that most bank business loans are on a collect note basis.

On installment loans, banks and other lenders usually charge interest on an *add-on* basis. This means that interest is added to the funds disbursed in order to determine the face value of the note. Suppose, in our example, that an installment loan were involved with 12 equal monthly installments and that the interest rate were 12 percent. The borrower would receive $10,000, and the face value of the note would be $11,200. Thus, $1,200 in interest is paid. However, the borrower has use of the full $10,000 for only 1 month and at the end of that month must pay one-twelfth of $11,200, or $933.33. Installments in that amount are due at the end of each of the subsequent 11 months until the note is paid. For the full year, then, the borrower has use of only about one-half of the $10,000. Instead of a 12 percent rate, the effective rate is nearly double that, about 22 percent with monthly compounding. Thus, add-on interest is paid on the initial amount of the loan and not on the declining balance as is customary with other types of loans.

Compensating Balances

In addition to charging interest on loans, commercial banks often require the borrower to maintain demand deposit balances at the bank in direct proportion to either the amount of funds borrowed or the amount of the commitment. These minimum balances are known as compensating balances. The amount required in the compensating balance varies according to competitive conditions in the market for loans and specific negotiations between the borrower and lender. Banks would like to obtain balances equal to at least 10 percent of a line of credit. If the line is $2 million, the borrower would be required to maintain average balances of at least $200,000 during the year. Another arrangement might be for the bank to require average balances of 5 percent of the line and 5 percent more on the amount owing when the line is in use. If a firm's line were $2 million and its borrowings averaged $600,000, it would be required to maintain $130,000 in compensating balances.

The effect of a compensating balance requirement is to raise the effective cost of borrowing if the borrower is required to maintain balances above the amount the firm would maintain ordinarily. If we borrow $1 million at 12 percent and are required to maintain $100,000 more in balances than we would ordinarily, we will then have use of only $900,000 of the $1 million loan. The effective annual interest cost is $120,000/$900,000 = 13.33 percent, rather than 12 percent.

The notion of compensating balances for loans may be weakening. Increasingly, banks are becoming profit as opposed to deposit oriented and accordingly are fine-tuning profitability analyses of customer relationships. With the rapid and significant fluctuations in the cost of funds to banks in recent years, as well as the accelerated competition among financial institutions, banks make some loans without compensating balance requirements. The interest rate charged is in line with the bank's incremental cost of obtaining funds. The movement toward sophisticated profitability analysis has driven banks to direct compensation for loans through interest rates and fees as opposed to indirect compensation through deposit balances.

SECURED LENDING ARRANGEMENTS

Many firms cannot obtain credit on an unsecured basis, either because they are new and unproven or because bankers do not highly regard the firms' ability to service debt. To make a loan, lenders require security that will reduce their risk of loss. With security, lenders have two sources of loan payment: the cash-flow ability of the firm to service the debt and, if that source fails for some reason, the collateral value of the security. Most lenders will not make a loan unless the firm has sufficient expected cash flows to make proper servicing of debt highly probable. To reduce their risk further, they require security.

Collateral Value

The excess of the market value of the security pledged over the amount of the loan determines the lender's margin of safety. If the borrower is unable to meet an obligation, the lender can sell the security to satisfy the claim. If the security is sold for an amount exceeding the amount of the loan and interest owed, the difference is remitted to the borrower. If the security is sold for less, the lender becomes a general, or unsecured, creditor for the amount of the difference. Because secured lenders do not wish to become general creditors, they usually seek security with a market value sufficiently above the amount of the loan to minimize the likelihood of their not being able to sell the security in full satisfaction of the loan. The degree of security protection a lender seeks varies with the creditworthiness of the borrower, the security the borrower has available, and the financial institution making the loan.

The value of the collateral to the lender varies according to several factors.

Perhaps the most important is marketability. If the collateral can be sold quickly in an active market without depressing the price, the lender is likely to be willing to lend an amount that represents a fairly high percentage of the collateral's stated value. On the other hand, if the collateral is a special-purpose machine designed specifically for a company and has no viable secondary market, the lender may choose to lend nothing at all. The life of the collateral also matters. If the collateral has a cash-flow life that parallels closely the life of the loan, it will be more valuable to the lender than collateral, which is much longer-term in nature. As the collateral is liquidated into cash, the proceeds may be used to pay down the loan. Still another factor is the basic riskiness associated with the collateral. The greater the fluctuation in its market value or the more uncertain the lender is concerning market value, the less desirable the collateral from the standpoint of the lender. Thus, marketability, life, and riskiness determine the attractiveness of various types of collateral to a lender and, hence, the amount of financing available to a company. Before taking up specific short-term secured lending arrangements, we take a brief look at how lenders protect themselves under the Uniform Commercial Code.

Article 9 of the Code deals with security interests of lenders, the specific aspect with which we are concerned. A lender who requires collateral of a borrower obtains a *security interest* in the collateral. The collateral may be accounts receivable, inventory, equipment, or other assets of the borrower. The security interest in the collateral is created by a *security agreement*, also known as a *security device*. This agreement is signed by the borrower and lender and contains a description of the collateral. To "perfect" a security interest in the collateral, the lender must file a copy of the security agreement or a financing statement with a public office of the state in which the collateral is located. Frequently, this office is that of the secretary of state. The filing gives public notice to other parties that the lender has a security interest in the collateral described. Before accepting collateral as security for a loan, a lender will search the public notices to see if the collateral has been pledged previously in connection with another loan. Only the lender with a valid security interest in the collateral has a prior claim on the assets and can sell the collateral in settlement of the loan.

RECEIVABLE LOANS

Assignment of Accounts Receivable

Accounts receivable are one of the most liquid assets of the firm; consequently, they make desirable security for a loan. From the standpoint of the lender, the major difficulties with this type of security are the cost of processing the collateral and the risk of fraud. To illustrate the nature of the arrangement, we trace through a typical assignment of accounts receivable loan. A company may seek a receivable loan from either a commercial bank or a finance company. Because a bank usually charges a lower interest rate than a finance company does, the firm generally will try first to borrow from a bank.

Quality and Size of Receivables.   In evaluating the loan request, the lender will analyze the quality of the firm's receivables to determine how much to lend against them. The higher the quality of the accounts the firm maintains, the higher the percentage the lender is willing to advance against the face value of the receivables pledged. A lender does not have to accept all the borrower's accounts receivable; usually, accounts that have low credit ratings or that are unrated will be rejected. Also, government and foreign accounts usually are ineligible unless special arrangements are made. Depending on the quality of the receivables accepted, a lender typically advances between 50 and 80 percent of their face value.

The lender is concerned not only with the quality of receivables but also with their size. The lender must keep records on each account receivable that is pledged; the smaller the average size of the accounts, the more it costs per dollar of loan to process them. Consequently, a firm that sells low-priced items on open account will generally be unable to obtain a receivable loan regardless of the quality of the accounts. The cost of processing the loan is simply too high. Sometimes a general assignment, known also as a "bulk" or "blanket" assignment, will be used to circumvent the problem of cost. With a general assignment, the lender does not keep track of the individual accounts but records only the total amounts in the accounts assigned and the payments received. Because preventing fraud is difficult with a general assignment, the percentage advance against the face value of receivables is likely to be low, perhaps 25 percent.

Procedure.   Suppose a lender has decided to extend credit to a firm on the basis of a 75 percent advance against the face value of accounts receivable assigned. The firm then sends in a schedule of accounts showing the name of the accounts, the dates of billing, and the amounts owed. The lender will sometimes require evidence of shipment, such as an invoice. Having received the schedule of accounts, the lender has the borrower sign a promissory note and a security agreement. The firm then receives 75 percent of the face value of the receivables shown on the schedule of accounts.

A receivable loan can be on either a nonnotification or a notification basis. Under the former arrangement, customers of the firm are not notified that their accounts have been pledged to the lender. When the firm receives payment on an account, it forwards this payment, together with other payments, to the lender. The lender checks the payments against its record of accounts outstanding and reduces the amount the borrower owes by 75 percent of the total payments. The other 25 percent is credited to the borrower's account. With a nonnotification arrangement, the lender must take precautions to make sure the borrower does not withhold a payment check. With a notification arrangement, the account is notified of the assignment, and remittances are made directly to the lender. Under this arrangement, the borrower cannot withhold payments. Most firms naturally prefer to borrow on a nonnotification basis; however, the lender reserves the right to place the arrangement on a notification basis.

An accounts receivable loan is a more or less continuous financing arrangement. As the firm generates new receivables that are acceptable to the lender, they are assigned, adding to the security base against which the firm is able to borrow. New receivables replace the old, and the security base and the amount of loan fluctuate accordingly. A receivable loan is a very flexible means of secured financing. As receivables build up, the firm is able to borrow additional funds to finance this buildup. Thus, it has access to "built-in" financing.

Factoring Receivables

Factoring. The selling of receivables to a financial institution, the factor, usually without recourse. This is a method of financing.

In the assignment of accounts receivable, the firm retains title to the receivables. When a firm **factors** its receivables, it actually sells them to a factor. The sale may be either with or without recourse, depending on the type of arrangement negotiated. The factor maintains a credit department and makes credit checks on accounts. Based on its credit investigation, the factor may refuse to buy certain accounts that it deems too risky. By factoring, a firm frequently relieves itself of the expense of maintaining a credit department and making collections. Any account that the factor is unwilling to buy is an unacceptable credit risk unless, of course, the firm wants to assume this risk on its own and ship the goods. Factoring arrangements are governed by a contract between the factor and the client. The contract frequently is for 1 year with an automatic provision for renewal and can be canceled only with prior notice of 30 to 60 days. Although it is customary in a factoring arrangement to notify customers that their accounts have been sold and that payments on the account should be sent directly to the factor, in many instances notification is not made. Customers continue to remit payments to the firm, which, in turn, endorses them to the factor. These endorsements frequently are camouflaged to prevent customers from learning that their accounts have been sold.

Factoring Costs. For bearing risk and servicing the receivables, the factor receives a commission, which typically is somewhat over 1 percent of the face value of the receivables. The commission varies according to the size of the individual accounts, the volume of receivables sold, and the quality of the accounts. Since receivables sold to the factor will not be collected from the various accounts for a period of time, the firm may wish to receive payment for the sale of its receivables before they are actually collected. On that advance, it must pay interest. Advancing payment is a lending function of the factor in addition to risk bearing and servicing the receivables. For this additional function, the factor requires compensation. If the receivables total $10,000 and the factoring fee is 2 percent, the factor will credit the firm's account with $9,800. If the firm wants to draw on this account before the receivables are collected, it will have to pay an interest charge—say, $1\frac{1}{2}$ percent a month—for the use of the funds. If it wishes a cash advance, and the receivables are collected, on the average, in 1 month, the interest cost will be approximately $.015 \times 9,800$, or $147.[2] Thus, the total cost of factoring is composed of a factoring fee plus an interest charge if the firm draws on its account before the receivables are collected. If the firm does not draw on its account until the receivables are collected, there is no interest charge. In a

---

[2] The actual cash advance would be $9,800 less the interest cost, or $9,653.

third alternative, the firm may leave its funds with the factor beyond the time when the receivables are collected, and it will receive interest on the account from the factor.

Flexibility.   The typical factoring arrangement is continuous. As new receivables are acquired, they are sold to the factor, and the firm's account is credited. The firm then draws on this account as it needs funds. Sometimes the factor will allow the firm to overdraw its account during periods of peak needs and thereby borrow on an unsecured basis. Under other arrangements, the factor may withhold a reserve from the firm's account as a protection against losses. The principal sources of factoring are commercial banks, factoring subsidiaries of bank holding companies, and certain old-line factors. Although some people attach a stigma to the company that factors, many others regard it as a perfectly acceptable method of financing. Its principal shortcoming is that it can be expensive. We must bear in mind, however, that the factor often relieves the firm of credit checkings, the cost of processing receivables, and collection expenses. For a small firm, the savings may be quite significant.

INVENTORY LOANS

Inventories also represent a reasonably liquid asset and are therefore suitable as security for loans. As with a receivable loan, the lender determines a percentage advance against the market value of the collateral. This percentage varies according to the quality of the inventory. Certain inventories, such as grains, are very marketable and when properly stored resist physical deterioration. The margin of safety required by the lender on a loan of this sort is fairly small, and the advance may be as high as 90 percent. On the other hand, the market for a highly specialized piece of equipment may be so narrow that a lender is unwilling to make any advance against its reported market value. Thus, not every kind of inventory can be pledged as security for a loan. The best collateral is inventory that is relatively standard and for which a ready market exists apart from the marketing organization of the borrower.

Lenders determine the percentage that they are willing to advance by considering marketability, perishability, market price stability, and the difficulty and expense of selling the inventory to satisfy the loan. The cost of selling some inventory may be very high. Lenders do not want to be in the business of liquidating collateral, but they do not want to assure themselves that collateral has adequate value in case the borrower defaults in the payment of principal or interest. As is true with most secured loans, however, the actual decision to make the loan will depend on the cash-flow ability of the borrower to service debt. There are a number of different ways a lender can obtain a secured interest in inventories, and we consider each in turn. In the first three methods (floating lien, chattel mortgage, and trust receipt), the inventory remains in the possession of the borrower. In the last two methods (terminal warehouse and field warehouse receipts), the inventory is in the possession of a third party.

Floating Lien

Floating lien. A general, or blanket, lien against a group of assets, such as receivables and inventories, without the assets being specifically identified.

Under the Uniform Commercial Code, the borrower may pledge inventories "in general" without specifying the specific inventory involved. Under this arrangement, the lender obtains a **floating lien** on all inventory of the borrower. This lien by its very nature is loose, and the lender may find it difficult to police. Frequently, a floating lien is requested only as additional protection and does not play a major role in determining whether or not the loan will be made. Even if the collateral is valuable, the lender usually is willing to make only a moderate advance because of the difficulty in exercising tight control over the collateral. The floating lien can be made to cover both receivables and inventories, as well as the collection of receivables. This modification gives the lender a lien on a major portion of a firm's current assets. In addition, the lien can be made to encompass almost any length of time so that it includes future as well as present inventory as security.

Chattel Mortgage

Chattel mortgage. A lien on property, usually equipment, backing a loan.

With a **chattel mortgage,** inventories are identified specifically by serial number or by some other means. While the borrower holds title to the goods, the lender has a lien on inventory. This inventory cannot be sold unless the lender consents. Because of the rigorous identification requirements, chattel mortgages are ill suited for inventory with rapid turnover or inventory that is not easily identified because of size or other reasons. Chattel mortgages are well suited for certain capital assets such as machine tools.

Trust Receipt Loans

Trust receipt. Used in secured lending, where the goods are held in trust for the lender.

Under a **trust receipt** financing arrangement, the borrower holds in trust for the lender the inventory and proceeds from its sale. This type of lending arrangement, also known as floor planning, has been used extensively by automobile dealers, equipment dealers, and consumer durable goods dealers. An automobile manufacturer will ship cars to a dealer who, in turn, may finance the payment for these cars through a finance company. The finance company pays the manufacturer for the cars shipped. The dealer signs a trust receipt security agreement, which specifies what can be done with the inventory. The car dealer is allowed to sell the cars but must turn the proceeds of the sale over to the lender in payment of the loan. Inventory in trust, unlike inventory under a floating lien, is specifically identified by serial number or by other means. In our example, the finance company periodically audits the cars the dealer has on hand. The serial numbers of these cars are checked against those shown in the security agreement. The purpose of the audit is to see if the dealer has sold cars without remitting the proceeds of the sale to the finance company.

As the dealer buys new cars from the automobile manufacturer, a new trust receipt security agreement is signed taking account of the new inventory. The dealer then borrows against this new collateral, holding it in trust. Although there is tighter control over collateral with a trust receipt agreement than with a floating lien, there is still the risk of inventory's being sold without the proceeds being turned over to the lender. Consequently, the lender must exercise judgment in deciding to lend under this arrangement. A dishonest dealer can devise numerous ways to fool the lender.

Many durable goods manufacturers finance the inventories of their distributors or dealers. Their purpose is to encourage dealers or distributors to carry reasonable stocks of goods. It is reasoned that the greater the stock, the more likely the dealer or distributor is to make a sale. Because the manufacturer is interested in selling its product, financing terms often are more attractive than they are with an "outside" lender.

Terminal Warehouse Receipt Loans

A borrower secures a **terminal warehouse receipt loan** by storing inventory with a public, or terminal, warehousing company. The warehouse company issues a warehouse receipt, which evidences title to specific goods that are located in the warehouse. An example of a warehouse receipt is shown in Fig. 12-2. The warehouse receipt gives the lender a security interest in the goods, against which a loan can be made to the borrower. Under such an arrangement, the warehouse can release the collateral to the borrower only when authorized to do so by the lender. Consequently, the lender is able to maintain strict control over the collateral and will release collateral only when the borrower pays a portion of the loan. For protection, the lender usually requires the borrower to take out an insurance policy with a loss-payable clause in favor of the lender.

Terminal warehouse receipt loan. A loan secured by goods held in a public warehouse for which the lender holds the receipt.

Warehouse receipts may be either nonnegotiable or negotiable. A nonnegotiable warehouse receipt is issued in favor of a specific party—in this case, the lender—who is given title to the goods and has sole authority to release them. A negotiable warehouse receipt can be transferred by endorsement. Before goods can be released, the negotiable receipt must be presented to the warehouse operator. A negotiable receipt is useful when title to the goods is transferred from one party to another while the goods are in storage. With a nonnegotiable receipt, the release of goods can be authorized only in writing. Most lending arrangements are based on nonnegotiable receipts.

Field Warehouse Receipt Loans

In a terminal warehouse receipt loan, the goods are located in a public warehouse. Another arrangement, known as **field warehousing,** permits loans to be made against inventory that is located on the borrower's premises. Under this arrangement, a field warehousing company sets off a designated storage area on the borrower's premises for the inventory pledged as collateral. The field warehousing company has sole access to this area and is supposed to maintain strict control over it. (The goods that serve as collateral are segregated from the borrower's other inventory.) The field warehousing company issues a warehouse receipt as described in the preceding section, and the lender extends a loan based

Field warehousing. A means of secured financing where goods are segregated at the place of the borrower and the lender has a lien on them.

LAWRENCE SYSTEMS, INC.

NOT INSURED

ORIGINAL WAREHOUSE RECEIPT
NON NEGOTIABLE

RECEIVED FROM:
FOR STORAGE IN
LOCATED AT (STREET)

SUBJECT TO ALL THE TERMS AND CONDITIONS CONTAINED HEREIN AND ON THE REVERSE SIDE HEREOF FOR THE ACCOUNT OF AND TO BE DELIVERED WITHOUT SURRENDER OF THIS WAREHOUSE RECEIPT UPON WRITTEN INSTRUCTION OF

FILL IN ▶ ______________________________
WAREHOUSE RECEIPT HOLDER

					24178	**Depositor's Declared Values for which the Warehouseman Assumes No Responsibility.**
REPT TYPE	REG CODE	WAREHOUSE NO	HOLDER NO	DATE	RECEIPT NO	

CODE NO.	ITEM	NO. OF UNITS	SAID TO BE OR CONTAIN	UNIT VALUES	EXTENSION (BJH)
			SPECIMEN COPY		BJZ

CAUTION: LAWRENCE SYSTEMS, INC. WILL NOT BE RESPONSIBLE FOR THE QUANTITIES SHOWN HEREON UNLESS TOTAL NUMBER OF UNITS IS TYPED BELOW.

TOTAL ▶

Stored under field warehousing arrangement. Subject to lien for storage, handling and other charges as per contract and lease with the industry served. A general lien is claimed for charges and expenses in regard to other goods deposited by the same depositor. Transfers of merchandise not complete unless made on the books of the warehouse company.

"By agreement goods of same kind or grade may be commingled and where authorized by law unlike units shall be deemed fungible and treated as equivalents."

LAWRENCE SYSTEMS, INC.

BY ▶

BONDED WAREHOUSE MANAGER

(Do not accept this warehouse receipt if any corrections or erasures appear hereon.)

FIGURE 12-2
Sample warehouse receipt

SOURCE: *Lawrence Systems, Inc. Reprinted by permission.*

on the collateral value of the inventory. The field warehouse arrangement is a useful means of financing when it is not desirable, either because of the expense or because of the inconvenience, to place the inventory in a public warehouse. Field warehouse receipt lending is particularly appropriate when a borrower must make frequent use of inventory. Because of the need to pay the field warehousing company's expenses, the cost of this method of financing can be relatively high.

The warehouse receipt, as evidence of collateral, is only as good as the issuing warehousing company. When administered properly, a warehouse receipt loan affords the lender a high degree of control over the collateral; however, sufficient examples of fraud show that the warehouse receipt does not always evidence actual value. The warehouse operator must exercise strict control. A grain elevator that is alleged to be full may, in fact, be empty. Upon close examination, we may find that barrels reported to contain chemical concentrate actually contain water.[3]

COMPOSITION OF SHORT-TERM FINANCING

In this and the preceding chapter we considered various sources of short-term financing. Because the total amount of short-term financing was assumed to have been determined according to the framework presented in Chapter 8, only determination of the best combination need be considered in this chapter. The appropriate mix, or the weighting, of alternative sources will depend on considerations of cost, availability, timing, flexibility, and the degree to which the assets of the firm are encumbered. Central to any meaningful analysis of alternative sources of funds is a comparison of their costs, and inextricably related to the question of cost is the problem of timing. Differentials in cost among various alternatives are not necessarily constant over time. Indeed, they fluctuate in keeping with changing financial market conditions. Thus, timing bears heavily on the question of the most appropriate mix of short-term financing.

Naturally, the availability of financing is important. If a firm cannot borrow through commercial paper or through a bank because of its low credit standing, it must turn to alternative sources. The lower the credit standing of the firm, of course, the fewer the sources of short-term financing available to it. Flexibility with respect to short-term financing pertains to the ability of the firm to pay off a loan as well as to its ability to renew it or increase it. With factoring and also with a bank loan, the firm can pay off the loan when it has surplus funds and thereby reduce its overall interest costs. For commercial paper, the firm must wait until final maturity before paying off the loan.

Flexibility relates also to how easily the firm can increase its loan on short notice. With a line of credit or revolving credit at a commercial bank, it is an

---

[3] For a lively discussion of the various ways frauds have taken place against secured lenders, see Monroe R. Lazere, "Swinging Swindles and Creepy Frauds," *Journal of Commercial Bank Lending*, 60 (September 1977), 44–52.

easy matter to increase borrowings, assuming the maximum has not been reached. With other forms of short-term financing, the firm is less flexible. Finally, the degree to which assets are encumbered bears on the decision. With secured loans, lenders obtain a lien on the assets of the firm. This secured position constrains the firm in future financing. Whereas receivables are actually sold under a factoring arrangement, the principle is the same. In this case, the firm sells one of its most liquid assets, thus reducing its creditworthiness in the minds of creditors.

All of these factors influence the firm in deciding on the most appropriate mix of short-term financing. Because cost is perhaps the key factor, differences in other factors should be compared with differences in cost. What is the cheapest source of financing from the standpoint of explicit costs may not be the cheapest source when flexibility, timing, and the degree to which assets are encumbered are considered. Although it would be desirable to express sources of short-term financing in terms of both explicit and implicit costs, the latter are hard to quantify. A more practical approach is to list available sources according to their explicit costs and then consider the other factors to see if they change the ranking as it relates to total desirability. Because the financing needs of the firm change over time, multiple sources of short-term financing should be explored on a continuous basis.

SUMMARY

Commercial paper is used only by well-established, high-quality companies. The evidence of debt is an unsecured short-term promissory note that is sold in the money market. Commercial paper is sold either through dealers or directly to investors. Rather than "stand-alone" paper, a firm may issue "bank-supported" paper, in which case a bank guarantees the creditworthiness of the paper. The principal advantage of commercial paper is that its yield is less than the rate of interest a company would have to pay on a bank loan. Bankers' acceptance financing is another type of money market credit. Usually associated with a foreign trade transaction, the acceptance is highly marketable and can be a very desirable source of short-term funds.

Short-term loans can be divided into two types: unsecured and secured. Unsecured credit usually is confined to bank loans under a line of credit, under a revolving-credit agreement, or on a transaction basis. Typically, banks require balances to compensate for a lending arrangement. If the borrower is required to maintain balances above those that it would maintain ordinarily, the effective cost of borrowing is increased. Interest rates on business loans are a function of the cost of funds to banks, the existing prime rate, the creditworthiness of the borrower, and the profitability of the relationship for the bank.

Many firms unable to obtain unsecured credit are required by the lender to pledge security. In giving a secured loan, the lender looks first to the cash-flow ability of the company to service debt and, if this source of loan repayment might fail, to the collateral value of the security. To provide a margin of safety, a lender usually will advance somewhat less than the market value of the collateral. The percentage advance varies according to the quality of the collateral pledged and the control the lender has over this collateral.

Accounts receivable and inventory are the principal assets used to secure short-term business loans. Receivables may either be pledged to secure a loan or sold to a factor. Inventory loans can be under a general lien, a chattel mortgage, a trust receipt, or terminal warehouse or field warehouse receipt arrangements. The most appropriate mix of short-term financing will depend on consideration of relative cost, availability, flexibility, timing, and the degree to which the assets of the firm are encumbered.

QUESTIONS

1. Why is the rate on commercial paper usually less than the prime rate charged by bankers and more than the Treasury bill rate?
2. Why would a firm borrow bank funds at higher rates instead of issuing commercial paper?
3. Who is able to issue commercial paper and for what purpose?
4. How do bankers' acceptances differ from commercial paper as a means of financing?
5. Compare and contrast a line of credit and a revolving credit.
6. If you were a borrower, would you rather have your loan on a collect basis or a discount basis, all other things being the same? as a lender?
7. What determines whether a lending arrangement is unsecured or secured?
8. As a lender, how would you determine the percentage you are willing to advance against a particular type of collateral?
9. As a financial consultant to a company, how would you go about recommending whether to use an assignment of accounts receivable or a factoring arrangement?
10. Why might a company prefer an unsecured source of funds such as a line of credit or a revolving credit agreement to some form of secured financing such as a receivable loan or chattel mortgage, even if the latter source is less expensive?
11. List assets that you would accept as collateral on a loan in your order of preference. Justify your priorities.
12. Inventory and accounts receivable are among the most liquid assets a firm owns. Does this liquidity make them the safest security available to the lender? Explain.
13. Which of the methods of short-term financing considered in this chapter would be most likely to be used by the following? Explain your reasoning.
    a. A raw materials processor such as a mining or lumber company

b. A retail sales concern such as an appliance retailer or high-fidelity equipment dealer

c. An international company

d. A consumer durable goods dealer such as an automobile sales agency

14. What reaction might a firm expect from trade creditors when it pledges its receivables to secure a bank loan?

15. In choosing the composition of short-term financing, what factors should be considered?

SELF-CORRECTION PROBLEMS

1. The Sphinx Supply Company needs to increase its working capital by $10,000,000. The following three alternatives of financing are available:

a. Forgo cash discounts, granted on a basis of 3/10, net 30.

b. Borrow from the bank at 15 percent. This alternative would necessitate maintaining a 12 percent compensating balance.

c. Issue commercial paper at 12 percent. The cost of placing the issue would be $100,000 each 6 months.

Assuming that the firm would prefer the flexibility of bank financing, provided the additional cost of this flexibility was no more than 2 percent per annum, which alternative should Sphinx select?

2. The Barnes Corporation has just acquired a large account. As a result, it needs an additional $75,000 in working capital immediately. It has been determined that there are three feasible sources of funds:

a. Trade credit: the company buys about $50,000 of materials per month on terms of 3/30, net 90. Discounts are taken.

b. Bank loan: the firm's bank will loan $100,000 at 13 percent. A 10 percent compensating balance will be required.

c. A factor will buy the company's receivables ($100,000 per month), which have a collection period of 60 days. The factor will advance up to 75 percent of the face value of the receivables at 12 percent on an annual basis. The factor also will charge a 2 percent fee on all receivables purchased. It has been estimated that the factor's services will save the company a credit department expense and bad-debts expense of $1,500 per month.

Which alternative should Barnes select on the basis of percentage cost?

3. The Kedzie Cordage Company needs to finance a seasonal bulge in inventories of $400,000. The funds are needed for 6 months. The company is considering the following possibilities:

a. Warehouse receipt loan from a finance company. Terms are 12 percent annualized with an 80 percent advance against the value of the inventory. The warehousing costs are $7,000 for the 6-month period. The residual financing requirement, which is $400,000 less the amount advanced, will need to be financed by forgoing cash discounts on its payables. Standard terms are 2/10, net 30; however, the company feels that it can postpone payment until the fortieth day without adverse effect.

b.   A floating lien arrangement from the supplier of the inventory at an effective interest rate of 20 percent. The supplier will advance the full value of the inventory.

c.   A field warehouse loan from another finance company at an interest rate of 10 percent annualized. The advance is 70 percent, and field warehousing costs amount to $10,000 for the 6-month period. The residual financing requirement will need to be financed by forgoing cash discounts on payables as in the first alternative.

Which is the least costly method of financing the inventory needs of the firm?

PROBLEMS

1.   Burleigh Mills Company has $5 million revolving credit agreement with First State Bank of Arkansas. Being a favored customer, the rate is set at 1 percent over the bank's cost of funds, where the cost is the rate on negotiable certificates of deposit (CDs). In addition, there is a $\frac{1}{2}$ percent commitment fee on the unused portion of the revolving credit. If the CD rate is expected to average 9 percent for the coming year and if the company expects to utilize, on average, 60 percent of the total commitment, what is the expected annual dollar cost of this credit arrangement? What is the percentage cost when both the interest rate and the commitment fee paid are considered? What happens to the percentage cost if, on average, only 20 percent of the total commitment is utilized?

2.   Bork Corporation wishes to borrow $100,000 for 1 year. It has the following alternatives available to it.

a.   An 8 percent loan on a discount basis with 20 percent compensating balances required.

b.   A 9 percent loan on a discount basis with 10 percent compensating balances required.

c.   A $10\frac{1}{2}$ percent loan on a collect basis with no compensating balance requirement.

Which alternative should Bork Corporation choose if it is concerned with the effective interest rate?

3.   Commercial paper has no stipulated interest rate. It is sold on a discount basis, and the amount of the discount determines the interest cost to the issuer. On the basis of the following information, determine the percentage interest cost on an annual basis for each of the following issues (assume a 360-day year):

ISSUE	FACE VALUE	PRICE	TIME TO MATURITY
(a)	$25,000	$24,500	60 days
(b)	100,000	96,500	180 days
(c)	50,000	48,800	90 days
(d)	75,000	71,300	270 days
(e)	100,000	99,100	30 days

4. The Selby Gaming Manufacturing Company has experienced a severe cash squeeze and needs $200,000 over the next 90 days. The company already has pledged its receivables in support of a loan. However, it does have $570,000 in unencumbered inventories. Determine the best financing alternative from the following two that are available.

 a. The Cody National Bank of Reno will lend against finished goods provided that they are placed in a public warehouse under its control. As the finished goods are released for sale, the loan is reduced by the proceeds of the sale. The company currently has $300,000 in finished goods inventory and would expect to replace finished goods that are sold out of the warehouse with new finished goods, so that it could borrow the full $200,000 for 90 days. The interest rate is 10 percent, and the company will pay quarterly warehousing costs of $3,000. Finally, it will experience a reduction in efficiency as a result of this arrangement. Management estimates that the lower efficiency will reduce quarterly before-tax profits by $4,000.

 b. The Zarlotti Finance Company will lend the company the money under a floating lien on all of its inventories. The rate is 23 percent, but no additional expenses will be incurred.

5. The Bone Company has been factoring its accounts receivable for the past 5 years. The factor charges a fee of 2 percent and will lend up to 80 percent of the volume of receivables purchased for an additional $1\frac{1}{2}$ percent per month. The firm typically has sales of $500,000 per month, 70 percent of which are on credit. By using the factor, two savings are effected:

 a. $2,000 per month that would be required to support a credit department

 b. A bad-debt expense of 1 percent on credit sales

 The firm's bank has recently offered to lend the firm up to 80 percent of the face value of the receivables shown on the schedule of accounts. The bank would charge 15 percent per annum interest plus a 2 percent monthly processing charge per dollar of receivables lending. The firm extends terms of net 30, and all customers who pay their bills do so by the thirtieth day. Should the firm discontinue its factoring arrangement in favor of the bank's offer if the firm borrows, on the average, $100,000 per month on its receivables?

6. Fritz-Polakoff Finance Company makes a variety of secured loans. Both the percentage of advance and the interest rate charged vary with the mar-

ketability, life, and riskiness of the collateral. It has established the following advances and interest rate charges for certain types of equipment:

ITEM	ADVANCE AGAINST APPRAISAL VALUE	INTEREST RATE
1. Forklift truck	75%	18%
2. Backhoe truck	80	18
3. Drill press	50	20
4. Bottle filler	40	22
5. Turret lathe	60	20

L. Bradford Company has used equipment of this sort with appraised values of $13,000, $19,000, $6,000, $38,000 and $24,000, respectively. How much can it borrow? What will be the total annual interest cost in dollars? as a percentage? (Assume that the company owns only one item of each.)

7. Vesco-Zultch Corporation is a chain of appliance stores in Chicago. It needs to finance all of its inventories, which average the following during the four quarters of the year (in thousands):

Quarter	1	2	3	4
inventory level (in thousands)	$1,600	$2,100	$1,500	$3,200

Vesco-Zultch presently utilizes a finance company loan secured by a floating lien. The interest rate is the prime rate plus $7\frac{1}{2}$ percent, but no additional expenses are incurred. The Boundary Illinois National Bank of Chicago is bidding for the Vesco-Zultch business. It has proposed a trust receipt financing arrangement. The interest rate will be $2\frac{1}{2}$ percent above the prime rate, with servicing costs of $20,000 each quarter. Should the company switch financing arrangements?

8. The Coral Machine Tool Company had the following balance sheet at the close of its fiscal year last month:

Cash	$ 14,000	Accounts payable	$240,000
Receivables	196,000	Bank loan	170,000
Inventories	170,000	Current liabilities	$410,000
Current assets	$380,000	Mortgage loan	240,000
Fixed assets	473,000	Common stock	50,000
		Retained earnings	153,000
	$853,000		$853,000

The company had the following income statement for the year:

Sales		$2,000,000
Cost of goods sold		
Purchases	$960,000	
Wages	600,000	
Depreciation	60,000	1,620,000
Gross profit		$ 380,000
Expenses		310,000
Profit before taxes		$ 70,000
Taxes		33,000
Profit		$ 37,000

The company has approached the bank to increase its loan so that the company can become more current in the trade and avail itself of certain cash discounts. Suppliers are becoming very difficult. Paying higher prices and being unable to take cash discounts, Coral estimates that its costs are $40,000 more per year than they would be if its average payable were 30 days in length.

a. How much additional financing is necessary to bring the average payable collection period to 30 days?

b. What are some of the problems from the standpoint of the bank? Is it likely to extend the additional credit on an unsecured basis?

SOLUTIONS TO SELF-CORRECTION PROBLEMS

1. a. $\dfrac{3}{97} \times \dfrac{360}{20} = 55.67\%$

b. $\dfrac{\$1,500}{\$8,800} = 17.05\%$ (000 omitted)

c. $\dfrac{\$1,200 + \$100 + \$100}{\$10,000} = 14\%$ (000 omitted)

The bank financing is approximately 3 percent more expensive than the paper; the latter, therefore, should be issued.

2. a. Cost of trade credit: if discounts are not taken, up to $97,000 can be raised after the second month. The cost would be

$$\frac{3}{97} \times \frac{360}{60} = 18.56\%$$

b. Cost of bank loan: assuming that the compensating balance would not otherwise be maintained, the cost would be

$$\frac{13}{90} = 14.44\%$$

c. Cost of factoring: factor fee for the year would be 2% × $1,200,000 = $24,000. The savings effected, however, would be $18,000, giving a net factoring cost of $6,000. Borrowing $75,000 on the receivables would thus cost:

$$\frac{12\%(\$75,000) + \$6,000}{\$75,000} = \frac{\$9,000 + \$6,000}{\$75,000} = 20.00\%$$

Bank borrowing would be the cheapest source of funds.

3. a. 12% of 80 percent of $400,000 for 6 months = $19,200
        Warehousing cost = 7,000
        Cash discount forgone to extend payables
        from 10 days to 40 days:

$$\left(\frac{2}{98} \times \frac{360}{30}\right)(\$80,000)(\tfrac{1}{2}\text{ year}) = .2449 \times 80,000 \times .5 =$$ 9,796

        Total cost $35,996

    b. $400,000 × 20% × $\tfrac{1}{2}$ year = $40,000

    c. 10% of 70% of $400,000 for 6 months = $14,000
        Field warehousing cost 10,000
        Cash discount forgone to extend payables
        from 10 days to 40 days:

$$\left(\frac{2}{98} \times \frac{360}{30}\right)(\$120,000)(\tfrac{1}{2}\text{ year}) = .2449 \times 120,000 \times .5 =$$ 14,694

        Total cost $38,694

        The warehouse receipt results in the lowest cost.

SELECTED REFERENCES

DENONN, LESTER E., "The Security Agreement," *Journal of Commercial Bank Lending*, 50 (February 1968), 32–40.

HARRINGTON, DIANA R., and BRENT D. WILSON, *Corporate Financial Analysis*, Plano, Tex: Business Publications, 1983, chap. 2.

LAZERE, MONROE R., "Swinging Swindles and Creepy Frauds," *Journal of Commercial Bank Lending*, 60 (September 1977), 44–52.

MCDANIEL, MOREY W., "Are Negative Pledge Clauses in Public Debt Issues Obsolete?" *Business Lawyer*, 38 (May 1983), 867–81.

QUARLES, J. CARSON, "The Floating Lien," *Journal of Commercial Bank Lending*, 53 (November 1970), 51–58.

STONE, BERNELL K., "The Design of a Company's Banking System," *Journal of Finance*, 38 (May 1983), 373–85.

C H A P T E R 13

Capital Budgeting

Now that we are deeply profound in matters of working capital, we are going to look at some decisions that have longer-term consequences to a company. These decisions involve both spending and financing, the first of which we take up in this chapter.

When a business firm makes a capital investment, it incurs a current cash outlay in the expectation of future benefits. Usually, these benefits extend beyond 1 year in the future. Examples include investment in assets such as equipment, buildings, and land, as well as the introduction of a new product, a new distribution system, or a new program for research and development. Thus, the firm's future success and profitability depend on investment decisions made currently.

An investment proposal should be judged in relation to whether it provides a return equal to, or greater than, that required by investors.[1] To simplify our investigation of the methods of **capital budgeting** in this chapter, we assume the required rate of return is given and is the same for all investment projects. This assumption implies that the selection of any investment project does not alter the **business-risk** complexion of the firm as perceived by suppliers of capital. In Chapter 15 we investigate how to determine the required rate of return, and in Chapter 14 we allow for the fact that different investment projects have different degrees of business risk. As a result, the selection of an investment project may affect the business-risk complexion of the firm, which, in turn, may affect the rate of return required by investors. For purposes of introducing capital budgeting in this chapter, however, we hold risk constant.

Capital budgeting. The allocation of capital to long-term capital investments used in the production of a good or service.

Business risk. The operating risk of the company due to the business it is in, as distinct from its financial risk.

INFORMATION REQUIRED

Capital budgeting involves

1. Generation of investment proposals
2. Estimate of cash flows for the proposals
3. Evaluation of cash flows
4. Selection of projects based on an acceptance criterion
5. Continual reevaluation of investment projects after their acceptance

Starting with the first, investment proposals can emanate from a variety of sources. For purposes of analysis, projects may be classified into one of five categories:

1. New products or expansion of existing products
2. Replacement of equipment or buildings
3. Research and development
4. Exploration
5. Others

The fifth category comprises miscellaneous items such as the expenditure of

[1] The development of this chapter assumes the reader has covered Chapter 4, on the mathematics of finance.

funds to comply with certain health standards or the acquisition of a pollution-control device. For a new product, the proposal usually originates in the marketing department. On the other hand, a proposal to replace a piece of equipment with a more sophisticated model usually emanates from the production area of the firm. In each case, efficient administrative procedures are needed for channeling investment requests.

Most firms screen proposals at multiple levels of authority. For a proposal originating in the production area, the hierarchy of authority might run from (1) section chiefs to (2) plant managers to (3) the vice-president for operations to (4) a capital expenditures committee under the financial manager to (5) the president to (6) the board of directors. How high a proposal must go before it is finally approved usually depends on its size. The greater the capital outlay, the greater the number of screens usually required. Plant managers may be able to approve moderate-sized projects on their own, but only higher levels of authority approve larger ones. Because the administrative procedures for screening investment proposals vary greatly from firm to firm, it is not possible to generalize. The best procedure will depend on the circumstances. It is clear, however, that companies are becoming increasingly sophisticated in their approach to capital budgeting.

Estimating Cash Flows

One of the most important tasks in capital budgeting is estimating future cash flows for a project. The final results we obtain are only as good as the accuracy of our estimates. Since cash, not income, is central to all decisions of the firm, we express whatever benefits we expect from a project in terms of cash flows rather than income. The firm invests cash now in the hope of receiving cash returns in a greater amount in the future. Only cash receipts can be reinvested in the firm or paid to stockholders in the form of dividends. In capital budgeting, good guys may get credit, but effective managers get cash. In setting up the cash flows for analysis, a computer spreadsheet program is invaluable. It allows one to change assumptions and quickly produce a new cash-flow stream. In the supplement, *Financial Management Computer Applications*, a program format for this purpose is presented.

For each investment proposal, we need to provide information on expected future cash flows on an after-tax basis. In addition, the information must be provided on an *incremental* basis, so that we analyze only the difference between the cash flows of the firm with and without the project. For example, if a firm contemplates a new product that is likely to compete with existing products, it is not appropriate to express cash flows in terms of the estimated sales of the new product. We must take into account probable "cannibalization" of existing products, and we must make our cash-flow estimates on the basis of incremental sales. The key is to analyze the situation with and without the new investment. Only incremental cash flows matter.

In this regard, sunk costs must be ignored. One is concerned with incremental costs and benefits, and the recovery of past costs is irrelevant. They are bygones and should not enter into the decision process. Also, we must be mindful that certain costs do not necessarily involve a dollar outlay. If we have allocated plant space to a project and this space can be used for something else, its **opportunity cost** must be included in the project's evaluation. If a presently unused building can be sold for $300,000, that amount should be treated as a cash outlay at the outset of the project. Thus, in deriving cash flows we must consider appropriate opportunity costs.

Opportunity cost. The return available on the next best investment alternative.

To illustrate the information needed for a capital budgeting decision, consider the following situation. A firm is considering the introduction of a new product. To launch the product, it will need to spend $150,000 for special equipment and the initial advertising campaign. The marketing department envisions the product life to be 6 years and expects incremental sales revenue to be

YEAR 1	YEAR 2	YEAR 3	YEAR 4	YEAR 5	YEAR 6
$60,000	$120,000	$160,000	$180,000	$110,000	$50,000

Cash outflows include labor and maintenance costs, materials costs, and various other expenses associated with the product. As with sales, these costs must be estimated on an incremental basis. In addition to these outflows, the firm will need to pay higher taxes if the new product generates higher profits; and this incremental outlay must be included. Suppose that on the basis of these considerations the firm estimates total incremental cash outflows to be

YEAR 1	YEAR 2	YEAR 3	YEAR 4	YEAR 5	YEAR 6
$40,000	$70,000	$100,000	$100,000	$70,000	$40,000

Because depreciation is a noncash expense, it is not included in these outflows. The expected net cash flows from the project are

	INITIAL COST	YEAR 1	YEAR 2	YEAR 3	YEAR 4	YEAR 5	YEAR 6
Cash inflows		$60,000	$120,000	$160,000	$180,000	$110,000	$50,000
Cash outflows	$150,000	40,000	70,000	100,000	100,000	70,000	40,000
Net cash flows	−$150,000	$20,000	$ 50,000	$ 60,000	$ 80,000	$ 40,000	$10,000

Thus, for an initial cash outflow of $150,000, the firm expects to generate net cash flows of $20,000, $50,000, $60,000, $80,000, $40,000, and $10,000 over the next 6 years. These cash flows represent the relevant information we need in order to judge the attractiveness of the project.

Patterns of Cash Flows. The net cash flows for this example are plotted in the top panel of Fig. 13-1. We notice that the initial cash outlay, or invest-

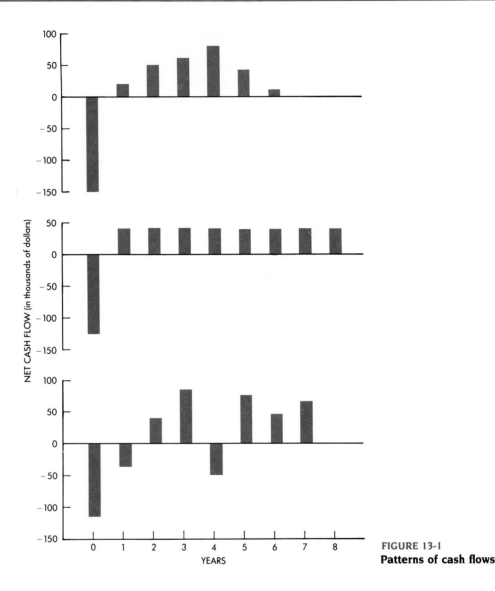

FIGURE 13-1
Patterns of cash flows

ment, is followed by positive and increasing net cash flows through year 4, after which they drop off as the project becomes older. Many other patterns are possible, both with respect to the life of the project and to the annual cash flows. In the middle panel, the initial cash outlay is followed by a stream of eight equal net cash inflows. From Chapter 4, we recognize this pattern to be an *annuity*. In the bottom panel, two distinct investment phases are shown. The first is at time 0 and continues into year 1 where there are heavy advertising and promotion expenses. In year 4, additional investment is needed to upgrade production capability and to promote the product some more. These outlays more than offset operating cash inflows, so there is a net cash outflow for the year. In the next 2 years, the project generates net cash inflows. Finally, the project terminates at the end of year 7. At that time, a salvage value is realized that results in a higher net cash inflow than in year 6. These examples illustrate that the patterns of expected net cash flows can vary considerably over time, depending on the project.

Replacement Decisions and Depreciation

To go to a somewhat more complicated replacement decision example involving taxes, suppose that we are considering the purchase of a new machine to replace an old lathe and that we need to obtain cash-flow information in order to evaluate the attractiveness of this project. The purchase price of the new machine is $18,500, and it will require an additional $1,500 to install, bringing the total cost to $20,000. We can sell the old machine for its depreciated book value of $2,000. The initial net cash outflow for the investment project, therefore, is $18,000. The new machine should cut labor and maintenance costs and affect other cash savings totaling $7,100 a year before taxes for each of the next 5 years, after which it will probably not provide any savings, nor will it have a salvage value. These savings represent the net savings to the firm if it replaces the old machine with the new. In other words, we are concerned with the difference between the cash flows resulting from the two alternatives: continuing with the old machine or replacing it with a new one.

Because a machine of this sort has a useful life in excess of 1 year, we cannot charge its cost against income for tax purposes but must depreciate it. We then deduct depreciation from income in order to compute taxable income. As discussed in Chapter 2, capital assets fall into defined cost recovery classes of 3, 5, 10, 15, 20, and $27\frac{1}{2}$ years, depending on their nature. The property class in which an asset falls determines its depreciable life for tax purposes. For ease of understanding, suppose for now that the machine we are considering falls into the 5-year property category and that the firm employs straight-line depreciation.

As a result, the annual depreciation charge is 20 percent of the total depreciable cost of $20,000, or $4,000 a year. Assume additionally that the corporate income tax rate is 40 percent. Moreover, assume that the old machine has a remaining depreciable life of 5 years, that there is no expected salvage value at the end of this time, and that the machine also is subject to straight-line depreciation. Thus, the annual depreciation charge on the old machine is 20 percent of its depreciated book value of $2,000, or $400 a year. Because we are interested in the incremental impact of the project, we must subtract depreciation charges on the old machine from depreciation charges on the new one to obtain the incremental depreciation charges associated with the project. Given the information cited, we now are able to calculate the expected net cash flow (after taxes) resulting from the acceptance of the project. It is shown in Table 13-1.

In figuring the net cash flow, we simply deduct the additional cash outlay for federal income taxes from the annual cash savings. The expected annual net cash inflow for this replacement proposal is $5,700 for each of the next 5 years; this figure compares with additional income after taxes of $2,100 a year. The cash-flow and net profit figures differ by the amount of additional depreciation. Because our concern is not with income, as such, but with cash flows, we are interested in the right-hand column. For an initial cash outlay of $18,000, then, we are able to replace an older machine with a new one that is expected to result in

TABLE 13-1
Determining the net cash flow

	BOOK ACCOUNT	CASH-FLOW ACCOUNT
Annual cash savings	$7,100	$7,100
Depreciation on new machine	4,000	
Less: Depreciation on old machine	400	
Additional depreciation charge	$3,600	
Additional income before taxes	3,500	
Income tax (40%)	1,400	1,400
Additional income after taxes	$2,100	
Annual net cash flow		$5,700

net cash savings of $5,700 a year over the next 5 years. As in the previous example, the relevant cash-flow information for capital budgeting purposes is expressed on an incremental, after-tax basis.

METHODS FOR EVALUATING PROJECTS

Once we have collected the necessary information, we are able to evaluate the attractiveness of the various investment proposals under consideration. The investment decision will be either to accept or to reject the proposal. In this section, we evaluate four methods of capital budgeting:

1. Average rate of return
2. Payback
3. Internal rate of return
4. Net present value

The first two are approximate methods for assessing the economic worth of a project. For simplicity, we assume throughout that the expected cash flows are realized at the end of each year.

Average Rate of Return on Investment

This accounting method represents the ratio of the average annual profits after taxes to the average investment in the project. In our previous example, the average annual book earnings for the 5-year period are $2,100, and the net investment in the project is $18,000. Therefore,

$$\text{Average rate of return} = \frac{\$2,100}{\$18,000} = 11.67\% \qquad (13\text{-}1)$$

Once the average rate of return for a proposal has been calculated, it may be compared with a required rate of return to determine if a particular proposal should be accepted or rejected.

The principal virtue of the average rate of return method is its simplicity; it makes use of readily available accounting information. Once the average rate of return for a proposal has been calculated, it may be compared with a required, or cutoff, rate of return to determine if a particular proposal should be accepted or rejected. The principal shortcomings of the method are that it is based on accounting income rather than on cash flows and that it fails to take account of the timing of cash inflows and outflows. The time value of money is ignored; benefits in the last year are valued the same as benefits in the first year.

Suppose that we have three investment proposals, each costing $9,000 and each having an economic and depreciable life of 3 years. Assume that these proposals are expected to provide the following book profits and cash flows over the next 3 years:

	PROJECT A		PROJECT B		PROJECT C	
PERIOD	Book Profit	Net Cash Flow	Book Profit	Net Cash Flow	Book Profit	Net Cash Flow
1	$3,000	$6,000	$2,000	$5,000	$1,000	$4,000
2	2,000	5,000	2,000	5,000	2,000	5,000
3	1,000	4,000	2,000	5,000	3,000	6,000

Each proposal will have the same average rate of return: $2,000/$9,000, or 22 percent; however, few, if any, firms would be equally favorable to all three projects. Most would prefer project A, which provides a larger portion of total cash benefits in the first year. For this reason, the average rate of return leaves much to be desired as a method for project selection.

Payback Method

The **payback period** of an investment project tells us the number of years required to recover our initial cash investment. It is the ratio of the initial fixed investment over the annual cash inflows for the recovery period. For our example,

$$\text{Payback period} = \frac{\$18,000}{\$5,700} = 3.16 \text{ years} \qquad (13\text{-}2)$$

Payback period. The length of time before the cumulative expected cash flows from an investment project equal its cost.

If the annual cash inflows are not equal, the job of calculation is somewhat more difficult. Suppose that annual cash inflows are $4,000 in the first year, $6,000 in the second and third years, and $4,000 in the fourth and fifth years. In the first 3 years, $16,000 of the original investment will be recovered, followed by $4,000 in the fourth year. With an initial cash investment of $18,000, the payback period is 3 years + ($2,000/$4,000), or $3\frac{1}{2}$ years.

If the payback period calculated is less than some maximum acceptable payback period, the proposal is accepted; if not, it is rejected. If the required payback period were 4 years, the project in our example would be accepted. The major shortcoming of the payback method is that it fails to consider cash flows after the payback period; consequently, it cannot be regarded as a measure of profitability. Two proposals costing $10,000 each would have the same payback period if they both had annual net cash inflows of $5,000 in the first 2 years, but one project might be expected to provide no cash flows after 2 years, whereas the other might be expected to provide cash flows of $5,000 in each of the next 3 years. Thus, the payback method can be deceptive as a yardstick of profitability. In addition to this shortcoming, the method does not take account of the magnitude or timing of cash flows during the payback period; it considers only the recovery period as a whole.

The method does give a rough indication of the liquidity of a project. Many managers use it also as a crude measure of risk; but as we shall see in the subsequent chapter, other analytical approaches do a much better job. While the payback method may provide useful insights, it is best employed as a supplement to the internal rate of return or net present value methods.

Internal Rate of Return Method

Because of the various shortcomings in the average rate of return and payback methods, it generally is felt that discounted cash-flow methods provide a more objective basis for evaluating and selecting investment projects. These methods take account of both the magnitude and the timing of expected cash flows in each period of a project's life. In any economy in which capital has value, the time value of money is an important concept. Stockholders place a higher value on an investment project that promises returns over the next 5 years than on a project that promises identical returns for years 6 through 10. Consequently, the timing of expected future cash flows is extremely important in the investment decision.

Internal rate of return. The rate of discount that equates the present value of cash inflows with the present value of cash outflows.

Discounted cash-flow methods enable us to isolate differences in the timing of cash flows for various projects by discounting these cash flows to their present values. The two discounted cash-flow methods are the **internal rate of return** method and the present-value method, and we consider each in turn. This presentation builds on the foundations established in Chapter 4 when we covered the mathematics of finance and in Chapter 5 when we took up the returns on common stocks.

The internal rate of return for an investment proposal is the discount rate that equates the present value of the expected cash outflows with the present value of the expected inflows. If the initial cash outlay or cost occurs at time 0, it is represented by that rate, r, such that

$$X_0 = \frac{X_1}{(1 + r)} + \frac{X_2}{(1 + r)^2} + \cdots + \frac{X_n}{(1 + r)^n} \qquad (13\text{-}3)$$

Thus, r is the rate that discounts the stream of future cash flows—X_1 through X_n—to equal in present value the initial outlay at time 0—X_0. For our example, the problem can be expressed as

$$\$18,000 = \frac{\$5,700}{(1 + r)} + \frac{\$5,700}{(1 + r)^2} + \frac{\$5,700}{(1 + r)^3} + \frac{\$5,700}{(1 + r)^4} + \frac{\$5,700}{(1 + r)^5} \quad (13\text{-}4)$$

Solving for the internal rate of return, r, sometimes involves a trial-and-error procedure using present-value tables. Fortunately, there are computer programs and programmed calculators for solving for the internal rate of return, and these eliminate the arduous computations involved in the trial-and-error procedure. Still, there are times when, by necessity, one must resort to the latter method. To illustrate, consider again our example. The cash-flow stream is represented by an even series of cash flows of $5,700, to be received at the end of each of the next 5 years. We want to determine the discount factor that, when multiplied by $5,700, equals the cash outlay of $18,000 at time 0. Suppose that we start with the discount rates—14 percent, 16 percent, and 18 percent—and calculate the present value of the cash-flow stream. For the different discount rates, we find, using Table B in the appendix at the end of the book,

DISCOUNT RATE	DISCOUNT FACTOR	CASH FLOW EACH YEAR	PRESENT VALUE OF STREAM
18%	3.1272	$5,700	$17,825.04
16%	3.2743	5,700	18,663.51
14%	3.4331	5,700	19,568.67

When we compare the present value of the stream with the initial outlay of $18,000, we see that the internal rate of return necessary to discount the stream to $18,000 falls between 16 and 18 percent, being closer to 18 than to 16 percent. To approximate the actual rate, we interpolate between 17 and 18 percent as follows:

	DISCOUNT RATE	PRESENT VALUE
	17%	$18,236.01
	18	17,825.04
Difference	1%	$ 410.97
$\frac{236.01}{410.97} = .57$	17% + .57% = 17.57%	

Thus, the internal rate of return necessary to equate the present value of the cash inflows with the present value of the outflows is approximately 17.57 percent. Note that interpolation gives only an approximation of the exact percentage; the relationship between the two discount rates is not linear with respect to present value.

When, as above, the cash-flow stream is an even series, and the initial outlay occurs at time 0, there really is no need for trial and error. We simply divide the initial outlay by the cash flow and search for the nearest discount factor. Using our example, we divide $18,000 by $5,700, obtaining 3.1579. The nearest discount factor on the 5-year row in Table B at the end of the book is 3.1272, and this figure corresponds to a discount rate of 18 percent. Inasmuch as 3.1579 is more than 3.1272, we know that the actual rate lies between 17 and 18 percent, and we interpolate accordingly. When the cash-flow stream is an uneven series, the task is more difficult, and here we must resort to trial and error. With practice, a person can come surprisingly close in selecting discount rates from which to start.

Acceptance Criterion.   The acceptance criterion generally employed with the internal rate of return method is to compare the internal rate of return with a required rate of return, known also as the cutoff, or **hurdle, rate.** If the internal rate of return exceeds the required rate, the project is accepted; if not, it is rejected. If the required rate of return is 12 percent and this criterion is used, the investment proposal will be accepted. If the required rate of return is the return investors expect the firm to earn on the project, accepting a project with an internal rate of return in excess of the required rate of return should result in an increase in the market price of the stock, because the firm accepts a project with a return greater than that required to maintain the present market price per share. In Chapter 15 we will say much more about relating the investment decision to the objective of the firm. We assume for now that the required rate of return is given.

Hurdle rate. The minimum required rate of return on investment in capital assets. The rate at which a project is acceptable.

Net Present Value Method

Like the internal rate of return method, the present-value method is a discounted cash-flow approach to capital budgeting. Recall from Chapter 4 that with the present-value approach, all cash flows are discounted to present value, using the required rate of return. The **net present value** of an investment proposal is

Net present value. The present value of the cash inflows minus the present value of the cash outflows.

$$NPV = X_0 + \frac{X_1}{(1 + k)} + \frac{X_2}{(1 + k)^2} + \cdots + \frac{X_n}{(1 + k)^n} \qquad (13\text{-}5)$$

where k is the required rate of return. If the sum of these discounted cash flows is zero or more, the proposal is accepted; if not, it is rejected. Another way to express the acceptance criterion is to say that the project will be accepted if the present value of cash inflows exceeds the present value of cash outflows. The rationale behind the acceptance criterion is the same as that behind the internal rate of return method. If the required rate of return is the return investors expect the firm to earn on the investment proposal, and the firm accepts a proposal with a net present value greater than zero, the market price of the stock should rise. Again, the firm is taking on a project with a return greater than that necessary to leave the market price of the stock unchanged.

If we assume a required rate of return of 12 percent after taxes, the net present value of our example problem is

$$NPV = -\$18{,}000 + \frac{\$5{,}700}{(1.12)} + \frac{\$5{,}700}{(1.12)^2} + \frac{\$5{,}700}{(1.12)^3} + \frac{\$5{,}700}{(1.12)^4} + \frac{\$5{,}700}{(1.12)^5}$$

$$= -\$18{,}000 + \$20{,}547$$

$$= \$2{,}547 \tag{13-6}$$

Again, we can solve the problem by computer, by calculator, or by reference to the appropriate present-value table at the end of the book. Using Table B, because an annuity is involved, we find the appropriate discount factor 3.6048 and multiply $5,700 by it to obtain $20,547. Subtracting the initial outlay of $18,000, we obtain $2,547. Inasmuch as the net present value of this proposal is greater than 0, the proposal should be accepted, using the present-value method.

With the internal rate of return method, we are given the cash flows, and we solve for the rate of discount that equates the present value of the cash inflows with the present value of outflows. We then compare the internal rate of return with the required rate of return to determine whether the proposal should be accepted. With the present-value method, we are given the cash flows and the required rate of return, and we solve for the net present value. The acceptability of the proposal depends on whether the net present value is zero or more.

Mutual Exclusion and Dependency

In evaluating a group of investment proposals, we have to determine whether they are independent of each other. A proposal is said to be *mutually exclusive* if the acceptance of it precludes the acceptance of one or more other proposals. For example, if the firm is considering investment in one of two temperature-control systems, acceptance of one system will rule out acceptance of the other. Two mutually exclusive proposals cannot both be accepted.

A *contingent* or *dependent* proposal is one whose acceptance depends on the acceptance of one or more other proposals. The addition of a large machine may necessitate construction of a new wing to house it. Contingent proposals must be part of our thinking when we consider the original, dependent proposal. Recognizing the dependency, we can make investment decisions accordingly.

Profitability Index

The **profitability index,** or benefit-cost ratio, of a project is the present value of future net cash flows over the initial cash outlay. It can be expressed as

Profitability index. The present value of future cash flows of a project divided by its cost.

$$PI = \frac{\sum\limits_{t=1}^{n} X_t/(1 + k)^t}{X_0} \tag{13-7}$$

where Σ means the sum of discounted cash flows from period 1 through period n. For our example,

$$PI = \frac{\$20,547}{\$18,000} = 1.14 \qquad (13\text{-}8)$$

As long as the profitability index is 1.00 or greater, the investment proposal is acceptable. For any given project, the net present value method and the profitability index give the same accept-reject signals. If we must choose between mutually exclusive projects, the net present value measure is preferred because it expresses in absolute terms the expected economic contribution of the project. In contrast, the profitability index expresses only the relative profitability.[2]

COMPARISON OF PRESENT-VALUE
AND INTERNAL RATE OF RETURN METHODS

In general, the net present value and internal rate of return methods lead to the same acceptance or rejection decision. In Fig. 13-2 we illustrate graphically the two methods applied to a typical investment project. The figure shows the curvilinear relationship between the net present value of a project and the discount rate employed. When the discount rate is 0, net present value is simply the total cash inflows less the total cash outflows of the project. Assuming that total inflows exceed total outflows and that outflows are followed by inflows, the typical project will have the highest net present value when the discount rate is 0. As the discount rate increases, the present value of future cash inflows decreases relative to the present value of cash outflows. At the intercept, the net present value of the project is 0. The discount rate at that point represents the internal rate of return that equates the present value of cash inflows with the present value of cash outflows. For discount rates greater than the internal rate of return, the net present value of the project is negative.

If the required rate of return is less than the internal rate of return, we would accept the project using either method. Suppose that the required rate were 10 percent. As seen in Fig. 13-2, the net present value of the project then would be Y. Inasmuch as Y is greater than 0, we would accept the project, using the present-value method. Similarly, we would accept the project using the internal rate of return method because the internal rate exceeds the required rate. For required rates greater than the internal rate of return, we would reject the project under either method. Thus, we see that the internal rate of return and present-value methods give us identical answers with respect to the acceptance or rejection of an investment project.

[2] See Bernhard Schwab and Peter Lusztig, "A Comparative Analysis of the Net-Present Value and the Benefit-Cost Ratio as Measures of the Economic Desirability of Investments," *Journal of Finance*, 24 (June 1969), 507–16.

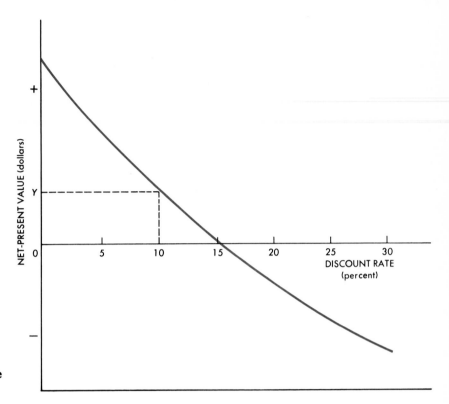

FIGURE 13-2
Relation between discount rate and net present value

Compounding Differences

We must identify important differences between the methods. When two invest-ment proposals are mutually exclusive, so that we can select only one, the two methods may give contradictory results. To illustrate the nature of the problem, suppose a firm had two mutually exclusive investment proposals that were ex-pected to generate the following cash flows:

	CASH FLOWS				
Year	0	1	2	3	4
Proposal A	−$23,616	$10,000	$10,000	$10,000	$10,000
Proposal B	− 23,616	0	5,000	10,000	32,675

Internal rates of return for proposals A and B are 25 percent and 22 percent, re-spectively. If the required rate of return is 10 percent, however, and we use this figure as our discount rate, the net present values of proposals A and B are $8,083 and $10,347, respectively. Thus, proposal A is preferred if we use the in-ternal rate of return method, whereas proposal B is preferred if we use the present-value method. If we can choose but one of these proposals, we obviously have a conflict.

The conflict between these two methods is due to different assumptions with respect to the reinvestment rate on funds released from the proposals. The internal rate of return method implies that funds are reinvested at the internal rate of return over the remaining life of the proposal. For proposal A, the assumption is that cash flows of $10,000 at the end of years 1, 2, and 3 can be reinvested to earn a return of 25 percent, compounded annually. The present-value method implies reinvestment at a rate equivalent to the required rate of return used as the discount rate. Because of these differing assumptions, the two methods can give different rankings of investment proposals, as we have seen.

To illustrate further the nature of the problem, consider two additional mutually exclusive proposals with the following cash flows:

	CASH FLOWS			
Time	0	1	2	3
Proposal C	−$155.22	$100.00	0	$100.00
Proposal D	− 155.22	0	0	221.00

The net present value of each of these proposals is $10.82 if we assume a required rate of return of 10 percent. However, we would be indifferent between the two proposals only if the firm had opportunities for reinvestment at a rate of 10 percent.

This concept is illustrated in Fig. 13-3, where the functional relationship between net present value and the discount rate is graphed for the two proposals. The intercepts on the 0 horizontal line represent the internal rates of return of the two proposals that equate their net present values with 0. For proposal C, the internal rate of return is 14 percent; for proposal D, it is 12.5 percent. The intercepts on the vertical axis represent total undiscounted cash inflows less total cash outflows for the two proposals. We see that proposal D ranks higher than proposal C if the reinvestment rate is below 10 percent and lower if it is above 10 percent. At the point of intersection, 10 percent, the proposals have identical net present values. This point represents the crossover rate. Given a reinvestment rate of 10 percent, then, the two proposals would have equal ranking. For reinvestment rates other than this percentage, we would prefer one proposal to the other. In a similar manner, other mutually exclusive investment proposals can be evaluated according to the intersections.

Scale of Investment

In addition to the problem of different implicit compounding rates, a problem arises if the initial cash outlays are different for two mutually exclusive investment proposals. Because the results of the internal rate of return method are ex-

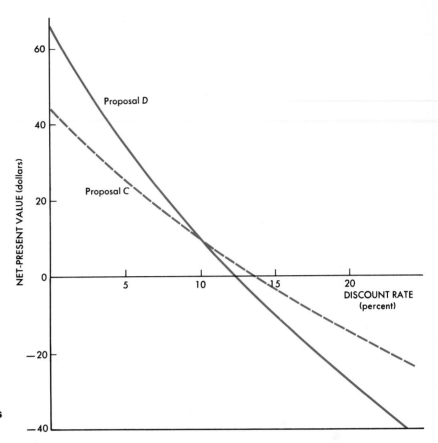

FIGURE 13-3
Relation between discount rate and net present values, proposals C and D

pressed as a percent, the scale of investment is ignored. Without allowance for this factor, a 50 percent return on a $100 investment would always be preferred to a 25 percent return on a $500 investment. In constrast, the results of the present-value method are expressed in absolute terms. If the investment proposals were each for 1 year, we would have the following, assuming a required rate of return of 10 percent:

| | CASH FLOWS | | IRR | NPV (10%) |
	Year 0	Year 1		
Proposal X	−$100	$150	50%	$36.36
Proposal Y	− 500	625	25	68.18

With respect to absolute returns, the second proposal is superior, despite the fact that its internal rate of return is less. The reason is that the scale of investment is greater, affording a greater net present value.

Multiple Rates of Return

A final problem with the internal rate of return method is that multiple internal rates of return are possible. A necessary, but not sufficient, condition for this occurrence is that the cash-flow stream changes sign more than once. All of our examples depicted situations where a cash outflow was followed by one or more cash inflows. In other words, there was but one change in sign, which ensured a unique internal rate of return. However, some projects involve multiple changes in sign. At the end of the project, there may be a requirement to restore the environment. This often happens in the extractive industry where the land must be reclaimed at the end of the project. With a chemical plant, there are sizable dismantling costs. Whatever the cause, these costs result in a cash outflow at the end of the project and, hence, in more than one change in sign in the cash-flow series.

Whether these changes in sign cause more than one internal rate of return depends also on the magnitudes of the cash flows. As the relationship is complicated and requires illustration, we address the problem in detail in Appendix A at the end of the chapter. While most projects have but one change in sign in the cash-flow stream, some have more. When this occurs, the financial manager must be alert to the possibility of multiple internal rates of return. As shown in Appendix A, no one internal rate of return makes sense economically when there are multiple internal rates of return, and an alternative method of analysis must be used.

With multiple IRR situations, calculators and computer programs often are fooled and produce only one IRR. Perhaps the best way to determine if a problem exists is to calculate the net present value of a project at various discount rates. If the discount rate were increased from zero in 25 percent increments up to, say, 1,000 percent, the NPV could be plotted on a graph similar to that shown in Fig. 13-3. If the NPV line connecting the dots crosses the 0 NPV line more than once, you have a multiple IRR problem.

Summary of Shortcomings of the IRR Method

We have seen that the present-value method always provides correct rankings of mutually exclusive investment projects, whereas the internal rate of return method sometimes does not. With the latter method, the implied reinvestment rate will differ depending on the cash-flow stream for each investment proposal under consideration. For proposals with a high internal rate of return, a high reinvestment rate is assumed; for proposals with a low internal rate of return, a low reinvestment rate is assumed. Only rarely will the internal rate of return calculated represent the relevant rate for reinvestment of intermediate cash flows. With the present-value method, however, the implied reinvestment rate—namely, the required rate of return—is the same for each proposal. In essence, this reinvestment rate represents the minimum return on opportunities available to the firm.

In addition, the net present value method takes account of differences in the scale of investment. If our objective is truly value maximization, the only theoretically correct opportunity cost of funds is the required rate of return. It is consistently applied with the net present value method, thereby avoiding the reinvestment rate and scale of investment problems. Finally, the possibility of multiple rates of return hurts the case for the internal rate of return method.

With all these criticisms, why is it used at all? The reason is that many managers find the internal rate of return easier to visualize and interpret than they do the net present value measure. One does not have to specify a required rate of return in the calculations. To the extent that the required rate of return is but a rough estimate, the internal rate of return method may permit a more satisfying comparison of projects for the typical manager. Put another way, managers feel comfortable with a return measure as opposed to an absolute net present value figure. As long as the company is not confronted with many mutually exclusive projects or with unusual projects having multiple sign changes in the cash-flow stream, the internal rate of return method may be used with reasonable confidence. When this is not the case, the shortcomings just discussed must be borne in mind. Either modifications in the internal rate of return method or a switch to the net present value method needs to occur.

ADDITIONAL FACTORS INFLUENCING CASH FLOWS

In our machine replacement example, we assumed straight-line depreciation, the depreciable life of the asset equaling its economic life, no investment tax credit, no salvage value, and no working capital requirement. We wanted to keep the example simple so that we could analyze the methods for evaluating expected profitability. We need now to digress for a while in order to examine the effect of the foregoing considerations on the magnitude and timing of cash flows. We also shall examine the question of mutually exclusive projects with different lives.

Method of Depreciation

In our earlier example, we assumed straight-line depreciation when computing cash flows. However, a more advantageous method of depreciation is available for tax purposes. Under the 1986 Tax Reform Act, there are seven property classes for cost recovery (depreciation) purposes. As described in Chapter 2, the property category in which an asset falls determines its depreciable life for tax purposes. As also described in that chapter, half-year conventions are observed in the first and in the year following the last year of the property class. As a result, depreciation allowed is less in those years.

The Treasury publishes depreciation percentages of original cost for each property class. For the first four property classes, they are the following:

RECOVERY YEAR	3-YEAR	5-YEAR	7-YEAR	10-YEAR
1	33.33%	20.00%	14.29%	10.00%
2	44.44	32.00	24.29	18.00
3	14.82	19.20	17.49	14.40
4	7.41	11.52	12.49	11.52
5		11.52	8.93	9.22
6		5.76	8.93	7.37
7			8.92	6.56
8			4.46	6.55
9				6.55
10				6.55
11				3.28

These percentages correspond to the principles taken up in Chapter 2, and they should be used for determining depreciation.

Setting Up the Cash Flows

In most cases, the capital recovery (depreciation) period is shorter than the economic life of the asset. To illustrate how we might go about using depreciation tables and setting up the cash flows for analysis, suppose that a company were considering an asset costing $100,000 that fell in the 5-year property class. The asset was expected to produce annual before-tax cash savings of $32,000 in each of the first 2 years, $27,000 in each of the next 2 years, $22,000 in both the fifth and the sixth years, and $20,000 in the seventh and last year. Assume further a 40 percent tax rate (federal and state) and no salvage value. Setting up the cash flows is facilitated greatly with a spreadsheet program like Lotus 1-2-3. The annual net cash flows are

	0	1	2	3	4	5	6	7
1. Cost	(100,000)							
2. Annual savings		32,000	32,000	27,000	27,000	22,000	22,000	20,000
3. Depreciation		20,000	32,000	19,200	11,520	11,520	5,760	
4. Income		12,000	0	7,800	15,480	10,480	16,240	20,000
5. Taxes (40%)		4,800	0	3,120	6,192	4,192	6,496	8,000
6. Net cash flow (1) + (2) − (5)	(100,000)	27,200	32,000	23,880	20,808	17,808	15,504	12,000

We see that the tax shield occurs only in the first 6 years, after which the full cash savings are subject to taxation. As a result, the cash flow is lower. This shift in timing over what would occur with straight-line depreciation over the life of the asset has a favorable present-value effect. To determine the net present value of the project, we discount the cash flows shown in row 6 by the required rate of return and sum them. If the required rate of return were 12 percent, the net present value would be $3,405, whereas the internal rate of return is 13.25 percent, both measures indicating acceptance of the project. Similarly, cash flows for other projects can be set up in the manner shown.

Salvage Value and Taxes

The cash-flow pattern will change toward the better if the asset is expected to have a salvage, or scrap, value at the end of the project. As the asset will be fully depreciated at that time, the salvage value realized is subject to taxation at the ordinary income tax rate. Suppose that the asset were sold for $10,000 at the end of year 7. With a 40 percent tax rate, the company will realize cash proceeds of $6,000 at the end of the last year. This amount then would be added to the net cash inflow previously determined to give the total cash flow in the last year.

Salvage value. The value of a capital asset at the end of the planning period. Also known as scrap value.

If the asset is sold before it is fully depreciated, the tax treatment is different. In general, if an asset is sold for more than its depreciated book value but for less than its cost, the firm pays taxes at the full corporate rate. If the asset is sold for more than its cost, this excess is subject to the capital gains tax treatment, which sometimes is more favorable. As such calculations are complicated, the reader is referred to the tax code and/or a tax attorney when faced with the tax treatment of a sale of an asset.

Working Capital Requirement

In addition to the investment in a fixed asset, it is sometimes necessary to carry additional cash, receivables, or inventories. This investment in working capital is treated as a cash outflow at the time it occurs. For example, if $15,000 in working capital is required in connection with our example, there would be an additional cash outflow of $15,000 at time 0, bringing the total outflow to $105,000. At the end of the project's life, the working capital investment presumably is returned. Therefore, there would be a $15,000 cash inflow at the end of year 7. As a result, the cash inflow in that year would be $27,000 instead of $12,000.

This switching of cash flows obviously is adverse from a present-value stand-point: $15,000 is given up at time 0 and is not gotten back until 7 years later. Again using 12 percent as the required rate of return, the net present value of row 6 of our previous example, rearranged as suggested, is −$4,810. The internal rate of return is now 10.57 percent. These figures compare with $3,405 and 13.25 percent determined before. Thus, an initial working capital investment of $15,000 causes the project to be unacceptable, whereas before it was acceptable. While total cash flows are not affected, their timing is affected.

CAPITAL RATIONING

Capital rationing occurs any time there is a budget ceiling, or constraint, on the amount of funds that can be invested during a specific period, such as a year. Such constraints are prevalent in a number of firms, particularly in those that

Capital rationing. A fixed ceiling on the annual amount of capital expenditures that forces the rationing of capital.

have a policy of financing all capital expenditures internally. Another example of capital rationing occurs when a division of a large company is allowed to make capital expenditures only up to a specified budget ceiling, over which the division usually has no control. With a capital rationing constraint, the firm attempts to select the combination of investment proposals that will provide the greatest profitability.

Your firm may have the following investment opportunities, ranked in descending order of profitability indexes (the ratio of the present value of future net cash flows over the initial cash outlay):

Proposal	4	7	2	3	6	5	1
Profitability index	1.25	1.19	1.16	1.14	1.09	1.05	.97
Initial outlay	$400,000	$100,000	$175,000	$125,000	$200,000	$100,000	$150,000

If the budget ceiling for initial outlays during the present period is $1 million, and the proposals are independent of each other, you would select proposals in descending order of profitability until the budget was exhausted. With capital rationing, you would accept the first five proposals, totaling $1 million in initial outlays. In other words, you do not necessarily invest in all proposals that increase the net present value of the firm; you invest in an acceptable proposal only if the budget constraint allows such an investment. You will not invest in proposal 5, even though the profitability index in excess of 1 would suggest its acceptance. The critical aspect of the capital rationing constraint illustrated is that capital expenditures during a period are strictly limited by the budget ceiling, regardless of the number of attractive investment opportunities.

A budget ceiling carries its cost, too, when it bars us from taking advantage of any opportunity beyond the cutoff. In our example, the opportunity forgone by the $1 million budget ceiling is proposal 5, which has a profitability index of 1.05. Although all cash flows are discounted at the required rate of return, we do not necessarily accept proposals that provide positive net present values. We see which proposals we can accept before we exhaust the budget. In so doing, we may reject projects that provide positive net present value, as was shown by proposal 5.

Capital rationing usually results in an investment policy that is less than optimal. In some periods, the firm accepts projects down to its required rate of return; in others, it rejects projects that would provide returns substantially in excess of the required rate. If the firm actually can raise capital at that approximate real cost, should it not invest in all projects yielding more than the required rate of return? If it rations capital and does not invest in all projects yielding more than the required rate, is it not forgoing opportunities that would enhance the market price of its stock?

From a theoretical standpoint, a firm should accept all projects yielding more than the required rate of return.[3] By so doing, it will increase the market price per share, because it is taking on projects that will provide a return higher than that necessary to maintain the present market price per share. This proposition assumes that the firm actually can raise capital, within reasonable limits, at the required rate of return. Certainly, unlimited amounts of capital are not available at any one cost. However, most firms are involved in a more or less continual process of making decisions to undertake capital expenditures and to finance these expenditures. Given these assumptions the firm should accept all proposals yielding more than the required rate of return and raise capital to finance these proposals at that approximate real cost. Certainly, there are circumstances that complicate the use of this rule. In general, however, this policy should tend to maximize the market price of the stock over the long run. If the firm rations capital and rejects projects that yield more than the required rate of return, then the firm's investment policy, by definition, is less than optimal. Management could increase the value of the firm to the shareholders by accepting these projects.

SUMMARY

Capital budgeting involves the outlay of current funds in anticipation of cash-flow benefits. Capital budgeting decisions by corporations have an important impact on capital formation and on a country's economic growth. In this chapter we first considered the collection of cash-flow information for the evaluation of investment proposals. The key is to measure incremental cash flows with and without the investment proposal being analyzed. Depreciation under the accelerated cost recovery system (1986 Tax Reform Act) has a significant effect on the pattern of cash flows and, hence, on present value. Also affecting the pattern of cash flows is the presence of salvage value and a working capital requirement.

Capital budgeting methods, including the average rate of return and payback methods, were evaluated under the assumption that the acceptance of any investment proposal does not change the total business-risk complexion of the firm. The two discounted cash-flow methods—internal rate of return and net present value—are the only appropriate means by which to judge the economic contribution of an investment proposal.

The important distinctions between the internal rate of return method and the present-value method are the implied compounding rate, the scale of investment, and the possibility of multiple internal rates of return. Depending on the situation, contrary answers can be given with respect to the acceptance of mutually exclusive investment proposals. On theoretical grounds, a case can be made for the superiority of the present-value method, though in practice the internal rate of return method is popular. The problem of capital rationing was examined, and we concluded that such a policy is likely to result in investment decisions that are less than optimal.

---

[3] We shall examine the rationale for this criterion in Chapter 15.

APPENDIX A
Multiple Internal Rates of Return

In a well-known article, Lorie and Savage pointed out that certain streams of cash flows may have more than one internal rate of return.[4] To illustrate the problem, suppose that we had the following stream of cash flows corresponding to the "pump" proposal of Lorie and Savage:

YEAR	0	1	2
Cash flow	−$1,600	$10,000	−$10,000

In this example, a new, more effective pump is substituted for an existing pump. On an incremental basis, there is an initial outlay followed by net cash inflows resulting from the increased efficiency of the new pump. If the quantity of oil, for example, is fixed, the new pump will exhaust this supply more quickly than the old pump would. Beyond this point of exhaustion, the new pump alternative would result in an incremental outflow, because the old pump would still be productive.

When we solve for the internal rate of return for the cash-flow stream, we find that it is not one rate but two: 25 percent and 400 percent. This unusual situation is illustrated in Fig. 13-4, where the discount rate is plotted along the horizontal axis and net present value along the vertical axis. At a zero rate of discount, the net present value of the project is simply the sum of all the cash

[4] See James H. Lorie and Leonard J. Savage, "Three Problems in Rationing Capital," *Journal of Business*, 28 (October 1955), 229–39.

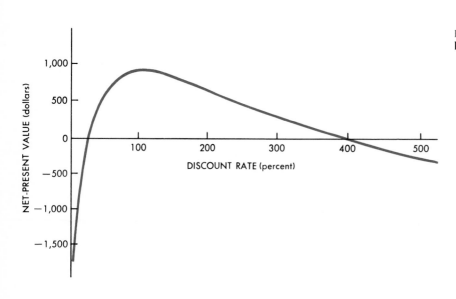

FIGURE 13-4
Dual rates of return

flows. It is −$1,600 because total cash outflows exceed total cash inflows. As the discount rate increases, the present value of the second-year outflow diminishes with respect to the first-year inflow, and the present value of the proposal becomes positive when the discount rate exceeds 25 percent. As the discount rate increases beyond 100 percent, the present value of all future cash flows (years 1 and 2) diminishes relative to the initial outflow of −$1,600. At 400 percent, the present value of all cash flows again becomes 0.

This type of proposal differs from the usual case, shown in Fig. 13-2, in which net present value is a decreasing function of the discount rate, and in which there is but one internal rate of return that equates the present value of all inflows with the present value of all outflows. An investment proposal may have any number of internal rates of return, depending upon the cash-flow pattern. Consider the following series of cash flows:

YEAR	0	1	2	3
Cash flow	−$1,000	$6,000	−$11,000	$6,000

In this example, discount rates of 0, 100 percent, and 200 percent result in the net present value of all cash flows equaling 0.

The number of internal rates of return is limited to the number of reversals of sign in the cash-flow stream. In the example, we have three reversals and three internal rates of return. Although a multiple reversal in signs is a necessary condition for multiple internal rates of return, it is not sufficient for such an occurrence. The occurrence of multiple internal rates of return also depends on the magnitude of cash flows. For the following series of cash flows, there is but one internal rate of return (32.5 percent), despite two reversals of sign:

YEAR	0	1	2
Cash flow	−$1,000	$1,400	−$100

When confronted with a proposal having multiple rates of return, how does one decide which is the correct rate? In our dual-rate example, is the correct rate 25 percent or 400 percent? Actually, neither rate is correct, because neither is a measure of investment worth. In essence, the firm has "borrowed" $10,000 from the project at the end of the year 1 and will pay it back at the end of year 2. The relevant question is: What is it worth to the firm to have the use of $10,000 for one year? This question, in turn, depends on the rate of return on investment opportunities available to the firm for that period of time. If the firm could earn 20 percent on the use of these funds and realize these earnings at the end of the period, the value of this opportunity would be $2,000, to be received at the end of year 2. This amount would then be compared with the initial outlay of $1,600 to determine whether the project is worthwhile. Similarly, other proposals can be evaluated in this manner to determine whether they are worthwhile.

In general, holding risk constant a company wishes to lend at as high a rate as possible and to borrow at as low a rate as possible. In the case of a project having multiple changes in signs, both lending and borrowing are involved. The best way to tackle the problem is to separate cash flows into their lending and borrowing components and then to use the net present value approach. In this way, the appropriate minimum required rate of return can be used on the lending side and the appropriate borrowing rate on that side.

APPENDIX B
Inflation and Capital Budgeting

In general, the presence of inflation in the economy distorts capital budgeting decisions. The principal reason is that depreciation charges are based on original rather than replacement costs. As income grows with inflation, an increasing portion is taxed, with the result that real cash flows do not keep up with inflation. To illustrate, consider an investment proposal costing $24,000 under the assumptions that no inflation is expected, depreciation is straight line over four years, and the tax rate is 50 percent. The following cash flows are expected to occur:

YEAR	CASH SAVINGS	DEPRECIATION	TAXES	CASH FLOW AFTER TAXES
1	$10,000	$6,000	$2,000	$8,000
2	10,000	6,000	2,000	8,000
3	10,000	6,000	2,000	8,000
4	10,000	6,000	2,000	8,000

Depreciation is deducted from cash savings to obtain taxable income, on which taxes of 50 percent are based.[5] Without inflation, depreciation charges represent the "cost" of replacing the investment as it wears out. Because nominal income on which taxes are paid represents real income, the last column represents real cash flows after taxes. The internal rate of return that equates the present value of the cash inflows with the cost of the project is 12.6 percent.

Consider now a situation in which inflation is at a rate of 7 percent per annum, and cash savings are expected to grow at this overall rate of inflation. The after-tax cash flows become the following.

[5] This example is similar to one in John A. Tatom and James E. Turley, "Inflation and Taxes: Disincentives for Capital Formation," *Review of the Federal Reserve Bank of St. Louis,* 60 (January 1978), 2–8.

YEAR	CASH SAVINGS	DEPRECIATION	TAXES	CASH FLOW AFTER TAXES
1	$10,700	$6,000	$2,350	$8,350
2	11,449	6,000	2,725	8,724
3	12,250	6,000	3,125	9,125
4	13,108	6,000	3,554	9,554

Although these cash flows are larger than before, they must be deflated by the inflation rate if one is concerned with the real as opposed to the nominal rate of return. Therefore, the last column becomes

	YEAR			
	1	2	3	4
Real after-tax cash flow	$7,804	$7,620	$7,449	$7,289

As we see, the real after-tax cash flows are less than before, and they decline steadily over time. The reason is that depreciation charges do not change in keeping with inflation, so that an increasing portion of the tax savings is subject to taxation. As taxes increase at a rate faster than inflation, real after-tax cash flows must decline. The internal rate of return based on real after-tax cash flows is 9.9 percent compared with 12.6 percent without inflation.

Therefore, the presence of inflation results in lower real rates of return. Consequently, there is less incentive for companies to undertake capital investments. While the cash-flow situation is improved with accelerated depreciation, the same unfavorable comparisons hold. There simply is a disincentive for companies to undertake capital expenditures, with the result that the amount invested typically is less than would be the case in the absence of inflation. It follows also that there will be an incentive to seek investments with faster paybacks (shorter economic lines) and that industry will become less capital intensive.

The Bias in Cash-Flow Estimates

In estimating cash flows, each company must take anticipated inflation into account. Often there is a tendency to assume that price levels will remain unchanged throughout the life of the project. Frequently, this assumption is imposed unknowingly: future cash flows are estimated on the basis of existing prices. However, a bias arises in the selection process, in that the required rate of return for the project usually is based on current capital costs, which in turn embody a premium for anticipated inflation.[6]

Assume a situation in which the hurdle rate for a project is its required rate of return as perceived by investors and creditors. (The ways by which it is measured are taken up in Chapter 15.) There is general agreement that security prices are influenced by inflation. As we discovered in Chapter 3, the relationship is far from simple and it is not stable over time.

The key factor is that if the acceptance criterion, namely, the required rate of return, includes a premium for anticipated inflation, then the estimated cash flows also must reflect inflation. Such cash flows are affected in several ways. If cash inflows ultimately arise from the sale of a product, expected future prices affect these inflows. As for cash outflows, inflation affects both expected future wages and material costs. Note that future inflation does not affect depreciation charges on existing assets. Once the asset is acquired, these charges are known with certainty. The effect of anticipated inflation on cash inflows and cash outflows will vary with the nature of the project. In some cases, cash inflows through price increases, will rise faster than cash outflows; in other cases, the opposite will hold. No matter what the relationship, it is a vital part of the cash-flow estimates. Otherwise, a bias of the type described before arises.

Illustration of Inflation Bias.   A project that cost $100,000 at time 0 was under consideration and was expected to provide cash-flow benefits over the next 5 years. Straight-line depreciation was $20,000 a year, and the corporate tax rate (federal and state) was 50 percent. Cash flows were estimated on the basis of price levels at time 0, with no consideration to the effect of future inflation upon them, and these estimates were

| | PERIOD | | | | |
	1	2	3	4	5
Expected cash inflow, I_t	$30,000	$40,000	$50,000	$50,000	$30,000
Expected cash outflow, O_t	10,000	10,000	10,000	10,000	10,000
	$20,000	$30,000	$40,000	$40,000	$20,000
Times (1 − tax rate)	.50	.50	.50	.50	.50
	$10,000	$15,000	$20,000	$20,000	$10,000
Depreciation × tax rate	10,000	10,000	10,000	10,000	10,000
Net cash flow	$20,000	$25,000	$30,000	$30,000	$20,000

If the project's required rate of return were 14 percent, the net present value of the project would be −$14,821. As this figure is negative, the project would be rejected.

The results are biased in the sense that the discount rate embodies an element attributable to anticipated future inflation, whereas the cash-flow estimates do not. Suppose that the existing rate of inflation, as measured by changes in the

[6] This section is based on James C. Van Horne, "A Note on Biases in Capital Budgeting Introduced by Inflation," *Journal of Financial and Quantitative Analysis*, 6 (January 1971), 653–58.

price-level index, were 10 percent, and that this rate was expected to prevail over the next 5 years. If both cash inflows and cash outflows were expected to increase at this rate, the net present value of the project would be

$$NPV_0 = \sum_{t=1}^{5} \frac{[I_t(1.10)^t - O_t(1.10)^t][1 - .5] + 20,000_t[.5]}{(1.14)^t} - 100,000$$

$$= \$1,615 \qquad\qquad\qquad\qquad (13B\text{-}1)$$

where I_t is the cash inflow in year t, O_t is the cash outflow in year t, and $20,000 is the annual depreciation in year t, which is multiplied by the tax rate to give the tax-shield cash savings. Because the net present value is positive, the project would now be acceptable, whereas before it was not. To reject it under the previous method of estimating cash flows would result in an opportunity loss to stockholders, for the project provides a return somewhat in excess of that required by investors.

This example serves to illustrate the necessity of taking anticipated inflation into account explicitly when estimating future cash flows. Too often there is a tendency not to consider its effect in these estimates. Because anticipated inflation is embodied in the required rate of return, not to take account of it in the cash-flow estimates will result in a biased appraisal of the project and, in turn, the possibility of a less than optimal allocation of capital.

It is essential, then, to compare apples with apples or oranges with oranges. If a nominal required return is used, which usually is the case, then nominal cash flows should be employed, and these cash flows should take account of expected future inflation. If a real required rate of return is used, then the cash-flow estimates should not be adjusted for inflation. Consistency is critical, as illustrated in our example. More exact inflation adjustment procedures for capital investment are described elsewhere, but consistency in assumptions is the important lesson to be learned.

QUESTIONS

1. Explain what is meant by the time value of money. Why is a bird in the hand worth two (or so) in the bush? Which capital budgeting approaches ignore this concept? Are they optimal?

2. In evaluating the return from investments, why is depreciation included in the cash flows from a project and not deducted as are other expenses such as wages and taxes?

3. In capital budgeting for a new machine, should the following be added or subtracted from the new machine's purchase price?
   a. The market value of the old machine is $500.
   b. An investment in inventory of $2,000 is required.
   c. The book value of the old machine is $1,000.
   d. $200 is required to ship the new machine to the plant site.

    e. A concrete foundation for the new machine will cost $250.

    f. Training of the machine operator will cost $300.

    g. There is an investment tax credit on the new machine.

4. Why does the payback period bias the process of asset selection toward short-lived assets?

5. Contrast the internal rate of return with the net present value. Why might these two time value approaches to asset selection give conflicting decision rules?

6. In determining the expected cash flows from a new investment project, why should past sunk costs be ignored in the estimates?

7. The payback period, although it is conceptually unsound, is very popular in business as a criterion for assigning priorities to investment projects. Why is it unsound, and why is it popular?

8. Why are capital budgeting procedures not applied to working capital decisions?

9. Discuss the adjustments in the capital budgeting decision that should be made to compensate for expected inflation. (See Appendix B.)

10. What is a mutually exclusive investment project? a dependent project?

11. Is the economic efficiency of a country enhanced by the use of modern capital budgeting techniques? Why?

12. What is the purpose of requiring more levels of approval, the larger the capital expenditure? Is more information also required in support of the request?

13. If capital rationing is not optimal, why would any company use it?

14. The internal rate of return method implies that intermediate cash flows are reinvested at the internal rate of return. Under what circumstances is this assumption likely to lead to a seriously biased measure of the economic return from the project?

15. What is the difference between a product expansion and an equipment replacement type of investment?

SELF-CORRECTION PROBLEMS

1. Briarcliff Stove Company is considering a new product line to supplement its range line. It is anticipated that the new product line will involve cash investments of $700,000 at time 0 and $1.0 million in year 1. After-tax cash inflows of $250,000 are expected in year 2, $300,000 in year 3, $350,000 in year 4, and $400,000 each year through year 10. While the product line might be viable after year 10, the company prefers to be conservative and end all calculations at that time.

    a. If the required rate of return is 15 percent, what is the net present value of the project? Is it acceptable?

b. What is its internal rate of return?

c. What would be the case if the required rate of return were 10 percent?

d. What is the project's payback period?

2. Carbide Chemical Company is considering the replacement of two old machines with a new, more efficient machine. The old machines could be sold for $70,000 in the secondary market. Their depreciated book value is $120,000, with a remaining useful and depreciable life of 8 years. Straight-line depreciation is used on these machines. The new machine can be purchased and installed for $480,000. It has a useful life of 8 years, at the end of which a salvage value of $40,000 is expected. The machine falls into the 5-year property class for accelerated cost recovery (depreciation) purposes. Due to its greater efficiency, the new machine is expected to result in incremental annual savings of $120,000. The company's corporate tax rate is 34 percent, and if a loss occurs in any year on the project it is assumed that the company will receive a tax credit of 34 percent of such loss.

a. What are the incremental cash inflows over the 8 years and what is the incremental cash outflow at time 0?

b. What is the project's net present value if the required rate of return is 14 percent?

3. The Platte River Perfect Cooker Company is evaluating three investment situations: (1) produce a new line of aluminum skillets, (2) expand its existing cooker line to include several new sizes, and (3) develop a new higher-quality line of cookers. If only the project in question is undertaken, the expected present values and the amounts of investment required after taking all investment tax credits are

PROJECT	INVESTMENT REQUIRED	PRESENT VALUE OF FUTURE CASH FLOWS
1	$200,000	$290,000
2	115,000	185,000
3	270,000	400,000

If projects 1 and 2 are jointly undertaken, there will be no economies; the investment required and present values will simply be the sum of the parts. With projects 1 and 3, economies are possible in investment because one of the machines acquired can be used in both production processes. The total investment required for projects 1 and 3 combined is $440,000. If projects 2 and 3 are undertaken, there are economies to be achieved in marketing and producing the products but not in investment. The expected present value of future cash flows for projects 2 and 3 is $620,000. If all three projects are undertaken simultaneously, the economies noted above will still hold. However, a $125,000 extension on the plant will be necessary, as space is not available for all three projects. Which project or projects should be chosen?

PROBLEMS

1. Lobears, Inc., has two investment proposals, which have the following characteristics:

	PROJECT A			PROJECT B		
PERIOD	Cost	Profit after Taxes	Net Cash Flow	Cost	Profit after Taxes	Net Cash Flow
0	$9,000	—	—	$12,000	—	—
1		$1,000	$5,000		$1,000	$5,000
2		1,000	4,000		1,000	5,000
3		1,000	3,000		4,000	8,000

For each project, compute its average rate of return, its payback period, and its net present value, using a discount rate of 15 percent.

2. In Problem 1, what criticisms may be offered against the average rate of return as a capital budgeting method? What criticisms may be offered against the payback method?

3. The following are exercises on internal rates of return:

   a. An investment of $1,000 today will return $2,000 at the end of 10 years. What is its internal rate of return?

   b. An investment of $1,000 will return $500 at the end of each of the next 3 years. What is its internal rate of return?

   c. An investment of $1,000 today will return $900 at the end of 1 year, $500 at the end of 2 years, and $100 at the end of 3 years. What is its internal rate of return?

   d. An investment of $1,000 will return $130 per year forever. What is its internal rate of return?

4. Two mutually exclusive projects have projected cash flows as follows:

PERIOD	0	1	2	3	4
A	−$2,000	$1,000	$1,000	$1,000	$1,000
B	− 2,000	0	0	0	6,000

   a. Determine the internal rate of return for each project.

   b. Determine the net present value for each project at discount rates of 0, 5, 10, 20, 30, and 35 percent.

   c. Plot a graph of the net present value of each project at the different discount rates.

d. Which project would you select? Why? What assumptions are inherent in your decision?

5. Zaire Electronics can make either of two investments at time 0. Assuming a required rate of return of 14 percent, determine for each project (a) the payback period, (b) the net present value, (c) the profitability index, and (d) the internal rate of return. Assume the accelerated cost recovery system for depreciation and that the asset falls in the 5-year property class and the corporate tax rate is 34 percent.

PROJECT	INVESTMENT	1	2	3	4	5	6	7
A	$28,000	$8,000	$8,000	$8,000	$8,000	$8,000	$8,000	$8,000
B	20,000	5,000	5,000	6,000	6,000	7,000	7,000	7,000

6. Thoma Phamaceutical Company may buy DNA testing equipment costing $60,000. This equipment is expected to reduce clinical staff labor costs by $20,000 annually. The equipment has a useful life of 5 years, but falls in the 3-year property class for cost recovery (depreciation) purposes. No salvage value is expected at the end. The corporate tax rate for Thoma is 38 percent, and its required rate of return is 15 percent. (If profits after taxes on the project are negative in any year, the firm will receive a tax credit of 38 percent of the loss in that year.) On the basis of this information, what is the net present value of the project? Is it acceptable?

7. In problem 6, suppose that 6 percent inflation in labor cost savings is expected over the last 4 years, so that savings in the first year are $20,000, savings in the second year are $21,200, and so forth.

   a. If the required rate of return is still 15 percent, what is the net present value of the project? Is it acceptable?

   b. If a working capital requirement of $10,000 were required in addition to the cost of the equipment, and this additional investment were needed over the life of the project, what would be the effect on net present value? (All other things are the same as in Problem 7, part a.)

8. The Lake Tahoe Ski Resort is comparing a half-dozen capital improvement projects. It has allocated $1 million for capital budgeting purposes. The following proposals and associated profitability indexes have been determined. The projects themselves are independent of one another.

PROJECT	AMOUNT	PROFITABILITY
1. Extend ski lift 3	$500,000	1.22
2. Build a new sports shop	150,000	.95
3. Extend ski lift 4	350,000	1.20
4. Build a new restaurant	450,000	1.18
5. Build addition to housing complex	200,000	1.20
6. Build an indoor skating rink	400,000	1.05

a. With strict capital rationing, which of the investments should be undertaken?

b. Is this an optimal strategy?

9. The City of San Jose must replace a number of its concrete mixer trucks with new trucks. It has received several bids and has evaluated closely the performance characteristics of the various trucks. The Patterbilt truck, which costs $74,000, is top-of-the-line equipment. The truck has a life of 8 years, assuming that the engine is rebuilt in the fifth year. Maintenance costs of $2,000 a year are expected in the first 4 years, followed by total maintenance and rebuilding costs of $13,000 in the fifth year. During the last 3 years, maintenance costs are expected to be $4,000 a year. At the end of 8 years the truck will have an estimated scrap value of $9,000.

A bid from Bulldog Trucks, Inc., is for $59,000 a truck. Maintenance costs for this truck will be higher. In the first year they are expected to be $3,000, and this amount is expected to increase by $1,500 a year through the eighth year. In year 4 the engine will need to be rebuilt, and this will cost the company $15,000 in addition to maintenance costs in that year. At the end of 8 years the Bulldog truck will have an estimated scrap value of $5,000.

The last bidder, Best Tractor and Trailer Company, has agreed to sell trucks at $44,000 each. Maintenance costs in the first 4 years are expected to be $4,000 the first year and to increase by $1,000 a year. For the city's purposes, the truck has a life of only 4 years. At that time it can be traded in for a new Best Truck, which is expected to cost $52,000. The likely trade-in value of the old truck is $15,000. During years 5 through 8 the second truck is expected to have maintenance costs of $5,000 in year 5, and these are expected to increase by $1,000 each year. At the end of 8 years the second truck is expected to have a resale or salvage value of $18,000.

a. If the City of San Jose's opportunity cost of funds is 8 percent, which bid should it accept? Ignore tax considerations, as the city pays no taxes.

b. If its opportunity cost were 15 percent, would your answer change?

Appendix B Problem

10. Rioka Corporation can invest in a project that costs $100,000 and has a useful life of 5 years. The expected cash flows from the project are

		YEAR		
1	2	3	4	5
$20,000	$40,000	$40,000	$30,000	$20,000

The company's tax rate is 50 percent, and its cost of capital based on present conditions in the financial markets is 12 percent. The company uses straight-line depreciation. For simplicity, assume no investment tax credit.

a. Compute the net present values of the project without the consideration of inflation.

b. If inflation of 7 percent per annum is expected over the life of the project and cash flows are adjusted upward, what is the project's net present value?

SOLUTIONS TO SELF-CORRECTION PROBLEMS

1. a.

YEAR	CASH FLOW	DISCOUNT FACTOR (15%)	PRESENT VALUE
0	$ (700,000)	1.00000	$(700,000)
1	(1,000,000)	.86957	(869,570)
2	250,000	.75614	189,035
3	300,000	.65752	197,256
4	350,000	.57175	200,113
5–10	400,000	2.1638*	865,520
		Net present value =	$(117,646)

*5.0188 for 10 years − 2.8550 for 4 years.

As the net present value is negative, the project is unacceptable.

b. Internal rate of return is 13.21 percent.
If the trial-and-error method were used, we would have the following:

YEAR	CASH FLOW	14% DISCOUNT FACTOR	14% PRESENT VALUE	13% DISCOUNT FACTOR	13% PRESENT VALUE
0	$ (700,000)	1.0000	$(700,000)	1.0000	$(700,000)
1	(1,000,000)	.87719	(877,190)	.88496	(884,960)
2	250,000	.76947	192,368	.78315	195,788
3	300,000	.67497	202,491	.69305	207,915
4	350,000	.59208	207,228	.61332	214,662
5–10	400,000	2.3024	920,960	2.4517	980,680
		Net present value	$(54,143)		$ 14,085

Interpolating gives us

$$13\% + \frac{14,085}{54,143 + 14,085} = 13.21\%$$

As the internal rate of return is less than the required rate of return, the project would not be acceptable.

c. The project would be acceptable.

d. Payback period = 6 years. −$700,000 − $100,000 + $250,000 + $300,00 + $350,000 + $400,000 +$400,000 = 0.

2. a. Incremental cash inflows:

	1	2	3	4	5	6	7	8
1. Savings	$120,000	$120,000	$120,000	$120,000	$120,000	$120,000	$120,000	$120,000
2. Depreciation, new	96,000	153,600	92,160	55,296	55,296	27,648		
3. Depreciation, old	15,000	15,000	15,000	15,000	15,000	15,000	15,000	15,000
4. Incremental depreciation	81,000	138,600	77,160	40,296	40,296	12,648	(15,000)	(15,000)
5. Profit before tax (1) − (4)	39,000	(18,600)	42,840	79,704	79,704	107,352	135,000	135,000
6. Taxes (34%)	13,260	(6,324)	14,566	27,099	27,099	36,500	45,900	45,900
7. Operating cash flow (1) − (6)	106,740	126,324	105,434	92,901	92,901	83,500	74,100	74,100
8. Salvage value × (1 − .34)								26,400
9. Net cash flow	$106,740	$126,324	$105,434	$ 92,901	$ 92,901	$ 83,500	$ 74,100	$100,500

Incremental cash outflow:

$$\text{Cost} - \frac{\text{Sale of old}}{\text{machines}} - \text{Tax savings on book loss}$$

$$\$480,000 - \quad \$70,000 \quad - .34(\$120,000 - \$70,000) = \$393,000$$

b. Net present value of $393,000 outflow and net cash inflows on line 9 at 14 percent = $75,139.
The project is acceptable.

3.

PROJECT	INVESTMENT REQUIRED	PRESENT VALUE OF FUTURE CASH FLOWS	NET PRESENT VALUE
1	$200,000	$290,000	$ 90,000
2	115,000	185,000	70,000
3	270,000	400,000	130,000
1, 2	315,000	475,000	160,000
1, 3	440,000	690,000	250,000
2, 3	385,000	620,000	235,000
1, 2, 3	680,000	910,000	230,000

Projects 1 and 3 should be chosen as they provide the highest net present value.

SELECTED REFERENCES

BACON, PETER W., "The Evaluation of Mutually Exclusive Investments," *Financial Management*, 6 (Summer 1977), 55–58.

BIERMAN, HAROLD, JR., and SEYMOUR SMIDT, *The Capital Budgeting Decision*, 6th ed., New York: Macmillan, 1984.

GITMAN, LAWRENCE J., and VINCENT A. MERCURIO, "Cost of Capital Techniques Used by Major U.S. Firms," *Financial Management*, 11 (Winter 1982), 21–29.

HERBST, ANTHONY, "The Unique, Real Internal Rate of Return: Caveat Emptor!" *Journal of Financial and Quantitative Analysis*, 13 (June 1978), 363–70.

HONG, HAI, "Inflation and the Market Value of the Firm: Theory and Tests," *Journal of Finance*, 32 (September 1977), 1031–48.

KEANE, SIMON M., "The Internal Rate of Return and the Reinvestment Fallacy," *Journal of Accounting and Business Studies*, 15 (June 1979), 48–55.

KIM, SUK H., "A Summary of Empirical Studies on Capital Budgeting Practices," *Business and Public Affairs*, 13 (Fall 1986), 21–25.

LOGUE, DENNIS E., and T. CRAIG TAPLEY, "Performance Monitoring and the Timing of Cash Flows," *Financial Management*, 14 (Autumn 1985), 34–39.

LORIE, JAMES H., and LEONARD J. SAVAGE, "Three Problems in Rationing Capital," *Journal of Business*, 28 (October 1955), 229–39.

McCONNELL, JOHN J., and CHRIS J. MUSCARELLA, "Corporate Capital Expenditure Decisions and the Market Value of the Firm," *Journal of Financial Economics*, 14 (September 1985), 399–422.

PINCHES, GEORGE E., "Myopia, Capital Budgeting and Decision Making," *Financial Management*, 11 (Autumn 1982), 6–19.

RAPPAPORT, ALFRED, and ROBERT A. TAGGART, JR., "Evaluation of Capital Expenditure Proposals Under Inflation," *Financial Management*, 11 (Spring 1982), 5–13.

SCHWAB, BERNHARD, and PETER LUSZTIG, "A Comparative Analysis of the Net Present Value and the Benefit-Cost Ratios as Measures of the Economic Desirability of Investments," *Journal of Finance*, 24 (June 1969), 507–16.

TATOM, JOHN A., and JAMES E. TURLEY, "Inflation and Taxes: Disincentives for Capital Formation," *Review of the Federal Reserve Bank of St. Louis*, 60 (January 1978), 2–8.

VAN HORNE, JAMES C., "A Note on Biases in Capital Budgeting Introduced by Inflation," *Journal of Financial and Quantitative Analysis*, 6 (January 1971), 653–58.

———, "The Variation of Project Life as a Means for Adjusting for Risk," *Engineering Economist*, 21 (Spring 1976), 151–58.

WEINGARTNER, H. MARTIN, "Capital Rationing: n Authors in Search of a Plot," *Journal of Finance*, 32 (December 1977), 1403–31.

C H A P T E R 14

Risk and Capital Budgeting

In the dictionary, risk is defined as exposure to possible loss or injury. For the financial manager, it is the likelihood of an unfavorable outcome. Different investment projects have different degrees of risk. The project that is expected to provide a high return may be so risky that it causes a significant increase in the perceived risk of the firm. In turn, this may cause a decrease in the firm's value, despite the project's considerable potential. In this chapter we consider various ways by which management can gauge the risk of a project or a group of projects. Our ultimate objective is to come to an understanding of how risk affects value. First we must measure project risk under a variety of circumstances, and that is the purpose of this chapter.

Given information about the expected risk of an investment proposal or proposals, together with information about the expected return, management must then evaluate this information and reach a decision. As the decision to accept or reject an investment proposal depends on the risk-adjusted return required by suppliers of capital, we defer consideration of the evaluation of risky investments until we consider required rates of return in the next chapter. In this chapter we develop the information necessary to evaluate risky investments. In Chapter 15 we examine the use of this information in reaching capital budgeting decisions consistent with an objective of maximizing shareholder wealth. We begin this chapter with a discussion of the overall operating risk of the firm. We then move on to a general introduction to project risk, followed by the consideration of its specific measurement. Again, a spreadsheet program, such as Lotus 1-2-3, should be used whenever appropriate in setting up the cash flows for analysis.

OPERATING LEVERAGE AND RISK

The overall business risk of a firm is related to its **operating leverage.** Operating leverage is simply the employment of an asset for which the firm pays a fixed cost. Expressed differently, operating leverage occurs any time a firm has fixed costs that must be met, regardless of volume. In the very long run, of course, all costs are variable. Consequently, our analysis necessarily involves the short run. We employ assets with a fixed cost in the hope that volume will produce revenues more than sufficient to cover all fixed and variable costs. One of the more dramatic examples of operating leverage is in the airline industry, where a large portion of total costs is fixed. Beyond a certain break-even load factor, each additional passenger represents essentially straight profit to the airline.

The essential thing is that fixed costs do not vary as volume changes. These costs include things such as depreciation of buildings and equipment, insurance, property taxes, part of the overall utility bills, and a portion of the cost of management. On the other hand, variable costs vary directly with the level of output. These costs include raw materials, direct labor costs, part of the overall utility bills, direct selling commissions, and certain parts of general and administrative expenses. With fixed costs, the percentage change in profits accompanying a change in volume is greater than the percentage change in volume. This phenomenon is known as operating leverage.

We should recognize that operating leverage is but one component of the

Operating leverage. The employment of fixed assets that magnify variations in profits.

overall business risk of the firm. The principal factors giving rise to business risk are variability or uncertainty of sales and production costs. Operating leverage magnifies the impact of these factors on the variability of profits; however, operating leverage is not the source of the variability, per se. Consequently, the degree of operating leverage of a firm should not be taken to represent its business risk. Because of the underlying variability of sales and costs, however, increases in operating leverage will increase the total variability of profits and, hence, magnify the company's business risk.

Analyzing Operating Leverage

Our firm produces a quality testing machine that sells for $50 a unit. We have annual fixed costs of $100,000 and variable costs of $25 a unit, regardless of the volume sold. We wish to study the relationship between total costs and total revenues. One way to do that is shown in the break-even chart in Fig. 14-1, which depicts the relationship among profits, fixed costs, variable costs, and volume. By *profits*, we mean operating profits before taxes. This definition purposely excludes interest on debt and preferred stock dividends. These costs are not part of

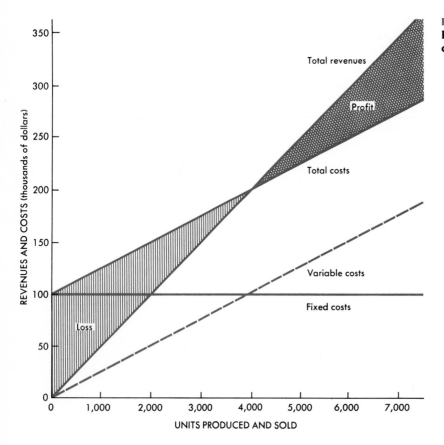

FIGURE 14-1
Break-even analysis: original conditions

the total fixed costs of the firm when it comes to analyzing operating leverage. They are taken into account when we analyze financial leverage in the next part.

The intersection of the total costs line with the total revenue line represents the break-even point. The fixed costs that must be recovered from the sales dollar after the deduction of variable costs determine the volume necessary to break even. In Fig. 14-1 this break-even point is 4,000 units of output. At the break-even point, variable costs plus fixed costs equal total revenue:

$$F + V(X) = P(X) \qquad (14\text{-}1)$$

where F = fixed costs
V = variable costs per unit
X = volume of output (in units)
P = price per unit.

Rearranging Eq. (14-1), the break-even point is

$$X = F/(P - V)$$
$$= 100{,}000/(50 - 25)$$
$$= 4{,}000$$

For each additional increment of volume above the break-even point, there is increasing profit represented by the crosshatched area in the figure. Likewise, as volume falls below the break-even point, there are increasing losses, represented by the lined area. Table 14-1 shows the profit for various levels of volume. We see that the closer the volume to the break-even point, the greater the percentage change in profit in relation to a percentage change in volume. The fact that fixed costs equal variable costs at the break-even point is attributable to the nature of the example. Because price less variable costs equals $50 - \$25 = \$25$, this amount is the same as variable costs per unit. As total price less variable costs must equal fixed costs at the break-even point, so, too, do total variable costs. As the example is changed in the subsequent section, this situation no longer holds.

Change in Factors.   A break-even chart like that in Fig. 14-1 tells us the relationship between operating profits and volume. The greater the ratio of price to variable costs per unit, the greater the absolute sensitivity of profits to volume and the greater the degree of operating leverage for all levels of output. A change

TABLE 14-1
Relation between profit and volume—original case

Volume (in thousands of units)	0	1	2	3	4	5	6	7
Operating profit (in thousands of dollars)	−$100	−$75	−$50	−$25	0	$25	$50	$75

in volume is not the only factor that affects profits, however; a change in selling price, in variable cost per unit, or in fixed costs also affects profits. In the light of Fig. 14-1, we examine a favorable change in each of these factors, all other factors held constant.

An increase in price lowers the break-even point. For example, an increase in price from $50 to $65 per unit would result in the following break-even point (in units):

$$X = 100,000/(65 - 25) = 2,500$$

Table 14-2 shows the relationship between profits and volume for five levels of output. The original situation is shown in the second column; the situation with a $65 price is in the third column. Profits, of course, are $15 per unit greater for each level of volume.

A decrease in fixed costs also lowers the break-even point; indeed, that is the whole idea behind operating leverage. If fixed costs were lowered from $100,000 to $50,000, the break-even point would be

$$X = 50,000/(50 - 25) = 2,000$$

With this change, profits for various levels of volume are shown in the fourth column of Table 14-2.

Finally, a decrease in variable costs again lowers the break-even point. If the change were from $25 to $20 per unit, the break-even point would be

$$X = 100,000/(50 - 20) = 3,333$$

Profits are $5 per unit greater, and the relationship of profits with volume is shown in column 5 of Table 14-2.

The last column of the table shows the relationship between profits and volume if all three of the changes occur simultaneously. Although we have considered only a favorable change in each case, it should be clear that a decrease in price, an increase in fixed costs, and an increase in variable costs will result in a

TABLE 14-2
Relation between profits and volume—
changing assumptions

VOLUME (IN UNITS)	PROFITS (IN THOUSANDS)				
	Original Case	Price ($65)	Fixed Costs ($50,000)	Variable Costs ($20)	All Three
0	−$100	−$100	−$ 50	−$100	−$ 50
2000	− 50	− 20	0	− 40	40
4,000	0	60	50	20	130
6,000	50	140	100	80	220
8,000	100	220	150	140	310

higher break-even point and lower profits. In both directions, the closer the volume to the break-even point, the greater the percentage change in profit for a percentage change in volume.

Thus, operating leverage magnifies the overall risk of the firm. It is not the underlying cause of risk, for that depends on the variability of demand for the product plus the variability of various costs. However, increases in operating leverage increase the variability of profits that accompany the underlying fluctuations mentioned earlier. With this in mind, we turn now to the measurement of risk for investment projects.

THE PROBLEM OF PROJECT RISK

We define the riskiness of an investment project as the variability of its cash flows from those that are expected. The greater the variability, the riskier the project is said to be. For each project under consideration, we can make estimates of the future cash flows. Rather than estimate only the most likely cash-flow outcome for each year in the future as we did in Chapter 4, we estimate a number of possible outcomes. In this way we are able to consider the range of possible cash flows for a particular future period rather than just the most likely cash flow.

An Illustration

To illustrate the formulation of multiple cash-flow forecasts for a future period, suppose that we had two investment proposals under consideration. Suppose further that we were interested in making forecasts for the following states of the economy: normal, deep recession, mild recession, major boom, and minor boom. After assessing the future under each of these possible states, we estimate the following cash flows for the next year:

	ANNUAL CASH FLOWS	
STATE	Proposal A	Proposal B
Deep recession	$3,000	$2,000
Mild recession	3,500	3,000
Normal	4,000	4,000
Minor boom	4,500	5,000
Major boom	5,000	6,000

We see that the dispersion of possible cash flows for proposal B is greater than that for proposal A; therefore, we could say that it was riskier. To quantify our analysis of risk, however, we need additional information. More specifically, we need to know the likelihood of the various states of the economy occurring. Suppose our estimate of the odds for a deep recession is 10 percent, of a mild recession 20 percent, of a normal economy 40 percent, of a minor economic boom 20 percent, and of a major economic boom 10 percent. Given this information, we now are able to formulate a probability distribution of possible cash flows for proposals A and B:

PROPOSAL A		PROPOSAL B	
Probability	Cash Flow	Probability	Cash Flow
.10	$3,000	.10	$2,000
.20	3,500	.20	3,000
.40	4,000	.40	4,000
.20	4,500	.20	5,000
.10	5,000	.10	6,000

We can graph these probability distributions, and the results are shown in Fig. 14-2. As we see, the dispersion of cash flows is greater for proposal B than it is for proposal A, despite the fact that the most likely outcome is the same for both investment proposals: $4,000. According to the discussion in Chapter 13, the firm would rank the proposals equally. The critical question is whether dis-

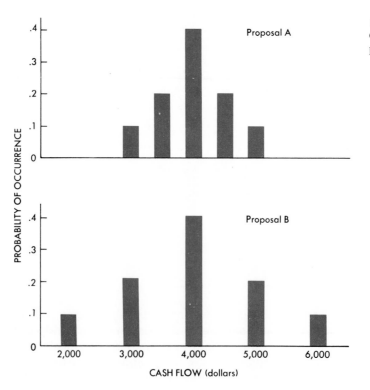

FIGURE 14-2
Comparison of two proposals

person should be considered. If risk is associated with the probability distribution of possible cash flows, such that the greater the dispersion the greater the risk, proposal B would be the riskier investment. If management, stockholders, and creditors are averse to risk, proposal A then would be preferred to proposal B.

Measurement of Dispersion

Rather than always having to resort to graph paper, we need a measure of the dispersion of a probability distribution. The tighter the distribution, the lower this measure should be; the wider the distribution, the greater it should be. The conventional measure of dispersion is the **standard deviation,** which will be presented first mathematically and then illustrated with the previous example. The standard deviation can be expressed mathematically as

Standard deviation. A statistical measure of the dispersion or wideness of a distribution.

$$\sigma = \sqrt{\sum_{x=1}^{n} (A_x - \overline{A})^2 P_x} \qquad (14\text{-}2)$$

where A_x is the cash flow for the xth possibility, P_x is the probability of occurrence of that cash flow, and $\overline{A}$ is the expected value of cash flows, to be defined in Eq. (14-3). Σ means the sum of the bracketed amounts from possibility 1 through possibility n. In other words, n is the total number of possibilities—five in our example. The square-root sign, $\sqrt{}$, indicates that we take the square root of the calculated amount. While all of this seems rather formidable, in fact the standard deviation can be computed rather easily with the aid of a calculator. The **expected value,** $\overline{A}$, of a probability distribution is defined as

Expected value. The weighted average of possible outcomes, with the weights being the probabilities of occurrence.

$$\overline{A} = \sum_{x=1}^{n} A_x P_x \qquad (14\text{-}3)$$

It is simply a weighted average of the possible cash flows, with the weights being the probabilities of occurrence.

The standard deviation is simply a measure of the tightness of a probability distribution. For a normal, bell-shaped distribution, approximately 68 percent of the total area of the distribution falls within one standard deviation on either side of the expected value. This means that there is only a 32 percent chance that the actual outcome will be more than one standard deviation from the mean. The probability that the actual outcome will fall within two standard deviations of the expected value of the distribution is approximately 95 percent, and the probability that it will fall within three standard deviations is over 99 percent. A table showing the area of a normal distribution that is so many standard deviations to the right or left of the expected value is given in Appendix B to this chapter. As we shall see later in the chapter, the standard deviation is used to assess the likelihood of an event's occurring.

An Illustration.   To illustrate the derivation of the expected value and standard deviation of a probability distribution of possible cash flows, consider again our previous example. The expected value of the distribution for proposal A is

$$\overline{A}_a = .10(3,000) + .20(3,500) + .40(4,000) + .20(4,500) + .10(5,000) = 4,000$$

which is the same as that for proposal B:

$$\overline{A}_b = .10(2,000) + .20(3,000) + .40(4,000) + .20(5,000) + .10(6,000) = 4,000$$

However, the standard deviation for proposal A is

$$\sigma_a = [.10(3,000 - 4,000)^2 + .20(3,500 - 4,000)^2 + .40(4,000 - 4,000)^2$$
$$+ .20(4,500 - 4,000)^2 + .10(5,000 - 4,000)^2]^{1/2} = [300,000]^{1/2} = 548$$

where $[\ ]^{1/2}$ is simply the square root, the same as $\sqrt{}$. Note also that when we square a minus number, such as $(3,000 - 4,000)^2$, it becomes positive. The standard deviation for proposal B is

$$\sigma_b = [.10(2,000 - 4,000)^2 + .20(3,000 - 4,000)^2 + .40(4,000 - 4,000)^2$$
$$+ .20(5,000 - 4,000)^2 + .10(6,000 - 4,000)^2]^{1/2} = [1,200,000]^{1/2} = 1,095$$

Thus, proposal B has a higher standard deviation, indicating a greater dispersion of possible outcomes, and so we would say it had greater risk.

Coefficient of Variation.   A measure of relative dispersion is the coefficient of variation, which simply is the standard deviation of a probability distribution over its expected value. For proposal A, the coefficient of variation is

$$CV_a = 548/4,000 = .14$$

while that for proposal B is

$$CV_b = 1,095/4,000 = .27$$

Because the coefficient of variation for proposal B exceeds that for proposal A, we would say that it had a greater degree of risk. One might question the use of the coefficient of variation when in our example it was obvious that proposal B had greater risk owing to its larger standard deviation. In our example, however, the expected values of the probability distributions of possible cash flows for the two proposals were the same. What if they were different? Here we need a measure of relative dispersion, and the coefficient of variation is such a measure. Frequent reference to the expected value, standard deviation, and coefficient of variation will be made in the remainder of this chapter.[1]

RISK FOR THE INDIVIDUAL PROJECT

If investors and creditors are risk averse—and all available evidence suggests that they are—it behooves management to incorporate the risk of an investment proposal into its analysis of the proposal's worth. Otherwise, capital budgeting decisions are unlikely to be in accord with an objective of maximizing share price. Having established the need for taking risk into account, we proceed to measure it for individual investment proposals. But remember that the riskiness of a stream of cash flows for a project can, and usually does, change with the length of time in the future. In other words, the probability distributions are not necessarily the same from one period to the next.

This notion is illustrated in Fig. 14-3 for a hypothetical investment project. The distributions are like those shown in Fig. 14-2 except that they are continuous instead of being discrete bars. This means that a cash-flow outcome is assigned to each possible state of the economy, and a continuous line is drawn. As before, the tighter and more peaked the distribution, the less the risk. The expected value of each of the distributions is depicted by the horizontal dashed

[1] We assume that risk can be judged solely in relation to the expected value and standard deviation of a probability distribution. Implied is that the shape of the distribution is unimportant. This holds when the distribution is relatively symmetric, or "bell-shaped." However, if it is significantly skewed to the right or left, management may wish to take account of this fact as well. Although it is possible to incorporate a skewness measure into our analysis of risk, it is difficult mathematically to do so. For simplicity, we shall deal with only the expected value and standard deviation of a normal probability distribution.

FIGURE 14-3
Changing risk over time

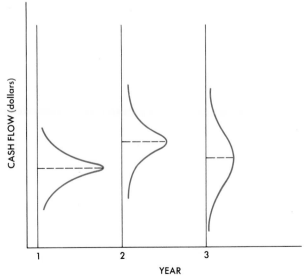

line. We see that both the expected value of cash flow and the dispersion of the probability distribution change over time. We must come to grips with this factor so that we can quantify the risk of a prospective investment proposal.

Use of a Probability Tree

One way of approaching the problem is with a probability tree. Here we specify the likely future cash flows of a project as they relate to the outcomes in previous periods. If a project turns out to be good in the first period, it may well turn out to be good in subsequent periods. While there frequently is a link between what happens in one period and what happens in the next, this is not always the case. If cash flows are believed to be independent from period to period, we simply specify a probability distribution of cash-flow outcomes for each period. If there is a link, we should take this dependence into account.

With a probability tree we attempt to unfold future events as they might occur. Figure 14-4 shows a probability tree for a three-period case. Here we see that if the outcome in period 1 is the upper branch, it results in a different set of possible outcomes in period 2 than if the lower branch occurred in period 1. The same thing applies to going from period 2 to period 3. Therefore, at time 0 the probability tree represents our best estimate of what is likely to occur in the future, contingent upon what occurs before. For each of the branches in the figure, a cash flow as well as a probability is attached.

For the first period, the cash-flow outcome does not depend on what happened before. Therefore, the probabilities associated with the two branches are said to be *initial probabilities*. For the second and third periods, however, cash-flow outcomes depend on what happened before. Therefore, the probabilities involved in these periods are said to be *conditional probabilities*. Finally, the *joint probability* is the probability that a particular sequence of cash flows might oc-

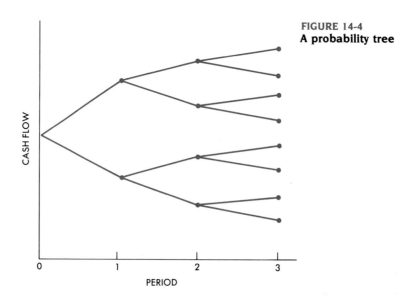

FIGURE 14-4
A probability tree

cur. For example, one sequence is the top branches in each of the three periods. The joint probability is the product of the initial probability and the two conditional probabilities for the top branches. Rather than continue to discuss probability trees in the abstract, let us proceed to an example.

An Illustration for a Project

Suppose that we were considering the investment in a project costing $240 at time 0 that was expected to generate the possible cash flows shown in Table 14-3. Given a cash flow of −$100 in period 1, the probability is .40 that this negative flow will become −$400 in period 2, .40 that it will remain at −$100, and .20 that it will be $200. The joint probability that a −$100 cash flow in period 1 will be followed by a −$400 cash flow in period 2 is simply the product of the initial probability and the conditional probability, or .25 × .40 = .10.

TABLE 14-3
Illustration of a probability tree*

	PERIOD I		PERIOD 2	
Initial Probability P(1)	Net Cash Flow	Conditional Probability P(2/1)	Net Cash Flow	Joint Probability P(1, 2)
.25	−$100	.40	−$400	.10
		.40	− 100	.10
		.20	200	.05
.50	200	.20	− 100	.10
		.60	200	.30
		.20	500	.10
.25	500	.20	200	.05
		.40	500	.10
		.40	800	.10

*Initial investment at time 0 = $240.

Similarly, the joint probability that a cash flow of −$100 in period 1 will be followed by a cash flow of −$100 in period 2 is .25 × .40 = .10, and the probability that a −$100 cash flow in period 1 will be followed by a $200 cash flow in period 2 is .25 × .20 = .05. If the cash flow in period 1 turns out to be $200, there is a .20 probability that it will become −$100 in period 2, .60 it will remain at $200 in period 2, and .20 it will become $500. In the same manner as before, we can calculate the joint probabilities for this branch, and they are found to be .10, .30, and .10, respectively. Similarly, the joint probabilities for the last branch, where a $500 net cash flow in period 1 occurs, can be determined.

Discounting to Present Value.   In discounting the various cash flows to their present value, one should employ the risk-free rate. This rate is used because we attempt to isolate the time value of money by discounting, and then we analyze risk separately. To include a premium for risk in the discount rate would result in double counting with respect to our evaluation. We would compensate for risk in the discounting process and then again in our analysis of the dispersion of the distribution of possible net present values. For this reason, we use the risk-free rate for discounting purposes.

For our example problem, the expected value of the probability distribution of possible net present values is

$$\overline{NPV} = -\$240 + \sum_{x=1}^{z} NPV_x P_x \qquad (14\text{-}4)$$

where NPV_x is the net present value for series x of net cash flows, covering all periods, P_x is the probability of occurrence of that series, and z is the total number of cash-flow series. For our example, there are nine possible series of net cash flows, so z = 9. The first series is represented by a cash flow of −$100 in period 1, followed by a −$400 cash flow in period 2. The probability of occurrence of that cash flow is .10. If the risk-free rate used as the discount rate is 8 percent, the net present value of this series is

$$NPV_1 = -240 - \frac{100}{(1.08)} - \frac{400}{(1.08)^2} = -\$676$$

The second cash-flow series is represented by a cash flow of −$100 in period 1, followed by a −$100 cash flow in period 2. The net present value of this series is

$$NPV_2 = -240 - \frac{100}{(1.08)} - \frac{100}{(1.08)^2} = -\$418$$

In the same manner, the net present values for the seven other cash-flow series can be determined. When these values are multiplied by their respective probabilities of occurrence (the last column in Table 14-3) and summed, we obtain the

TABLE 14-4
Calculation of expected value of net present value
for example problem

(1) CASH FLOW SERIES	(2) NET PRESENT VALUE	(3) PROBABILITY OF OCCURRENCE	(4) (2) × (3)
1	−$676	.10	−$68
2	− 418	.10	− 42
3	− 161	.05	− 8
4	− 141	.10	− 14
5	117	.30	35
6	374	.10	37
7	394	.05	20
8	652	.10	65
9	909	.10	91
		Weighted average =	$116

expected value of net present value of the probability distribution of possible net present values (rounded to the nearest dollar). The calculations are shown in Table 14-4, and we see that the expected value of net present value is $116.

Calculating the Standard Deviation.   The standard deviation of the probability distribution of possible net present values can be determined by

$$\sigma = \sqrt{\sum_{x=1}^{z} (NPV_x - \overline{NPV})^2 P_x} \tag{14-5}$$

where the symbols are the same as for Eq. (14-4). The standard deviation for our example problem is

$$\sigma = [.10(-676 - 116)^2 + .10(-418 - 116)^2$$
$$+ .05(-161 - 116)^2 + .10(-141 - 116)^2$$
$$+ .30(117 - 116)^2 + .10(374 - 116)^2$$
$$+ .05(394 - 116)^2 + .10(652 - 116)^2$$
$$+ .10(909 - 116)^2]^{1/2} = [197,277]^{1/2} = \$444$$

Rounding to the nearest dollar, the project has an expected value of net present value of $116 and a standard deviation of $444. Although the mathematical calculation of the standard deviation is feasible for simple cases, it is not for complex situations. Here, one should resort to simulation to approximate the standard deviation. The technique is explained in Appendix A to this chapter, where the Hertz model for evaluating risky investments is considered.

Use of Information

The expected value and the standard deviation of the probability distribution of possible net present values, whether derived by a probability tree or some other means, give us a considerable amount of information by which to evaluate the risk of the investment proposal. If the probability distribution is approximately normal, we are able to calculate the probability of the proposal's providing a net present value of less or more than a specified amount. The probability is found by determining the area under the curve to the left or to the right of a particular point of interest. To go on with our previous illustration, suppose we wish to determine the probability that the net present value will be zero or less. To determine this probability, we first calculate the difference between 0 and the expected value of net present value for the project.

In our example, this difference is −$116. We then standardize this difference by dividing it by the standard deviation of possible net present values. The formula is

$$S = \frac{X - \overline{NPV}}{\sigma} \tag{14-6}$$

where X is the outcome in which we are interested, $\overline{NPV}$ is the expected value of net present value, and σ is the standard deviation of the probability distribution. In our case

$$S = \frac{0 - 116}{444} = -.26$$

This figure tells us that a net present value of 0 lies .26 standard deviation to the left of the expected value of the probability distribution of possible net present values.

To determine the probability that the net present value of the project will be 0 or less, we consult a normal probability distribution table found in most statistics texts or in Appendix B at the end of this chapter. We find that for the normal distribution, there is a .4013 probability that an observation will be less than −.25 standard deviations from the expected value of that distribution and a .3821 probability that it will be less than −.30 standard deviations from the expected value. Interpolating, we find that there is approximately a 40 percent probability that the net present value of the proposal will be zero or less. We know also that there is a 60 percent probability that the net present value of the project will be greater than zero. With a normal distribution, .68 of the distribution falls within one standard deviation on either side of the expected value. We know then that there is approximately a two-thirds probability that the net present value of the proposal will be between $116 − $444 = −$328 and $116 + $444 = 560. By expressing differences from the expected value in terms of standard deviations, we are able to determine the probability that the net present value for an investment proposal will be greater or less than a particular amount.[2]

This information tells us that the dispersion of possible outcomes for the project is rather wide. There is a 40 percent probability that the net present value will be zero or less and about a one-sixth probability that it will be −$328 or worse. (The latter is simply the area of a curve that is greater than one standard deviation to the left of the expected value.)

Knowledge of these probabilities is fundamental for a realistic assessment of risk. Suppose that the firm is considering another investment proposal, call it Y. The probability distribution for this proposal is shown in Fig. 14-5, as is that for our example problem, which we call proposal X. We see that the expected value of net present value for proposal Y is $200, which is higher than that for proposal X, $116. Moreover, there is less dispersion with proposal Y than there is with proposal X. Therefore, we would say that proposal Y dominates proposal X on the basis of both risk and return. Whether proposal Y or both projects should be accepted depends on the risk tolerances of management. We address ourselves to this question in the next chapter. In this chapter we want to learn how to measure risk.

---

[2] In these examples we have assumed normal probability distributions. Although this property is very desirable for purposes of calculation, it is not necessary for use of the above approach. Even when the distribution is not normal, we usually are able to make relatively strong probability statements by using Chebyshev's inequality.

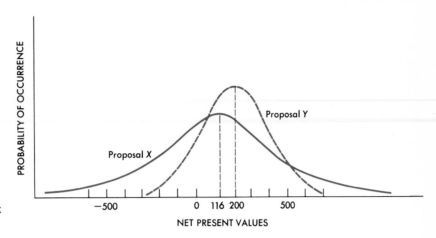

FIGURE 14-5
Probability distributions of net present values for two projects

RISK IN A PORTFOLIO SENSE

In the last section we measured risk for a single investment proposal. When multiple investment projects are involved and we have a combined risk, the measurement procedure differs from that for a single project. The approach we take corresponds to the portfolio approach in security analysis. Portfolio theory was discussed in Chapter 5; here we apply the approach to capital investment projects. The limited circumstances under which the approach is feasible are taken up in Chapter 15, when we examine the acceptance criteria for risky investments. Our purpose here is only to show how to measure risk for combinations of risky investments, assuming that such a measure is desired.

If a firm adds a project whose future cash flows are likely to be highly correlated with those of existing assets, the total risk of the firm will increase more than if it adds a project that has a low degree of correlation with existing assets. The idea is that projects can be combined to reduce relative risk.

Figure 14-6 shows the expected cash-flow patterns for two projects over time. Proposal A is cyclical, while proposal B is mildly countercyclical. By combining the two projects, we see that total cash-flow dispersion is reduced, and the dispersion of the return on investment is reduced even more. The combination of projects to reduce risk is known as diversification, and the principle is the same as diversification in securities. One attempts to reduce deviations in return from the expected value of return.

Measurement of Portfolio Risk

The standard deviation of the probability distribution of possible net present values is more difficult to calculate for a portfolio than for a single investment. It is not the summation of the standard deviations of the individual projects making up the portfolio, but

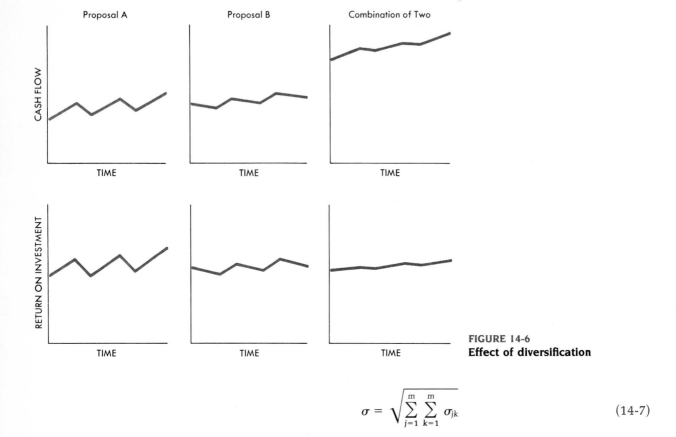

FIGURE 14-6
Effect of diversification

$$\sigma = \sqrt{\sum_{j=1}^{m} \sum_{k=1}^{m} \sigma_{jk}} \qquad (14\text{-}7)$$

where j refers to project j, k to project k, m is the total number of projects in the portfolio, and σ_{jk} is the covariance between possible net present values for projects j and k. (This rather formidable expression will be illustrated shortly.)

The covariance term in Eq. (14-7) is

$$\sigma_{jk} = r_{jk}\sigma_j\sigma_k \qquad (14\text{-}8)$$

Correlation coefficient. A measure that describes how closely two variables move together over time.

where r_{jk} is the expected **correlation coefficient** between possible net present values for projects j and k, σ_j is the standard deviation for project j, and σ_k is the standard deviation for project k. The standard deviations of the probability distributions of possible net present values for projects j and k are determined by the methods taken up in the previous section. When $j = k$ in Eq. (14-8), the correlation coefficient is 1.0, and $\sigma_j\sigma_k$ becomes σ_j^2 (that is, the standard deviation squared of the probability distribution of possible net present values for investment project j).

An Illustration

To illustrate these concepts, suppose that a firm has a single existing investment project, 1, and that it is considering investing in an additional project, 2. Assume

354

further that the projects have the following expected values of net present value, standard deviations, and correlation coefficients:

	EXPECTED VALUE OF NET PRESENT VALUE	STANDARD DEVIATION	CORRELATION COEFFICIENT
Project 1	$12,000	$14,000	1.00
Project 2	8,000	6,000	1.00
Projects 1 and 2			.40

The expected value of the net present value of the combination of projects is simply the sum of the two separate net present values.

$$NPV = \$12,000 + \$8,000 = \$20,000$$

The standard deviation for the combination, using Eqs. (14-7) and (14-8), is

$$\sigma = \sqrt{r_{11}\sigma_1^2 + 2r_{12}\sigma_1\sigma_2 + r_{22}\sigma_2^2}$$
$$= \sqrt{(1.00)(14,000)^2 + (2)(.40)(14,000)(6,000) + (1.00)(6,000)^2}$$
$$= \$17,297$$

Thus, the expected value of net present value of the firm increases from $12,000 to $20,000 and the standard deviation of possible net present values from $14,000 to $17,297 with the acceptance of project 2. The coefficient of variation (standard deviation over expected value of net present value) is 14,000/12,000 = 1.17 without project 2 and 17,297/20,000 = .86 with the project. If we employ the coefficient of variation as a measure of relative business risk, we conclude that acceptance of project 2 would lower the business risk of the firm.

By accepting projects with relatively low degrees of correlation with existing projects, a firm diversifies and in so doing may be able to lower its overall business risk. We note that the lower the degree of positive correlation, r_{12}, the lower the standard deviation of possible net present values, all other things being equal. Whether the coefficient of variation declines when an investment project is added depends also on the expected value of net present value for the project.

Correlation Between Projects

Estimating the correlation between possible net present values for two projects in Eq. (14-8) is the key ingredient in analyzing risk in a portfolio context. When two projects are similar to projects with which the company has had experience, it may be feasible to compute the correlation coefficients using historical data. For other investments, estimates of the correlation coefficients must be based solely on an assessment of the future.

Management might have reason to expect only slight correlation between investment projects involving research and development for an electronic tester and a new food product. On the other hand, it might expect high positive correlation between investments in a milling machine and a turret lathe if both machines were used in the production of industrial lift trucks. The profit from a machine to be used in a production line will be highly, if not completely, correlated with the profit for the production line itself.

The correlation between expected net present values of various investments may be positive, negative, or 0, depending on the nature of the association. A correlation coefficient of 1.00 indicates that the net present values of two investment proposals vary directly in exactly the same proportional manner; a correlation coefficient of -1.00 indicates that they vary inversely in exactly the same proportional manner; and a 0 correlation coefficient indicates that they are independent or unrelated. For most pairs of investments, the correlation coefficient lies between 0 and 1.00. The reason for the lack of negatively correlated investment projects is that most investments are correlated positively with the economy.

Estimates of the correlation coefficients must be as objective as possible if the total standard deviation figure obtained in Eq. (14-7) is to be realistic. It is not unreasonable to expect management to make fairly accurate estimates of these coefficients. When actual correlation differs from expected correlation, the situation can be a learning process, and estimates on other projects can be revised.

Combinations of Risky Investments

We now have a procedure for determining the total expected value and the standard deviation of a probability distribution of possible net present values for a combination of investments. For our purposes, we define a *combination* as including all existing investment projects and one or more proposals under consideration. We assume, then, that the firm has existing investment projects and that these projects are expected to generate future cash flows. Thus, existing projects constitute a subset that is included in all combinations. We denote this portfolio of projects by the italic letter *E*.

A firm has under consideration four investment proposals, which are independent of one another; that is, they are not contingent or mutually exclusive. If these proposals are labeled 1, 2, 3, and 4, we have the following possible combinations of risky investments:

E	E, 1	E, 1, 2	E, 1, 2, 3	E, 1, 2, 3, 4
	E, 2	E, 1, 3	E, 1, 2, 4	
	E, 3	E, 1, 4	E, 1, 3, 4	
	E, 4	E, 2, 3	E, 2, 3, 4	
		E, 2, 4		
		E, 3, 4		

Thus, 16 combinations of projects are possible, with one possibility being the rejection of all of the proposals under consideration, so that the firm is left with only its existing projects, E. The expected value of net present value and standard deviation for each of these combinations can be computed in the manner described previously. The results can then be graphed.

Figure 14-7 is a scatter diagram of the 16 possible combinations. Here the expected value of net present value is along the horizontal axis, and the standard deviation is on the vertical axis. Each dot represents a combination. Collectively, these dots constitute the total set of feasible combinations of investment opportunities available to the firm.

We see that certain dots dominate others in the sense that they represent a higher expected value of net present value and the same standard deviation, a lower standard deviation and the same expected value of net present value, or both a higher expected value and a lower standard deviation. The dominating dots are those that are farthest to the right in the figure. Four of them have been identified specifically—combinations B, H, L, and P. (The dot E represents all existing investment projects.)

Although the selection process itself is deferred until Chapter 15, we observe here that the combination ultimately chosen determines the new investment proposal or proposals that will be accepted. If combination H were selected and it consisted of E, 1, and 4, investment proposals 1 and 4 would be accepted. Those investment proposals not in the combination finally selected would be rejected. In our case, they would be proposals 2 and 3. If the combination finally selected consisted of only existing investment projects, E, all investment proposals under consideration would be rejected. The selection of any other combination implies the acceptance of one or more of the investment proposals under consideration.

The incremental expected value of net present value and standard deviation can be determined by measuring on the horizontal and vertical axes the distance from dot E to the dot representing the combination finally selected. These

FIGURE 14-7
Opportunity set of combinations of projects

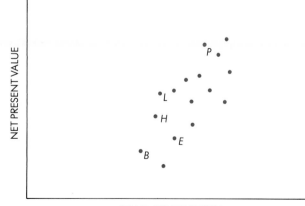

NET PRESENT VALUE

STANDARD DEVIATION

distances can be thought of as the incremental contribution of expected value of net present value and standard deviation to the firm as a whole. In Chapter 15, we explore how the actual selection can be made and under what circumstances this approach is appropriate. Our purpose here has been to measure risk for combinations of risky investments in order to provide management with such information.

SUMMARY

Operating leverage may be defined as the employment of an asset with a fixed cost in the hope that sufficient revenue will be generated to cover all fixed and variable costs. We study the operating leverage of a firm by using a break-even graph, which enables us to analyze the relationship among profits, volume, fixed costs, variable costs, and prices. By varying these factors, management may determine the sensitivity of profits and, in so doing, obtain a better understanding of the operating risk of the firm.

The risk of an investment project can be defined as the deviation in actual cash flows from those that were expected. Expressing the future in terms of probability distributions of possible cash flows, we can express risk quantitatively as the standard deviation of the distribution. The coefficient of variation is simply the standard deviation of a probability distribution over its expected value, and it serves as a relative measure of risk. Business risk is the risk associated with the operations of the firm, and it can be expressed in terms of the coefficient of variation.

One approach to the evaluation of risky investments is the direct analysis of the probability distribution of possible net present values of a project. Given the expected value and standard deviation of the distribution, management can determine the probability that the actual net present value will be lower than some amount such as zero. This type of information is extremely valuable in judging the risk of a project. The use of a probability tree was illustrated for taking account of changing risk over time.

Investment projects also can be judged with respect to their portfolio risk. Here we are concerned with the marginal risk of a project to the firm as a whole. By diversifying into projects not having high degrees of correlation with existing assets, a firm is able to reduce the standard deviation of its probability distribution of possible net present values relative to the expected value of the distribution. The likely degree of correlation between projects is the key to measuring portfolio risk.

Our purpose in this chapter has been to explore the means by which risk can be quantified for investment proposals and combinations of proposals. With this information, together with information about the expected profitability of the investment, we should reach much more informed, better decisions. In Chapter 15 we consider how this information can be employed in the decision process.

APPENDIX A
Simulation Approach to Risky Investments

In considering risky investments, we can use simulation to approximate the expected return and dispersion about the expected return for an investment proposal. By *simulation*, we mean testing the results of an investment decision before it actually occurs. The testing itself is based on a model coupled with probabilistic information. A simulation model proposed by Hertz considers the following factors in deriving a project's earnings stream:

MARKET ANALYSIS

1. Market size
2. Selling price
3. Market growth rate
4. Share of market (which results in physical sales volume)

INVESTMENT COST ANALYSIS

5. Investment required
6. Residual value of investment

OPERATING AND FIXED COSTS

7. Operating costs
8. Fixed costs
9. Useful life of facilities[3]

Probability distributions are assigned to each of these factors, based on management's assessment of the probable outcomes. Thus, the possible outcomes are charted for each factor according to their probability of occurrence. Once the probability distributions are determined, the next step is to determine the average rate of return that will result from a random combination of the nine factors just listed. To illustrate the simulation process, assume that the market-size factor had the following probability distribution:

Market size (in thousands of units)	450	500	550	600	650	700	750
Probability	.05	.10	.20	.30	.20	.10	.05

Now suppose that we have a roulette wheel with 100 numbers, on which num-

---

[3] David B. Hertz, "Risk Analysis in Capital Investment," *Harvard Business Review*, 42 (January –February 1964), 95–106.

bers 1 to 5 represent a market size of 450,000 units, 6 to 15 represent a market size of 500,000, 16 to 35, a market size of 550,000 units, and so on through 100. As in roulette, we spin the wheel, and the ball falls in one of the 100 slots: number 26. For this trial, then, we simulate a market size of 550,000 units. Fortunately, we do not need a roulette wheel to undertake a simulation; the same type of operation can be carried out on a computer in a much more efficient manner.

Simulation trials are undertaken for each of the other eight factors. The first four factors (market analysis) give us the annual sales per year; factors 7 and 8 give us the operating costs and fixed costs per year. Together, these six factors enable us to calculate the annual earnings per year. When trial values for these six factors are combined with trial values for the required investment, the useful life, and the residual value of the project, we have sufficient information to calculate the return on investment for that trial run. Thus, the computer simulates trial values for each of the nine factors and then calculates the return on investment based on the values simulated. The process is repeated a number of times: each time we obtain a combination of values for the nine factors and the return on investment for that combination. When the trial is repeated often enough, the rates of return can be plotted in a frequency distribution like that shown in Fig. 14-8.

From this frequency distribution we are able to evaluate the expected return and the dispersion about this expected return, or risk, in the same manner as before; in other words, we can determine the probability that an investment will provide a return greater or less than a certain amount. By comparing the probability distribution of rates of return for one proposal with the probability distribution of rates of return for another, management is able to evaluate the respective merits of different risky investments.

Two points should be mentioned with respect to Hertz's simulation method. Although it computes the average rate of return on investment, the method could easily be modified to calculate the internal rate of return, the net present value, or the profitability index. In addition, although Hertz allows for

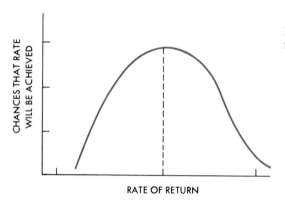

FIGURE 14-8
Probability distribution for rate of return

CHANCES THAT RATE WILL BE ACHIEVED

RATE OF RETURN

dependency among the nine factors, the model presented treats the factors as though they were independent. To the extent that dependency exists among factors, it must be taken into account in determining the probability distributions. For example, there is likely to be significant correlation between the market size and the selling price. These interrelationships add considerable complexity to the estimating procedure. Notwithstanding the added complexity of estimating and specifying in the model the relationships among factors, it must be done if the model is to provide realistic results. These estimates may be based on empirical testing when such testing is feasible. Once the relationships are incorporated in the model, those factors that are correlated would then be simulated jointly. Rates of return for the simulated trials would be calculated and a frequency distribution of simulated trials formed in the same manner as before.

APPENDIX B
Normal Probability Distribution Table

Table 14B-1 shows the area of the normal distribution that is X standard deviations to the left or to the right of the mean. The test is "one tail" in the sense that we are concerned with one side of the distribution or the other. If we wished to know the area of the curve, or probability, that was 1.5 standard deviations or more from the arithmetic mean on the right, it would be depicted by the colored area in Fig. 14-9. In Table 14B-1 we see that this corresponds to 6.68 percent of the total area of the normal distribution. Thus, we would say that there was a 6.68 percent probability that the actual outcome would exceed the mean by 1.5 standard deviations. In a similar manner, the table can be used to determine the probability associated with other distances from the mean.

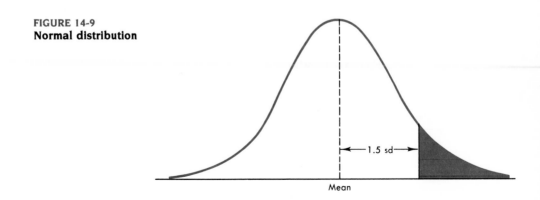

FIGURE 14-9
Normal distribution

TABLE 14B-1
Area of normal distribution that is X standard deviations to the left or right of the mean

NUMBER OF STANDARD DEVIATIONS FROM MEAN (X)	AREA TO THE LEFT OR RIGHT (ONE TAIL)	NUMBER OF STANDARD DEVIATIONS FROM MEAN (X)	AREA TO THE LEFT OR RIGHT (ONE TAIL)
.00	.5000	1.55	.0606
.05	.4801	1.60	.0548
.10	.4602	1.65	.0495
.15	.4404	1.70	.0446
.20	.4207	1.75	.0401
.25	.4013	1.80	.0359
.30	.3821	1.85	.0322
.35	.3632	1.90	.0287
.40	.3446	1.95	.0256
.45	.3264	2.00	.0228
.50	.3085	2.05	.0202
.55	.2912	2.10	.0179
.60	.2743	2.15	.0158
.65	.2578	2.20	.0139
.70	.2420	2.25	.0122
.75	.2264	2.30	.0107
.80	.2119	2.35	.0094
.85	.1977	2.40	.0082
.90	.1841	2.45	.0071
.95	.1711	2.50	.0062
1.00	.1577	2.55	.0054
1.05	.1469	2.60	.0047
1.10	.1357	2.65	.0040
1.15	.1251	2.70	.0035
1.20	.1151	2.75	.0030
1.25	.1056	2.80	.0026
1.30	.0968	2.85	.0022
1.35	.0885	2.90	.0019
1.40	.0808	2.95	.0016
1.45	.0735	3.00	.0013
1.50	.0668		

QUESTIONS

1. Why should we be concerned with risk in capital budgeting? Why not just work with the expected cash flows as we did in Chapter 13?

2. Define the concept of *operating leverage*.

3. Classify the following short-run manufacturing costs as either typically fixed or typically variable. Which costs are variable at management's discretion? Are any of these costs fixed in the long run?

   a. Insurance   c. Property taxes   e. R & D
   b. Direct labor   d. Interest expense   f. Advertising

g. Raw materials   j. Depreciation

h. Bad-debt loss   k. Maintenance

i. Depletion

4. What would be the effect on the break-even point of the following?

a. Increased selling price

b. Increase in the minimum wage

c. Change from straight-line to accelerated depreciation

d. Increased sales

e. A 5 percent surtax on corporate profits

f. A liberalized credit policy

5. Is the standard deviation an adequate measure of risk? Can you think of a better measure?

6. How do you go about standardizing the dispersion of a probability distribution to make generalizations about the risk of a project?

7. Risk in capital budgeting can be judged by analyzing the probability distribution of possible returns. What shape distribution would you expect to find for a safe project whose returns were absolutely certain? for a very risky project?

8. If project A has an expected value of net present value of $200 and a standard deviation of $400, is it more risky than project B whose expected value is $140 and standard deviation is $300?

9. In a probability tree, what are initial, conditional, and joint probabilities?

10. Why should the risk-free rate be used for discounting cash flows to their present value when evaluating risky capital investments?

11. What are the benefits of using simulation to evaluate capital investment projects?

12. What role does the correlation between net present values play in the risk of a portfolio of investment projects?

13. What is meant by dominance in a portfolio sense?

14. What determines whether a project is accepted or rejected using a portfolio approach?

15. Is there any business that is risk free?

SELF-CORRECTION PROBLEMS

1. Knoble Specialty Paint Company has fixed costs of $3 million a year, including advertising. Variable costs are $1.75 per half-pint of paint produced and the average selling price is $2 per half-pint.

a. What is the annual break-even point in half-pints? in dollars of sales?

b. If variable costs decline to $1.68 per half-pint, what would happen to the break-even point?

c.   If fixed costs increase to $3.75 million per year, what would be the effect on the break-even point?

2.   Ponape Lumber Company is evaluating a new saw with a life of 2 years. The saw costs $3,000 and future after-tax cash flows depend on demand for the company's products. The probability tree of possible future cash flows associated with the new saw is

YEAR 1		YEAR 2		
Initial Probability	Cash Flow	Conditional Probability	Cash Flow	BRANCH
		.3	$1,000	1
.4	$1,500	.4	1,500	2
		.3	2,000	3
		.4	$2,000	4
.6	$2,500	.4	2,500	5
		.2	3,000	6

a.   What are the joint probabilities of occurrence of the various branches?

b.   If the risk-free rate is 10 percent, what is the expected value and standard deviation of the probability distribution of possible net present values?

c.   Assuming a normal distribution, what is the probability the actual net present value will be less than zero?

3.   Zello Creamery Company would like to develop a new product line—puddings. The expected value and standard deviation of the probability distribution of possible net present values for the product line are $12,000 and $9,000, respectively. The company's existing lines are ice cream, cottage cheese, and yogurt. The expected values of net present value and standard deviation for these product lines are

	NET PRESENT VALUE	σ
Ice cream	$16,000	$8,000
Cottage cheese	20,000	7,000
Yogurt	10,000	4,000

The correlation coefficients between products are

	ICE CREAM	COTTAGE CHEESE	YOGURT	PUDDING
Ice cream	1.00			
Cottage cheese	.90	1.00		
Yogurt	.80	.84	1.00	
Pudding	.40	.20	.30	1.00

a. Compute the expected value and the standard deviation of the probability distribution of possible net present values for a combination consisting of existing products.

b. Compute the expected value and standard deviation for a combination consisting of existing products plus pudding. Compare your results in parts a and b. What can you say about the pudding line?

PROBLEMS

1. R. A. Rice, Inc., can invest in one of two mutually exclusive projects. The two proposals have the following discrete probability distributions of net cash flows for period p:

A		B	
Probability	Cash Flow	Probability	Cash Flow
.20	$2,000	.10	$2,000
.30	4,000	.40	4,000
.30	6,000	.40	6,000
.30	8,000	.10	8,000

a. Without calculating a mean and a coefficient of variation, can you select the better proposal, assuming a risk-averse management?

b. Verify your intuitive determination.

2. The Madison Company earns monthly, after taxes, $2,400 on sales of $88,000. The average tax rate of the company is 40 percent. The company's only product sells for $20, of which $15 is variable cost.

a. What is the monthly fixed cost of the Madison Company?

b. What is the break-even point in units? in dollars?

(Hint: Determine profit before taxes, total costs before taxes, and units produced and variable costs before you derive fixed costs.)

3. What would be the effect of the following on the break-even point of the Madison Company (Problem 2)?

   a. An increase in price of $5 per unit (assume that volume is constant)

   b. A decrease in fixed costs of $2,000

   c. A decrease in variable costs of $1 per unit and an increase in fixed costs of $6,000.

4. The D. T. Crazy Horse Hotel has a capacity to stable 50 horses. The fee for stabling a horse is $100 per month. Maintenance, depreciation, property taxes, and other fixed costs total $1,200 per month. Variable costs per horse are $12 per month for hay and bedding and $8 per month for grain. Income is taxed at a 40 percent rate.

   a. Determine the break-even point.

   b. Compute the monthly profits after taxes if an average of 40 horses are stabled.

5. The Hume Corporation is faced with several possible investment projects. For each, the total cash outflow required will occur in the initial period. The cash outflows, expected net present values, and standard deviations are given in the following table. All projects have been discounted at the risk-free rate, and it is assumed that the distributions of their possible net present values are normal.

PROJECT	COST	NET PRESENT VALUE	STANDARD DEVIATION
A	$100,000	$10,000	$20,000
B	50,000	10,000	30,000
C	200,000	25,000	10,000
D	10,000	5,000	10,000
E	500,000	75,000	75,000

   a. Ignoring size, are there some projects that are clearly dominated by others with respect to the coefficient of variation? (For the coefficient, use cost plus net present value in the denominator.)

   b. May size be ignored?

   c. What is the probability that each of the projects will have a net present value greater than or equal to zero?

6. The probability distribution of possible net present values for project X has an expected value of $20,000 and a standard deviation of $10,000. Assuming a normal distribution, calculate the probability that the net present value will be zero or less, that it will be greater than $30,000, and that it will be less than $5,000.

7. Xonics Graphics, Inc., is evaluating a new technology for its reproduction equipment. The technology will have a 3-year life, it will cost $1,000, and its impact on cash flows is subject to risk. Management estimates that there is a 50:50 chance that the technology will either save the company $1,000 in the first year or save it nothing at all. If nothing at all, savings in the last 2 years would be zero as well. Even here there is some possibility that in the second year an additional outlay of $300 would be required to convert back to the original process, for the new technology may decrease efficiency. Management attaches a 40 percent probability to this occurrence if the new technology "bombs out" in the first year. If the technology proves itself, it is felt that second-year cash flows will be $1,800, $1,400 and $1,000, with probabilities of .20, .60, and .20, respectively. In the third year, cash flows are expected to be $200 greater or $200 less than the cash flow in period 2, with an equal chance of occurrence. (Again, these cash flows depend on the cash flow in period 1 being $1,000.)

   a. Set up a probability tree to depict the cash-flow possibilities.

   b. Calculate a weighted net present value for each 3-year possibility, using a risk-free rate of 5 percent.

   c. What is the risk of the project?

8. The Windrop Company will invest in two of three possible proposals, the cash flows of which are normally distributed. The expected net present value (discounted at the risk-free rate) and the standard deviation for each proposal are given as follows:

	1	2	3
Expected net present value	$10,000	$8,000	$6,000
Standard deviation	4,000	3,000	4,000

Assuming the following correlation coefficients for each possible combination, which combination dominates the others?

PROPOSALS	CORRELATION COEFFICIENTS
1	1.00
2	1.00
3	1.00
1 and 2	.60
1 and 3	.40
2 and 3	.50

9. The Plaza Corporation is confronted with various combinations of risky investments.

COMBINATION	NET PRESENT VALUE	STANDARD DEVIATION
A	$100,000	$200,000
B	20,000	80,000
C	75,000	100,000
D	60,000	150,000
E	50,000	20,000
F	40,000	60,000
G	120,000	170,000
H	90,000	70,000
I	50,000	100,000
J	75,000	30,000

a. Plot the above portfolios.

b. Which combinations dominate the others?

Appendix A Problem

10. The Bertz Company uses a simulation approach to judge investment projects. Three factors are employed: market demand, in units; price per unit minus cost per unit; and investment required at time 0. These factors are felt to be independent of one another. In analyzing a new consumer product, Bertz estimates the following probability distributions:

ANNUAL DEMAND		PRICE MINUS COST PER UNIT		INVESTMENT REQUIRED	
Probability	Units	Probability	Dollars	Probability	Dollars
.05	10,000	.10	$3.00	.30	$1,800,000
.10	20,000	.20	4.50	.40	2,000,000
.20	30,000	.40	6.00	.30	2,300,000
.30	45,000	.20	7.00		
.20	60,000	.10	8.00		
.10	75,000				
.05	90,000				

a. Using a random number table or some other random process, simulate 20 or more trials for these three factors and compute the return on investment for each trial. (Note: return = profit/investment.)

b. Approximately what is the most likely return? How risky is the project?

SOLUTIONS TO SELF-CORRECTION PROBLEMS

1. a. $x = \dfrac{3,000,000}{2.00 - 1.75} = 12,000,000$ half-pints

   $\$2 \times 12$ million half-pints $= \$24$ million in annual sales

   b. $x = \dfrac{3,000,000}{2.00 - 1.68} = 9,375,000$ half-pints

   c. $x = \dfrac{3,750,000}{2.00 - 1.75} = 15,000,000$ half-pints

   Any decrease in fixed costs, decrease in variable costs, or increase in price lowers the break-even point, and vice versa.

2. a.

BRANCH	1	2	3	4	5	6	Total
Joint probability	.12	.16	.12	.24	.24	.12	1.00

   b. Present value of cash flows at 10 percent (with rounding), NPV and standard deviation:

YEAR 0	YEAR 1	YEAR 2	BRANCH	NET PRESENT VALUE
		$ 826	1	−$ 810
	$1,364	1,240	2	− 396
		1,653	3	17
−$3,000				
		1,653	4	926
	2,273	2,066	5	1,339
		2,479	6	1,752

$\overline{NPV} = .12(-\$810) + .16(-\$396) + .12(\$17) + .24(\$926) + .24(\$1,339) + .12(1,752) = \$595$

S.D. $= [.12(-\$810 - \$595)^2 + .16(-\$396 - \$595)^2 + .12(\$17 - \$595)^2 + .24(\$926 - \$595)^2$
$+ .24(\$1,339 - \$595)^2 + .12(\$1,752 - \$595)^2]^{1/2} = \$868$

   c. Standardizing the difference from zero, we have $\$595/\$868 = .685$. Looking in Table 14B-1 in Appendix B of this chapter, we find that .685 corresponds to an area of approximately .25. Therefore, there is approximately one chance out of four that the net present value will be zero or less.

3. a. Net present value $= \$16,000 + \$20,000 + \$10,000 = \$46,000$

   Standard deviation $= [(\$8,000)^2 + (2)(.9)(\$8,000)(\$7,000) + (2)(.8)(\$8,000)(\$4,000) + (\$7,000)^2 + (2)(.84)(\$7,000)(\$4,000) + (\$4,000)^2]^{1/2} = [\$328,040,000]^{1/2} = \$18,112$

b. Net present value = $46,000 + $12,000 = $58,000
Standard deviation = $[\$328{,}040{,}000 + (\$9{,}000)^2 +$
$(2)(.4)(\$9{,}000)(\$8{,}000) + (2)(.2)(\$9{,}000)(\$7{,}000) +$
$(2)(.3)(\$9{,}000)(\$4{,}000)]^{1/2} = [\$513{,}440{,}000]^{1/2} = \$22{,}659.$
The coefficient of variation for existing projects (σ/NPV) =
$18,112/$46,000 = .39. The coefficient of variation for existing projects
plus puddings = $22,659/$58,000 = .39. While the pudding line has a
higher coefficient of variation ($9,000/$12,000 = .75) than existing
projects, indicating a higher degree of risk, the correlation of this product
line with existing lines is sufficiently low as to bring the coefficient of variation for all products including puddings in line with that for only existing
products.

SELECTED REFERENCES

BEY, ROGER P., "Capital Budgeting Decisions When Cash Flows and Project Lives Are Stochastic and Dependent," *Journal of Financial Research*, 6 (Fall 1983), 175–87.

HAYES, ROBERT H., and DAVID A. GARVIN, "Managing as if Tomorrow Mattered," *Harvard Business Review*, 60 (May–June 1982), 71–79.

HERTZ, DAVID B., "Risk Analysis in Capital Investment," *Harvard Business Review*, 42 (January–February 1964), 95–106.

———, "Investment Policies That Pay Off," *Harvard Business Review*, 46 (January–February 1968), 96–108.

HILLIER, FREDERICK S., "The Derivation of Probabilistic Information for the Evaluation of Risky Investments," *Management Science*, 9 (April 1963), 443–57.

MAGEE, J. F., "How to Use Decision Trees in Capital Investment," *Harvard Business Review*, 42 (September–October 1964), 79–96.

ROBICHEK, ALEXANDER A., "Interpreting the Results of Risk Analysis," *Journal of Finance*, 30 (December 1975), 1384–86.

———, and JAMES VAN HORNE, "Abandonment Value and Capital Budgeting," *Journal of Finance*, 22 (December 1967), 557–89; EDWARD A. DYL and HUGH W. LONG, "Comment," *Journal of Finance*, 24 (March 1969), 88–95; and ROBICHEK and VAN HORNE, "Reply," ibid., 96–97.

SICK, GORDON A., "A Certainty-Equivalent Approach to Capital Budgeting," *Financial Management*, 15 (Winter 1986), 23–32.

SCHALL, LAWRENCE D., and GARY L. SUNDEM, "Capital Budgeting Methods and Risk: A Further Analysis," *Financial Management*, 9 (Spring 1980), 7–11.

TRIGEORGIS, LENOS, and SCOTT P. MASON, "Valuing Managerial Flexibility," *Midland Corporate Finance Journal*, 5 (Spring 1987), 14–21.

VAN HORNE, JAMES, "Capital-Budgeting Decisions Involving Combinations of Risky Investments," *Management Science*, 13 (October 1966), 84–92.

———, "The Analysis of Uncertainty Resolution in Capital Budgeting for New Products," *Management Science*, 15 (April 1969), 376–86.

———, "Capital Budgeting Under Conditions of Uncertainty as to Project Life," *Engineering Economist*, 17 (Spring 1972), 189–99.

———, "Variation of Project Life as a Means for Adjusting for Risk," *Engineering Economist*, 21 (Summer 1976), 151–58.

CHAPTER 15

Required Returns on Capital Investments

The acceptance criterion for capital investments is perhaps the most difficult and controversial topic in finance. We know in theory that it should be the rate of return on a project that will leave the market price of the company's stock unchanged. The difficulty is in determining this rate in practice. Because predictng the effect of decisions on stock prices is an inexact science (some would call it an art form), estimating the appropriate required rate of return is inexact as well. Rather than skirt the issue, we address it head on and propose a general framework for measuring the required rate of return. The idea is a simple one. We try to determine the opportunity cost of a capital investment project by relating it to a financial market investment with the same risk.

CREATION OF VALUE

If the return on the project exceeds what the financial markets require, it is said to earn an excess return. This excess return, as we define it, represents the creation of value. Simply put, the project earns more than its economic keep.

Industry Attractiveness

Value creation has several sources, but perhaps the most important are industry attractiveness and competitive advantage. These are the things that give rise to positive net present value projects, ones that provide expected returns in excess of what the financial markets require. Favorable industry characteristics include the growth phase of a product cycle, barriers to entry, and other protective devices such as patents, temporary monopoly power, and/or oligopoly pricing where nearly all competitors are profitable. Industry attractiveness has to do with the relative position of an industry in the spectrum of return-generating possibilities.

Competitive Advantage

Competitive advantage involves the relative position of a company within an industry. The company could be multidivisional, in which case competitive advantage needs to be judged industry by industry. The avenues to competitive advantage are several: cost advantage, marketing and price advantage, and superior organizational capability (corporate culture).[1] Competitive advantage is eroded with competition. Relative cost or marketing superiority, for example, is conspicuous and will be attacked. As before, the mark of a successful company is one that continually identifies and exploits opportunities for excess returns. Only with a sequence of short-run advantages can any overall competitive advantage be sustained.

Thus, industry attractiveness and competitive advantage are principal

[1] For an extensive discussion of this concept, and much more, see Michael E. Porter, *Competitive Advantage* (New York: Free Press, 1985).

sources of value creation. The more favorable these are, the more likely the company is to have expected returns in excess of what the financal markets require for the risk involved.

In what follows, we endeavor to measure what the financial markets require. We begin with the required rate of return for the company as a whole and then move on to consider the required rate of return for individual projects and for various subsets of an enterprise such as divisions.

OVERALL COST OF CAPITAL OF THE FIRM

For a company as a whole, there is an aggregation of assets. As a result, the use of an overall **cost of capital** as the acceptance criterion for investment decisions is appropriate only under certain circumstances. These circumstances are that the assets of the firm are homogeneous with respect to risk and that investment proposals under consideration are of the same character. If investment proposals vary widely with respect to risk, the required rate of return for the company as a whole is not appropriate as an acceptance criterion. The advantage of using it is, of course, its simplicity. Once it is computed, projects can be evaluated using a single rate that does not change unless underlying conditions, both business and financial market, change. This avoids the problem of computing individual required rates of return for each investment proposal. However, it is important that if the firm's overall required rate of return is used as an acceptance criterion, projects correspond in general to the foregoing conditions. Otherwise, one should determine an acceptance criterion for each project, a topic we take up in the latter part of this chapter.

Cost of capital. The explicit or implied return required on various types of financing. The overall cost of capital is a weighted average of the individual costs.

The overall cost of capital of a firm is composed of the costs of the various components of financing. The cost of equity capital is the most difficult to measure, and it will occupy most of our attention. We consider also the costs of debt and preferred stock. Our concern throughout will be with the *marginal* cost of a specific source of financing. The use of marginal costs follows from the fact that we use the cost of capital to decide whether to invest in new projects. Past costs of financing have no bearing on this decision. All costs will be expressed on an after-tax basis, to conform to the expression of investment project cash flows on an after-tax basis. Once we have examined the explicit costs of various sources of financing, we shall combine these costs to obtain an overall cost of capital to the firm. We assume in the development of this chapter that the reader has covered the foundation materials in Chapters 4 and 5 on the mathematics of finance and on valuation.

Cost of Debt

Although the liabilities of a company are varied, our focus is only on nonseasonal debt that bears an explicit interest cost. We ignore accounts payable, accruals, and other obligations not having an explicit interest cost. For the most part, our concern is with long-term debt. However, continuous short-term debt, such as an accounts receivable loan, also qualifies. (A bank loan to finance seasonal inventory requirements would not qualify.) The assumption is that the firm will finance a capital project, whose benefits extend over a number of years, with financing of the same general sort.

The explicit cost of debt can be derived by solving for the discount rate, k, that equates the net proceeds of the debt issue with the present value of interest plus principal payments, then adjusting the explicit cost obtained for the tax effect. The discount rate, k, known as the yield to maturity, is solved with the formula

$$P_0 = \sum_{t=1}^{n} \frac{I_t + P_t}{(1 + k)^t} \tag{15-1}$$

where P_0 is the initial cash inflow to the firm; Σ denotes the summation for periods 1 through n, the final maturity; I_t is the interest payment in period t; and P_t is the payment of principal in period t. If principal payments occur only at final maturity, only P_n will appear. By solving for k, the rate of discount that equates the present value of cash outflows with the initial cash inflow, we obtain the before-tax cost of debt. All of this should be familiar from our discussion of bond valuation in Chapter 5. The after-tax cost of debt, which we denote by k_i, can be approximated by

$$k_i = k(1 - t) \tag{15-2}$$

where k is the internal rate of return or yield and t is the company's marginal tax rate. Because interest charges are tax deductible, the after-tax cost of debt is substantially less than the before-tax cost. If the before-tax cost, k, in Eq. (15-1) were found to be 11 percent and the tax rate (federal and state) were 40 percent

$$k_i = 11.00(1 - .40) = 6.60\%$$

We note that the 6.60 percent after-tax cost in our example represents the marginal, or incremental, cost of additional debt. It does not represent the cost of debt funds already employed.

The explicit cost of debt is considerably cheaper than the cost of another source of financing having the same k but where the financial charges are not deductible for tax purposes. Implied in the calculation of an after-tax cost of debt is the fact that the firm is profitable. Otherwise, it does not gain the tax benefit associated with interest payments. The explicit cost of debt for an unprofitable firm is the before-tax cost, k.

Cost of Preferred Stock

The cost of preferred stock is a function of its stated dividend. As we discuss in Chapter 22, this dividend is not a contractual obligation of the firm but is payable at the discretion of the board of directors. Consequently, unlike debt, it does not create a risk of legal bankruptcy. To holders of common stock, however, preferred stock is a security interest that takes priority over theirs. Most corporations that issue preferred stock intend to pay the stated dividend. As preferred stock has no maturity date, its cost may be represented as

$$k_p = \frac{D}{I_0} \qquad (15\text{-}3)$$

where D is the stated annual dividend and I_0 represents the proceeds of the preferred stock issue. If a company were able to sell a 10 percent preferred stock issue ($50 par value) and realize net proceeds of $49 a share, the cost of the preferred stock would be $5/$49 = 10.20 percent. Note that this cost is not adjusted for taxes because the preferred stock dividend is paid after taxes. Thus, the explicit cost of preferred stock is greater than that for debt.

However, the preferred stock has a desirable feature to the corporate investor. The tax law provides that 80 percent of the dividends received by one corporation from another are exempt from taxation. This attraction on the demand side usually results in yields on preferred stocks being slightly below those on bonds of the same company. It is only after taxes that debt financing becomes more attractive.

Cost of Equity Capital

The cost of equity capital is by far the most difficult cost to measure. In theory, it may be defined as the minimum rate of return that the company must earn on the equity-financed portion of an investment project in order to leave unchanged the market price of the stock. If the firm invests in projects having an expected return less than this required return, the market price of the stock over the long run will suffer.

In the context of the dividend discount models (DDM) presented in Chapter 5, the cost of equity capital can be thought of as the rate of discount that equates the present value of all expected future dividends per share, as perceived by investors at the margin, with the current market price per share. Recall from Chapter 5 that

$$P_0 = \frac{D_1}{(1 + k_e)} + \frac{D_2}{(1 + k_e)^2} + \cdots + \frac{D\infty}{(1 + K_e)^\infty}$$

$$P_0 = \sum_{t=1}^{\infty} \frac{D_t}{(1 + k_e)^t} \qquad (15\text{-}4)$$

where P_0 is the value of a share of stock at time 0, D_t is the dividend per share expected to be paid in period t, k_e is the appropriate rate of discount, and Σ represents the sum of discounted expected future dividends from period 1 through infinity, depicted by the symbol ∞.

Estimating Future Dividends.   If we can successfully estimate the stream of future dividends that the market expects, it is an easy matter to solve for the rate of discount that equates this stream with the current market price of the stock. Because expected future dividends are not directly observable, they must be estimated. Herein lies the major difficulty in estimating the cost of equity capital. For reasonably stable patterns of past growth, one might project this trend into the future. However, we must temper the projection to take account of current market sentiment. Insight into such sentiment can come from reviewing various analyses about the company in financial newspapers and magazines.

If, for example, dividends were expected to grow at an 8 percent annual rate into the foreseeble future, the perpetual growth model presented in Chapter 5 might be used to determine the required rate of return. If the expected dividend in the first year were $2 and the present market price per share were $27, we would have

$$k_e = \frac{\$2}{\$27} + .08 = .154 = 15.4\%$$

This rate would then be used as an estimate of the firm's required return on equity capital. The important thing, then, is to measure the growth in dividends per share as perceived by investors at the margin.

Nonlinear Growth Patterns.   If the growth in dividends is expected to taper off in the future, the perpetual growth model will not do. As explained in Chapter 5, a modification of Eq. (15-4) is in order. Frequently, the transition in growth is from an above-normal growth rate to one that is considered normal. If dividends were expected to grow at a 15 percent compound rate for 5 years, at a 10 percent rate for the next 5 years, and then grow at a 5 percent rate, we would have

$$P_0 = \sum_{t=1}^{5} \frac{D_0(1.15)^t}{(1 + k_e)^t} + \sum_{t=6}^{10} \frac{D_5(1.10)^{t-5}}{(1 + k_e)^t} + \sum_{t=11}^{\infty} \frac{D_{10}(1.05)^{t-10}}{(1 + k_e)^t} \qquad (15\text{-}5)$$

We see that the current dividend, D_0, is the base on which the expected growth in future dividends is built. By solving for k_e, we obtain the cost of equity capital as defined. One would use the method illustrated in Chapter 5 to solve for k_e. For example, if the current dividend, D_0, were $2 a share and market price per share, P_0, were $70, k_e in Eq. (15-5) would be 10.42 percent. For other patterns of expected future growth, the equation can be easily modified to deal with the situation.

The more growth segments we specify, of course, the more the growth pattern will approximate a curvilinear relationship. From Chapter 5, we learned how to determine the terminal value at the beginning of the last growth segment. This terminal value can be based on expected future dividends, as in Eq. (15-5), in which case the perpetual dividend growth model is used, or on earnings per share multiplied by an assumed price/earnings ratio.

Capital-Asset Pricing Model Approach

Rather than estimating the future dividend stream of the firm and then solving for the cost of equity capital, we may approach the problem directly by estimating the required rate of return on the company's equity. From our discussion of the capital-asset pricing model (CAPM) in Chapter 5, we know that it implies the following required rate of return for a stock:

$$R_j = i + (\bar{R}_m - i)\beta_j \qquad (15\text{-}6)$$

where i is the risk-free rate, $\bar{R}_m$ is the expected return for the market portfolio, and β_j is the beta coefficient for stock j. From Chapter 5, we know that because of the market's aversion to systematic risk, the greater the beta of a stock, the greater its required return. The risk-return relationship is described by the security market line (see Fig. 5-7 in Chapter 5). It implies that in market equilibrium, security prices will be such that there is a linear trade-off between the required rate of return and systematic risk.

Beta Relationship.   Beta, then, is a measure of the responsiveness of the excess returns for security j (in excess of the risk-free rate) to those of the market, using some broad-based market index such as Standard & Poor's 500-stock index as a surrogate for the market portfolio. If the historical relationship between security returns and those for the market portfolio is believed to be a reasonable proxy for the future, one can use past returns to compute the beta for a stock. This was illustrated in Chapter 5, where a characteristic line was fitted to the relationship between returns in excess of risk-free rate for the stock and those for the market index. *Beta* is defined as the slope of this line. To free us of the need to calculate beta information directly, several services provide historical beta information on a large number of publicly traded stocks. These services allow us to obtain the beta for a stock with ease, thereby facilitating greatly the calculation of the cost of equity capital.

Again, if the past is thought to be a good proxy for the future, we can use Eq. (15-6) to compute the cost of equity capital for a company. To illustrate, suppose that the beta for the Silva-Chin Company were found to be 1.20, based on monthly excess return data over the last 5 years. This coefficient tells us that the stock's excess return goes up or down by a somewhat greater percentage than does the excess return for the market. (A beta of 1.00 means that excess returns for the stock vary proportionally with excess returns for the market portfolio.) Thus, the stock of Silva-Chin company has more unavoidable, or systematic, risk than does the market as a whole. But management believes that this past relationship is likely to hold in the future. Furthermore, a rate of return of about 17 percent on stocks in general is expected to prevail and a risk-free rate of 12 percent is expected.

This is all the information we need in order to compute the required rate of return on equity for Silva-Chin Company. Using Eq. (15-6), the cost of equity capital would be

$$R_j = .12 + (.17 - .12)1.20 = 18\%$$

Thus, the estimated required rate of return on equity for Silva-Chin Company is approximately 18 percent. In essence, we are saying that this is the rate of return that investors expect the company to earn on its equity.

Risk-Free Rate and Market Return.   In addition to beta, it is important that the numbers used for the risk-free rate and the market return in the formula be the best estimates of the future possible. The former is controversial, not as to the security that should be used but the maturity. Most agree that the proper instrument is a Treasury security. But the proper maturity is another matter. As the CAPM is a one-period model, some contend a short-term rate, such as that for 3-month Treasury bills, is in order. Others argue that because capital investment projects are long-lived, a long-term Treasury bond rate should be used. Still others, myself included, feel more comfortable with an intermediate-term rate, such as that on 1- or 2-year Treasury notes. This is a middle position in a rather murky area. With an upward-sloping yield curve (the relationship between yield and maturity), the longer the maturity the higher the risk-free rate but also the less the variability of interest rates.

For the expected return on the market portfolio of stocks, as usually depicted by Standard & Poors' 500-stock index, one can use consensus estimates of security analysts, economists, and others who regularly predict such returns. Goldman Sachs, Merrill Lynch, and other investment banks make these predictions, often on a monthly basis. These estimated annual returns are for the immediate future. The expected return on the market portfolio has exceeded the risk-free rate by anywhere from 3 to 7 percent in recent years. Expressed differently, the "before-hand" or ex ante market risk premium has ranged from 3 to 7 percent. This is not the range of risk premiums actually realized over some holding period but the expected risk premium for investing in the market portfolio as opposed to the risk-free asset. Due to changes in inflation, in interest rates, and in the degree of investor risk aversion in society, both the risk-free rate and the expected market return change over time. Therefore, the 18 percent computed earlier would be an estimate of the required return on equity at only a moment in time.

If measurement were exact and certain assumptions held,[2] the cost of equity capital determined by this method would be the same as that provided by a dividend-capitalization model. Recall that the latter estimate is the rate of discount that equates the present value of the stream of expected future dividends with the current market price of the stock. By now it should be apparent that we can hope only to approximate the cost of equity capital. We believe that the methods suggested enable such an approximation more or less accurately, depending on the situation. For a large company whose stock is actively traded on the New York Stock Exchange and whose systematic risk is close to that of the market as a whole, we can usually estimate more confidently than we can for a moderate-sized company whose stock is inactively traded in the over-the-counter market and whose systematic risk is very large. We must live with the inexactness involved in the measurement process and try to do as good a job as possible.

---

[2] As discussed in Chapter 5, the capital-asset pricing model assumes the presence of perfect capital markets. When this assumption is relaxed to take account of real-world conditions, the residual risk of a stock may take on a degree of importance. We know that the total risk of a security is composed of its systematic as well as its residual risk. The assumption of the capital-asset pricing model is that residual risk can be completely diversified away, leaving us with only systematic risk.

If imperfections exist in the capital markets, these may impede efficient diversification by investors. (One example of an imperfection is the presence of significant bankruptcy costs.) The greater the imperfections that are believed to exist, the greater the allowance that must be made for residual risk. As a result, it will be necessary to adjust upward the required rate of return. For amplification of this point, see James C. Van Horne, *Financial Management and Policy*, 8th ed. (Englewood Cliffs, N.J.: Prentice-Hall, 1989), chaps. 7–8.

Debt Cost as the Base.   Rather than estimate the required return in this manner, some people use the company's debt cost as a basis for estimating its equity cost. A firm's before-tax cost of debt will exceed the risk-free rate by a risk premium. The greater the risk of the firm, the greater this premium and the more interest the firm must pay in order to borrow. The relationship is illustrated in Fig. 15-1. On the horizontal axis, the firm's debt is shown to have systematic risk equal to β_d. As a result, its required return is k_d, which exceeds the risk-free rate of i.

In addition to this risk premium, the common stock of a company must provide a higher expected return than the debt of the same company. The reason is that there is more systematic risk involved. This phenomenon also is illustrated in the figure. We see that for a beta of β_e, an expected return of k_e is required and that this percentage exceeds the company's cost of debt, k_d. The historical risk premium in expected return for stocks over corporate bonds has been around 3 percent. If this seemed reasonable for a particular company, one could use the firm's before-tax cost of debt as a base and add to it a premium of around 3 percent to estimate its cost of equity capital. To illustrate, suppose Valkury Corporation's bonds sell in the market to yield 15 percent. Using the approach just outlined, its approximate cost of equity would be

$$k_e = k_d + \begin{matrix} \text{Stock over debt} \\ \text{risk premium} \end{matrix} = 15\% + 3\% = 18\%$$

This percentage then would be used as the cost of equity capital. The advantage of the approach is that one does not have to use beta information and make the calculation involved in Eq. (15-6). The disadvantage is that it does not allow for changing risk premiums over time; and because the 3 percent is for companies overall, the approach is not as accurate as the direct estimate of the required return on equity capital for a specific company. However, it does offer an alternative method of estimating the cost of equity capital within the overall framework of the capital-asset pricing model.

FIGURE 15-1
The security market line with debt and stock

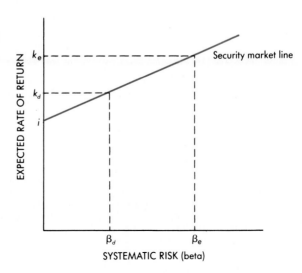

Weighted Average Cost of Capital

Once we have computed costs of individual components of the capital structure,[3] we would weigh them according to some standard and calculate a weighted average cost of capital. The firm's overall cost of capital may be expressed as

$$\text{Cost of capital} = \sum_{x=1}^{n} k_x w_x \tag{15-7}$$

where k_x is the after-tax cost of the xth method of financing, w_x is the weight given to that method as a percentage of the firm's total financing, and Σ denotes the summation for financing methods 1 through n. To illustrate the calculations involved, suppose that a firm had the following capital structure at the latest statement date, where the amounts shown represent market values:

	AMOUNT	PROPORTION
Debt	$ 30 million	30%
Preferred stock	10 million	10%
Common stock equity	60 million	60%
	$100 million	100%

Common stock equity includes both common stock issues and retained earnings. In calculating proportions, it is important that we use market value as opposed to book-value weights. Because we are trying to maximize the value of the firm to its shareholders, only market-value weights are consistent with our objective. Market values are used in the calculation of costs of the various components of financing, so market-value weights should be used in determining the weighted average cost of capital.

To continue with our illustration, suppose that the firm computed the following after-tax costs for the component methods of financing:

	COST
Debt	6.6%
Preferred stock	10.2
Common stock equity	18.0

Again we emphasize that these costs must be present-day costs based on current

---

[3] While equity, debt, and preferred stocks are the major types of financing, there are other types. These include leasing, convertible securities, warrants, and options. Because determining the costs of these methods of financing involves some special and rather complex valuation issues, we treat them in individual chapters where we are able to give such issues proper attention. For our purposes in this chapter, knowing the costs of equity, debt, and preferred stock financing is sufficient for illustrating the overall cost of capital of a company. When costs are determined for other types of financing, they can be inserted in the weighting scheme to be discussed now.

financial market conditions. Past embedded costs of financing have no bearing on the required rate of return. Given the costs shown, the weighted average cost of capital for this example problem is

	(1) PROPORTION	(2) COST	(3) WEIGHTED COST (1) × (2)
Debt	30%	6.6%	1.98%
Preferred stock	10	10.2	1.02
Common stock equity	60	18.0	10.80
			13.80%

Thus, with the assumptions of this example, 13.8 percent represents the weighted average cost of the component methods of financing, where each component is weighted according to market-value proportions.

Some Limitations

With the calculation of a weighted average cost of capital, the critical question is whether the figure represents the firm's real cost of capital. The answer depends on how accurately we have measured the individual marginal costs, on the weighting system, and on certain other assumptions. Assume for now that we are able to measure accurately the marginal costs of the individual sources of financing, and let us examine the importance of the weighting system.

Weighting System.   The critical assumption in any weighting system is that the firm will in fact raise capital in the proportions specified. Because the firm raises capital *marginally* to make a *marginal* investment in new projects, we need to work with the marginal cost of capital to the firm as a whole. This rate depends on the package of funds employed to finance investment projects. In other words, our concern is with new or incremental capital, not with capital raised in the past. In order for the weighted average cost of capital to represent a marginal cost, the weights employed must be marginal; that is, the weights must correspond to the proportions of financing inputs the firm intends to employ.

If they do not, capital is raised on a marginal basis in proportions other than those used to calculate this cost. As a result, the real weighted average cost of capital will differ from that calculated and used for capital investment decisions. An obvious bias results. If the real cost is greater than that which is measured, certain investment projects will be accepted that will leave investors worse off than before. On the other hand, if the real cost is less than the measured cost, projects will be rejected that could increase shareholder wealth. Therefore, the 13.8 percent weighted average cost of capital computed in our example is realistic only if the firm intends to finance in the future in the same proportions as its existing capital structure.

Raising capital is "lumpy," and strict proportions cannot be maintained. For example, a firm would have difficulty financing each project with 30 percent debt, 10 percent preferred stock, and 60 percent retained earnings. In practice, it may finance with debt in one instance and with preferred stock or retained earnings in another. Over time, most firms are able to finance in roughly a proportional manner. It is in this sense that we try to measure the marginal cost of capital for the package of financing employed.

Flotation costs. The costs associated with issuing securities.

Flotation Costs.   Flotation costs involved in the sale of common stock, preferred stock, or a debt instrument affect the profitability of a firm's investments. In many cases, the new issue must be priced below the market price of existing financing; in addition, there are out-of-pocket flotation costs. Owing to flotation costs, the amount of funds the firm receives is less than the price at which the issue is sold. The presence of flotation costs in financing requires an adjustment be made in the evaluation of investment proposals.

That adjustment is made by adding flotation costs of financing to the project's intial cash outlay. Suppose that an investment proposal costs $100,000 and that to finance the project the company must raise $60,000 externally. Both debt and common stock are involved, and flotation costs come to $4,000. Therefore, $4,000 should be added to $100,000, bringing the total intial outlay to $104,000. In this way, the proposal is properly "penalized" for the flotation costs associated with its financing. The expected future cash flows associated with the project are discounted at the weighted average cost of capital. If the project were expected to provide annual cash inflows of $24,000 forever and the weighted average cost of capital were 20 percent, the project's net present value would be

$$NPV = \frac{\$24,000}{.20} - \$104,000 = \$16,000$$

This amount contrasts with a net present value of $20,000 if no adjustment is made for flotation costs.

Thus, the adjustment for flotation costs should be made in the project's cash flows and not in the cost of capital.[4] To adjust the cost of capital results in an excessive "penalty" wherever the net present value of the project is positive. In our previous example, $4,000 in flotation costs represents 4 percent of the $100,000 investment, so the "adjusted" cost of capital would be 20 percent/$(1 - .04)$ = 20.83 percent.

Therefore, the net present value of the project would be

$$NPV = \frac{\$24,000}{.2083} - \$100,000 = \$15,218$$

As we see, the use of an adjusted cost of results in a biased, low estimate of the net present value of a project whenever this value is positive. The appropriate procedure is to adjust the project's initial cash outlay and to use the weighted

[4] For a defense of the procedure, see Simon E. Keane, "The Investment Discount Rate—In Defense of the Market Rate of Interest," *Accounting and Business Research* (Summer 1976), 234; and John R. Ezzell and R. Burr Porter, "Flotation Costs and the Weighted Average Cost of Capital," *Journal of Financial and Quantitative Analysis*, 11 (September 1976), 403–13.

average "unadjusted" cost of capital as the discount rate. However, in many circumstances the bias involved in adjusting the cost of capital for flotation costs is small. In such cases, the latter method is suitable.

Rationale for Weighted Average Cost

The rationale behind the use of a weighted average cost of capital is that by financing in the proportions specified and accepting projects yielding more than the weighted average required return, the firm is able to increase the market price of its stock. This increase occurs because investment projects accepted are expected to return more on their equity-financed portions than the cost of equity capital, k_e. Once these expectations are apparent to the marketplace, the market price of the stock should rise, all other things the same, because expected future earnings per share (and dividends per share) are higher than those expected before the projects were accepted. The firm has accepted projects that are expected to provide a return greater than that required by investors at the margin, based on the risk involved.

We must return to the critical assumption that over time the firm finances in the proportions specified. If it does so, the financial risk of the company remains roughly unchanged. As we shall see in Chapter 17, the "implicit" costs of financing are embodied in the weighted average cost of capital by virtue of the fact that a firm has to supplement nonequity financing with equity financing. It does not raise capital continually with supposedly cheaper debt funds without increasing its equity base. The firm's capital structure need not be optimal for the firm to employ the weighted average cost of capital for capital budgeting purposes. The important consideration is that the weights used be based on the future financing plans of the company. If they are not, the weighted average cost of capital calculated does not correspond to the actual cost of funds obtained; as a result, capital budgeting decisions are likely to be suboptimal.

The use of a weighted average cost of capital figure must be qualified also for the points raised earlier. It assumes that the investment proposals being considered do not differ in systematic, or unavoidable, risk from that of the firm and that the residual risk of the proposals does not provide any diversification benefits to the firm. Only under these circumstances is the cost of capital figure obtained appropriate as an acceptance criterion. These assumptions are extremely binding. They imply that the projects of a firm are completely homogeneous with respect to risk and that only projects of the same risk will be considered.

In practice, of course, the issue is one of degree. If the conditions noted are approximately met, then the company's weighted average cost of capital may be used as the acceptance criterion. If a firm produced only one product and all proposals considered were in conjunction with the marketing and production of that product, the use of the firm's overall cost of capital as the acceptance criterion probably would be appropriate. (Even here, however, there may be significant enough differences in risk among investment proposals to warrant separate consideration.) For a multiproduct firm with investment proposals of varying risk, the use of an overall required rate of return is inappropriate. Here the required rate of return for the specific proposal should be used, as determined with the methods proposed in the next section. The key, then, is the homogeneity with respect to risk of existing investment projects and investment proposals under consideration.

THE CAPM: PROJECT-SPECIFIC AND GROUP-SPECIFIC REQUIRED RETURNS

When the existing investment projects of the firm and investment proposals under consideration are not homogeneous with respect to risk, the use of the firm's cost of capital as an acceptance criterion will not do. In these cases, we must formulate a specific acceptance criterion for the particular project involved. One means for doing so is with the capital-asset pricing model, and this approach is described in this section.

Capital-Asset Pricing Model Approach to Projects

Essentially, the capital-asset pricing model approach is the same as that for determining the cost of equity capital of the firm. However, instead of the expected relation between excess returns for the stock (returns in excess of the risk-free rate) and those for the market portfolio, one is concerned with the expected relation of excess returns for the project and those for the market portfolio. The required return for an equity-financed project would be

$$R_k = i + (\overline{R}_m - i)\beta_k \qquad (15\text{-}8)$$

where β_k is the slope of the characteristic line that describes the relationship between excess returns for project k and those for the market portfolio. As can be seen, this equation is identical to Eq. (15-6) except for the substitution of the project return and its beta for those of the stock.

Assume that the firm intends to finance a project entirely with equity. The acceptance criterion then would be to invest in the project if its expected return exceeded the required return, R_k, as determined with Eq. (15-8). To illustrate the acceptance criterion for projects using this concept, we turn to Fig. 15-2. All projects with internal rates of return lying on or above the line should be accepted, for they provide expected excess returns. Acceptable projects are depicted by x's. All projects lying below the line, shown by the o's, would be rejected. Note that the greater the systematic risk of a project, the greater the return that is required. If the project had no risk, only the risk-free rate would be required. For projects with more risk, however, a risk premium is demanded, and it increases with the degree of systematic risk of the project. The goal of the firm in this context is to search for investment opportunities lying above the line.

Application of the Model—The Use of Proxy Companies.   The difficulty in applying this approach is in estimating the beta for a project. Recall from Chapter 5 that derivation of the characteristic line is based on changes in

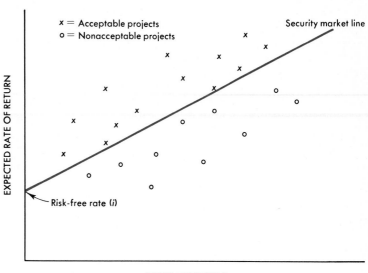

FIGURE 15-2
The security market line as applied to risky investment

market value for a stock and those for the market portfolio. It is, therefore, necessary to estimate changes in the market value of the project over time in relation to changes in value for the market portfolio. The values of nontraded assets are not directly observable, so we cannot calculate the beta in the manner presented earlier for a publicly traded stock.

However, in many cases the project is sufficiently similar to a company whose stock is publicly held so that we can use that company's beta in deriving the required rate of return on equity for the project. For large projects, such as new products, one frequently can identify publicly traded companies that are engaged entirely, or almost entirely, in the same type of operation. The important thing is to identify a company or companies with systematic risk characteristics similar to those of the project in question.

Suppose that a chemical company is considering the formation of a real estate subsidiary. As there are a number of real estate companies with publicly traded stocks, one simply could determine the beta for one of those companies or a group of them and use it in Eq. (15-6) to derive the required rate of return for the project. Note that the relevant required rate of return is not that for the chemical company but that for other real estate firms. Stated differently, the market views the chemical company's venture in the same way it views other firms engaged solely in real estate. By concentrating on companies in the same line as the firm desires to enter, we can find surrogates that approximate the systematic risk of the project. An exact duplication of the project's risk is unlikely, but reasonable approximations frequently are possible.

To illustrate the calculations, suppose that the average beta for a sample of real estate companies whose stocks were publicly traded and whose basic businesses were similar to the venture contemplated by the chemical company was 1.6. We can use this beta as a surrogate for the beta of the project. If we expect the average return on the market portfolio of stocks to be 13 percent and the risk-free rate to be 8 percent, the required return on equity for the project would be

385

$$R_k = .08 = (.13 - .08)1.6 = 16\%$$

So 16 percent would be used as the required equity return for the project.

Finding Proxy Companies.   One should endeavor to identify companies of a similar nature to the project in question. The search for similars usually is industry based. Sometimes one will turn to the SIC (Standard Industrial Classification) code to determine an initial sample. When a project falls in a single industry classification, the job is relatively easy. From the sample of proxy companies, their betas are arrayed. If outliers are felt not to be comparable to the project in question, they might be culled. Rather than compute an arithmetic average of the sample betas, I find it better to use a modal or median value. The idea is to come up with a beta that broadly portrays the business risk of the investment project. One can only hope to approximate, given the data problems.

When there are no companies whose stocks are publicly traded and so we cannot find proxies for the project, the task becomes much more difficult. Even here, however, there sometimes exists information on the market value of the project in question. For machine tools, a secondary market of sorts exists, where prices are established for used machines of various ages. Other assets have similar markets where prices can be determined. Given these prices, we can measure the market return for a particular period and then use such information to derive an estimate of beta for the project.[5] The approach is hampered, however, by a number of measurement problems. Unless one is able to use a company or companies whose stock is publicly traded as a proxy for the project, the derivation of a beta for a specific project is a difficult matter. For this reason we will restrict our attention to the use of proxy company information.

The Required Return with Leverage.   If the firm consistently finances projects with equity, we would use R_k as the required rate of return for the project. If some debt financing is employed, however, we need to determine a weighted average required return. Here the weighting system is similar to that illustrated earlier for the firm's overall cost of capital. Rather than vary the proportion of debt financing project by project, most companies apply the same weights to all projects. Presumably these weights will correspond to the proportions with which the firm intends to finance over time. If the firm intends to finance with one part debt for every two parts equity, and the after-tax cost of debt is 6.60 percent while the required return on equity for the project is 16 percent, the overall required return for the project is

$$R_k = .066(1/3) + .16(2/3) = 12.87\%$$

If the project were expected to provide an internal rate of return in excess or equal to this rate, the project would be accepted. If not, it would be rejected. Thus, the acceptance criterion is specifically related to the systematic risk of the project through the cost of equity capital.

---

[5] For such an example, see Van Horne, *Financial Management and Policy*, chap. 7.

Group-Specific Required Returns

Rather than determine project-specific required returns, some companies categorize projects into roughly homogeneous groups and then apply the same required return to all projects emanating from that group. One advantage is that it is not as time consuming as computing required returns for each project. Another is that it often is easier to find proxy companies for a group than it is for an individual project. By group, we mean some subunit of the company that carries on a set of activities that can be differentiated from the other activities of the firm. Usually these activities are differentiated along product or service lines as well as along management lines. Frequently the subunits are divisions or subsidiaries of the company, though a group is not restricted to this definition.

If the products or service of the group are homogeneous with respect to risk, and new proposals are of the same sort, a group-specific required return is an appropriate acceptance criterion. It represents the transfer price of capital from the company to the group. Stated differently, it is the rate of return the company expects the group to earn on its capital investments. The greater the systematic risk of the group, the greater its required return.

The computation of the required rate of return is the same as that for the specific project. For each group, proxy companies whose stocks are publicly traded are identified. On the basis of these surrogates, betas are derived for each group and from these a required return on equity capital is calculated.[6] If debt is used, a weighted average required return for the group is derived in the same manner as in the previous section. Once group-specific required returns are computed, capital is allocated, or transferred, throughout the firm on a risk-adjusted returns basis. The approach provides a consistent framework for allocating capital among groups with greatly different risks.

The approach is illustrated in Fig. 15-3. Here, the bars represent the required return for four groups. The weighted average cost of capital for the firm as a whole is depicted by the dashed line. Projects providing expected return above the bars should be accepted; those below the bars rejected. Note that this criterion means that for the two "safer" groups, some accepted projects may provide expected returns below the firm's overall cost of capital but above the required return for the group. For the two "riskier" groups, rejected projects may have provided returns greater than the overall cost of capital but less than the group's required return. Indeed, capital is allocated on a risk-return basis specific to the systematic risk of the group.[7]

[6] For illustrations of this approach with actual companies, see James C. Van Horne, "An Application of the Capital Asset Pricing Model to Divisional Required Returns," *Financial Management*, 9 (Spring 1980), 14–19; and Diana R. Harrington, "Stock Prices, Beta and Strategic Planning," *Harvard Business Review*, 61 (May–June 1983), 157–64. For a different approach to determining divisional required returns by an actual company, see Benton E. Gup and Samuel W. Norwood III, "Divisional Cost of Capital: A Practical Approach," *Financial Management*, 11(Spring 1982), 20–24. Finally, for an excellent overall discussion of the application of the CAPM to divisional required returns, see Barr Rosenberg and Andrew Rudd, "The Corporate Use of Beta," *Issues in Corporate Finance* (Stern, Stewart, Putnam & Macklis, Inc., 1983), pp 42–52.

[7] Russell J. Fuller and Halbert S. Kerr, "Estimating the Divisional Cost of Capital: An Analysis of the Pure-Play Technique," *Journal of Finance*, 36 (December 1981), 997–1009, collected proxy company betas for the various divisions of some 60 multidivision firms. The authors found that an appropriately weighted average of the betas of the proxy firms closely approximated the beta of the multidivision firm.

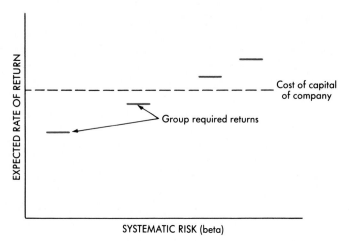

FIGURE 15-3
Group-specific required returns

Some Qualifications

Whether the required returns are project specific or group specific, there are certain problems in the application of the CAPM. For one thing, the amount of nonequity financing that is assigned to a project is an important consideration. For the procedure to hold, it should approximate the same relative amount as that used by the proxy company. In other words, the proportion of nonequity financing allocated to a project should not be significantly out of line with that for the proxy company being used. Otherwise, one will not get a reasonable proxy for the systematic risk of the project. Where the proportions are not nearly the same, the proxy company's beta should be adjusted before it is used as the cost of equity capital for the project. A procedure for adjusting the beta is presented in the appendix to this chapter. Using this procedure, one can approximate the beta for the proxy company, assuming that it had the same relative proportion of nonequity financing as that contemplated for the project. The cost of equity capital for the project can then be determined in the same manner as before.

In addition to the practical problems, there is an underlying assumption in the capital-asset pricing model approach that must be questioned. As we know, this assumption is that only the systematic risk of the firm is important. However, the probability of a firm's becoming insolvent depends on its total risk, not just its systematic risk. When insolvency or bankruptcy costs are significant, investors may be served by the firm's paying attention to the impact of a project on the total risk of the firm. The total risk is composed of both systematic and unsystematic risk. The variability of cash flows is what determines the possibility of a company's going insolvent, and this variability depends on the firm's total risk, not just its systematic risk.[8] For this reason, a company may wish to estimate the impact of a new project on both systematic and total risk.

---

[8] When there are significant bankruptcy costs, these work to the detriment of stockholders as residual owners of the company. It, therefore, may be important for the firm to keep the probability of becoming bankrupt within reasonable bounds. To do so, it must consider the impact of the project on the firm's total risk (systematic and residual). This approach is taken up in the last section of the chapter. See Chapter 27 for details on bankruptcy costs.

Allocating Debt Funds

When allocating debt funds to a division, most people use the company's overall borrowing cost. However, the notion that equity costs differ according to a division's underlying risk applies also to the cost of debt funds. Both types of costs are determined in capital markets according to a risk-return trade-off. The greater the risk, the greater the interest rate that will be required. While a case can be made for differentiating debt costs among divisions according to their systematic risks, few companies do it. For one thing, there are mechanical difficulties in computing the beta, for the market index must include debt instruments. Conceptually, the division itself is not ultimately responsible for its debt. The company as a whole is responsible. Because of diversification of cash flows among divisions, the probability of payment for the whole may be greater than the sum of the parts. For these reasons, few companies have tried to apply the CAPM to divisional debt cost as they have to equity costs. Still, it may be appropriate to vary debt costs for divisions depending on their risk, even though the adjustment is partly subjective.

If one division is allocated a much higher proportion of debt, it will have a lower overall required return on paper. But is it truly lower? Should one division be allowed to significantly lower its required return simply by taking on more leverage? Is this fair to other divisions? Apart from the incentive issue, what are the problems to the company as a whole?

High leverage for one division may cause the cost of debt funds for the overall company to rise. This marginal increase should not be allocated across divisions, but rather it should be pinpointed to the division responsible. Second, the high leverage incurred by the division may increase the uncertainty of the tax shield associated with debt for the company as a whole. Finally, high leverage for one division increases the volatility of returns to stockholders of the company, together with the possibility of insolvency and bankruptcy costs being incurred. In turn, this will cause them to increase the required return on equity to compensate for the increased risk. (The way this comes about will be taken up in Chapter 17.)

For these reasons, the "true" cost of debt for the high leverage division may be considerably greater than originally imagined. If this is the case, some type of premium should be added to the divisions's required return in order to reflect more accurately the true cost of capital for the division. The difficulty is in deciding on what premium is appropriate; and adjustments usually are partly subjective. Still it is possible to get a reasonable handle on incremental interest cost and perhaps some crude approximation of the probability that the tax shield may be postponed or lost. While crude, it is best to make some adjustment in overall divisional required returns when significantly different costs and/or proportions of debt financing are involved.

EVALUATION OF PROJECTS ON THE BASIS OF THEIR TOTAL RISK

When for either theoretical or practical reasons it is not appropriate to compute a required rate of return for a project or group using the CAPM, or when we simply want to supplement the model for the reasons just described, we turn to more subjective means for evaluating risky investments. Many firms deal with the problem in very informal ways. Decision makers simply try to incorporate risk into their judgment on the basis of their "feel" for the projects being evaluated. This "feel" can be improved upon by discussions with others familiar with the proposals and the risks inherent in them. Frequently, such discussions center on "what if" types of questions. In a general way, then, an allowance can be made for risk in capital expenditure decisions. The problem with informal approaches to risk, of course, is that the information developed usually is sketchy, and the treatment of it is not consistent from project to project or over time.

We know from our discussion in Chapter 14 that expected return and risk can be quantified in a consistent manner. Given this information, the question is whether a project should be accepted or rejected. We will begin by examining how management might evaluate a single investment proposal and then move on to combinations of risky investments. These methods are firm-risk oriented in the sense that management does not consider explicitly the effect of the project on investors' portfolios. The focus is on total risk, the sum of systematic and residual risk. Management assesses the likely effect of the project on the variability of cash flows and earnings of the firm. From this assessment, it then can estimate the likely effect on share price. The critical factor from the standpoint of valuation is how accurately management is able to link share price with risk-profitability information for an investment proposal. As we shall see, the linkage tends to be subjective, which detracts from the accuracy of the approaches.

Evaluation of a Proposal

You will recall from Chapter 14 that the information generated for an investment proposal was the probability distribution of possible net present values. We saw also that by standardizing the dispersion in terms of so many standard deviations from the expected value of the distribution, we can determine the probability that the net present value of the project will be zero or less. In the evaluation of a single proposal, it is unlikely that management would accept an investment proposal having an expected value of net present value of zero unless the probability distribution had no dispersion. In this special case the proposal, by definition, would be riskless. For risky investments, the net present value would have to exceed zero. How much it would have to exceed zero before acceptance were warranted depends on the amount of dispersion of the probability distribution and the utility preferences of management with respect to risk.

To facilitate project selection as well as to make it consistent over time, management may wish to formulate maximum risk profiles. To express the probability distributions in relative instead of absolute terms, we can convert the net present value probability distribution into a distribution of possible profitability indexes. (Recall that the profitability index is simply the present value of future net cash flows over the initial cash outlay.) Suppose we had a proposal costing $10,000 where the expected value of the probability distribution of possible net present values was $1,200. The profitability index for this expected value would be ($1,200 + $10,000)/$10,000 = 1.12. The profitability index for zero net present value is (0 + $10,000)/$10,000 = 1.00. Similarly, we can convert the entire distribution of possible profitability indexes. An example of such distribution is shown in Fig. 15-4.

If management has specified maximum risk profiles for various expected values of profitability indexes, one would simply compare the proposal shown in Fig. 15-4 with the maximum risk profile for an expected value of profitability index of 1.12. If the dispersion of the proposal is less than that for the risk profile, the proposal will be accepted. If not, it will be rejected. The maximum level of dispersion permitted, as depicted by the risk profile, will increase with the expected value of profitability index. For a profitability index of 1.02, the dispersion of the maximum risk profile will be narrower than that for a profitability index of 1.10. Some hypothetical risk profiles are shown in Fig. 15-5. We note that the greater the expected value of profitability index, the greater the dispersion that is tolerable to management. To illustrate their application, compare the probability distribution in Fig. 15-4 with that shown in the third row, first column, of Fig. 15-5. The latter is for a profitability index of 1.12. We see that the dispersion of the probability distribution for the hypothetical project (Fig. 15-4) is somewhat wider than the dispersion tolerable to management for that level of expected profitability, Therefore, the proposal would be rejected according to this method.

Some Qualifications.   The real problem with this approach is that the link with share price is not direct. Management is presented with information about the expected return and risk of a project; and on the basis of this information it reaches a decision. However, there is no direct link to the likely reaction of well-diversified investors. This link depends entirely on the perceptiveness of management in judging investors' trade-off between profitability and risk. Moreover, there is no analysis of the impact of the project on the overall risk of the firm; as we know, this factor becomes important if capital markets are less than perfect. In essence, the project is evaluated in isolation of investors and of existing investment projects.

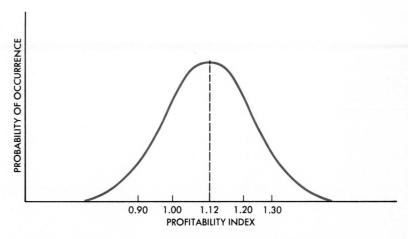

FIGURE 15-4
Probability distribution of profitability indexes, proposal X

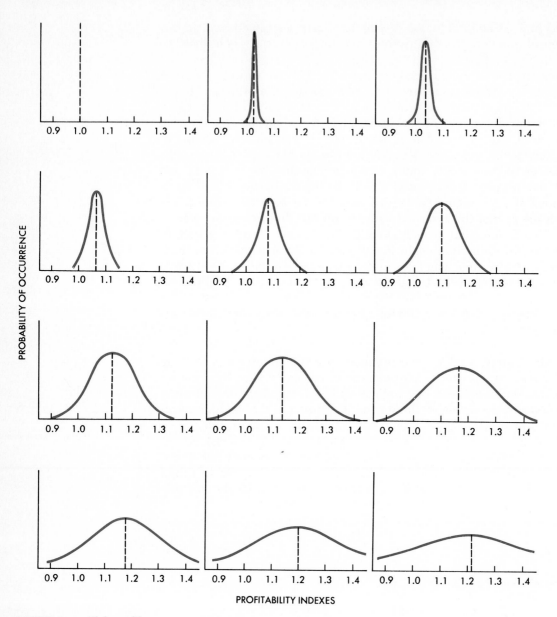

FIGURE 15-5   **Risk profiles**

For these reasons, the approach leaves much to be desired. Still, we must recognize that in practice most investment decisions are made by management in this or some similar way. By providing management with information about the dispersion of possible outcomes, more informed decisions are possible than in the conventional capital budgeting analysis, which considers only the expected values of cash flows.

Combinations of Risky Investments

From Chapter 14 we know that the marginal risk of an individual proposal to the firm as a whole depends on its correlation with existing projects as well as its correlation with proposals under consideration that might be accepted. The appropriate information is the standard deviation and expected value of the probability distribution of possible net present values for all feasible combinations of existing projects and investment proposals under consideration. Assume for now that management is interested only in the marginal impact of an investment proposal on the risk complexion of the firm as a whole.

The selection of the most desirable combination of investments will depend on management's risk preferences with respect to net present value and variance, or standard deviation. Figure 15-6 shows various combinations of risky investments available to the firm. This figure is the same as Fig. 14-7 in Chapter 14. Each dot represents a combination of proposals under consideration and existing investment projects for the firm. We see that certain dots dominate others in the sense that they represent a higher expected value of net present value and the same standard deviation, a lower standard deviation and the same expected value of net present value, or both a higher expected value and a lower standard deviation. The dots that dominate others are those that are farthest to the right. With information of this sort before it, management can eliminate most combinations of risky investments simply because they are dominated by other combinations.

In this case, management would probably consider only three combinations of risky investments—B, L, and P. From these it would choose the one that it felt offered the best combination of expected return and risk. If it were moderately averse to risk, it might choose combination L. While combination P provides a somewhat higher expected value of net present value, it also has a higher standard deviation. Combination B has lower risk but also lower expected value of net present value.

FIGURE 15-6
Opportunity set of combinations of projects

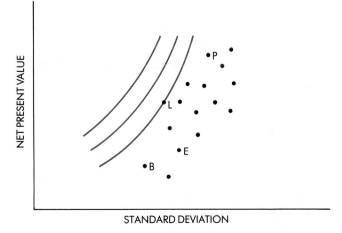

As discussed in Chapter 14, the final selection determines the new investment proposal or proposals that will be accepted. An exception would occur only when the combination selected was composed of existing projects. In this situation, no investment proposals under consideration would be accepted. If the portfolio of existing projects were represented by combination E in the figure, the selection of any of the four outlying combinations would imply the acceptance of one or more new investment proposals. Investment proposals under consideration that were not in the combination finally selected would, of course, be rejected.

Conceptual Implications

On the basis of the information presented, management determines which investment proposals under consideration offer the best marginal contribution of expected value of net present value and standard deviation to the firm as a whole. In determining the standard deviation for a combination, management must consider the correlation between an investment proposal and the set of existing and other new proposed investments. This evaluation suggests that the total risk of the firm is what is important; investment decisions are made in light of their marginal impact on total risk.

This approach implies that from the standpoint of stockholders, management should be concerned with the firm's solvency. As discussed, such solvency depends on the total risk of the firm. Owing to less than perfect correlation with each other, certain projects have diversification properties. As a result, the total risk of the firm will be less than the sum of the parts. Management presumably will endeavor to accept investment proposals in a way that will keep the probability of insolvency within reasonable bounds while maximizing net present value.

As indicated before, the problem with this approach is that it ignores the fact that investors can diversify the portfolios of common stocks they hold. They are not dependent on the firm to diversify away risk. Therefore, diversification by the firm may not be a thing of value in the sense of doing something for investors that they cannot do for themselves. To the extent that investors are concerned only with the unavoidable or systematic risk of a project, the capital-asset pricing model approach illustrated earlier should be used.

It may be reasonable to use both approaches. The CAPM approach might serve as the foundation for judging the valuation implications of an investment project. To the extent that the possibility of insolvency exists and the bankruptcy costs that result are considerable, the project also would be judged in a total firm-risk context. If both approaches give clear accept or reject signals, those signals should be followed. The obvious problem occurs if one approach gives an accept signal while the other gives a reject signal. In this case, management should place more weight on one or the other signal, depending on which approach is more applicable.

If the stock of a large company is publicly held, and if the possibility of insolvency is remote, a strong case can be made for using the signal given by the capital-asset pricing model. If the stock is traded in a market with high transaction and information costs, if the possibility of insolvency is significant, and if the expression of project returns in terms of market-based returns is crude, greater reliance should be placed on the total firm-risk approach. Even here, one should recognize that a portion of the residual risk can be diversified away.

SUMMARY

In theory, the required rate of return for an investment project should be the rate that leaves the market price of the stock unchanged. If an investment project earns more than what financial markets require it to earn for the risk involved, value is created. The sources of such value creation are industry attractiveness and competitive advantage.

If existing investment projects and investment proposals under consideration are homogeneous with respect to risk, it is appropriate to use the overall cost of capital of a company as the acceptance criterion. This can be a weighted average cost of the various instruments with which the company intends to finance. By far the most difficult cost to measure is the cost of equity capital. Using a dividend-capitalization model, this cost is the rate of discount that equates the present value of the stream of expected future dividends with the market price of the stock. Approaching the problem directly, we can estimate the cost of equity capital with the capital-asset pricing model.

Given the measurement of marginal costs of debt, preferred stock, and equity, a weighted average cost of capital can be computed. The weights employed should correspond to the proportions with which the firm intends to finance. Once computed, the weighted average cost is used as a basis for accepting or rejecting investment proposals. The rationale for its use was discussed, as were certain qualifications. When investment projects, both existing and new, are widely variant with respect to risk, use of the company's overall cost of capital as an acceptance criterion is not appropriate.

In such cases, we should determine an acceptance criterion for each investment project or group of projects under consideration. One means for computing a risk-adjusted required rate of return for a proposal is with the CAPM. Here the idea is to identify publicly traded companies whose lines of business and systematic risk closely parallel the group's. These companies then are proxies for developing beta information, which may be adjusted for leverage. (See the appendix.) Once a representative beta is computed, the required return on equity can easily be determined. If debt financing is employed, a weighted average required return for the project is calculated, based on the proportions the firm uses in its financing. In the same manner, a group-specific required return may be determined for a division, a subsidiary, or some other subunit of the firm. Certain problems arising from the differential utilization of nonequity financing among groups of a company were explored.

A practical means for evaluating risky investment is to analyze the expected value and standard deviation of the probability distribution of possible returns for an investment proposal and, on the basis of this information, reach a decision. The greater the dispersion of the distribution, the greater the expected value that presumably would be required by management. The problem with this approach is that the link between the investment decision and share price is not direct.

Finally, we examined the marginal impact of an investment project on the total risk of the firm. This becomes a concern if there is a possibility of insolvency. By analyzing the expected return and risk of various possible combinations of existing projects and investment proposals under consideration, management is able to select the best one, usually on the basis of dominance. The selection itself determines which proposals will be accepted and which will be rejected. With this approach, the diversification properties of a project are recognized in the computation of the standard deviation for a combination. Again, this is important if one is concerned with the impact of investment proposals accepted on the total risk of the firm as opposed to only its systematic risk.

APPENDIX
Adjusting the Beta for Leverage

The systematic risk of a stock is due to both the business and the financial risk of the company. In the calculation of a project's or group's cost of equity capital, the external company used as a proxy for the business risk of the project or group will sometimes have a significantly different proportion of debt than that used by the firm. As a result, it may be desirable to adjust the beta of the proxy company for this difference in relative debt. In what follows, we present a procedure for making such an adjustment under the assumptions of the capital-asset pricing model. In the end, we will qualify the results for the considerations to be taken up in Chapter 17.

With corporate income taxes, interest payments are deductible for tax purposes. Under these circumstances, Hamada, as well as others, has demonstrated that the required rate of return for a stock is[9]

$$R_j = i + \left(\frac{R_m - i}{\sigma_m^2}\right)(r_{ju,m}\sigma_{ju}\sigma_m)\left[1 + \frac{D}{S}(1 - T_c)\right] \tag{15A-1}$$

where i = risk-free rate
  R_m = the expected return on the market portfolio
  σ_m = standard deviation of the probability distribution of possible market returns
  σ_{ju} = standard deviation of the probability distribution of possible returns for security j *in the absence of leverage*
  $r_{ju,m}$ = correlation coefficient between returns for security j *in the absence of leverage* and the market portfolio
  D/S = the debt-to-equity ratio in market value terms
  T_c = corporate tax rate.

[9] Robert S. Hamada, "Portfolio Analysis, Market Equilibrium and Corporation Finance," *Journal of Finance*, 24 (March 1969), 19–30.

The important thing to note is that the covariance between returns, which is the second bracketed term in the equation, is as if the company had an all-equity capital structure.

Equation (15A-1) can be expressed in terms of the more familiar beta:

$$R_j = i + (R_m - i)\beta_{ju}\left[1 + \frac{D}{S}(1 - T_c)\right] \qquad (15A\text{-}2)$$

where β_{ju} is the beta measuring the responsiveness of the excess return for the security *in the absence of leverage* to the excess return for the market portfolio. Thus the overall required rate of return is composed of the risk-free rate, i, plus a premium for business risk, $(R_m - i)\beta_{ju}$, and a premium for financial risk

$$(R_m - i)\beta_{ju}\left[\frac{D}{S}(1 - T_c)\right]$$

The measured beta for the stock, β_j, embodies both risks and it is simply

$$\beta_j = \beta_{ju}\left[1 + \frac{D}{S}(1 - T_c)\right] \qquad (15A\text{-}3)$$

Rearranging, the beta for the stock *in the absence of leverage* is

$$\beta_{ju} = \frac{\beta_j}{\left[1 + \dfrac{D}{S}(1 - T_c)\right]} \qquad (15A\text{-}4)$$

Given these expressions, we were able to derive the beta *in the absence of leverage* for a particular stock. Suppose the measured beta, β_j, for security j were 1.4; the debt-to-equity ratio, D/S, were .70; and the tax rate were 40 percent. Therefore the beta *in the absence of leverage* would be

$$\beta_{ju} = \frac{1.4}{[1 + .7(.6)]} = 0.99$$

If we now wished to determine the beta for a different amount of leverage, we would use Eq. (15A-3). Suppose that we were interested in using security j as a proxy for the systematic risk of our project or group. However, we employ a debt-to-equity ratio of .3 as opposed to the .7 for security j. Therefore, the adjusted beta would be

$$\text{Adjusted } \beta_j = 0.99[1 + .3(.6)] = 1.17$$

This beta contrasts with 0.99 for security j *in the absence of leverage* and with 1.40 for security j with a debt-to-equity ratio .70.

In summary, we are able to derive an adjusted beta for a security under the assumption of a different proportion of debt than what occurs. We first estimate the beta for the stock *in the absence of leverage* and then adjust this figure for the proportion of leverage we wish to employ. The final result is an approximation of the beta that would prevail if the external company were to employ the desired proportion of debt.

Note that the adjustment procedure assumes that all the tenets of the capital asset pricing model hold, except for the presence of corporate taxes. With corporate taxes, value increases in a linear manner with leverage, as shown in the formulations above. Chapter 17 introduces additional imperfections in an overall assessment of the impact of capital structure on valuation. Therefore, the adjustment procedure presented provides an approximate beta when the proportion of debt is varied, but it is only an approximation. For large beta adjustments, the procedure is crude.

QUESTIONS

1. Why is it important to use marginal weights in calculating a weighted average cost of capital?

2. Under what circumstances is it appropriate to use the weighted average cost of capital as an acceptance criterion?

3. Do the funds provided by sources such as accounts payable and accruals have a cost of capital? Explain.

4. What will happen to the cost of debt funds for cost of capital purposes if a company should go into a period of negligible profits and pay no taxes?

5. With a dividend-capitalization model, how do you estimate the cost of equity capital? What is the critical variable in this model?

6. What is the critical assumption inherent in the capital-asset pricing model as it relates to the acceptance criterion for risky investments?

7. Instead of using the expected return on the market portfolio and the risk-free rate in a CAPM approach to estimating the required return on equity, how would one use the firm's debt cost in a CAPM approach?

8. What is the purpose of proxy companies in the application of the capital-asset pricing model to estimating required returns?

9. Distinguish a project-specific from a group-specific required return.

10. In evaluating a project on the basis of its total risk, who determines whether the project is acceptable? How? Is share price likely to be maximized?

11. What is the distinction between evaluating the expected value and standard deviation for an individual investment project and for a group or combination of projects?

12. Should companies in the same industry have approximately the same required rates of return on investment projects? Why or why not?

13. If you use debt funds to finance a project, why is not their cost the required

return for the project? As long as the project earns more than enough to pay interest and service the principal, does it not benefit the firm?

14. If the cost of bankruptcy proceedings (attorney fees, trustee fees, delays, inefficiencies, and so on) were to rise substantially, would this occurrence have an effect on a company's required rate of return and on the way it looks at investment opportunities?

15. Should a company with multiple divisions establish separate required rates of return, or costs of capital, for each division as opposed to using the company's overall cost of capital?

16. For a corporation investing in capital projects, how is value created by using required return calculations?

17. What are the sources of value creation through capital investment decisions?

SELF-CORRECTION PROBLEMS

1. Silicon Wafer Company presently pays a dividend of $1 per share and has a share price of $20.

   a. If this dividend were expected to grow at a 12 percent rate forever, what is the firm's expected, or required, return on equity using a dividend-capitalization model approach?

   b. Instead of the situation in part a, suppose that the dividend were expected to grow at a 20 percent rate for 5 years and at 10 percent annum thereafter.

2. Determine the required return on equity for the following situations, using the capital-asset pricing model.

SITUATION	EXPECTED RETURN MARKET PORTFOLIO	RISK-FREE RATE	BETA
1	15%	10%	1.00
2	18	14	.70
3	15	8	1.20
4	17	11	.80
5	16	10	1.90

What generalizations can you make?

3. Norvella-Hays Company has two divisions: Health Foods and Specialty Metals. Each division employs debt equal to 30 percent and preferred stock equal to 10 percent of its total requirements, with equity capital used for the remainder. The current borrowing rate is 15 percent, and the company's tax rate is 40 percent. Presently, preferred stock can be sold yielding 13 percent.

Norvella-Hays wishes to establish a minimum return standard for each division based on the risk of that division. This standard then would serve as the transfer price of capital to the division. The company has thought about using the capital-asset pricing model in this regard. It has identified two samples of companies, with modal value betas of .90 for Health Foods and 1.30 for Specialty Metals. The risk-free rate is presently 12 percent and the expected return on the market portfolio 17 percent. Using the CAPM approach, what weighted average required returns on investment would you recommend for these two divisions?

4. You are evaluating two separate projects as their effect on the total risk and return of your corporation. The projects are expected to result in the following:

	NET PRESENT VALUE OF COMPANY (IN THOUSANDS)	STANDARD DEVIATION (IN THOUSANDS)
Existing projects only	$6,000	$3,000
Plus project 1	7,500	4,500
Plus project 2	8,200	5,000
Plus projects 1 and 2	9,700	6,100

a. Would you invest in one or both projects?
b. What would you do if a capital-asset pricing model approach to the problem suggested a different decision?

PROBLEMS

1. Zapata Enterprises is financed by two sources of funds: bonds and common stock. The cost of capital for funds provided by bonds is K_i and K_e is the cost of capital for equity funds. The capital structure consists of amount B of bonds and S of stock. Compute the weighted average of cost of capital, K_o.

2. Assume that B (Problem 1) is $3 million and S is $7 million. The bonds have a 14 percent cost, and the stock is expected to pay $500,000 in dividends this year. The growth rate of dividends has been 11 percent and is expected to continue at the same rate. Find the cost of capital, if the corporate tax rate on income is 40 percent.

3. On March 10, International Copy Machines (ICOM), one of the favorites of the stock market, was priced at $300 per share. This price was based on an expected annual growth rate of at least 20 percent for quite some time in the future. In July, economic indicators turned down, and investors revised downward to 15 percent their estimate for future growth of ICOM. What should happen to the price of the stock? Assume the following:

a. A perpetual growth valuation model is a reasonable representation of the way the market values ICOM.

b. The firm does not change its dividend, the risk complexion of its assets, or its degree of financial leverage.

c. The expected dividend at the end of the first year is $3 per share.

4. K-Far Stores has launched an expansion program that should result in the saturation of the Bay Area marketing region of California in 6 years. As a result, the company is predicting a growth in earnings of 12 percent for 3 years and 6 percent for years 4 through 6, after which it expects constant earnings forever. The company expects to increase its dividends per share, now $2, in keeping with this growth pattern. Currently, the market price of the stock is $25 per share. Estimate the company's cost of equity capital.

5. The Manx Company was recently formed to manufacture a new product. It has the following capital structure in market value terms:

13% Debentures of 2005	$ 6,000,000
12% Preferred stock	2,000,000
Common stock (320,000 shares)	8,000,000
	$16,000,000

The company has a marginal tax rate of 40 percent. A study of publicly held companies in this line of business suggests that the required return on equity is about 17 percent. (The capital-asset pricing model approach was used to determine the required rate of return.) Compute the firm's present weighted average cost of capital.

6. The Tumble Down D Ranch in Montana would like a new mechanized barn, which will cost $600,000. The barn is expected to provide annual cash savings of $90,000 indefinitely (for practical purposes of computation, forever). The ranch, which is incorporated and has a public market for its stock, has a weighted average cost of capital of 14.5 percent. For this project, Howard Kelsey, the president, intends to use $200,000 in retained earnings and to finance the balance half with debt and half with a new issue of common stock.

Flotation costs on the debt issue amount to 2 percent of the total debt raised, whereas flotation costs on the new common stock issue come to 15 percent of the issue. What is the net present value of the project after allowance for flotation costs? Should the ranch invest in the new barn?

7. Cohn and Sitwell, Inc., may begin to manufacture special drill bits and other equipment for oil rigs. This is currently regarded as complementary, and the company has certain expertise by virtue of its having a large mechanical engineering staff. Because of the large outlays required to get into the business, management is concerned that Cohn and Sitwell earn a proper return. Since the new venture is believed to be sufficiently different from the company's existing operations, management feels that a required rate of return other than the company's present one should be employed.

The financal manager's staff has identified several companies engaged solely in the manufacture and sale of oil-drilling equipment whose stocks are publicly traded. Over the last 5 years, the average beta for these companies has been 1.28. The staff believes that 18 percent is a reasonable estimate of the average return on stocks in general for the foreseeable future and that the risk-free rate will be around 12 percent. In financing projects, Cohn and Sitwell uses 40 percent debt and 60 percent equity. The after-tax cost of debt is 8 percent.

a. On the basis of this information, determine a required rate of return for the project, using the capital-asset pricing model approach.

b. Is the figure obtained likely to be a realistic estimate of the required rate of return on the project?

8. Acosta Sugar Company has estimated that the overall return for Standard & Poor's 500-stock index will be 15 percent the next 10 years. The company also feels that the interest rate on Treasury securities will average 10 percent over this interval. The company is thinking of expanding into a new product line: almonds. It has no experience in this line but has been able to obtain information on various companies involved in producing and processing nuts. Although no company examined produces only almonds, Acosta's management feels that the beta for such a company would be 1.10, once the almond operation was ongoing. There is some uncertainty about the beta that will actually prevail. Management has attached the following probabilities to possible outcomes:

Probability	.2	.3	.2	.2	.1
Beta	1.00	1.10	1.20	1.30	1.40

a. What is the required rate of return for the project using the mode beta of 1.10?

b. What is the range of required rates of return?

c. What is the expected value of required rate of return?

9. After a careful study of the risk preferences of its management, the Henken Aviation Company has determined certain risk profiles for investment projects. These risk profiles depict the maximum standard deviation of profitability index that is tolerable for a particular expected value of profitability index. (The profitability index is the present value of future cash flows of a project divided by the initial cash outlay.) The risk profiles for various profitability indexes are as follows:

Expected profitability index	1.00	1.05	1.10	1.15	1.20	1.25
Maximum standard deviation	0	.04	.10	.15	.21	.26

The company is considering two new investment proposals, which are expected to have the following characteristics:

PROPOSAL X COST = $2 MILLION		PROPOSAL Y COST = $5 MILLION	
Net Present Value	Probability of Occurrence	Net present Value	Probability of Occurrentce
−$ .5 million	.10	−$ .4 million	.10
0	.20	.1 million	.15
.5 million	.40	.5 million	.50
1.0 million	.20	.9 million	.15
1.5 million	.10	1.4 million	.10

Given the risk profiles of the company, should either or both of the two proposals be accepted?

10. Benzo Tube Company wishes to evaluate three new investment proposals. It is concerned with the impact of the proposals on its total risk. Consequently, it has determined expected values and standard deviations of the probability distributions of possible net present values for the possible combinations of existing projects, E, and investment proposals under consideration:

COMBINATION	EXPECTED VALUE OF NET PRESENT VALUE (IN THOUSANDS)	STANDARD DEVIATION (IN THOUSANDS)
E	$6,500	$5,250
E, 1	6,800	5,000
E, 2	7,600	8,000
E, 3	7,200	6,500
E, 1, 2	7,900	7,500
E, 1, 3	7,500	5,600
E, 2, 3	8,300	8,500
E, 1, 2, 3	8,600	9,000

Which combination do you feel is most desirable? Which proposals should be accepted? Which should be rejected?

Appendix Problem

11. Willie Sutton Bank Vault Company has a debt-to-equity ratio (market value) of .75. Its present cost of debt funds is 15 percent, and it has a marginal tax rate of 40 percent. Willie Sutton Bank Vault is eyeing the automated bank teller business, a field that involves electronics and is consider-

ably different from its own, so the company is looking for a benchmark or proxy company. The Peerless Machine Company, whose stock is publicly traded, produces only automated teller equipment. Peerless has a debt-to-equity ratio of .25, a beta of 1.15, and an effective tax rate of .40.

a.   If Willie Sutton Bank Vault Company wishes to enter the automated bank teller business, what systematic risk (beta) is involved if it intends to employ the same amount of leverage in the new venture as it presently employs?

b.   If the risk-free rate presently is 13 percent and the expected return on the market portfolio is 17 percent, what return should the company require for the project if it uses a capital-asset pricing model approach?

SOLUTIONS TO SELF-CORRECTION PROBLEMS

1.   a. $k_e = \dfrac{D_1}{P_0} + g \qquad D_1 = D_0(1.12) = \$1(1.12) = \$1.12$

$k_e = \dfrac{\$1.12}{\$20} + 12\% = 17.6\%$

b.   Through the trial-and-error approach illustrated in Chapters 4 and 5, one ends up using 18 percent and 19 percent as discount rates:

END OF YEAR	DIVIDEND PER SHARE	PRESENT VALUE AT 18%	PRESENT VALUE AT 19%
1	$1.20	$1.02	$1.01
2	1.44	1.03	1.02
3	1.73	1.05	1.03
4	2.07	1.07	1.03
5	2.49	1.09	1.04
Present value, 1–5 years		$5.26	$5.13

Year 6 dividend = $2.49(1.10) = $2.74
Market prices at the end of year 5 using a perpetual growth dividend valuation model:

$$P_5 = \frac{\$2.74}{.18 - .10} = \$34.25, \qquad P_5 = \frac{\$2.74}{.19 - .10} = \$30.44$$

Present value at time 0 for amounts received at end of year 5:

$$\$34.25 \text{ at } 18\% = \$14.97, \qquad \$30.44 \text{ at } 19\% = \$12.76$$

	18%	19%
Present value of 1–5 years	$ 5.26	$ 5.13
Present value of 6–∞ years	$14.97	$12.76
Present value of all dividends	$20.23	$17.89

Therefore, the discount rate is closer to 18 percent than it is to 19 percent. Interpolating.

$$k_e = 18\% + \frac{\$.23}{\$20.23 - \$17.89} = 18.10\%$$

and this is the estimated return on equity that the market requires.

2.

SITUATION	EQUATION	REQUIRED RETURN
1	10% + (15% − 10%)1.00	15.0%
2	14% + (18% − 14%)0.70	16.8
3	8% + (15% − 8%)1.20	16.4
4	11% + (17% − 11%)0.80	15.8
5	10% + (16% − 10%)1.90	21.4

The greater the risk-free rate, the greater the expected return on the market portfolio, and the greater the beta, the greater will be the required return on equity, all other things being the same. In addition, the greater the market risk premium ($\overline{R}_m - i$), the greater the required return, all other things being the same.

3. Cost of debt = 15%(1 − .4) = 9%
Cost of preferred stock = 13%
Cost of equity for Health Foods division = .12 + (.17 − .12).90 = 16.5%
Cost of equity for Specialty Metals division
    = .12 + (.17 − .12)1.30 = 18.5%
Weighted average required return for Health Foods division
    = .3(9%) + .1(13%) + .6(16.5%) = 13.9%
Weighted average required return for Specialty Metals division
    = .3(9%) + .1(13%) + .6(18.5%) = 15.1%
As mentioned in the text, a conceptual case can be made for adjusting the nonequity costs of financing of the two divisions for differences in systematic risks. However, we have not done so.

4. a. The coefficients of variation (standard deviation/NPV) for the alternatives are

Existing projects	.50
Plus project 1	.60
Plus project 2	.61
Plus projects 1 and 2	.63

The coefficient of variation increases with either or both investments. A reasonably risk-averse decision maker will prefer the existing projects to any combination of new project additions to existing projects. If this is the case, both new projects will be rejected. The actual decision will depend on your risk preferences. Presumably, these preferences will be influenced by the presence of bankruptcy costs.

b. If the CAPM approach gives an opposite decision, the key to deciding would be the importance of market imperfections. As indicated earlier, if a company's stock is traded in imperfect markets, if the possibility of insolvency is substantive, and if bankruptcy costs are significant, more reliance should be placed on a total variability approach because it recognizes residual plus systematic risk. If things point to the opposite direction, more reliance should be placed on the CAPM results.

SELECTED REFERENCES

ANG, JAMES S., and WILBUR G. LEWELLEN, "Risk Adjustment in Capital Investment Project Evaluations," *Financial Management*, 11 (Summer 1982), 5–14.

ARDITTI, FRED D., and HAIM LEVY, "The Weighted Average Cost of Capital as a Cutoff Rate: A Critical Analysis of the Classical Textbook Weighted Averge," *Financial Management*, 6 (Fall 1977), 24–34.

CHAMBERS, DONAL R., ROBERT S. HARRIS, and JOHN J. PRINGLE "Treatment of Financing Mix in Analyzing Investment Opportunities," *Financial Management*, 11 (Summer 1982), 24–41.

CONINE, THOMAS E., JR., and MAURY TAMARKIN, "Division Cost of Capital Estimation: Adjusting for Leverage," *Financial Management*, 14 (Spring 1985), 54–58.

FULLER, RUSSELL J., and HALBERT S. KERR, "Estimating the Divisional Cost of Capital: An Analysis of the Pure-Play Technique," *Journal of Finance*, 36 (December 1981), 997–1009.

GREENFIELD, ROBERT L., MAURY R. RANDALL, and JOHN C. WOODS, "Financial Leverage and Use of the Net Present Value Investment Criterion," *Financial Management*, 12 (Autumn 1983), 40–44.

GUP, BENTON E., and SAMUEL W. NORWOOD III, "Divisional Cost of Capital: A Practical Approach," *Financial Management*, 11 (Spring 1982), 20–24.

HARRINGTON, DIANA R., "Stock Prices, Beta and Strategic Planning," *Harvard Business Review*, 61 (May–June, 1983), 157–64.

HARRIS, ROSBET S., and JOHN J. PRINGLE, "Risk-Adjusted Discount Rates—Extensions from the Average-Risk Case," *Journal of Financial Research*, 8 (Fall 1985), 237–44.

HOWE, KEITH M., "A Note on Flotation Costs and Capital Budgeting," *Financial Management*, 11 (Winter 1982), 30–33.

KEANE, SIMON E., "The Investment Discount Rate—In Defence of the Market Rate of Interest," *Accounting and Business Research*, Summer 1976, 228–36.

LESSARD, DONALD R., and RICHARD S. BOWER, "An Operational Approach to Risk Screening," *Journal of Finance*, 27 (May 1973), 321–38.

LEWELLEN, WILBUR G., and DOUGLAS R. EMERY, "Corporate Debt Management and the Value of the Firm," *Journal of Financial and Quantitative Analysis*, 21 (December 1986), 415–25.

MILES, JAMES A., and JOHN R. EZZELL, "The Weighted Average Cost of Capital, Perfect Capital Markets, and Project Life: A Clarification," *Journal of Financial and Quantitative Analysis*, 15 (September 1980), 719–30.

_____, "Reformulating Tax Shield Valuation: A Note," *Journal of Finance*, 40 (December 1985), 1485–92.

MYERS, STEWART C., "Determinants of Corporate Borrowing," *Journal of Financial Economics*, 5 (November 1977), 147–75.

_____, and RICHARD RUBACK, "Discounting Rules for Risky Assets," working paper, Sloan School, MIT (January 1987).

ROSENBERG, BARR, and ANDREW RUDD, "The Corporate use of Beta," *Issues in Corporate Finance* (Stern, Stewart, Putnam & Macklis, Inc., 1983), pp. 42–52.

SHAPIRO, ALAN C., and SHERIDAN TITMAN, "An Integrated Approach to Corporate Risk Management," *Midland Corporate Finance Journal*, 3 (Summer 1985), 41–56.

VAN HORNE, JAMES C., "An Application of the Capital Asset Pricing Model to Divisional Required Returns," *Financial Management*, 9 (Spring 1980), 14–19.

CHAPTER 16

Leveraging the Firm

Financial leverage involves the use of funds for which the firm pays a fixed cost in the hope of increasing the return to its common stockholders. Since increases in leverage also increase the risk of the earnings stream to common stockholders, we face the familiar trade-off between risk and expected return. Higher expected return leads to higher stock prices, all other things being the same. Greater risk results in lower stock prices, again holding all else constant. With respect to financial leverage, the goal is to strike a happy balance between risk and expected return, maximizing the market price of the firm's stock.

> **Leveraged.** The use of debt having a fixed return to magnify the earnings available to common stockholders. Also known as gearing and in general simply describes borrowing.

In this chapter we are going to explore ways a company may evaluate the impact of leverage on expected return and risk. Our purpose here is to show how we might approach the problem in practice. In the next chapter, we shall explore the conceptual underpinnings to the problem. The additional discussion in that chapter will provide a richer insight into the problem and reinforce the presentation in this chapter. Thus, the two chapters are closely related. Before proceeding further, however, let us take a moment to define financial risk.

FINANCIAL RISK

Broadly speaking, financial risk encompasses both the risk of possible insolvency and the variability in earnings available to common stockholders. As a firm increases the proportion of debt, lease financing, and preferred stock in its capital structure, fixed charges increase. As a result, the probability of cash insolvency increases. To illustrate this notion, suppose that two firms have different degrees of leverage but are identical in every other respect. Each has expected annual cash earnings of $80,000 before interest and taxes. Firm A has no debt; Firm B has $200,000 worth of 15 percent perpetual bonds outstanding. Thus, the total annual financial charges for Firm B are $30,000, whereas Firm A has no financial charges. If cash earnings for both firms happen to be 75 percent lower than expected, namely, $20,000, Firm B will be unable to cover its financial charges with cash earnings. We see, then, that the probability of cash insolvency increases with the financial charges incurred by the firm.

The second aspect of financial risk involves the relative dispersion of income available to common stockholders. Suppose that the expected future annual operating incomes over the next 5 years for Firms A and B were subjective random variables where the expected values of the probability distributions were each $80,000 and the standard deviations, $40,000. As before, assume that Firm A has no debt, while Firm B has $200,000 in 15 percent bonds. If, for simplicity, we neglect federal income taxes, the expected value of earnings available to common stockholders would be $80,000 for Firm A and $50,000 for Firm B. Because the standard deviation about the expected values is the same for both firms, the relative dispersion of expected earnings available to common stockholders is greater for Firm B than for Firm A. For Firm A the coefficient of variation, which is simply the standard deviation divided by the expected value, is

$$\text{Coefficient of variation} = \frac{\$40,000}{\$80,000} = .50$$

while for Firm B it is

$$\text{Coefficient of variation} = \frac{\$40,000}{\$50,000} = .80$$

Graphically, the relationship is shown in Fig. 16-1. We see that the degree of dispersion from the expected value of earnings available to common stockholders is the same for both firms, but the expected value of these earnings is greater for Firm A than for Firm B. As a result, the relative dispersion, as measured by the coefficient of variation, is less for Firm A.

The dispersion in earnings available to common stockholders is to be distinguished from the dispersion of operating income, known as business risk. In our example, both firms had the same degree of business risk, as defined, because the coefficient of variation of expected future operating income was the same.

$$\text{Coefficient of variation} = \frac{\$40,000}{\$80,000} = .50$$

Only in the degree of financial risk do the two firms differ. In summary, we regard financial risk as encompassing the volatility of earnings available to common stockholders as well as the probability of insolvency. Both aspects are related directly to the dispersion of expected operating income, or the business risk, of the firm.

EBIT-EPS RELATIONSHIPS

EPS. Earnings per share.

EBIT. The earnings before interest and taxes of a company.

To analyze the appropriate degree of financial leverage for a firm, we need, among other things, to understand the sensitivity of earnings per share **(EPS)** to earnings before interest and taxes **(EBIT)** for various financing alternatives. EBIT does not depend on financial leverage but rather is a result of the operations and the business risk of the firm. We must know what happens to a firm's earnings per share under various financing options as changes in EBIT occur.

Calculation of Earnings per Share

To illustrate an EBIT-EPS analysis of leverage, suppose Cherokee Tire Company with long-term capitalization of $10 million consisting entirely of common stock wishes to raise another $5 million for expansion through one of three possible financing plans. The company may finance with (1) all common stock, (2) all debt at 12 percent interest, or (3) all preferred stock with an 11 percent dividend. Present annual earnings before interest and taxes are $2 million, the income tax rate is 40 percent, and 200,000 shares of stock are now outstanding. Common stock can be sold at $50 per share under financing option 1, which translates into 100,000 additional shares of stock.

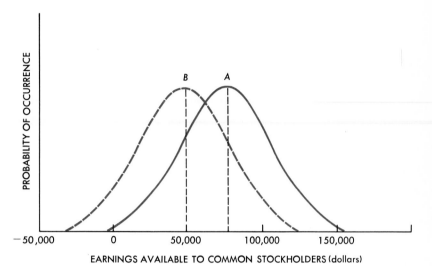

FIGURE 16-1
Probability distribution of earnings available to common stockholders

To determine the EBIT break-even, or indifference, points among the various financing alternatives, we begin by calculating earnings per share for some hypothetical level of EBIT. Suppose we wished to know what earnings per share would be under the three financing plans if EBIT were $2.4 million. The calculations are shown in Table 16-1. We note that interest on debt is deducted before taxes, while preferred stock dividends are deducted after taxes. As a result, earnings available to common stockholders are higher under the debt alternative than they are under the preferred stock alternative, despite the fact that the interest rate on debt is higher than the preferred stock dividend rate.

Break-Even, or Indifference, Analysis

Given the information in Table 16-1, we are able to construct a break-even or indifference, chart similar to what we did for operating leverage. On the horizontal axis we plot earnings before interest and taxes and on the vertical axis, earnings per share. For each financing alternative, we must draw a straight line to reflect EPS for all possible levels of EBIT. To do so, we need two data points for each alternative. The first is the EPS calculated for some hypothetical level of EBIT. For $2.4 million in EBIT, we see in Table 16-1 that earnings per share are $4.80, $5.40, and $4.45 for the common, debt, and preferred stock financing alternatives. We simply plot these earnings per share at the $2.4 million mark in EBIT. Note that it does not matter which hypothetical level of EBIT we choose for calculating EPS. On good graph paper, one level is as good as the next.

The second datum point is simply the EBIT necessary to cover all fixed financial costs for a particular financing plan, and it is plotted on the horizontal axis. For the common stock alternative, there are no fixed costs, so the intercept on the horizontal axis is zero. For the debt alternative, we must have EBIT of $600,000 to cover interest charges; so $600,000 becomes the horizontal axis intercept. For the preferred stock alternative, we must divide total annual divi-

Break-even analysis. Analysis of the effect of financing alternatives on earnings per share. The break-even point is the EBIT level where EPS is the same for two alternatives.

TABLE 16-1
Calculations of earnings per share under three financing alternatives

	COMMON	DEBT	PREFERRED
Earnings before interest and taxes (hypothetical)	$2,400,000	$2,400,000	$2,400,000
Interest	—	600,000	—
Earnings before taxes	$2,400,000	$1,800,000	$2,400,000
Income taxes	960,000	720,000	960,000
Earnings after taxes	$1,440,000	$1,080,000	$1,440,000
Preferred stock dividend	—	—	550,000
Earnings available to common stock holders	$1,440,000	$1,080,000	$ 890,000
Number of shares	300,000	200,000	200,000
Earnings per share	$4.80	$5.40	$4.45

dends by one minus the tax rate in order to obtain the EBIT necessary to cover these dividends. Thus, we need $916,667 million in EBIT to cover $550,000 in preferred stock dividends, assuming a 40 percent tax rate. Again, preferred dividends are deducted after taxes, so it takes more in before-tax earnings to cover them than it does to cover interest. Given the horizontal axis intercepts and earnings per share for some hypothetical level of EBIT, we draw a straight line through the two sets of points. The break-even, or indifference, chart for Cherokee Tire Company is shown in Fig. 16-2.

We see from the figure that the earnings per share indifference point between the debt and common stock financing alternatives is $1.8 million in EBIT. If EBIT is below that point, the common stock alternative will provide higher earnings per share; above that point the debt alternative is best. The indifference point between the preferred stock and the common stock alternative is $2.75 million in EBIT. Above it, the preferred stock alternative is favored with respect to earnings per share; below it, the common stock alternative is best. We note

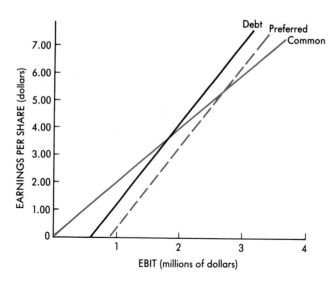

FIGURE 16-2
Indifference chart for three financing alternatives

that there is no indifference point between the debt and preferred stock alternatives. The debt alternative dominates for all levels of EBIT and by a constant amount of earnings per share, namely, $0.95.

Indifference Point Mathematically.   The difference point between two methods of financing can be determined mathematically by

$$\frac{(EBIT^* - C_1)(1 - t)}{S_1} = \frac{(EBIT^* - C_2)(1 - t)}{S_2} \qquad (16\text{-}1)$$

where EBIT* = the EBIT indifference point between the two methods of financing for which we solve

C_1, C_2 = annual interest expenses or preferred stock dividends on a before-tax basis for financing methods 1 and 2 (with preferred stock, the dividend is divided by $1 - t$)

t = corporate tax rate

S_1, S_2 = number of shares of common stock to be outstanding after financing for methods 1 and 2.

Suppose that we wished to determine the indifference point between the common stock and the debt-financing alternative in our example. We would have

$$\frac{(EBIT^* - 0)(.6)}{300,000} = \frac{(EBIT^* - 600,000)(.6)}{200,000} \qquad (16\text{-}2)$$

Rearranging, we obtain

$$.6(EBIT^*)(200,000) = .6(EBIT^*)(300,000)$$

$$-.6(600,000)(300,000)$$

$$60,000 \ EBIT^* = 108,000,000,000$$

$$EBIT^* = \$1,800,000$$

The indifference point in EBIT, where earnings per share for the two methods of financing are the same, is $1.8 million. This amount can be verified graphically in Fig. 16-2. Thus, indifference points for financial leverage can be determined either graphically or mathematically.

Effect on Risk

So far our concern has been only with what happens to the return to common stockholders. We have seen in our example that if EBIT is above $1.8 million, debt financing is the preferred alternative from the standpoint of earnings per share. We know from our earlier discussion, however, that the impact on expected return is only one side of the coin. The other side is the effect of leverage on risk. An EBIT-EPS chart does not permit a precise answer to this question; nevertheless, certain generalizations are possible. For one thing, the financial manager should compare the indifference point between debt and common stock financing with the most likely level of EBIT. The higher the level of EBIT, assuming that it exceeds the indifference point, the stronger the case that can be made for debt financing, all other things the same.

In addition, the financial manager should assess the likelihood of EBITs falling below the indifference point. Suppose that the EBIT in our example is $3 million. Given the business risk of the company and the resulting possible fluctuations in EBIT, the financial manager should assess the probability of EBITs falling below $1.8 million. If the probability is negligible, the use of the debt alternative will be supported. On the other hand, if EBIT presently is only slightly above the indifference point and the probability of EBIT's falling below this point is high, the financial manager may conclude that the debt alternative is too risky.

This notion is illustrated in Fig. 16-3, where two probability distributions of possible EBITs are superimposed on the indifference chart shown in Fig. 16-2. In Fig. 16-3, however, we focus on only the debt and common stock alternatives. For the "safe" distribution, there is virtually no probability that EBIT will fall below the indifference point. Therefore, we might conclude that debt should be used, because the effect on shareholder return is substantial, whereas risk is negligible. For the "risky" distribution, there is a significant probability that EBIT will fall below the indifference point. In this case, the financial manager may conclude that the debt alternative is too risky.

In summary, the greater the level of EBIT above the indifference point and the lower the probability of downside fluctuation, the stronger the case that can

FIGURE 16-3
Indifference chart with EBIT probability distributions

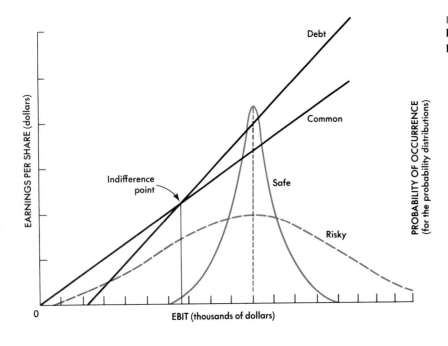

be made for the use of debt financing. EBIT-EPS analysis is but one of several methods for determining the appropriate amount of debt a firm might carry. No one method of analysis is satisfactory by itself. When several methods are undertaken simultaneously, however, generalizations are possible.[1] Let us examine the other methods for analyzing the appropriate degree of financial leverage for a firm.

CASH-FLOW ABILITY TO SERVICE DEBT

When considering the appropriate capital structure, we would analyze also the cash-flow ability of the firm to service fixed charges. The greater the dollar amount of senior securities the firm issues and the shorter their maturity, the greater the fixed charges of the firm. These charges include principal and interest payments on debt, lease payments, and preferred stock dividends. Before assuming additional fixed charges, the firm should analyze its expected future cash flows, for fixed charges must be met with cash. The inability to meet these charges, with the exception of preferred stock dividends, may result in financial insolvency. The greater and more stable the expected future cash flows of the firm, the greater the debt capacity of the company.

Coverage Ratios

Among the ways in which we can gain knowledge about the debt capacity of a firm is through the use of coverage ratios. In the computation of these ratios, one typically uses earnings before interest and taxes as a rough measure of the cash flow available to cover debt-servicing obligations. Perhaps the most widely used coverage ratio is *times interest earned*, which is simply

$$\text{Times interest earned} = \frac{\text{EBIT}}{\text{Interest on debt}} \qquad (16\text{-}3)$$

Suppose that the most recent annual earnings before interest and taxes for a company were $4 million and interest payments on all debt obligations were $1.5 million. Therefore, times interest earned would be 2.67 times. This tells us that EBIT can drop by as much as 62.5 percent and the firm still will be able to cover its interest payments out of earnings.

A coverage ratio of only one indicates that earnings are *just* sufficient to satisfy the interest burden. Although generalizations about what is an appropriate interest coverage ratio are difficult, one usually is concerned when the ratio gets much below 3:1. Circumstances differ however. In a highly stable industry, a relatively low times-interest-earned ratio may be appropriate, whereas it is not appropriate in a highly cyclical industry.

Note that the times-interest-earned ratio tells us nothing about the firm's

---

[1] For an extension of break-even analysis that brings in valuation concepts, see Haim Levy and Robert Brooks, "Financial Break-Even Analysis and the Value of the Firm," *Financial Management*, 15 (Autumn 1986), 22–26.

ability to meet principal payments on its debt. The inability to meet a principal payment constitutes the same legal default as failure to meet an interest payment. Therefore, it is useful to compute the coverage ratio for the full debt-service burden. This ratio is

$$\text{Debt-service coverage} = \frac{\text{EBIT}}{\text{Interest} + \dfrac{\text{Principal payments}}{1 - \text{Tax rate}}} \qquad (16\text{-}4)$$

Here principal payments are adjusted upward for the tax effect. The reason is that EBIT represents earnings before taxes. Because principal payments are not deductible for tax purposes, they must be paid out of after-tax earnings. Therefore, we must adjust principal payments so that they are consistent with EBIT. If principal payments in our previous example were $1 million per annum and the tax rate were 40 percent, the debt-service coverage ratio would be

$$\text{Debt-service coverage} = \frac{\$4 \text{ million}}{\$1.5 \text{ million} + \dfrac{\$1 \text{ million}}{1 - .4}} = 1.26$$

A coverage ratio of 1.26 means that EBIT can fall by only 21 percent before earnings coverage is insufficient to service the debt.[2] Obviously, the closer the ratio is to 1.0, the worse things are, all other things the same. However, even with the coverage ratio of less than one, a company may still meet its obligations if it can renew some of its debt when it comes due.

The financial risk associated with leverage should be analyzed on the basis of the firm's ability to service total fixed charges. While lease financing is not debt per se, its impact on cash flows is exactly the same as the payment of interest and principal on a debt obligation. (See Chapter 20 for an analysis of lease financing.) Annual lease payments, therefore, should be added to the numerator and denominator of Eq. (16-4) in order to reflect properly the total cash-flow burden associated with financing.

As with the times-interest-earned ratio, exact rules of thumb are lacking for what constitutes a good or bad debt-service ratio. It varies according to the business risk of the firm. This is illustrated in Fig. 16-4, which shows the probability distributions of EBIT for two hypothetical companies. The expected value of EBIT is the same for both companies, as is the debt-service burden as described by the denominator in Eq. (16-4). Therefore, the debt-service coverage ratios also are the same, $100/$60 = 1.67. Company A, however, has much more business risk. The probability that EBIT will fall below the debt-service burden is depicted by the shaded areas in the figure. We see that this probability is much greater for Company A than it is for Company B. While a debt-service coverage ratio of 1.67 may be appropriate for Company B, it may not be appropriate for Company A. Simply put, a company with stable cash flows is able to take on relatively more fixed charges. This explains why electric utility companies have low coverage ratios when compared with manufacturing companies.

[2] This percent is determined by $1 - (1/1.26) = .21$.

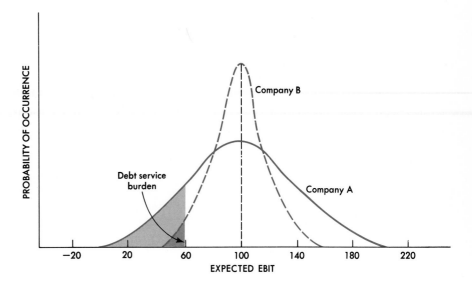

FIGURE 16-4
Possible EBIT in relation to debt-service burden

As discussed in Chapter 6 on financial ratios, two comparisons should be undertaken with a coverage ratio. First, it should be compared with past and expected future ratios of the same company. Called trend analysis, the comparison determines if there has been an improvement or deterioration in coverage over time. The second comparison is with similar companies, perhaps in the same industry. The idea here is to try to isolate business risk as nearly as possible by comparing like companies. Sources of data and types of analysis possible are described in Chapter 6, so we do not dwell on them here.

Ultimately, one wants to make generalizations about the appropriate amount of debt (and leases) for a firm to have in its capital structure. It is clear that over the long run the wherewithal to service debt for the going concern is earnings. Therefore, coverage ratios are an important tool of analysis. However, they are but one tool by which a person is able to reach conclusions with respect to appropriate capital structure for the firm. Coverage ratios are subject to certain limitations and, consequently, cannot be used as a sole means for determining a capital structure. The fact that EBIT falls below the debt-service burden does not spell immediate doom for the company. Often alternative sources of funds, including renewal of the loan, are available, and these sources must be considered.

Probability of Cash Insolvency

The vital question for the firm is not so much whether a coverage ratio will fall below one but what the chances of **insolvency** are. The answer depends on whether all sources of payment—EBIT, cash, a new financing arrangement, or the sale of assets—are collectively deficient. A coverage ratio tells only part of the story. To address the broader question of cash insolvency, we must obtain information on the possible deviation of actual cash flows from those that are expected. As we discussed in Chapter 7, cash budgets can be prepared for a range

Insolvency. The inability to meet contractual financial obligations.

of possible outcomes, with a probability attached to each. This information is extremely valuable to the financial manager in evaluating the ability of the firm to meet fixed obligations. Not only expected earnings are taken into account in determining this ability, but other factors as well: the purchase or sale of assets, the liquidity of the firm, dividends, seasonal patterns, and any other factors impacting on cash flows. Given the probabilities of particular cash-flow sequences, the financial manager is able to determine the amount of fixed charges and debt the company can undertake while still remaining within insolvency limits tolerable to management.

Management may feel that a 5 percent probability of being out of cash is the maximum it can tolerate and that this probability corresponds to a cash budget prepared under pessimistic assumptions. In this case, debt might be undertaken up to the point where the cash balance under the pessimistic cash budget is just sufficient to cover the fixed charges associated with the debt. In other words, debt would be increased to the point at which the additional cash drain would cause the probability of cash insolvency to equal the risk tolerance specified by management. Note that the method of analysis simply provides a means for assessing the effect of increases in debt on the risk of cash insolvency. On the basis of this information, management would arrive at the most appropriate level of debt.

Donaldson has proposed a similar type of analysis.[3] He suggests that the ultimate concern of a company is whether cash balances during some future period will be involuntarily reduced below zero. Therefore, he advocates examining the cash flows of the company under the most adverse circumstances, that is, in his definition, under recession conditions. These conditions may or may not be the most adverse; however, in keeping with the spirit of his proposal, the firm should evaluate its cash flows under adverse circumstances. Donaldson defines the net cash balance during a recession as

$$CB_r = CB_0 + NCF_r \qquad (16\text{-}5)$$

where CB_0 = cash balance at start of recession and NCF_r = net cash flows during recession. Donaldson then calculates a probability distribution of expected net cash flows,[4] and analyzes the cash-flow behavior of a firm during recession. Combining the beginning cash balances, CB_0, with the probability distribution of recession cash flows, NCF_r, he prepares a probability distribution of cash balances during the recession—CB_r.

To ascertain its debt capacity, a firm first would calculate the fixed charges associated with additional increments of debt. For each addition, the firm then would determine the probability of being out of cash. As before, management could set tolerance limits on the probability of being out of cash. Suppose that

---

[3] Gordon Donaldson, *Corporate Debt Capacity* (Boston: Division of Research, Harvard Business School, 1961). See also Donaldson, "Strategy for Financial Emergencies," *Harvard Business Review*, 47 (November–December 1969), 67–79.

[4] The determinants of net cash flows with which he works are sales collections, other cash receipts, payroll expenditures, raw material expenditures, and nondiscretionary cash expenditures. By analyzing each of these determinants, he determines the range and probability of recession net cash flows.

the firm is considering issuing $20 million in additional debt and that the annual fixed charges are $4 million. By subtracting $4 million from the expected cash balances shown for the probability distribution of CB_r, we obtain the probability distribution of CB_r with the addition of $20 million in debt. If the probability of being out of cash with this increment of debt is negligible, Donaldson would contend that the company has unused debt capacity. Therefore, it would be possible to increase the amount of debt until the probability of being out of cash equaled the risk tolerance of management.

Donaldson extends his analysis to calculate the probability of cash inadequacy. Our discussion before was in terms of cash insolvency, which is defined as lack of cash after all nonessential expenditures have been cut. Cash inadequacy is said to occur if the firm is out of cash after making certain desired expenditures such as dividends, R&D expenditures, and capital expenditures. Thus, cash insolvency is the extreme form of cash inadequacy.

The analysis of the cash-flow ability of the firm to service fixed charges is perhaps the best way to analyze financial risk, but there is some question as to whether the external market analyzes a company in this manner. Sophisticated lenders and institutional investors certainly analyze the amount of fixed charges and evaluate financial risk in keeping with the ability of the firm to service these charges, but individual investors may judge financial risk more by the book-value proportions of debt to equity. There may or may not be a reasonable correspondence between the ratio of debt to equity and the amount of fixed charges relative to the firm's cash-flow ability to service these charges. Some firms may have relatively high ratios of debt to equity but substantial cash-flow ability to service debt. Consequently, the analysis of debt-to-equity ratios alone can be deceiving, and an analysis of the magnitude and stability of cash flows relative to fixed charges is extremely important in determining the appropriate capital structure for the firm.

OTHER METHODS OF ANALYSIS

Comparison of Capital Structure Ratios

Another method of analyzing the appropriate capital structures for a company is to evaluate the capital structure of other companies having similar business risk. Companies used in this comparison may be those in the same industry. If the firm is contemplating a capital structure significantly out of line with that of similar companies, it is conspicuous in the marketplace. This is not to say that the firm is wrong. Other companies in the industry may be too conservative in their use of debt. The optimal capital structure for all companies in the industry might call for a higher proportion of debt to equity than the industry average. As a result, the firm may well be able to justify more debt than the industry average. If the firm is noticeably out of line in either direction, it should be prepared to justify its position, because investment analysts and creditors tend to evaluate companies by industry.

There are wide variations in the use of financial leverage among business firms. A good deal of the variation is removed if one goes to industry classifications, because there is a tendency for the firms in an industry to cluster when it comes to debt ratios. For selected industries, the total liabilities-to-net-worth ratios are as follows.

INDUSTRY	DEBT TO NET WORTH
General building contractors	5.3
Dairy products	1.1
Air transportation	2.1
Drugs	.8
Motor vehicles and equipment	1.6
General merchandise stores	1.7
Real estate investment trusts	3.4
Newspapers	.6

Whereas general contractors make extensive use of debt in financing projects, drug companies and newspapers do not employ much leverage. Compare apples with apples as opposed to apples with oranges. Look at other companies in the same industry.

Surveying Investment Analysts and Lenders

The firm may profit also by talking with investment analysts, institutional investors, and investment houses to obtain their views on appropriate amounts of leverage. These analysts examine many companies and are in the business of recommending stocks. They, therefore, have an influence on the market, and their judgments with respect to how the market evaluates leverage may be very worthwhile. Similarly, a firm may wish to interview lenders to see how much debt it can undertake before the cost of borrowing is likely to rise. Finally, the management of a company may develop a "feel" for what has happened to the market price of the stock when they have issued debt in the past.

Security Ratings

Whenever a company sells a debt or preferred stock issue to public investors, as opposed to private lenders such as banks, it must have the issue rated by one or more rating services. The principal rating agencies are Moody's Investors Service and Standard & Poor's. The issuer of a new corporate security contracts with the agency to evaluate and rate the issue as to quality, as well as to update the rating throughout the life of the instrument. For this service, the issuer pays a fee. In addition, the rating agency charges subscribers to its rating publications. While the assignment of a rating for a new issue is current, changes in ratings of existing securities tend to lag the events that prompt the change.

Both agencies use much the same letter grading. The ratings used by Moody's, as well as brief descriptions, are shown in Table 16-2. In their ratings, the agencies attempt to rank issues according to their probability of default. The first four grades are considered investment-quality issues, whereas other rated securities are considered speculative. The highest grade securities, whose risk of default is felt to be negligible, are rated triple A. For each rating category a modifier of 1, 2, or 3 is applied. For example, Aa-1 means that a security is in the higher end of the Aa rating category. Baa-3 indicates that a security is in the lower end of the Baa category. The ratings by the agencies are widely respected and are recognized by various government regulatory agencies as measures of default risk. In fact, many investors accept them without further investigation of the risk of default.

TABLE 16-2
Security ratings by Moody's Investors Service

GRADE	DESCRIPTION
Aaa	Best quality
Aa	High quality
A	Upper-medium grade
Baa	Medium grade
Ba	Low-medium grade; possesses specualive elements
B	lowest-medium grade; generally lacks characteristics of desirable investment
Caa	Poor standing; may be in default
Ca	Speculative in a high degree; often in default
C	Lowest grade; very poor prospects

The rating agencies look at a number of things before assigning a grade: trends in ratios of liquidity, debt, profitability, and coverage; the firm's business risk, both historically and expected; present and likely future capital requirements; specific features associated with the instrument being issued; the relative proportion of debt; and, perhaps most important, the cash-flow ability to service principal and interest payments. If a public security offering is contemplated, the financial manager must be mindful of ratings when determining how much leverage is appropriate. If taking on additional debt lowers your firm's security rating from Baa to B, a noninvestment grade for many institutional investors, you will want to factor this into account before making a decision.[5] It may well be that the advantages of debt outweigh the lower security rating. However, a

---

[5] For a further discussion of security ratings and default risk, see James C. Van Horne, *Financial Market Rates and Flows*, 2nd ed. (Englewood Cliffs, N.J.: Prentice-Hall, 1984), chap. 8.

significant lowering of a security rating usually is a manifestation of fundamental problems, which may raise the implicit as well as the explicit cost of leverage. Therefore, you will want to consider the likely effect of a change in capital structure on your company's security rating.

COMBINATION OF METHODS

We have discovered a number of methods of analysis that can be brought to bear on the question: What is an appropriate degree of leverage for our company? These include EBIT-EPS analysis, cash-flow ability to service debt, the leverage ratio of our firm relative to others, regression analysis and simulation, survey of investment analysts and lenders, and an evaluation of the effect of a decision on our security rating. In addition to these factors, you will want to know the changing interest cost for various levels of debt. The maturity structure of the debt is important as well, but we take this up later in the book. We focus here only on the broad issue of the degree of leverage to employ. All of the analyses should be guided by the conceptual framework presented in the next chapter.

The implicit cost of leverage, that is, the effect on a stock's value in the marketplace, is not easy to determine. Nevertheless, by undertaking a variety of analyses, the financial manager should be able to determine, within some range, the appropriate capital structure. By necessity, the final decision has to be somewhat subjective, but it can be based on the best information available. To put the matter in the proper conceptual perspective, we turn to the next chapter.

SUMMARY

Financial leverage involves the use of funds for which the firm agrees to pay a fixed charge. The greater the financial leverage of a firm, the greater the fluctuation in earnings available to common stockholders, all other things the same. Therefore, the advantage of higher expected returns to common stockholders must be balanced against the risks to them.

By using an indifference chart, we can study the relationship between earnings before interest and taxes and earnings per share under alternative methods of financing. The degree of sensitivity of EPS to EBIT depends on the explicit cost of the method of financing, the number of shares of common stock to be issued, and the nearness to the indifference point. It is important in this analysis to evaluate the indifference point in relation to the level of EBIT as well as in relation to likely fluctuations in EBIT.

In addition, the cash-flow ability of the firm to service debt should be evaluated. The firm's debt capacity can be assessed by analyzing coverage ratios and the probability of cash insolvency under various levels of debt. In this manner, the financial manager is better able to estimate the debt capacity of the firm. Of all the methods of analysis, assessing the cash-flow ability to service debt is perhaps the most important.

Other methods of analysis include a comparison with debt ratios of like companies, such as those within the same industry, and discussions with investment analysts, investment bankers, and lenders. Security ratings on public issues of debt and preferred stock necessarily are of concern to the financial manager and are a part of any decision. In deciding on an appropriate capital structure, all these factors should be considered. In addition, certain concepts involving valuation should guide the decision. These concepts are discussed in the next chapter.

QUESTIONS

1. Define the concept of *financial leverage*.
2. Discuss the similarities and differences of financial and operating leverage (discussed in Chapter 14).
3. Can the concept of financial leverage be analyzed quantitatively? Explain.
4. The EBIT-EPS chart suggests that the higher the debt ratio, the higher the earnings per share for any level of EBIT above the indifference point. Why do firms sometimes choose financing alternatives that do not maximize EPS?
5. Why is the percentage of debt for an electric utility higher than that for the typical manufacturing company?
6. Is the debt-to-equity ratio a good proxy for financial risk as represented by the cash-flow ability of a company to service debt? Why or why not?
7. How can a company determine in practice if it has too much debt? Too little debt?
8. How can coverage ratios be used to determine an appropriate amount of debt to employ? Are there any shortcomings to the use of these ratios?
9. In financial leverage, why not simply increase leverage as long as the firm is able to earn more on the employment of the funds than they cost? Would not earnings per share increase?
10. Describe how a company could determine its debt capacity by increasing its debt hypothetically until the probability of running out of cash reached some degree of tolerance.
11. How might a company's bond rating influence a capital structure decision?

SELF-CORRECTION PROBLEMS

1. Dorsey Porridge Company presently has $3 million in debt outstanding bearing an interest rate of 12 percent. It wishes to finance a $4 million expansion program and is considering three alternatives: additional debt at 14

percent interest, preferred stock with a 12 percent dividend, and the sale of common stock at $16 per share. The company presently has 800,000 shares of common stock outstanding and is in a 40 percent tax bracket.

a. If earnings before interest and taxes are presently $1.5 million, what would be earnings per share for the three alternatives, assuming no immediate increase in profitability?

b. Develop a break-even, or indifference, chart for these alternatives. What are the approximate indifference points? To check one of these points, what is the indifference point mathematically between debt and common stock?

c. Which alternative do you prefer? How much would EBIT need to increase before the next alternative would be best?

2. Torstein Torque and Gear Company has $7.4 million in long-term debt having the following schedule:

	AMOUNT (IN THOUSANDS)
15% serial bonds, payable $100,000 in principal annually	$2,400
13% first mortgage bonds, payable $150,000 in principal annually	3,000
18% subordinated debentures, interest only until maturity in 10 years	2,000
	$7,400

Torstein's common stock has a book value of $8.3 million and a market value of $6 million. The corporate tax rate, federal and state, is 50 percent. Torstein is in a cyclical business: its expected EBIT is $2 million, with a standard deviation of $1.5 million. The average debt-to-equity ratio of other companies in the industry is .47.

a. Determine the times interest earned and the debt-service coverage of the company.

b. What are the probabilities that these two ratios will go below 1:1?

c. Does Torstein have too much debt?

3. Aberez Company and Vorlas Vactor, Inc., have the following financial characteristics:

	ABEREZ		VORLAS VACTOR	
	Company	Industry Norm	Company	Industry Norm
Debt to equity	1.10	1.43	.78	.47
Bond rating	A-1	A-2	Baa-3	Baa-1
Times interest earned	4.7	4.4	5.3	5.1
Cash and marketable securities to total assets	.08	.07	.10	.13

On the basis of these data, which company has the greater degree of financial risk?

PROBLEMS

1. The Lemaster Company is a new firm that wishes to determine an appropriate capital structure. It can issue 16 percent debt or 15 percent preferred stock. The total capitalization of the company will be $5 million, and common can be sold at $20 per share. The company is expected to have a 50 percent tax rate. The possible capital structures are

PLAN	DEBT	PREFERRED	EQUITY
1	0%	0%	100%
2	30	0	70
3	50	0	50
4	50	20	30

a. Construct an EBIT-EPS chart for the four plans.
b. Determine the relevant indifference points.
c. Using Eq. (16-1), verify the indifference points on your graph for the dominant plans.
d. Which plan is best?

2. Hi Grade Regulator Company currently has 100,000 shares of common stock outstanding with a market price of $60 per share. It also has $2 million in 6 percent bonds. The company is considering a $3 million expansion program that it can finance with (a) all common stock at $60 a share, (b) straight bonds at 8 percent interest, (c) preferred stock at 7 percent, and (d) half common stock at $60 per share and half 8 percent bonds.

a. For a hypothetical EBIT level of $1 million after the expansion program, calculate the earnings per share for each of the alternative methods of financing. Assume a corporate tax rate of 50 percent.
b. Construct an EBIT-EPS chart. What are the indifference points between alternatives? What is your interpretation of them?

3. Hi Grade Regulator Company (see Problem 2) expects the EBIT level after the expansion program to be $1 million, with a two-thirds probability that it will be between $600,000 and $1,400,000.

a. Which financing alternative do you prefer? Why?
b. Suppose that the expected EBIT level were $1.5 million and that there were a two-thirds probability that it would be between $1.3 million and $1.7 million. Which financing alternative would you prefer? Why?

4. Fazio Pump Corporation presently has 1.1 million shares outstanding and $8 million in debt bearing an interest rate of 10 percent on average. It is considering a $5 million expansion program financed either with (a) com-

mon stock at $20 per share being realized, (b) debt at an interest rate of 11 percent, or (c) preferred stock with a 10 percent dividend rate. Earnings before interest and taxes (EBIT) after the new funds are raised are expected to be $6 million, and the company's tax rate is 35 percent.

a. Determine likely earnings per share after financing for each of the three alternatives.

b. What would happen if EBIT were $3 million? $4 million? $8 million?

c. What would happen under the original conditions if the tax rate were 46 percent? if the interest rate on new debt were 8 percent and the preferred stock dividend rate were 7 percent? if the common could be sold for $40 per share?

5. Cornwell Real Estate Speculators, Inc., and the Northern California Electric Utility Company have the following EBIT and debt-servicing burden:

	CORNWELL	NORTHERN CALIFORNIA
Expected EBIT	$5,000,000	$100,000,000
Annual interest	1,600,000	45,000,000
Annual principal payments on debt	2,000,000	35,000,000

The tax rate for Cornwell is 40 percent; for Northern California Electric Utility, 36 percent. Compute the times-interest-earned ratio and the debt-service coverage ratio for the two companies. With which company would you feel more comfortable if you were a lender? Why?

6. Gamma Tube Company plans to undertake a $7.5 million capital improvement program and is considering how much debt to use. It feels that it could obtain debt financing at the following interest rates (assume that this debt is perpetual):

Amounts (in millions)	First $3	Next $2	Next $1.5	Next $1
Interest cost	10%	11%	12%	13%

The company has made projections of its net cash flows (exclusive of new financing) during a period of adversity such as a recession. In a recession, it expects a net cash flow of $3 million with a standard deviation of $2 million (assume a normal distribution). Its beginning cash balance is $1 million. If the company is willing to tolerate only a 5 percent probability of running out of cash during a recession, what is the maximum proportion of the $7.5 million capital improvement program that can be financed with debt? (Use the probability concepts discussed in Chapter 14 and the table in Appendix B to that chapter.)

7. The debt ratios of four companies are as follows.

COMPANY	TOTAL DEBT/ TOTAL ASSETS	LONG-TERM DEBT/ TOTAL CAPITALIZATION
A	.56	.43
B	.64	.66
C	.47	.08
D	.42	.26

The companies are part of the following industries: supermarket, chemical, apparel making, and airline (not in order). Match the company with the industry.

SOLUTIONS TO SELF-CORRECTION PROBLEMS

(000 omitted)

	DEBT	PREFERRED STOCK	COMMON STOCK
EBIT	$1,500	$1,500	$1,500
Interest on existing debt	360	360	360
Interest on new debt	560	—	—
Profit before taxes	$ 580	$1,140	$1,140
Taxes	232	456	456
Profit after taxes	$ 348	$ 684	$ 684
Preferred stock dividend	—	480	—
Earnings available to common stockholders	$ 348	$ 214	$ 684
Number of shares	800	800	1,050
Earnings per share	$ .435	$ .268	$ .651

b.

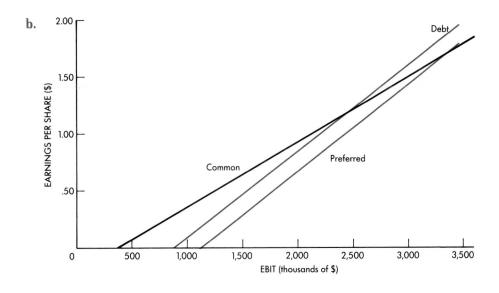

427

Approximate indifference points:

Debt and common: $2.7 million in EBIT

Preferred and common: $3.6 million in EBIT

Debt dominates preferred by the same margin throughout. There is no indifference point.

Mathematically, the indifference point between debt and common (000 omitted) is

$$\frac{(\text{EBIT}^* - \$920)(1 - .4)}{800} = \frac{(\text{EBIT}^* - \$360)(1 - .4)}{1,050}$$

$$.6(\text{EBIT}^*)(1,050) - .6(\$920)(1,050) = .6(\text{EBIT}^*)(800) - .6(\$360)(800)$$

$$630(\text{EBIT}^*) - 480(\text{EBIT}^*) = \$579,600 - \$172,800$$

$$150(\text{EBIT}^*) = \$406,800$$

$$\text{EBIT}^* = \$2,712$$

Note that for the debt alternative, the total before-tax interest is $920, and this is the intercept on the horizontal axis. For the preferred stock alternative, we divide $480 by $(1 - .4)$ to get $800. When this is added to $360 in interest on existing debt, the intercept becomes $1,160.

c. For the present EBIT level, common is clearly preferable. EBIT would need to increase by $2,712,000 − $1,500,000 = $1,212,000 before an indifference point with debt is reached. One would want to be comfortably above this indifference point before a strong case for debt should be made. The lower the probability that actual EBIT will fall below the indifference point, the stronger the case that can be made for debt, all other things the same.

2. a. Total annual interest (in thousands)

15% of $2.4 million =	$ 360
13% of $3.0 million =	390
18% of $2.0 million =	360
	$1,110

Total annual principal payments = $100 + $150 = $250

EBIT necessary to service = $250/(1 − .5) = $500

Times interest earned = $2,000/$1,110 = 1.80

Debt-service coverage = $2,000/$1,610 = 1.24

b. Deviation from mean before ratio is 1 to 1:

Times interest earned: $2,000 − $1,110 = $890

Debt-service coverage: $2,000 − $1,610 = $390

Standardizing the deviation and using Table 14B-1 in Chapter 14:

	TIMES INTEREST EARNED	DEBT-SERVICE COVERAGE
Standardized deviation ratio	$890/$1,500	$390/$1,500
Standardized deviation	.593	.260
Probability of occurrence (Table 14B-1)	.28	.40

The probabilities that the two ratios will be less than 1:1 are approximately 28 percent and 40 percent. These probabilities assume that the distribution of possible EBITs is normal.

c. There is a substantial probability, 40 percent, that the company will fail to cover its interest and principal payments. Its debt ratio of $7.4 million/$8.3 million = .89 is much higher than the industry norm of .47. Its ratio of book value of debt to market value of stock is even higher. Although the information is limited, based on what we have, it would appear that Torstein has too much debt. However, other factors, such as liquidity, may mitigate against this conclusion.

3. Aberez has a lower debt ratio than its industry norm; Vorlas has a higher ratio relative to its industry. Both companies exceed modestly their industry norms with respect to times interest earned. The lower debt ratio and higher times interest earned for Vorlas's industry suggests that its industry might have more business risk than the industry of which Aberez is a part. The liquidity ratio of Aberez is higher than the industry norm while that for Vorlas is lower than the industry norm. Although all three financial ratios for Vorlas are better than are those for Aberez, they are lower relative to the industry norm. Finally, the bond rating of Aberez is much better than is that of Vorlas, being in the upper part of the A grade and slightly higher than the industry norm. The bond rating of Vorlas is the very lowest of that for investment-grade bonds. It is also lower than the typical company's bond rating in the industry. If the industry norms are reasonable representations of underlying business and financial risk, we would say that Vorlas had the greater degree of risk.

SELECTED REFERENCES

DONALDSON, GORDON, *Corporate Debt Capacity*. Boston: Division of Research, Harvard Business School, 1961.

———, "Strategy for Financial Emergencies," *Harvard Business Review*, 47 (November–December 1969), 67–79.

FERRI, MICHAEL G., and WESLEY H. JONES, "Determinants of Financial Structure: A New Methodological Approach," *Journal of Finance*, 34 (June 1979), 631–44.

HONG, HAI, and ALFRED RAPPAPORT, "Debt Capacity, Optimal Capital Structure, and Capital Budgeting," *Financial Management*, 7 (Autumn 1978), 7–11.

LEVY, HAIM, and ROBERT BROOKS, "Financial Break-Even Analysis and the Value of the Firm," *Financial Management*, 15 (Autumn 1986), 22–26.

MYERS, STEWART C., "Capital Structure Puzzle," *Journal of Finance*, 39 (July 1984), 575–92.

PIPER, THOMAS R., and WOLF A. WEINHOLD, "How Much Debt is Right for Your Company," *Harvard Business Review*, 60 (July–August 1982), 106–14.

SCOTT, DAVID R., JR., and JOHN D. MARTIN, "Industry Influence on Financial Structure," *Financial Management*, 4 (Spring 1975), 67–73.

CHAPTER 17

Conceptual Aspects of Capital Structure

Capital structure. The proportion or mix of securities used to finance the firm.

We have just observed a company approaching the question of how much debt it should have in its **capital structure.** The incremental expected return and risk to common stockholders are very much a part of the answer. Now we explore the valuation underpinnings to the question of capital structure. As we shall see, much controversy surrounds the issue. Despite the unsettled nature of the matter, we hope that this presentation will provide the conceptual backdrop necessary to guide the financial manager in capital structure decisions.

Throughout our discussion, we assume that the investment and dividend decisions of the firm are held constant. We wish to determine the effect of a change in financing mix on share price. The focus is different from before in that we are concerned with how security prices are determined in the overall financial markets. That is, how do suppliers of capital value a company in relation to other companies when it changes its capital structure? We shall see that financial market imperfections play a major role. For simplicity, we consider only debt versus equity financing, though the principles taken up apply to preferred stock financing as well.

INTRODUCING THE THEORY

The key question with which we are concerned is whether a firm can affect its total valuation (debt plus equity) and its cost of capital by changing its financing mix. Changes in the financing mix are assumed to occur by issuing debt and repurchasing stock or by issuing stock and retiring debt. In what follows, our attention is directed to what happens to the total valuation of the firm and to its overall required return when the ratio of debt to equity, or degree of leverage, is varied.

For ease of illustration, let us assume that we are concerned with a company whose operating earnings are not expected to grow and that pays out all of its earnings to stockholders in the form of dividends. Moreover, suppose that we live in a world where, happily, there are no income taxes. Later this assumption will be relaxed to consider the issue in the real, and perhaps cruel, world of taxes. For now, the issue can be best understood if we assume no taxes and later treat taxes as a market imperfection.

In the subsequent discussion we are concerned with the three different rates of return. The first is

$$k_i = \frac{F}{B} = \frac{\text{Annual interest charges}}{\text{Market value of debt outstanding}} \qquad (17\text{-}1)$$

In this equation, k_i is the yield on the company's debt, assuming this debt to be perpetual. The second rate of return with which we are concerned is

$$k_e = \frac{E}{S} = \frac{\text{Earnings available to common stockholders}}{\text{Market value of stock outstanding}} \qquad (17\text{-}2)$$

With our assumptions of a firm whose earnings are not expected to grow and that has a 100 percent dividend-payout ratio, the earnings/price ratio represents the market rate of discount that equates the present value of the stream of expected future dividends with the current market price of the stock.[1] This is not to say that it should be used as a general rule to depict the required return on equity. (See Chapter 15.) We use it only because of its simplicity in illustrating the theory of capital structure. The final rate we consider is

$$k_o = \frac{O}{V} = \frac{\text{Net operating earnings}}{\text{Total market value of the firm}} \tag{17-3}$$

where $V = B + S$. Here, k_o is an overall **capitalization rate** for the firm. It is defined as the weighted average cost of capital and may also be expressed as

Capitalization rate. The discount rate used to determine the value of a stream of expected future cash flows.

$$k_o = k_i\left(\frac{B}{B + S}\right) + k_e\left(\frac{S}{B + S}\right) \tag{17-4}$$

We want to know what happens to k_i, k_e, and k_o when the degree of leverage, as denoted by the ratio B/S, increases.

Net Operating Income Approach

One approach to the valuation of the earnings of a company is known as the net operating income approach. To illustrate it, assume that a firm has $1,000 in debt at 10 percent interest, that the expected value of annual net operating earnings is $1,000, and that the overall capitalization rate, k_o, is 15 percent. Given this information, we may calculate the value of the firm as

O	Net operating income	$1,000
k_o	Overall capitalization rate	.15
V	Total value of firm	$6,667
B	Market value of debt	1,000
S	Market value of stock	$5,667

The earnings available to common stockholders, E, is simply net operating income minus interest payments or $1,000 − $100 = $900. The implied required return on equity is

$$k_e = \frac{E}{S} = \frac{\$900}{\$5,667} = 15.88\%$$

With this approach, net operating income is capitalized at an overall capitalization rate to obtain the total market value of the firm. The market value of the debt then is deducted from the total market value to obtain the market value of

---

[1] In Chapter 5 we saw that the price of a security that is expected to pay a fixed payment of C forever is $P = C/k$, where k is the yield required on a perpetual investment. Rearranging, we have $k = C/P$, which is the same as Eq. (17-2).

the stock. Note that with this approach the overall capitalization rate, k_o, as well as the cost of debt funds, k_i, stay the same regardless of the degree of leverage. The required return on equity, however, increases linearly with leverage.

To illustrate, suppose that the firm increases the amount of debt from $1,000 to $3,000 and uses the proceeds of the debt issue to repurchase stock. The valuation of the firm then is

O	Net operating income	$1,000
k_o	Overall capitalization rate	.15
V	Total value of firm	$6,667
B	Market value of debt	3,000
S	Market value of stock	$3,667

The implied required return on equity is

$$k_e = \frac{E}{S} = \frac{\$700}{\$3,667} = 19.09\%$$

We see that the required equity return, k_e, rises with the degree of leverage. This approach implies that the total valuation of the firm is unaffected by its capital structure. Figure 17-1 shows the approach graphically. Not only is the total value of the firm unaffected but so too is share price. To illustrate, assume in our example that the firm with $1,000 in debt has 100 shares of common stock outstanding. Thus, the market price per share is $56.67 ($5,667/100). The firm issues $2,000 in additional debt and, at the same time, repurchases $2,000 of stock at $56.67 per share, or 35.29 shares in total if we permit fractional shares. It then

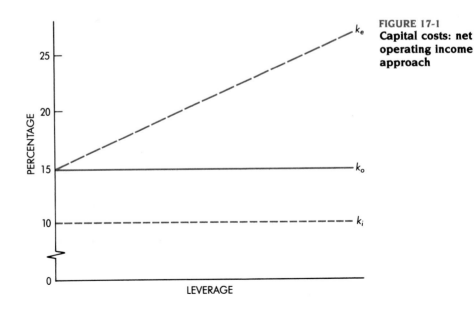

FIGURE 17-1
Capital costs: net operating income approach

has $100 - 35.29$ shares = 64.71 shares outstanding. We saw in the example that the total market value of the firm's stock after the change in capital structure is $3,667. Therefore, the market price per share is $3,667/64.71 = $56.67, the same as before the increase in leverage and recapitalization.

The critical assumption with this approach is that k_o is constant regardless of the degree of leverage. The market capitalizes the value of the firm as a whole; as a result, the breakdown between debt and equity is unimportant. An increase in the use of supposedly "cheaper" debt funds is offset exactly by the increase in the required equity return, k_e. Thus, the weighted average of k_e and k_i remains unchanged for all degrees of leverage. As the firm increases its degree of leverage, it becomes increasingly more risky, and investors penalize the stock by raising the required equity return directly in keeping with the increase in the debt-to-equity ratio. As long as k_i remains constant, k_e is a constant linear function of the debt-to equity ratio. Because the cost of capital of the firm, k_o, cannot be altered through leverage, the net operating income approach implies that there is no one optimal capital structure.

So far, our discussion of the net operating income approach has been purely definitional; it lacks behavioral significance. Modigliani and Miller offered behavioral support for the independence of the total valuation and the cost of capital of the firm from its capital structure.[2] Before taking up the implications of their position, however, we examine the traditional approach to valuation.

Traditional Approach

The traditional approach to valuation and leverage assumes that there is an optimal capital structure and that the firm can increase the total value of the firm through the judicious use of leverage. The approach suggests that the firm initially can lower its cost of capital and raise its total value through leverage. Although investors raise the required rate of return on equity, the increase in k_e does not offset entirely the benefit of using "cheaper" debt funds. As more leverage occurs, investors increasingly penalize the firm's required equity return until eventually this effect more than offsets the use of "cheaper" debt funds.

In one variation of the traditional approach, shown in Fig 17-2, k_e is assumed to rise at an increasing rate with leverage, whereas k_i is assumed to rise only after significant leverage has occurred. At first, the weighted average cost of capital declines with leverage because the rise in k_e does not offset entirely the use of cheaper debt funds. As a result, the weighted average cost of capital, k_o, declines with moderate use of leverage. After a point, however, the increase in k_e more than offsets the use of cheaper debt funds in the capital structure, and k_o begins to rise. The rise in k_o is supported further, once k_i begins to rise. The optimal capital structure is the point at which k_o bottoms out. In the figure, this optimal capital structure is point X. Thus the traditional position implies that the cost of capital is not independent of the capital structure of the firm and that there is an optimal capital structure.

[2] Franco Modigliani and Merton H. Miller, "The Cost of Capital, Corporation Finance and the Theory of Investment," *American Economic Review*, 48 (June 1958), 261–97.

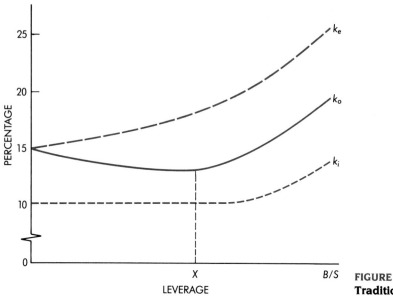

FIGURE 17-2
Traditional approach

TOTAL-VALUE PRINCIPLE

Modigliani and Miller (MM), in their original position, advocate that the relationship between leverage and the cost of capital is explained by the net operating income approach. They make a formidable attack on the traditional position by offering behavioral justification for having the firm's overall capitalization rate, k_o, remain constant throughout all degrees of leverage.

MM argue that the total risk for all security holders of a firm is not altered by changes in its capital structure. Therefore, the total value of the firm must be the same, regardless of its financing mix. Simply put, the Modigliani-Miller position is based on the idea that no matter how you divide up the capital structure of a firm among debt, equity, and other claims, there is a conservation of investment value.[3] That is, because the total investment value of a corporation depends on its underlying profitability and risk, it is invariant with respect to relative changes in the firm's financial capitalization. Thus, the total pie does not change as it is divided into debt, equity, and other securities. The sum of the parts must equal the whole; so regardless of financing mix, the total value of the firm stays the same, according to MM.

The support for this position rests on the idea that investors are able to substitute personal for corporate leverage, thereby replicating any capital structure the firm might undertake. Because the firm is unable to do something for its stockholders (leverage) that they cannot do for themselves, capital structure changes are not a thing of value in the perfect capital market world that MM assume. Therefore, two firms alike in every respect except for capital structure

---

[3] This idea was first espoused by John Burr Williams, *The Theory of Investment Value* (Amsterdam: North-Holland, 1938), pp. 72–73.

must have the same total value. If not, **arbitrage** will be possible, and its occurrence will cause the two firms to sell in the market at the same total value. In other words, arbitrage precludes perfect substitutes from selling at different prices in the same market.

Arbitrage. The sale of an overvalued asset in one market and the purchase of an undervalued like asset in another market to give a riskless profit.

Arbitrage Support Illustrated

Consider two firms identical in every respect except that Company A is not levered, while Company B has $30,000 of 12 percent bonds outstanding. According to the traditional position, Company B may have a higher total value and lower average cost of capital than Company A. The valuation of the two firms is assumed to be the following:

		COMPANY A	COMPANY B
O	Net operating income	$10,000	$10,000
F	Interest on debt		3,600
E	Earnings available to common stockholders	$10,000	$ 6,400
k_e	Required equity return (divide by)	.15	.16
S	Market value of stock	$66,667	$40,000
B	Market value of debt		30,000
V	Total value of firm	$66,667	$70,000
k_o	Implied overall capitalization rate	15%	14.3%
B/S	Debt-to-equity ratio	0	75.0%

MM maintain that this situation cannot continue, for arbitrage will drive the total values of the two firms together. Company B cannot command a higher total value simply because it has a financing mix different from Company A's. MM argue that by investing in Company A, investors in Company B are able to obtain the same dollar return with no increase in financial risk. Moreover, they are able to do so with a smaller investment outlay.[4] Because investors would be better off with the investment requiring the lesser outlay, they would sell their shares in Company B and buy shares in Company A. These arbitrage transactions would continue until Company B's shares declined in price and Company A's shares increased in price enough to make the total value of the two firms identical.

If you are a rational investor who owns 1 percent of the stock of Company B, the levered firm, worth $400 (market value), you should

1. Sell the stock in Company B for $400.
2. Borrow $300 at 12 percent interest. This personal debt is equal to 1 percent of the debt of Company B, your previous proportional ownership of the company.
3. Buy 1 percent of the shares of Company A, the unlevered firm, for $666.67.

Prior to this series of transactions, your expected return on investment in Company B's stock was 16 percent on a $400 investment, or $64. Your expected

[4] This arbitrage proof appears in Franco Modigliani and Merton H. Miller, "Reply to Heins and Sprenkle," *American Economic Review*, 59 (September 1969), 592–95.

return on investment in Company A is 15 percent on a $666.67 investment, or $100. From this return, you must deduct the interest charges on your personal borrowings, so your net dollar return is

Return on investment in Company A	$100
Less: Interest ($300 × .12)	36
Net return	$ 64

Your net dollar return, $64, is the same as it was for your investment in Company B; however, your cash outlay of $366.67 ($666.67 less personal borrowings of $300) is less than the $400 investment in Company B, the levered firm. Because of the lower investment, you would prefer to invest in Company A under the conditions described. In essence, you "lever" the stock of the unlevered firm by taking on personal debt.

The action of a number of investors undertaking similar arbitrage transactions will tend to drive up the price of Company A shares and lower its k_e, and drive down the price of Company B and increase its k_e. This arbitrage process will continue until there is no further opportunity for reducing one's investment outlay and achieving the same dollar return. At this equilibrium, the total value of the two firms must be the same. As a result, their average costs of capital, k_o, also must be the same.

The important thing is the presence of rational investors in the market who are willing to substitute personal, or "homemade," leverage for corporate leverage. The analysis can be extended further to cross risk classes and include general equilibrium in the capital markets. Here, however, we must take account of differences in business-risk premiums. On the basis of the arbitrage process illustrated, MM conclude that a firm cannot change its total value or its weighted average cost of capital by leverage. Consequently, the financing decision does not matter from the standpoint of our objective of maximizing market price per share. One capital structure is as suitable as the next.

PRESENCE OF MARKET IMPERFECTIONS AND INCENTIVE ISSUES

With perfect capital markets, the arbitrage argument ensures the validity of MM's thesis that the cost of capital and total valuation of a firm are independent of its capital structure. To dispute the MM position, we need to look for reasons why the arbitrage process may not work perfectly. The following are the major arguments against the MM arbitrage process.

Bankruptcy Costs

If there is a possibility of bankruptcy, and if administrative and other costs associated with bankruptcy are significant, the levered firm may be less attractive to investors than the unlevered one. With perfect capital markets, zero bankruptcy costs are assumed. If the firm goes bankrupt, assets presumably can be sold at their economic values with no liquidating or legal costs involved. Proceeds from the sale are distributed according to the priority of claims on assets described in Chapter 27. If capital markets are less than perfect, however, there may be administrative costs, and assets may have to be liquidated at less than their economic values. These costs and the "shortfall" in liquidating value from economic value represent a drain in the system from the standpoint of debt and equity holders.

In the event of bankruptcy, security holders as a whole receive less than they would in the absence of bankruptcy costs. To the extent that the levered firm has a greater possibility of bankruptcy than the unlevered one, it would be a less attractive investment, all other things being the same. The possibility of bankruptcy is not a linear function of the debt-equity ratio but increases at an increasing rate beyond some threshold. As a result, the expected cost of bankruptcy increases in this manner and would be expected to have a corresponding negative effect upon the value of the firm.

Put another way, investors are likely to penalize the price of the stock as leverage increases. The nature of the penalty is illustrated in Fig. 17-3 for the case of a no-tax world. Here the required rate of return for investors, k_e, is broken down into its component parts. There is the risk-free rate, i, plus a premium for business risk. This premium is depicted on the vertical axis by the difference between the required rate of return for an all-equity capital structure and the risk-free rate. As debt is added, the required rate of return rises, and this increment represents a financial-risk premium. In the absence of bankruptcy costs, the required return would rise in a linear manner according to Modigliani-Miller, and this relationship is shown. However, with bankruptcy costs and an increasing probability of bankruptcy with leverage, the required rate of return would be expected to rise at an increasing rate beyond some point. At first there

FIGURE 17-3
Required rate of return for equity capital when bankruptcy costs exist

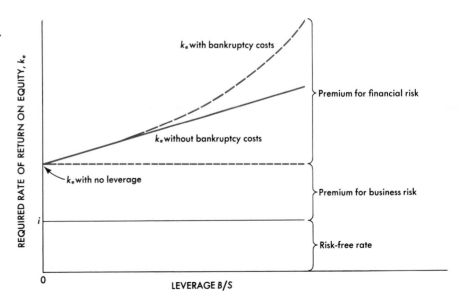

might be a negligible probability of bankruptcy, so there would be little or no penalty. As leverage increases, so does the penalty; for extreme leverage, the penalty becomes very substantial indeed.

Agency Costs

Agency costs. The cost of monitoring management so that it and the firm behave in ways consistent with contractual agreements with stockholders and lenders. Example: auditing fees.

Closely related to bankruptcy costs with respect to impact are **agency costs.** We may think of management as agents of the owners of the company, the stockholders. These stockholders, hoping that the agents will act in their best interests, delegate decision-making authority to them. For management to make optimal decisions in the stockholders' behalf, it is important that they not only have the right incentives (salary, bonuses, stock options, and perquisites) but that they be monitored. Monitoring can be done by such things as bonding the agent, auditing financial statements, appraising assets as to value, and explicitly restricting management decisions. Creditors monitor the behavior of management and stockholders by imposing protective covenants in the loan agreement between the borrower and lender. (See Chapter 20.) The monitoring activities described necessarily involve costs.

Michael C. Jensen and William H. Meckling have expounded a sophisticated theory of agency costs.[5] Among other things, they show that regardless of who makes the monitoring expenditures, the cost is ultimately borne by stockholders. For example, debt holders, anticipating monitoring expenditures, charge higher interest. The greater the probable monitoring costs, the higher the interest rate and the lower the value of the firm to its shareholders, all other things staying the same. The presence of monitoring costs acts as a disincentive to the issuance of debt, particularly beyond a prudent amount. It is likely that the amount of monitoring required by debtholders increases with the amount of debt outstanding. When there is little or no debt, lenders may engage in only limited monitoring, whereas with a great deal of debt, they may insist on extensive monitoring. Monitoring costs, like bankruptcy costs, would tend to rise at an increasing rate with leverage, as illustrated in Fig. 17-3.

Debt and the Incentive to Manage Efficiently

Working in the other direction is the notion that high debt levels create incentives for management to be more efficient.[6] By taking on the cash-flow obligation to service debt, it is claimed that management's "feet are held close to the fire." As a result there is said to be an incentive not to squander funds in wasteful activities, whether it be an investment, a perquisite, a company plane, or whatever. The idea is that levered companies may be leaner because management cuts the fat. Contrarily, the company with little debt and significant free cash flow, after

---

[5] Michael C. Jensen and William H. Meckling, "Theory of the Firm: Managerial Behavior, Agency Costs and Ownership Structure," *Journal of Financial Economics,* 3 (October 1976), 305–60.

[6] A number of people have made this argument, but it is articulated perhaps best in Michael C. Jensen, "The Takeover Controversy: Analysis and Evidence," *Midland Corporate Finance Journal,* 4 (Summer 1986), 12–21.

investing in all worthwhile projects, may have a tendency to squander funds. In the absence of other incentives, "running scared" to make debt payments may have a salutary effect on efficiency.

Differences in Corporate and Personal Leverage

The perceived risks of personal leverage and corporate leverage may differ. Despite the implication in the MM analysis that personal and corporate leverage are perfect substitutes, in the case of corporate borrowings the individual has only limited liability. If the levered company goes bankrupt, the investors' losses are limited to their investments in the stock. They are not liable for the debts of the company. If they borrow personally and default, lenders can claim assets in addition to the stock. Therefore, their total risk exposure is greater with personal leverage and investment in the unlevered company than it is with a straight investment in the levered company.

In addition to greater risk, there are other reasons why investors may have a greater aversion to personal leverage than they do to corporate leverage. If investors borrow personally and pledge their stock as collateral, they are subject to possible margin calls. Many investors view this possibility with considerable alarm. Moreover, personal leverage involves a certain amount of inconvenience for investors, which they do not experience with corporate leverage. For these reasons, personal leverage may not be a perfect substitute for corporate leverage in the minds of many investors. Owing to market imperfections, the risk-adjusted cost of borrowing may be higher for the individual than for the corporation. If so, the levered company could have a somewhat greater total value than the unlevered firm for this reason alone.

Institutional Restrictions

Restrictions on investment behavior may retard the arbitrage process. Many institutional investors, such as pension funds and life insurance companies, are not allowed to engage in the "homemade" leverage that was described. Regulatory bodies often restrict stock and bond investments to a list of companies meeting certain quality standards such as only a "safe" amount of leverage. If a company breaches that amount, it may be removed from the acceptable list, thereby precluding certain institutions from investing in it. This reduction in investor demand can have an adverse effect on the market value of the company's financial instruments. Moreover, if there are enough restrictions on lenders, a firm may find that credit is unavailable to it beyond a certain degree of leverage.

Transaction Costs

Transaction costs tend to restrict the arbitrage process. Arbitrage will take place only up to the limits imposed by transaction costs, after which it is no longer profitable. As a result, the levered firm could have a slightly higher or slightly lower total value. The direction of the net effect of this imperfection is not predictable.

With the exception of the incentive to manage efficiently and transactions costs, the factors listed above limit the amount of debt that a firm will want to undertake. In particular, extreme leverage will be burdened by a number of costs and restrictions. If market imperfections systematically affect the arbitrage process, then capital structure decisions may matter. To develop a complete picture, we must include the important role of taxes, to which we now turn.

THE EFFECT OF TAXES

When we allow for taxes, most agree that the use of leverage can have a favorable impact on a company's total valuation if used judiciously. We must consider two taxes—corporate and personal—and because their effects are very different, we take them up separately. In the end, we will draw together their separate effects along with those of the market imperfections previously considered. For now, we assume that there are no market imperfections other than the presence of corporate taxes.

Corporate Taxes

The advantage of debt in a world of corporate taxes is that interest payments are deductible as an expense. They elude taxation at the corporate level, whereas dividends or retained earnings associated with stock are not deductible by the corporation for tax purposes. Consequently, the total amount of payments available for both debt holders and stockholders is greater if debt is employed.

To illustrate, suppose that the earnings before interest and taxes are $2,000 for companies X and Y, and they are alike in every respect except in leverage. Company Y has $5,000 in debt at 12 percent interest, whereas Company X has no debt. If the tax rate (federal and state) is 40 percent for each company, we have

	COMPANY X	COMPANY Y
Earnings before interest and taxes	$2,000	$2,000
Interest—income to debt holders	0	600
Profit before taxes	2,000	1,400
Taxes	800	560
Income available to stockholders	$1,200	$ 840
Income to debt holders plus income to stockholders	$1,200	$1,440

Thus, total income both to debt holders and stockholders is larger for levered Company Y than it is for unlevered Company X. The reason is that debt holders receive interest payments without the deduction of taxes at the corporate level, whereas income to stockholders is after corporate taxes have been paid. In essence, the government pays a subsidy to the levered company for the use of debt. Total income to all investors increases by the interest payment times the tax rate. In our example, this amounts to $600 \times .40 = \$240$. This figure represents a tax shield that the government provides the levered company. If the debt employed by a company is permanent, the present value of the tax shield using the perpetuity formula is

$$\text{Present value of tax shield} = \frac{t_c rB}{r} = t_c B \qquad (17\text{-}5)$$

where t_c is the corporate tax rate, r is the interest rate on the debt, and B is the market value of the debt. For Company Y in our example,

$$\text{Present value of tax shield} = .40(\$5,000) = \$2,000$$

What we are saying is that the tax shield is a thing of value and that the overall value of the company will be $2,000 more if debt is employed than if the company has no debt. This increased valuation occurs because the stream of income to all investors is $240 per year greater. The present value of $240 per year discounted at 12 percent is $240/.12 = \$2,000$. Implied is that the risk associated with the tax shield is that of the stream of interest payments, so the appropriate discount rate is the interest rate on the debt. Thus, the value of the firm is

$$\text{Value of firm} = \begin{array}{c}\text{Value if}\\\text{unlevered}\end{array} + \begin{array}{c}\text{Value of}\\\text{tax shield}\end{array} \qquad (17\text{-}6)$$

For our example, suppose that the required equity return for Company X, which has no debt, is 16 percent. Therefore, the value of the firm if it were unlevered would be $1,200/.16 = \$7,500$. The value of the tax shield is $2,000, so the total value of Company Y, the levered firm, is $9,500. We see in Eqs. (17-5) and (17-6) that the greater the amount of debt, the greater the tax shield and the greater value of the firm, all other things staying the same. By the same token, the greater the leverage, the lower the cost of capital of the firm. Thus, the original MM proposition as subsequently adjusted for corporate taxes suggests that an optimal strategy is to take on a maximum amount of leverage.[7] This implies a capital structure consisting almost entirely of debt. Since this is not consistent with the behavior of corporations, we must seek alternative explanations.

Tax Shield Uncertainty

The tax savings associated with the use of debt usually are not certain, as implied in the treatment above. If reported income should be low or turn negative, the tax shield on debt is reduced or even eliminated. Moreover, if the firm

---

[7] Franco Modigliani and Merton H. Miller, "Corporate Income Taxes and the Cost of Capital: A Correction," *American Economic Review*, 64 (June 1963), 433–42.

should go bankrupt and liquidate, the future tax savings associated with debt would stop altogether. Not only is there uncertainty as to the tax shield associated with debt, but those associated with other tax shelters as well. These tax shelters compete with debt and compound the overall uncertainty. Finally, there is uncertainty that the Congress will change the corporate tax rate.

All of these things make the tax shield associated with debt financing less than certain. As leverage increases, the uncertainty associated with the debt tax shield becomes more important. As a result, this factor may reduce the value of the corporate tax shield shown in Eq. (17-6). With extreme leverage, the diminution in value of the corporate tax shield may be rather significant.

Corporate Plus Personal Taxes

Apart from tax shield uncertainty, the presence of taxes on personal income may reduce or possibly eliminate the corporate tax advantage associated with debt financing. With the combination of corporate taxes and personal taxes on both debt and stock income, the present value of the corporate tax shield shown in Eq. (17-5) may change. The equation becomes[8]

$$\text{Present value of tax shield} = \left[1 - \frac{(1 - t_c)(1 - t_{ps})}{1 - t_{pd}} \right] B \qquad (17\text{-}7)$$

where t_{ps} is the personal income tax rate applicable to common stock income to the investor, t_{pd} is the personal tax rate applicable to income from the company's debt, and B is the market value of the firm's debt. We see that as long as t_{pd} is greater than t_{ps}, the tax advantage of debt is less than $t_c B$, which we determined to be the advantage in a world of corporate but not personal taxes.

If the income from holding a common stock consists only of dividends and if dividends and interest both are taxed as ordinary income, t_{ps} would equal t_{pd}. As a result, the tax advantage in Eq. (17-7) would reduce to $t_c B$, which is the same as appears in Eq. (17-5) for the valuation of a levered firm with corporate income taxes but no personal income taxes. Suppose, however, that part of the income from holding a stock consists of capital gains. Such gains often are taxed at a lower rate than ordinary income. Sometimes the differential is explicit in that the tax rate is less. Even when capital gains are taxed at the same rate as ordinary income, however, there is an advantage to the capital gain. For one thing it is postponed until the security is sold. For those who give securities as gifts to charitable causes, the tax may be largely avoided as it is if a person dies. Finally, some states tax capital gains at a more favorable rate.

For these reasons, the effective tax on capital gains in a present value sense is less than that on interest and dividend incomes, even when the federal tax

---

[8] Merton H. Miller, "Debt and Taxes," *Journal of Finance*, 32 (May 1977), 266–68. See also Donald E. Farrar and Lee L. Selwyn, "Taxes, Corporate Financial Policies and Returns to Investors," *National Tax Journal*, 20 (December 1967), 444–54; and M. J. Brennan, "Taxes, Market Valuation and Corporate Financial Policy," *National Tax Journal*, 23 (December 1970), 417–27.

rates are the same. Suppose for now we assume that overall stock income (dividends and capital gains) is taxed at a somewhat lower personal tax rate than debt income (interest). That is, t_{ps} is less than t_{pd} in Eq. (17-7). As a result, the tax advantage associated with leverage would be less than $t_c B$.

In other words, investors overall must hold both a company's common stock and its debt instruments. If the tax on debt income is greater than that on common stock income, increases in a company's debt ratio result in an increase in the personal income taxes that must be paid. Therefore the existence of personal income taxes, together with differential tax rates on ordinary income and capital gains, will reduce the corporate income tax advantage associated with leverage.[9]

Suppose that the marginal corporate tax rate is 34 percent, the marginal personal tax rate on debt income is 28 percent, and the market value of DSS Corporation's perpetual debt is $1 million. Now suppose the effective marginal personal tax rate on stock income is 24 percent (owing to postponement and other present-value considerations). As a result, the present value of the tax shield is

$$\text{Present value of tax shield} = \left[1 - \frac{(1 - .34)(1 - .24)}{(1 - .28)} \right] \$1 \text{ million}$$

$$= \$303{,}333$$

If the effective personal tax rate on stock income is .20 instead of .24, we have

$$\text{Present value of tax shield} = \left[1 - \frac{(1 - .34)(1 - .20)}{(1 - .28)} \right] \$1 \text{ million}$$

$$= \$266{,}667$$

Thus, the corporate tax advantage associated with debt is less if the effective personal tax rate on debt income exceeds that on stock income. Moreover, the greater the personal tax on debt income relative to stock income, the lower the corporate tax shield.

The magnitude of net tax shield is an empirical question. Perhaps the only evidence that bears directly on the issue comes from the study of changes in value when companies significantly recapitalize their capital structures. These changes occur when a company exchanges one type of security for another. Unfortunately, there have been few such studies and the evidence from them is

---

[9] Miller, "Debt and Taxes," 261–75, argues that the tax advantage of corporate debt is eliminated in market equilibrium. If this were the case, the value of the firm and its cost of capital would be independent of its capital structure even with taxes. Essentially his argument is based on corporations adjusting the supply of corporate debt to take advantage of clienteles of investors with different tax brackets. In market equilibrium, Miller claims that $(1 - t_c)(1 - t_{ps}) = (1 - t_{pd})$, so that the term in brackets in Eq. (17-7) is zero. This provocative claim has been challenged by a number of authors who argue that the tax on stock income is positive, that empirical relationships between market instruments are inconsistent with the claim, and that Miller's position is deficient theoretically. Space does not permit a review of these articles, but the reader should appreciate the controversy generated by Miller's position.

fragmentary.[10] Those available, and before the 1986 Tax Act, show that the net tax shield is less than the corporate tax shield, being in the neighborhood of .25. That is, if there is a $1 increment in corporate debt, the net tax advantage is 25 cents. Again, such estimates must be taken as very crude.

The tax advantage associated with leverage is reduced but not eliminated when we allow for different personal tax rates. As a result, an optimal leverage strategy would still call for the corporation to have a large proportion of debt. This is despite the fact that tax shield uncertainty may lessen the net tax effect with extreme leverage. As corporations overall are not highly levered, we must search for other factors affecting the valuation of the corporation when it alters the proportion of debt in its capital structure.

TAXES AND MARKET IMPERFECTIONS COMBINED

This statement brings us back to the influence of the various market imperfections considered earlier. Only if in some way they restrict the use of debt financing can the observed capital structure behavior of corporations be explained.

Bankruptcy Costs, Agency Costs, and Taxes

If one allows for bankruptcy costs, and if the probability of bankruptcy increases at an increasing rate with the degree of leverage, extreme leverage is likely to be penalized by lenders and investors. (As discussed earlier, bankruptcy costs represent a drain on the system to security holders.) In a world of both taxes and bankruptcy costs, there would likely be an optimal capital structure even if all of the other behavioral tenets of the MM position held. The cost of capital of a firm would decline as leverage was first employed because of the net tax advantage of debt (corporate less tax shield uncertainty and personal). Gradually, however, the prospect of bankruptcy would become increasingly important, causing the cost of capital to decrease at a decreasing rate as leverage increased. As leverage became extreme, the bankruptcy effect might more than offset the tax effect, causing the cost of capital of the firm to rise.

The presence of agency, or monitoring, costs accentuates this rise. Again, with increases in leverage beyond some threshold, agency costs increase at an increasing rate. The combined influence of bankruptcy and agency costs serves to limit the range over which the net tax shield has a positive effect on share price. Therefore, the value of the firm is

---

[10] Ronald W. Masulis, "The Effects of Capital Structure Change on Security Prices: A Study of Exchange Offers," *Journal of Financial Economics,* 8 (June 1980), 139–78; J. J. McConnell and R. Schlarbaum, "Evidence on the Impact of Exchange Offers on Security Prices: The Case of Income Bonds," *Journal of Business,* 54 (January 1981), 65–85; and Ronald W. Masulis, "The Impact of Capital Structure Change on Firm Value: Some Estimates," *Journal of Finance,* 38 (March 1983), 107–26. For an indirect study of the effect, see David Flath and Charles R. Knoeber, "Taxes, Failure Costs, and Optimal Industry Capital Structure," *Journal of Finance,* 35 (March 1980), 99–117.

$$\begin{array}{c} \text{Value of} \\ \text{firm} \end{array} = \begin{array}{c} \text{Value if} \\ \text{unlevered} \end{array} + \begin{array}{c} \text{Value of} \\ \text{tax shield} \end{array} - \begin{array}{c} \text{Present value} \\ \text{of bankruptcy and} \\ \text{agency costs} \end{array} \qquad (17\text{-}8)$$

As leverage is increased, the second term on the right increases so that the value of the firm also increases. With more and more leverage, tax shield uncertainty gradually lessens the increment in value that occurs. Despite this occurrence, if we look only at the net tax effect, a high proportion of debt would be optimal.

This effect is illustrated in Fig. 17-4 by the solid line. We see that tax shield uncertainty causes the cost-of-capital line to curve up slightly as more and more leverage occurs. Still the net tax effect of corporate and personal taxes has a favorable effect on the cost of capital and on share value. When the firm has little debt, bankruptcy and agency costs are seen to be insignificant. As more debt is employed, these costs eventually become significant, as reflected by the dashed line. Increasingly, they offset the net tax shield. At the point where marginal bankruptcy–agency costs equal the marginal tax shield benefit, cost of capital is minimized and share price maximized. By definition, this represents the optimal capital structure, as denoted by the mark along the horizontal axis. To visualize the effect of leverage on share price, substitute share value for cost of capital on the vertical axis and turn the figure upside down.

Impact of Additional Imperfections

If other imperfections and behavioral factors dilute the MM position further, the point at which the cost of capital line turns up would be earlier than that depicted in the figure. Consider now the cost of borrowing. After some point of leverage, the interest rate charged by creditors usually rises. The greater the leverage, of course, the higher the interest rate charged. As a result, the cost of debt would turn up after a point. This phenomenon was illustrated earlier in

FIGURE 17-4
Cost of capital with taxes, bankruptcy, and agency costs

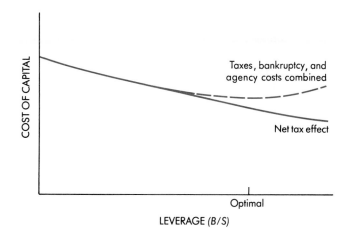

Fig. 17-2. In turn, this factor exerts upward influence on the overall cost of capital line. Institutional restrictions on lenders also might cause the cost of capital line to turn up sooner than it does in Fig. 17-4. If, because of extreme leverage, a company no longer is able to sell debt securities to institutions, it must seek out unrestricted investors, and they will demand even higher interest rates. If institutional imperfections are serious enough, debt funds may not be available beyond a point of leverage, in which case there would be a discontinuity in Fig. 17-4.

Other capital-market imperfections work to hamper the arbitrage process so that "homemade" leverage is not a perfect substitute for corporate leverage. Recall that these imperfections include transaction costs, higher costs of borrowing for individuals than for corporations, and imperfections in information. The greater the importance one attaches to these factors, the less effective the arbitrage process becomes, and the stronger the case that can be made for an optimal capital structure.

There are a number of reasons for believing that an optimal capital structure exists in theory. Depending on one's view as to the strengths of the various capital-market and behavioral imperfections, the expected optimal capital structure may occur earlier or later along the scale of possible leverage.

FINANCIAL SIGNALING

Closely related to monitoring costs and agency relationships is the notion of signaling. Because strict managerial contracts are difficult to enforce, managers may use capital structure changes to convey information about the profitability and risk of the firm. The implication is that insiders know something about the firm that outsiders do not. As a manager, your pay and benefits may depend on the firm's market value. That gives you an incentive to let investors know when the firm is undervalued. You could make an announcement, "Our firm is undervalued," but you are more sophisticated than that, and you know that investors would probably be as convinced as if you were boasting about your child. So you alter your firm's capital structure by issuing more debt. Increased leverage implies a higher probability of bankruptcy, and since you would be penalized contractually if bankruptcy occurred, investors conclude that you have good reason to believe that things really are better than the stock price reflects. Your actions speak louder than words. Increased leverage is a positive sign.

This is not to say that capital structure changes cause changes in valuation. Rather, it is the signal conveyed by the change which is significant. This signal pertains to the underlying profitability and risk of the firm, as that is what is important when it comes to valuation. Financial signaling is a topic of considerable interest in the writing on finance, but the various models are difficult to evaluate. Unless the managerial contract is very precise, the manager is tempted to give false signals. Moreover, there simply may be more effective and less costly ways to convey information than by altering the firm's capital structure. We shall have more to say about this phenomenon when we consider dividend policy in Chapter 18.

SUMMARY

Much controversy has developed over whether the capital structure of a firm, as determined by its financing decision, affects its cost of capital. Traditionalists argue that the firm can lower its cost of capital and increase market value per share by the judicious use of leverage. Modigliani and Miller, on the other hand, argue that in the absence of taxes and other market imperfections, the total value of the firm and its cost of capital are independent of capital structure. This position, which is the same as the net operating income approach, is based on the notion that there is a conservation of investment value. No matter how you divide the pie between debt and equity claims, the total pie or investment value of the firm stays the same. Therefore, leverage is said to be irrelevant. We saw that behavioral support for the MM position was based on the arbitrage process.

In a world of corporate income taxes, there is a substantial advantage to the use of debt, and we can measure the present value of the tax shield. This advantage is lessened with tax shield uncertainty, particularly if leverage is high. When we allow for personal income taxes and a higher personal tax rate on debt income than on stock income, we find the tax advantage of debt to be further reduced. Bankruptcy and agency costs work to the disadvantage of leverage, particularly extreme leverage. A combination of net tax effect with bankruptcy and agency costs will result in an optimal capital structure. Other market imperfections—such as differences between corporate and "homemade" leverage and institutional restrictions on lender and stock investor behavior—impede the equilibrium of security prices according to expected return and risk. As a result, leverage may affect the value of the firm because of these reasons.

Financial signaling occurs when capital structure changes convey information to security holders. It assumes an asymmetry in information between management and stockholders. Management behavior results in debt issues being regarded as "good news" by investors, whereas stock issues are regarded as "bad news." Empirical evidence seems to be consistent with this notion.

For the financial manager to make proper capital structure decisions, these decisions must be rooted in theory. Every effort should be made to judge an alternative with respect to the imperfections described. In practice, such analysis can be accomplished with the tools taken up in the preceding chapter.

QUESTIONS

1. Contrast the net operating income approach with the Modigliani-Miller approach to the theory of the capital structure.
2. Why is the net income approach not likely to be a fair representation of the valuation process when it comes to capital structure decisions?
3. Why might you suspect that the optimal capital structure would differ significantly from one industry to another? Would the same factors produce differing optimal capital structures within all industry groupings?

4. What factors determine the interest rate a firm must pay for debt funds? Is it reasonable to expect this rate to rise with an increasing debt-to-equity ratio? Why?

5. What is the total-value principle as it applies to capital structure?

6. Define the notion of arbitrage. How does it affect the issue of capital structure?

7. If there were not imperfections in financial markets, what capital structure should the firm seek? Why are market imperfections important in finance? Which imperfections are most important?

8. Why do the effects of corporate taxes and personal taxes tend to be in opposite directions when it comes to the capital structure issue?

9. What are bankruptcy costs? agency costs? How do they affect the valuation of the firm when it comes to leverage?

10. Why do institutional lenders no longer lend money to a corporation when it takes on too much debt?

11. Suppose that a company were to earn negligible profits and pay no taxes. How would this affect its optimal capital structure?

12. If the corporate tax rate were cut in half, what would be the effect on debt financing?

13. Dividends presently are taxed twice. The corporation must pay taxes on its earnings and then stockholders must pay taxes on the dividends distributed. What would be the effect on corporate financing if this double taxation were eliminated by permitting companies to deduct dividend payments as an expense?

14. Why might capital structure changes speak louder than words if management believed its stock were undervalued? What is the likely direction of the financial signal?

SELF-CORRECTION PROBLEMS

1. Abacus Calculation Company and Zoom Calculators, Inc., are identical except for capital structures. Abacus has 50 percent debt and 50 percent equity, while Zoom has 20 percent debt and 80 percent equity. (All percentages are in market-value terms.) The borrowing rate for both companies is 13 percent in a no-tax world, and capital markets are assumed to be perfect.

   a. If you own 2 percent of the stock of Abacus, what is your dollar return if the company has net operating income of $360,000 and the overall capitalization rate of the company, k_o, is 18 percent? What is the implied required return on equity?

   b. Zoom has the same net operating income as Abacus. What is the implied required equity return of Zoom? Why does it differ from that of Abacus?

2. Massey-Moss Corporation has earnings before interest and taxes of $3 million and a 40 percent tax rate. It is able to borrow at an interest rate of 14

percent, whereas its required equity return in the absence of borrowing is 18 percent.

   a. In the absence of personal taxes, what is the value of the company in an MM world with no leverage? with $4 million in debt? with $7 million in debt?

   b. Personal as well as corporate taxes now exist. The marginal personal tax rate on common stock income is 25 percent, and the marginal personal tax rate on debt income is 30 percent. Determine the value of the company using Eq. (17-7) for each of the three debt alternatives in part a. Why do your answers differ?

3. L'Etoile du Nord Resorts is considering various levels of debt. Presently, it has no debt and a total market value of $15 million. By undertaking leverage, it believes that it can achieve a net tax advantage (corporate and personal combined) equal to 20 percent of the amount of the debt. However, the company is concerned with bankruptcy and agency costs as well as lenders increasing their interest rate if it borrows too much. The company believes that it can borrow upwards of $5 million without incurring any of these costs. However, each additional $5 million increment in borrowing is expected to result in the three costs mentioned being incurred. Moreover, they are expected to increase at an increasing rate with leverage. The present value cost is expected to be the following for various levels of debt:

Debt (in millions)	$5	$10	$15	$20	$25	$30
PV cost of bankruptcy, agency, and increased interest rate (in millions)	0	.6	1.2	2.0	3.2	5.0

Is there an optimal amount of debt for the company?

PROBLEMS

1. The E. W. Lambert Company has net operating earnings of $10 million and $20 million of debt with a 7 percent interest charge. In all cases, assume no taxes.

   a. With a required return on equity of $12 \frac{1}{2}$ percent at that level of debt, compute the total value of the firm and the implied overall capitalization rate. (*Hint:* Capitalize earnings.)

   b. Next, assume that the firm issues an additional $10 million in debt and uses and proceeds to retire stock; the interest rate and required equity return remain the same. Compute the new total value of the firm and overall capitalization rate.

   c. Using the net operating income approach and an overall capitalization rate of 11 percent, compute the total market value, the stock market value, and the implied required equity return for the E. W. Lambert Company prior to the sale of additional debt.

  d. Determine the answers to part c if the company were to sell the additional $10 million in debt.

2. The Kelly Company and the Green Company are identical in every respect except that the Kelly Company is not levered, while the Green Company has $2 million in 12 percent bonds outstanding. There are no taxes, and capital markets are assumed to be perfect. The valuation of the two firms is the following:

	KELLY	GREEN
Net operating income	$ 600,000	$ 600,000
Interest on debt	0	240,000
Earnings to common stockholders	$ 600,000	$ 360,000
Required equity return	.15	.16
Market value of stock	$4,000,000	$2,250,000
Market value of debt	0	2,000,000
Total value of firm	$4,000,000	$4,250,000
Implied overall capitalization rate, k_o	15.00%	14.12%
Debt/equity ratio, B/S	0	.89

  a. You own $22,500 worth of Green stock. Show the process and the amount by which you could reduce your outlay through the use of arbitrage.

  b. When will this arbitrage process cease?

3. The C. T. Carlisle Corporation has a $1 million capital structure and will always maintain this book-value amount. Carlisle currently earns $250,000 per year before taxes of 50 percent, has an all-equity capital structure of 100,000 shares, and pays all earnings in dividends. The company is considering issuing debt in order to retire stock. The cost of the debt and the price of the stock at various levels of debt are given in the following table. It is assumed that the new capital structure would be reached all at once by purchasing stock at the current price. In other words, the table is a schedule at a point in time.

AMOUNT OF DEBT	AVERAGE PRETAX COST OF DEBT	PRICE OF STOCK
$ 0	—	$10.00
100,000	10.0%	10.00
200,000	10.0	10.50
300,000	10.5	10.75
400,000	11.0	11.00
500,000	12.0	10.50
600,000	14.0	9.50

a.   By observation, what do you think is the optimal capital structure?

b.   Construct a graph in terms of k_e, k_i, and k_o based on the data given.

c.   Are your feelings in part a confirmed?

4.   Zapatta Cottonseed Oil Company has $1 million in earnings before interest and taxes. Currently it is all equity financed. It may issue $3 million in perpetual debt at 15 percent interest in order to repurchase stock, thereby recapitalizing the corporation. There are no personal taxes.

a.   If the corporate tax rate is 40 percent, what is the income to all security holders if the company remains all equity financed? If it is recapitalized?

b.   What is the present value of the debt tax shield?

c.   The required equity return for the company's stock is 20 percent while it remains all equity financed. What is the value of the firm? What is the value if it is recapitalized?

5.   Petroles Vintage Wine Company is presently family owned and has no debt. The Petroles family is considering going public by selling some of their stock in the company. Investment bankers tell them the total market value of the company is $10 million if no debt is employed. In addition to selling stock, the family wishes to consider issuing debt that, for computational purposes, would be perpetual. The debt then would be used to purchase stock, so the size of the company would stay the same. Based on various valuation studies, the present value of tax shield is estimated at 22 percent of the amount borrowed when both corporate and personal taxes are taken into account. The investment banker has estimated the following present values for bankruptcy costs associated with various levels of debt:

DEBT (IN MILLIONS)	PRESENT VALUE OF BANKRUPTCY COSTS
$1	0
2	$ 50,000
3	100,000
4	200,000
5	400,000
6	700,000
7	1,100,000
8	1,600,000

Given this information, what amount of debt should the family choose?

6.   Acme-Menderhall Corporation is trying to determine an appropriate capital structure. It knows that as its leverage increases, its cost of borrowing will eventually increase as will the required rate of return on its common stock. The company has made the following estimates for various leverage ratios.

DEBT/(DEBT + EQUITY)	INTEREST RATE ON BORROWINGS	REQUIRED RATE OF RETURN ON EQUITY	
		Without Bankruptcy Costs	With Bankruptcy Costs
0	—	10 %	10 %
.10	8 %	$10\frac{1}{2}$	$10\frac{1}{2}$
.20	8	11	$11\frac{1}{4}$
.30	$8\frac{1}{2}$	$11\frac{1}{2}$	12
.40	9	$12\frac{1}{4}$	13
.50	10	$13\frac{1}{4}$	$14\frac{1}{2}$
.60	11	$14\frac{1}{2}$	$16\frac{1}{4}$
.70	$12\frac{1}{2}$	16	$18\frac{1}{2}$
.80	15	18	21

a. At a tax rate of 50 percent, what is the weighted average cost of capital of the company at various leverage ratios in the absence of bankruptcy costs? What is the optimal capital structure?

b. With bankruptcy costs, what is the optimal capital structure?

7. Archer-Deloitte Company wishes to finance a $15 million expansion program and is trying to decide between debt and equity. Management believes the market does not appreciate the company's profit potential and that the stock is undervalued. What security do you suppose it will use in financing and what will be the market's reaction? What if management felt the stock were overvalued?

SOLUTIONS TO SELF-CORRECTION PROBLEMS

1. a.

Net operating income	$ 360,000
Overall capitalization rate	.18
Total value of firm	$2,000,000
Market value of debt (50%)	$1,000,000
Market value of stock (50%)	$1,000,000
Net operating income	$ 360,000
Interest on debt (13%)	130,000
Earnings to common stockholders	$ 230,000
2% of $230,000 = $4,600	

Implied required equity return = $230,000/$1,000,000 = 23%

b.

Total value of firm	$2,000,000
Market value of debt (20%)	400,000
Market value of equity (80%)	1,600,000
Net operating income	$ 360,000
Interest on debt (13%)	52,000
Earnings to common stockholders	$ 308,000

Implied required equity return = $308,000/$1,600,000 = 19.25%

It is lower because Zoom uses less debt in its capital structure. As the equity capitalization is a linear function of the debt-to-equity ratio when we use the net operating income approach, the decline in required equity return offsets exactly the disadvantage of not employing so much in the way of "cheaper" debt funds.

2. a. Value if unlevered (000 omitted):

EBIT	$ 3,000	
Profit before taxes	3,000	
Taxes	1,200	
Profit after taxes	$ 1,800	
Required equity return (divide by)	.18	
Value if unlevered	$10,000	($10 million)

Value with $4 million in debt:

Value = value if unlevered + value of tax shield

Value = $10,000 + .40($4,000) = $11,600

Value with $7 million in debt:

Value = $10,000 + .40($7,000) = $12,800

Due to the tax subsidy, the firm is able to increase its value in a linear manner with more debt.

b. Value if unlevered (000 omitted): the same as before, namely, $10,000 ($10 million). Value with $4 million in debt:

$$\text{Value} = \$10,000 + \left[1 - \frac{(1 - .40)(1 - .25)}{1 - .30}\right]\$4,000$$

$$= \$11,429$$

Value with $7 million in debt:

$$\text{Value} = \$10,000 + \left[1 - \frac{(1 - .40)(1 - .25)}{1 - .30}\right]\$7,000$$

$$= \$12,500$$

The presence of personal taxes reduces the tax advantage associated with corporate debt. As long as the personal tax on stock income is less than that on debt income, however, the net tax advantage to debt is positive. As a result, the value of the firm rises with more debt, but not as rapidly if there were no personal taxes or if the personal tax rate on stock and debt income were the same.

3. (In millions):

(1) LEVEL OF DEBT	(2) FIRM VALUE UNLEVERED	(3) PV OF TAX SHIELD (1) × .20	(4) PV OF BANKRUPTCY, AGENCY AND INCREASED INTEREST COSTS	VALUE OF FIRM (2) + (3) − (4)
0	$15	0	0	$15.0
$ 5	15	$1	0	16.0
10	15	2	$ .6	16.4
15	15	3	1.2	16.8
20	15	4	2.0	17.0
25	15	5	3.2	16.8
30	15	6	5.0	16.0

The market value of the firm is maximized with $20 million in debt.

SELECTED REFERENCES

ARDITTI, FRED D., "The Weighted Average Cost of Capital: Some Questions on Its Definition, Interpretation, and Use," *Journal of Finance*, 28 (September 1973), 1001–9.

BAXTER, NEVINS D., "Leverage, Risk of Ruin, and the Cost of Capital," *Journal of Finance*, 22 (September 1967), 395–404.

BRADLEY, MICHAEL, GREGG A. JARRELL, and E. HAN KIM, "On the Existence of an Optimal Capital Structure: Theory and Evidence," *Journal of Finance*, 39 (July 1984), 857–77.

CASTANIAS, RICHARD, "Bankruptcy Risk and Optimal Capital Structure," *Journal of Finance*, 38 (December 1983), 1617–35.

CHEN, ANDREW H., and E. HAN KIM, "Theories of Corporate Debt Policy: A Synthesis," *Journal of Finance*, 34 (May 1979), 371–84.

DEANGELO, HARRY, and RONALD W. MASULIS, "Optimal Capital Structure Under Corporate and Personal Taxation," *Journal of Financial Economics*, 8 (March 1980), 3–29.

HAUGEN, ROBERT A., and LEMMA W. SENBERT, "Corporate Finance and Taxes: A Review," *Financial Management*, 15 (Autumn 1986), 5–21.

HAUGEN, ROBERT A., and LEMMA W. SENBET, "The Irrelevance of Bankruptcy Costs to the Theory of Optimal Capital Structure," *Journal of Finance*, 33 (June 1978), 383–94.

HEINS, A. JAMES, and CASE M. SPRENKLE, "A Comment on the Modigliani-Miller Cost of Capital Thesis," *American Economic Review*, 59 (September 1969), 590–92.

JENSEN, MICHAEL C., and WILLIAM E. MECKLING, "Theory of the Firm: Managerial Behavior, Agency Cost and Ownership Structure," *Journal of Financial Economics*, 3 (October 1976), 305–60.

———, and CLIFFORD W. SMITH, JR., "Stockholder, Manager, and Creditor Interests: Applications of Agency Theory," In Edward I. Altman and Marti G. Subrahmanyam, eds., *Recent Advances in Corporate Finance* (Homewood, Ill.: Richard D. Irwin, 1985), chap. 4.

LEE, WAYNE L., ANJAN V. THAKOR, and GUATAM VORA, "Screening, Market Signalling, and Capital Structure Theory," *Journal of Finance*, 38 (December 1983), 1507–18.

LITZENBERGER, ROBERT H., "Some Observations on Capital Structure and the Impact of Recent Recapitalizations on Share Prices," *Journal of Financial and Quantitative Analysis*, 21 (March 1986), 47–58.

———, and JAMES C. VAN HORNE, "Elimination of the Double Taxation of Dividends and Corporate Financial Policy," *Journal of Finance*, 33 (June 1978), 737–49.

MASULIS, RONALD W., "The Impact of Capital Structure Change on Firm Value: Some Estimates," *Journal of Finance*, 38 (March 1983), 107–26.

MILES, JAMES A., and JOHN R. EZZELL, "Reformulating Tax Shield Valuation: A Note," *Journal of Finance*, 40 (December 1985), 1485–92.

MILLER, MERTON H., "Debt and Taxes," *Journal of Finance*, 32 (May 1977), 266–68.

MODIGLIANI, FRANCO, and M. H. MILLER, "The Cost of Capital, Corporate Finance, and the Theory of Investment," *American Economic Review*, 48 (June 1958), 261–97.

———, "The Cost of Capital Corporation Finance, and the Theory of Investment: Reply," *American Economic Review*, 51 (September 1959), 655–69; "Taxes and the Cost of Capital: A Correction," *American Economic Review*, 53 (June 1963), 433–43; "Reply," *American Economic Review*, 55 (June 1965), 524–27; "Reply to Heins and Sprenkel," *American Economic Review*, 59 (September 1969), 592–95.

MYERS, STEWART C., "Capital Structure Puzzle," *Journal of Finance*, 39 (July 1984), 575–92.

———, and NICHOLAS S. MAJLUF, "Corporate Financing and Investment Decisions When Firms Have Information That Investors Do Not Have," *Journal of Financial Economics*, 13 (June 1984), 187–222.

SMITH, CLIFFORD W., JR., "Investment Banking and the Capital Acquisition Process," *Journal of Financial Economics*, 15 (January/February 1986), 3–29.

VAN HORNE, JAMES C., "Optimal Initiation of Bankruptcy Proceedings by Debt Holders," *Journal of Finance*, 31 (1976), 897–910.

CHAPTER 18

Dividend Policy and Retained Earnings

Over the years, business corporations have relied heavily on retained earnings as a source of financing. Since the dividend-payout ratio, the percentage of earnings paid to stockholders in cash, reduces the amount of earnings the firm retains, a dividend decision necessarily involves a financing decision. The dividend-payout ratio is a major aspect of the dividend policy of the firm, which may affect the value of the firm to the stockholder. But other aspects are also a part of the firm's overall dividend policy: stability of dividends, certain factors that influence the payout ratio from the standpoint of the firm, stock dividends and stock splits, the repurchase of stock, and procedural and legal elements. We are going to turn to these now.

DIVIDEND-PAYOUT RATIO

The first questions before us are whether the payment of cash dividends can affect shareholder wealth and, if it can, what dividend-payout ratio will maximize shareholder wealth. Again, we assume that business risk is held constant. To evaluate the question of whether the dividend-payout ratio affects shareholder wealth, it is necessary to examine first the firm's policy solely as a financing decision involving the retention of earnings. As long as the firm's investment projects have returns that exceed the required return, it will use retained earnings—and the amount of senior securities the increase in equity base will support—to finance these projects. If the firm has retained earnings left over after financing all acceptable investment opportunities, these earnings will be distributed to stockholders in the form of cash dividends. (We rule out share repurchase for now.) If not, there will be no dividends. If the number of acceptable investment opportunities involves a total dollar amount that exceeds the amount of retained earnings plus the senior securities these retained earnings will support, the firm will finance the excess with a combination of a new equity issue and senior securities.

When we treat dividend policy strictly as a financing decision, the payment of cash dividends is a passive residual. The amount of dividend payout will fluctuate from period to period in keeping with fluctuations in the amount of acceptable investment opportunities available to the firm. If these opportunities abound, the percentage of dividend payout is likely to be zero. On the other hand, if the firm is unable to find profitable investment opportunities, dividend payout will be 100 percent. For situations between these two extremes, the payout will be a fraction between 0 and 1.

Dividends as a Passive Residual

To illustrate dividend policy as a financing decision determined solely by the profitability of investment opportunities available, let us examine Walter's formula.[1] His model was one of the earlier dividend models, and certain later models correspond to this one. His formula is as follows.

[1] James E. Walter, "Dividend Policies and Common Stock Prices," *Journal of Finance*, 11 (March 1956), 29–41.

$$P = \frac{D + \frac{r}{\rho}(E - D)}{\rho} \tag{18-1}$$

where P = market price per share of common stock
D = dividends per share
E = earnings per share
r = return on investment
ρ = market capitalization rate.

Suppose that r = 24 percent, ρ = 20 percent, E = \$4, and D = \$2. The market price per share would be

$$P = \frac{2 + (.24/.20)(4 - 2)}{.20} = \$22$$

The optimal dividend-payout ratio is determined by varying D until you obtain the maximum market price per share. Under a strict interpretation of the Walter formula, the optimal dividend-payout ratio should be 0 if r is greater than ρ. Thus, in our example,

$$P = \frac{0 + (.24/.20)(4 - 0)}{.20} = \$24$$

With a payout ratio of 0, market price per share is maximized. Similarly, if r is less than ρ, the optimal payout ratio should be 100 percent. Suppose that r = .16, ρ = .20, E = \$4, and D = \$2. The market price per share then would be

$$P = \frac{2 + (.16/.20)(4 - 2)}{.20} = \$18$$

However, with a dividend-payout ratio of 100 percent

$$P = \frac{4 + (.16/.20)(4 - 4)}{.20} = \$20$$

Thus, market price per share can be maximized with a complete distribution of earnings. If $r = \rho$, market price per share is insensitive to the payout ratio.

The treatment of dividend policy as a passive residual determined solely by the availability of acceptable investment proposals implies that dividends are irrelevant; investors are indifferent between dividends and retention by the firm. If investment opportunities promise a return greater than their required return, investors would prefer to have the company retain earnings. If the return is equal to the required return, they would be indifferent between retention and dividends. Contrarily, if the return were less than the required return, they would prefer dividends. Supposedly, if the firm can earn more on projects than the required return, investors are perfectly happy to let the firm retain as much in earnings as it needs to finance the investments. With irrelevance, the required return is invariant with respect to changes in dividend payout. Are dividends more than just a means of distributing unused funds? Should dividend policy in any way be an active decision variable? To answer these questions, we must examine more thoroughly the argument that dividends are irrelevant, so that changes in the payout ratio (holding investment opportunities constant) do not affect shareholder wealth.

Irrelevance of Dividends

Modigliani and Miller's 1961 article[2] is the most comprehensive argument for the irrelevance of dividends. They assert that, given the investment decision of the firm, the dividend-payout ratio is a mere detail. It does not affect the wealth of shareholders. MM argue that the value of the firm is determined solely by the earning power of the firm's assets, or its investment policy, and that the manner in which the earnings stream is split between dividends and retained earnings does not affect this value. As in the previous chapter, when we considered the capital structure decision, MM assume perfect capital markets where there are no transaction costs, no flotation costs to companies issuing securities, and no taxes. Moreover, the future profits of the firm are assumed to be known with certainty. (Later this assumption is removed.)

Dividends versus Terminal Value.   The crux of MM's position is that the effect of dividend payments on shareholder wealth is offset exactly by other means of financing. Consider first selling additional stock in lieu of retaining earnings. When the firm has made its investment decision, it must decide whether to retain earnings or to pay dividends and sell new stock in the amount of these dividends in order to finance the investments. MM suggest that the sum of the discounted value per share after financing and dividends paid is equal to the market value per share before the payment of dividends. In other words, the stock's decline in market price because of the dilution caused by external financing offsets exactly the payment of the dividend. Thus, the stockholder is said to be indifferent between dividends and the retention of earnings.

One might ask: How does this correspond to our earlier chapters, when we said that dividends are the foundation for the valuation of common stocks? Although it is true that the market value of a share of stock is the present value of all expected future dividends, the timing of the dividends can vary. The irrelevance position simply argues that the present value of future dividends remains unchanged even though dividend policy changes their timing. It does not argue that dividends, including liquidating dividends, are never paid, only that their postponement is a matter of indifference when it comes to market price per share.

[2] Merton H. Miller and Franco Modigliani, "Dividend Policy, Growth, and the Valuation of Shares," *Journal of Business*, 34 (October 1961), 411–33.

Conservation of Value.   Given MM's assumptions of perfect certainty as well as their other assumptions, the irrelevance of dividends follows. As with our example for corporate leverage in the previous chapter, the total-value principle ensures that the sum of market value plus current dividends of two firms identical in all respects other than dividend-payout ratios will be the same.

Investors are able to replicate any dividend stream the corporation might pay. If dividends are less than desired, investors can sell portions of their stock to obtain the desired cash distribution. If dividends are more than desired, investors can use dividends to purchase additional shares in the company. Thus, investors are able to manufacture "homemade" dividends in the same way they devise "homemade" leverage in capital structure decisions. For a corporate decision to be a thing of value, the company must be able to do something for stockholders that they cannot do for themselves. Because investors can manufacture "homemade" dividends, which are perfect substitutes for corporate dividends under the preceding assumptions, dividend policy is irrelevant. As a result, one dividend policy is as good as the next. The firm is unable to create value simply by altering the mix of dividends and retained earnings. As in capital structure theory, there is a conservation of value so that the sum of the parts is always the same. The total size of the pie is what will be eaten, and it is unchanged in the slicing.

Arguments for Relevance

A number of arguments have been advanced in support of the contrary position, namely, that dividends are relevant under conditions of uncertainty. In other words, investors are not indifferent to whether they receive their returns on investment in dividend income or stock price appreciation. We shall examine these arguments under conditions of uncertainty.

Preference for Dividends.   Certain investors in the market may have a preference for dividends over capital gains. The payment of dividends may resolve uncertainty in their minds. It might be argued that because dividends are received on a current, ongoing basis, whereas the prospect of capital gains is off in the future, investors in a dividend-paying company resolve their uncertainty earlier than do those investing in a nondividend paying company. To the extent investors prefer the early resolution of uncertainty, they may be willing to pay a higher price for the stock that offers the greater current dividend, all other things held constant. If, in fact, investors can manufacture "homemade" dividends, such a preference is irrational. Nonetheless, sufficient statements from investors make it difficult to dismiss the argument. Perhaps, for either psychological or inconvenience reasons, investors prefer not to manufacture "homemade" dividends but to get the "real thing" directly from the company.

Taxes on the Investor.   When we allow for taxes, there are a variety of effects. To the extent that the personal tax rate on capital gains is less than that on dividend income, there may be an advantage to the retention of earnings. While the 1986 Tax Act brought these two rates together, the capital gains tax is deferred until the actual sale of stock. Effectively, the stockholder is given a valuable timing option when the firm retains earnings as opposed to paying dividends. As brought out in Chapter 17, the capital gains tax may be avoided if appreciated securities are given as gifts to charitable causes or if the person dies. Finally, some states tax capital gains at a more favorable rate than dividend income. For these reasons, the effective (present-value) tax on capital gains is less than that on dividend income, even when the federal tax rate on the two types of income is the same. This would suggest that a dividend-paying stock will need to provide a higher expected before-tax return than will a nondividend-paying stock of the same risk. According to this notion, the greater the dividend yield of a stock, the higher the before-tax return required, all other things being the same.

However, investors do not necessarily experience the same taxation on the two types of income. Institutional investors, such as retirement and pension funds, pay no tax on either dividends or capital gains. For corporate investors intercompany dividends are taxed at a rate below that applicable to capital gains. For example, if Laurel Corporation owns 100 shares of Hardy Corporation, which pays $1 per share dividend, 80 percent of the dividend income is tax exempt. In other words, Laurel Corporation would pay taxes on $20 of dividend income at the corporate tax rate. The overall tax effect will be less than if Hardy Corporation had share appreciation of $100 and all of this were taxed at the capital gains rate. Accordingly, there may be a preference for current dividends on the part of corporate investors. Also, there are a growing number of tax-free institutional investors. For these investors, there is no tax on either dividends or capital gains. Other parties not having a differential tax include brokers and dealers. For them, both dividends and capital gains are taxed as ordinary income. Despite these exceptions, for many investors there exists a present-value differential in taxes between a dollar of dividends and a dollar of capital gains.

Still it is not clear that there is a before-tax return effect of the type described. If there were clienteles of investors having dividend preferences, corporations could adjust their dividend payout to take advantage of the situation. Suppose that two-fifths of all investors prefer a zero dividend payout, one-fifth prefer a 25 percent payout, and the remaining two-fifths prefer a 50 percent payout. If most companies pay out 25 percent of their earnings in dividends, there will be excess demand for the shares of companies paying zero dividends and for the shares of companies whose dividend payout ratio is 50 percent. Presumably, a number of companies will recognize this excess demand and adjust their payout ratios in order to increase share price. The action of these companies eventually will eliminate the excess demand. In equilibrium, the dividend payouts of corporations will match the desires of investor groups. At this point, no company would be able to affect its share price by altering its dividend. As a result, even with taxes, dividend payout would be irrelevant.

We are left with an unsettled situation in which the effect of taxes on dividends is not clear. Even if there is an effect, however, it was lessened with the 1986 Tax Act. As a result of the act, we might expect demand for higher yielding stocks to increase. Before examining empirical evidence on the subject, we must look at other factors that may influence the payment of dividends.

Flotation Costs.   The irrelevance of dividend payout is based on the idea that in accordance with the investment policy of the firm, funds paid out of the firm must be replaced by funds acquired through external financing. The introduction of flotation costs favors the retention of earnings in the firm. For each dollar paid out in dividends, the firm nets less than a dollar after flotation costs per dollar of external financing.

Transaction Costs and Divisibility of Securities.   Transaction costs involved in the sale of securities tend to restrict the arbitrage process in the same manner as that described for debt. Stockholders who desire current income must pay brokerage fees on the sale of portions of their stocks if the dividend paid is not sufficient to satisfy their current desire for income. This fee varies inversely, per dollar of stock sold, with the size of the sale. For a small sale, the brokerage fee can be rather significant. As a result of this fee, stockholders with consumption desires in excess of current dividends will prefer the company to pay additional dividends. Perfect capital markets also assume that securities are infinitely divisible. The fact that the smallest integer is one share may result in "lumpiness" with respect to selling shares for current income. This, too, acts as a deterrent to the sale of stock in lieu of dividends. On the other hand, stockholders not desiring dividends for current consumption purposes will need to reinvest their dividends. Here, again, transaction costs and divisibility problems work to the disadvantage of the stockholder, although in the opposite direction. Thus, transaction costs and divisibility problems cut both ways, and one is not able to draw directional implications regarding dividends versus retained earnings.

Institutional Restrictions.   The law limits the types of common stock that certain institutional investors may buy. The prescribed list of eligible securities is determined in part by the duration over which dividends have been paid. If a company does not pay dividends or has not paid them over a sufficiently long period, certain institutional investors are not permitted to invest in the stock.

Universities, on the other hand, sometimes have restrictions on the expenditure of capital gains from their endowments. Also, a number of trusts have a prohibition against the liquidation of principal. In the case of common stocks, the beneficiary is entitled to the dividend income, but not to the proceeds from the sale of stock. As a result of this stipulation, the trustee who manages the investments may feel constrained to pay particular attention to dividend yield and seek stocks paying reasonable dividends. Though the two influences described are small in aggregate, they work in the direction of a preference for dividends as opposed to retention and capital gains.

Financial Signaling

This argument is different from the other arguments in that it depends on imperfections in the market for financial information. It suggests that dividends have an impact on share price because they communicate information, or signals, about the firm's profitability. Presumably, firms with good news about their future profitability will want to tell investors. Rather than make a simple announcement, dividends may be increased to add conviction to the statement. When a firm has a target payout ratio that is stable over time and it changes this ratio, investors may believe that management is announcing a change in the expected future profitability of the firm. The signal to investors is that management and the board of directors truly believe things are better than the stock price reflects.

Accordingly, the price of the stock may react to this change in dividends. The idea here is that the reported accounting earnings of a company may not be a proper reflection of its economic earnings. To the extent that dividends provide information on economic earnings not provided by reported earnings, share price will respond. Put another way, dividends speak louder than words. Thus, dividends are said to be used by investors as predictors of the firm's future performance; they convey management's expectations of the future.

A Summing Up

A company should endeavor to establish a dividend policy that will maximize shareholder wealth. Most everyone agrees that if a company does not have sufficiently profitable investment opportunities, it should distribute any excess funds to its stockholders. The firm need not pay out the exact unused portion of earnings every period. Indeed, it may wish to stabilize the absolute amount of dividends paid from period to period. But over the longer run the total earnings retained, plus the senior securities the increasing equity base will support, will correspond to the amount of profitable investment opportunities. Dividend policy still would be a passive residual determined by the amount of investment opportunities.

To pay a larger dividend requires faith that shareholder wealth somehow will be enhanced. Empirical testing of dividend policy has focused primarily on the tax effect and on financial signaling. Results have been mixed as to whether there is a tax effect that requires a higher, before-tax return the greater the dividend.[3] Certain evidence suggests such an effect, whereas other studies are consistent with neutrality. No studies support a positive dividend effect in the sense of a net preference for dividends more than offsetting the differential taxation of dividends and capital gains. Whether there is a negative or neutral effect is in an unsettled state empirically. If the taxation of dividends and capital gains remains the same (as enacted under the 1986 Tax Act), any "yield tilt" effect, requiring higher dividend-paying stocks to provide higher before-tax expected returns will be difficult to detect in future empirical studies. In contrast to the results for a tax effect on financial signaling the evidence is consistent in support of a dividend announcement effect: increases in dividends leading to positive excess stock returns and decreases to negative excess returns. Therefore, dividends would appear to convey information.

---

[3] For a detailed review of the empirical evidence, see James C. Van Horne, *Financial Management and Policy*, 8th ed. (Englewood Cliffs, N.J.: Prentice-Hall, 1989), chap. 11.

For the firm to be justified in paying a dividend larger than that dictated by the amount left over after profitable investment opportunities, there must be a net preference for dividends in the market. Only institutional restrictions and some investors' preference for dividends argue for dividends. The other arguments suggest either a neutral effect or a systematic bias favoring retention. There does appear to be some positive value associated with a modest dividend as opposed to none at all. This occurrence may be due to institutional restrictions and a signaling effect. Beyond that, the picture is very cloudy, and some argue that even a modest dividend has no effect on valuation. Few academic scholars argue that dividends significantly in excess of what a passive policy would dictate will lead to share price improvement. Rather, the arguments are for either a neutral effect or a negative effect owing to tax reasons. Before making a final observation, let us look at some practical things to consider in approaching a dividend-payout decision.

MANAGERIAL CONSIDERATIONS IN DETERMINING A DIVIDEND PAYOUT

So far we have discussed only the theoretical aspects of dividend policy. Yet when a company establishes a policy, it looks at a number of things. These considerations should be related back to the theory of dividend payout and the valuation of the firm. In what follows, we take up various factors that firms in practice can and should analyze when approaching a dividend decision.

Funds Needs of the Firm

Perhaps the place to begin is with an assessment of the funds needs of the firm. In this regard, cash budgets and projected source-and-use-of-funds statements (topics taken up in Chapter 7) are of particular use. The expected operating cash flows of the firm, expected future capital expenditures, any likely buildups in receivables and inventories, scheduled reductions in debt, and any other thing that affects the cash position of the firm should be taken into account. The key is to determine the likely cash flows and cash position of the company in the absence of a change in dividend. In addition to looking at expected outcomes, we should factor in business risk, so that we may obtain a range of possible cash flow outcomes, a procedure spelled out in Chapter 7.

In keeping with our earlier discussion of the theory of dividend payout, the firm wishes to determine if anything is left over after servicing its funds needs, including profitable investment projects. In this regard, the firm should look at its situation over a reasonable number of future years, to iron out fluctuations. The likely ability of the firm to sustain a dividend should be analyzed relative to the probability distributions of possible future cash flows and cash positions. On the basis of this analysis, a company can determine its likely future residual funds.

Liquidity

The liquidity of a company is a prime consideration in many dividend decisions. Because dividends represent a cash outflow, the greater the cash position and overall liquidity of a company, the greater its ability to pay a dividend. A company that is growing and profitable may not be liquid, for its funds may go into fixed assets and permanent working capital. Because the management of such a company usually desires to maintain some liquidity cushion to give it flexibility and a protection against uncertainty, it may be reluctant to jeopardize this position in order to pay a large dividend. The liquidity of the company, of course, is determined by the firm's investment and financing decisions. The investment decision determines the rate of asset expansion and the firm's need for funds; and the financing decision determines the way in which this need will be financed.

Ability to Borrow

A liquid position is not the only way to provide for flexibility and thereby protect against uncertainty. If a firm has the ability to borrow on comparatively short notice, it may be relatively flexible. This ability to borrow can be in the form of a line of credit or a revolving credit from a bank, or simply the informal willingness of a financial institution to extend credit. In addition, flexibility can come from the ability of a firm to go to the capital markets with a bond issue. The larger and more established a company, the better its access to the capital markets. The greater the ability of the firm to borrow, the greater its flexibility and the greater its ability to pay a cash dividend. With ready access to debt funds, management should be less concerned with the effect that a cash dividend has on its liquidity.

Assessment of Any Valuation Information

To the extent there are insights into the effect of a dividend on valuation, they should be gathered. Most companies look at the dividend-payout ratios of other companies in the industry, particularly those having about the same growth. It may not matter that a company is out of line with similar companies, but it will be conspicuous and usually a company will want to justify its position. Finally, a company should judge the informational effect of a dividend. What do investors expect? Here security analysts and security reports are useful. The company should ask itself what information it is conveying with its present dividend and what it would convey with a possible change in dividend. As much of this was discussed in the previous section, we limit our remarks here.

Control

If a company pays substantial dividends, it may need to raise capital at a later time through the sale of stock in order to finance profitable investment opportunities. Under such circumstances, the controlling interest of the company may be diluted if controlling stockholders do not or cannot subscribe for additional shares. These stockholders may prefer a low dividend payout and the financing of investment needs with retained earnings. Such a dividend policy may not maximize overall shareholder wealth, but it still may be in the best interests of those in control.

Control can work two ways, however. When a company is being sought by another company or by individuals, a low dividend payout may work to the advantage of the "outsiders" seeking control. The outsiders may be able to convince stockholders that the company is not maximizing shareholder wealth and that they (the outsiders) can do a better job. Consequently, companies in danger of being acquired may establish a high dividend payout in order to please stockholders.

Restrictions in Bond Indenture or Loan Agreement

The protective covenants in a bond indenture or loan agreement often include a restriction on the payment of dividends. This restriction is employed by the lenders to preserve the company's ability to service debt. Usually, it is expressed as a maximum percentage of cumulative earnings. When such a restriction is in force, it naturally influences the firm's dividend policy. Sometimes the management of a company welcomes a dividend restriction imposed by lenders, because then it does not have to justify to stockholders the retention of earnings. It need only point to the restriction.

Some Final Observations

In determining a dividend payout, the typical company will analyze a number of the factors just described. These factors largely dictate the boundaries within which a dividend can be paid. When a company pays a dividend in excess of its residual funds, it implies that management and the board of directors believe the payment has a favorable effect on shareholder wealth. The frustrating thing is that we have so little in the way of clear generalizations from the empirical evidence. The lack of firm footing for predicting the long-run effect of a specific dividend policy on valuation makes the dividend decision more difficult in many ways than either the investment or financing decisions.

Considerations taken up in this section allow a company to determine with reasonable accuracy what would be an appropriate passive dividend strategy. An active dividend policy involves an act of faith, because it demands that a portion of the cumulative dividends ultimately be replaced with common stock financing. Such a strategy is undertaken in a foggy area, but one in which most academics have difficulty believing shareholder wealth will be enhanced.

Notwithstanding, many companies profess a belief that dividend payout affects share price and behave in a manner consistent with dividends mattering.

DIVIDEND STABILITY

In addition to the percentage of dividend payout, stability is attractive to investors. By stability, we mean maintaining its position in relation to a trend line, preferably one that is upward-sloping. All other things being the same, a stock may be higher in price if it pays a stable dividend over time than if it pays out a fixed percentage of earnings. Suppose that Company A has a long-run dividend-payout ratio of 50 percent of earnings. It pays out this percentage every year, despite the fact that its earnings are cyclical. The dividends of Company A are shown in Fig. 18-1. Company B, on the other hand, has exactly the same earnings and a long-run dividend-payout ratio of 50 percent, but it maintains a relatively stable dividend over time. It changes the absolute amount of dividend only in keeping with the underlying trend of earnings. The dividends of Company B are shown in Fig. 18-2.

Over the long run, the total amount of dividends paid by these two firms is the same; however, the market price per share of Company B may be higher than that of Company A, all other things being the same. Investors may well place a positive utility on dividend stability and pay a premium for the company that offers it. To the extent that investors value dividend stability, the overall dividend policy of Company B would be better than that of Company A. This policy includes not only the percentage of dividend payout in relation to earnings but also the manner in which the actual dividends are paid. Rather than vary dividends directly with changes in earnings per share, Company B raises the dividend only when reasonably confident a higher dividend can be maintained.

FIGURE 18-1
Hypothetical dividend policy of Company A

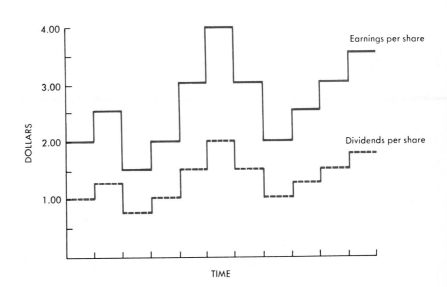

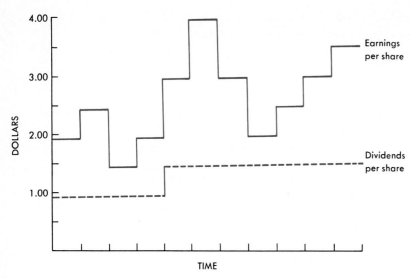

FIGURE 18-2
Hypothetical dividend policy of Company B

Valuation of Stability

Investors may be willing to pay a premium for stable dividends because of the informational content of dividends, the desire of investors for current income, and certain legal considerations.

Informational Content.   When earnings drop and a company does not cut its dividend, the market may have more confidence in the stock than it would have if the dividend were cut. The stable dividend may convey management's view that the future of the company is better than the drop in earnings suggests. Thus, management may be able to affect the expectations of investors through the informational content of dividends. Management will not be able to fool the market permanently. If there is a downward trend in earnings, a stable dividend will not convey forever an impression of a rosy future. Moreover, if a firm is in an unstable business with wide swings in earnings, a stable dividend cannot give the illusion of underlying stability.

Current Income Desires.   A second factor may favor stable dividends. Investors who desire a specific periodic income will prefer a company with stable dividends to one with unstable dividends, even though both companies may have the same pattern of earnings and long-run dividend payout. Although investors can always sell a portion of their stock for income when the dividend is not sufficient to meet their current needs, many investors have an aversion to dipping into principal. Moreover, when a company reduces its dividend, earnings usually are down and the market price of the stock depressed. Overall, income-conscious investors place a positive utility on stable dividends, even though they can always sell a few shares of stock for income.

Legal Considerations.   A stable dividend may be advantageous from the legal standpoint of permitting certain institutional investors to buy the stock. Various governmental bodies prepare legal lists of securities in which pension funds, savings banks, trustees, insurance companies, and certain others may invest. To qualify, a company must have an uninterrupted pattern of dividends. A cut in the dividend may result in the removal of a company from these legal lists.

The arguments presented in support of the notion that stable dividends have a positive effect on the market price of the stock are only suggestive. Little empirical evidence sheds light on the question. Although studies of individual stocks often suggest that stable dividends buffer the market price of the stock when earnings turn down, there have been no comprehensive studies of a large sample of stocks dealing with the relationship between dividend stability and valuation. Nevertheless, most companies strive for stability in their dividend payments. This is consistent with a belief that stable dividends have a positive effect on value.

Target Payout Ratios

A number of companies appear to follow the policy of a target dividend-payout ratio over the long run. Lintner contends that dividends are adjusted to changes in earnings, but only with a lag.[4] When earnings increase to a new level, a company increases dividends only when it feels it can maintain the increase in earnings. Companies are also reluctant to cut the absolute amount of their cash dividend. Both of these factors explain the lag in dividend changes behind changes in earnings. In an economic upturn, the lag relationship becomes visible when **retained earnings** increase in relation to dividends. In a contraction, retained earnings will decrease relative to dividends.

Retained earnings. The cumulative earnings of the company after dividends.

The case of Coleman Company illustrates the use of a target payout ratio and stable dividends. Coleman makes outdoor camping equipment, sports marine products, and central heating and air-conditioning units. Business is somewhat cyclical, with resulting swings in earnings, but the company maintains stable and increasing dividends over time; it raises dividends when management and the board of directors are confident that earnings can be sustained. The dividends per share and earnings per share for the company are shown in Fig. 18-3.

Regular and Extra Dividends

One way for a company to increase its cash distribution in periods of prosperity is to declare an *extra* dividend in addition to the *regular* quarterly or semiannual dividend. By declaring an extra dividend, the company warns investors that the

---

[4] See John Lintner, "Distribution of Income of Corporations," *American Economic Review*, 46 (May 1956), 97–113.

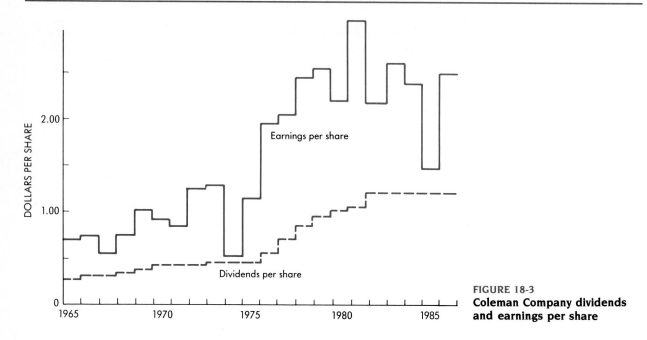

FIGURE 18-3
Coleman Company dividends and earnings per share

dividend is not an increase in the established dividend rate. The declaration of an extra dividend is suitable particularly for companies with fluctuating earnings. General Motors, for example, has declared extra dividends in good years. The use of the extra dividend enables the company to maintain a stable record of regular dividends but also to distribute to stockholders some of the rewards of prosperity. If a company pays extra dividends continuously, it defeats its purpose. The extra becomes the expected. When properly labeled, however, an extra or special dividend still conveys positive information to the market concerning the firm's present and future performance.

STOCK DIVIDENDS AND STOCK SPLITS

Stock dividends and stock splits typically are used for different purposes; nevertheless, in an economic sense the two are very similar. Only from an accounting standpoint is there a significant difference. Accounting principles treat a stock distribution in excess of 25 percent of the shares outstanding as a stock split, whereas lesser distributions can be classified stock dividends.

Stock Dividends

Stock dividend. A dividend paid in additional stock as opposed to cash.

A **stock dividend** is simply the payment of additional stock to stockholders. It represents nothing more than a recapitalization of the company; a stockholder's proportional ownership remains unchanged. Chen Industries had the following capital structure before issuing a stock dividend:

Common stock ($5 par, 400,000 shares)	$ 2,000,000
Paid-in capital	1,000,000
Retained earnings	7,000,000
Net worth	$10,000,000

Chen pays a 5 percent stock dividend, amounting to 20,000 additional shares of stock. The fair market value of the stock is $40 a share. For each 20 shares of stock owned, the stockholder receives an additional share. The balance sheet of the company after the stock dividend would be

Common stock ($5 par, 420,000 shares)	$ 2,100,000
Paid-in capital	1,700,000
Retained earnings	6,200,000
Net worth	$10,000,000

With a stock dividend, $800,000 is transferred ($40 × 20,000 shares) from retained earnings to the common stock and paid-in capital accounts. Because the par value stays the same, the increase in number of shares is reflected in a $100,000 increase in the common stock account ($5 × 20,000 shares). The residual of $700,000 goes into the paid-in capital account. The net worth of the company remains the same.

Because the number of shares of stock outstanding is increased by 5 percent, earnings per share of the company are reduced proportionately. Total net profit after taxes is $1 million. Before the stock dividend, earnings per share were $2.50 ($1 million/400,000). After the stock dividend, earnings per share would be $2.38 (1 million/420,000). Thus, stockholders have more shares of stock but lower earnings per share. Their proportion of total earnings available to common-stock holders remains unchanged.

Stock Splits

With a **stock split,** the number of shares is increased through a proportional reduction in the par value of the stock. A lumber company has the following capital structure before a stock split:

Common stock ($5 par, 400,000 shares)	$ 2,000,000
Paid-in capital	1,000,000
Retained earnings	7,000,000
Net worth	$10,000,000

Stock split. An increase in the number of shares outstanding by reducing the par value of the stock. Example: a 2-for-1 stock split where par value per share is reduced by one-half.

After the split, the capital structure is as follows.

Common stock ($2.50 par, 800,000 shares)	$ 2,000,000
Paid-in capital	1,000,000
Retained earnings	7,000,000
Net worth	$10,000,000

With a stock dividend, the par value is not reduced, whereas with a split, it is. As a result, the common stock, paid-in capital, and retained-earnings accounts remain unchanged. The net worth, of course, also stays the same; the only change is in the par value of the stock. Except in accounting treatment, the stock dividend and stock split are very similar. A stock split, however, is usually reserved for occasions when a company wishes to achieve a substantial reduction in the market price per share. A principal purpose of a split is to place the stock in a more popular trading range, thereby attracting more buyers.

Very seldom will a company maintain the same cash dividends per share before and after a split, but it might increase the effective dividends to stockholders. A company may split its stock 2 for 1 and establish a dividend rate of $1.20 a share, whereas before, the rate was $2 a share. A stockholder owning 100 shares before the split would receive $200 in cash dividends per annum. After the split, the stockholder would own 200 shares and would receive $240 in dividends.

Value to Investors of Stock Dividends and Splits

Theoretically, a stock dividend or stock split is not a thing of value to investors. They receive additional stock certificates, but their proportionate ownership of the company is unchanged. The market price of the stock should decline proportionately, so that the total value of their holdings stays the same. To illustrate with a stock dividend, suppose that you held 100 shares of stock worth $40 per share or $4,000 in total. After a 5 percent stock dividend, share price should drop by $40(1 - 1.00/1.05), or by $1.90. The total value of your holdings then would be $38.10 × 105, or $4,000. Under these conditions, the stock dividend does not represent a thing of value to you. You merely have an additional stock certificate evidencing ownership.

To the extent that the investor wishes to sell a few shares of stock for income, the stock dividend may make it easier to do so. Without the stock dividend, of course, stockholders also could sell a few shares of their original holdings for income. In either case, the sale of stock represents the sale of principal and is subject to the capital gains tax. It is probable that certain investors do not look at the sale of a stock dividend as a sale of principal. To them, the stock dividend represents a windfall gain; they can sell it and still retain their original holdings. The stock dividend may have a favorable psychological effect on these stockholders.

Effect on Cash Dividends.   The stock dividend or stock split may be accompanied by an increased cash dividend. For the former, suppose that an investor owns 100 shares of a company paying a $1 dividend. The company declares a 10 percent stock dividend and, at the same time, announces that the cash dividend per share will remain unchanged. The investor then will have 110 shares, and total cash dividends will be $110 rather than $100, as before. In this case, a stock dividend increases the total cash dividends. Whether this increase in cash dividend has a positive effect on shareholder wealth will depend on the trade-off between current dividends and retained earnings, which we discussed earlier. Clearly, the stock dividend in this case represents a decision by the firm to increase modestly the amount of cash dividends.

Sometimes a stock dividend is employed to conserve cash. Instead of increasing the cash dividend as earnings rise, a company may desire to retain a greater portion of its earnings and declare a stock dividend. The decision then is to lower the dividend-payout ratio; for as earnings rise and the dividend remains the same, the payout ratio will decline. Whether shareholder wealth is increased by this action will depend on considerations discussed previously. The decision to retain a higher proportion of earnings, of course, could be accomplished without a stock dividend. However, the stock dividend may tend to please certain investors by virtue of its psychological impact. However, the substitution of stock for cash dividends involves a sizable administrative cost. Stock dividends simply are much more costly to administer than are cash dividends, and this out-of-pocket expense works to their disadvantage.

Informational Content. The declaration of a stock dividend or a stock split may convey information to investors. As taken up earlier, there may be asymmetric information between management and investors. Instead of a press announcement, a stock dividend or split may connote more convincingly management's belief about the favorable prospects of the company. Whether these signals are more convincing is an empirical question, and here the evidence is overwhelming: there is a statistically significant and positive stock price reaction around the announcement of a stock dividend or a stock split.[5] The information effect is that the stock is undervalued and should be higher priced. Of course, the company must eventually deliver improved earnings if the stock is to remain higher. The underlying cause for the increase in market price is perceived growth, not the stock dividend or split itself.

Reverse Stock Split

Rather than increase the number of shares of stock outstanding, a company may want to reduce the number. It can accomplish this with a **reverse split.** In our stock-split example before, had there been a 1-to-4 reverse split instead of the 2-for-1 straight stock split, for each four shares held, the stockholder would receive one share in exchange. The par value per share would become $20, and

Reverse split. A stock split where the stockholder receives one share for a specified number held.

[5] A classic earlier study is by Eugene F. Fama, Lawrence Fisher, Michael Jensen, and Richard Roll, "The Adjustment of Stock Prices to New Information," *International Economic Review*, 10 (February 1969), 1–21. Other studies include Guy Charest, "Split Information, Stock Returns and Market Efficiency," *Journal of Financial Economics*, 6 (June–September 1978), 265–96; J. Randall Woolridge, "Stock Dividends as Signals," *Journal of Financial Research*, 6 (Spring 1983), 1–12; and Mark S. Grinblatt, Ronald W. Masulis, and Sheridan Titman, "The Valuation Effects of Stock Splits and Stock Dividends," *Journal of Financial Economics*, 13 (December 1984), 461–90.

there would be 100,000 shares outstanding rather than 400,000. Reverse stock splits are employed to increase the market price per share when the stock is considered to be selling at too low a price. Many companies have an aversion to seeing their stock fall significantly below $10 per share. If financial difficulty or some other depressant lowers the price into this range, it can be increased with a reverse split.

As with stock dividends and straight stock splits, there is likely to be an information or signaling effect associated with the announcement. Usually the signal is negative, such as would accompany the admission by a company that it is in financial difficulty. However, this need not be the case; the company simply may want to place the stock in a higher trading range where trading costs and servicing expenses are lower. Nonetheless, the empirical evidence is consistent with a statistically significant decline in share price around the announcement date, holding other things constant.[6] The decline is tempered by the company's past earnings performance, but a healthy company should think twice before undertaking a reverse stock split. There are too many bad apples in the barrel not to be tainted by association.

REPURCHASE OF STOCK

In recent years a number of companies have repurchased a portion of their outstanding common stock. Some companies repurchase stock in order to have it available for stock options. In this way, the total number of shares is not increased with the exercise of the options. Another reason for **stock repurchase** is to have shares available for the acquisition of other companies. In certain cases, companies no longer wishing to be publicly owned "go private" by purchasing all of the stock of the outside stockholders. In still other situations, stock is repurchased with the full intention of retiring it. Under these circumstances, repurchase of stock may be treated as a part of the firm's dividend decision.

Stock repurchase. The repurchase of stock by a company, either in the secondary market or by tender offer. A means for distributing excess funds.

Method of Repurchase

Tender offer. An offer to the stockholders of a company to purchase their shares at a specified price. Tender can be made by the company or by others.

The two most common methods of repurchase are through a **tender offer** and through the purchase of stock in the marketplace. With a tender offer, the company makes a formal offer to stockholders to purchase so many shares, typically at a set price. This bid price is above the current market price; stockholders can elect either to sell their stock at the specified price or to continue to hold it. Typically the tender offer period is between 2 and 3 weeks. If stockholders tender more shares than originally sought by the company, the company may elect to purchase all or part of the excess. It is under no obligation to do so. In general, the transaction costs to the firm in making a tender offer are higher than those incurred in the purchase of stock in the open market. The principal costs in-

---

[6] See J. Randall Woolridge and Donald R. Chambers, "Reverse Splits and Shareholder Wealth," *Financial Management*, 12 (Autumn 1983), 5–15; and R. C. Radcliffe and W. Gillespie, "The Price Impact of Reverse Splits," *Financial Analysts Journal*, 35 (January–February 1979), 63–67.

volve the fee paid to the investment banker who manages the repurchase and the fees paid to soliciting dealers.

In open-market purchases, a company buys its stock as any other investor does—through a brokerage house. Usually, the brokerage fee is negotiated. Certain Securities and Exchange Commission rules restrict the manner in which a company bids for its shares. As a result, it takes an extended period of time for a company to accumulate a relatively large block of stock. For this reason, the tender offer is more suitable when the company seeks a large amount of stock.

Before the company repurchases stock, stockholders must be informed of the company's intentions. In a tender offer, these intentions are announced by the offer itself. Even here, the company must not withhold other information. It would be unethical for a mining company, for example, to withhold information of a substantial ore discovery while making a tender offer to repurchase shares. In open-market purchases, especially, it is necessary to disclose the company's repurchase intentions. Otherwise, stockholders may sell their stock not knowing about a repurchase program that will increase earnings per share. Given full information about the amount of repurchase and the objective of the company, the stockholders can sell their stock if they so choose. Without proper disclosure, the selling stockholder may be penalized. When the amount of stock repurchased is substantial, a tender offer is particularly suitable, for it gives all stockholders equal treatment.

Repurchasing as Part of a Dividend Decision

If a firm has excess cash and insufficient profitable investment opportunities to justify the use of these funds, it may be in the shareholders' interests to distribute the funds. The distribution can be accomplished either by the repurchase of stock or by paying the funds out in increased dividends. In the absence of personal income taxes and transaction costs, the two alternatives, theoretically, should make no difference to stockholders. With repurchase, fewer shares remain outstanding, and earnings per share and, ultimately, dividends per share rise. As a result, the market price per share should rise as well. In theory, the capital gain arising from repurchase should equal the dividend that otherwise would have been paid.

Deuce Hardware Company has the following earnings and market price per share:

Net profit after taxes	$2,000,000
Number of shares outstanding	500,000
Earnings per share	$4
Market price per share, after distribution	$60
Price/earnings ratio	15

The company is considering the distribution of $1.5 million, either in cash dividends or in the repurchase of its own stock. If investors are expecting the cash dividend, the value of a share of stock before the dividend is paid will be $63, that is, $3 a share in expected dividends ($1.5 million/500,000) plus the $60 market price. The firm chooses to repurchase its stock, however, and makes a tender offer to stockholders at $63 a share. It then will be able to repurchase $1.5 million/$63, or 23,810 shares. Earnings per share will be

$$EPS = \$2,000,000/476,190 = \$4.20$$

If the price/earnings ratio stays at 15, the total market price per share will be $63 (4.20 × 15), the same total value as under the dividend alternative. Thus, the amount of distribution to stockholders is $3 per share, whether dividends or repurchase of stock (and subsequent capital gain) is used.

With a differential tax rate on dividends and capital gains, repurchase of stock offers a tax advantage over payment of dividends to the taxable investor. The market price increase resulting from a repurchase of stock is subject to the capital gains tax, whereas dividends are taxed at the higher ordinary income tax rate.[7] At times in our tax laws, capital gains have been taxed at a more favorable rate; at other times, at the same rate. Even here the tax is postponed until the stock is sold, whereas with dividends the tax must be paid on a current basis.

The repurchase of stock seems particularly appropriate when the firm has a large amount of unused funds to distribute. To pay the funds out through an extra dividend would result in a nonpostponable tax to stockholders. The tax effect could be alleviated somewhat by paying the funds out as extra dividends over a period of time, but this action might result in investors' counting on the extra dividend. The firm must be careful not to undertake a steady program of repurchase in lieu of paying dividends. The Internal Revenue Service will regard such a program as dividend income and not allow stockholders redeeming their shares the capital gains tax advantage.[8] Hence, it is important that the repurchase of stock be a "one-shot" transaction and not be used as a substitute for regular dividends or even for recurring extra dividends.

Investment or Financing Decision?

Some regard the repurchase of stock as an investment decision instead of a dividend decision. Indeed, in a strict sense, it is, even though stock held in the treasury does not provide an expected return as other investments do. No company can exist by investing only in its own stock. The decision to repurchase should involve distribution of unused funds when the firm's investment opportunities are not sufficiently attractive to employ those funds, either now or in the foresee-

---

[7] See Edwin J. Elton and Martin J. Gruber, "The Effect of Share Repurchases on the Value of the Firm," *Journal of Finance*, 23 (March 1968), 135–50.

[8] The tax consequences involved in the repurchase of stock are complex and, in places, ambiguous. In most cases, the monies received by stockholders who tender their shares are subject to the capital gains tax. Under certain circumstances, however, the distribution can be treated as ordinary income to the redeeming stockholder. If the stockholders' percentage of ownership of the company after the tender is greater than .80 of their percentage prior to the tender, the repurchase can be treated as ordinary income by the Internal Revenue Service. This problem can be avoided if the company obtains an advance ruling from the IRS that the repurchase of stock is not equivalent to a dividend.

able future. The repurchase of stock cannot be treated as an investment decision as we define the term.

Repurchase may be regarded as a financing decision, however, provided its purpose is to alter the capital structure proportions of the firm. By issuing debt and repurchasing stock, a firm can immediately change its debt-to-equity ratio toward a greater proportion of debt. In this case, the repurchase of stock is a financing decision, because the alternative is to not pay out dividends. Only when there is excess cash can the repurchase of stock be treated as a dividend decision.

Possible Signaling Effect

In addition to the factors considered, stock repurchases may have a signaling effect. For example, a positive signal might be sent to the market if management believed the stock were undervalued and they were constrained in not being able to tender shares they owned individually. According to this line of reasoning, the premium in repurchase price over existing share price would reflect management's belief about the degree of undervaluation. The idea is that concrete actions speak louder than words. In separate empirical studies Dann and Vermaelen find evidence supporting the signaling effect, particularly for tender offers as opposed to open-market purchases.[9]

While dividends and repurchases are similar informationally in that they are paid with cash, they also are somewhat different. The regular cash dividend provides ongoing reinforcement of the underlying ability of the firm to generate cash. It is like a quarterly news release and can be habit forming. In contrast, share repurchase is not a regular event. It may be viewed more as an "extra" used on occasions when management believes the stock is greatly undervalued.[10] Because both dividends and repurchases are done with cash, management has a disincentive to give false signals and implicitly pledges itself to provide cash-flow results consistent with the signal.

ADDITIONAL CONSIDERATIONS

Procedural Aspects

When the board of directors of a corporation declares a cash dividend, it specifies a **record date.** At the close of business that day, a list of stockholders is drawn up from the stock transfer books of the company. Stockholders on the list

Record date. The date set for determining whether a person who buys a stock is entitled to a dividend, a right, or something else.

---

[9] Larry Y. Dann, "Common Stock Repurchases: An Analysis of Returns to Bondholders and Stockholders," *Journal of Financial Economics*, 9 (June 1981), 113–38; and Theo Vermaelen, "Common Stock Repurchases and Market Signalling," *Journal of Economics*, 9 (June 1981), 139–83.

[10] See Paul Asquith and David W. Mullins, Jr., "Signalling with Dividends, Stock Repurchases, and Equity Issues," *Financial Management*, 15 (Autumn 1986), 27–44.

are entitled to the dividend, whereas stockholders who come on the books after the date of record are not entitled to the dividend. When the board of directors of United Chemical Company met on May 8, it declared a dividend of 25 cents a share payable June 15 to stockholders of record on May 31. Jennifer Doakes owned the stock on May 31, so she is entitled to the dividend even though she might sell her stock prior to the dividend actually being paid on June 15.

A problem can develop in the sale of stock in the days immediately prior to the date of record. The buyer and the seller of the stock have several days to settle, that is, to pay for the stock or to deliver it, in the case of the seller. As a result, the company may not be notified of the stock transfer in sufficient time. For this reason, the brokerage community has a rule whereby new stockholders are entitled to dividends only if they purchase the stock four business days prior to the date of record. If the stock is purchased after that time, the stockholder is not entitled to the dividend. The date itself is known as the **ex-dividend** date. In our example, the date of record was May 31. If this were a Friday, four business days before would be May 27, and this would be the ex-dividend date. To receive the dividend, a new stockholder must purchase the stock on May 26 or before. If purchased on May 27 or after, the stock is said to be ex-dividend. That is, it is without the 25-cent dividend.

Once a dividend is declared, stockholders become general creditors of the company until the dividend is actually paid; the declared but unpaid dividend is a current liability of the company coming out of retained earnings.

Ex-dividend. The date at which a purchaser of a stock is no longer entitled to the declared dividend.

Automatic Dividend Reinvestment Plans.   A number of large companies have instigated automatic dividend reinvestment plans (ADR plans). Under these plans, stockholders can reinvest the dividends that they would receive in the stock of the company. The stock involved can be either existing stock or newly issued stock. If it is existing stock, a bank acting as trustee accumulates funds from all stockholders wishing to reinvest and then purchases shares in the open market. The stockholder must bear the brokerage costs, but these costs are relatively low because the trustee buys stock in volume.

Some plans provide for purchase at a discount from the current market price of the stock. Normally the discount is 5 percent, and it serves as an inducement for reinvestment. Even though reinvested, the dividend is taxable to the stockholder as ordinary income, and this is a major disadvantage to the taxable stockholder. (The exception is public utilities stocks, where reinvested dividends are not immediately taxed.) Companies offering such plans have found that shareholder participation is around 20 percent. The number of companies using dividend reinvestment plans has increased steadily from their origination in the early 1970s. Utilities are the dominant user, followed by banks. Industrial companies have made only limited use of such plans.

Legal Restrictions

Capital Restriction.   Although state laws vary considerably, most states prohibit the payment of dividends if these dividends impair capital. *Capital* is defined in some states as the par value of the common stock. If a firm had 1 million shares outstanding with a $2 par value, total capital would be $2 million. If the net worth of a company were $2.1 million, the company could not pay a cash dividend totaling $200,000 without impairing capital.

Other states define *capital* to include not only the par value of the common stock but also the paid-in capital. Under such statutes, dividends can be paid only out of retained earnings. The purpose of the capital-impairment laws is to protect creditors of a corporation, and they may have some effect when a corporation is relatively new. With established companies that have been profitable in the past and have built up retained earnings, substantial losses will usually have been incurred before the restriction has an effect. By this time, the situation may be sufficiently hopeless that the restriction gives creditors little protection.

Insolvency.   Some states prohibit the payment of cash dividends if the company is insolvent. *Insolvency* is defined either in a legal sense, as liabilities exceeding assets, or in a technical sense, as the firm's being unable to pay its creditors as obligations come due. As the ability of the firm to pay its obligations is dependent on its liquidity rather than on its capital, the technical insolvency restriction gives creditors a good deal of protection. When cash is limited, a company is restricted from favoring stockholders to the detriment of creditors.

Excess Accumulation of Cash.   The Internal Revenue Code prohibits the undue retention of earnings. Although *undue retention* is defined vaguely, it usually is thought to be retention significantly in excess of the present and future investment needs of the company. The purpose of the law is to prevent companies from retaining earnings for the sake of avoiding taxes. For example, a company might retain all its earnings and build up a substantial cash and marketable securities position. The entire company then could be sold, and stockholders would be subject only to a capital gains tax, which is postponed relatively to what would occur if dividends were paid. If the IRS can prove unjustified retention, it can impose penalty tax rates on the accumulation. Whenever a company does build up a substantial liquid position, it has to be sure that it can justify the retention of these funds to the IRS. Otherwise, it may be in order to pay the excess funds out to stockholders as dividends.

SUMMARY

The critical question in dividend policy is whether dividends have an influence upon the value of the firm, given its investment decision. If dividends are irrelevant, as Modigliani and Miller believe, the firm should retain earnings only in keeping with its investment opportunities. If there are not sufficient investment opportunities to provide expected returns in excess of those required, the unused funds should be paid out as dividends. The key issue is whether dividends are more than just a means of distributing unused funds. With perfect capital markets and an absence of taxes, stockholders can manufacture "homemade" dividends, making dividend payout irrelevant. With differential taxes on dividends and capital gains, there seemingly is a bias in favor of retention. However, different investors are affected differently. The market imperfection of flotation costs biases things in favor of retention because retention is less expensive than the common stock financing used to replace the dividend. Restrictions on the investment behavior of financial institutions work in the direction of a preference for dividends. Other imperfections also are part of the picture.

Empirical testing of dividend policy has focused on whether there is a tax effect and whether dividends serve as signals in conveying information. The evidence is conflicting with respect to the former, ranging from a neutral effect to a negative effect. However, there seems to be agreement that dividends provide financial signals. In the final analysis, we are unable to state whether the dividend payout of the firm should be more than a passive decision variable. Most academics think not. Admittedly, many companies behave as if dividend policy is relevant, but the case for it is not conclusive.

When a company is faced with a dividend decision, managerial considerations include the funds needs of the firm, business risk, liquidity, ability to borrow, assessment of any valuation information, control, and restrictions in a bond indenture or loan agreement. Many people feel that the stability of dividends has a positive effect on the market price of the stock. Stable dividends may tend to resolve uncertainty in the minds of investors, particularly when earnings per share drop. Stable dividends also may have a positive utility to investors interested in current periodic income. Many companies appear to follow the policy of a target dividend-payout ratio, increasing dividends only when they feel that an increase in earnings can be sustained. The use of an extra dividend permits a cyclical company to maintain a stable record of regular dividends while paying additional dividends whenever earnings are unusually high.

A stock dividend pays additional stock to stockholders. It is used frequently to conserve cash and to reduce the cash dividend-payout ratio of the firm. Theoretically, the stock dividend is not a thing of value to the stockholder unless cash dividends per share remain unchanged or are increased. A more effective device for reducing market price per share is a stock split. With a split, the number of shares is increased by the terms of the split; for example, 3-for-1 split means that the number of shares is tripled. Both stock dividends and stock splits appear to have an informational or signaling effect. When other things are held constant, share price tends to rise around the time of the announcement, consistent with a positive signal. In a reverse stock split, the number of shares outstanding is reduced and the signal to the market usually is negative.

A company's repurchase of its own stock should be treated as a dividend decision when the firm has funds in excess of present and foreseeable future investment needs. It may distribute these funds either as dividends or by the repurchase of stock. In the absence of a tax differential between dividends and capital gains, the monetary value of the two alternatives should be about the same. With the tax differential, there is a tax advantage to the repurchase of stock. Because of objections by the Internal Revenue Service, repurchase of stock cannot be used in lieu of regular dividends. Finally, we examined various procedural aspects associated with paying dividends as well as certain legal restrictions.

QUESTIONS

1. What weakness do you see in the Walter formula as the indicator of an optimal dividend policy? Consider carefully the firm's investment opportunities and optimal capital structure before you answer.

2. Contrast a passive dividend-payout policy with an active one.

3. How does an investor manufacture "homemade" dividends? What is the effect of the actions of a number of investors doing so, all other things held constant?

4. How do taxes affect the return to investors? Are they a consideration in the dividend-payout decision?

5. Why do companies with high growth rates tend to have low dividend-payout ratios and companies with low growth rates high payout ratios?

6. What is financial signaling as it relates to cash dividends, stock dividends and splits, and repurchase of stock?

7. From a managerial standpoint, how does the firm's liquidity and ability to borrow affect the dividend-payout ratio?

8. As the firm's financial manager, would you recommend to the board of directors that the firm adopt as policy a stable dividend payment per share or a stable payout ratio? What are the disadvantages of each? Would the firm's industry influence your decision? Why?

9. What is a target dividend-payout ratio? An extra cash dividend?

10. Define a stock dividend and a stock split. What is their impact on share value?

11. Are regular stock dividends valuable to investors? Why or why not?

12. If we wish to raise share price, is not it a good idea to have a reverse stock split?

13. As an investor, would you prefer the firm to repurchase its stock by means of a tender offer or through open market operations? Why?

14. If repurchase of stock has a favorable tax effect, why would a company ever want to pay a cash dividend?

15. When earnings turn bad, why are boards of directors of companies reluctant to reduce the dividend?

16. Why do lenders frequently place a formal restriction in the loan agreement or the indenture on the amount of dividends that can be paid?

17. What is an automatic dividend reinvestment plan and how might it help stockholders?

18. Is the dividend decision really a financing decision in disguise?

SELF-CORRECTION PROBLEMS

---

1. The Beta-Alpha Company expects with some degree of certainty to generate the following net income and to have the following capital expenditures during the next 5 years (in thousands):

YEAR	1	2	3	4	5
Net income	$2,000	$1,500	$2,500	$2,300	$1,800
Capital expenditures	1,000	1,500	2,000	1,500	2,000

The company currently has 1 million shares of common stock outstanding and pays dividends of $1 per share.

a. Determine dividends per share and external financing required in each year if dividend policy is treated as a residual decision.

b. Determine the amounts of external financing in each year that will be necessary if the present dividend per share is maintained.

c. Determine dividends per share and the amounts of external financing that will be necessary if a dividend payout ratio of 50 percent is maintained.

d. Under which of the three dividend policies are aggregate dividends maximized? external financing minimized?

2. Do-Re-Me Corporation makes musical instruments and experiences only moderate growth. The company has just paid a dividend and is contemplating a dividend of $1.35 per share 1 year hence. The present market price per share is $15, and stock price appreciation of 5 percent per annum is expected.

a. If the required equity return were 14 percent and we lived in a no-tax world, what would be the market price per share at the end of the year using the Miller-Modigliani model? What would be the price if no dividend were paid?

b. Jose Hernandez, a stockholder, is in a 30 percent tax bracket for ordinary income, but his effective tax rate for capital gains is 26 percent. If he were to hold the stock one year, what would be his expected after-tax return in dollars for each share held?

3. Darcy Dip Doodle Company's earnings per share over the last 10 years were the following:

YEAR	1	2	3	4	5	6	7	8	9	10
EPS ($)	1.70	1.82	1.44	1.88	2.18	2.32	1.84	2.23	2.50	2.73

a. Determine annual dividends per share under the following policies:
   (1) A constant dividend-payout ratio of 40 percent (to the nearest cent).
   (2) A regular dividend of 80 cents and an extra dividend to bring the payout ratio to 40 percent if it otherwise would fall below.
   (3) A stable dividend that is occasionally raised. The payout ratio may range between 30 percent and 50 percent in any given year, but it should average approximately 40 percent.

b. What are the valuation implications of each of these policies?

4. The Kleidon King Company has the following stockholders' equity account:

Common stock ($8 par value)	$ 2,000,000
Paid-in capital	1,600,000
Retained earnings	8,400,000
Total net worth	$12,000,000

The current market price of the stock is $60 per share.

a. What will happen to this account and to the number of shares outstanding with a 20 percent stock dividend?
b. With a 2-for-1 stock split?
c. With a 1-for-2 reverse stock split?
d. In the absence of an informational or signaling effect, at what share price should the common sell after the 20 percent stock dividend? What might happen if there were a signaling effect?

PROBLEMS

1. The Peters Company's equity account (book value) is as follows:

The Peters Company equity accounts December 31, 19x8

Common stock ($5 par, 1,000,000 shares)	$ 5,000,000
Paid-in capital	5,000,000
Retained earnings	$15,000,000
Total net worth	$25,000,000

Currently, Peters is under pressure from stockholders to pay some dividends. Peters's cash balance is $500,000, all of which is needed for transactions purposes. The stock is trading for $7 a share.

a. What is the legal limit that can be paid in cash dividends?

    b. Compute the equity account if the company pays a 20 percent stock dividend.

    c. Compute the equity account if the company declares a 6-for-5 stock split.

2. Malkor Instruments Company treats dividends as a residual decision. It expects to generate $2 million in net earnings after taxes in the coming year. The company has an all-equity capital structure, and its cost of equity capital is 15 percent. The company treats this cost as the opportunity cost of retained earnings. Because of flotation costs and underpricing, the cost of common stock financing is higher. It is 16 percent.

    a. How much in dividends (out of the $2 million in earnings) should be paid if the company has $1.5 million in projects whose expected returns exceed 15 percent?

    b. How much in dividends should be paid if it has $2 million in projects whose expected returns exceed 15 percent?

    c. How much in dividends should be paid if it has $3 million in projects whose expected returns exceed 16 percent? What else should be done?

3. The Mann Company belongs to a risk class for which the appropriate capitalization rate is 15 percent. It currently has outstanding 100,000 shares selling at $100 each. The firm is contemplating the declaration of a $5 dividend at the end of the current fiscal year, which just began. Answer the following questions based on the Modigliani and Miller model and the assumption of no taxes.

    a. What will be the price of the stock at the end of the year if a dividend is not declared? What will it be if one is?

    b. Assuming that the firm pays the dividend, has net income of $1 million, and makes new investments of $2 million during the period, how many new shares must be issued?

    c. Is the MM model realistic with respect to valuation? What factors might mar its validity?

4. For each of the companies described here, would you expect it to have a medium, high, or a low dividend-payout ratio? Explain why.

    a. A company with a large proportion of inside ownership, all of whom are high-income individuals

    b. A growth company with an abundance of good investment opportunities

    c. A company that has high liquidity and much unused borrowing capacity and is experiencing ordinary growth

    d. A dividend-paying company that experiences an unexpected drop in earnings from a trend

    e. A company with volatile earnings and high business risk

5. Forte Papers Corporation and Great Southern Paper Company are in the same industry, both are publicly held with a large number of stockholders, and they have the following characteristics:

	FORTE	GREAT SOUTHERN
Expected annual cash flow (in thousands)	$ 50,000	$35,000
Standard deviation of cash flows (in thousands)	30,000	25,000
Annual capital expenditures (in thousands)	42,000	40,000
Cash and marketable securities (in thousands)	5,000	7,000
Existing long-term debt (in thousands)	100,000	85,000
Unused short-term line of credit (in thousands)	25,000	10,000
Flotation costs and underpricing on common stock issues as a percent of proceeds	.05	.08

On the basis of this information, which company is likely to have the higher dividend payout ratio? Why?

6. The Axalt Corporation and the Baxalt Corporation have had remarkably similar earnings patterns over the last 5 years. In fact, both firms have had identical earnings per share. Further, both firms are in the same industry, produce the same product, and face the same business and financial risks. In short, these firms are carbon copies of each other in every respect but one: Axalt paid out a constant percentage of its earnings (50 percent) in dividends, while Baxalt has paid a constant cash dividend. The financial manager of the Axalt Corporation has been puzzled by the fact that the price of his firm's stock has been generally lower than the price of Baxalt's stock, even though in some years Axalt's dividend was substantially larger than Baxalt's.

   a. What might account for the condition that has been puzzling the financial manager of Axalt?

   b. What might be done by both companies to increase the market prices of their stock?

	AXALT			BAXALT		
YEARS	EPS	Div.	Mkt Price	ESP	Div.	Mkt Price
1	$1.00	.50	$6	$1.00	.23	4\frac{7}{8}$
2	.50	.25	4	.50	.23	4$\frac{3}{8}$
3	−.25	nil	2	−.25	.23	4
4	.30	.15	3	.30	.23	4$\frac{1}{4}$
5	.50	.25	3$\frac{1}{2}$	.50	.23	4$\frac{1}{2}$

7. The Canales Copper Company declared a 25 percent stock dividend on March 10 to stockholders of record on April 1. The market price of the stock is $50 per share. You own 160 shares of the stock.

a. If you sold your stock on March 20, what would be the price per share, all other things the same (no signaling effect)?

b. After the stock dividend is paid, how many shares of stock will you own?

c. At what price would you expect the stock to sell on April 2, all other things the same (no signaling effect)?

d. What will be the total value of your holdings before and after the stock dividend, all other things the same?

e. If there were an informational or signaling effect, what would be the effect on share price?

8. The Sherill Corporation capital structure December 30, 19x3

Common stock ($1 par, 1,000,000 shares)	$1,000,000
Paid-in capital	300,000
Retained earnings	1,700,000
Net worth	$3,000,000

The firm earned $300,000 after taxes in 19x3 and paid out 50 percent of these earnings as cash dividends. The price on the firm's stock on December 30 was $5.

a. If the firm declared a stock dividend of 3 percent of December 31, what would be the reformulated capital structure?

b. Assuming the firm paid no stock dividend, how much would earnings per share be for 19x3? dividends per share?

c. Assuming a 3 percent stock dividend, what would happen to EPS and DPS for 19x3?

d. What would the price of the stock be after the 3 percent stock dividend if there were no signaling or other effects?

9. Johore Trading Company has 2.4 million shares of common stock outstanding, and the present market price per share is $36. Its equity capitalization is as follows:

Common stock, $2.00 par	$ 4,800,000
Paid-in capital	5,900,000
Retained earnings	87,300,000
Net worth	$98,000,000

a. If the company were to declare a 12 percent stock dividend, what would happen to these accounts? a 25 percent stock dividend? a 5 percent stock dividend?

b. If, instead, the company declared a 3-for-2 stock split, what would happen to the accounts? a 2-for-1 stock split? a 3-for-1 split?

c. What would happen if there were a reverse stock split of 1-for-4? 1-for-6?

10. The T. N. Cox Company is owned by several wealthy Texans. The firm earned $3,500,000 after taxes this year. With 1 million shares outstanding, earnings per share were $3.50. The stock recently has traded at $72 per share, among the current stockholders. Two dollars of this value is accounted for by investor anticipation of a cash dividend. As financial manager of T. N. Cox, you have contemplated the alternative of repurchasing the company stock by means of a tender offer at $72 per share.

a. How much stock could the firm repurchase if this alternative were selected?

b. Ignoring taxes, which alternative should be selected?

c. Considering taxes, which alternative should be selected?

11. On February 2, 1989, the board of directors of International Zinc and Iron Corporation met and declared a 20 cent per share cash dividend payable March 20 to stockholders of record on March 1.

a. If you wished to buy the stock before it went ex-dividend, by what date would you need to make your purchase?

b. If you already own the stock but the company declares bankruptcy on March 10, what happens to your dividend?

c. If there are 8 million shares outstanding, what will happen to cash, the dividend-payable account (current liabilities), and to retained earnings on February 2? on March 20?

SOLUTIONS TO
SELF-CORRECTION PROBLEMS

1. **a.**

YEAR	INCOME AVAILABLE FOR DIVIDENDS	DIVIDENDS PER SHARE	EXTERNAL FINANCING
1	$1,000	$1.00	0
2	0	0	0
3	500	0.50	0
4	800	0.80	0
5	0	0	$200
	$2,300		$200

b.

YEAR	(1) NET INCOME	(2) DIVIDENDS	(3) CAPITAL EXPENDITURES	(4) EXTERNAL FINANCING (2) + (3) − (1)
1	$2,000	$1,000	$1,000	0
2	1,500	1,000	1,500	$1,000
3	2,500	1,000	2,000	500
4	2,300	1,000	1,500	200
5	1,800	1,000	2,000	1,200
		$5,000		$2,900

c.

YEAR	(1) NET INCOME	(2) DIVIDENDS	(3) DIVIDENDS PER SHARE	(4) CAPITAL EXPENDITURES	(5) EXTERNAL FINANCING (2) + (4) − (1)
1	$2,000	$1,000	$1.00	$1,000	0
2	1,500	750	.75	1,500	$ 750
3	2,500	1,250	1.25	2,000	750
4	2,300	1,150	1.15	1,500	350
5	1,800	900	.90	2,000	1,100
		$5,050			$2,950

d. Aggregate dividends are highest under alternative C, which involves a 50 percent dividend payout. However, they are only slightly higher than that which occurs under alternative B. External financing is minimized under alternative A, the residual dividend policy.

2. **a.** According to Modigliani-Miller, the payment of any dividend must be offset by equity financing if capital structure is to be held constant. Thus, $P_1 = P_0(1 + \rho) − D_1$, where P_0 is the market price per share at time 0, P_1 is share price at time 1, ρ is the capitalization rate for the firm, and D_1 is the dividend per share at time 1. With a dividend, $P_1 = \$15(1 + .14) − \$1.35 = \$15.75$. Without a dividend, $P_1 = \$15(1 + .14) − 0 = \$17.10$. For the $15.75, the dividend of $1.35 brings total value at time 1 to $17.10. Thus, the investor would have the same total value either way.

	AMOUNT	TAX RATE	TAX	AFTER-TAX AMOUNT
Dividend	$1.35	30%	$.405	$ .945
Capital gain	.75	26	.195	.555
Total after-tax return				$1.500

$75,000,000

Northern California Public Utility Company
13¾% FIRST MORTGAGE BONDS DUE 2019

Interest payable September 1 and March 1. The bonds are redeemable on 30 days' notice at the option of the company at 113.75% to and including March 1, 1990, at decreasing prices thereafter to and including March 1, 2011, and thereafter at 100%. Due March 1, 2019.

Application will be made to list the bonds on the New York Stock Exchange.

THESE SECURITIES HAVE NOT BEEN APPROVED OR DISAPPROVED BY THE SECURITIES AND EXCHANGE COMMISSION NOR HAS THE COMMISSION PASSED UPON THE ACCURACY OR ADEQUACY OF THIS PROSPECTUS. ANY REPRESENTATION TO THE CONTRARY IS A CRIMINAL OFFENSE.

	Price to Public (1)	Underwriting Discounts and Commissions (2)	Proceeds to Company (1) (3)
Per unit	99.750%	0.875%	98.875%
Total	$74,812,500	$656,250	$74,156,250

(1) Plus accrued interest from March 1, 1989 to date of delivery and payment.
(2) The company has agreed to indemnify the several purchasers against certain civil liabilities.
(3) Before deducting expenses payable by the company estimated at $200,000.

The new bonds are offered by the several purchasers named herein subject to prior sale, when, as and if issued and accepted by the purchasers and subject to their right to reject any orders for the purchase of the new bonds, in whole or in part. It is expected that the new bonds will be ready for delivery on or about March 12, 1989 in New York City.

HENDERSHOTT, KANE AND KAUFMAN

ELTON AND GRUBER   LITZENBERGER, MCDONALD, PARKER
                                        AND PORTERFIELD
BRENNAN, KRAUS AND SCHWARTZ   UPSTAIRS AND DOWNING
                        CARLETON, PINCHES, REILLY, AND YAWITZ
BLACK, MERTON AND SCHOLES   MODIGLIANI, MILLER, KIM,
                                        ROLL AND SHARPE

The date of this prospectus is March 5, 1989.

FIGURE 19-1
Sample cover of a prospectus

ment bankers are invited into syndicates, and their participations are determined primarily on the basis of their ability to distribute securities. For this function, an investment banker is rewarded by a selling concession of so many dollars a bond. In the Northern California Public Utility offering, the selling concession was $5 per bond, or 57 percent of the total spread of $8.75. The ultimate seller can be either a member of the underwriting syndicate or a qualified outside security dealer. To earn the full concession, however, the seller must be a member of the syndicate. An outside security dealer must purchase bonds from a member and will obtain only a dealer concession, which is less than the full selling concession. In our example, the outside dealer concession was $2.50 per bond out of a total selling concession of $5.00.

Best efforts offering. A security offering where the investment bank agrees to do its best to sell it. No guarantee of sale as occurs with an underwriting.

Best Efforts Offering.   Instead of underwriting a security issue, investment bankers may sell the issue on a **best efforts** basis. Under this arrangement, the investment bankers agree to sell only as many securities as they can at an established price. They have no responsibility for securities that are unsold. In other words, they bear no risk. Investment bankers frequently are unwilling to underwrite a security issue of smaller, nontechnological companies. For these companies, the only feasible means by which to place securities may be through a best efforts offering.

Making a Market.   On occasion, the underwriter will make a market for a security after it is issued. In the first public offering of common stock, making a market is important to investors. In making a market, the underwriter maintains a position in the stock, quotes bid and asked prices, and stands ready to buy and sell it at those prices. These quotations are based on underlying supply and demand conditions. With a secondary market, the stock has greater liquidity to investors; this appeal enhances the success of the original offering.

Shelf Registrations

The distinguishing feature of the traditional underwriting is that the registration process with the Securities and Exchange Commission takes at least several weeks to complete. (The process itself is described later in the chapter.) Often two or more months elapse between the time a company decides to finance and the time the security offering actually takes place. As a result of this time lapse as well as the fixed costs associated with a registration, there is an incentive for having a large as opposed to a small security offering.

Shelf registration. Rule 415 of the Securities and Exchange Commission permitting a corporation to file one registration statement covering a number of successive security issues.

    Large corporations, whose securities are listed on an exchange, are able to shortcut the registration process by filing only a brief statement under Rule 415. This rule, which was initiated in 1982, permits what is known as a **shelf registration**. Here a company files an amendment to its detailed SEC filing every time it wishes to sell new securities. Mostly this amendment contains details about the specific security being offered. Information about the company and risks inherent in its operations is found in the regular required SEC report, which provides the authority under which the individual shelf registrations occur. By using a shelf registration, a company is able to go to market with a new issue in a matter of days as opposed to weeks or months. As a result, it has the flexibility to time issues to market conditions, and the issues themselves need not be large.

Flotation Costs and Other Repercussions.   In effect, a corporation places securities it expects to use in financing over the next two years on the "shelf," and from time to time it auctions off some of them. Therein lies the second major distinction between a shelf registration and a traditional underwriting. Obviously, the company will select the low-cost bidder. In this regard, large corporations are able to play investment bankers off against each other, and the resulting competition is left in reduced spreads. For example, a typical spread on a traditional underwriting of corporate bonds is $7.50 or $8.75 per bond; the spread on a shelf registration might be $2 or $3 a bond. Flotation costs for a large common stock issue, again using a traditional underwriting, might run 3 to 4 percent of the gross proceeds.[1] With a shelf registration, an SEC study indicated that these costs would run about 2 to 3 percent. In addition, the fixed costs of public debt issues (legal and administrative) are lower with a shelf registration because there is but one registration. Therefore, it is not surprising that large corporations have turned to shelf registrations.

For the somewhat smaller corporation, which must resort to a traditional underwriting, the widespread use of shelf registrations may work to their disadvantage. While there are far fewer traditional underwritings than before, the spreads for these underwritings do not appear to have widened. Mostly investment banks have absorbed the lower profitability associated with shelf registrations in reduced overall underwriting profitabilty. However, the amount of free advice available to a company is less than before. When overall underwriting profits were large, investment banks competed with all kinds of free advisory services, concerning such things as conditions and timing in the capital markets and financial strategy. As the lucrative underwriting business suffered, investment banks cut back on the free services they offered. Overall, then, shelf registrations have had a profound effect on the way in which securities, particularly debt instruments, are distributed, on the number of traditional underwritings, and on the function of investment banks.

RIGHTS OFFERINGS

Instead of selling a security issue to new investors, many firms offer the securities first to existing shareholders on a **privileged subscription** basis. This type of offering is known as a rights offering. Frequently, the corporate charter requires that a new issue of common stock or an issue of securities convertible into common be offered first to existing shareholders because of their preemptive right.

Privileged subscription. The sale of security to existing stockholders. Also known as a rights offering.

---

[1] For smaller issues, flotation costs, as a percentage of the gross proceeds of the issue, are higher.

Preemptive Right

Preemptive right. The right given to common stockholders to purchase new issues of common stock, or securities convertible into common, in order to preserve their proportional ownership.

Under a preemptive right, existing common stockholders have the right to preserve their proportionate ownership in the corporation. If the corporation issues additional common stock, they must be given the right to subscribe to the new stock so that they maintain their pro rata interest in the company. You may own 100 shares of a corporation that decides to make a new common stock offering for the purpose of increasing outstanding shares by 10 percent. If you have a preemptive right, you must be given the option to buy 10 additional shares so that you can preserve your proportionate ownership in the company. Various states have different laws regarding preemptive rights, but most of them provide that a stockholder has a preemptive right unless the corporate charter otherwise denies it.

Terms of Offering

When a company offers its securities for sale by privileged subscription, it mails to its stockholders one right for each share of stock they hold. With a common stock offering, the rights give stockholders the option to purchase additional shares according to the terms of the offering. The terms specify the number of rights required to subscribe for an additional share of stock, the subscription price per share, and the expiration date of the offering. The holder of rights has three choices: (1) exercise them and subscribe for additional shares; (2) sell them, because they are transferable; or (3) do nothing and let them expire. The last usually occurs only if the value of a right is negligible or if the stockholder owns but a few shares of stock. Generally, the subscription period is 3 weeks or less. A stockholder who wishes to buy a share of additional stock but does not have the necessary number of rights may purchase additional rights. If you now own 85 shares of stock in a company, and the number of rights required to purchase 1 additional share is 10, your 85 rights would allow you to purchase only 8 full shares of stock. If you would like to buy the ninth share, you may do so by purchasing an additional 5 rights.

In a rights offering, the board of directors establishes a date of record. Investors who buy the stock prior to that date receive the right to subscribe to the new issue. The stock is said to sell **with rights on** prior to the date of record. After the date of record, the stock is said to sell *ex-rights;* that is, the stock is traded without the rights attached. An investor who buys the stock after this date does not receive the right to subscribe to additional stock.

Rights on. Security traded with rights.

Value of Rights

The market value of a right is a function of the present market price of the stock, the subscription price, and the number of rights required to purchase an additional share of stock. The theoretical market value of one right after the offering is announced but while the stock is still selling rights-on is

$$R_o = \frac{P_o - S}{N + 1} \qquad (19\text{-}1)$$

where R_o = market value of one right when stock is selling rights-on
$\quad P_o$ = market value of a share of stock selling rights-on
$\quad S$ = subscription price per share
$\quad N$ = number of rights required to purchase one share of stock.

If the market price of a stock is \$100 a share, the subscription price is \$90 a share, and it takes 4 rights to buy an additional share of stock, the theoretical value of a right when the stock is selling rights-on is

$$R_o = \frac{100 - 90}{4 + 1} = \$2 \qquad (19\text{-}2)$$

We note that the market value of the stock with rights on contains the value of one right.

When the stock goes **ex-rights**, the market price theoretically declines, for investors no longer receive the right to subscribe to additional shares. The theoretical value of one share of stock when it goes ex-rights is

Ex-rights. The date at which a purchaser of a stock is no longer entitled to subscription rights to buy new shares.

$$P_x = \frac{(P_o \times N) + S}{N + 1} \qquad (19\text{-}3)$$

where P_x = market price of stock when it goes ex-rights. For our example,

$$P_x = \frac{(100 \times 4) + 90}{4 + 1} = \$98$$

From this example, we see that, theoretically, the right does not represent a thing of value to the stockholder, whose stock is worth \$100 before the date of record; after the date of record, it is worth \$98 a share. The decline in market price is offset exactly by the value of the right. Thus, theoretically, the stockholder does not benefit from a rights offering; the right represents merely a return of capital.

The theoretical value of a right when the stock sells ex-rights is

$$R_x = \frac{P_x - S}{N} \qquad (19\text{-}4)$$

where R_x = the market value of one right when the stock is selling ex-rights. If, in our example, the market price of the stock is \$98 when it goes ex-rights,

$$R_x = \frac{98 - 90}{4} = \$2$$

or the same value as before.

We should be aware that the actual value of a right may differ somewhat from its theoretical value on account of transaction costs, speculation, and the irregular exercise and sale of rights over the subscription period. However, arbitrage limits the deviation of actual value from theoretical value. If the price of a right is significantly higher than its theoretical value, stockholders will sell their rights and purchase the stock in the market. Such action will exert downward pressure on the market price of the right and upward pressure on its theoretical value. The latter occurs because of the upward pressure on the market price of the stock. If the price of the right is significantly lower than its theoretical value, arbitragers will buy the rights, exercise their option to buy stock, and then sell the stock in the market. This occurrence will exert upward pressure on the market price of the right and downward pressure on its theoretical value. These arbitrage actions will continue as long as they are profitable.

Success of the Offering

One of the most important aspects of a successful rights offering is the subscription price. If the market price of the stock should fall below the subscription price, stockholders obviously will not subscribe to the stock, for they can buy it in the market at a lower price. Consequently, a company will set the subscription price at a value lower than the current market price to reduce the risk of the market price's falling below it. We know that the stock should fall in price when it goes ex-rights. Its new theoretical value is determined by Eq. (19-3); and we see that it strongly depends on N, the number of rights required to purchase one share of stock. The greater the N, the less the theoretical price decline when the stock goes ex-rights. Thus, the risk that the market price will fall below the subscription price is inversely related to N.[2] To illustrate, suppose the following were true:

	COMPANY A	COMPANY B
Market value per share rights-on, P_o	$60.00	$60.00
Subscription price, S	$46.00	$46.00
Number of rights needed to purchase one share, N	1	10
Theoretical value of one share ex-rights, P_x	$53.00	$58.73

We see that Company A will have a greater decline in value per share when its stock goes ex-rights than will Company B. All other things being the same, there is a greater probability, or risk, that Company A's stock will fall below the subscription price of $46 than there is that Company B's stock will fall below it.

Apart from the number of rights required to purchase one share, the risk that the market price of a stock will fall below the subscription price is a function of the volatility of the company's stock, the tone of the market, expectations

---

[2] See Haim Levy and Marshall Sarnat, "Risk, Dividend Policy, and the Optimal Pricing of a Rights Offering," *Journal of Money, Credit, and Banking*, 3 (November 1971), 840–49.

of earnings, and other factors. To avoid all risk, a company can set the subscription price so far below the market price that there is virtually no possibility that the market price will fall below it. The greater the discount from the current market price, the greater the value of the right, and the greater the probability of a successful sale of stock. As long as stockholders do not allow their rights to expire, theoretically they neither gain nor lose by the offering. In other words, the subscription price is irrelevant if stockholders exercise their rights and subscribe for more shares or if they sell them. Therefore, it might seem feasible to set the subscription price at a substantial discount in order to assure a successful sale.

The greater the discount, however, the more shares that will have to be issued to raise a given amount of money, and the greater the dilution in earnings per share. This dilution may be of practical concern, for the investment community analyzes closely the growth trend in earnings per share. Significant underpricing of the new issue will dampen the growth trend in earnings per share. Although theoretically the stockholders are equally well off regardless of the subscription price set, in practice the market value of their stock holdings may suffer if investors in any way are fooled by the dilution in reported earnings per share. Obviously this would be an imperfection in the market, but imperfections on occasion can make a difference. There is no empirical evidence, however, to support the view that the amount of dilution in a rights offering matters.

If the firm wishes to maintain the same dividend per share, underpricing, which will result in more shares issued, will increase the total amount of dividends the company will need to pay and lower its coverage ratio. The disadvantages of underpricing must be balanced against the risk of the market price's falling below the subscription price. The primary consideration in setting the subscription price is to reduce the probability of this occurrence to a tolerable level. If, then, the subscription price appears to result in excessive dilution and this dilution seems to matter, the company should consider a public issue, wherein the amount of underpricing usually is less. For most rights offerings, the subscription price discount from the current market price ranges between 10 and 20 percent.

Standby Arrangement and Oversubscriptions

A company can ensure the complete success of a rights offering by having an investment banker or group of investment bankers "stand by" to underwrite the unsold portion of the issue. For this standby commitment, the underwriter charges a fee that varies with the risk involved in the offering. Often the fee consists of two parts: a flat fee and an additional fee for each unsold share of stock that the underwriter has to buy. From the standpoint of the company issuing the stock, the greater the risk of an unsuccessful sale, the more desirable a **standby arrangement,** although it also is more costly. In view of the high costs of a standby arrangement relative to the number of times they are needed, it is surprising that so many companies have their rights offerings underwritten.

Another means to increase the probability that the entire issue will be sold is through oversubscriptions. This device gives stockholders not only the right to subscribe for their proportional share of the total offering, but also the right to

Standby arrangement. Occurs in a rights issue where an underwriter agrees to purchase any unsold stock.

oversubscribe for any unsold shares. Oversubscriptions are then awarded on a pro rata basis relative to the number of unsold shares. Stockholders may subscribe to 460,000 shares of a 500,000-share rights offering. Perhaps some of them would like to purchase more shares, and their oversubscriptions total 100,000 shares. As a result, each stockholder oversubscribing is awarded four-tenths of a share for each share oversubscribed. This results in the entire issue being sold. Although the use of oversubscriptions increases the chances that the issue will be entirely sold, it does not ensure this occurrence, as does the standby agreement. It is possible that the combination of subscriptions and oversubscriptions will fall short of the amount of stock the company desires to sell.

Privileged Subscription versus Underwritten Issue

By offering stock first to existing stockholders, the company taps investors who are familiar with its operations. As a result, a successful sale is more probable. The principal sales tool is the discount from the current market price, whereas with a public issue, the major selling tool is the investment banking organization. Because the issue is not underwritten, the flotation costs of a rights offering are lower than the costs of an offering to the general public. Moreover, many stockholders feel that they should be given the first opportunity to buy new common shares.

Offsetting these advantages in the minds of some is that a rights offering will have to be sold at a lower price than will an issue to the general public. If a company goes to the equity market with reasonable frequency, this means that there will be somewhat more dilution with rights offerings than there will be with public issues. Even though this consideration is not relevant theoretically, many companies wish to minimize dilution and will choose the public offering. To the extent that there are information, legal, and institutional imperfections that influence this choice, existing shareholder wealth may be enhanced by a decision to go the public issue route. Examples of imperfections include financial reporting that masks the "true" trend in earnings per share, restraints on a company's issuing stock at below its book value, and possible institutional incentives for a company to sell stock at as high a price per share as possible. Also, a public offering will tend to result in a wider distribution of shares, which may be desirable to the company.

Although these factors may have an effect on shareholder wealth, we would expect their effect to be slight. The issue remains as to why so many companies incur the costs associated with underwriting when they could sell securities through a privileged subscription (without a standby arrangement) at less cost. Several explanations have been offered, including the concentration of stock ownership affecting the merchandising expense of a security issue and heterogeneous expectations causing an information effect.[3] Still the greater flotation

---

[3] For the former argument, see Robert S. Hansen and John M. Pinkerton, "Direct Equity Financing: A Resolution of a Paradox," *Journal of Finance*, 17 (June 1982), 651–65; for the latter, John Parsons and Artur Raviv, "Alternative Methods for Floating New Issues: Price Effects and the Benefits of an Underwritten Offering," Research paper, Kellogg School of Management, Northwestern University, Evanston, Ill., November 1982.

cost associated with an underwritten issue must be weighted carefully in reaching a financing decision.

REGULATION OF SECURITY OFFERINGS

Both the federal and state governments regulate the sale of new securities to the public, but federal authority is far more encompassing in its influence.

Federal Regulation

With the collapse of the stock market in 1929 and the subsequent depression, there came a cry to protect investors from misinformation and fraud. Congress undertook extensive investigations and proposed federal regulation of the securities industry. The *Securities Act of 1933* dealt with the sale of new securities and required the full disclosure of information to investors. The *Securities Exchange Act of 1934* dealt with the regulation of securities already outstanding. Moreover, it created the **Securities and Exchange Commission** to enforce the two acts.

Securities and Exchange Commission. The U.S. government agency responsible for policing the sale of securities and the organized exchanges.

Most corporations selling securities to the public must register the issue with the SEC. Certain types of corporations, such as railroads, are exempt because they are regulated by other authorities. In addition, a corporation selling $1.5 million or less in new securities is required to file only a limited amount of information with the SEC under Regulation A. Also, if the issue is entirely sold to citizens of a single state, it does not necessarily fall under the SEC. Most corporations, however, must file a detailed registration statement, which contains information such as the nature and history of the company, the use of the proceeds of the security issue, financial statements, the management and directors and their security holdings, competitive conditions and risks, legal opinions, and a description of the security being issued. Along with the registration statement, the corporation must file a copy of the *prospectus* (see Fig. 19-1). which is a summary of the essential information in the registration statement. The prospectus must be available to prospective investors and others who request it.

The SEC reviews the registration statement and the prospectus to see that all the required information is presented and that it is not misleading. If the SEC is satisfied with the information, it approves the registration, and the company is then able to issue a final prospectus and sell the securities. If not, the SEC issues a *stop order*, which prevents the sale of the securities. Most deficiencies can be corrected by the company, and approval will usually be given eventually, except in cases of fraud or misrepresentation. For serious violations of the 1933 Securities Act, the SEC is empowered to go to court and seek an injunction. It should be pointed out that the SEC is not concerned with the investment value of the securities being issued, only with the presentation of complete and accurate information of all material facts regarding the security. Investors must make their own decisions based on that information. The security being issued may well be a highly speculative one subject to considerable risk. As long as the information is correct, the SEC will not prevent its sale.

The minimum period required between the time a registration statement is filed and the time it becomes effective is 20 days. The usual time lapse, however, is around 40 days. As we discussed earlier, large corporations are able to use shelf registrations. Once a detailed report is filed covering a block of securities, the company is able to sell off the shelf by filing a simple amendment. The lapse in time in this case is very short—perhaps a day.

The SEC regulates the sale of securities in the secondary markets in addition to the sale of new issues. In this regard, it regulates the activities of the security exchanges, the over-the-counter market, investment bankers and brokers, the National Association of Security Dealers, and investment companies. It requires monthly reports on inside stock transactions by officers, directors, and large stockholders. Whenever an investor or group obtains 5 percent or more of the stock, it must file Form 13D, which alerts all to the accumulation and to subsequent changes in ownership. In its regulatory capacity, the SEC seeks to prevent manipulative practices by investment dealers and by officers and directors of the company, abuses by insiders (officers and directors) in transactions involving the company's stock, fraud by any party, and other abuses affecting the investing public.

State Regulation

Individual states have security commissions that regulate the issuance of new securities in their states. Like the SEC, these commissions seek to prevent the fraudulent sale of securities. The laws providing for state regulation of securities are known as blue-sky laws, because they attempt to prevent the false promotion and sale of securities representing nothing more than blue sky. State regulations are particularly important when a security issue is sold entirely to people within the state and is not subject to SEC scrutiny. In addition, it can be important when the amount of the issue is less than $1.5 million and subject to only limited SEC scrutiny. Unfortunately, the laws of the individual states vary greatly in their effectiveness. Some states are strict, others are fairly permissive, with the result that misrepresentative promotion can thrive.

PRIVATE PLACEMENTS

Rather than sell securities to the public or to existing stockholders through a privileged subscription, a corporation can sell the entire issue to a single institutional investor or a small group of such investors. This type of sale is known as a private or direct placement, for the company negotiates directly with the investor over the terms of the offering, eliminating the function of the underwriter. In what follows, we focus on the private placement of debt issues. Equity placements involving venture capitalists will be discussed later.

Features

One of the more frequently mentioned advantages of a private placement is the speed of the commitment. A public issue must be registered with the SEC, documents must be prepared and printed, and extensive negotiations undertaken; all this requires lead time. In addition, the public issue always involves risks with respect to timing. With a private placement, the terms can be tailored to the needs of the borrower, and the financing can be consummated quickly. However, the large corporation also can quickly tap the public market through a shelf registration.

Because the private placement of debt is negotiated, the exact timing in the market is not a critical problem. The fact that there is but a single investor or small group of investors is attractive if it becomes necessary to change any of the terms of the issue. It is much easier to deal with a single investor than with a large group of public security holders. A possible disadvantage in this regard, however, is that a single investor may monitor the company's operations in much greater detail than will a trustee for the purchasers of a public issue.

Another advantage of a privately placed debt issue is that the actual borrowing does not necessarily have to take place all at once. The company can enter into an arrangement whereby it can borrow up to a fixed amount over a period of time. For this nonrevolving credit arrangement, the borrower usually will pay a commitment fee. This type of arrangement gives the company flexibility, allowing it to borrow only when it needs the funds. Because the private placement does not have to be registered with the SEC, the company avoids making available to the public the detailed information required by the SEC.

Private placements allow medium-sized and sometimes small companies to sell a bond issue that they could not sell by public offering because flotation costs would be prohibitive. Institutional investors are willing to invest in bonds of these smaller companies, provided that the company is creditworthy. It is doubtful that institutional investors would seek an issue of less than $250,000 (and many insist upon a higher minimum), but we must remember that a $10 million bond issue is considered small as a public offering. The dominant lender in the private placement market is the life insurance category, though private and public pension funds are active as well.

Despite these advantages, the private placement market is less now than what it used to be. There are two reasons. The first is the shelf registration process described previously, which permits large companies to borrow quickly. The second is the development of the junk bond market. Before, lower grade companies (Ba and below) were not able to borrow in the public market. However, the junk bond market now permits their access, and many companies have substituted public debt for private placements.

Cost of Issue

There are two costs to consider in comparing a private placement of debt with a public offering: the initial costs and the interest cost. As the negotiations usually are direct, private placement involves no underwriting or selling expenses, except, perhaps, for services of an investment banker, whom companies frequently consult about planning and negotiating the issue. Nevertheless, the initial total cost of a private placement is usually significantly less than that of a public offering.

The second aspect of the cost of a private placement of debt is the interest cost. Fragmentary evidence indicates that the yield on private placements is above that on public offerings. In addition to interest costs, institutional investors sometimes will request an equity "sweetener," such as warrants, to entice them to invest in the debt issue of a company. While the exact cost of this "sweetener" is difficult to measure, it certainly adds to the total cost of a private placement. For a long-term debt issue, the total cost is likely to be somewhat higher for a private placement than for a public offering (initial and interest costs). Moreover, the difference in cost will vary somewhat over time as interest rates, in general, change. The difference in cost between the private placement and the public markets must be balanced against the advantages of the private placement.

SIGNALING EFFECTS

When a company announces a security issue, there may be an information effect that causes a stock market reaction. Holding constant market movements, scholars have found negative stock price reactions (or abnormal returns) to a common stock or convertible security issue.[4] Straight debt and preferred stock announcements do not tend to show a statistically significant effect. A typical reaction for stock-issue announcements is shown in Fig. 19-2, where days around the event are on the horizontal axis and the cumulative average abnormal return, after isolating overall market-movement effects, is along the vertical axis. As seen, a stock price reduction occurs around the announcement date and it tends to average about 3 percent.

Expectations of Future Cash Flows

Several explanations have been offered for this phenomenon. For one thing, the security issue announcement may be telling us something about future cash flows. When a company announces a security issue, the implication is that these funds will go to one or more purposes: investment in assets, reduction of debt, stock repurchase or increased dividends, or to make up for lower than expected operating cash flows. To the extent an unexpected security sale is associated with the last, the event will be bad news and the stock price accordingly may suffer.

---

[4] For an excellent synthesis of the empirical evidence, see Clifford W. Smith, Jr., "Investment Banking and the Capital Acquisition Process," *Journal of Financial Economics*, 15 (January–February 1986), 3–29. See also Paul Asquith and David W. Mullins, Jr., "Signalling with Dividends, Stock Repurchases, and Equity Issues," *Financial Management*, 15 (Autumn 1986), 27–44.

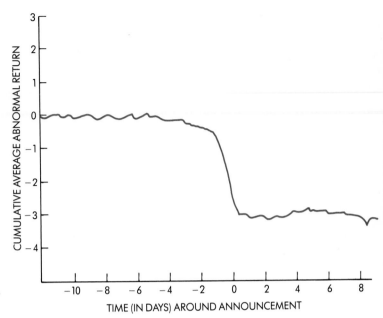

FIGURE 19-2
Relative stock returns around the announce-ment of a new equity issue

Asymmetric Information

A second effect has to do with asymmetric information between investors and management. The idea here is that potential investors in securities have less information than management, and that management tends to issue securities when the market's assessment of their value is higher than management's assessment.[5] This would be particularly true with common stock, where investors have only a residual claim to income and assets. Because cash flows are affected when a new security is offered, an asymmetric information effect is difficult to sort out using new issue data.

With an exchange offering of one security for another, however, cash flows are not affected. When empirical studies on exchange offers are categorized into those that increase leverage and those that decrease leverage, the results are striking.[6] Leverage-increasing transactions are accompanied by positive abnormal stock returns in the two days prior to announcement, while leverage-reducing transactions are accompanied by negative returns. The effect is greatest for debt-for-common exchanges (positive return) and common-for-debt exchanges (negative return), followed by preferred-for-common (positive return)

[5] See Stewart C. Myers and Nicholas S. Majluf, "Corporate Financing and Investment Decisions When Firms Have Information That Investors Do Not Have," *Journal of Financial Economics,* 13 (June 1984), 187–221.

[6] Again, the source of this categorization is Smith, "Investment Banking and the Capital Acquisition Process," 10–12. Included in exchange offers are pairwise combinations of debt, convertibles, preferred stock, and common stock.

and preferred-for-debt (negative return). Thus, the evidence is consistent with an asymmetric information effect. In other words, managers are more likely to issue debt or preferred when they believe the common stock is underpriced in the market and to issue common when they believe it is overpriced.

In summary, the issuance of new securities as well as exchange offerings appears to cause information effects that impact stock prices. The financial manager must be mindful of these potential effects before a decision is reached.

SUMMARY

When companies finance their long-term needs externally, they may obtain funds from the capital markets or directly from a single institutional investor or a small group of them. If the financing involves a public offering, the company often will use the services of an investment banking firm. The investment banker's principal functions are risk bearing, or underwriting, and selling the securities. For these functions, the investment banking firm is compensated by the spread between the price it pays for the securities and the price at which it resells the securities to investors. The offering itself can be either a traditional underwriting or, in the case of a large corporation, a shelf registration. With a shelf registration, a company sells securities "off the shelf" without the delays associated with a lengthy registration process. Instead, only an amendment is filed with the Securities and Exchange Commission. Not only is the shelf registration faster, but the cost of the issue is a good deal less.

A company may give its existing stockholders the first opportunity to purchase a new security issue on a privileged subscription basis. This type of issue is known as a rights offering, because existing stockholders receive one right for each share of stock they hold. A right represents an option to buy the new security at the subscription price; and it takes a specified number of rights to purchase the security. Depending on the relationship between the current market price of the stock and the subscription price, a right will usually have a market value. Security offerings to the general public and offerings on a privileged subscription basis must comply with federal and state regulations. The enforcement agency for the federal government is the Securities and Exchange Commission, whose authority encompasses both the sale of new securities and the trading of existing securities in the secondary market.

Rather than offering securities to existing stockholders or the general public, a company may place them privately with an institutional investor. With a private placement, the company negotiates directly with the investor; there is no underwriting and no registration of the issue with the SEC. The private placement has the virtue of flexibility and affords the medium-sized and even the small company the opportunity to sell its securities.

The announcement of a debt or stock issue may be accompanied by a stock market reaction. For one thing, the announcement may connote information about future cash flows of the company, or the reaction may be due to asymmetric information between investors and management. The latter presumes management will finance with stock when it believes the stock is overvalued and with debt when it believes the stock is undervalued. Empirical evidence is consistent with both of these notions, so the financial manager must recognize the likelihood of an information effect when issuing securities.

QUESTIONS

1. What is the difference between a public and a private issue of securities?
2. How does a traditional underwriting differ from a shelf registration?
3. Is the selling function or the risk-bearing function more highly rewarded on a bond issue that is underwritten?
4. As a best efforts offering is cheaper than an underwriting, why don't more companies make use of it?
5. In issuing a new bond issue, the firm may decide to sell the bonds through a private placement or through a public issue. Evaluate these two alternatives.
6. There exists an inverse relationship between flotation costs and the size of the issue being sold. Explain the economic forces that cause this relationship.
7. Should the preemptive right be required of all companies that issue common stock or securities convertible into common?
8. Many major U.S. corporations, notably Exxon and American Telephone & Telegraph, have extensively used rights offerings in the past decade. Why do you feel these corporations have chosen to raise funds with a rights offering rather than a new equity issue, especially when a fair percentage of the rights (2 to 5 percent) is never exercised?
9. What role does the subscription price play in a rights offering?
10. Define a standby arrangement; an oversubscription. Why are they used? Which is used more often?
11. What is the principal regulatory authority when it comes to security offerings? What is its function?
12. Which of the following companies would you expect to use a private placement of long-term debt as opposed to a public offering?
    a. An electric utility serving Chicago
    b. A $13 million annual volume maker of electronic components
    c. A consortium of oil companies to finance an oil discovery in the Arctic
    d. A tennis shoe retreading company serving northern California
13. In general, how do the costs of a private placement of a debt issue differ from those of a traditional underwriting?
14. Has the availability of shelf registrations reduced the importance of private placements? Why?

15. Why is it that a security offering of new stock or debt often is accompanied by a stock price reaction around the time of the announcement?

SELF-CORRECTION PROBLEMS

1. The Homex Company wishes to raise $5 million in additional equity capital through a traditional underwriting. After considering the potential difficulty of selling the shares, the investment banker decides that the selling concession should be between 3 and 4 percent of the value of the issue. When the risks of underwriting are evaluated, it is decided that the selling concession should constitute between 50 and 60 percent of the gross spread. If the management fee (which constitutes part of the underwriting profit) is taken to be 15 percent of the gross spread, answer the following questions:

   a. Assuming that the selling concession is set at 4 percent of gross proceeds and 50 percent of the gross spread, what would be the dollar value of the management fee, net underwriting profit, selling concession, and gross spread on the Homex underwriting?

   b. Rework part a, assuming that the selling concession was set at 3 percent of gross proceeds and 60 percent of the gross spread.

   c. Assuming that the managing underwriter underwrote 25 percent and sold 20 percent of the issue, what would be the manager's total compensation under part a? under part b?

2. The stock of the Dunbar Company is selling for $150 per share. The company issues rights to subscribe for one additional share of stock at $125 a share, for each nine held. Compute the theoretical value of the following:

   a. A right when the stock is selling rights-on

   b. One share of stock when it goes ex-rights

   c. A right when the stock sells ex-rights and the actual market price goes to $143 per share

3. Zum Restaurants, Inc., must decide between a public issue of intermediate-term notes and the private placement of debt with an insurance company. In both cases, the funds needed are $6 million over 6 years with no principal payment until the end. With a public issue, the interest rate will be 15 percent, the underwriting spread $10 per note, and the notes priced to the public at $1,000 apiece. To realize $6 million in proceeds, the company will need to issue some additional notes to offset the spread. Legal, printing, and other initial costs come to $195,000 with the public issue. For the private issue, the interest rate will be $15\frac{1}{2}$ percent, and initial costs will come to only $20,000.

   a. Ignoring the time value of money, which method has the higher total costs over the 6 years? In words, which method would be helped if we considered the time value of money?

   b. What if the maturity were 12 years, and all other things stayed the same?

PROBLEMS

1. Caldacci Copper Company, a risky company, needs to raise $75 million in long-term debt funds. The company is negotiating the offering through First Columbia Corporation. First Columbia believes it can bring together a syndicate of investment bankers to underwrite and sell the issue. The bonds will be given a coupon rate so that they may be priced to the public at their face value of $1,000. The selling concession will be $6 per bond; in addition, administrative expenses of $115,000 will be incurred. Typically, First Columbia requires a manager's fee of 15 percent of the total spread. To sell this issue, it feels that the underwriting commission, net of expenses and management fees, must be 25 percent of the total spread.

    a. What will be the total spread? the total spread per bond?

    b. What will be the net proceeds of the issue of Caldacci Copper?

    c. What is the selling concession as a percent of the total spread?

    d. What are the total costs of issuing the securities as a percentage of the net proceeds to the company?

2. Black Telecommunications Company needs to raise $1.8 billion (face value) of debt funds over the next 2 years. If it were to use traditional underwritings, the company would expect to have six underwritings over the 2-year span. The underwriter spread would likely be $7.50 per bond, and out-of-pocket expenses paid by the company would total $350,000 per underwriting. With shelf registrations, the average size of offering would probably be $75 million. Here the estimated spread is $3.00 per bond, and out-of-pocket expenses of $40,000 per issue are expected.

    a. Ignoring interest costs, what are the total absolute costs of flotation over the 2 years for the traditional underwriting method of offering securities?

    b. For the shelf registration method?

    c. Which is lower?

3. The Ville Platte Artists School will issue 200,000 shares of common stock at $40 per share through a subscription issue. The 800,000 shares of stock currently outstanding have a market price of $50 per share.

    a. Compute the number of rights required to buy a share of stock at $40.

    b. Compute the value of a right.

    c. Compute the value of the stock ex-rights.

4. The stock of the American Corporation is selling for $50 per share. The company then issues rights to subscribe for 1 new share at $40 for each 5 rights held.

    a. What is the theoretical value of a right if the stock is selling rights-on?

    b. What is the theoretical value of one share of stock when it goes ex-rights?

    c. What is the theoretical value of a right when the stock sells ex-rights at $50?

5. Two different companies are considering rights offerings. The current market price per share is $48 in both cases. To allow for fluctuations in market price, Company X wants to set a subscription price of $42 while Company Y feels a subscription price of $41½ is in order. The number of rights necessary to purchase an additional share is 14 in the case of Company X and 4 in the case of Company Y.

   a. Which company has the larger stock issue relatively? Is it the larger stock issue in absolute terms?

   b. In which case is there less risk that the market price will fall below the subscription price?

6. Doubletree Foods, Inc., is considering either a new stock issue or a new debt issue to raise capital. What is the likely information effect and stock market reaction that accompanies the announcement of a stock issue? of a debt issue? Why?

7. Obtain a prospectus on a recent security issue of a corporation. Analyze it according to

   a. The type of security being offered. Are there any special features? If a bond, is it secured? How is it secured?

   b. The size of the issue and the type of company involved. How sound is the company financially? How stable are its earnings? What is the growth potential? Is the size of the issue appropriate?

   c. The flotation cost. What is the underwriter spread? Is it too high a percentage of gross proceeds? What portion of the spread is in support of underwriting? in support of selling? What is the dealer concession? Under what conditions may it be earned?

   d. The underwriting syndicate. How many underwriters are there? What is the maximum participation? the minimum participation? Who is the manager? Are there provisions made for support of the price during the distribution period?

   e. The pricing. Is the issue priced properly from the standpoint of the company? of the investor? of the underwriter? How successful was the issue?

SOLUTIONS TO SELF-CORRECTION PROBLEMS

1.a.

Selling commission	= 4% of gross proceeds =	50% of gross spread
Gross spread	= 8% of $5,000,000	= $400,000
Selling commission	=	$200,000
Management fee	= 15% of $400,000	= $ 60,000
Net underwriting profit =		$140,000

b.

Selling commission	= 3% of gross proceeds =	60% of gross spread
Gross spread	= 5% of $5,000,000	= $250,000
Selling commission	=	$150,000
Management fee	= 15% of $250,000	= $37,500
Net underwriting profit =		$62,500

c. Case A: $60,000 + .25($140,000) + .20($200,000) = $135,000
Case B: $37,500 + .25($62,500) + .20($150,000) = $83,125

2.a. $R_o = \dfrac{P_o - S}{N + 1}$

$= \dfrac{\$150 - \$125}{9 + 1} = \dfrac{\$25}{10} = \$2.50$

b. $P_x = \dfrac{(P_o \times N) + S}{N + 1} = \dfrac{(\$150 \times 9) + \$125}{9 + 1}$

$= \dfrac{\$1,350 + \$125}{10} = \dfrac{\$1,475}{10} = \$147.50$

c. $R_x = \dfrac{P_x - S}{N} = \dfrac{\$143 - 125}{9} = \dfrac{\$18}{9} = \$2$

3.a. Public issue:

Number of $1,000 face value notes to be issued to raise $6 million (to nearest note) = $6,000,000/$990 = 6,061 or $6,061,000 in notes
Total interest cost (nearest 000) = $6,061,000 × 15% × 6 years = $5,455,000
Total costs = $5,455,000 + $195,000 = $5,650,000

Private issue:

Total interest cost = $6,000,000 × $15\frac{1}{2}$% × 6 years = $5,580,000
Total costs = $5,580,000 + $20,000 = $5,600,000

As the interest payments are spread out over the 6 years, the time value of money effect would be to enhance the private issue. The differential out-of-pocket expense occurs at the beginning.

b. Public issue:

Total interest cost = $6,061,000 × 15% × 12 years = $10,910,000
Total costs = $11,105,000

Private issue:

Total interest cost = $6,000,000 × $15\frac{1}{2}$% × 12 years = $11,160,000
Total costs = $11,180,000

With a longer-term loan, the differential in interest rate becomes more important.

SELECTED REFERENCES

ASQUITH, PAUL, and DAVID MULLINS, Jr., "Equity Issues and Offering Dilution," *Journal of Financial Economics*, 15 (January–February 1986), 61–90.

———, "Signalling with Dividends, Stock Repurchases, and Equity Issues," *Financial Management*, 15 (Autumn 1986), 27–44.

BACON, PETER W., "The Subscription Price in Rights Offerings," *Financial Management*, 1 (Summer 1972), 59–64.

BHAGAT, SANJAI, "The Effect of Pre-emptive Right Amendments on Shareholder Wealth," *Journal of Financial Economics*, 12 (November 1983), 289–310.

FUNG, W. K. H., and ANDREW RUDD, "Pricing New Corporate Bond Issues: An Analysis of Issue Cost and Seasoning Effects," *Journal of Finance*, 41 (July 1986), 633–42.

HANSEN, ROBERT S., and JOHN M. PINKERTON, "Direct Equity Financing: A Resolution of a Paradox," *Journal of Finance*, 37 (June 1982), 651–65.

HEINKEL, ROBERT, and EDUARDO S. SCHWARTZ, "Rights versus Underwritten Offerings: An Asymmetric Information Approach," *Journal of Finance*, 41 (March 1986), 1–18.

HESS, ALAN C., and PETER A. FROST, "Tests for Price Effects of New Issues of Seasoned Securities," *Journal of Finance*, 37 (March 1982), 11–26.

KEANE, SIMON M., "The Significance of the Issue Price in Rights Issues," *Journal of Business Finance*, 4 (1972), 40–45.

LEVY, HAIM, and MARSHALL SARNAT, "Risk, Dividend Policy, and the Optimal Pricing of a Rights Offering," *Journal of Money, Credit and Banking*, 3 (November 1971), 840–49.

MYERS, STEWART C., and NICHOLAS S. MAJLUF, "Corporate Financing and Investment Decisions When Firms Have Information That Investors Do Not Have," *Journal of Financial Economics*, 13 (June 1984), 187–221.

RITTER, JAY R., "The Costs of Going Public," *Journal of Financial Economics*, forthcoming.

SMITH, CLIFFORD W., JR., "Investment Banking and the Capital Acquisition Process," *Journal of Financial Economics*, 15 (January–February 1986), 3–29.

VAN HORNE, JAMES C., "Implied Fixed Costs in Long-term Debt Issues," *Journal of Financial and Quantitative Analysis*, 8 (December 1973), 821–34.

———, *Financial Market Rates and Flows*, 2nd ed. Englewood Cliffs, N.J.: Prentice-Hall, 1984.

WHITE R. W., and P. A. LUSZTIG, "The Price Effects of Rights Offerings," *Journal of Financial and Quantitative Analysis*, 15 (March 1980), 25–40.

ZWICK, BURTON, "Yields on Privately Placed Corporate Bonds," *Journal of Finance*, 35 (March 1980), 23–29.

CHAPTER 20

Term and Lease Financing

The principal characteristic of short-term loans is that they are self-liquidating in less than a year. Frequently, they finance seasonal and temporary funds requirements. Term financing, on the other hand, finances more permanent funds requirements, such as fixed assets and underlying buildups in receivables and inventories. The loan is usually paid with the generation of cash flows over a period of years. As a result, most of these loans are paid in regular, periodic installments. We regard term financing as involving final maturities of 1 to 7 years. These boundaries are arbitrary, although the 1-year boundary is rather commonly accepted. In this chapter we examine various types of term debt as well as lease financing.

TERM LOANS

Term loan. A loan from a bank or insurance company with a maturity of more than 1 year.

Commercial banks are a primary source of term financing. Two features of a bank **term loan** distinguish it from other types of business loans. First, it has a final maturity of more than 1 year; second, it most often represents credit extended under a formal loan agreement. For the most part, these loans are repayable in periodic installments: quarterly, semiannually, or annually. The payment schedule of the loan usually is geared to the borrower's cash-flow ability to service the debt. Typically, this schedule calls for equal periodic installments, but it may specify irregular amounts or repayment in a lump sum at final maturity. Sometimes the loan is amortized in equal periodic installments except for the final payment, known as a "balloon" payment, which is larger than any of the others.

Most bank term loans are written with original maturities in the 3- to 5-year range. The final maturity of a term loan does not always convey the length of time the loan is likely to remain outstanding. In some cases the bank and the company expect the loan to be renewed successively with maturity. These evergreen loans are typically characterized by credit to companies in growth phases. Despite the expectation of evergreen refunding upon maturity, the bank is not legally obligated to extend the loan. As a result, most requests for extensions and additional credit are analyzed afresh based on changed conditions from the time of the original loan. What was thought to be an evergreen loan may turn out to be a "deciduous" one if the financial condition and performance of the borrower deteriorate.

Costs and Benefits

Generally, the interest rate on a term loan is higher than the rate on a short-term loan to the same borrower. If a firm could borrow at the prime rate on a short-term basis, it might pay 0.25 percent to 0.50 percent more on a term loan. The interest rate on a term loan can be set in two ways: (1) a fixed rate that is effective over the life of the loan may be established at the outset, or (2) a variable rate may be set, to be adjusted in keeping with changes in the prime rate. Sometimes a ceiling or a floor rate is established, limiting the range within which the rate may fluctuate.

In addition to interest costs, the borrower is required to pay the legal expenses that the bank incurs in drawing up the loan agreement. Also, **a commitment fee** may be charged for the time during the commitment period when the loan is not taken down. For an ordinary term loan, these additional costs usually are rather small in relation to the total interest cost of the loan. A typical fee on the unused portion of a commitment is 0.50 percent, with a range of 0.25 percent to 0.75 percent. This means that if the commitment fee were 0.50 percent on a commitment of $1 million, and the company took down all of the loan 3 months after the commitment, it would owe the bank $1 million $\times$ .005 $\times \frac{3}{12} =$ $1,250.

Commitment fee. The fee charged by a lender for making a contractual commitment to lend the company money.

The principal advantage of an ordinary bank term loan is flexibility. The borrower deals directly with the lender, and the loan can be tailored to the borrower's needs through direct negotiation. The bank usually has had previous experience with the borrower, so it is familiar with the company's situation. Should the firm's requirements change, the terms and conditions of the loan may be revised. In many instances, bank term loans are made to small businesses that do not have access to the capital markets and cannot readily float a public issue. The ability to set a public issue varies over time in keeping with the tone of the capital markets, whereas access to term loan financing is more dependable. Even large companies that are able to go to the public market may find it more convenient to seek a bank term loan than to float a public issue.

Revolving Credits

As we said in Chapter 12, a revolving credit is a formal commitment by a bank to lend up to a certain amount of money to a company over a specified period of time. The actual notes evidencing debt are short term, usually 90 days, but the company may renew them or borrow additionally, up to the specified maximum, throughout the duration of the commitment. Many revolving credit commitments are for 3 years, although it is possible for a firm to obtain a shorter commitment. As with an ordinary term loan, the interest rate is usually 0.25 to 0.50 percent higher than the rate at which the firm could borrow on a short-term basis under a line of credit. When a bank makes a revolving credit commitment, it is legally bound under the loan agreement to have funds available whenever the company wants to borrow. The borrower usually must pay for this availability in the form of a commitment fee, perhaps 0.50 percent per annum, on the difference between the amount borrowed and the specified maximum.

This borrowing arrangement is particularly useful at times when the firm is uncertain about its funds requirements. The borrower has flexible access to funds over a period of uncertainty and can make more definite credit arrangements when the uncertainty is resolved. Revolving credit agreements can be set up so that at the maturity of the commitment, borrowings then owing can be converted into a term loan at the option of the borrower. Someday your company may introduce a new product and face a period of uncertainty over the next several years. To provide maximum financial flexibility, you might arrange a 3-year revolving credit that is convertible into a 5-year term loan at the expiration of the revolving credit commitment. At the end of 3 years, the company should know its funds requirements better. If these requirements are permanent, or nearly so, the firm might wish to exercise its option and take down the term loan.

Insurance Company Term Loans

In addition to banks, life insurance companies and certain other institutional investors lend money on a term basis, but with differences in the maturity of the loan extended and in the interest rate charged. In general, life insurance companies are interested in term loans with final maturities in excess of 7 years. Because these companies do not have the benefit of compensating balances or other business from the borrower, and because their loans usually have a longer maturity than bank term loans, typically, the rate of interest is higher. To the insurance company, the term loan represents an investment and must yield a return commensurate with the costs involved in making the loan, the risk, the maturity, and prevailing yields on alternative investments. Because an insurance company is interested in keeping its funds employed without interruption, it normally has a prepayment penalty, whereas usually the bank does not. Insurance company term loans generally are not competitive with bank term loans. Indeed, they are complementary, for they serve different maturity ranges.

LOAN AGREEMENTS

When a lender makes a term loan or revolving credit commitment, it provides the borrower with available funds for an extended period. Much can happen to the financial condition of the borrower during that period. To safeguard itself, the lender requires the borrower to maintain its financial condition and, in particular, its current position at a level at least as favorable as when the commitment was made. The provisions for protection contained in a loan agreement are known as protective **covenants.**

Covenant. A restriction on a borrower imposed by a lender, such as the former must maintain a minimum amount of working capital.

Loan agreement. A legal agreement specifying the terms of loan and obligations of the borrower.

The **loan agreement** itself simply gives the lender legal authority to step in should the borrower default under any of the provisions. Otherwise, the lender would be locked into a commitment and would have to wait until maturity before being able to effect corrective measures. The borrower who suffers losses or other adverse developments will default under a well-written loan agreement; the lender then will be able to act. The action usually takes the form of working with the company to straighten out its problems. Seldom will a lender demand immediate payment, despite the legal right to do so in cases of default. More typically, the condition under which the borrower defaults is waived or the loan agreement is amended. The point is that the lender has the authority to act, even though negotiation with the borrower may be instituted to resolve the problem.

Formulation of Provisions

The formulation of the different restrictive provisions should be tailored to the specific loan situation. The lender fashions these provisions for the overall protection of the loan. No one provision is able by itself to provide the necessary safeguards; but together with the other provisions, it is designed to ensure over-all liquidity and ability to pay a loan. The important protective covenants of a loan agreement may be classified as follows: (1) general provisions used in most loan agreements, which are variable to fit the situation; (2) routine provisions used in most agreements, which usually are not variable; and (3) specific provisions that are used according to the situation. Although we focus on a loan agreement, the protective covenants used and the philosophy underlying their use are the same for a bond indenture, which is described in Chapter 21.

General Provisions.   The *working capital requirement* probably is the most commonly used and most comprehensive provision in a loan agreement. Its purpose is to preserve the company's current position and ability to pay the loan. Frequently, a straight dollar amount, such as $6 million, is set as the minimum working capital the company must maintain during the duration of the commitment. When the lender feels that it is desirable for a specific company to build working capital, it may increase the minimum working capital requirement throughout the duration of the loan. The establishment of a working capital minimum normally is based on the amounts of present working capital and projected working capital, allowing for seasonal fluctuations. The requirement should not restrict the company unduly in the ordinary generation of profit. Should the borrower incur sharp losses or spend too much for fixed assets, purchase of stock, dividends, redemption of long-term debt, and so forth, it would probably breach the working capital requirement.

The *cash dividend and repurchase of stock restriction* is another major restriction in this category. Its purpose is to limit cash going outside the business, thus preserving the liquidity of the company. Most often, cash dividends and repurchase of stock are limited to a percentage of net profits on a cumulative basis after a certain base date, frequently the last fiscal year end prior to the date of the term loan agreement. A less flexible method is to restrict dividends and repurchase of stock to an absolute dollar amount each year. In most cases the prospective borrower must be willing to undergo a cash dividend and repurchase of stock restriction. If tied to earnings, this restriction still will allow adequate dividends as long as the company is able to generate satisfactory profits.

The *capital expenditures limitation* is third in the category of general provisions. Capital expenditures may be limited to a fixed dollar amount yearly or, probably more commonly, either to depreciation or to a percentage thereof. The capital expenditures limitation is another tool the lender uses to ensure the maintenance of the borrower's current position. By limiting capital expenditures directly, the bank can be surer that it will not have to look to liquidation of fixed assets for payment of its loan. Again, the provision should not be so restrictive that it prevents the adequate maintenance and improvement of facilities.

A *limitation on other indebtedness* is the last general provision. This limitation may take a number of forms, depending on the circumstances. Frequently, a loan agreement will prohibit a company from incurring any other long-term debt. This provision protects the lender, inasmuch as it prevents future lenders from obtaining a prior claim on the borrower's assets. Usually a company is permitted to borrow within reasonable limits for seasonal and other short-term purposes arising in the ordinary course of business.

Routine Provisions.   The second category of restrictions includes routine, usually invariable provisions found in most loan agreements. Ordinarily, the loan agreement requires the borrower to furnish the bank with financial statements and to maintain adequate insurance. Additionally, the borrower normally must not sell a significant portion of its assets and must pay, when due, all taxes and other liabilities, except those it contests in good faith. A provision forbidding the pledging or mortgaging of any of the borrower's assets is almost always included in a loan agreement; this important provision is known as a **negative pledge clause.**

> **Negative pledge clause.** A protective covenant whereby the borrower agrees not to allow a lien on any of its assets.

Ordinarily, the company is required not to discount or sell its receivables. Moreover, the borrower generally is prohibited from entering into any leasing arrangement of property, except up to a certain dollar amount of annual rental. The purpose of this provision is to prevent the borrower from taking on a substantial lease liability, which might endanger its ability to pay the loan. A lease restriction also prevents the firm from leasing property instead of purchasing it and thereby getting around the limitations on capital expenditures and debt. Usually, too, there is a restriction on other contingent liabilities. The provisions in this category appear as a matter of routine in most loan agreements. Although somewhat mechanical, they close many loopholes and provide a tight, comprehensive loan agreement.

Special Provisions.   In specific loan agreements, the lender uses special provisions to achieve a desired total protection of its loan. A loan agreement may contain a definite understanding regarding the use of the loan proceeds, so that there will be no diversion of funds to purposes other than those contemplated when the loan was negotiated. A provision for limiting loans and advances often is found in a term loan agreement. Closely allied to this restriction is a limitation on investments, which is used to safeguard liquidity by preventing certain nonliquid investments.

If one or more executives are essential to a firm's effective operation, a lender may insist that the company carry life insurance on them. Proceeds of the insurance may be payable to the company or directly to the lender, to be applied to the loan. An agreement may also contain a management clause, under which certain key individuals must remain actively employed in the company during the time the loan is owing. Aggregate executive salaries and bonuses sometimes are limited in the loan agreement, to prevent excessive compensation of executives, which might reduce profits. This provision closes another loophole; it prevents large stockholders who are officers of the company from increasing their own salaries in lieu of paying higher dividends, which are limited under the agreement.

Negotiation of Restrictions

The provisions just described represent the most frequently used protective covenants in a loan agreement. From the standpoint of the lender, the aggregate impact of these provisions should be to safeguard the financial position of the borrower and its ability to pay the loan. Under a well-written agreement, a borrower cannot get into serious financial difficulty without defaulting under an agreement, thereby giving the lender legal authority to take action. Although the lender is instrumental in establishing the restrictions, the restrictiveness of protective covenants is subject to negotiation between borrower and lender. The final result will depend on the relative bargaining power of each of the parties involved.

EQUIPMENT FINANCING

Equipment represents another asset of the firm that may be pledged to secure a loan. If the firm either has equipment that is marketable or is purchasing such equipment, it is usually able to obtain some sort of secured financing. Because such loans usually are for more than a year, we take them up in this chapter rather than under short-term secured loans. As with other secured loans, the lender evaluates the marketability of the collateral and will advance a percentage of the market value, depending on the quality of the equipment. Frequently, the repayment schedule for the loan is set in keeping with the economic depreciation schedule of the equipment. In setting the repayment schedule, the lender wants to be sure that the market value of the equipment always exceeds the balance of the loan.

The excess of the expected market value of the equipment over the amount of the loan is the margin of safety, which will vary according to the specific situation. The rolling stock of a trucking company is movable collateral and reasonably marketable. As a result, the advance may be as high as 80 percent. Less marketable equipment, such as that with a limited use, will not command as high an advance. A certain type of lathe may have a thin market, and a lender might not be willing to advance more than 50 percent of its reported market value. Some equipment is so specialized that it has no value as collateral.

Sources and Types of Equipment Financing

Commercial banks, finance companies, and the sellers of equipment are among the sources of equipment financing. Because the interest charged by a finance company on an equipment loan usually is higher than that charged by a commercial bank, a firm will turn to a finance company only if it is unable to obtain the loan from a bank. The seller of the equipment may finance the purchase either by holding the secured note itself or by selling the note to its captive finance subsidiary. The interest charge will depend on the extent to which the seller uses financing as a sales tool. The seller who uses financing extensively may charge only a moderate interest rate, but may make up for part of the cost of carrying the notes by charging higher prices for the equipment. The borrower must consider this possibility in judging the true cost of financing. Equipment loans may be secured either by a chattel mortgage or by a conditional sales contract arrangement.

A *chattel mortgage* is a **lien** on property other than real property. The borrower signs a security agreement that gives the lender a lien on the equipment

Lien. A legal claim on certain assets. Used to secure a loan.

specified in the agreement. To perfect the lien, the lender files a copy of the security agreement or a financing statement with a public office of the state in which the equipment is located. Given a valid lien, the lender can sell the equipment if the borrower defaults in the payment of principal or interest on the loan.

Conditional sales contract. A means of financing provided by the seller of equipment, who holds title to it until the financing is paid off.

With a **conditional sales contract** arrangement, the seller of the equipment retains the title to it until the purchaser has satisfied all the terms of the contract. The buyer signs a conditional sales contract security agreement to make periodic installment payments to the seller over a specified period of time. These payments usually are monthly or quarterly. Until the terms of the contract are satisfied completely, the seller retains title to the equipment. Thus, the seller receives a down payment and a **promissory note** for the balance of the purchase price upon the sale of the equipment. The note is secured by the contract, which gives the seller the authority to repossess the equipment if the buyer does not meet all the terms of the contract.

Promissory note. A legal promise to pay a sum of money to a lender.

The seller may either hold the contract or sell it, simply by endorsing it, to a commercial bank or finance company. The bank or finance company then becomes the lender and assumes the security interest in the equipment. If the buyer should default under the terms of the contract, the bank or finance company could repossess the equipment and sell it in satisfaction of its loan. Often, the vendor will sell the contract to a bank or finance company with recourse. Under this arrangement, the lender has the additional protection of recourse to the seller in case the buyer defaults.

LEASE FINANCING

Lease. The economic use of an asset for which the lessee agrees to pay the owner, the lessor, a series of periodic lease payments.

A **lease** is a contract whereby the owner of an asset (the lessor) grants to another party (the lessee) the exclusive right to use the asset, usually for an agreed period of time, in return for the payment of rent. Most of us are familiar with leases of houses, apartments, offices, or telephones. Recent decades have seen an enormous growth in the leasing of business assets such as cars and trucks, computers, machinery, and even manufacturing plants. An obvious advantage to the lessee is the use of an asset without having to buy it. For this advantage, the lessee incurs several obligations. First and foremost is the obligation to make periodic lease payments, usually monthly or quarterly and in advance. Also, the lease contract specifies who is to maintain the asset. Under a *maintenance lease*, the lessor pays for maintenance, repairs, taxes, and insurance. Under a **net lease,** the lessee pays these costs.

Net lease. A lease where the lessee maintains and insures the asset.

The lease may be *cancellable* or *noncancellable*. When cancellable, there sometimes is a penalty. An **operating lease** for office space, for example, is relatively short term and is cancellable with proper notice. The term of this type of lease is shorter than the asset's economic life. In other words, the lessor does not recover its investment during the first least period. It is only in re-leasing the space over and over, either to the same party or to others, that the lessor recovers its cost. Other examples of operating leases include the leasing of copying machines, certain computer hardware, word processors, and automobiles. In contrast, a *financial lease* is longer term in nature and is noncancellable. The lessee

Operating lease. A short-term lease that is cancellable.

is obligated to make lease payments until the lease's expiration, which corresponds to the useful life of the asset. These payments not only amortize the cost of the asset but provide the lessor an interest return. Our focus in this chapter is on financial as opposed to operating leases.

Finally, the lease contract typically specifies some kind of option to the lessee at expiration. It may involve renewal, where the lessee has the right to renew the lease for another lease period, either at the same rent or at a different, usually lower, rent. The option might be to purchase the asset at expiration. For tax reasons, the purchase price must not be significantly lower than what the asset would fetch from another party in the market. If the lessee does not exercise its option, the lessor takes possession of the asset and is entitled to any *residual value* associated with it.

Forms of Lease Financing

Virtually all lease financing arrangements fall into one of three main types of lease financing: a sale and leaseback arrangement, the direct acquisition of an asset under a lease, and leveraged leasing. In this section we briefly describe these categories; in the subsequent section we present a framework for the analysis of lease financing.

Sale and Leaseback.   Under a sale and leaseback arrangement a firm sells an asset to another party, and this party leases it back to the firm. Usually the asset is sold at approximately its market value. The firm receives the sales price in cash and the economic use of the asset during the basic lease period. In turn, it contracts to make periodic lease payments and give up title to the asset. As a result, the lessor realizes any residual value the asset might have at the end of the lease period, whereas before, this value would have been realized by the firm. The firm may realize an income tax advantage if the asset involves a building on owned land. Whereas land is not depreciable if owned outright, lease payments are tax deductible, so the firm indirectly is able to amortize the value of the land. Lessors engaged in sale and leaseback arrangements include insurance companies, other institutional investors, finance companies, and independent leasing companies.

> **Sale and leaseback.** The sale of an asset with the agreement to lease it back for an extended period of time with specified payments.

Direct Leasing.   Under direct leasing, a company acquires the use of an asset it did not own previously. A firm may lease an asset from the manufacturer: IBM leases computers; Xerox Corporation leases copiers. Indeed, capital goods are abundantly available today on a lease-financed basis. A wide variety of direct leasing arrangements meet various needs of firms. The major types of lessors are manufacturers, finance companies, banks, independent leasing companies, special-purpose leasing companies, and partnerships. For leasing arrangements involving all but manufacturers, the vendor sells the asset to the lessor who, in turn, leases it to the lessee. As in any lease arrangement, the lessee has use of the asset, along with a contractual obligation to make lease payments to the lessor.

Leverage leasing. A lease arrangement where the lessor borrows a portion of the funds necessary.

Leveraged Leasing.   A special form of leasing became popular in the financing of assets requiring large capital outlays. This device is known as *leveraged leasing*. In contrast to the two parties involved in the forms of leasing previously described, there are three parties involved in leveraged leasing: (1) the lessee, (2) the lessor, or equity participant, and (3) the lender. We examine each in turn.

From the standpoint of the lessee, there is no difference between a leveraged lease and any other type of lease. The lessee contracts to make periodic payments over the basic lease period and, in return, is entitled to the use of the asset over that period of time. The role of the lessor, however, is changed. The lessor acquires the asset in keeping with the terms of the lease arrangement and finances the acquisition in part by an equity investment of, say, 20 percent (hence the name *equity participant*). The remaining 80 percent is provided by a long-term lender or lenders. Usually, the loan is secured by a mortgage on the asset, as well as by the assignment of the lease and lease payments. The lessor is the borrower.

As owner of the asset, the lessor is entitled to deduct all depreciation charges associated with the asset. The cash-flow pattern for the lessor typically involves (1) a cash outflow at the time the asset is acquired, which represents its equity participation; (2) a period of cash inflows represented by lease payments and tax benefits, less payments of the debt (principal and interest); and (3) a period of net cash outflows during which, because of declining tax benefits, the sum of lease payments and tax benefits falls below the debt payments due. If there is any residual value at the end of the lease period, this of course represents a cash inflow to the lessor. Although the leveraged lease may seem the most complicated of the three forms of leasing we have described, it reduces to certain basic concepts. From the standpoint of the lessee, which is our stance, the leveraged lease can be analyzed in the same manner as any other lease. Therefore, we will not treat it separately in the rest of this chapter.

Accounting Treatment

Accounting for leases has changed dramatically over time. A number of years ago lease financing was attractive to some because the obligation did not appear on the company's financial statements. As a result, leasing was regarded as a "hidden" or "off-balance-sheet" method of financing. However, accounting requirements have changed so that now many leases must be shown on the balance sheet as a capitalized asset with the associated liability being shown as well. For these leases, the reporting of earnings is affected. Other leases must be fully disclosed in footnotes to the financial statement. As the accounting treatment of leases is involved, we discuss it in the appendix to this chapter, in order to maintain the chapter's continuity. The main point is that it no longer is possible for a firm to "fool" investors and creditors by using lease as opposed to debt financing. The full impact of the lease obligation is apparent to any supplier of capital who makes the effort to read the financial statements.

Tax Treatment

For tax purposes, the lessee can deduct the full amount of the lease payment. The Internal Revenue Service wants to be sure that the lease contract truly represents a lease and not an installment purchase of the asset. To assure itself that a "true" lease in fact is involved, it may check on whether there is a meaningful **residual value** at the end of the lease term. Usually this is construed to mean that the term of the lease cannot exceed 90 percent of the useful life of the asset. In addition to this criterion, the lessee must not be given an option to purchase the asset or to release it at a nominal price at the end of the lease period. Any option must be based on fair market value at the lease's expiration, such as would occur with an outside offer. The lease payments must be reasonable in that they provide the lessor not only a return of principal but a reasonable interest return as well. In addition, the lease term must be less than 30 years, or it will be construed as a purchase of the asset.

> **Residual value.** The value of a leased asset at the end of the lease period.

In essence, the IRS wants to ensure itself that the lease contract is not, in effect, a purchase of the asset, for which payments are much more rapid than would be allowed with depreciation. As lease payments are deductible for tax purposes, such a contract would allow the lessor effectively to "depreciate" the asset more quickly than allowed under a straight purchase. If the lease contract meets the conditions described, the full lease payment is deductible for tax purposes.

With leasing, the cost of any land is amortized in the lease payments. By deducting the lease payments as an expense for federal income tax purposes, in essence, the lessee is able to write off the original cost of the land. If the land is purchased, the firm cannot depreciate it for tax purposes. When the value of land represents a significant portion of the asset acquired, lease financing can offer a tax advantage to the firm. Offsetting this tax advantage is the likely residual value of land at the end of the basic lease period. The firm also may gain certain tax advantages in a sale and leaseback arrangement when the assets are sold for less than their depreciated value.

Economic Foundation to Leasing Industry

The principal reason for the existence of leasing is that companies, financial institutions, and individuals derive different tax benefits from owing assets. The marginally profitable company may not be able to reap the full benefit of accelerated depreciation, whereas the high income, and taxed, corporation or individual is able to realize such. The former may be able to obtain a greater portion of the overall tax benefits by leasing the asset from the latter party as opposed to buying it. Because of competition among lessors, part of the tax benefits may be passed on to the lessee in the form of lower lease payments than would otherwise be the case.

Another tax disparity has to do with the alternative minimum tax (AMT). For a company subject to the AMT, accelerated depreciation is a preference item, whereas a lease payment is not so classified. Such a company may prefer to lease, particularly from another party that pays taxes at a higher effective rate. The greater the divergence in abilities of various parties in society to realize the tax benefits associated with owning an asset, the greater the attraction of lease financing overall. It is not the existence of taxes per se that gives rise to leasing but divergences in the abilities of various parties to realize the tax benefits.

Another consideration, albeit it a minor one, is that lessors enjoy a somewhat superior position in bankruptcy proceedings over what would be the case if they were secured lenders. The riskier the firm that seeks financing, the greater the incentive for the supplier of capital to make the arrangement a lease rather than a loan.

In addition to these reasons, there may be others that explain the existence of lease financing. For one thing, the lessor may enjoy economies of scale in the purchase of assets that are not available to individual lessees. Also, the lessor may have a different estimate of the life of the asset, its salvage value, or of the discount rate than the lessee. Finally, the lessor may be able to provide expertise to its customers in equipment selection and maintenance. While all of these factors may give rise to leasing, we would not expect them to be nearly as important as the tax reason.

EVALUATING LEASE FINANCING IN RELATION TO DEBT FINANCING

To evaluate whether or not a lease financing proposal is a good thing, compare it with financing the asset with debt. Whether leasing or borrowing is best will depend on the patterns of cash outflows for each financing method and on the opportunity cost of funds. To illustrate a method of analysis, we compare lease financing with debt financing, using a hypothetical example. We assume that the firm has decided to invest in a project on the basis of considerations that were discussed in Part IV. In other words, the investment worthiness of the project is evaluated separately from the specific method of financing to be employed. We assume also that the firm has determined an appropriate capital structure and has decided to finance the project with a fixed-income type of instrument—either debt or lease financing. We turn now to examining the two alternatives.

Example for Analyses

Suppose that Kennedy Electronics, Inc., has decided to acquire a piece of equipment costing $148,000 to be used in the fabrication of microprocessors. If it were to lease finance the equipment, the manufacturer will provide such financing over 7 years. The terms of the lease call for the annual payment of $27,500. As is customary, lease payments are made in advance, that is, at the end of the year prior to each of the 7 years. The lessee is responsible for maintenance of the equipment, insurance, and taxes.

Embodied in the lease payments is an implied interest return to the lessor.

If we ignore possible residual value, this before-tax return can be found by solving the following equation for R:

$$\$148,000 = \sum_{t=0}^{6} \frac{\$27,500}{(1 + R)^t} \qquad (20\text{-}1)$$

Because lease payments are made in advance, we solve for the internal rate of return that equates the cost of the asset with one lease payment at time 0, plus the present value of six lease payments at the end of each of the next 6 years. When we solve for R, we find it to be 9.79 percent. If instead of this return, the lessor wished a return of 11 percent, it would need to obtain annual lease payments of x in the following equation:

$$\$148,000 = \sum_{t=0}^{6} \frac{x}{(1.11)^t}$$

$$\$148,000 = x + 4.2305x$$

$$x = \frac{\$148,000}{5.2305} \qquad (20\text{-}2)$$

$$= \$28,296$$

In the equation, 4.2305 is the present-value discount factor for an even stream of cash flows for 6 years, discounted at 11 percent (see Appendix Table B at the back of the book). Therefore, the annual lease payment would be $28,296.

If the asset is purchased, Kennedy Electronics would finance it with a 7-year term loan at 12 percent. The company is in a 40 percent tax bracket. The asset falls in the 5-year property class for accelerated cost recovery (depreciation) purposes. Accordingly, the schedule discussed in Chapter 2 is used:

Year	1	2	3	4	5	6
Depreciation	20.00%	32.00%	19.20%	11.52%	11.52%	5.76%

The cost of the asset is then depreciated at these rates, so that first-year depreciation is .20 × $148,000 = $29,600 and so forth. At the end of the 7 years, the equipment is expected to have a scrap value of $15,000. Kennedy Electronics Company is entitled to this residual value, as it would be the owner of the asset under the purchase alternative.

Present Value For Lease Alternative

By comparing the present values of cash outflows for leasing and borrowing, we are able to tell which method of financing should be used. It is simply the one with the lowest present value. Remember that the company will make annual lease payments of $27,500 if the asset is leased. Because these payments are an expense, they are deductible for tax purposes, but only in the year for which the payment applies. The $27,500 payment at the end of year 0 represents a prepaid expense and is not deductible for tax purposes until year 1. Similarly, the other six payments are not deductible until the following year.

As leasing is analogous to borrowing, an appropriate discount rate for discounting the after-tax cash flows might be the after-tax cost of borrowing. For our example, the after-tax cost of borrowing is 12%(1 − .40) = 7.2%. The reason for using this rate as our discount rate is that the difference in cash outflows between lease financing and debt financing involes little risk. Therefore, it is not appropriate to use the company's overall cost of capital, which embodies a risk premium for the firm as a whole, as the discount rate.

Given the foregoing information, we are able to compute the present value of cash outflows. The computations are shown in the last column of Table 20-1. We see that the present value of the total cash outflows under the leasing alternative is $98,904. This figure, then, must be compared with the present value of cash outflows under the borrowing alternative.

TABLE 20-1
Schedule of cash outflows: leasing alternative

END OF YEAR	(1) LEASE PAYMENT	(2) TAX SHIELD (1)(.4)	(3) CASH OUTFLOW AFTER TAXES (1) − (2)	(4) PRESENT VALUE OF CASH OUTFLOWS (7.2%)
0	$27,500	—	$27,500	$27,500
1–6	27,500	$11,000	16,500	78,165
4		11,000	(11,000)	(6,761)
				$98,904

Present Value For Borrowing Alternative

If the asset is purchased, Kennedy Electronics is assumed to finance it entirely with a 12 percent unsecured term loan, its payment schedule being of the same configuration as the lease payment schedule. In other words, loan payments are assumed to be payable at the beginning, not the end, of each year. This assumption places the loan on an equivalent basis with the lease and allows us to compare apples with apples, as most lease arrangements call for payment in advance. A loan of $148,000 is taken out at time 0 and is payable over 7 years with annual payments of $28,955 at the beginning of each year.[1] The proportion of interest in each payment depends on the unpaid principal amount owing during the year. The principal amount owing during year 1 is $148,000 minus the payment at the very start of the year of $28,955, which is equal to $119,045. The an-

---

[1] This amount is computed in the same manner as in Eq. (20-2), using 12 percent instead of 11 percent.

TABLE 20-2
Schedule of debt payments

END OF YEAR	LOAN PAYMENT	PRINCIPAL AMOUNT OWING AT END OF YEAR	ANNUAL INTEREST
0	$28,955	$119,045	$ 0
1	28,955	104,375	14,285
2	28,955	87,945	12,525
3	28,955	69,544	10,553
4	28.955	48,934	8,345
5	28,955	25,851	5,872
6	28,953	0	3,102

nual interest for the first year is $119,045 \times 12\% = \$14,285.$[2] As subsequent payments are made, the interest component increases. Table 20-2 shows these components over time.

To compute the cash outflows after taxes for the debt alternative, we must determine the tax effect. This requires knowing the amounts of annual interest and annual depreciation. Using the cost recovery schedule for the 5-year property class listed earlier, the annual depreciation charges are shown in the third column of Table 20-3. Because both depreciation and interest are deductible expenses for tax purposes, they provide a tax shield equal to their sum times the tax rate of 40 percent. This is shown in column 4 of the table. When this shield is deducted from the debt payment, we obtain the cash outflow after taxes at the end of each year, column 5. At the end of year 7, the asset is expected to have a residual value of $15,000. This amount is subject to the corporate tax rate of 40 percent for the company, which leaves an expected after-tax cash inflow of

[2] For ease of illustration, we round to the nearest dollar throughout. This results in the final debt payment in Table 20-2 being slightly less than would otherwise be the case.

TABLE 20-3
Schedule of cash outflows: debt alternative

END OF YEAR	(1) LOAN PAYMENT	(2) INTEREST	(3) DEPRECIATION	(4) TAX SHIELD [(2) + (3)] .4	(5) CASH OUTFLOWS AFTER TAXES (1) − (4)	(6) PRESENT VALUE OF CASH OUTFLOWS (7.2%)
0	$28.955	$ 0	$ 0	$ 0	$28,955	$28,955
1	28,955	14,285	29,600	17,554	11,401	10,635
2	28,955	12,525	47,360	23,954	5,001	4,352
3	28,955	10,553	28,416	15,588	13,367	10,851
4	28,955	8,345	17,050	10,158	18,797	14,233
5	28,955	5,872	17,050	9,169	19,786	13,976
6	28,953	3,102	8,524	4,650	24,303	16,013
7	(15,000)			(6,000)	(9,000)	(5,532)
						$93,484

$9,000. Finally we compute the present value of all of these cash flows at a 7.2 percent discount rate and find that they total $93,484.

This present value of cash outflow is less than that for the lease alternative, $98,904. Therefore, the analysis suggests that the company use debt as opposed to lease financing in acquiring use of the asset. This conclusion arises despite the fact that the implied interest rate embodied in the lease payments, 9.79 percent, is less than the explicit cost of debt financing, 12 percent. However, if the asset is bought, the company is able to avail itself of accelerated cost recovery depreciation, and this helps the situation from a present-value standpoint. Moreover, the residual value at the end of the project is a favorable factor, whereas this value goes to the lessor with lease financing.

Another factor that favors the debt alternative is the deductibility of interest payments for tax purposes. Because the amount of interest embodied in a "mortgage-type" debt payment is higher at first and declines with successive payments, the tax benefits associated with these payments follow the same pattern over time. From a present-value standpoint, this pattern benefits the firm relative to the pattern of lease payments, which typically are constant over time. These positive factors to purchase and debt financing more than offset the implied interest rate advantage to lease financing. The lease payment terms simply are not attractive enough to give up the tax and other benefits associated with ownership.

Other Considerations

The decision to borrow rests on the relative timing and magnitude of cash flows under the two financing alternatives, as well as on the discount rate employed. We have assumed that the cash flows are known with certainty. While this is reasonable for the most part, there is some uncertainty that, on occasion, can be important. The residual value of an asset at the end is usually subject to considerable uncertainty, for example.

As we can see, deciding between leasing and borrowing can involve some rather extensive calculations. Each situation requires a separate analysis. The analysis is complicated if the two alternatives involve different amounts of financing. If we finance less than the total cost of the asset by borrowing, but finance 100 percent of the cost by leasing, we must consider the difference in the amount of financing both from the standpoint of explicit as well as implicit costs. These considerations and the others mentioned throughout this chapter can make the evaluation of lease financing rather detailed.

SUMMARY

Term financing generally is thought to include maturities of 1 to 7 years. There are a number of sources of such financing. Commercial banks, insurance companies, and other institutional investors make term loans to business firms. Banks also provide financing under a revolving credit arrangement, which represents a formal commitment on the part of the bank to lend up to a certain amount of money over a specified period of time. Lenders who offer unsecured credit usually impose restrictions on the borrower. These restrictions are called protective covenants and are contained in a loan agreement. If the borrower defaults under any of the provisions of the loan agreement, the lender may initiate immediate corrective measures. On a secured basis, firms can obtain intermediate-term financing by pledging equipment that they own or are purchasing. Banks, finance companies, and sellers of the equipment are active in providing this type of secured financing.

In lease financing, the lessee agrees to pay the lessor, periodically, for economic use of the lessor's asset. Because of this contractual obligation, leasing is regarded as a method of financing similar to borrowing. Leasing can involve the direct acquisition of an asset under a lease, a sale and leaseback arrangement, or a leveraged lease. The accounting treatment of leases and the tax implications were discussed.

One of the principal economic reasons for leasing is the inability of a firm to utilize all the tax benefits associated with ownership of an asset. This can arise not only because of unprofitable operations but because earnings are not of sufficient size to effectively utilize all of the possible tax benefits. One means for analyzing lease financing in relation to debt financing is to discount to present value the net cash outflows after taxes under each alternative, using the after-tax cost of borrowing as the discount rate. The preferred alternative is the one that provides the lower present value.

APPENDIX
Accounting Treatment of Leases

The accounting treatment of leases has undergone sweeping change over the past three decades. Where once leases were not disclosed, gradually disclosure was required in the footnotes to the financial statement. With only minimal disclosure, leasing was attractive to certain firms as an "off-balance-sheet" method of financing. There was no evidence that such financing had a favorable effect on valuation, all other things the same; nevertheless, many a company proceeded on the assumption that "off-balance sheet" financing was a good thing. Then came the Financial Accounting Standards Board Statement No. 13 in 1976 with an explicit ruling which called for the capitalization on the balance sheet of certain types of leases.[3] In essence, this statement says that if the lessee acquires essentially all of the economic benefits and risks of the leased property, then the

---

[3] *Statement of Financial Accounting Standards No. 13, Accounting for Leases* (Stamford, Conn.: Financial Accounting Standards Board, November 1976).

value of the asset along with the corresponding lease liability must be shown on the balance sheet.

Capital and Operating Leases

Leases that conform in principle to this definition are called *capital leases*. More specifically, a lease is regarded as a capital lease if it meets any one of the following conditions:

1. The lease transfers title to the asset to the lessee by the end of the lease period.
2. The lease contains an option to purchase the asset at a bargain price.
3. The lease period is equal to or greater than 75 percent of the estimated economic life of the asset.
4. At the beginning of the lease the present value of the minimum lease payments equals or exceeds 90 percent of the fair value of the leased property to the lessor.

If any of these conditions is met, the lessee is said to have acquired most of the economic benefits and risks associated with the leased property; therefore, a capital lease is involved. If a lease does not meet any of these conditions, it is classified as an *operating lease*. Essentially, operating leases give the lessee the right to use the leased property over a period of time, but they do not give the lessee all of the benefits and risks that are associated with the asset.

Recording the Value of a Capital Lease.   With a capital lease, the lessee must report the value of the leased property on the asset side of the balance sheet. The amount reflected is the present value of the minimum lease payments over the lease period. If executory costs, such as insurance, maintenance, and taxes, are a part of the total lease payment, these are deducted and only the remainder is used for purposes of calculating the present value. As required by the accounting rules, the discount rate employed is the lower of (1) the lessee's incremental borrowing rate or (2) the lessor's implicit interest rate if, in fact, that rate can be determined.

The present value of the lease payments should be recorded as an asset on the lessee's balance sheet. (If the fair value of the leased property is lower than the present value of the minimum lease payments, then the fair value would be shown). The associated lease obligation would be shown on the liability side of the balance sheet, with the present value of payments due within 1 year being reflected as current liabilities and the present value of payments due after 1 year being shown as noncurrent liabilities. The leased property may be combined with similar information on assets that are owned, but there must be a disclosure in a footnote with respect to the value of the leased property and its amortization. A hypothetical balance sheet might look like the following:

ASSETS		LIABILITIES	
Gross fixed assets*	$3,000,000	Current	
Less: accumulated		Obligations under	
depreciation and		capital leases	$ 90,000
amortization	1,000,000	Noncurrent	
Net fixed assets	$2,000,000	Obligations under	
		capital leases	$270,000

*Gross fixed assets include leased property of $500,000. Accumulated depreciation and amortization includes $140,000 in amortization associated with such property.

Here we see in the footnote that the capitalized value of leases of the company is $500,000 less $140,000 in amortization, or $360,000 in total. The liability is split with $90,000 current and $270,000 due beyond 1 year. In addition to this information, more details are required in footnotes. Relevant information here includes the gross amounts of leased property by major property categories (these can be combined with categories of owned assets), the total future minimum lease payments, a schedule by years of future lease payments required over the next 5 years, the total minimum sublease rentals to be received, the existence and terms of purchase or renewal options and escalation clauses, rentals that are contingent on some factor other than the passage of time, and any restrictions imposed in the lease agreement.

Disclosure of Operating Leases.   For operating leases, as for capital leases, some of the same disclosure is required, but it can be in footnotes. For noncancellable leases having remaining terms in excess of 1 year, the lessee must disclose total future minimum lease payments, a schedule by year for the next 5 years, the total sublease rentals to be received, the basis for contingent rental payments, the existence and terms of purchase and renewal options and escalation clauses, and any lease agreement restrictions. The last two categories are included in a general description of the leasing arrangement.

Amortizing the Capital Lease and Reducing the Obligation

A capital lease must be amortized and the liability reduced over the lease period. The method of amortization can be the lessee's usual depreciation method for assets that are owned. It should be pointed out that the period of amortization is always the lease term, even if the economic life of the asset is longer. If the latter occurs, the asset would have an expected residual value, which would go to the lessor. FASB No. 13 also requires that the capital lease obligation be reduced over the lease period by the "interest" method. Under this method, each lease payment is separated into two components: the payment of principal and the payment of interest. The obligation is reduced by the amount of the principal payment.

Reporting Earnings.   For income-reporting purposes, FASB No. 13 requires that both the amortization of the leased property and the annual interest embodied in the lease payment be treated as an expense. This expense then is deducted in the same way that any expense is, to obtain net income. This treatment differs from that for the operating lease, for which only the lease payment itself is deductible as an expense. It also differs from the way all leases were treated prior to FASB No. 13, when only the lease payment was deductible. As you can appreciate, the accounting for leases can become quite complicated.

QUESTIONS

1. What reasons can you cite for a firm's use of intermediate-term debt? Why isn't long-term debt substituted in its place? short-term debt?

2. Why do insurance companies not compete more actively with banks for short- and intermediate-term financing?

3. What is the purpose of protective covenants in a term loan agreement?

4. How does a revolving credit agreement differ from a line of credit?

5. How should a lender go about setting the working capital protective covenant in a loan agreement? the capital expenditure covenant?

6. As a borrower, how would you negotiate over the working capital and capital expenditure restrictions a lender wished to impose?

7. What are the key financial institutions providing intermediate-term financing to business firms?

8. How does a chattel mortgage differ from a conditional sales contract when it comes to financing equipment?

9. Chapter 1 suggests that the decision-making processes of investing funds (buying assets) and of raising funds (financing assets) are two separate and distinct functions of the financial manager. This chapter suggests that, at least in the case of leasing, the decision-making processes cannot be separated. Discuss the problems raised by this sort of situation.

10. How does a financial lease differ from an operating lease? a maintenance lease from a net lease?

11. Contrast a sale and leaseback with direct leasing.

12. In general, how is lease financing treated from an accounting standpoint vis-à-vis debt financing?

13. Discuss the probable impact that a sale and leaseback arrangement will have on
    a. Liquidity ratios
    b. Return on investment
    c. Return on equity
    d. The risk class of the corporation's stock
    e. The price of the stock

14. Some businesspeople consider that the risk of obsolescence and inflexibility is being transferred from the lessee to the lessor. How is the lessor induced to accept higher risk and greater inflexibility?

15. In your opinion, would the following factors tend to favor borrowing or leasing as a financing alternative? Why?

    a. Increased corporate tax rate

    b. Accelerated depreciation

    c. Rising price level

    d. Increased residual value of the leased asset

    e. An increase in the risk-free interest rate

SELF-CORRECTION PROBLEMS

1. Sir Toby Ales is expanding its chain of retail liquor stores. This program will require a capital expenditure of $3 million, which must be financed. The company has settled on a 3-year revolving credit of $3 million, which may be converted into a 3-year term loan at the expiration of the revolving credit commitment. The commitment fee for both credit arrangements is .50 percent of the unused portions. The bank has quoted Sir Toby Ales an interest rate of 1 percent over prime for the revolving credit and $1\frac{1}{2}$ percent over prime for the term loan, if that option is taken. The company expects to borrow $1.4 million at the outset and another $1.6 million at the very end of the first year. At the expiration of the revolving credit, the company expects to take down the full-term loan. At the end of each of the fourth, fifth, and sixth years, it expects to make principal payments of $1 million.

    a. For each of the next 6 years, what is the expected commitment fee in dollars?

    b. What is the expected dollar interest cost above the prime rate?

2. Assuming that annual lease payments are in advance and that there is no residual value, solve for the unknown in each of the following situations:

    a. Purchase price of $46,000, implicit interest rate of 11 percent, a 6-year lease period, solve for the annual lease payment.

    b. Purchase price of $210,000, a 5-year lease period, annual lease payments of $47,030, solve for the implied interest rate.

    c. Implied interest rate of 8 percent, a 7-year lease period, annual lease payments of $16,000, solve for the purchase price.

    d. Purchase price of $165,000, implied interest rate of 10 percent, annual lease payments of $24,412, solve for the lease period.

3. Cordillera Pisco Company wishes to acquire a $100,000 press, which has a useful life of 8 years. At the end of this time, its scrap value will be $8,000. The asset falls into the 5-year property class for cost recovery (depreciation) purposes. The company can use either lease or debt financing. Lease pay-

ments of $16,000 at the beginning of each of the 8 years would be required. If debt financed, the interest rate would be 14 percent and debt payments would be due at the beginning of each of the 8 years. (Interest would be amortized as a mortgage type of debt instrument.) The company is in a 40 percent tax bracket. Which method of financing has the lower present value of cash outflows?

PROBLEMS

1. Zenda Fashions Corporation wishes to borrow $600,000 on a 5-year term basis. Oysterman's National Bank is willing to make such a loan at a 14 percent rate, provided the loan is completely amortized over the 5-year period. Payments are due at the end of each of the 5 years. Set up an amortization schedule of equal annual loan payments that will satisfy these conditions. Be sure to show both the principal and interest components of each of the overall payments.

2. On January 1, Sharpe Razor Corporation is contemplating a 4-year, $3 million term loan from the Fidelity First National Bank. The loan is payable at the end of the fourth year and would involve a loan agreement that would contain a number of protective covenants. Among these restrictions are that the company must maintain working capital of $3 million at all times, that it cannot take on any more long-term debt, that its total liabilities cannot be more than .6 of its total assets, and that capital expenditures in any year are limited to depreciation plus $3 million. The company's balance sheet at December 31, before the term loan, is

Current assets	$ 7 million	Current liabilities	3 million
Net fixed assets	10 million	Long-term debt	
		(due in 5 years)	5
		Net worth	9
	$17 million		$17 million

The proceeds of the term loan will be used in increase Sharpe's investment in inventories and receivables in response to introducing a new "closer-to-the-face" razor blade. The company anticipates a subsequent need to grow at a rate of 24 percent a year, equally divided between current assets and net fixed assets. Profits after taxes of $1.5 million are expected this year, and these profits are expected to grow by $250,000 per year over the subsequent 3 years. The company pays no dividends and does not intend to pay any over the next 4 years. Depreciation in the past year was $2.5 million, and this is predicted to grow over the next 4 years at the same rate as the increase in net fixed assets.

Under the loan agreement, will the company be able to achieve its growth objective?

3. Given the following information, compute the annual lease payment (paid in advance) that a lessor will require:

   a. Purchase price of $260,000, interest rate of 13 percent, 5-year lease period, and no residual value

   b. Purchase price of $138,000, interest rate of 6 percent, 9-year lease period, and a near-certain residual value of $20,000

   c. Purchase price of $773,000, interest rate of 9 percent, 10-year lease period, and no residual value

4. Bork Electronics Company is considering leasing one of its products in addition to selling it outright to customers. The product, the Zeus Tester, sells for $18,600 and has an economic life of 8 years.

   a. To earn 12 percent interest, what annual lease payment must Bork require as lessor? (Assume that lease payments are payable in advance.)

   b. If the product has a salvage value (known with certainty) of $4,000 at the end of 8 years, what annual lease payment will be required?

5. Fez Fabulous Fabrics wishes to acquire a $100,000 multifacet cutting machine. The machine has a useful life of 8 years, after which there is no expected salvage value. If it were to lease finance the machine over 8 years, annual lease payments of $16,000 would be required, payable in advance. The company also could borrow at a 12 percent rate. The asset falls in the 5-year property class for cost recovery (depreciation) purposes, and the company has a 35 percent tax rate. What is the present value of cash outflows for each of these alternatives, using the after-tax cost of debt as the discount rate? Which alternative is preferred?

6. Valequez Ranches, Inc., wishes to acquire a mechanized feed spreader that costs $80,000. The ranch company intends to operate the equipment for 5 years, at which time it will need to be replaced. However, it is expected to have a salvage value of $10,000 at the end of the fifth year. The asset will be depreciated on a straight-line basis ($16,000 per year) over the 5 years, and Valequez Ranches is in a 30 percent tax bracket. Two means for financing the feed spreader are available. A lease arrangement calls for lease payments of $19,000 annually, payable in advance. A debt alternative carries an interest cost of 10 percent. Debt payments will be at the start of each of the 5 years using mortgage type of debt amortization. Using the present-value method, determine the best financing alternative.

Appendix Problem

7. Lucky Locker Corporation has just leased a metal bending machine that calls for annual lease payments of $30,000 payable in advance. The lease period is 6 years, and the lease is classified as a capital asset for accounting purposes. The company's incremental borrowing rate is 11 percent, whereas the lessor's implicit interest rate is 12 percent. Amortization of the lease in the first year amounts to $16,332. On the basis of this information, compute

   a. The accounting lease liability that will be shown on the balance sheet immediately after the first lease payment.

b. The annual lease expense (amortization plus interest) in the first year as it will appear on the accounting income statement. (The interest expense is based on the accounting value determined in part a.)

c. The annual lease expense for tax purposes.

SOLUTIONS TO SELF-CORRECTION PROBLEMS

1. **a, b.**

	YEAR					
	Revolving Credit			Term Loan		
	1	2	3	4	5	6
Amount borrowed during year (in thousands)	$ 1,400	$ 3,000	$ 3,000	$ 3,000	$ 2,000	$ 1,000
Unused portion (in thousands)	1,600	0	0	0	1,000	2,000
Commitment fee (.005)	8,000	0	0	0	5,000	10,000
Interest cost above prime (1% first 3 years and $1\frac{1}{2}$% in last 3)	14,000	30,000	30,000	45,000	30,000	15,000

2. **a.** Using Eq. (20-2) as the formula throughout

$$\$46,000 = \sum_{t=0}^{5} \frac{x}{(1.11)^t}$$

$$\$46,000 = x + 3.6959x$$

$$x = \frac{\$46,000}{4.6959} = \$9,795.78$$

b. $\$210,000 = \sum_{t=0}^{4} \frac{\$47,030}{(1 + x)^t}$

$210,000/\$47,030 = 4.4652$

Subtracting 1 from this gives 3.4652. Looking in Appendix Table B across the year 4 row, we find that 3.4652 is very near the 3.4651 shown for 6 percent. Therefore, the implied interest rate is approximately 6 percent.

c.

$$x = \sum_{t=0}^{6} \frac{\$16,000}{(1.08)^t}$$

$$x = \$16,000(1 + 4.6229)$$

$$= \$89,966.40$$

d. $$\$165,000 = \sum_{t=0}^{x} \frac{\$24,412}{(1.10)^t}$$

$\$165,000/\$24,412 = 6.759$

Substracting 1 from this gives 5.759. Looking in Appendix Table B down the 10 percent column, we find that 5.759 corresponds to year 9. Therefore, the lease period is 9 + 1, or 10 years.

3. Lease cash outflows:

END OF YEAR	(1) LEASE PAYMENT	(2) TAX SHIELD (1)(.40)	(3) CASH OUTFLOWS AFTER TAXES (1) − (2)	(4) PRESENT VALUE OF CASH OUTFLOWS (8.4%)
0	$16,000	—	$16,000	$16,000
1–7	16,000	$6,400	9,600	49,305
8	—	6,400	(6,400)	(3,357)
			Present value of cash outflows =	$61,948

The discount rate is the before-tax cost of borrowing, 14 percent, times 1 minus the tax rate.

Debt cash outflows:

$$\text{Annual debt payment: } \$100,000 = \sum_{t=0}^{7} \frac{x}{(1.14)^t}$$

$$\$100,000 = x + 4.2883x$$

$$x = \frac{\$100,000}{5.2883} = \$18,910$$

END OF YEAR	DEBT PAYMENT	PRINCIPAL AMOUNT OWING AT END OF YEAR	ANNUAL INTEREST
0	$18,910	$81,090	$ 0
1	18,910	73,533	11,353
2	18,910	64,917	10,295
3	18,910	55,096	9,088
4	18,910	43,899	7,713
5	18,910	31,135	6,146
6	18,910	16,584	4,359
7	18,906	0	2,322

The last payment is slightly lower due to rounding throughout.

Present value of cash flows:

END OF YEAR	(1) DEBT PAYMENT	(2) INTEREST	(3) DEPRECIATION	(4) TAX SHIELD (3 + 4).40	(5) AT CASH FLOW (2) − (5)	(6) PV OF CASH FLOWS (8.4%)
0	$18,910	$ 0	$ 0	$ 0	$18,910	$18,910
1	18,910	11,353	20,000	12,541	6,369	5,875
2	18,910	10,295	32,000	16,918	1,992	1,695
3	18,910	9,088	19,200	11,315	7,595	5,962
4	18,910	7,713	11,520	7,693	11,217	8,124
5	18,910	6,146	11,520	7,066	11,844	7,913
6	18,910	4,359	5,760	4,048	14,862	9,160
7	18,906	2,322		929	17,977	10,222
8	(8,000)	Residual value		(3,200)	(4,800)	(2,518)
		Present value of cash outflows				$65,344

As the lease alternative has the lower present value of cash outfflows, it is preferred.

SELECTED REFERENCES

ARNOLD, JASPER H., III, "How to Negotiate a Term Loan," *Harvard Business Review*, 60 (March–April, 1982), 131–38.

BIERMAN, HAROLD, JR., *The Lease versus Buy Decision*. Englewood Cliffs, N.J.: Prentice-Hall, 1982.

BOWER, RICHARD S., "Issues in Lease Financing," *Financial Management*, 2 (Winter 1973), 25–34.
_____, and GEORGE S. OLDFIELD, JR., "Of Lessees, Lessors, and Discount Rates and Whether Pigs Have Wings," *Journal of Business Research*, 9 (March 1981), 29–38.

BOWER, RICHARD S., FRANK C. HERRINGER, and J. PETER WILLIAMSON, "Lease Evaluation," *Accounting Review*, 41 (April 1966), 257–65.

FABOZZI, FRANK J., *Equipment Leasing: A Comprehensive Guide for Executives*. Homestead, Ill.: Dow Jones-Irwin, 1981.

GILL, RICHARD C., "Term Loan Agreements," *Journal of Commercial Bank Lending*, 62 (February 1980), 22–27.

HULL, JOHN C., "The Bargaining Positions of the Parties to a Lease Agreement," *Financial Management*, 11 (Autumn 1982), 71–79.

JOHNSON, ROBERT W., and WILBUR G. LEWELLEN, "Analysis of the Lease-or-Buy Decision," *Journal of Finance*, 27 (September 1972), 815–23.

LEWELLEN, WILBUR G., and DOUGLAS R. EMERY, "On the Matter of Parity Among Financial Obligations," *Journal of Finance*, 36 (March 1981), 97–111.

LEWELLEN, WILBUR G., MICHAEL S. LONG, and JOHN J. McCONNELL, "Asset Leasing in Competitive Capital Markets," *Journal of Finance*, 31 (June 1976), 787–98.

McCONNELL, JOHN J., and JAMES S. SCHALLHEIM, "Valuation of Asset Leasing Contracts," *Journal of Financial Economics*, 12 (August 1983), 237–61.

McDANIEL, MOREY W., "Are Negative Pledge Clauses in Public Debt Issues Obsolete?" *Business Lawyer*, 38 (May 1983), 867–81.

MILLER, MERTON H., and CHARLES W. UPTON, "Leasing, Buying, and the Cost of Capital Services," *Journal of Finance*, 31 (June 1976), 787–98.

MYERS, STEWART C., DAVID A. DILL, and ALBERTO J. BAUTISTA, "Valuation of Financial Lease Contracts," *Journal of Finance*, 31 (June 1976), 799–820.

O'BRIEN, THOMAS J., and BENNIE H. NUNNALLY, JR., "A 1982 Survey of Corporate Leasing Analysis," *Financial Management*, 12 (Summer 1983), 30–36.

SMITH, BRUCE D., "Accelerated Debt Repayment in Leverage Leases," *Financial Management*, 11 (Summer 1982), 73–80.

SMITH, CLIFFORD W., JR., and JEROLD B. WARNER, "On Financial Contracting: An Analysis of Bond Covenants," *Journal of Financial Economics*, 7 (June 1980), 117–61.

VAN HORNE, JAMES, "A Linear-Programming Approach to Evaluating Restrictions under a Bond Indenture or Loan Agreement," *Journal of Financial and Quantitative Analysis*, 1 (June 1966), 68–83.

———, "The Cost of Leasing with Capital Market Imperfections," *Engineering Economist*, 23 (Fall 1977), 1–12.

WEINGARTNER, H. MARTIN, "Leasing, Asset Lives and Uncertainty: Guides to Decision Making," *Financial Management*, 16 (Summer 1987), 5–12.

ZIMMERMAN, CHARLES S., "An Approach to Writing Loan Agreement Covenants," *Journal of Commercial Bank Lending*, 58 (November 1975), 2–17.

CHAPTER 21

Long-term Liabilities

As we continue our stroll through the financing of a company, we take up long-term debt in this chapter. We first explore the features of such debt, move on to various types of instruments, and then examine the nature and value of the call provision. Also, we analyze the profitability of refunding an existing bond issue with a new one. Finally, we investigate the pension fund liability of a company, an extremely important contractual obligation for many a firm.

FEATURES OF BONDS

The long-term debt issues of a corporation have a number of features, many of which are quite interesting. Some are more mundane, and while we have your attention, we will start with them. The fixed return of a long-term debt issue is denoted by the *coupon rate*. A 13 percent debenture indicates that the issuer will pay bondholders $130 per annum for every $1,000-face-value bond they hold. The *yield to maturity* on a bond is determined by solving for the rate of discount that equates the present value of principal and interest payments with the current market price of the bond. (See Chapter 4 for the mathematics of bond interest.)

A company issuing bonds to the public designates a qualified *trustee* to represent the interests of the bondholders. The obligations of a trustee are specified in the Trust Indenture Act of 1939, administered by the Securities and Exchange Commission. The trustee's responsibilities are to authenticate the bond issue's legality at the time of issuance, to watch over the financial condition and behavior of the borrower to make sure all contractual obligations are carried out, and to initiate appropriate actions if the borrower does not meet any of these obligations. The trustee is compensated directly by the corporation, a compensation that adds to the costs of borrowing.

The legal agreement between the corporation issuing the bonds and the trustee, who represents the bondholders, is defined in the **indenture**. The indenture contains the terms of the bond issue as well as the restrictions placed on the company. These restrictions, known as *protective covenants*, are very similar to those contained in a term loan agreement. Because we analyzed protective covenants in Chapter 20, it is not necessary to describe them here. The terms contained in the indenture are established jointly by the borrower and trustee. If the issue is a negotiated underwriting, the underwriter also will be involved. If the corporation defaults under any of the provisions of the indenture, the trustee, on behalf of the bondholders, can take action to correct the situation. If not satisfied, the trustee then can call for the immediate payment of all outstanding bonds.

> **Indenture.** A formal agreement establishing the terms of a bond issue and the relationship among borrower, bondholders, and trustee.

Bond Ratings

The creditworthiness of a publicly traded debt instrument often is judged by investors in terms of the credit rating assigned to it by investment agencies. The principal rating agencies are Moody's Investors Service and Standard & Poor's. The issuer of a new corporate bond contracts with the agency to evaluate and rate the bond, as well as to update the rating throughout the bond's life. For this service, the issuer pays a fee. In addition, the rating agency charges subscribers to its rating publications.

Based on their evaluations of a bond issue, the agencies give their opinion in the form of letter grades, which are published for use by investors. In their ratings, the agencies attempt to rank issues according to the probability of default. The highest grade issues, whose risk of default is felt to be negligible, are rated triple A, followed by double A, single A, B double a, and so forth through C and D, which are the lowest grades of the two agencies, respectively. The first four grades mentioned are considered to represent investment-quality issues, whereas other rated bonds are considered speculative. For each rating category, a modifier of 1, 2, or 3 is applied. For example, Aa-1 means that a security is in the higher end of the Aa rating category. Baa-3 indicates that a security is in the lower end of the Baa category. The ratings by the two agencies are widely respected as measures of default risk. In fact, many investors do not separately analyze the default risk of a company.

Junk Bonds

Junk bond. A bond with a rating of Ba or less.

During the 1980s an active market developed for noninvestment grade bonds. These are bonds with a grade of Ba or less, and they are called "junk" or "high-yield" bonds. The market was promulgated by the investment banking firm of Drexel Burnham Lambert, and is still dominated by that firm. A number of companies now use this market to raise billions and billions of dollars of capital each year. In addition, junk bonds have been used in acquisitions (a topic taken up in Chapter 24).

The principal investors include pension funds, "high-yield" bond mutual funds, and a limited number of savings and loan associations. A secondary market of sorts exists, but in any kind of financial panic or "flight to quality" by investors, such liquidity would dry up. So far, the default losses on junk bonds have been low, no more than $1\frac{1}{2}$ percent in lost return above that for investment grade bonds. However, the market is too new to have a good long-term picture of their true default risk. After all, it takes a fairly severe economic downturn to get a proper perspective.

On a public policy level there is concern that junk bond financing has led to speculative froth, and proposals have been advanced to restrict their issuance. Such proposals have mainly to do with bonds used to finance takeover and not with the regular raising of capital. For many companies—including medium-sized and/or newer companies—junk bonds have become a viable means of financing. Their issuance is conditional on stable or improving financial market conditions. In an unstable market, few investors are to be found.

Sinking fund. Fund established to retire a bond issue before maturity. The corporation is required to make periodic sinking-fund payments to a trustee.

Sinking Funds

The majority of corporate bond issues carry a provision for a **sinking fund** that requires the corporation to make periodic sinking-fund payments to a trustee, in order to retire a specified face amount of bonds each period. The sinking-fund retirement of a bond issue can take two forms: (1) The corporation can make a cash payment to the trustee, which in turn calls the bonds for redemption at the sinking-fund call price. (This usually is lower than the regular call price of a bond, which we will discuss shortly.) The bonds themselves are called on a lottery basis by their serial numbers, which are published in the *Wall Street Journal* and other papers. (2) The corporation can purchase bonds in the open market and pay the trustee by delivering to it a given number of bonds.

The corporation should purchase the bonds in the open market as long as the market price is less than the sinking-fund call price; when the market price exceeds the call price, it should make cash payments to the trustee. Because of the orderly retirement of debt as well as the liquidity provided by the regular purchase activity, many investors find the sinking-fund provision valuable. In general, sinking-fund bonds yield less than comparable bond issues that have no sinking-fund provision, partly because of the shorter duration. Many sinking funds begin not at the time of issuance of the bond but after a period of 5 or 10 years. Also, sinking-fund payments do not necessarily retire the bond issue. There can be a "balloon" payment at final maturity.

Some corporations, in purchasing bonds for sinking-fund payment, find that *accumulators* have got there first. Accumulators are institutional or other investors who buy bonds in advance of the corporation's going into the market to acquire them for sinking funds. If supply is sufficiently restricted, the corporation will be able to purchase bonds only by bidding up the price. In this way, the accumulator hopes to sell the bonds at an inflated price, knowing the corporation must purchase them in order to satisfy the sinking-fund requirement.

For example, an accumulator might buy bonds at a price of $810 per bond to yield 14.9 percent and sell them to the corporation for $890, which corresponds to a yield of 13.3 percent. While the price is significantly above the previous going market price, imperfections allow the accumulator to partially corner the market, thereby forcing the corporation to pay the inflated price. Although perfectly legal, accumulators are not looked on with great favor by financial managers. Only when the bonds sell at a discount from the sinking-fund call price, of course, does accumulation occur. Otherwise, the corporation will make a cash payment to the trustee, which will purchase bonds at the call price.

Floating Rate Notes

Instead of a fixed interest rate over the life of the debt instrument, the interest rate can float with some short-term rate, such as the Treasury bill or commercial paper rate. With the high and volatile interest rate environment of the early 1980s, many corporations were reluctant to commit to long-term debt. Floating rate notes (FRN) were looked to as a way to reduce some of the risk of volatile interest rates. A typical FRN might have a 5-year maturity with the interest rate adjusted every 3 months in keeping with changes in the Treasury bill rate. An initial interest rate is set for the first 3 months, but after that the instrument might provide an interest rate 0.5 percent above the 3-month Treasury bill rate.

Often a minimum or floor rate is specified, and there may be some special features such as options, a declining spread, or even a fixed-rate provision after a specified change in rates. The FRN is a financial innovation that came about in response to volatile interest rates. During such times its use is widespread.

TYPES OF DEBT INSTRUMENTS

Debentures

Debenture. An unsecured, long-term debt instrument.

The word **debenture** usually applies to the unsecured bonds of a corporation. Investors look to the earning power of the corporation as their security. Because these general credit bonds are not secured by specific property, in the event of liquidation the holder becomes a general creditor. Although the bonds are unsecured, debenture holders are protected by the restrictions imposed in the indenture, particularly the negative pledge clause, which precludes the corporation from pledging its assets to other creditors. This provision safeguards the investor in that the borrower's assets will not be impaired in the future. Because debenture holders must look to the general credit of the borrower to meet principal and interest payments, only well-established and creditworthy companies are able to issue debentures.

Subordinated Debentures

Subordination. A debt issue giving a lower claim on assets and income than other classes of debt. Known as junior debt.

Subordinated debentures represent debt that ranks behind debt senior to these debentures with respect to the claim on assets. In the event of liquidation, subordinated debenture holders usually only receive settlement if all senior creditors are paid the full amount owed them. These holders still would rank ahead of preferred and common stockholders in the event of liquidation. The existence of **subordination** may work to the advantage of senior bondholders because senior holders are able to assume the claims of the subordinated debenture holders. To illustrate: a corporation is liquidated for $600,000. It had $400,000 in straight debentures outstanding, $400,000 in subordinated debentures outstanding, and $400,000 in obligations owed to general creditors. One might suppose that the straight debenture holders and the general creditors would have an equal and prior claim in liquidation, that each would receive $300,000. The fact is that the straight debenture holders are entitled to the subordinated debenture holders' claims, giving them $800,000 in total claims. As a result, they are entitled to two-thirds of the liquidating value, or $400,000, whereas general creditors are entitled to only one-third or $200,000.

Because of the nature of the claim, a straight subordinated debenture issue has to provide a yield significantly higher than does a regular debenture issue in order to be attractive to investors. Frequently, subordinated debentures are convertible into common stock and, therefore, may sell at a yield that actually is less than what the company would have to pay on an ordinary debenture. From the standpoint of a creditor, the equity base of the firm is the same whether the issue remains as subordinated debentures or is converted into common stock.

Mortgage Bonds

A **mortgage bond** issue is secured by a lien on specific assets of the corporation—usually fixed assets. The specific property securing the bonds is described in detail in the mortgage, which is the legal document giving the bondholder a lien on a property. As with other secured lending arrangements, the market value of the collateral should exceed the amount of the bond issue by a reasonable margin of safety. If the corporation defaults in any of the provisions of the bond indenture, the trustee, on behalf of the bondholders, has the power to foreclose. In a foreclosure, the trustee takes over the property and sells it, using the proceeds to pay the bonds. If the proceeds are less than the amount of the issue outstanding, the bondholders become general creditors for the residual amount.

Mortgage bond. A bond issue secured by a mortgage.

A company may have more than one bond issue secured by the same property. A bond issue may be secured by a *second mortgage* on property already used to secure another bond issue under a *first mortgage*. In the event of foreclosure, the first-mortgage bondholders must be paid the full amount owed them before there can be any distribution to the second-mortgage bondholders.

Income Bonds

A company is obligated to pay interest on an **income bond** only when it is earned. There may be a cumulative feature in the issue where unpaid interest in a particular year accumulates. If the company does generate earnings, it will have to pay the cumulative interest to the extent that earnings permit. However, the cumulative obligation usually is limited to no more than 3 years. As should be evident, this type of security offers the investor a rather weak promise of a fixed return. Nevertheless, the income bond is still senior to preferred and common stock, as well as to any subordinated debt. Unlike preferred stock dividends, the interest payment is deductible for tax purposes. Because income bonds are not popular with investors, they have been used principally in reorganizations.[1]

Income bonds. A bond where the payment of interest is contingent upon the earnings of the firm.

Equipment Trust Certificates

Although equipment trust financing is a form of lease financing, the certificates themselves represent an intermediate- to long-term fixed-income investment. This method of financing is used by railroads to finance the acquisition of rolling stock. Under this method, the railroad arranges with a trustee to purchase equipment from a manufacturer. The railroad signs a contract with the manufacturer for the construction of specific equipment. When the equipment is delivered, equipment trust certificates are sold to investors. The proceeds of this sale, together with the down payment by the railroad, are used to pay the manufacturer.

---

[1] For an extensive analysis of income bonds, see John J. McConnell and Gary G. Schlarbaum, "Returns, Risks, and Pricing of Income Bonds," *Journal of Business*, 54 (January 1981), 33–57.

Title to the equipment is held by the trustee, which in turn leases the equipment to the railroad. Lease payments are used by the trustee to pay a fixed return on the certificates outstanding—actually a dividend—and to retire a specified portion of the certificates at regular intervals. Upon the final lease payment by the railroad, the last of the certificates is retired, and title to the equipment passes to the railroad.

The duration of the lease varies according to the equipment involved, but 15 years is rather common. Because rolling stock is essential to the operation of a railroad and has a ready market value, equipment trust certificates enjoy a very high standing as fixed-income investments. As a result, railroads are able to acquire cars and locomotives on favorable financing terms. Airlines, too, use a form of equipment trust certificate to finance jet aircraft. Though these certificates are usually sold to institutional investors, some issues are sold to the public.

Project Financing

The term *project financing* describes various financing arrangements for large, individual investment projects. Often a separate legal entity is formed to own the project. Suppliers of capital then look to the earnings stream of the project for repayment of their loan or for the return on their equity investment. Often the project involves energy: not only large explorations of gas, oil, and coal but also tankers, port facilities, refineries, and pipelines. Other projects include alumina plants, fertilizer plants, and power plants. These projects require huge amounts of capital, which a single company cannot usually supply. Many times a consortium of companies is formed to spread risk and to finance the project. Part of the funds comes from equity participations by the companies, and the rest comes from lenders or lessors.

If the loan or lease is on a nonrecourse basis, the lender or lessor pays exclusive attention to the size of the equity participation and to the economic feasibility of the project. In other words, the lender or lessor can look only to the project for payout, so the larger the equity cushion and the more confidence that can be placed in the projections, the better the project. In another type of arrangement, each sponsor may guarantee its share or the project's obligations. Under these circumstances, the lender or lessor places emphasis on the creditworthiness of the sponsors as well as on the economic feasibility of the project.

For the sponsors of the project, there are several types of sharing rules. In a "take-or-pay" type of arrangement, each sponsor agrees to purchase a specific percentage of the output of the project and to pay that percentage of the operating costs of the project plus debt-servicing charges. In a "throughput" arrangement, which frequently involves pipelines, each sponsor is required to ship through the facility a certain amount, or percentage, or product. If the total shipped is insufficient to cover the expenses of running the facility, sponsors are assessed additional amounts to cover the shortfall. The amount of assessment is proportional to their participation. The maturity of the loan or lease corresponds to the likely ability of the project to generate cash over time. While the financing need not be long term, in most cases it extends over 8 or more years.

Actually, the term *project financing* conveys nothing more than the financing of a large project. The methods of financing are no different from those we have studied. They include debt and lease financing. What is different is the size and complexity of the financing. It is tailored to the needs of the sponsors as well as to the needs of potential suppliers of capital. Tax considerations rank very high in tailoring the financing to the best advantage of all parties. The key is that the project stands alone in the sense that the sponsoring companies are liable for no more than their equity participations and their obligations under a "throughput" arrangement if such exists.

CALL PROVISION

Most corporate bond issues provide for a call feature, which gives the corporation the option to buy back the bonds at a stated price before their maturity. Not all bond issues are callable; in times of low interest rates in particular, some corporations issue noncallable, or "noncall-life," bonds as they are known. When a bond is callable, the **call price** usually is above the par value of the bond and decreases over time. A bond with 20 years to maturity might be callable at $110 ($1,100 per $1,000-face-value bond) the next 2 years, $109 the following 2 years, and so on until the final 2 years, when it is callable at $101. Frequently, the call price in the first year is established at 1 year's interest above the face value of the bond. If the coupon rate is 14 percent, the initial call price may be $114 ($1,140 per $1,000 face value).

Call price. The price the company must pay for a security when it wishes to redeem it.

There are two types of call provisions, according to when they can be exercised. The security may be immediately callable, which simply means that the instrument may be bought back by the issuer at the call price at any time. Rather than being immediately callable, the call provision may be deferred for a period of time. The most widely used deferred call periods are 5 years for public utility bonds and 10 years for industrial bonds. During this deferment period, the investor is protected from a call by the issuer. In recent years, virtually all issues of corporate bonds have involved a deferred call as opposed to an immediate call feature.

The call provision gives the company flexibility in its financing. If interest rates should decline significantly, it can call the bonds and refinance the issue at a lower interest cost. Thus, the company does not have to wait until the final maturity to refinance. In addition, the provision may be advantageous to the company if it finds any of the protective covenents in the bond indenture to be unduly restrictive. By calling the bonds before maturity, the company can eliminate these restrictions. Of course, if the issue is refinanced with bonds, similar restrictions may be imposed.

Value of Call Privilege

Although the call privilege is beneficial to the issuing corporation, it works to the detriment of investors. If interest rates fall and the bond issue is called, they can invest in other bonds only at a sacrifice in yield to maturity. Consequently, the call privilege usually does not come free to the borrower. Its cost, or value, is measured at the time of issuance by the difference in yield on the callable bond and the yield that would be necessary if the security were noncallable. This value is determined by supply and demand forces in the market for callable securities.

When interest rates are high and expected to fall, the call feature is likely to have significant value. Investors are unwilling to invest in callable bonds unless such bonds yield more than bonds that are noncallable, all other things the same. In other words, they must be compensated for assuming the risk that the bonds might be called. On the other hand, borrowers are willing to pay a premium in yield for the call privilege in the belief that yields will fall and that it will be advantageous to refund the bonds.

When interest rates are low and are expected to rise, the call privilege may have a negligible value in that the company might pay the same interest rate if there were no call privilege. For the privilege to have value, interest rate expectations must make it seem possible that the issue will be called. If interest rates are low and are not expected to fall further, there is little probability that the bonds will be called. The key factor is that the borrower has to be able to refund the issue at a profit; and that cannot be done unless interest rates drop significantly, for the issuer must pay the call price—which is usually at a premium above par value—as well as the flotation costs involved in refinancing. If there is no probability that the borrower can refund the issue at a profit, the call privilege is unlikely to have a value.

The announcement of a call may convey information to investors about the future of the company. If the call changes the capital structure of the company, for example, investors may react to the leverage change apart from whether or not the bond issue is refunded at a lower interest cost. As we discussed in Chapters 17 and 19, the leverage change may convey information about an unanticipated change in the earnings prospects of the company—positive for increases in leverage and negative for decreases.

REFUNDING A BOND ISSUE

Refunding. The replacement of one debt issue with another, usually to realize a lower interest cost.

In this section, we analyze the profitability of a company's refunding a bond issue before its maturity. By **refunding**, we mean calling the issue and replacing it with a new issue of bonds. In this regard, we focus our attention on only one reason for refunding—profitability—which, in turn, is due to interest rates' having declined since the bonds were issued.

A Refunding Example

The refunding decision can be regarded as a form of capital budgeting: There is an initial cash outlay followed by future interest savings. These savings are represented by the difference between the annual net cash outflow required under the old bonds and the net cash outflow required on the new, or refunding, bonds. Calculating the initial cash outlay is more complex. Consequently, it is best to show an example of this method of evaluation.[2]

A company currently has a $20 million, 12 percent debenture issue outstanding, and the issue still has 20 years to final maturity. Because interest rates are significantly lower than at the time of the original offering, the company can now sell a $20 million issue of 20-year bonds at a coupon rate of 10 percent that will net it $19,600,000 after the underwriting spread.

For federal income tax purposes, the unamortized issuing expense of the old bonds, the **call premium**, and the unamortized discount of the old bonds, if they were sold at a discount, are deductible as expenses in the year of the refunding. The old bonds were sold 5 years ago at a $250,000 discount from par value, so the unamortized portion now is $200,000. Moreover, the legal fees and other issuing expenses involved with the old bonds have an unamortized balance of $100,000. The call price on the old bonds is $109, issuing expenses on the new bonds are $150,000, the income tax rate is 40 percent, and there is a 30-day period of overlap. The period of overlap is the lag between the time the new bonds are sold and the time the old bonds are called. This lag occurs because most companies wish to have the proceeds from the new issue in hand before they call the old issue. Otherwise, there is a certain amount of risk associated with calling the old issue and being at the "mercy" of the bond market in raising new funds. During the period of overlap, the company pays interest on both bond issues.

Call premium. The excess of the call price of a security over its par value.

Framework for Analysis. With this rather involved background information in mind, we can calculate the initial cash outflow and the future cash benefits. The net cash outflow at the time of the refunding is as follows:

Cost of calling old bonds (call price $109)		$21,800,000
Net proceeds of new bond issue		19,600,000
Difference		$ 2,200,000
Expenses		
Issuing expense of new bonds	$ 150,000	
Interest expense on old bonds during overlap period	200,000	
Gross cash outlay		350,000
		$ 2,550,000
Less: Tax savings		
Interest expense on old bonds during overlap period	200,000	
Call premium	1,800,000	
Unamortized discount on old bonds	200,000	
Unamortized issuing expenses on old bonds	100,000	
Total	$2,300,000	
Tax savings (40% of amount above)		920,000
Net cash outflow		$ 1,630,000

For ease of presentation, we ignore any interest that might be earned by investing the refunding bond proceeds in marketable securities during the 30-day pe-

---

[2] This section draws upon Oswald D. Bowlin, "The Refunding Decision: Another Special Case in Capital Budgeting," *Journal of Finance*, 21 (March 1966), 55–68. Its development assumes that the reader has covered Chapter 13.

riod of overlap. The annual net cash benefits may be determined by calculating the difference between the net cash outflow required on the old bonds and the net cash outflow required on the new or refunding bonds. We assume for simplicity that interest is paid but once a year, at year end. The annual net cash outflow on the old bonds is

Interest expense 12%		$2,400,000
Less: Tax savings		
Interest expense	$2,400,000	
Amortization of bond discount ($200,000/20)	10,000	
Amortization of issuing costs ($100,000/20)	5,000	
Total	$2,415,000	
Tax savings (40% of amount above)		966,000
Annual net cash outflow, old bonds		$1,434,000

For the new bonds, the bond discount as well as the issuing costs may be amortized for tax purposes in the same manner as were the old bonds. The annual net cash outflow on the new bonds is shown in the following table.

Interest expense 10%		$2,000,000
Less: Tax savings		
Interest expense	$2,000,000	
Amortization of bond discount ($400,000/20)	20,000	
Amortization of issuing costs ($150,000/20)	7,500	
Total	$2,027,500	
Tax savings (40% of amount above)		811,000
Annual net cash outflow, new bonds		$1,189,000
Difference between annual net cash outflows ($1,434,000 − $1,189,000)		$ 245,000

Discounting.   Thus, for an initial net cash outflow of **$1,630,000**, the company can achieve annual net cash benefits of **$245,000** over the next 20 years. Because the net cash benefits occur in the future, they must be discounted back to present value. But what discount rate should be used? Certain authors advocate the use of the cost of capital. However, a refunding operation differs from other investment proposals. Once the new bonds are sold, the net cash benefits are known with certainty. From the standpoint of the corporation, the refunding operation is essentially a riskless investment project. The only risk associated with the cash flows is that of the firm's defaulting in the payment of principal or interest. Because a premium for default risk is embodied in the market rate of interest the firm pays, the appropriate discount rate might be the after-tax cost of borrowing on the refunding bonds. Using this cost, 10%(1 − .40) = 6 percent, as our discount factor, the refunding operation would be worthwhile if the net present value were positive.[3] For our example, the net present value is

[3] Recall from Chapter 13 that the net present value is the present value of net cash benefits less the initial cash outflow.

$1,180,131, indicating that the refunding operation is worthwhile. The internal rate of return is 13.92 percent, indicating again that the refunding is worthwhile, because the internal rate of return exceeds the required rate of 6 percent.[4]

Other Considerations

Just because a refunding operation is found to be worthwhile, it should not necessarily be undertaken right away. If interest rates are declining, and this decline is expected to continue, management may prefer to delay the refunding. At a later date, the refunding bonds can be sold at an even lower rate of interest, making the refunding operation even more worthwhile. The decision concerning timing must be based on expectations of future interest rates.

Several points should be raised with respect to the calculations in our example. First, most firms refund an existing issue with a new bond issue of a longer maturity. In our example, we assumed that the new bond issue had the same maturity as that of the old bond issue. Our analysis needs to be modified slightly when the maturity dates are different. The usual procedure is to consider only the net cash benefits up to the maturity of the old bonds. A second assumption in our example was that neither issue involved sinking-fund bonds or serial bonds. If either issue calls for periodic reduction of the debt, we must adjust our procedure for determining future net cash benefits. Finally, the annual cash outflows associated with the refunding bonds usually are less than those associated with the refunded bonds. As a result, there is a decrease in the leverage of the firm. While this effect is likely to be small, on occasion it can be a significant consideration.

PENSION FUND LIABILITY

Although it does not appear on the balance sheet, many companies have a contractual obligation to make present and future pension payments. Under the Employee Retirement Income Security Act of 1974 (ERISA), this liability is every bit as binding a claim as a federal tax lien and is senior to all other claims. In other words, it is extremely important and goes to the head of the line of creditors if the firm were to be liquidated. In the aggregate, corporate pension fund liabilities have grown enormously during the last two decades, representing a huge source of investment funds. For some companies this liability exceeds tangible assets. As a financial manager, you will be involved in any pension fund your company might have, so a basic understanding is essential.

---

[4] An alternative method of analysis is to replicate the cash outflows of the old bond issue and then determine the present value of this stream using as the discount rate the interest rate at which new bonds could be sold in the current market. If this present value exceeds the call price of the old bonds, the refunding would be worthwhile. Among others using this approach are Jess B. Yawitz and James A . Anderson, "The Effect of Bond Refunding on Shareholder Wealth," *Journal of Finance*, 32 (December 1979), 1738–46.

Types of Pension Plans

Corporate pension plans may be one of two types. A *defined benefit plan* either pays a retired employee so many dollars per month or it pays the individual a percentage of his or her final salary. Either way the benefits are what is specified. Typically, these payments are flat, with no provision for increases with inflation. Under ERISA, a person who leaves a company prior to regular retirement age will qualify for pension benefits, provided he or she has been with the firm a sufficient time. This provision is known as **vesting.** A plan must be 100 percent vested after a certain period of employment, the maximum length a company may take before full vesting an employee being 10 years.

Vesting. Employee being entitled to part or all of his or her pension upon departure prior to the official retirement age.

The second type of plan is a *defined contribution plan.* Here a company agrees to make a specified monthly or annual payment to the pension plan. All contributions to the plan are a tax-deductible expense by the corporation. (Usually, these payments may be augmented by the employee making individual contributions on a voluntary basis.) The contributions are invested, and at retirement the employee is entitled to the cumulative total of contributions plus investment earnings on those contributions. Only when the employee retires and actually receives payment are taxes paid on the benefits. In the accumulation/investment phase, no taxes are paid. Actual future benefits paid to an employee are not known with certainty; they depend on what can be earned by investing the contributions. As most corporate employees are covered by defined benefit plans, we concentrate on the former type of plan.

Funded and Unfunded Liabilities

The pension liability of a company with a defined benefit plan is composed of two parts. There is the liability to currently retired employees. The present value of this obligation depends on their average life expectancy as well as the discount rate used. The second obligation is to employees not yet retired. This obligation is further subdivided into (1) the benefits earned by employees by virtue of past employment and (2) likely benefits to be earned based on future service. The latter is a forecast, and obviously subject to error. The total pension liability of a company must be valued, usually by an actuary. The idea is to determine the amount of funds necessary for a company to be able to make good on its pension obligations. The *present value of liabilities* is calculated by discounting to present-value likely future benefits to be paid, where these benefits are based on past service as well as on expected future service.

The magnitude of present-value liability obviously is sensitive to the discount rate employed—the higher the rate, the lower the liability. However, the rate must correspond to a realistic return on investment in stocks, bonds, and other assets. Usually actuaries are conservative in the rate they use. This may make sense, inasmuch as they typically ignore the effect of inflation on future salaries and wages. By changing actuarial assumptions, companies sometimes are able to reduce pension fund liabilities in relation to assets. However, the change is an accounting one and usually does not affect the obligation in an economic sense. Moreover, auditors and government agencies restrict the degree to which "creative" actuarial changes can occur.

Once the liabilities are valued, the assets must be valued. This valuation process also consists of two parts. The first involves past corporate contributions. These contributions are paid to a trust or insurance company and invested in a diversified portfolio of assets. The market value of this portfolio then is its value, though some actuaries value the portfolio using historical costs. The second part involves the present value of expected future contributions by the company for future service by employees. Again this is an estimate, and this total also is sensitive to the discount rate. The *present value of assets* is the sum of the two parts.

It is desirable, of course, for the present value of the assets to equal the present value of the pension liabilities. This seldom is the case. When the former is less than the latter, there is said to be an unfunded liability, which is simply

Unfunded liability = *PV* of pension liabilities − *PV* of pension assets

If a company has an unfunded liability, it must be reported in a footnote to the balance sheet. For some companies, the unfunded liability is large and is a matter of concern to creditors. Why? Because it represents a claim that ultimately must be paid. If the underfunded plan is terminated, the company is responsible for the deficit up to 30 percent of its net worth. Credit- and bond-rating agencies are mindful of this obligation and analyze it closely before assigning a rating.

We must recognize that the unfunded liability of a company is not a precise figure. It is an actuary's estimate and is subject to a number of assumptions. However, suppliers of capital should watch closely a company's unfunded liability and dig into the assumptions. For many a company, it simply is too large a potential liability to be ignored, despite problems of estimation. In fact, for some companies the unfunded pension liability dwarfs all other liabilities.

Other Aspects

If a company should go into bankruptcy and there not be enough on hand to meet its pension obligations, the Pension Benefit Guarantee Corporation (PBGC) makes good on most of the total obligation. This government agency is funded by premiums paid to it by companies with pension plans. Because the premium is invariant with respect to default risk, there is gamesmanship to it. From the standpoint of the stockholders of a company, the bias is for the pension fund to invest in risky assets. If the investments go well, they gain in enhanced share value; if badly, the PBGC is left holding the bag. Another variant is that when interest rates decline and actuarial assumptions result in a plan being overfunded, many companies voluntarily terminate their plans and start new ones. The "excess overfunding" in the old plan then reverts to the company, boosting earnings and net worth. Whether wealth is expropriated in favor of the company's equity holders depends on the circumstances, but some sizable increases in share price have been found around the time of the reversion. Obviously, the

PBGC would like to reduce the "games" played against it, but its legislated tools to do so are limited.

Throughout our discussion, we have dealt with pensions for nonunion employees. Unions have their own pension plans, and the labor contracts they negotiate with corporations include contributions to the union pension fund. Union employees look to this fund and not to the company's for their retirement income.

An important responsibility of the financial manager is to oversee the management of the pension fund's investments. This involves determining asset allocations, choosing investment managers, and monitoring their investment performance. These responsibilities are in addition to analyzing actuarial assumptions, determining the proper funding of a plan, and overseeing the record keeping. These topics as well as those discussed could occupy an entire book. We have just skimmed the surface, but in so doing have, we hope, conveyed the importance of pension plans and of the unfunded liability to suppliers of capital. The interested reader is referred to more detailed discussions and analyses.[5]

SUMMARY

The principal features of debt include the fixed or floating rate return, the final maturity, the priority of claim on assets, the credit quality (going from the highest investment grade to junk bonds), the call privilege, and the presence or absence of a sinking-fund provision. Types of debt financing include debentures, subordinated debentures, mortgage bonds, collateral trust bonds, income bonds, equipment trust certificates, and project financing.

In financing with long-term debt, the company must bargain with investors over the terms of the debt instrument. If the company wishes to include terms that are not beneficial to investors, it must be prepared to pay a higher yield in order to sell the instrument. If debentures are subordinated, investors will demand a higher yield than if the issue involves straight debentures. Another interesting aspect of the bargaining process between the borrower and the investors relates to the call privilege. If interest rate expectations in the market lead investors to think that the issue may be called, the company will have to pay a higher yield for the privilege of being able to call it.

A method was proposed for analyzing the refunding of an existing bond issue before maturity. By refunding, we mean calling the old issue and replacing it with a new, refunding bond issue. The method proposed treats the refunding operation as a riskless capital budgeting project.

The financial manager necessarily is involved in the company's pension plan. Most corporate plans involve defined benefits, and the present value of the pension liability must be compared with the present value of assets earmarked to meet that obligation. If the former exceeds the latter, the company has an unfunded liability. The magnitude of this liability should be watched closely by suppliers of capital, for pensions are a prior claim in the event of liquidation.

[5] See, for example, Daniel M. McGill, *Fundamentals of Private Pensions*, 5th ed. (Philadelphia: Pension Research Council, University of Pennsylvania, 1984); and Lawrence J. Kotlikoff and Daniel E. Smith, *Pensions in the American Economy* (Chicago: University of Chicago Press, 1983).

QUESTIONS

1. What is the role of rating services when it comes to a company's bond issues?
2. Contrast serial bonds and bonds requiring a sinking fund.
3. There are two ways in which sinking-fund payments may be used by the trustee. What are the benefits and drawbacks of each to the bondholders and the company?
4. How does an income bond differ from a mortgage bond issue?
5. Explain why a commercial bank loan officer would be particularly concerned with subordinated debt owed to the principal stockholders or officers of a company.
6. What are "junk bonds"? How might they be used in financing a corporation?
7. In issuing long-term debt, which types of instruments would be most used by railroads? by public utilities? by industrial firms?
8. Why do callable bonds typically have a higher yield to maturity than noncallable bonds, holding all other things constant? Is the yield differential likely to be constant over time? If not, why not?
9. In the refunding decision, differential cash flows are discounted at the after-tax cost of debt. Explain why these cash flows are not discounted at the average cost of capital.
10. Are refundings by corporations likely to occur steadily over time? If not, when are waves of refundings likely to occur?
11. Contrast a defined benefit pension plan with a defined contribution plan.
12. Why should a supplier of capital be concerned with the way a company handles its pension plan?

SELF-CORRECTION PROBLEMS

1. The Lemand Corporation has $8 million of 10 percent mortgage bonds outstanding under an open-end indenture. The indenture allows additional bonds to be issued as long as all of the following conditions are met:
   a. Pretax interest coverage [(income before taxes + bond interest)/bond interest] remains greater than 4.
   b. Net depreciated value of mortgage assets remains twice the amount of mortgage debt.
   c. Debt/equity ratio remains below .5.

   The Lemand Corporation has net income after taxes of $2 million and a 50 percent tax rate, $40 million in equity, and $30 million in depreciated assets, covered by the mortgage. Assuming that 50 percent of the proceeds of a new issue would be added to the base of mortgaged assets and that the company has no sinking-fund payments until next year, how much more

10 percent debt could be sold under each of the three conditions? Which protective covenant is binding?

Northern California Public Service Company is considering refunding its preferred stock. The dividend rate on this stock is $6, and it has a par value of $50 a share. The call price is $52 a share, and 500,000 shares are outstanding. George Arroya, vice-president, finance, feels the company can issue new preferred stock in the current market at an interest rate of 11 percent. With this rate, the new issue could be sold at par; the total par value of the issue would be $25 million. Flotation costs of $780,000 are tax deductible, but the call premium is not tax deductible; the company's marginal tax rate is 30 percent. A 90-day period of overlap is expected between the time the new preferred stock is issued and the time the old preferred stock is retired. Should the company refund its preferred stock? (Preferred stock dividends are assumed to be paid forever unless the issue is called. These dividends are not deductible as an expense for corporate tax purposes. The problem may be set up in the same way as a bond refunding, except for the qualifications noted above.)

PROBLEMS

1. Bragon Manufacturing Company has in its capital structure $20 million of $13\frac{1}{2}$ percent sinking-fund debentures. The sinking fund call price is $1,000 per bond, and sinking-fund payments of $1 million in face amount of bonds are required annually. Presently, the yield to maturity on the debentures in the market is 12.21 percent. To satisfy the sinking-fund payment, should the company deliver cash to the trustee or bonds? What if the yield to maturity were 14.60 percent?

2. The Hirsch Corporation is in bankruptcy. Mortgaged assets have been sold for $5 million, and other assets have yielded $10 million. Hirsch has $10 million in mortgage bonds, $5 million in subordinated (to the mortgage bonds) debentures, $15 million owed to general creditors, and $10 million par value of common stock. How would the $15 million distribution in bankruptcy be made?

3. Five years ago, Zapada International issued $50 million of 10 percent, 25-year debentures at a price of $990 per bond to the public. The call price was originally $1,100 per bond the first year after issuance, and this price declined by $10 each subsequent year. Zapada now is calling the bonds in order to refund them at a lower interest rate.

   a. Ignoring taxes, what is the bondholder's return on investment for the 5 years? (Assume that interest is paid once a year and that the investor owns one bond.)

   b. If the bondholder now can invest $1,000 in a 20-year security of equivalent risk that provides 8 percent interest, what is the overall return over the 25-year holding period? How does this compare with the return on the Zapada bonds had they not been called? (Assume again that interest is paid once a year. Both rates of return can be approximated using the present-value tables at the end of the book.)

4. The U.S. Zither Corporation has $50 million of 14 percent debentures out-standing, which are due in 25 years. USZ could refund these bonds in the current market with new 25-year bonds, sold to the public at par ($1,000 per bond) with a 12 percent coupon rate. The spread to the underwriter is 1 percent, leaving $990 per bond in proceeds to the company. The old bonds have an unamortized discount of $1 million, unamortized legal fees and other expenses of $100,000, and a call price of $1,140 per bond. The tax rate is 40 percent. There is a 1-month overlap during which both issues are outstanding, and issuing expenses are $200,000. Compute the present value of the refunding, using the after-tax rate on the new bonds as the discount rate. Is the refunding worthwhile?

5. Crakow Machine Company wishes to borrow $10 million for 10 years. It can issue either a noncallable bond at 11.40 percent interest or a bond callable at the end of 5 years for 12 percent. For simplicity, we assume that the bond will be called only at the end of year 5. The interest rate that is likely to prevail 5 years hence for a 5-year straight bond can be described by the following probability distribution:

Interest rate	9%	10%	11%	12%	13%
Probability	0.1	0.2	0.4	0.2	0.1

Issuing and other costs involved in selling a bond issue 5 years hence will total $200,000. The call price is assumed to be par.

a. What is the total absolute amount of interest payments for the non-callable issue over the 10 years? (Do not discount.) What is the ex-pected value of total interest payments and other costs if the company issues callable bonds? (Assume that the company calls the bonds and issues new ones only if there is a savings in interest costs after issuing expenses.) On the basis of total costs, should the company issue non-callable or callable bonds?

b. What would be the outcome if the probability distribution of interest rates 5 years hence were the following?

Interest rate	7%	9%	11%	13%	15%
Probability	0.2	0.2	0.2	0.2	0.2

Assume that all other conditions stay the same.

6. Solie Sod and Seed Company (SSS) has a defined benefit pension plan for its salaried employees. The balance sheet of the plan has the following for-mat:

Value of existing pension fund assets	PV of expected benefits to retired employees
PV of expected future contributions	PV of expected benefits for future service
Total assets	Total pension fund liabilities

Presently, the fund has an unfunded liability. Determine in general the effect of each of the following on the appropriate balance sheet item and on the unfunded liability:

a. Sal Zambrano joins the firm and is expected to be entitled to a pension of $25,000 a year starting in 20 years.

b. In a good earnings year, SSS buys $400,000 in bonds and contributes them to the plan over and above its regular contribution.

c. In view of inflation, SSS raises the monthly pension of existing retirees by $10 per month.

d. As interest rates have risen, the discount rate used for determining present values is raised by 1 percent.

7. Research project: Obtain copies of several bond indentures. Pay particular attention to the restrictive covenants concerning things such as dividends, working capital, additional debt, and nature of the business. Try to relate the cost of debt to the firm to the relative restrictiveness of these provisions. How would you go about finding a measure of the degree of restriction so that trade-offs with interest could be made?

SOLUTIONS TO SELF-CORRECTION PROBLEMS

1. (dollars in millions) Let x = the number of millions of dollars of new debt which can be issued.

a. $$\frac{\$4.8}{\$.8 + .10x} = 4$$

$$4(\$.8) + 4(.10x) = \$4.8$$

$$.40x = \$1.6$$

$$x = \$4$$

b. $$\frac{\$30 + .5x}{\$8 + x} = 2$$

$$2(\$8) + 2(x) = \$30 + .5x$$

$$1.5x = \$14$$

$$x = \$9.333$$

c. $$\frac{\$10 + x}{\$40} = .5$$

$$.5(\$40) = \$10 + x$$

$$x = \$10$$

Condition a is binding, and it limits the amount of new debt to $4 million.

2. *Net cash outflow*

Cost of calling old preferred ($52)	$26,000,000
Net proceeds of new issue: $25 million −	
flotation costs of $780,000	24,220,000
Difference	$ 1,780,000
Preferred stock dividends on old	
preferred during overlap	750,000
Gross cash outlay	$ 2,530,000
Less: Tax savings on flotation costs,	
$780,000(.30)	234,000
Net cash outflow	$ 2,296,000

Annual net cash outflow on old preferred

Preferred stock dividend	$ 3,000,000

Annual net cash outflow on new preferred

Preferred stock dividend	$ 2,750,000

Difference = $3,000,000 − $2,750,000 = $250,000
Discounted at a rate of 11 percent for a perpetuity:

$$PV = \frac{\$250,000}{.11} = \$2,272,727$$

The preferred stock issue should not be refunded. The net benefit is negative ($2,272,727 − $2,296,000). The same analysis mechanics apply to refunding a preferred stock issue as apply to refunding a bond issue.

SELECTED REFERENCES

ALDERSON, MICHAEL J., and K. C. CHEN, "Excess Asset Reversions and Shareholder Wealth," *Journal of Finance*, 41 (March 1986), 225–41.

ANG, JAMES S., "The Two Faces of Bond Refunding," *Journal of Finance*, 30 (June 1975), 869–74.

BLACK, FISCHER, "The Tax Consequences of Long Run Pension Policy," *Financial Analysts Journal*, 36 (July–August 1980), 21–28.

BODIE, ZVI, JAY O. LIGHT, RANDALL MORCK, and ROBERT A. TAGGART, JR., "Corporate Pension Policy: An Empirical Investigation," *Financial Analysts Journal*, 41 (September–October 1985), 10–16.

BOWLIN, OSWALD D., "The Refunding Decision: Another Special Case in Capital Budgeting," *Journal of Finance*, 21 (March 1966), 55–68.

DYL, EDWARD A., and MICHAEL D. JOEHNK, "Sinking Funds and the Cost of Corporate Debt," *Journal of Finance*, 34 (September 1979), 887–94.

EMERY, DOUGLAS R., and WILBUR G. LEWELLEN, "Refunding Noncallable Debt," *Journal of Financial and Quantitative Analysis*, 19 (March 1984), 73–82.

GUJARATHI, MAHENDRA, and CARMELO GIACCOTTO, "Cash Flow Analysis for Bond Refunding," research paper, University of Connecticut, 1986.

KALOTAY, ANDREW J., "On the Management of Sinking Funds," *Financial Management*, 10 (Summer 1981), 34–40.

KOTLIKOFF, LAWRENCE J., and DANIEL E. SMITH, *Pensions in the American Economy*. Chicago: University of Chicago Press, 1983.

McCONNELL, JOHN J., and GARY G. SCHLARBAUM, "Returns, Risks, and Pricing of Income Bonds, 1956–76," *Journal of Business*, 54 (January 1981), 33–57.

McDANIEL, MOREY W., "Are Negative Pledge Clauses in Public Debt Issues Obsolete?" *Business Lawyer*, 38 (May 1983), 867–81.

―――, "Bondholders and Corporate Governance," *Business Lawyer*, 41 (February 1986), 413–60.

McGILL, DANIEL M., *Fundamentals of Private Pensions*, 5th ed. Philadelphia: Pension Research Council, University of Pennsylvania, 1984.

MARSHALL, WILLIAM J., and JESS B. YAWITZ, "Optimal Terms of the Call Provision on a Corporate Bond," *Journal of Financial Research*, 2 (Fall 1980), 203–11.

OFER, AHARON R., and ROBERT A. TAGGART, JR., "Bond Refunding: A Clarifying Analysis," *Journal of Finance*, 32 (March 1977), 21–30.

SORENSEN, ERIC H., "On the Seasoning Process of New Bonds: Some Are More Seasoned Than Others," *Journal of Financial and Quantitative Analysis*, 17 (June 1982), 195–208.

SMITH, CLIFFORD W., JR., and JEROLD B. WARNER, "On Financial Contracting; An Analysis of Bond Covenants," *Journal of Financial Economics*, 7 (June 1979), 117–61.

TEPPER, IRWIN, "Taxation and Corporate Pension Policy," *Journal of Finance*, 36 (March 1981), 1–14.

VAN HORNE, JAMES C., "Implied Fixed Costs in Long-term Debt Issues," *Journal of Financial and Quantitative Analysis*, 8 (December 1973).

―――, "Called Bonds: How Does the Investor Fare?" *Journal of Portfolio Management*, 6 (Summer 1980), 58–61.

―――, *Financial Market Rates and Flows*. 2nd ed., Englewood Cliffs, N.J.: Prentice-Hall, 1984, chaps. 8 and 9.

CHAPTER 22

Preferred Stock and Common Stock

In this chapter we take up two forms of equity financing—preferred stock and common stock. Although they both fall under the same general heading, their differences are far more pronounced than their similarities. From the standpoint of the ultimate owners of the corporation—namely, the common stockholders—preferred stock is a form of leverage to be evaluated much like debt. Because the theory behind the use of these securities was discussed in Chapter 18, this chapter is devoted primarily to examining their features.

PREFERRED STOCK AND ITS FEATURES

Preferred stock is a hybrid form of financing, combining features of debt and common stock. In the event of liquidation, a preferred stockholder's claim on assets comes after that of creditors but before that of common stockholders. Usually, this claim is restricted to the par value of the stock. If the par value of a share of preferred stock is $100, the investor will be entitled to a maximum of $100 in settlement of the principal amount. Although preferred stock carries a stipulated dividend, the actual payment of a dividend is a discretionary rather than a fixed obligation of the company. The omission of a dividend will not result in a default of the obligation or insolvency of the company. The board of directors has full power to omit a preferred stock dividend if it so chooses.

The maximum return to preferred stockholders usually is limited to the specified dividend, and these stockholders ordinarily do not share in the residual earnings of the company. Thus, if you own 100 shares of $10\frac{1}{2}$ percent preferred stock, $50 par value, the maximum return you can expect in any year is $525, and this return is at the discretion of the board of directors. The corporation cannot deduct this dividend on its tax return; this fact is the principal shortcoming of preferred stock as a means of financing. In view of the fact that interest payments on debt are deductible for tax purposes, the company that treats a preferred stock dividend as a fixed obligation finds the explicit cost to be rather high.

Cumulative Feature

Almost all preferred stocks have a cumulative feature, providing for unpaid dividends in any single year to be carried forward. Before the company can pay a dividend on its common stock, it must pay the dividends *in arrears* on its preferred stock. A board of directors may omit the preferred stock dividend on a company's 8 percent cumulative preferred stock for 3 consecutive years. If the stock has a $100 par value, the company is $24 per share in arrears on its preferred stock. Before it can pay a dividend to its common stockholders, it must pay preferred stockholders $24 for each share of preferred stock held. It should be emphasized that just because preferred stock dividends are in arrears, there is no guarantee that they ever will be paid. If the corporation has no intention of paying a common stock dividend, there is no need to clear up the **arrearage** on the preferred. The preferred stock dividend typically is omitted for lack of earn-

Arrearage. A late or overdue payment, which may be cumulative.

ings, but the corporation does not have to pay a dividend if earnings are restored.

If the preferred stock dividends are in arrears, and the company wishes to pay a common stock dividend, it may choose not to clear up the arrearage but to make an exchange offering to preferred stockholders. Say that the **cumulative dividends** on an issue of $100 par value preferred stock are $56 and that the market price of the stock is $38 a share. The company might offer preferred stockholders common stock in the company, valued at $90, for each share of preferred stock held. Although theoretically the preferred stockholders are asked to give up $156 ($100 par value plus $56 dividend arrearages), the exchange offering promises them $90 relative to a current preferred stock market value of only $38 per share. To eliminate the preferred stock, the company must obtain the approval of a required percentage of the stock outstanding, often two-thirds. Consequently, it probably will make its exchange offering contingent on obtaining the required acceptance.

If a preferred stock is noncumulative, dividends not paid in 1 year do not carry forward. As a result, a company can pay a common stock dividend without regard to any dividends it did not pay in the past on its preferred stock. From the standpoint of an investor, a noncumulative preferred stock is little more than an income bond. In fact, there is somewhat less uncertainty with income bonds, for the conditions under which interest will be paid are specified clearly, and bondholders have a prior claim on assets. Because of the obvious disadvantage to investors, noncumulative preferred stock issues are rare, although they may be used in reorganizations.

Cumulative dividends. A feature that requires that all cumulative unpaid dividends on the preferred be paid before a dividend may be paid on the common stock.

Participating Feature

A participating feature allows preferred stockholders to participate in the residual earnings of the corporation according to some specified formula. The preferred stockholder might be entitled to share equally with common stockholders in any common stock dividend beyond a certain amount. Suppose that a 6 percent preferred stock ($100 par value) were **participating preferred,** so that the holders were entitled to share equally in any common stock dividends in excess of $6 a share. If the common stock dividend is $7, the preferred stockholder will receive $1 in extra dividends for each share of stock owned. The formula for participation can vary greatly. The essential feature is that preferred stockholders have a prior claim on income and an opportunity for additional return if the dividends to common stockholders exceed a certain amount. Unfortunately for the investor, practically all preferred stock issues are nonparticipating, with the maximum return limited to the specified dividend rate.

Participating preferred stock. Stock where the holder is allowed to participate in increasing dividends if the common stockholders receive increasing dividends.

Voting Power

Because of their prior claim on assets and income, preferred stockholders normally are not given a voice in management unless the company is unable to pay preferred stock dividends during a specified period. Arrearages on four quarterly dividend payments might constitute such a default; under such circumstances, preferred stockholders as a class would be entitled to elect a specific number of directors. Usually, the number of directors is rather small in relation to the total; and, by the time the preferred stockholders obtain a voice in management, the company probably is in considerable financial difficulty. Consequently, the voting power that preferred stockholders are granted may be virtually meaningless.

Depending on the agreement between the preferred stockholders and the company, they may obtain voting power under other conditions as well. The company may default under restrictions in the agreement that are similar to those found in a loan agreement or a bond indenture. One of the more frequently imposed restrictions is that dividends on common stock are prohibited if the company does not satisfy certain financial ratios. We note, however, that default under any of the provisions of the agreement between the corporation and its preferred stockholders does not result in the obligation's becoming immediately payable, as does default under a loan agreement or bond indenture. The preferred stockholders merely are given a voice in management and assurance that common stock dividends will not be paid during the period of default. Thus, preferred stockholders do not have nearly the same legal power in default as do debt holders.

Retirement of Preferred Stock

The fact that preferred stock, like common stock, has no maturity does not mean that most preferred stock issues will remain outstanding forever, because provision for retirement of the stock invariably is made.

Call Feature.   Almost all preferred stock issues have a stated call price, which is above the original issuance price and may decrease over time. Like the call feature on bonds, the call feature on preferred stock affords the company flexibility. Because the market price of a straight preferred stock tends to fluctuate in keeping with interest rate cycles, the value of the preferred stock call feature is determined by the same considerations as is the call feature for bonds, which we discussed in Chapter 21. Long-term debt, unlike preferred stock, has a final maturity that ensures the eventual retirement of the issue. Without a call feature on preferred stock, the corporation would be able to retire the issue only by the more expensive and less efficient methods of purchasing the stock in the open market, inviting *tenders* of the stock from preferred stockholders at a price above the market price, or offering the preferred stockholders another security in its place.

Sinking Fund.   Many preferred stock issues provide for a sinking fund, which partially ensures an orderly retirement of the stock. Like bond issues, a preferred stock sinking fund is advantageous to investors because the retirement process exerts upward pressure on the market price of the remaining shares. Also, the coverage ratio on the preferred stock dividend is improved as the number of shares outstanding is reduced.

Use in Financing

Nonconvertible preferred stock is not used extensively as a means of long-term financing; only public utilities employ it with any degree of regularity. One of the drawbacks is the fact that the preferred dividend is not tax deductible by the issuer. For the corporate investor, however, preferred stock may be more attractive than debt instruments because 80 percent of the dividends received by the corporation is not subject to taxation.

The attraction has given rise to *adjustable rate preferred stock* (ARPS) in 1982 and later to *money market preferred stock* to serve the marketable security needs of corporations. As explained in Chapter 9, for the ARPS, the quarterly dividend rate "floats" with movements in Treasury security interest rates. Typically, the benchmark Treasury security is the higher in yield of (1) the 3-month Treasury bill rate, (2) the rate on a 10-year Treasury security, or (3) the rate on a 20-year Treasury security. Also, there usually are floor and ceiling interest rates, which bracket the prevailing yield when the preferred stock is offered. While the ceiling works to the detriment of the investor, it protects the issuing corporation in times of rising interest rates. Money market preferred stock (MMP), also explained in Chapter 9 is like ARPS except that an auction occurs every 49 days. As a result, the dividend rate is set by market forces in keeping with money market rates. The MMP has largely displaced the ARPS in popularity with corporate investors.

One advantage of preferred stock financing is that it is a flexible financing arrangement; the dividend is not a legal obligation of the corporation issuing the securities. If earnings turn bad and the financial condition of the company deteriorates, the dividend can be omitted. With debt financing, interest must be paid regardless of whether earnings are good or bad. To be sure, companies that are accustomed to paying dividends on their common stock certainly regard the preferred dividend as a fixed obligation. Nevertheless, under dire circumstances, a company that omits its common stock dividend can also omit its preferred dividend.

Another advantage of a straight preferred stock issue is that it has no final maturity; in essence, it is a perpetual loan. From the standpoint of creditors, preferred stock adds to the equity base of the company and thereby strengthens its financial condition. The additional equity base enhances the ability of the company to borrow in the future. Although the explicit, after-tax cost of preferred stock is considerably higher than that of bonds, the implied benefits just discussed may offset this cost. In addition, the implicit cost of preferred stock financing, from the standpoint of investors' penalizing the **price/earnings ratio** of the common stock, may be somewhat less than that of debt financing.[1] To the extent that investors are apprehensive over legal bankruptcy, they would regard

Price/earnings ratio. The market price per share divided by the most recent 12 months of earnings per share.

---

[1] Gordon Donaldson, in "In Defense of Preferred Stock," *Harvard Business Review*, 40 (July–August 1962), 123–36, defends rigorously the use of preferred stock as a means of financing under certain circumstances. He argues that when a company has utilized its debt capacity, it may be able to finance further with preferred stock because the preferred stock capacity of a company is distinct from its debt capacity.

debt as a riskier form of leverage. Unlike creditors, preferred stockholders cannot force a company into legal bankruptcy.

COMMON STOCK AND ITS FEATURES

The common stockholders of a corporation are its residual owners; collectively, they own the company and assume the ultimate risk associated with ownership. Their liability, however, is restricted to the amount of their investment. In the event of liquidation, these stockholders have a residual claim on the assets of the company after the claims of all creditors and preferred stockholders are settled in full. Common stock, like preferred stock, has no maturity date; and holders can liquidate their investments by selling their stocks in the secondary market.

Authorized, Issued, and Outstanding Shares

The corporate charter of a company specifies the number of *authorized shares* of common stock, the maximum that the company can issue without amending its charter. Although amending the charter is not a difficult procedure, it does require the approval of existing stockholders, which takes time. For this reason, a company usually likes to have a certain number of shares that are authorized but unissued. These unissued shares allow flexibility in granting stock options, pursuing mergers, and splitting the stock. When authorized shares of common stock are sold, they become issued stock. *Outstanding stock* is the number of shares issued and actually held by the public; the corporation can buy back part of its issued stock and hold it as **treasury stock.**

Treasury stock. Common stock that has been repurchased and is held by the company.

Par Value

Par value. The stated value of a security, such as bonds having a par value of $1,000. The same as face value.

A share of common stock can be authorized either with or without **par value.** The par value of a stock is merely a stated figure in the corporate charter and is of little economic significance. A company should not issue stock at a price less than par value, because stockholders who bought stock for less than par would be liable to creditors for the difference between the price they paid and the par value. Consequently, the par values of most stocks are set at fairly low figures relative to their market values. Suppose that a company sold 10,000 shares of new common stock at $45 a share and that the par value of the stock was $5 per share. The equity portion of the balance sheet would be

Common stock ($5 par value)	$ 50,000
Paid-in capital	400,000
Net worth	$450,000

Stock can be authorized without par value and carried on the books at the market price or some stated value. The difference between the issuing price and the stated value is reflected as **paid-in capital.**

Paid-in capital. Funds received by a company in a sale of common stock that are in excess of the par value of the stock.

Book Value and Liquidating Value

The **book value** of a share of stock is the net worth of a corporation less the par value of preferred stock outstanding divided by the number of shares outstanding. Suppose in the case above that the company is now 1 year old and has generated $80,000 in after-tax profit, but pays no dividend. The net worth is now $450,000 + $80,000 = $530,000, and book value per share is $530,000/ 10,000 = $53.

Book value. The accounting value of an asset. In the case of common stock, net worth divided by the number of shares.

Although one might expect the book value of a share of stock to correspond to the liquidating value (per share) of the company, frequently it does not. Often assets are sold for less than their book values, particularly when liquidating costs are involved. In some cases, certain assets—notably land and mineral rights—have book values that are modest in relation to their market values. For the company involved, liquidating value may be higher than book value. Thus, book value may not correspond to liquidating value and, as we shall see, it often does not correspond to market value.

Market Value

Market value per share is the current price at which the stock is traded. For actively traded stocks, market price quotations are readily available. For the many inactive stocks that have thin markets, prices are difficult to obtain. Even when obtainable, the information may reflect only the sale of a few shares of stock and not typify the market value of the firm as a whole. For companies of this sort, care must be taken in interpreting market price information.

The market value of a share of common stock usually will differ from its book value and its liquidating value. It is a function of the current and expected future dividends of the company and the perceived risk of the stock on the part of investors. Because these factors bear only a partial relationship to the book value and liquidating value of the company, the market value per share may not be tied closely to these values.

Typically, the shares of a newer company are traded in the *over-the-counter (OTC) market*, where one or more security dealers maintain an inventory in the stock and buy and sell it at bid and ask prices they quote. As a company grows in financial stature, number of stockholders, and volume of transactions, it may qualify for **listing** on a stock exchange, such as the New York Stock Exchange. However, many firms prefer to remain a part of the OTC marketplace. The NASDAG quotations system (National Association of Securities Dealers) for many of these stocks provides significant marketability to the investor.

Listed security. A security that is traded on an organized exchange.

RIGHTS OF STOCKHOLDERS

Right to Income

Common stockholders are entitled to share in the earnings of the company only if cash dividends are paid. Stockholders prosper from the market-value appreciation of their stock, but they are entirely dependent on the board of directors for the declaration of dividends that give them income from the company. Thus, we see that the position of a common stockholder differs markedly from that of a creditor. If the company fails to pay contractual interest and principal payments to creditors, the creditors are able to take legal action to ensure that payment is made or the company is liquidated. Stockholders, on the other hand, have no legal recourse to a company for not distributing profits. Only if management, the board of directors, or both are engaged in fraud may stockholders take their case to court and possibly force the company to pay dividends.

Voting Power

Inasmuch as the common stockholders of a company are its owners, they are entitled to elect a board of directors. In a large corporation, stockholders usually exercise only indirect control through the board of directors they elect. The board, in turn, selects the management, and management actually controls the operations of the company. In a proprietorship, partnership, or small corporation, the owners usually control the operations of the business directly. In a large corporation, there may be times when the goals of management differ from those of the common stockholders. The only recourse of a stockholder to management is through the board of directors.

Because common stockholders often are widely dispersed geographically and therefore disorganized, management can often exercise effective control of a large corporation if it controls only a small percentage of the stock outstanding. By proposing a slate of directors that is favorable to its own interests, management is able to maintain control.

Proxies and Proxy Contests

Proxy. A document giving one person the authority to act in behalf of another. Example: a proxy for management to vote the shares of a stockholder. Can also mean the substitution of one for another. Example: a proxy company.

Common stockholders are entitled to one vote for each share of stock they own. Because most stockholders do not attend the annual meeting, they may vote by **proxy,** a form by which stockholders assign their right to vote to another person. The SEC regulates the solicitation of proxies and also requires companies to disseminate information to its stockholders through proxy mailings. Prior to the annual meeting, management solicits proxies from stockholders to vote for the recommended slate of directors and for any other proposals requiring stockholder approval. If stockholders are satisfied with the company, they generally sign the proxy in favor of management, giving written authorization to management to vote their shares. If some stockholders do not vote their shares, the number of shares voted at the meeting and the number needed to constitute a majority are lower. Because of the proxy system and the fact that management is able to mail information to stockholders at the company's expense, management has a distinct advantage in the voting process.

But the fortress is not invulnerable. Outsiders can seize control of a company through a proxy contest. Obviously, they would not attempt a takeover if management controlled a large percentage of shares outstanding. When an outside group undertakes a proxy raid, it is required to register its proxy statement with the Securities and Exchange Commission to prevent the presentation of misleading or false information. Despite the fact that the insurgents usually are unsuccessful, the undertaking of a proxy contest often is associated with a higher share price performance than otherwise would be the case. Apparently, the challenge itself is sufficient to change investor expectations about management in the future behaving more in keeping with maximizing shareholder wealth.

Voting Procedures

Depending on the corporate charter, the board of directors is elected either under a *majority voting system* or under a **cumulative voting system.** Under the majority system, stockholders have one vote for each share of stock they own, and they must vote for each director position that is open. A stockholder who owns 100 shares will be able to cast 100 votes for each director's position open. Because each person seeking a position on the board must win a majority of the total votes cast for that position, the system precludes minority interests from electing directors. If management can obtain proxies for over 50 percent of the shares voted, it can select the entire board.

Cumulative voting. A method for electing corporate directors, whereby a shareholder may cast up to the shares held times the number of directors to be elected for a single director.

Under a cumulative voting system, a stockholder is able to accumulate votes and cast them for less than the total number of directors being elected. The total number of votes is the number of shares the stockholder owns times the number of directors being elected. If you are a stockholder who owns 100 shares, and 12 directors are to be elected, you may cast 1,200 votes for whatever number of directors you choose, the maximum being 1,200 votes for 1 director.

A cumulative voting system, in contrast to the majority system, permits minority interests to elect a certain number of directors. The minimum number of shares necessary to elect a specific number of directors is determined by

$$\frac{\text{Total shares outstanding} \times \text{Specific number of directors sought}}{\text{Total number of directors to be elected} + 1} + 1 \qquad (22\text{-}1)$$

If there are 3 million shares outstanding, the total number of directors to be elected is 14, and if a minority group wishes to elect 2 directors, it will need at least the following number of shares:

$$\frac{3,000,000 \times 2}{14 + 1} + 1 = 400,001$$

Cumulative voting gives minority interests a better opportunity to be represented on the board of directors of a corporation. Because the system is more democratic, a number of states require that companies in the state elect directors in this way. Even with cumulative voting, however, management can reduce the number of directors and sometimes preclude minority interests from obtaining a seat on the board. Suppose that the minority group actually owns 400,001 shares. With 14 directors to be elected, the group can elect 2 directors. If the board is reduced to 6 members, the minority group can elect no directors because the minimum number of shares needed to elect a single director is

$$\frac{3,000,000 \times 1}{6 + 1} + 1 = 428,572$$

Another method of thwarting a minority interest from obtaining representation is to stagger the terms of the directors so that only a portion is elected each year. If a firm has 12 directors and the term is 4 years, only 3 are elected each year. As a result, a minority group needs considerably more shares voted in its favor to elect a director than it would need if all 12 directors came up for election each year.

CLASSIFIED COMMON STOCK

A company may have more than one class of common stock. Its common stock can be classified according to the claim on income and voting power. Class A common of a company may have no voting privilege but may be entitled to a prior claim to dividends, whereas the Class B common has voting rights but a lower claim to dividends. Usually, the promoters of a corporation and its management will hold the Class B common stock, whereas the Class A common is sold to the public. Actually, the Class A shares in this example are no more than a form of preferred stock. Usually, Class A stock is given some voting power but not as much as the Class B stock per dollar of investment.

Suppose that the Class A and Class B common stockholders of a company are entitled to one vote per share, but that the Class A stock is issued at an initial price of $20 a share. If $2 million is raised in the original offering through the issuance of 80,000 shares of Class A common for $1.6 million and 200,000 shares of Class B common for $400,000, the Class B stockholders will have over twice as many votes as Class A holders have, although their original investment is only one-fourth as large. Thus, the Class B holders have effective control of the company. Indeed, this is the purpose of classified stock.

For this control, the Class B holders must be willing to give up something in order to make Class A stock attractive to investors. Usually, they take a lower claim both to dividends and assets. An appropriate balance must be struck between voting power and the claim to dividends and assets if the company is to bargain effectively for Class A equity funds.[2] Sometimes, the Class B common simply is given to the promoters of a corporation without any cash investment on their part. Perhaps the most famous example of a company with classified common stock is the Ford Motor Company. The Class B stock is owned by members of the Ford family and the Class A stock is held by the general public. Regardless of the number of Class A stock issued, the Class B common constitutes 40 percent of the total voting power of the company. Thus, members of the Ford family retain substantial voting power in the company, despite the fact that they hold far fewer shares than does the general public.

SUMMARY

Preferred stock is a hybrid form of security having characteristics both of debt and common stock. The payment of dividends is not a legal but a discretionary obligation, although many companies regard the obligation as fixed. Preferred stockholders' claims on assets and income come after those of creditors but before those of common stockholders. The return on their investment is almost always limited to the specified dividend; very seldom do preferred stockholders participate in the residual earnings of the company. Although they may have some voting power, this power generally is restricted to situations in which the company has evolved itself into financial difficulty.

Because preferred stock has no final maturity, almost all issues have call features that give the corporation financial flexibility. Retirement of the preferred stock can be accomplished also by a sinking fund, convertibility, or an exchange offering. Because of the 80 percent exemption of dividends to the corporate investor, preferred stock typically has a lower yield than corporate bonds. Particularly popular for marketable security portfolios is money market preferred stock. The principal disadvantage of preferred stock is that the dividend is not tax deductible.

The common stockholders of a corporation are its owners. As such, they are entitled to share in the residual earnings of the company if cash dividends are paid. As owners, however, they have only a residual claim on assets in the event of liquidation. Common stockholders are also entitled to a voice in management through the board of directors they elect. These directors can be elected under a majority voting system or a cumulative voting system. The cumulative system allows minority interests to obtain representation on the board of directors. Differences between authorized, issued, and outstanding shares were explained, as were differences in par value, book value, liquidating value, and

[2] In perhaps the most extensive testing of classified common stock, Ronald C. Lease, John J. McConnell, and Wayne H. Mikkelson, "The Market Value of Control in Publicly-traded Corporations," *Journal of Financial Economics*, 11 (April 1983), 439–71, test whether differences in voting control affect common stock value. By and large, the evidence revealed that classified common stock that had superior voting rights enjoyed a premium in market price. See also Harry DeAngelo and Linda DeAngelo, "Managerial Ownership of Voting Rights: A Study of Public Corporations with Dual Classes of Common Stock," *Journal of Financial Economics*, 14 (March 1985), 33–70, for further analysis of the control issue.

market value. The use of different classes of common stock allows the promoters and management of a corporation to retain voting control without having to make a large capital contribution.

QUESTIONS

1. Because the dividend payments on preferred stock are not a tax-deductible expense, the explicit cost of this form of financing is high. What are some of the offsetting advantages to the firm and to the investor that enable this type of security to be sold?

2. From the standpoint of the preferred stock issuer, why is it desirable to have a call feature?

3. How does a money market preferred stock differ from regular preferred stock?

4. Why do most preferred stock issues have a cumulative feature? Would not the company be better off with a noncumulative feature?

5. If not otherwise stated, what would you assume as usual with respect to the following features for a preferred stock: cumulative, participation, voting power, call feature, claim on assets?

6. What advantages to the firm are there from broad share distribution? Is the preemptive right in conflict with an objective of broad share distribution?

7. Why would a company ever wish to use classified common stock in its financing instead of straight common stock?

8. Why does most common stock have a low par value in relation to its market value?

9. Why does book value per share of common stock change over time?

10. The common stockholder is considered the residual owner of a corporation. What does this mean in terms of risk and return?

11. Why does the number of authorized shares usually exceed the number that is actually outstanding?

12. In any proxy attempt by an outside group to gain control of a company, the advantage lies with management. What are the reasons for this advantage?

13. If Congress were to eliminate the double taxation of dividends so that a company could deduct dividend payments in the same way it does interest payments for tax purposes, what would be the effect on preferred stock and common stock financing?

SELF-CORRECTION PROBLEMS

1. Alvarez Apparel, Inc., could sell preferred stock with a dividend cost of 12 percent. If it were to sell bonds in the current market, the interest rate cost would be 14 percent. The company is in a 40 percent tax bracket.

a. What is the after-tax cost of each of these methods of financing?

b. Setlec Corporation holds a limited number of preferred stocks in its marketable security portfolio. It is in a 36 percent tax bracket. If it were to invest in the preferred stock of Alvarez Apparel, what would be its after-tax return? What would be its after-tax return if it were to invest in the bonds?

2. Caroline Islands Resorts has 1,750,000 shares of authorized common stock, having a $1 par value. Over the years, it has issued 1,532,000 shares, but presently 63,000 are held as treasury stock. The paid-in capital of the company is presently $5,314,000.

a. How many shares are now outstanding?

b. If the company were able to sell stock at $19 per share, what is the maximum amount it could raise under its existing authorization, including treasury shares?

c. What would be its common stock and paid-in capital accounts after the financing?

3. The Berkeley Brass Company has a 9-person board and has 2 million shares of common stock outstanding. It is chartered with a cumulative voting rule. Jane Irwin, a granddaughter of the founder, controls directly or indirectly 482,000 shares. As she disagrees with present management, she wants a slate of her own directors on the board.

a. If all directors are elected once a year, how many directors can she elect?

b. If director terms are staggered so that only 3 are elected each year, how many can she elect?

PROBLEMS

1. The Riting Railroad needs to raise $9.5 million for capital improvements. One possibility is a new preferred stock issue: 8 percent, $100 par value stock that would yield 9 percent to investors. Flotation costs for an issue this size amount to 5 percent of the total amount of preferred stock sold; these costs are deducted from gross proceeds in determining the net proceeds to the company. (Ignore any tax considerations.)

a. At what price per share will the preferred stock be offered to investors? (Assume the issue never will be called.)

b. How many shares must be issued to raise $9.5 million for Riting Railroad?

2. Lost Horizon Silver Mining Company has 200,000 shares of $7 cumulative preferred stock outstanding, $100 par value. The preferred stock has a participating feature. If dividends on the common stock exceed $1 per share, preferred stockholders receive additional dividends per share equal to one-half of the excess. In other words, if the common stock dividend were $2, preferred stockholders would receive an additional dividend of $.50. The

company has 1 million shares of common outstanding. What would dividends per share be on the preferred stock and on the common stock if earnings available for dividends in three successive years were (a) $1,000,000, $600,000, and $3,000,000; (b) $2,000,000, $2,400,000, and $4,600,000; and (c) $1,000,000, $2,500,000, and $5,700,000. (Assume that all of the available earnings are paid in dividends, but nothing more is paid.)

3. D. Sent, a disgruntled stockholder of the Zebec Corporation, desires representation on the board. The Zebec Corporation, which has 10 directors, has 1 million shares outstanding.

   a. How many shares would Sent have to control to be assured of one directorship under a majority voting system?

   b. Recompute part a, assuming a cumulative voting system.

   c. Recompute parts a and b, assuming that the number of directors was reduced to 5.

4. The stock of the Moribund Corporation is currently selling in the market for $45 per share, yet it has a liquidation value of $70 per share. The Raid Corporation has decided to make a tender offer for the shares of Moribund. Raid feels that it must obtain at least 50 percent of the shares in order to effect the liquidation. Assuming that Raid makes its tender offer on the expected relationship shown in the following table, at what price should the tender be made?

PRICE PER SHARE	EXPECTED PERCENTAGE OF SHARES TENDERED
$55	50%
57	60
59	70
62	80
67	90
72	100

SOLUTIONS TO SELF-CORRECTION PROBLEMS

1. a. After-tax cost:
       Preferred stock = 12.00%
       Bonds = 14%(1 − .40) = 8.40%

   b. The dividend income to a corporate investor is 80 percent exempt from taxation. With a corporate tax rate of 36 percent, we have for the preferred stock: after-tax return = 12%[1 − .20(.36)] = 11.14%. For the bonds, the after-tax return = 14%(1 − .36) = 8.96%.

2.   a.

Issued shares	1,532,000
Treasury shares	63,000
Outstanding shares	1,469,000

b.

Authorized shares	1,750,000
Outstanding shares	1,469,000
Available shares	281,000

281,000 shares × $19 = $5,339,000

c.

Common stock ($1 par)	$ 1,750,000
Paid-in capital*	10,372,000

*Consists of $18 × 281,000 shares plus $5,314,000.

3.   a.   Number of shares necessary to elect one director $= \dfrac{2{,}000{,}000 \times 1}{9 + 1} + 1$

= 200,001. She can elect two directors.

b.   Number of shares necessary to elect one director $= \dfrac{2{,}000{,}000 \times 1}{3 + 1} + 1$

= 500,001. She can elect no directors.

SELECTED REFERENCES

BHAGAT, SANJAI, "The Effect of Pre-emptive Right Amendments on Shareholder Wealth," *Journal of Financial Economics*, 12 (November 1983), 289–310.

DEANGELO, HARRY, and LINDA DEANGELO, "Managerial Ownership of Voting Rights: A Study of Public Corporations with Dual Classes of Common Stock," *Journal of Financial Economics*, 14 (March 1985), 33–70.

DODD, PETER, and JEROLD B. WARNER, "On Corporate Governance: A Study of Proxy Contests," *Journal of Financial Economics*, 11 (April 1983), 401–38.

DONALDSON, GORDON, "In Defense of Preferred Stock," *Harvard Business Review*, 40 (July–August 1962), 123–36.

_____ , "Financial Goals: Management vs. Stockholders," *Harvard Business Review*, 41 (May–June 1963), 116–29.

FINNERTY, JOHN D., "Preferred Stock Refunding Analysis: Synthesis and Extension," *Financial Management*, 13 (Autumn 1984), 22–28.

FOOLADI, IRAJ, and GORDON S. ROBERTS, "On Preferred Stock," *Journal of Financial Research*, 9 (Winter 1986), 319–24.

LEASE, RONALD C., JOHN J. McCONNELL, and WAYNE H. MIKKELSON, "The Market Value of Control in Publicly-traded Corporations," *Journal of Financial Economics*, 11 (April 1983), 439–71.

LEVY, HAIM, "Economic Evaluation of Voting Power of Common Stock," *Journal of Finance*, 38 (March 1983), 79–94.

McDANIEL, WILLIAM R., "Sinking Fund Preferred Stock," *Financial Management*, 13 (Spring 1984), 45–52.

SMITH, DAVID B., "A Framework for Analyzing Nonconvertible Preferred Stock Risk," *Journal of Financial Research*, 6 (Summer 1983), 127–40.

SOLDOFSKY, ROBERT M., "Classified Common Stock," *Business Lawyer* (April 1968), 899–902.

VAN HORNE, JAMES C., "New Listings and Their Price Behavior," *Journal of Finance*, 25 (September 1970), 783–94.

CHAPTER 23

Convertibles, Exchangeables, and Warrants

In addition to straight debt and equity instruments, a company may finance with an option, a contract giving its holder the right to buy common stock or to exchange something for it within a specific period of time. As a result, the value of the option instrument is strongly influenced by changes in value of the stock. In this chapter, we consider three specific types of options employed by business firms in their financing: the convertible security, the exchangeable bond, and the warrant. In the appendix to the chapter, a detailed discussion of option pricing theory appears.

CONVERTIBLE SECURITY FEATURES

Convertible security. A bond or a preferred stock that is convertible into a specified number of shares of common stock at the option of the holder.

Conversion price and ratio. The conversion ratio is the number of shares of stock into which a security may be converted. The conversion price is the face value of the security divided by the conversion ratio.

A **convertible security** is a bond or a share of preferred stock that can be converted at the option of the holder into common stock of the same corporation. Once converted into common stock, the stock cannot be exchanged again for bonds or preferred stock. The ratio of exchange between the convertible security and the common stock can be stated in terms of either a **conversion price** or a **conversion ratio.** McKesson Corporation's $9\frac{3}{4}$ percent convertible subordinated debentures ($1,000 face value) have a conversion price of $43.75, meaning that each debenture is convertible into 22.86 shares of common stock. We simply divide the face value of the security by the conversion price to obtain the conversion ratio, $1,000/$43.75 = 22.86 shares. The conversion privilege can be stated in terms of either the conversion price or the conversion ratio.

The conversion terms are not necessarily constant over time. Many convertible issues provide for increases or "step-ups" in the conversion price at periodic intervals. For example, a $1,000 face value bond might have a conversion price of $40 a share for the first 5 years, $45 a share for the second 5 years, $50 for the third 5, and so on. In this way, the bond converts into fewer shares of common stock as time goes by. Usually, the conversion price is adjusted for any stock splits or stock dividends that occur after the securities are sold. If the common stock were split 2 for 1, the conversion price would be halved. This provision protects the convertible bondholder and is known as an antidilution clause.

Conversion Value and Premium

The *conversion value* of a convertible security is the conversion ratio of the security times the market price per share of the common stock. If McKesson stock were selling for $50, the conversion value of one convertible subordinated debenture would be 22.86 × $50, or $1,143.

The convertible security provides the investor with a fixed return from a bond or with a specified dividend from preferred stock. in addition, the investor receives an option to convert the security into common stock and thereby participates in the possibility of capital gains associated with being a residual owner of the corporation. Because of this option, the company usually is able to sell the convertible security at a lower yield than it would have to pay on a straight bond or preferred stock issue.

At the time of issuance, the convertible security will be priced higher than its conversion value. The differential is known as the *conversion premium*. The McKesson convertible subordinated debentures were sold to the public for $1,000 a bond. The market price of the common stock at the time of issuance of the convertibles was approximately 38\frac{1}{2}$ per share. Therefore the conversion value of each bond was 22.86 × 38\frac{1}{2}$ = $880, and the differential of $120 between this value and the issuing price represented the conversion premium. Frequently, this premium is expressed as a percentage; in our example the conversion premium is $120/$880 = 13.6% For most issues of convertibles, the conversion premium ranges from 10 to 20 percent. For a growth company, the conversion premium can be in the upper part of this range, or perhaps even higher in the case of super-growth. For companies with more moderate growth, the conversion premium may be closer to 10 percent. The range itself is established mainly by market tradition, in keeping with the idea that the issuer should be in a position to force conversion within a reasonable period of time. (Forcing conversion will be illustrated shortly.)

Almost without exception, convertible securities provide for a *call price*. As was true with the straight bond or preferred stock, the call feature enables the corporation to call the security for redemption. Few convertible securities, however, are ever redeemed. Instead, the purpose of the call usually is to force conversion when the conversion value of the security is significantly above its call price.

Other Features

Almost all convertible bond issues are subordinated to other creditors. That fact permits the lender to treat convertible subordinated debt or convertible preferred stock as a part of the equity base when evaluating the financial condition of the issuer. In the event of liquidation, it makes no difference to the creditor if the issue is actually converted; in either case, the lender has a prior claim. The situation is different with a convertible bond that is not subordinate. As long as the bond is not converted, its holder would be a general creditor in the event of liquidation. For this reason, there is a strong incentive from other creditors for the company to make the issue subordinated.

Investors in a company's common stock tend to recognize the potential **dilution** in their position before actual conversion takes place. For accounting reporting purposes, a company with convertible securities or warrants outstanding is required to report earnings per share in such a way that the reader of the financial statement can visualize the potential dilution. More specifically, it must report earnings per share on two bases. The first is *primary* earnings per share, which are simply earnings available to common stockholders divided by the actual number of shares outstanding. The second is *fully diluted* earnings per share, which are earnings available to common stockholders divided by the total number of shares outstanding plus the number of shares that would be added if all warrants were exercised and all convertible securities were converted. For companies with sizable financing with convertibles and warrants, the difference between the two earnings per share figures can be substantial.

Dilution. Reduction in value or in proportion of income to a shareholder.

USE OF CONVERTIBLES

Convertible securities, in many cases, are employed as deferred common stock financing. Technically these securities represent debt or preferred stock, but in essence they are delayed common stock. Companies that issue convertibles expect them to be converted in the future. By selling a convertible security instead of common stock, they create less dilution in earnings per share, both now and in the future. The reason is that the conversion price on a convertible security is higher than the issuing price on a new issue of common stock.

The current market price of the common stock of the mythical ABC Corporation is $40 per share. If the company raises capital with an issue of common stock, it will have to underprice the issue in order to sell it in the market, but it can sell the stock through underwriters and realize net proceeds of $36 per share. If the company wishes to raise $18 million, the issue will involve 500,000 shares of additional stock. On the other hand, if ABC Corporation sells a convertible issue, it is able to set the conversion price above the current market price per share. If the conversion premium is 15 percent, the conversion price will be $46 per share. Assuming an $18 million issue of convertibles, the number of shares of additional stock after conversion will be

$$\frac{\$18 \text{ million}}{\$46} = 391,305$$

We see that potential dilution with a convertible issue is less than that with a common issue because fewer shares are being added.

Another advantage to the company in using convertible securities is that the interest rate or preferred dividend rate is lower than the rate the company would have to pay on a straight bond or a straight preferred stock issue. The conversion feature makes the issue more attractive to investors. The greater the value of the conversion feature to investors, the lower the yield the company will need to pay in order to sell the issue. The lower interest payments early on may be particularly useful to a company in a growth phase, for it allows it to keep more cash for growth. Moreover, companies with relatively low credit ratings but good prospects for growth may find it extremely difficult to sell a straight issue of bonds or preferred stock. The market may respond more favorably to a convertible issue of these companies, not because of its quality as a bond or as preferred stock but because of its quality as common stock.

Forcing or Stimulating Conversion

Companies usually issue convertible securities with the expectation that these securities will be converted within a certain length of time. Investors can exercise their options voluntarily at any time and exchange the convertible security for common stock; however, they may prefer to hold the security, for its price will increase as the price of the common stock increases. During this time, also, they receive regular interest payments or preferred stock dividends. For the security convertible to common stock that pays no dividend, it is to the holder's advantage never to convert voluntarily. In other words, the investor should delay conversion as long as possible. (When a company pays a common stock dividend, it may be in the interest of the convertible security holder to convert voluntarily.) On the other hand, it is in the company's interest, in behalf of existing stockholders, to force conversion as soon as possible. In this way, the cost of paying interest on the convertible debenture, or dividends on the convertible preferred stock, can be avoided.

To force conversion, companies issuing convertible securities usually must call the issue. If the call is to succeed, the market price of the security must be significantly higher than the call price, so that investors will convert rather than accept the lower call price. Many companies regard a 20 percent premium of conversion value over call price as a sufficient cushion for possible declines in market price and for enticing investors to convert their securities. The conversion price of a convertible debenture ($1,000 face value) might be $50 and the call price $1,080. For the conversion value of the bond to equal the call price, the market price of the stock must be $1,080/20, or $54 a share. If the bonds are called when the market price is $54, many investors might choose to accept the call price rather than convert. The company then would have to redeem many of the bonds for cash, in part defeating the purpose of the original financing. In order to ensure almost complete conversion, it might wait to call the debentures until the conversion value of the bond was 20 percent above the call price, a value that corresponds to a common stock market price of approximately $65 a share. At this price, the investor who accepts the call price suffers a significant opportunity loss. Studies show that companies tend to call their convertibles after a period of rise in their common stock price relative to the market. As a result, the opportunity loss to the holder for not converting is pronounced.

Market Price Reaction.   Upon announcement that a convertible bond issue is to be called, the market price of the company's common stock typically declines by a small but significant amount. This decline may be due to several reasons, though all are somewhat dubious. It is clear that the company will have lower interest expenses after conversion than before. As a result, it loses a tax shield, which, we know from Chapter 17, may have value to the common stockholders. However, this argument supposes that investors are surprised by the call and that they do not expect the company to replace the called debt. Another reason for the decline in share price might be the dilution in earnings per share, which results from an increased number of shares. However, the potential dilution surely is recognized in the marketplace before the convertible bond is called, although the timing of the call may be somewhat uncertain. Finally, there may be a wealth transfer from stockholders to senior security holders if the calling of the convertible bond issue is unexpected. The senior claims simply become more creditworthy with the elimination of a debt issue. Wayne H. Mikkelson tests these notions and finds convertible bond calls to result in a decline in share price at the announcement date, but convertible preferred stock calls not to result in a decline.[1] He speculates that there may be an information effect at

---

[1] Wayne H. Mikkelson, "Convertible Calls and Security Returns," *Journal of Financial Economics*, 9 (September 1981), 237–64; and Mikkelson, "Capital Structure Change and Decreases in Stockholders' Wealth: A Cross-Sectional Study of Convertible Security Calls," working paper, National Bureau of Economic Research, 1983.

play and that the calling of a convertible bond conveys unfavorable information about the company's earnings prospects.

Stimulating Conversion.   Other means are available to a company for "stimulating," as opposed to "forcing," conversion. By establishing an acceleration or "step-up" in the conversion price at steady intervals in the future, there is persistent pressure on bondholders to convert, assuming that the conversion value of the security is relatively high. If the conversion price is scheduled to increase from $50 to $56 at the end of next month, convertible bondholders have an incentive to convert prior to that time, all other things the same. If the holders wait, they receive fewer shares of stock. The step-up provision must be established at the time the convertible issue is sold; it cannot be used for purposes of stimulating conversion at a particular moment.

Another means for stimulating conversion is to increase the dividend on the common stock, thereby making the common more attractive. In certain cases, the dividend income available on the common may exceed interest income on the convertible security. Although the two stimulants enhance conversion, invariably a portion of the convertible bondholders will not convert, owing to the downside protection of the bond, the superior legal claim on assets, and other reasons. Consequently, calling the issue may be the only means for ensuring that the issue will be substantially converted.

Debt Plus Option Characteristic.   The simplistic view that a convertible bond is the best of all possible things because it offers a lower interest cost than straight debt and less dilution than equity financing overlooks the option nature of the contract. The convertible bond may be viewed as straight debt plus an option to purchase common stock. The greater the uncertainty, or risk, of the firm's cash flow, the less the value of the debt, all other things the same. Expressed differently, the greater the risk, the higher the interest rate necessary to attract lenders. On the other hand, the greater the uncertainty or volatility of cash flow, the greater the value of the option (see the appendix.)

Whereas the high-risk company may be unable to sell straight debt, the option characteristic makes the package attractive in the marketplace. Of course, there is no guarantee that the option will have value in the sense of the common stock being sufficiently high to make conversion worthwhile. The issue simply may remain overhanging as a debt instrument. Still, the potential realization of stock value at the time of issuance makes the convertible issue attractive. Thus, the convertible security serves an important role for the company faced with operating uncertainty.

VALUE OF CONVERTIBLE SECURITIES

As we know, the value of a convertible security to an investor is twofold: its value as a bond or preferred stock and its potential value as common stock. (Because the principles of valuation of a convertible bond and a convertible preferred stock are nearly the same, our subsequent discussion will refer to convertible bonds.) Investors obtain a hedge when they purchase a convertible bond. If the market price of the stock rises, the value of the convertible is determined largely by its conversion value. If the market for the stock turns down, the investor still holds a bond whose value provides a floor below which the price of the convertible is unlikely to fall.

Bond Value

The bond value of a convertible security is the price at which a straight bond of the same company would sell in the open market. For semiannual compounding, it can be determined by solving the following equation for B:

$$B = \sum_{t=1}^{2n} \frac{I}{\left(1 + \dfrac{r}{2}\right)^t} + \frac{F}{\left(1 + \dfrac{r}{2}\right)^{2n}} \tag{23-1}$$

where B = straight bond value of the convertible
I = semiannual interest payments determined by the coupon rate
F = face value of the bond
n = years to final maturity
r = market yield to maturity on a straight bond of the same company.

In the equation, we assume semiannual interest payments, which are typical with corporate bonds, so the total number of interest payments is two times the years to maturity, n, and the semiannual interest rate on a straight bond is r divided by 2.

Amos White Company has outstanding a 9 percent convertible debenture with a final maturity 20 years hence. If the company is to sell a straight 20-year debenture in the current market, the yield will have to be 12 percent to be attractive to investors. For a 20-year bond with a 9 percent coupon to yield 12 percent to maturity, the bond has to sell at a discount. Using Eq. (23-1) and rounding, we have

$$B = \sum_{t=1}^{40} \frac{\$45}{(1.06)^t} + \frac{\$1,000}{(1.06)^{40}} = \$774$$

Although it is possible to solve this equation using present-value tables, we need only consult a bond table to determine the market price. Thus the bond-value floor of Amos White Company's convertible bonds would be $774. This floor suggests that if the price of the common stock were to fall sharply so that the conversion feature had negligible value, the price of the convertible would fall only to $774. At that price, the security would sell as a straight bond in keeping with prevailing bond yields for that grade of security.

The bond-value floor of a convertible is not constant over time. It varies with (1) interest rate movements in the capital market and (2) changes in the financial risk of the company involved. If interest rates in general rise, the bond value of a convertible will decline. If the yield to maturity on a straight bond in our example increases from 12 to 14 percent, the bond value of the convertible will drop from $774 to $667. Moreover, the company's credit rating can either improve or deteriorate over time. If it improves, and the company is able to sell a straight bond at a lower yield to maturity, the bond value of the convertible security will increase, all other things held constant. If the company's credit standing deteriorates, and the yield on a straight bond increases, the bond-value floor will decline. Unfortunately for the investor, when the market price of the stock falls because of poor earnings and/or increased risk, its credit standing may suffer. As a result, the straight bond value of the convertible may decline along with the decline in its conversion value, giving investors less down-side protection than they might have expected originally.[2]

Premiums

Convertible securities frequently sell at premiums over both their bond value and their conversion value. Recall that the conversion value of a convertible is simply the current market price per share of the company's common stock times the number of shares into which the security is convertible. The fact that the convertible bond provides the investor with a degree of downside protection, given the qualifications mentioned, often results in its selling at a market price somewhat higher than its conversion value. In general, the more volatile the price movements of the stock, the more valuable is the downside protection afforded by the bond-value floor. For this reason as well as for additional reasons discussed later, the market price of a convertible security frequently is above its conversion value. The difference is known as the *premium-over-conversion value.*

Moreover, a convertible bond typically will sell at a *premium-over-bond value*, primarily because of the conversion feature. Unless the market price of the stock is very low relative to the conversion price, the conversion feature usually will have value, in that investors may eventually find it profitable to convert the securities. To the extent that the conversion feature does have value, the convertible will sell at a premium over its straight bond value. The higher the market price of the common relative to the conversion price, the greater this premium.

Relation Between Premiums

The trade-off between the two premiums depicts the value of the option to investors and is illustrated in Fig. 23-1. The market price of the common is on the horizontal axis; the value of the convertible security is on the vertical. It should be pointed out that the two axes are on different scales. The diagonal line, which starts at the origin, represents the conversion value of the bond. It is linear, as the conversion ratio is invariant with respect to the market price of the stock.

---

[2] Mathematically, the straight bond value of a convertible will rise over time, all other things held constant, if the face value of the convertible is above the straight bond value at the time of issuance. At final maturity the straight bond value will equal the face value of the convertible, assuming the company is not in default.

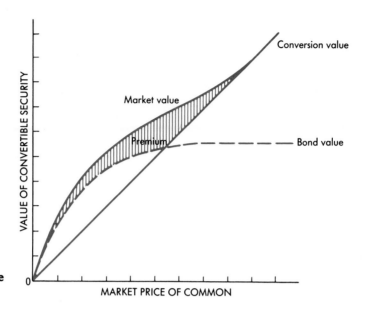

FIGURE 23-1
Relation between bond value and conversion-value premiums

The bond-value line, however, is related to the market price of the common. If a company is doing badly financially, the prices of both its common stock and its bonds are likely to be low. At the extreme, if the total value of the company were zero, both the bonds and the stock would have a value of zero. As the company becomes sounder financially and the common stock increases in price, bond value increases but at a decreasing rate. After a point, the bond-value line becomes flat, and further increases in common stock price are unrelated to it. At this point, the bond-value floor is determined by what other high-grade bonds sell for in the market. The upper curved line represents the market price of the convertible security. The distance between this line and the bond-value line is the premium over bond value, while the distance between the market-value line and the conversion-value line represents the premium over conversion value.

We see that at relatively high common stock price levels, the value of the convertible as a bond is insignificant. Consequently, its premium-over-bond value is high, whereas its premium-over-conversion value is negligible. The security sells mainly for its stock equivalent. Investors are unwilling to pay a significant premium-over-conversion value for the following reasons. First, the greater the premium of market price of the convertible over its bond value, the less valuable the bond-value protection is to the investor. Second, when the conversion value is high, the convertible may be called; if it is, the investor will want to convert rather than redeem the bond for the call price. Upon conversion, of course, the bond is worth only its conversion value.

On the other hand, when the market value of the convertible is close to its straight bond value, the conversion feature has little value. At this level, the convertible security is valued primarily as a straight bond. Under these circumstances, the market price of the convertible is likely to exceed its conversion value by a significant premium.

The principal reason for premiums in market price over both conversion value and bond value is the unusual appeal of a convertible as both a bond and an option on common stock. It offers the holder partial protection on the downside together with participation in upward movements in stock price. Thus, the distribution of possible outcomes is skewed to the right, and this characteristic finds favor with investors. Option pricing theory allows a deeper understanding of the valuation of this characteristic, and that is the subject of the appendix.

EXCHANGEABLE BONDS

An exchangeable bond is like a convertible bond, but the common stock involved is that of another corporation. In 1986, National Distillers and Chemical Corporation issued $49 million in 6 percent subordinated debentures exchangeable into stock of Cetus Corporation, a biotechnology firm. General Cinema has debt outstanding that is exchangeable into RJR Nabisco common stock. While still not a widespread means of financing, exchangeables are increasing in importance.

Features

Like the conversion price and conversion ratio for a convertible security, the *exchange price* and *exchange ratio* must be set at the time of issuance. The National Distillers debentures have an exchange price of $49, which translates into 20.41 shares of Cetus for each $1,000 face value debenture. At the time of issuance, Cetus was selling for $37.50 per share. Therefore, the *exchange premium* was 30.7 percent, which is very high as conversion premiums go. This reflected the nature of Cetus—good potential but little revenue and much uncertainty. The more variable the outcome, of course, the higher the option value. As with convertible bonds, there typically is a call feature with an exchangeable bond, and most issues are subordinated.

Use in Financing

Exchangeable bond issues usually occur only when the issuer owns common stock in the company in which the bonds can be exchanged. National Distillers, for example, owned 4 percent of the outstanding stock of Cetus Corporation. Exchange requests presumably will be satisfied from this holding, as opposed to acquiring stock in the open market. Therefore, the decision to go with an exchangeable bond issue may bring with it the reduction in or elimination of stock ownership in another company. A conscious decision of this sort is embraced in the financing.

Like the convertible, interest costs are lower because of the option value of the instrument. So far, most companies issuing exchangeables have been large and would not have experienced difficulty financing with a straight debt issue. The attraction is a lower interest cost together with the possibility of disposing of a common stock investment at a premium above the present price. Finally, some exchangeable issues of U.S. companies have been placed with investors outside the United States.

Valuation of an Exchangeable

The valuation of an exchangeable security is identical in most respects to that of a convertible security. However, there are differences. Instead of the bond and the common stock being in the same company, the bond is in one company and the stock in another. Therefore, the investor must analyze and track both components. One advantage is diversification; the bond-value floor and the stock value are not directly linked. Poor earnings and financial performance in one company will not lead to a simultaneous decline in bond-value floor and in the stock value. If the companies are in unrelated industries, the investor achieves diversification. With market imperfections, this may lead to a higher valuation for the exchangeable than for the convertible, all other things the same.

Because option values are driven by the volatility of the associated asset, differences in volatility may affect the choice between an exchangeable and a convertible bond issue. If the stock of the company in exchange is more volatile than that of the issuer, the option value will be greater with an exchangeable bond issue than it will with a convertible bond issue, all other things the same.

A relative disadvantage has to do with taxation. The difference between the market value of the stock at the time of exchange and the cost of the bond is treated as a capital gain for tax purposes. In the case of a convertible, this gain goes unrecognized until the stock is sold. The net effect of these factors is unclear. In summary, exchangeable securities are a variant of convertible securities that may increase in use what with the rapid innovation now occurring in corporate financing.

WARRANTS AND THEIR VALUATION

A **warrant** is an option to purchase a specified number of shares of common stock at a stated price. When holders exercise options, they surrender the warrants. Warrants often are employed as "sweeteners" to a public issue of bonds or debt that is privately placed. The investor obtains not only the fixed return associated with debt but also an option to purchase common stock at a stated price. If the market price of the stock should rise, this option can be valuable. As a result, the corporation should be able to obtain a lower interest rate than it would otherwise. For companies that are marginal credit risks, the use of warrants may spell the difference between being able and not being able to raise funds through a debt issue. In addition to being a "sweetener" to debt financing, warrants are used in the origination of a company as compensation to underwriters and venture capitalists.

Warrant. An option to purchase stock of a company at a specified exercise price over a specified period of time.

Features

The warrant itself contains the provisions of the option. It states the number of shares the holder can buy for each warrant. Frequently, a warrant will provide the option to purchase 1 share of common stock for each warrant held, but it might be 2 shares, 3 shares, or 2.54 shares. Another important provision is the price at which the warrant is exercisable, such as $12 a share. This means that in order to buy one share the warrant holder must put up $12. This exercise price may be either fixed or "stepped up" over time. For example, the exercise price might increase from $12 to $13 after 3 years and to $14 after another 3 years.

The warrant must specify the date the option expires unless it is perpetual, having no expiration date, such as warrants of Alleghany Corporation. Because a warrant is only an option to purchase stock, warrant holders are not entitled to any cash dividends paid on the common stock, nor do they have voting power. If the common stock is split or a stock dividend is declared, the option price of the warrant usually is adjusted to take this change into account.

Exercise of Warrants

Exercise price. The price that must be paid for a share of stock when either a call option or a warrant is exercised.

When warrants are exercised, the common stock of the company is increased. Moreover, the debt that was issued in conjunction with the warrants remains outstanding, assuming the warrants are detachable. At the time of the issue of the warrants, the **exercise price** usually is set in excess of the market price of the common stock. The premium often is 15 percent or so above the stock's value. If the share price is $40, this translates into an exercise price of $46.

To see how new capital can be infused with the exercise of warrants, let us take a company we shall call Westman Bodac. It has just raised $25 million in debt funds with warrants attached. The debentures carry an 11 percent coupon rate; and with each debenture ($1,000 face value) investors receive one warrant entitling them to purchase four shares of common stock at $30 a share. The capitalization of the company before financing, after financing, and after complete exercise of the options is as follows (in millions):

	BEFORE FINANCING	AFTER FINANCING	AFTER EXERCISE
Debentures		$25	$25
Common stock			
($10 par value)	$10	10	11
Paid-in capital			2
Retained earnings	40	40	40
Net worth	$50	$50	$53
Total capitalization	$50	$75	$78

The retained earnings of the company remain unchanged, and the debenture issue has neither matured nor been called. Exercising their options, the warrant holders purchase 100,000 shares of stock at $30 a share, or $3 million in total.

Consequently, the total capitalization of the company is increased by that amount.

A company cannot force the exercise of the warrant option as it can force the exercise of the conversion option by calling a convertible security. Consequently, it is unable to control when, if ever, the warrant will be exercised and there will be an infusion of new equity capital into the corporation. Only the expiration date sets a limit on how long the warrants can remain outstanding and unexercised. As with convertibles, it is necessary for companies to report earnings per share on a fully diluted basis. Full dilution means the maximum possible dilution if all convertible securities were converted into common stock and all warrants or options to purchase common stock were exercised. As a result of this requirement, the common stock investor is not likely to overlook the potential dilution inherent in a company's financing with convertible securities and warrants.

Valuation of Warrants

The theoretical value of a warrant can be determined by

$$NP_s - E \qquad\qquad (23\text{-}2)$$

where N = the number of shares that can be purchased with one warrant
  P_s = the market price of one share of stock
  E = the exercise price associated with the purchase of N shares.

The theoretical value of a warrant is the lowest level at which the warrant will generally sell. If, for some reason, the market price of a warrant were to go lower than its theoretical value, arbitragers would eliminate the differential by buying the warrants, exercising them, and selling the stock.

When the market value of the associated stock is less than the exercise price, the theoretical value of the warrant is zero and it is said to be trading "out of the money." When the value of the associated common stock is greater than the exercise price, the theoretical value of the warrant is positive, as depicted by the solid diagonal line in Fig 23-2. Under these circumstances, the warrant is said to be trading "in the money."

Premium Over Theoretical Value.   The primary reason that a warrant sells at a price higher than its theoretical value is the opportunity for leverage. To illustrate the concept of leverage, consider the Textron warrants. For each warrant held, one share of common stock can be purchased, and the exercise price is $10. If the stock were selling at $12 a share, the theoretical value of the warrant would be $2. Suppose, however, that the common stock increased by 25 percent in price to $15 a share. The theoretical value of the warrant would go from $2 to $5, a gain of 150 percent.

The opportunity for increased gain is attractive to investors when the common stock is selling near its exercise price. For a particular investment, the investor can buy more warrants than common stock. If the stock moves up in price

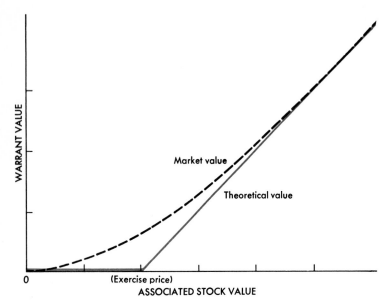

FIGURE 23-2
Relation between theoretical and actual values of a warrant

the investor will make more money on the warrants than on an equal investment in common stock. Of course, leverage works both ways; the percentage change can be almost as pronounced on the downside. However, there is a limit to how far the warrant can fall in price because it is bounded at zero. Moreover, for the market price to drop to zero, there would have to be no probability that the market price of the stock would exceed the exercise price during the exercise period. Usually there is some probability.

The market prices of many warrants are in excess of their theoretical values because of the potential for upside movements in the value of the warrant while, at the same time, downside movements are cushioned. In particular, this event occurs when the market price of the associated common stock is near the exercise price of the warrant.

Relationship Between Values.   The typical relationship between the market value of a warrant and the value of the associated common stock is shown in Fig. 23-2. The theoretical value of the warrant is represented by the solid line in the figure, and the actual market value by the dashed line. One might think of the theoretical value line as representing the values a warrant might take with only a moment to expiration. When there is a reasonable amount of time to expiration of the warrant, the relationship between warrant value and stock value is better depicted by the dashed line in Fig. 23-2. The greater the length of time to expiration, the more time the investor has in which to exercise the warrant and the more valuable it becomes. As a result, the further in the future the expiration date of the warrant, the higher the market-value line tends to be in relation to the theoretical-value line.

We note in the figure that when the market value of the associated common stock is low in relation to the exercise price, the actual market value of a warrant exceeds its theoretical values. As the market value of the associated stock rises, the market value of the warrant usually approaches its theoretical value. This simply suggests that a warrant has the greatest value, relative to its theoretical value, when it has the greatest potential percentagewise for upside movements and where the amount of funds invested is not all that great. The valuation of options, of which warrants are one form, is explored in more depth in the appendix to this chapter.

SUMMARY

Convertible securities, exchangeable securities, and warrants are options under which the holder can obtain common stock. The conversion or exchange feature enables the investor to transfer a debt instrument or preferred stock into common stock, whereas a warrant attached to a bond enables the holder to purchase a specified number of shares at a specified price. With a warrant, the exercise of the option does not result in the elimination of the bonds.

The convertible security can be viewed as a straight debt or preferred stock issue plus an option to buy common stock. For the corporation, convertibles often represent delayed common stock financing. For a given amount of financing, there will be less dilution with a convertible issue than with a common stock issue, assuming it eventually converts and is not "overhanging." As a hybrid security, the convertible security has a bond-value floor and a conversion, or stock, value. As a result, the distribution of possible returns is skewed to the right and there is a trade-off between the two factors.

An exchangeable bond may be exchanged for common stock in another corporation. It is like the convertible security in its valuation underpinnings with a couple of exceptions. This method of financing is applicable to companies that have stockholdings in another company.

Normally, warrants are employed as a "sweetener" for a public or private issue of debt. The market value of a warrant usually is higher than its theoretical value when the market value of the stock is close to the exercise price, because this situation gives the investor an opportunity for favorable leverage. When the market price of the stock is high relative to the exercise price, warrants tend to sell at about their theoretical values.

APPENDIX
Option Pricing

An **option** is simply a contract that gives the holder the right to buy or sell the common stock of a company at some specified price. Among a variety of option contracts, the most prevalent are the **call option** and the *put option*. The call option gives the holder the right to buy a share of stock at a specified price, known as the exercise price. We might have a call option to buy one share of ABC Corporation's common stock at $10 through December 31, which is the expiration date. The party who provides the option is known as the *writer*. In the case of a

Option. A contract that gives the option holder the right to buy or sell an asset at a stated price, known as the exercise price.

Call option. An option to buy an asset at a specified price, the exercise price, during a specified period of time.

call option, the writer must deliver stock to the option holder when the latter exercises the option.

As evident from our discussions in the chapter, a warrant is a form of call option, as is the convertible security, in that it gives the holder an option on the company's stock. In contrast to a call option, a put option gives the holder the right to sell a share of stock at a specified price up to the expiration date. It is the mirror image of a call option. In what follows, we will focus only on the valuation of call options.

Valuation on Expiration Date

Suppose that we were concerned with the value of a call option (hereafter simply called an option) on its expiration date. The value of the option is simply

$$V_o = \max(V_s - E, O) \tag{23A-1}$$

where V_s is the market price of one share of stock, E is the exercise price of the option, and max means the maximum value of $V_s - E$, or zero, whichever is greater. To illustrate the formula, suppose one share of Selby Corporation's stock is \$25 at the expiration date and that the exercise price of an option is \$15. The value of the option would be \$25 − \$15 = \$10. Note that the value of the option is determined solely by the value of the stock less the exercise price; however, the option cannot have a negative value. When the exercise price exceeds the value of the stock, the value of the option becomes zero.

This notion is illustrated graphically in Fig. 23-2, where the theoretical value of a warrant is shown. The expiration value of the option lies along the theoretical value line; the horizontal axis represents the price of a share of stock at the expiration date.

Valuation Prior to Expiration

Consider now the value of an option with one period to expiration. For simplicity, let us assume that it can be exercised only on the expiration date. The value of stock at the expiration date is not known, but rather is subject to probabilistic beliefs. As long as there is some time to expiration, it is possible for the market value of the option to be greater than its theoretical value. The reason is that the option *may* have value in the future. This was discussed for the warrant, so further discussion is not necessary. The actual value of the option might be described by the dashed line in Fig. 23-2.

The Effect of Time to Expiration.   In general, the longer the period of time to expiration, the greater the value of the option relative to its theoretical value. This makes sense in that there is more time in which the option may have value. Moreover, the further in the future one pays the exercise price, the lower its present value, and this too enhances the option's value. As the expiration date of an option approaches, the relationship between the option value and the stock value becomes more convex. This is illustrated in Fig. 23-3. Line 1 represents an option with a shorter time to expiration than that for line 2, and line 2 represents an option with a shorter time to expiration than that for line 3.

   The Influence of Volatility.   Usually the most important factor in the valuation of options is the price volatility of the associated stock. More specifically, the greater the possibility of extreme outcomes, the greater the value of the option to the holder, all other things the same. We may, at the beginning of a period, be considering options on two stocks that have the following probability distributions of possible values at the expiration of the option:

PROBABILITY OF OCCURRENCE	PRICE OF STOCK A	PRICE OF STOCK B
.10	$30	$20
.25	36	30
.30	40	40
.25	44	50
.10	50	60

The expected stock price at the end of the period is the same for both stocks:

FIGURE 23-3
Relation between stock price and option price for various expiration dates

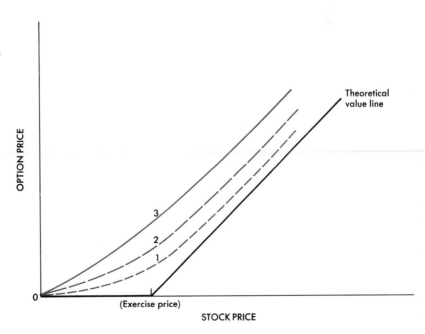

$40. For stock B, however, there is a much larger dispersion of possible outcomes. Suppose that the exercise prices of options to purchase stock A and stock B at the end of the period are also the same, say, $38. Thus, the two stocks have the same expected values at the end of the period, and the options have the same exercise price. The expected value of the option for stock A at the end of the period, however, is

$$\text{Option A} = 0(.10) + 0(.25) + (\$40 - \$38)(.30)$$
$$+ (\$44 - \$38)(.25) + (\$50 - \$38)(.10)$$
$$= \$3.30$$

whereas that for stock B is

$$\text{Option B} = 0(.10) + 0(.25) + (\$40 - \$38)(.30)$$
$$+ (\$50 - \$38)(.25) + (\$60 - \$38)(.10)$$
$$= \$5.80$$

Thus, the greater dispersion of possible outcomes for stock B leads to a greater expected value of option price on the expiration date. The reason is that values for the option cannot be negative. As a result, the greater the dispersion, the greater the magnitude of favorable outcomes as measured by the stock price minus the exercise price. Increases in the volatility of the stock therefore increase the magnitude of favorable outcomes for the option buyer and, hence, increase the value of the option.

Hedging With Options

Having two related financial assets—a stock and an option on that stock—we can set up a risk-free hedged position. Price movements in one of the financial assets will be offset by opposite price movements in the other. A hedged position can be established by buying the stock (holding it long) and by writing options. If the stock goes up in price, we gain in our long position, that is, in the stock we hold. We lose in the options we have written, because the price we must pay for the stock in order to deliver to the person exercising the option is higher than it was when the option was written. If the stock goes down in price, the opposite occurs. We lose on our long position, but gain on the options we have written.

Thus, when one holds a combination of stock and options written, movements upward or downward in the price of the stock are offset by opposite movements in the value of the option position written. If one does this properly, the overall position (long in stock, options written) can be made approximately risk free. In market equilibrium, one would expect to earn only the risk-free rate on a perfectly hedged position.

Black-Scholes Option Model

In a seminal paper, Fischer Black and Myron Scholes developed a precise model for determining the equilibrium value of an option.[3] This model is based on the hedging notion just discussed. Black-Scholes assume an option that can be exercised only at maturity, no transaction costs or market imperfections, a stock that pays no dividend, a known short-term interest rate at which market participants can both borrow and lend, and, finally, stock price movements that follow a random pattern.

Given these assumptions, we can determine the equilibrium value of an option. Should the actual price of the option differ from that given by the model, we could establish a riskless hedged position and earn a return in excess of the short-term interest rate. As arbitragers entered the scene, the excess return would eventually be driven out and the price of the option would equal that value given by the model.

To illustrate a hedged position, suppose that the appropriate relationship between the option and the stock of XYZ Corporation were that shown in Fig. 23-4. Suppose further that the current market price of the stock were $20 and the price of the option $7. At $20 a share, the slope of the line in Fig. 23-4 is one-half. A hedged position could be undertaken by buying a share of stock for $20 and writing two options at $7 each. The "net money" invested in this position would be $20 − 2($7) = $6.

This combination of holding one share of stock long and two options short leaves us essentially hedged with respect to risk. If the stock drops slightly in

[3] "The Pricing of Options and Corporate Liabilities," *Journal of Political Economy*, 81 (May–June 1973), 637–54.

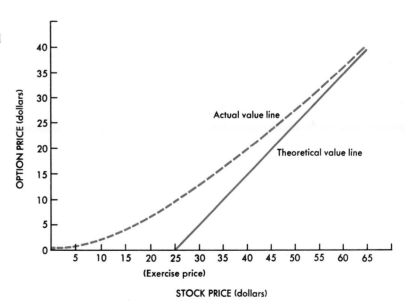

FIGURE 23-4
Relation between the option price and the stock price for XYZ Corporation

value, the value of the short position goes up by approximately an equal amount. We say *approximately* because with changes in the price of the common and with changes in time, the ideal hedge ratio changes. With a stock price increase, for example, the slope of the line in Fig. 23-4 increases. Therefore, fewer options would need to be written. If the stock price declines, the slope decreases and more options would need to be written to maintain a hedge. In addition, the line itself will shift downward as time goes on and the expiration date approaches. This is illustrated in Fig. 23-3.

Thus, one's short position in options must be continually adjusted for changes in the stock price and for changes in time if a riskless hedged position is to be maintained. The assumptions of the model make this possible; but in the real world, transaction costs make it impractical to adjust one's short position continuously. Even here, however, the risk that will appear as a result of moderate changes in stock price or of the passage of time will be small. Moreover, it can be diversified away. For practical purposes, then, it is possible to maintain a hedged position that is approximately risk free. Arbitrage will ensure that the return on this position is approximately the short-term, risk-free rate.

If the price of the option got out of line with that of the stock, it would be possible for a person to earn more than the short-term rate on a hedged position. In the example, the "net money" invested in the position was $6: $20 − 2($7). As the total hedged position is riskless, the "net money" invested should provide a return equal only to the short-term rate. If for some reason the prices on the two instruments got out of line with each other, it would be possible to earn a return on the total position in excess of the short-term rate times the "net money" invested. In other words, excess returns would be possible on a position perfectly hedged for risk.

As a result, arbitragers would enter the picture and would borrow large sums of money, establish hedged positions, and reap the excess returns available. This action would continue until the buying or selling pressure on the prices of the stock and the option drove such prices into "equilibrium" with each other. At such time, the return on the "net money" invested in a fully hedged position would once again be the short-term rate. Thus, there are equilibrating forces that cause a riskless hedge to provide a return equal to the short-term rate.

The Exact Formula and Implications. In this context, the equilibrium value of an option, V_o, that entitles the holder to buy one share of stock is shown by Black and Scholes to be

$$V_o = V_s N(d_1) - \left(\frac{E}{e^{rt}}\right) N(d_2) \tag{23A-2}$$

where V_s = the current price of the stock
E = the exercise price of the option
e = 2.71828
r = the short-term interest rate continuously compounded
t = the length of time in years to the expiration of the option

$N(d)$ = the value of the cumulative normal density function

$$d_1 = \frac{\ln (V_s/E + [r + \frac{1}{2}(\sigma^2)]t}{\sigma\sqrt{t}}$$

$$d_2 = \frac{\ln (V_s/E) + [r - \frac{1}{2}(\sigma^2)]t}{\sigma\sqrt{t}}$$

$\ln$ = the natural logarithm

σ = the standard deviation of the annual rate of return on the stock continuously compounded.

The important implication of this formula is that the value of the option is a function of the short-term interest rate, of the time to expiration, and of the variance rate of return on the stock, but it is not a function of the expected return on the stock. The value of the option in Eq. (23A-2) increases with the increase of the duration to expiration, t, the standard deviation, σ, and the short-term interest rate, r.

The reason for the first two relationships with option values is obvious from our earlier discussion. The last is not so obvious. Recall that a person is able to take a position in options that will provide the same dollar movements as the associated stock, but with a lower net investment. The "difference" in net money in the option relative to the stock may be invested in short-term market instruments. The greater the return on these investments, therefore, the greater the attraction of the option relative to the stock, and the greater its value. Another way to look at the matter is that the greater the interest rate, the lower the present value of exercise price that will need to be paid in the future if the option is exercised, and the greater the value of the option. Of the three factors affecting the value of the option, however, the short-term interest rate has the least impact.

In solving the formula, we know the current stock price, the time to expiration, the exercise price, and the short-term interest rate. The key unknown, then, is the standard deviation. This must be estimated. The usual approach is to use the past volatility of the stock's return as a proxy for the future. Black and Scholes as well as others have tested the model using standard deviations estimated from past data with some degree of success. Given the valuation equation for options, Black and Scholes derive the ratio of shares of stock to options necessary to maintain a fully hedged position. It is shown to be $N(d_1)$, which was defined earlier. Thus, the Black-Scholes model permits the quantification of the various factors that affect the value of an option. As we saw, the key factor is estimating the future volatility of the stock.

A Summing Up

In summary, it is possible to establish a riskless hedged position by buying a stock and by writing options. The hedge ratio determines the portion of stock held long in relation to the options that are written. In efficient financial markets, the rate of return on a perfectly hedged position would be the risk-free rate. If this is the case, it is possible to determine the appropriate value of the option at the beginning of the period. If the actual value is above or below this value, arbitrage should drive the price of the option toward the correct price.

The Black-Scholes option pricing model provides an exact formula for determining the value of an option based on the volatility of the stock, the price of the stock, the exercise price of the option, the time to expiration of the option, and the short-term interest rate. The model is based on the notion that investors are able to maintain reasonably hedged positions over time and that arbitrage will drive the return on such positions to the risk-free rate. As a result, the option price will bear a precise relationship to the stock price. The Black-Scholes model provides considerable insight into the valuation of contingent claims.

QUESTIONS

1. Define the conversion price of a convertible debenture, the conversion ratio, the conversion premium, the premium-over-conversion value, and the premium-over-bond value.

2. This chapter has argued that convertibles are a form of delayed equity financing allowing the sale of equity at a 10 to 20 percent premium over current market price. Yet most convertibles are finally called only if the current market price is well in excess of the conversion price. Would not the firm have been better off to wait and sell the common stock? Explain your position.

3. If convertible securities can be issued at a lower effective interest rate than long-term bonds, why would a company ever issue straight debt?

4. Why do warrants whose theoretical value is zero sell for positive prices?

5. Suppose you are the financial manager of a rather closely held small electronics firm. You have a favorable investment opportunity and are considering raising funds to finance it, using subordinated convertible debentures or straight bonds with warrants attached. Equity funds are not a possibility, as you feel the current stock price has been unnecessarily penalized for recent start-up expenses and the firm's high debt ratio (relative to the industry). If you expect additional large future funds requirements, which financing alternative would you adopt? Why?

6. Why might a convertible bondholder elect to convert voluntarily?

7. What reasons can you offer for the use of warrants by small, rapidly growing companies?

8. Why does the market price of an option such as a warrant usually exceed its value as common stock?

9. When a convertible security is converted into common stock, there is dilution in earnings per share. Would you expect the market price of the stock to decline as a result of this dilution?

10. If the desire of a company in selling convertible securities is delayed equity financing, would not it be wise to establish at the time the security is sold a "set-up" in conversion price every few years?

11. Why would an investor want to invest in warrants as opposed to common stock?

12. As a lender, how attractive are warrants to you as a "sweetener"? Will you give terms more favorable than you otherwise would?

13. Why is unlimited upside potential and a lower boundary of zero attractive to investors in a warrant? If the stock were highly volatile, would this be a good or a bad thing?

14. With option financing, such as convertible securities and debt issues with warrants attached, does the company get something (lower interest cost) for nothing?

15. How does an exchangeable bond differ from a convertible bond? How is it the same?

16. With respect to valuation, is the investor better off with an exchangeable bond or with a convertible bond?

SELF-CORRECTION PROBLEMS

The Charrier Boat Company has current earnings of $3 a share with 500,000 shares outstanding. The company plans to issue 40,000 shares of 7 percent, $50 par value convertible preferred stock at par. The preferred stock is convertible into two shares of common for each preferred share held. The common stock has a current market price of $21 per share.

a. What is the preferred stock's conversion value?

b. What is its conversion premium?

c. Assuming that total earnings stay the same, what will be the effect of the issue on earnings per share before conversion? on a fully diluted basis?

d. If profits after taxes increase by $1 million, what will be earnings per share before conversion? on a fully diluted basis?

2. Sadfield Manufacturing Company plans to issue $10 million in 10 percent convertible subordinated debentures. Currently, the stock price is $36 per share, and the company believes it could obtain a conversion premium (issuing price in excess of conversion value) of approximately 12 percent. The call price of the debenture in the first 10 years is $1,060 per bond, after which it drops to $1,030 in the next 10 years and to $1,000 in the last 10 years. To allow for fluctuations in the market price of the stock, the company does not want to call the debentures until their conversion value is at least 15 percent in excess of the call price. Earnings per share are expected to grow at an 8 percent compound annual rate in the foreseeable future, and the company envisions no change in its price/earnings ratio.

a. Determine the expected length of time that must elapse before the company is in a position to force conversion.

b. Is the issuance of a convertible security a good idea for the company?

3. Camelot Pizza has outstanding warrants, where each warrant entitles the holder to purchase two shares of stock at $24 per share. The market price per share of stock and market price per warrant were the following over the last year:

	OBSERVATION					
	1	2	3	4	5	6
Stock price	$20	$18	$27	$32	$24	$38
Warrant price	5	3	12	20	8	29

Determine the theoretical value per warrant for each of these observations. Plot the market value per warrant in relation to its theoretical value. At what price per common share is the warrant premium over theoretical value the greatest? Why?

PROBLEMS

1. The common stock of the Davidson Corporation earns $2.50 per share, has a 60 percent dividend payout, and sells at a P/E ratio of 10. Davidson wishes to offer $10 million of 9 percent, 20-year convertible debentures with an initial conversion premium of 20 percent and a call price of $105. Davidson currently has 1 million common shares outstanding and has a 50 percent tax rate.
   a. What is the conversion price?
   b. What is the conversion ratio per $1,000 debenture?
   c. What is the initial conversion value of each debenture?
   d. How many new shares of common must be issued if all debentures are converted?
   e. If Davidson can increase operating earnings (before taxes) by $1 million per year with the proceeds of the debenture issue, compute the new earnings per share and earnings retained before and after conversion.

2. Assume that the Davidson Corporation (in Problem 1) could sell $10 million in straight debt at 12 percent as an alternative to the convertible issue. Compute the earnings per share and earnings retained after issuance of the straight debt under the assumption of a $1 million increase in operating earnings and compare your answers with those obtained in Problem 1e.

3. Curran Consolidated Industries has outstanding a $7\frac{3}{4}$ percent, 20-year convertible debenture issue. Each $1,000 debenture is convertible into 25 shares of common stock. The company also has a straight debt issue outstanding of the same approximate maturity, so it is an easy matter to determine the straight bond value of the convertible issue. The market price of Curran stock is volatile. Over the last year, the following was observed:

	OBSERVATION				
	1	2	3	4	5
Market price per share	$ 40	$ 45	$ 32	$ 23	$ 18
Straight bond value	690	700	650	600	550
Market price of convertible debenture	1,065	1,140	890	740	640

   a. Compute the premium-over-conversion value (in dollars) and the premium-over-straight bond value for each of the observations.

   b. Compare the two premiums either visually or by graph. What do the relationships tell you with respect to the valuation of the convertible debenture?

4. The following year, Curran Consolidated Industries falls on further hard times. Its stock price drops to $10 per share and the market price of the convertible debentures to $440 per debenture. The straight bond value goes to $410. Determine the premium-over-conversion value and the premium-over-bond value. What can you say about the bond-value floor?

5. The Beruth Company needs to raise $10 million by means of a debt issue. It has the following alternatives: a 20-year, 8 percent convertible debenture issue with a $50 conversion price and $1,000 face value, or a 20-year, 12 percent straight debt issue. Each $1,000 bond has a detachable warrant to purchase four shares of stock for a total of $200. The company has a 50 percent tax rate, and its stock is currently selling at $40 per share. Its net income before interest and taxes is a constant 20 percent of its total capitalization, which currently appears as follows:

Common stock (par $5)	$ 5,000,000
Paid-in capital	10,000,000
Retained earnings	15,000,000
Total	$30,000,000

   a. Show the capitalizations resulting from each alternative, both before and after conversion or exercise (a total of four capitalizations).

   b. Compute earnings per share currently and under each of the four capitalizations determined in part a.

   c. If the price of Beruth stock went to $75, determine the theoretical value of each warrant issued under the second alternative.

6. Singapore Enterprises is considering an exchangeable bond issue where each bond can be exchanged for $16\frac{2}{3}$ shares of Malaysian Palm Oil Company. The latter company's stock is presently selling for $50 a share. At what premium-over-exchange value will the bonds be sold if they are sold for $1,000 a bond? Are there advantages to this type of financing versus a convertible issue?

7. Using Eq. (23-2), compute the theoretical value of each of the following warrants:

WARRANT	N	P_s	E
(a)	5	$100	$400
(b)	10	10	60
(c)	2.3	4	10
(d)	3.54	$27\frac{1}{8}$	35.40

8. Stanley Zinc Company called its 7 percent convertible subordinated debentures for redemption on March 25, 1989. The call price was $106. A holder of a $1,000 bond was entitled to convert into 34.7 shares of stock. At the time of the call announcement, the common stock of Stanley Zinc was selling at $43 per share.

   a. What is the approximate market price at which the debentures would be selling at the time of the announcement?

   b. By what percentage would market price per share need to drop before bondholders would rationally accept the call price?

9. Max Murphy, Inc., has warrants outstanding that allow the holder to purchase three shares of stock for a total $60 for each warrant that is held. Currently, the market price per share of Max Murphy common is $18. However, investors hold the following probabilistic beliefs about the stock 6 months hence.

Market price per share	$16	$18	$20	$22	$24
Probability	.15	.20	.30	.20	.15

   a. What is the present theoretical value of the warrant?

   b. What is the expected value of stock price 6 months hence?

   c. What is the expected theoretical value of the warrant 6 months hence?

   d. Would you expect the present market price of the warrant to equal its theoretical value? If not, why not?

10. Suppose you have just bought a warrant that entitles you to purchase two shares of stock for $45. The market price of the stock is $26 per share, whereas the market price of the warrant is $10 in excess of its theoretical value. One year later the stock has risen in price to $50 per share. The warrant now sells for $2 more than its theoretical value.

    a. If the common stock paid $1 in dividends for the year, what is the return on investment in the common?

    b. What is the return on investment in the warrant?

    c. Why do the two rates of return differ?

SOLUTIONS TO SELF-CORRECTION PROBLEMS

1. a. Conversion ratio × market price per share = 2 × \$21 = \$42
    b. (50/\$42) − 1 = 19.05%
    c. Earnings per share:

Total after tax earnings	
= \$3 × 500,000 shares =	\$1,500,000
Preferred stock dividend	140,000
Earnings available to common	
stockholders	\$1,360,000
Number of shares	500,000
Earnings per share	\$2.72
Total after-tax earnings	\$1,500,000
Number of shares (500,000 + 80,000)	580,000
Earnings per share	\$2.59

   d. Earnings per share after profit increase:

Total after-tax earnings	\$2,500,000
Preferred stock dividend	140,000
Earnings available to common	
stockholders	\$2,360,000
Number of shares	500,000
Earnings per share	\$4.72
Total after-tax earnings	\$2,500,000
Number of shares (500,000 + 80,000)	580,000
Earnings per share	\$4.31

2. a. Conversion price = \$36 × 1.12 = \$40.32
       Call price per share the first 10 years = \$40.32 × 1.06 = \$42.74
       Price to which the common must rise before company will be in a position to force conversion = \$42.74 × 1.15 = \$49.15
       Increase from present price = \$49.15/\$36 = 1.365

       At an 8 percent compound growth rate, earnings per share will grow to 1.36 in 4 years—this is simply $(1.08)^4$. If the price/earnings ratio stays the same, it will take approximately 4 years before the company will be in a position to force conversion.

    b. This period is somewhat longer than the 2 to 3 years that market participants have come to expect for the convertible security. Still it is not far out of line and the company may wish to go ahead. However, if uncertainty as to earnings per share increases with the length of time in the future, there may be considerable risk of an overhanging issue. This may cause the company to reconsider.

3. Market price of warrant and theoretical value at various common stock prices (in ascending order):

Common price	$18	$20	$24	$27	$32	$38
Warrant price	3	5	8	12	20	29
Theoretical value	0	0	0	6	16	28

When plotted, the relationship is of the same pattern as shown in Fig. 22-1. The maximum premium over theoretical value occurs when share price is $24, and the warrant has a theoretical value of zero. Here the greatest leverage occurs, and since volatility is what gives an option value, the premium-over-theoretical value tends to be greatest at this point.

SELECTED REFERENCES

ALEXANDER, GORDON J., and DAVID B. KUHNAU, "Market Timing Strategies in Convertible Debt Financing," *Journal of Finance*, 34 (March 1979), 143–56.

ALEXANDER, GORDON J., and ROGER D. STOVER, "The Effect of Forced Conversion on Common Stock Prices," *Financial Management*, 9 (Spring 1980), 39–45.

BLACK, FISCHER, and MYRON SCHOLES, "The Pricing of Options and Corporate Liabilities," *Journal of Political Economy*, 81 (May–June 1973), 637–54.

BRENNAN, MICHAEL J., and EDUARDO S. SCHWARTZ, "Convertible Bonds: Valuation and Optimal Strategies for Call and Conversion," *Journal of Finance*, 32 (December 1977), 1699–1715.

——— , "Analyzing Convertible Bonds," *Journal of Financial and Quantitative Analysis*, 15 (November 1980), 907–29.

FERRI, MICHAEL G., JOSEPH W. KREMER, and H. DENNIS OBERHELMAN, "An Analysis of Corporate Warrants," *Advances in Futures and Options Research*, 1 (1986), 201–26.

FINNERTY, JOHN D., "The Case for Issuing Synthetic Convertible Bonds," *Midland Corporate Finance Journal*, 4 (Fall 1986), 73–82.

GREEN, RICHARD C., "Investment Incentives, Debt, and Warrants," *Journal of Financial Economics*, 13 (March 1984), 115–36.

HAUGEN, ROBERT A., *Modern Investment Theory*. Englewood Cliffs, N.J.: Prentice-Hall, 1986, chaps. 17 and 18.

JONES, E. PHILIP, and SCOTT P. MASON, "Equity-Linked Debt," *Midland Corporate Finance Journal*, 3 (Winter 1986), 47–58.

MARR, M. WAYNE, and G. RODNEY THOMPSON, "The Pricing of New Convertible Bond Issues," *Financial Management*, 13 (Summer 1984), 31–37.

MIKKELSON, WAYNE H., "Convertible Calls and Security Returns," *Journal of Financial Economics*, 9 (September 1981), 237–64.

RUBINSTEIN, MARK, and JOHN C. COX, *Option Markets*. Englewood Cliffs, N.J.: Prentice-Hall, 1985.

SHARPE, WILLIAM F., *Investments*, 3rd ed. Englewood Cliffs, N.J.: Prentice-Hall, 1985, chap. 16.

VAN HORNE, JAMES C., "Warrant Valuation in Relation to Volatility and Opportunity Costs," *Industrial Management Review*, 10 (Spring 1969), 19–32.

CHAPTER 24

Mergers and Corporate Restructuring

Growth is an essential ingredient to the success and vitality of many a company. Without it, a company has difficulty generating dedication of purpose and attracting first-rate managers. Growth can be either internal or external. Up to now, we have considered only internal growth: A firm acquires specific assets and finances them by the retention of earnings or external financing. External growth, on the other hand, involves the acquisition of another company. In principle, growth by acquiring another company is little different from growth by acquiring a specific asset. Each requires an initial outlay, which is expected to be followed by future benefits.

Corporate restructuring embraces many things in addition to mergers. It can be construed as almost any change in capital structure, in operations, or in ownership that is outside the ordinary course of business. Such things as sell-offs, spin-offs, and leveraged buyouts are some examples. Others will follow. In mergers and in other forms of restructuring the idea is to create value.

SOURCES OF VALUE

There are various reasons why a company would wish to engage in corporate restructuring. The foundation in all cases is to create value for the stockholders, a theme that runs throughout this book. In this section, we consider various reasons for a restructuring but remember that they must be taken collectively.

Efficiency Gains

Often, operating economies can be achieved through a combination of companies. Duplicate facilities can be eliminated; marketing, accounting, purchasing, and other operations can be consolidated. The sales force may be reduced to avoid duplication of effort in a particular territory. In a railroad **merger,** the principal objective is to realize economies of operation through elimination of duplicate facilities and runs. When industrial companies merge, a firm with a product that complements an existing product line may fill out that line and increase the total demand for products of the acquiring company. The realization of such economies is known as synergism; the fused company is of greater value than the sum of the parts; that is, 2 + 2 = 5.

Merger. The combination of two companies where one loses its corporate identity.

In addition to operating economies, economies of scale may be possible with a merger of two companies. Economies of scale occur when average cost declines with increases in volume. Usually we think of economies of scale in production and overlook their possibilities in marketing, purchasing, distribution, accounting, and even finance. The idea is to concentrate a greater volume of activity into a given facility, into a given number of people, into a given distribution system, and so on. In other words, increases in volume permit a more efficient utilization of resources. Like anything else, it has limits. Beyond a point, increases in volume may cause more problems than they remedy, and a company actually may become less efficient. Economists speak of an "envelope curve" with economies of scale possible up to some optimal point, after which diseconomies occur.

With a divestiture, such as a sell-off or spin-off, reverse synergy may occur: $4 - 2 = 3$. That is, the operation may be more valuable to someone else in generating cash flows and positive net present value. As a result, it is willing to pay a higher price for the operation than its present value to you. In some situations, the operation may be a chronic loser and the owner is unwilling to commit the necessary resources to make it profitable. This was the case with Borg Warner Corporation when it decided to divest itself of York International, a maker of heating and air-conditioning equipment.

An allied reason for divestiture is a strategic change by the company. Periodically, most companies review their long-range plans in an effort to answer the eternal question, What businesses should we be in? Strategic considerations include internal capabilities (capital, plant, and people), the external product markets, and competitors. The market, as well as the competitive advantage of a company within a market, changes over time, sometimes very quickly. New markets emerge, as do new capabilities within the firm. What was once a good fit may no longer be a good fit. As a result, a decision may be reached to divest a particular operation. In the case of an acquisition of another company, not all of the parts may fit the strategic plan of the acquiring company. As a result, a decision may be reached to divest one or more of the parts. Strategic realignment is the most cited reason chief executive officers give to justify a divestiture.

Improved Management

Some companies are inefficiently managed, with the result that profitability is lower than it might be. To the extent the restructuring can provide better management, it may make sense for this reason alone. While a company can change management itself, the practical realities of entrenchment may be such that a pronounced restructuring is required for anything to happen. This motivation would suggest that poor-earning, low-return companies are ripe acquisition candidates, and there appears to be some evidence in support of this contention. However, there must be the potential for significantly better earnings through improved management. Some products and companies simply have little potential, and poor performance is due to things other than inefficient management.

Information Effect

Value also could occur if new information is conveyed as a result of the corporate restructuring. This notion implies asymmetric information between management (or the acquirer) and the general market for the stock. To the extent a stock is believed to be undervalued, a positive signal may occur via the merger announcement that causes share price to rise. The idea is that the merger/takeover event provides information on underlying profitability that otherwise cannot be convincingly conveyed. This argument has been examined elsewhere in the book and, in a nutshell, it is that specific actions speak louder than words.

In the case of a divestiture, its announcement may signal a change in investment strategy or in operating efficiency that, in turn, might have a positive effect on share price. On the other hand, if the announcement is interpreted as the sale of the most marketable subsidiary to deal with adversities elsewhere in the company, the signal will be negative. Whether a company is truly under- or overvalued is always questionable. Invariably, management believes it is undervalued, and in certain cases it has information that is not properly reflected in market price. There may be ways to convey effectively value other than by an irreversible corporate restructuring.

Wealth Transfers

Another reason for shareholder wealth to change is wealth transfers from them to debt holders, and vice versa. If a merger lowers the relative variability of cash flows, for example, debt holders benefit in having a more creditworthy claim. As a result, the market value of their claim should increase, all other things the same. If overall value does not change in other ways, their gain comes at the expense of stockholders.

    In contrast, if a company divests a portion of the enterprise and distributes the proceeds to stockholders, there will be a wealth transfer from debt holders to stockholders. The transaction reduces the probability that the debt will be paid, and it will have a lesser value. If the value of the debt declines by virtue of more default risk, the value of the equity will increase, assuming the total value of the firm remains unchanged. In essence, the stockholders have stolen away part of the enterprise, thereby reducing its collateral value to debt holders.

    In summary, any action that reduces the riskiness of cash flows, like a merger, may result in a wealth transfer from equity holders to debt holders. A restructuring that increases the relative riskiness, like a divestiture or leverage, may result in a transfer from debt holders to equity holders.

Tax Reasons

A motivation in many a merger is tax. In the case of a tax loss carryforward, a company with cumulative tax losses may have little prospect of earning enough in the future to utilize fully its tax loss carryforward.[1] By merging with a profitable company, it may be possible for the surviving company to utilize more effectively the carryforward. However, there are restrictions that limit its utilization to a percentage of the fair market value of the acquired company. Still, there can be an economic gain—at the expense of the government—that cannot be realized by either company separately.

    In addition, a merger permits a write-up in asset value of the acquired company to fair market value. As illustrated earlier in the chapter, this permits higher depreciation, which, in turn, means lower taxes being paid and higher cash flows. Certain rather technical changes in the 1986 Tax Act reduced the tax

---

[1] A loss is carried back 3 years and forward 15 years to offset taxable income in those years. It first must be applied to the earliest preceding year and then to the next 2 years in order. If the loss is not entirely offset by earnings in the 3 prior years, the residual is carried forward sequentially to reduce future profits, and taxes, in each of the next 15 years.

motivation of mergers. Because these changes are involved, we do not take them up.

Sometimes tax considerations enter into a decision to divest. If a company loses money and is unable to use a tax loss carryforward, divestiture in whole or in part may be the only way to realize value from this tax benefit. In other situations, the stepped-up basis for depreciable assets may be a factor. By sale of a division, for example, the assets may be marked up to their market values and higher depreciation charges taken by the new owner. This has positive cash-flow implications, which value can only be realized if there is an actual sales transaction.

Leverage Gains

Value also may arise from leverage. In many corporate restructurings, the degree of leverage changes, often increasing. When this occurs, value may be created for shareholders along the lines discussed in Chapter 17. There is a trade-off among the corporate tax effect, the personal tax effect, bankruptcy and agency costs, and incentive effects. As the valuation implications were presented in the earlier chapter, we will not repeat the discussion here. However, recognize that value may change simply because the restructuring action results in a change in leverage.

Hubris Hypothesis

Richard Roll argues that takeovers are motivated by bidders who get caught up in believing they can do no wrong and that their foresight is perfect.[2] Hubris refers to an animal-like spirit of arrogant pride and self-confidence. Such individuals are said not to have the rational behavior necessary to refrain from bidding. They get caught up in the "heat of the hunt" where the prey must be had regardless of cost. As a result, bidders pay too much for their targets. The hubris hypothesis suggests that the excess premium paid for the target company benefits those stockholders, but that stockholders of the acquiring company suffer a decrease in wealth.

Personal Reasons

In a tightly held company, the individuals who have controlling interest may want their company acquired by another company that has an established market for its stock. For estate tax purposes, it may be desirable for these individuals to hold shares of stock that are readily marketable and for which market price quotations are available. The owners of a tightly held company may have too much of their wealth tied up in the company. By merging with a publicly held company, they obtain a marked improvement in their liquidity, enabling them to sell some of their stock and diversify their investments.

[2] Richard Roll, "The Hubris Hypothesis of Corporate Takeovers," *Journal of Business*, 59 (April 1986), 197–216.

With these reasons in mind, let us consider various forms of corporate restructuring. We begin with mergers and then go on to divestitures and ownership structure changes.

IMPACT OF TERMS OF MERGER

When two companies are combined, a ratio of exchange occurs, denoting the relative weighting of the firms. In this section we consider the ratio of exchange with respect to the earnings, the market prices, and the book values of the stocks of the two companies involved. We assume that the combination is consummated in stock rather than in cash or debt. The objective in any merger should be to maximize the long-run wealth of existing stockholders. A successful merger, then, would be one that increased the market price of the firm's stock over the price it would have brought if the combination had not taken place.

Earnings Impact

In evaluating a possible acquisition, the acquiring firm must consider the effect the merger will have on the earnings per share of the surviving corporation. Company A is considering the acquisition, by stock, of Company B. The financial data on the acquisition at the time it is being considered are as follows:

	COMPANY A	COMPANY B
Present earnings	$20,000,000	$5,000,000
Shares	5,000,000	2,000,000
Earnings per share	$4.00	$2.50
Price per stock	$64.00	$30.00
Price/earnings ratio	16	12

Company B has agreed to an offer of $35 a share to be paid in Company A's stock. The exchange ratio, then, is $35/$64, or about .547 share of Company A's stock for each share of Company B's stock. In total 1,093,750 shares of Company A will need to be issued to acquire Company B. Assuming that the earnings of the component companies stay the same after the acquisition, earnings per share of the surviving company would be

	SURVIVING COMPANY A
Earnings	$25,000,000
Shares	6,093,750
Earnings per share	$4.10

Thus, there is an immediate improvement in earnings per share for Company A as a result of the merger. Company B's former stockholders experience a reduction in earnings per share, however. For each share of B's stock they had held, they now hold .547 share of A. Thus, the earnings per share on each share of Company B's stock they held is (.547)(4.10), or $2.24, compared with the previous $2.50.

Suppose that the price agreed upon for Company B's stock is $45 instead of $35 a share. The ratio of exchange, then, would be $45/$64, or about .703 share of A for each share of B. In total, 1,406,250 shares would have to be issued, and earnings per share after the merger would be

	SURVIVING COMPANY A
Earnings	$25,000,000
Shares	6,406,250
Earnings per share	$3.90

In this case, there is initial dilution in Company A's earnings per share on account of the acquisition of company B.[3] Dilution in earnings per share will occur any time the price/earnings ratio paid for a company exceeds the price/earnings ratio of the company doing the acquiring. In our example, the price/earnings ratio in the first case was $35/$2.50, or 14; in the second case it was $45/$2.50, or 18. Because the price/earnings ratio of Company A was 16, there was an increase in earnings per share in the first case and a decrease in the second.

Thus, both initial increases and decreases in earnings per share are possible. The *amount* of increase or decrease is a function of (1) the differential in price/earnings ratios and (2) the relative size of the two firms as measured by total earnings.[4] The higher the price/earnings ratio of the acquiring company in relation to that of the company being acquired and the larger the earnings of the acquired company in relation to those of the acquiring company, the greater the increase in earnings per share of the acquiring company. These relationships are illustrated in Fig. 24-1 for three different earnings relationships. The a subscript for total earnings, T_a, and for price/earnings ratio, P_a/E_a, denotes the acquiring company; the b subscript for T_b and P_b/E_b denotes the company being acquired.

Synergy. Economies realized in a merger where the whole is greater than the sum of the parts.

Future Earnings.   If the decision to acquire another company were based solely on the initial impact on earnings per share, an initial dilution in earnings per share would stop any company from acquiring another. This type of analysis, however, does not take into account the possibility of a future growth in earnings owing to the merger. This growth may be due to the expected growth in earnings of the acquired company as an independent entity and to any synergistic effects that result from the fusion of the two companies. If the earnings of

[3] Company B's former stockholders obtain an improvement in earnings per share. Earnings per share on each share of stock they had held are $2.74.

[4] See Walter J. Mead,"Instantaneous Merger Profit as a Conglomerate Merger Motive," *Western Economics Review,* 7 (December 1969), 295–306.

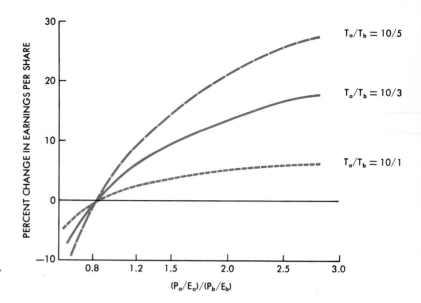

FIGURE 24-1
Relationship between earnings per share change and the price/earnings ratio differential and relative earnings

Company B are expected to grow at a faster rate than those of Company A, or if there is expected synergy, a high ratio of exchange for the stock may be justified, even though there is initial dilution in earnings per share for stockholders of Company A. The superior growth in earnings of the acquired company may result eventually in higher earnings per share for these stockholders relative to earnings per share without the merger.

It is useful to graph likely future earnings per share with and without the acquisition. Figure 24-2 shows this for a hypothetical merger. The graph tells us how long it will take for the dilution in earnings per share to be eliminated and for an accretion to take place. In this example, it is $1\frac{1}{2}$ years; earnings per share drop $.30 initially, but this relative dilution is eliminated by the middle of the second year. The greater the duration of dilution, the less desirable the acquisition is said to be from the standpoint of the acquiring company. Some companies set a ceiling on the number of years dilution will be tolerated, and this ceiling serves as a constraint in establishing the exchange ratio to be paid in the acquisition. When an acquisition is being considered, graphs should be prepared under differing assumptions of the exchange ratio. They also should be made under differing earnings assumptions for the combination; preparing such multiple graphs gives management greater information on which to base negotiations.

Market-Value Impact

The major emphasis in the bargaining process is on the ratio of exchange of market price per share. Judging the intrinsic value of a company, investors focus on the market price of its stock. That price reflects the earnings potential of the company, dividends, business risk, capital structure, asset values, and other factors that bear upon valuation. The ratio of exchange of market prices is simply

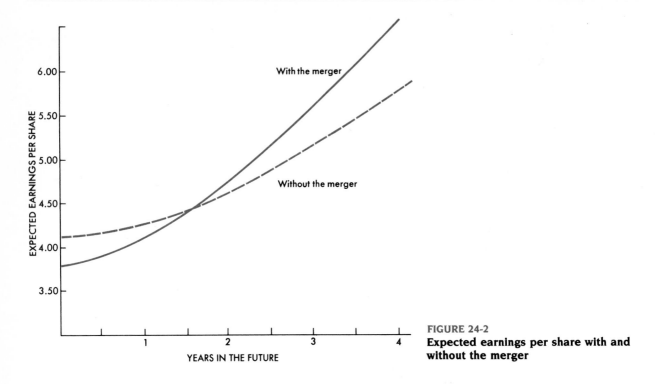

FIGURE 24-2
Expected earnings per share with and without the merger

$$\frac{\text{Market price per share of acquiring company} \times \text{Number of shares offered}}{\text{Market price per share of acquired company}}$$

If the market price of Acquiring Company is $60 per share and that of Bought Company is $30, and Acquiring Company offers a half share of its stock for each share of Bought Company, the ratio of exchange will be

$$\frac{\$60 \times .5}{\$30} = 1.00$$

In other words, the stocks of the two companies will be exchanged on a 1-to-1 market price basis. If the market price of the surviving company is relatively stable at $60 a share, stockholders of both companies are as well off as before with respect to market value. The company being acquired finds little enticement to accept a 1-to-1 market-value ratio of exchange, however. The acquiring company usually must offer a price in excess of the current market price per share of the company it wishes to acquire. Instead of a half share of stock, Acquiring Company might have to offer .667 share, or $40 a share in current market value.

Bootstrapping Earnings per Share.   In the absence of synergism, improved management, or the underpricing of Bought Company's stock in an efficient market, we would not expect it to be in the interest of Acquiring's stockholders to offer a price in excess of Bought Company's current market price. Acquiring stockholders could be better off if their company's price/earnings ratio is higher than Bought Company's and if somehow the surviving company is able to keep that same higher price/earnings ratio after the merger. Perhaps Company B has a price/earnings ratio of 10. The potential acquirer, on the other hand, has a price/earnings ratio of 18. Assume the following financial information:

	COMPANY A	COMPANY B
Present earnings	$20,000,000	$6,000,000
Shares	6,000,000	2,000,000
Earnings per share	$3.33	$3.00
Market price per share	$60.00	$30.00
Price/earnings ratio	18	10

With an offer of .667 share of Acquiring Company for each share of Bought Company, or $40 a share in value, the market price exchange ratio for Bought Company is

$$\frac{\$60 \times .667}{\$30} = 1.33$$

Stockholders of Bought Company are being offered a stock with a market value of $40 for each share of stock they own. Obviously, they benefit from the acquisition with respect to market price, because their stock was formerly worth $30 a share. Stockholders of Acquiring Company also stand to benefit, if the price/earnings of the surviving company stays at 18. The market price per share of the surviving company after the acquisition, all other things held constant, would be

	SURVIVING COMPANY
Total earnings	$26,000,000
Number of shares	7,333,333
Earnings per share	$3.55
Price/earnings ratio	18
Market price per share	$63.90

The reason for this apparent bit of magic whereby the stockholders of both companies benefit is the difference in price/earnings ratios.

Thus, companies with high price/earnings ratios supposedly would be able to acquire companies with lower price/earnings ratios and obtain an immediate increase in earnings per share, despite the fact that they pay a premium with respect to the market-value exchange ratio. The key factor is what happens to the price/earnings ratio after the merger. If it stays the same, the market price of the stock will increase. As a result, an acquiring company would be able to show a steady growth in earnings per share if it acquired a sufficient number of companies over time in this manner. This increase is not the result of operating economies or underlying growth but is due to the "bootstrap" increase in earnings per share through acquisitions. If the marketplace values this illusory growth, a company presumably could increase shareholder wealth through acquisitions alone.

In reasonably efficient capital markets, it is unlikely that the market will hold constant the price/earnings ratio of a company that cannot demonstrate growth potential in ways other than acquiring companies with lower price/earnings ratios. The acquiring company must be able to manage the companies it acquires and show some degree of synergism if the benefit of acquisitions is to be lasting. If the market is relatively free from imperfections and if synergism is not anticipated, we would expect the price/earnings ratio of the surviving firm to approach a weighted average of the two previous price/earnings ratios. Under these circumstances, the acquisition of companies with lower price/earnings ratios would not enhance shareholder wealth. For the acquiring company, share price would actually decline if the market-value exchange ratio were more than 1.00. If synergism and/or improved management were expected, however, shareholder wealth could be increased through the acquisition.

Empirical Evidence

In recent years, there have been a number of empirical studies on acquisitions, and these studies provide a wealth of information.[5] However, differences in samples, sample periods, and research methods render some of the valuation implications ambiguous. Nonetheless, with the ever-increasing number of studies, certain patterns emerge that make generalizations possible.

---

[5] These studies include Peter Dodd and Richard Ruback, "Tender Offers and Stockholder Returns," *Journal of Financial Economics*, 5 (1977), 351–73; Paul Asquith and E. Han Kim, "The Impact of Merger Bids on the Participating Firms' Security Holders," *Journal of Finance*, 37 (December 1982), 1209–28; Pieter T. Elgers and John J. Clark, "Merger Types and Shareholder Returns: Additional Evidence," *Financial Management*, 9 (Summer 1980), 66–72; Gershon Mendelker, "Risk and Return: The Case of Merging Firms," *Journal of Financial Economics*, 1 (December 1974), 303–35; Dennis C. Mueller, "The Effects of Conglomerate Mergers," *Journal of Banking and Finance*, 1 (December 1977), 315–47; Peter Dodd, "Merger Proposals, Management Discretion and Stockholder Wealth," *Journal of Financial Economics*, 8 (June 1980), 105–38; Michael Bradley, "Interfirm Tender Offers and the Market for Corporate Control," *Journal of Business*, 53 (October 1980), 345–76; Donald R. Kummer and J. Ronald Hoffmeister, "Valuation Consequences of Cash Tender Offers," *Journal of Finance*, 33 (May 1978), 505–16; Paul Asquith, "Merger Bids, Uncertainty, and Stockholder Returns," *Journal of Financial Economics*, 11 (April 1983), 51–84; Paul Asquith, Robert F. Bruner, and David W. Mullins, Jr., "The Gains to Bidding Firms from Merger," *Journal of Financial Economics*, 11 (April 1983), 121–40; Paul H. Malatesta, "The Wealth Effect of Merger Activity and the Objective Functions of Merging Firms," *Journal of Financial Economics*, 11 (April 1983), 155–82; Michael Bradley, Anand Desai, and E. Han Kim, "The Rationale Behind Interfirm Tender Offers: Information or Synergy," *Journal of Financial Economics*, 11 (April 1983), 183–206; Peter Dodd, "The Market for Corporate Control: A Review of the Evidence," *Midland Corporate Finance Journal*, 1 (Summer 1983), 6–20; Carol Ellen Eger, "An Empirical Test of the Redistribution Effect in Pure Exchange Mergers," *Journal of Financial and Quantitative Analysis*, 18 (December 1983), 547–72.

Michael Jensen and Richard S. Ruback, "The Market for Corporate Control: The Scientific Evidence," *Journal of Financial Economics* 11 (April 1983), 5–50; Michael C. Jensen, "The Takeover Controversy: Analysis and Evidence," *Midland Corporate Finance Journal*, 4 (Summer 1986), 6–32; Wayne H. Mikkelson and Richard S. Ruback, "An Empirical Analysis of the Interfirm Equity Investment Process," *Journal of Financial Economics*, 14 (December 1985), 523–54; Clifford G. Holderness and Dennis P. Sheehan, "Raiders or Saviors? The Evidence on Six Controversial Investors," *Journal of Financial Economics*, 14 (December 1985), 555–80; Debra K. Dennis and John J. McConnell, "Corporate Mergers and Security Returns," *Journal of Financial Economics*, 16 (June 1986), 143–88; Julian R. Franks and Robert S. Harris, "Shareholder Wealth Effects of Corporate Takeovers: The UK Experience," research paper, London Business School (November 1986).

For the successful, or completed, takeover, all studies show the target company stockholders' realizing appreciable increments in wealth relative to the market value of their holdings prior to any takeover activity. This wealth increment is due to the premium paid by the acquiring company, the size of which runs around 30 percent on average, though premiums as high as 80 percent occur. The market price of the target company's stock tends to rise once information about a potential takeover becomes available or rumors of such develop. Typically the stock price improvement begins prior to the takeover announcement, perhaps 1 month in advance. The pattern usually observed for the target or selling company is shown in Fig. 24-3.

For the buying, or acquiring, company, the evidence is less clear. In all cases of a successful takeover, a premium obviously is paid, and its justification must be expected synergy and/or more efficient management of the resources of the target company. The question is whether likely synergy and/or improved management will result in a wealth increment sufficient to offset the premium. Answers to this question from empirical studies are mixed. Some studies suggest stockholders of acquiring firms obtain a small improvement in share price, and others find no effect at all. The situation of no effect is illustrated in Fig. 24-3. Still others find that the stockholders of acquiring companies earn negative returns, holding constant other factors.[6] In the year following a takeover, negative returns are particularly evident.

Another explanation, of course, is that acquiring companies simply pay too much. This would agree with the hubris hypothesis, which predicts a decrease in value of the acquiring firm. In other words, potential synergy and management improvement are not enough to offset the premium paid. In certain bidding wars, the frenzy is such that rational decision making seems to disappear. In some contests the quest of the prize is so important that the premium is bid up beyond what synergy and/or improved management will justify. This is fueled in part by investment bankers who earn ever more handsome fees, the greater

[6] See Dodd, "Merger Proposals, Management Discretion and Stockholder Wealth"; Malatesta, "The Wealth Effect of Merger Activity and the Objective Function of Merging Firms"; Dodd, "The Market for Corporate Control"; and Eger, "An Empirical Test of the Redistribution Effect in Pure Exchange Mergers."

FIGURE 24-3
Relative stock returns around a successful takeover

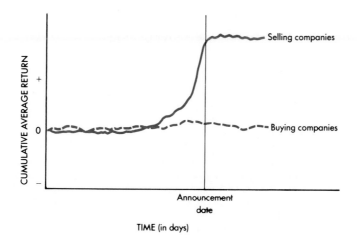

the price paid. Whether this phenomenon is widespread must await further studies, particularly those analyzing takeovers in recent years. One of the problems in testing is the fact that the typical acquiring firm is many times larger than the typical target firm. The return to the acquiring firm's stockholders, either positive or negative, may be hidden in statistical noise. Still, the fact that some studies show negative post-takeover returns should give acquiring companies pause for concern.

In summary, the evidence on returns to stockholders of acquiring companies is mixed. It is difficult to make an overall case for takeovers being a thing of value to the stockholders of the acquiring company. Clearly, some acquisitions are worthwhile, because of synergy and managerial improvement, and some are bad. The key for the financial manager is to be careful because, on average, a case cannot be made for corporations, overall, making consistently good acquisitions. For the acquired and the acquiring companies collectively, there is an increment in wealth associated with takeovers. This is primarily the result of the premium paid to the selling company's stockholders.

Only a limited number of studies deal with what happens to debt instrument returns around the time of a merger.[7] The results suggest that nonconvertible debt holders neither gain nor lose in a merger. For both acquiring and acquired companies, the abnormal returns at the time of the merger announcement do not differ significantly from zero.[8] Therefore, the wealth transfer hypothesis, which suggests that bondholders gain with a merger because of diversification leading to a reduction in default risk, is not supported.

ACQUISITIONS AND CAPITAL BUDGETING

From the standpoint of the buying corporation, acquisitions can be treated as another aspect of capital budgeting. In principle, the prospective acquisition may be evaluated in much the same manner as any capital budgeting project. There is an initial outlay and expected future benefits. Whether the outlay is cash or stock, the firm should attempt to allocate capital optimally in order to increase shareholder wealth over the long run. The main difference is that, with acquisitions, the initial cost may not be established; indeed, it usually is subject to bargaining. If it can be assumed that the acquiring company intends to maintain its existing capital structure over the long run, it is appropriate to evaluate the prospective acquisition without reference to the way it is financed.

Free Cash Flows and Their Value

In evaluating the prospective acquisition, the buying company should estimate the future cash income that the acquisition is expected to add after taxes. We are

[7] Asquith and Kim, "The Impact of Merger Bids on the Participating Firms' Security Holders"; Eger, "An Empirical Test of the Redistribution Effect in Pure Exchange Mergers"; E. Han Kim and John J. McConnell, "Corporate Merger and the Co-Insurance of Corporate Debt," *Journal of Finance*, 32 (May 1977), 349–65; and Dennis and McConnell, "Corporate Mergers and Security Returns."

[8] In an exception, Eger, op. cit, found evidence that bondholders experience slight but nonetheless statistically significant gains in the preannouncement period.

interested in what is known as *free cash flows*. These are the cash flows that remain after we subtract from expected revenues expected costs and the capital expenditures necessary to sustain, and hopefully improve, the cash flows. Expressed differently, free cash flow is the cash flow in excess of that required to finance all projects that have positive net present values when discounted at appropriate required rates of return.

The estimates of free cash flows should include consideration of any synergistic effects, for we are interested in the marginal impact of the acquisition. Moreover, the cash-flow estimates should be before any financial charges. The idea is to divorce the prospective acquisitions' financial structure from its overall worth as an investment. Our concern is with operating cash flows that arise from operating the acquired company, not with prospective net income after financial charges. On the basis of these considerations, suppose the following free cash flows are expected from a prospective acquisition:

	AVERAGE FOR YEARS (IN THOUSANDS)				
	1—5	6—10	11—15	16—20	21—25
Annual cash income after taxes from acquisition	$2,000	$1,800	$1,400	$800	$200
Net investment	600	300	—	—	—
Cash flow after taxes	$1,400	$1,500	$1,400	$800	$200

If the acquisition is not expected to increase or decrease the business-risk complexion of the firm as perceived by suppliers of capital, the appropriate discount rate would be the cost of capital. If this rate were 15 percent after taxes, the present value of the expected free cash flows shown would be $8,724,000. If the prospective acquisition has no debt, this figure suggests that the company can pay a maximum cash price of $8,724,000 for the acquisition and still be acting in the best interests of the company's stockholders. The actual price paid will be subject to negotiation. However, the present value of the prospective acquisition should represent an upper boundary for the acquiring company. Any price up to this amount should result in a worthwhile investment for the company. As a result, the market price per share of the firm's stock should increase over the long run. If the price paid is in excess of the acquisition's present value, this suggests that capital is less than optimally allocated.

Noncash Payments and Liability Assumption

Now what if the acquisition were for other than cash? In many cases, the buyer assumes the liabilities of the company it acquires. Moreover, payment to the acquired company's stockholders may involve common stock, preferred stock, debt, cash, or some combination of these. Does not this complicate the matter? It does, but we must keep our eye on the overriding valuation principle. That is the value of the incremental cash flows. The present-value figure obtained in our calculations, $8,724,000, represents the maximum "cash-equivalent" price to be paid. If securities other than cash are used in the acquisition, they should be converted to their cash-equivalent market values. If the acquiring firm assumes the liabilities of the acquired company, these too should be converted to their market value. Thus, the present value of incremental cash flows sets an upper limit on the market value of all securities, including cash, used in payment, together with the market value of any liabilities assumed in the acquisition. In this way, we are able to separate the investment worth of an acquisition from the way it is financed.

Estimating Cash Flows

In an acquisition, there are the usual problems with estimating future cash flows. The process may be somewhat easier than for a capital budgeting proposal because the company being acquired is a going concern. The acquiring company buys more than assets; it buys experience, an organization, and proven performance. The estimates of sales and costs are based on past results; consequently, they are likely to be more accurate than the estimates for a new investment proposal. Less uncertainty involved in the estimates means less dispersion of expected outcomes and lower risk, all other things held constant. An additional problem, however, is introduced when the acquisition is to be integrated into the acquiring company. Under these circumstances, the acquisition cannot be evaluated as a separate operation; the synergistic effects must be considered. Estimates of these effects are difficult, particularly if the organization that results from the acquisition is complex.

Cash-Flow versus the Earnings per Share Approach

The analysis of an acquisition on a free-cash-flow basis differs from that on an earnings per share basis. With an earnings per share approach, assuming common for common stock was involved, the question is whether there would be an earnings per share improvement now or in the future. In the cash-flow approach, the question is whether the expected net cash flows have a present value in excess of the acquisition's cost.

In general, the cash-flow approach looks at the valuation of an acquisition over the long run, whereas the earnings per share approach focuses on the short run. If a prospective acquisition does not result in a positive increment in earnings per share within a few years, it usually is ruled out if one relies only on the earnings per share approach. In contrast, the cash-flow approach looks at incremental cash flows likely to be generated from the acquisition for many years in the future. Thus, the earnings per share approach tends to bias the selection process in favor of companies with immediate growth prospects, but not necessarily long-term ones. Neither approach embodies in it a consideration for changes in business risk; however, this dimension can be incorporated into either method of analysis using the techniques discussed in Chapter 14.

Aside from risk, the question is which method—the cash-flow or the earnings per share method—should be used? Probably the best answer is that both methods should be employed. The cash-flow method is the more comprehensive with respect to the economic worth of an acquisition over the long run. If management is concerned with near-term growth in earnings per share and believes that this is what the market values, then a strong case can be made for the earnings per share method. In practice, it is difficult to imagine management ignoring the effect of an acquisition on earnings per share, no matter how sound the cash-flow approach is conceptually. By the same token, an earnings per share approach by itself may be too shortsighted and may bias things away from solid long-term growth prospects. Therefore, a strong case can be made for using a cash-flow method of analysis *in addition* to an earnings per share one.

BRINGING THE MERGER TO FRUITION

A merger or consolidation often begins with negotiations between the management of the two companies. Usually, the boards of directors of the companies are kept up to date on the negotiations. The acquirer evaluates many facets of a target company, as the rather exhaustive checklist shows in Fig. 24-4. Terms are agreed upon, initially, ratified by the respective boards, then approved by the common stockholders of both companies. Depending on the corporate charter, an established majority—usually two-thirds—of the total shares is required. After approval by the common stockholders, the merger or consolidation can take place once the necessary papers are filed with the states in which the companies are incorporated.

One hurdle remains. The Antitrust Division of the Department of Justice or the Federal Trade Commission could bring suit to block the combination. To block a merger or consolidation, the government, under Section 7 of the Clayton Act, must prove that a "substantial lessening of competition" might occur on account of it. Usually restraint of competition is interpreted as applying to either a geographic area, such as food stores in New Orleans, or to a line of commerce, such as aluminum ingot production. Broader interpretations are possible, and the combination of two large companies in unrelated lines of business and geographic areas sometimes is suspect simply because of "largeness" per se. Because the costs in executive time, legal expenses, and other expenses of waging an antitrust battle are so great, most companies, before going ahead with a combination, want to be reasonably sure that they will not be challenged.

Purchase of Assets or Purchase of Stock

A company may be acquired either by the purchase of its assets or common stock. The buying company may purchase all or a portion of the assets of another company and pay for them in cash or with its own stock. Frequently, the buyer acquires only the assets of the other company and does not assume its liabilities. If all the assets are purchased, the selling company is but a corporate shell. After the sale, its assets are composed entirely of cash or the stock of the buying company. The selling company can either hold the cash or stock or distribute it to its stockholders as a liquidating dividend, after which the company is dissolved.

General Information
- [ ] Exact corporate name
- [ ] Address
- [ ] Date and state of incorporation
- [ ] States in which the company is qualified to do business
- [ ] Location of minute books, by-laws, and certificate of incorporation
- [ ] History
- [ ] Description of products
- [ ] Fiscal year
- [ ] Capitalization
- [ ] Rights of each class of stock and other securities
- [ ] Stockholders' agreements and terms thereof
- [ ] Names of stockholders and holdings
- [ ] Bank depositaries and average bank balances
- [ ] Bank references
- [ ] Credit rating
- [ ] Location of company records
- [ ] Accountants: Name, address, and reputation
- [ ] Attorneys: Name and address

Personnel
- [ ] Directors and their affiliations
- [ ] Officers: For each — position, duties, age, health, salary, service, experience, personal plans for the future, other interests (including time devoted thereto), and stockholdings
- [ ] Organization chart
- [ ] Employee contracts: Terms, expiration date(s)
- [ ] Number of employees in production, sales, administration, etc.
- [ ] Union contracts: Terms, expiration dates
- [ ] Strike record, labor morale, handling of labor relations
- [ ] Labor market
- [ ] Pension, profit sharing, insurance, stock bonus, deferred compensation, and severance plans
- [ ] Comparison with industry as to number of employees, hours per week, and wage rates for the past five years and for the past twelve months

Operations
- [ ] Description, including significant changes in the past few years
   1. Capacity and per cent of utilization
   2. Production controls (scheduling and inventories)
   3. Shipping and receiving controls
   4. Accounting controls
- [ ] Principal suppliers and terms
- [ ] Distribution methods and terms (also, brokers or agents and compensation arrangements)
- [ ] Branch offices and their operations
- [ ] Subsidiaries, their operations and inter-company dealings
- [ ] Government contracts and subcontracts
- [ ] Seasonal factors
- [ ] Public and stockholder relations

Sales
- [ ] Description of market
- [ ] Number of customers and names of principal customers
- [ ] Gross and net sales for the past five years and for the past twelve months
   1. Penetration of market by product
   2. Possibilities of increase through existing lines and by diversification
- [ ] Sales comparison with the industry for the past five years and for the past twelve months
- [ ] Sales backlog, accounts receivable activity, customer continuity
- [ ] Sales correspondence
- [ ] Sales policies and method of compensation of sales personnel
- [ ] Pricing policies and fluctuations in the past five years
- [ ] Principal competitors
- [ ] Relative size in the industry
- [ ] Comparative advantages and disadvantages
- [ ] Anything significant in lines produced in the past few years
- [ ] Any nonrelated activities
- [ ] Missing product lines
- [ ] Advertising and other sales promotion programs: Cost and effectiveness in the past five years
- [ ] Research program: Cost, history, scope, potential, results, work by outsiders
- [ ] New developments
- [ ] Industry trends
- [ ] Current and future prospects

Earnings and Dividends
- [ ] Earnings record and budget for the past five years and the last twelve months, break-even point, gross profit margins and reasons for variations, nonrecurring income and expenses, changes in overabsorbed and underabsorbed burden
- [ ] Earnings comparison with the industry for the past five years
- [ ] Dividend and earnings record for the past five years in total and per share
- [ ] Potential economies
- [ ] Current and future prospects
- [ ] Analysis of selling and general and administrative expenses
- [ ] Contribution of company's effort to profit

Plant Facilities
- [ ] Location
- [ ] Shipping facilities
- [ ] Real estate taxes
- [ ] Land
   1. Acreage
   2. Cost
   3. Assessed value
   4. Fair market value

FIGURE 24-4

Acquisition evaluation checklist

PMM & Co./*Management Focus*/May-June 1980. Copyright Peat, Marwick, Mitchell & Co. Reprinted by permission.

- ☐ Buildings
  1. Description, including pictures, if available
  2. Age and condition
  3. Area
  4. Depreciation: Reserves, methods, rates, policies
  5. Assessed value
  6. Fair market value (recent appraisals)
  7. Fire insurance
- ☐ Title to realty and title policy
- ☐ Machinery and equipment
  1. Description
  2. Age, condition, efficiency, insurance coverage
  3. Depreciation: Reserves, methods, rates, policies
  4. Total acquisitions during the past five years
  5. Analysis of most recent additions
- ☐ Future plant, machinery, and equipment requirements
- ☐ Capitalization versus repair policies
- ☐ Capital expenditures and repairs for the past five years
- ☐ Percentage relationship of production costs and comparison with the industry
- ☐ Efficiency of operations
- ☐ Subcontracting done by others
- ☐ Certificates of necessity
- ☐ Facility contracts or leases
- ☐ Surplus or idle buildings or equipment

Assets
- ☐ Relationship of cash to current liabilities
- ☐ Age and number of accounts receivable (latest accounts receivable aging)
- ☐ Provision for bad debts
- ☐ Inventories for the past five years
  1. Relationship of inventories to current assets
  2. Location
  3. Finished goods by product
  4. Work in process by product
  5. Raw materials by product
  6. Pricing methods
  7. Accounting procedures and practices
  8. Provision for obsolete or slow-moving stock (latest inventory aging)
- ☐ Analysis of notes receivable
- ☐ Analysis of investments
- ☐ Subsidiaries
  1. Treatment on parent company's balance sheet
  2. Analysis (per check list) of significant items
- ☐ Analysis of other assets
- ☐ Patents held

Liabilities
- ☐ Renegotiable business
- ☐ Renegotiation status
- ☐ Current federal and state tax status and tax payments for the past three years
- ☐ Commitments for new buildings, machinery, inventories
- ☐ Long-term loans outstanding and terms
- ☐ Debentures outstanding and terms

- ☐ Dividend and interest arrearages
- ☐ Leases: Locations, areas, terms
- ☐ Insurance coverage, fidelity bonds, and amounts
- ☐ Pensions, etc.
- ☐ Contingent liabilities: Warranties; patent, etc., infringements; loss contracts; compensation for services
- ☐ Litigation record and present status

Financial Data
- ☐ Annual statements and audit reports for the past five years
- ☐ Tax returns for the past five years
- ☐ Surplus statements
- ☐ Disposition of funds statements
- ☐ Reports to Securities and Exchange Commission
- ☐ Explanation of how consolidations, if any, were effected and separate statement for each company involved
- ☐ Chart of accounts
- ☐ Book, net quick, liquidating, and market values for the past five years
- ☐ Working capital for the past five years and normal requirements based on trade practices, credit terms to customers, consignments, finished inventory, and raw inventory
- ☐ Net working capital ratios for the past five years
- ☐ Net quick position for the past five years
- ☐ Annual depreciation compared with capital additions for the past five years
- ☐ Inventory turnover for the past five years
- ☐ Cash, inventory, and working capital requirements for the past two years
- ☐ Interest charges for the past five years
- ☐ Exchange, if any, on which the company's stock is traded
- ☐ Recent stock sales and prices paid

Comparison with Comparable Companies
The following ratios for the subject company should be compared with those of comparable companies for the past five years and, if data are available, by quarters for the current year:
- ☐ Price to earnings
- ☐ Price to book value
- ☐ Sales to accounts receivable
- ☐ Sales to inventories
- ☐ Sales to fixed assets
- ☐ Earnings to book value

Terms of Acquisition
- ☐ Reasons for sale
- ☐ Price to be paid
- ☐ Terms of payment
- ☐ Financing
- ☐ Brokerage fees
- ☐ Tax considerations

Projected Financial Data
- ☐ Pro forma balance sheet
- ☐ Earnings forecast

FIGURE 24-4 (cont.)

Thus, when its assets are purchased, the selling company can continue to exist if it holds the cash or stock arising from the sale. If it has cash, it may invest in other assets, such as a division of another company. Obviously, if only a portion of its assets are sold, the selling company will continue as a corporate entity. When an acquiring company purchases the stock of another company, the latter is combined into the acquiring company. The company that is acquired ceases to exist, and the surviving company assumes all its assets and liabilities. As with a purchase of assets, the means of payment to the stockholders of the company being acquired can be either cash or stock. A purchase or assets is easier to effect than a purchase of stock, for all that is needed on the part of the buying company is approval by the board of directors. The selling company, however, needs the approval of its stockholders.

Taxable or Tax-Free Transaction

If the acquisition is made with cash or with a debt instrument, the transaction is taxable to the selling company or to its stockholders at that time. This means that they must recognize any capital gain or loss on the sale of the assets or the sale of the stock at the time of the sale. If payment is made with voting preferred or common stock, the transaction is not taxable at the time of the sale. The capital gain or loss is recognized only when the stock is sold. In addition to the requirement of voting stock, for a combination to be tax free, it must have a business purpose. In other words, it cannot be entirely for tax reasons. Moreover, in a purchase of assets the acquisition must involve substantially all of the assets of the selling company, and no less than 80 percent of those assets must be paid for with voting stock. In a purchase of stock, the buying company must own at least 80 percent of the selling company's stock immediately after the transaction.

In most cases, a tax-free transaction is preferred by the selling company and its stockholders because a postponable capital gain is involved. A tax-free combination allows the selling company—in a purchase of assets—or its stockholders—in a purchase of stock—to postpone taking the gain and paying taxes on it until it is desirable to do so. To qualify as a tax-free transaction, not only must preferred or common stock be used, but there must be a continuity of the surviving enterprise, the combination must not be solely for tax purposes, and the selling company stockholders must receive a significant and continuing equity stake in the acquiring company. While technical, the Internal Revenue Service wishes to discourage tax avoidance schemes that have no economic justification.

Another consideration is that with a taxable transaction the buying company is able to write up the value of the assets if their fair market value exceeds their book value. For example, Sanchez Metal Company acquires Baker Worm Gear, Inc., which has $800,000 in assets at book value. In market-value terms, these assets are worth $1 million. If Sanchez acquires the company through a taxable transaction, it is able to write up the assets to $1 million. The advantage, of course, is that Sanchez will be able to claim a higher depreciation expense for tax purposes. By paying lower taxes, greater after-tax cash flows occur—a desirable outcome. If the acquisition is a tax-free transaction, Sanchez is unable to write up the value of the assets and claim the higher depreciation charges.

Therefore, this consideration may make a taxable transaction more desirable from the standpoint of the buying company and cause it to pay a higher price than otherwise would be the case. Whether this factor significantly offsets the usual advantage to the seller of a tax-free transaction depends on the individual circumstances.

Accounting Treatment

From an accounting standpoint, a combination of two companies is treated either as a *purchase* or as a *pooling of interests*. In a purchase, the buyer treats the acquired company as an investment. If the buyer pays a premium above the fair market value of the assets, this premium must be reflected as **goodwill** on the buyer's balance sheet. Moreover, goodwill must be written off against future income, the logic being that it will be reflected in such income. An estimate must be made of the life of goodwill, as of any asset; and goodwill is amortized over this period, which cannot exceed 40 years. Thus, accounting earnings are reduced by the amount of the charge. Note that goodwill charges are not deductible for tax purposes. Therefore, the acquiring firm generally views as a disadvantage the reduction of reported future earnings associated with this accounting treatment.

> **Goodwill.** The intangible assets of the firm arising from paying more for them than their book value. Goodwill must be amortized.

In a pooling of interests, the balance sheets of the two companies are combined, with assets and liabilities simply being added together. As a result, goodwill is not reflected in the combination, and there is no charge against future income. Because reported earnings will be higher with the **pooling-of-interests** accounting treatment than they will be with the purchase treatment, many acquiring companies prefer it when the goodwill being acquired is substantial.

> **Pooling of interests.** A method of accounting treatment for a merger where the balance sheets of the two companies are simply combined.

The choice of accounting treatment does not rest entirely with the acquiring company, but rather is governed by the circumstances of the merger and the rules of the accounting profession. Only under the following rather restricted conditions can a merger be treated as a pooling of interests.[9]

1. Each of the combined companies must be autonomous for at least two years prior to the pooling and independent of the others in the sense that no more than 10 percent of the stock is owned.

2. The combination must be consummated in a single transaction or in accordance with a specific plan within one year after the plan is initiated. In this regard, no contingent payments are permitted.

3. The acquiring corporation can issue only common stock, with rights identical to those of the majority of outstanding voting stock, in exchange for *substantially* all of the voting common stock of another company. Here, "substantially" means 90 percent or more.

4. The surviving corporation must not later retire or reacquire common stock issued in connection with the combination, must not enter into an arrangement for the benefit of former stockholders, and must not dispose of a significant portion of the assets of the combining companies for at least 2 years.

---

[9] *Opinions of the Accounting Principles Board*, No. 16 (New York: American Institute of Certified Public Accountants, August 1970).

The most limiting condition is condition 3, which states that common must be exchanged for common. The next most limiting condition is the prohibition of contingent payments. The result of these conditions is a significant constraint on the number of poolings of interest.

ABC Company acquired XYZ Company in an exchange of stock valued at $2 million. XYZ Company had debt of $1 million and a net worth of $1.2 million prior to the merger, the net book value of its assets being $2.2 million. On the other hand, ABC Company, the acquirer, had a net worth of $10 million, debt of $5 million, and assets having a net book value of $15 million prior to the merger. The effects of the merger under the purchase and the pooling-of-interests methods of accounting treatment are as follows (in thousands):

	BEFORE MERGER		AFTER MERGER	
	ABC Company	XYZ Company	Purchase	Pooling
Net tangible assets	$15,000	$2,200	$17,200	$17,200
Goodwill	0	0	800	0
Total assets	$15,000	$2,200	$18,000	$17,200
Debt	$ 5,000	$1,000	$ 6,000	$ 6,000
Net worth	10,000	1,200	12,000	11,200
Total liabilities and net worth	$15,000	$2,200	$18,000	$17,200

With the purchase method, the total assets of the acquired company are written up by $800,000, which is the price paid in excess of book value. Moreover, this amount is reflected as goodwill and must be amortized in the manner described before. Under the pooling-of-interests accounting treatment, the assets shown for the surviving company are simply the sum of the book values of assets shown for the two companies before the merger.

So far we have considered only a case in which the acquiring company pays a price in excess of the book value of the assets. In many situations, the fair market value of the assets of the acquired company exceeds the book value of those assets. Under the purchase method of accounting, the tangible assets of the acquired company are written up to their fair market value. This write-up reduces the amount of goodwill. In our example, had the fair market value of the assets of the acquired company been $2.5 million instead of $2.2 million, net tangible assets of the surviving company would have been $17.5 million instead of $17.2 million, and goodwill would have been $500,000 instead of $800,000. The effects of the merger under the purchase and the pooling-of-interests methods of accounting treatment are shown (in thousands) in the foregoing table for the example described. If the purchase transaction is taxable, as defined in the previous section, the surviving company can claim a larger depreciation expense for tax purposes, which, in turn, enhances cash flows. This represents an advantage for purchase over pooling if the objective of the firm is to maximize the present value of after-tax cash flows. To the extent that the objective is maximizing accounting earnings, however, the purchase method loses its appeal as a greater amount of goodwill must be recorded.

Holding Companies

Instead of actually acquiring another company, a firm may purchase a portion of its stock and act as a holding company. By definition, a **holding company** owns sufficient voting stock to have a controlling interest in one or more other corporations. A holding company does not necessarily have to own 51 percent of the stock of another company in order to have control. For a widely held corporation, ownership of 20 percent or as little as 10 percent of the stock outstanding may constitute effective working control. The holding company had its origin in the latter part of the nineteenth century when the state of New Jersey first permitted corporations to exist for the sole purpose of owning stocks of other corporations.

> **Holding company.** A corporation that owns a controlling interest (common stock) in other companies.

One of the advantages of a holding company is that it allows a company to acquire control of another company by investing much less than would be necessary for a merger. Moreover, by acquiring only a portion of the stock, the holding company usually does not have to pay as high a price per share as it would if it sought to purchase all the stock. It may purchase the stock gradually without undue upward pressure on the market price of the stock. Another advantage is that formal approval from stockholders of the acquiring company is not required. It is an informal arrangement. A further advantage of a holding company is the possibility that, although limited, operating economies can be achieved through centralized management.

A principal disadvantage of the holding company is that 20 percent of the dividends paid to it by the subsidiary is subject to taxation.[10] Thus, the holding company must pay a partial tax on dividends, and stockholders of the holding company also must pay a tax on dividends they receive. The partial tax could be avoided, of course, if the stockholders owned the operating companies directly.

Through pyramiding a series of holding companies, it is possible to obtain considerable leverage with respect to assets controlled and earnings. Suppose that Holding Company A owns 20 percent of Holding Companies B, C, and D, which, in turn, own 20 percent controlling interest in nine operating companies. Thus, for every dollar of capital in each of the operating companies—$9 in all—Company A is able to control them with an investment of $.36, (.20 × .20 × $9), or 4 percent of the total capital of the operating companies. As long as the operating companies are profitable and are able to pay dividends to the holding companies, all may go well. In the 1920s there tended to be excessive pyramiding of holding companies, particularly in public utilities. In the 1930s, the leverage of these companies magnified the losses, and a number of the pyramids crumbled. Because of the many abuses of holding companies, the Public Utility Holding

---

[10] If the holding company owns 80 percent or more of the voting stock of the subsidiary, the dividend is not subject to taxation.

Company Act of 1935 was passed to restrict the operation of holding companies in the public utility field.

TAKEOVERS, TENDER OFFERS, AND DEFENSES

In our hypothetical examples, negotiations were confined to the managements and boards of directors of the companies involved. However, the acquiring company can make a tender offer directly to stockholders of the company it wishes to acquire. A tender offer is an offer to purchase shares of stock of another company at a fixed price per share from stockholders who "tender" their shares. The tender price usually is set significantly above the present market price, as an incentive. Use of the tender offer allows the acquiring company to bypass the management of the company it wishes to acquire and, therefore, serves as a threat in any negotiations with that management.

The tender offer can be used also when there are no negotiations but when one company simply wants to acquire another. It no longer is possible to surprise another company, because the Securities and Exchange Commission requires rather extensive disclosure. In both cash and stock tenders, the primary selling tool is the premium that is offered over the existing market price of the stock. In addition, brokers are often given attractive commissions for shares tendered through them. The tender offer itself is usually communicated through financial newspapers. Direct mailings are made to the stockholders of the company being bid for if the bidder is able to obtain a list of stockholders. Although a company is legally obligated to provide such a list, it usually is able to delay delivery long enough to frustrate the bidder.

Instead of one tender offer, some bidders make a two-tier offer. The first tier of stock usually represents control and, for example, might be 45 percent of the stock outstanding if the bidder already owned 5 percent. The first-tier offer is more attractive in terms of price and/or the form of payment than is the second-tier offer for the remaining stock. The differential is designed to increase the probability of successfully gaining control, by providing an incentive to tender early. The two-tier offer avoids the "free-rider" problem associated with a single tender offer where individual stockholders have an incentive to hold out in the hope of realizing a higher counteroffer by someone else. While the two-tier offer is controversial both within the acquisitions community and the Securities and Exchange Commission, it remains a popular device.

The company being bid for may use a number of defensive tactics. Management may try to persuade stockholders that the offer is not in their best interests. Usually, the argument is that the bid is too low in relation to the true, long-run value of the firm. Hearing that, stockholders may look at an attractive premium and find the long run too long. Some companies raise the cash dividend or declare a stock split in hopes of gaining stockholder support. Legal actions are often undertaken, more to delay and frustrate the bidder than with the expectation of winning. When the two firms are competitors, an antitrust suit may prove a powerful deterrent to the bidder. As a last resort, management of the company being bid for may seek a merger with a "friendly" company, known as a "white knight."

Antitakeover Amendments and Other Devices

In addition to defensive tactics, some companies use more formal methods that are put into place prior to an actual **takeover** attempt. Known as antitakeover or "shark-repellent" devices, they are designed to make a takeover more difficult. Before describing them, it is useful to consider their motivation. The managerial entrenchment hypothesis suggests that the barriers erected are to protect management jobs and that such actions work to the detriment of stockholders. On the other hand, the stockholders interest hypothesis implies that corporate control contests are dysfunctional and take management time away from profit-making activities. Therefore, antitakeover devices ensure more attention being paid to these activities and are in the interest of stockholders. Moreover, the barriers erected are said to cause individual stockholders not to accept a low offer price but to join other stockholders in a cartel response to any offer. This is particularly important in a dual offer, where, say, the first 51 percent of stock tendered receives one price and other stock tendered receives a lower price. Therefore, antitakeover devices would enhance shareholder wealth, according to this hypothesis.[11]

A handful of devices exist to make it more difficult for another party to take you over. As we know from Chapter 22, some companies *stagger the terms of their board of directors* so that fewer stand for election each year, and, accordingly, more votes are needed to elect a director. Sometimes, it is desirable to *change the state of incorporation*. Charter rules differ state by state, and many companies like to incorporate in a state with few limitations, such as Delaware. By so doing, it is easier for the corporation to install antitakeover amendments as well as to defend itself legally if a takeover battle ensues. Some companies put into place a *super-majority merger approval provision*. Instead of an ordinary majority being needed for approval of a merger, a higher percentage is required, often two-thirds. The percentage may be even higher; 80 percent is used in a number of instances. The ability to install this provision depends on the state of incorporation.

Another device is a *fair merger price provision*. Here the bidder must pay noncontrolling stockholders a price at least equal to a "fair price," which is established in advance. Usually, this minimum price is linked to earnings per share through a price/earnings ratio, but it may simply be a stated market price. Often the fair price provision is coupled with a supermajority provision. If the stated minimum price is not satisfied, the combination can only be approved if a supermajority of stockholders votes in favor of it.

To discourage potential acquirers, some companies instigate a distribution of rights to stockholders, allowing them to purchase a new series of securities, often convertible preferred stock. However, the security offering is triggered only if an outside party acquires some percentage, frequently 20 percent, of the company's stock. The idea is to have available a security offering that is unpalatable

Takeover. The acquisition of another company where management of the target firm opposes the merger.

---

[11] See Harry DeAngelo and Edward M. Rice, "Antitakeover Charter Amendments and Stockholder Wealth," *Journal of Financial Economics,* 11 (April 1983), 329–60; Scott C. Linn and John J. McConnell, "An Empirical Investigation of the Impact of Antitakeover Amendments on Common Stock Prices," *Journal of Financial Economics,* 11 (April 1983), 361–99; and Michael C. Jensen, "The Takeover Controversy: Analysis and Evidence," *Midland Corporate Finance Journal,* 4 (Summer 1986), 6–32, for a discussion of these hypotheses and of the various antitakeover devices.

Poison pill. A device used by a company to make it less attractive as a takeover candidate.

to the acquirer. This can be with respect to voting rights, with respect to a low exercise price paid for the security (a bargain), or with respect to precluding a control transaction unless a substantial premium, often several hundred percent, is paid. Known as a **poison pill,** the provision is meant to force the potential acquirer into negotiating directly with the board of directors. It has been used by such companies as Atlantic Richfield, Household Finance, and Tandem Computers. The board reserves the ability to redeem the rights at any time for a token amount. Thus, the poison pill puts power in the hands of the board to dissuade a takeover, which may or may not be in the interest of stockholders overall.

A *lockup provision* is used in conjunction with other provisions. This provision requires supermajority stockholder approval to modify the corporate charter and any previously passed antitakeover provisions. In addition to these charter amendments, many companies enter into *management contracts* with their top management. Typically, high compensation is triggered if the company is taken over. Known as a "golden parachute," these contracts effectively increase the price the acquiring company must pay in an unfriendly takeover. Their nuisance value may serve as a deterrent, but golden parachutes are so common that most acquiring companies have grown used to coping with them.

Despite these devices, outside groups do acquire blocks of stock in a corporation preparatory to either a takeover attempt or the sale of their stock to someone else who poses such a threat. Indication of unusual accumulation of stock comes from watching trading volume and stock transfers. If a group acquires more than 5 percent of a company, it is required to file a *13-D form* with the Securities and Exchange Commission. This form describes the people involved with the group, its holdings, and its intention. The standard response to the last is, "we bought it only as an investment," so little information is really conveyed. Each time the group acquires an additional 1 percent of the stock, it must file an amendment to the 13-D form. Therefore, a company can accurately track the amount of stock accumulated.

Sometimes the company will negotiate a *standstill agreement* with the outside party. Such an agreement is a voluntary contract where, for a period of several years, the substantial stockholder group agrees not to increase its stockholdings. Often this limitation is expressed as a maximum percentage of stock the group may own. The agreement also specifies that the group will not participate in a control contest against management and that it gives the right of first refusal to the company if it should decide to sell its stock. For this agreement, the group often negotiates a premium if the stock is sold to the company. The standstill agreement, together with the other provisions discussed, serves to reduce competition for corporate control. For the most part, legal obstacles have not proven particularly effective in thwarting takeovers, so we must not make too much of them. Whether they are in the interests of stockholders is taken up in the next section, where we review the empirical evidence.

As a last resort, some companies make a *premium buy-back offer* to the threatening party. As the name implies, the repurchase of stock is at a premium over its market price and usually is in excess of what the accumulator paid. Moreover, the offer is not extended to other stockholders. Known as *greenmail,* the idea is to get the threatening party off management's back by making it attractive for the party to leave. Of course the premium paid to one party may work to the disadvantage of stockholders left "holding the bag." Greenmail is a controversial topic that has led to cries for reform, the simplest version of which is simply to require that the same offer be made to all stockholders.

Evidence on Antitakeover Devices

There have been various tests of the two hypotheses discussed earlier. The empirical results are mixed. For the most part, the evidence does not indicate that a significant share price effect occurs when various antitakeover amendments are adopted. However, standstill agreements appear to have a negative effect on shareholder wealth, as do stock repurchases by a company from a large block owner. The latter often are associated with "greenmail," where the large block owner threatens the company with a hostile takeover, and the company buys the owner out at a favorable price to eliminate the threat. Unfortunately there is a wealth transfer away from nonparticipating stockholders. (See the articles already footnoted for references.)

DIVESTITURE

In a merger, two or more enterprises are put together. However, there are other aspects to corporate restructuring. A company may divest itself of a portion of the enterprise or liquidate entirely. In this section, we consider various methods of **divestiture.**

Divestiture. The divestment of a portion of the enterprise or the firm as a whole.

Liquidating the Overall Firm

The decision to sell a firm in its entirety should be rooted in value creation for the stockholders. Assuming the situation does not involve financial failure, which we address in Chapter 27, the idea is that the assets may have a higher value in **liquidation** than the present value of the expected cash-flow stream emanating from them. By liquidating, the seller is able to sell the assets to multiple parties, which may result in a higher value being realized than if they had to be sold as a whole, as occurs in a merger. With a complete liquidation, the debt of the company must be paid off at its face value. If the market value of the debt was previously below this, debt holders realize a wealth gain, which ultimately is at the expense of equity holders.

Liquidation. The sale of assets of a firm, either voluntarily or in bankruptcy.

Partial Sell-offs

In the case of a **sell-off,** only part of the company is sold. When a business unit is sold, payment generally is in the form of cash or securities. The decision should result in some positive net present value to the selling company. The key is

Sell-offs. The sale of a division of a company, known as a partial sell-off, or the company as a whole, known as a voluntary liquidation.

whether the value received is more than the present value of the stream of expected future cash flows if the operation were to be continued.

Corporate Spin-offs

Spin-off. The distribution to shareholders of stock in a subsidiary, after which the subsidiary becomes an independent company.

Similar to a sell-off, a **spin-off** involves a decision to divest a business unit such as a stand-alone subsidiary or division. In a spin-off, the business unit is not sold for cash or securities. Rather, common stock in the unit is distributed to the stockholders of the company on a pro rata basis, after which the operation becomes a completely separate company. For example, in 1986, Borg Warner Corporation spun off its York heating and air conditioning subsidiary, following a period of chronic losses. Physical assets as well as people were involved in the spin-off. There is no tax to the stockholder at the time of the spin-off; taxation occurs only when the stock is sold. After the spin-off, York International operated as a completely independent company with its stock traded on the New York Stock Exchange.

The motivations for a spin-off are similar in some ways to those for a sell-off. In the case of a spin-off, however, another company will not operate it. Therefore, there is no opportunity for synergy in the usual sense of the term. It is possible that as an independent company with different management incentives the operation will be better run. In this sense, an economic gain may be achieved from the transaction. However, costs are involved. New shares must be issued, and there are the ongoing costs of servicing stockholders, together with new agency costs involving auditors and other monitoring devices. Thus, there is duplication of costs in having two public companies as opposed to one. The net case for economic gain is not clear.

Other reasons would appear to have more substance. The previously cited argument of a wealth transfer from debt holders to equity holders might be applicable. Another factor from our earlier discussion is any information effect associated with the spin-off.

Also with a spin-off it may be possible to obtain flexibility in contracting. With a separate operation, one sometimes can rearrange labor contracts, get out from under tax regulations, or skirt regulatory constraints that no longer are directly applicable. Another type of contract involves management. With a spin-off, there is a separation of the business unit's management from that of the parent. As a result, it may be possible to restructure incentives in order to gain improved managerial productivity. Finally, the spin-off may permit greater flexibility in debt contracts when it comes to protective covenants imposed.[12] All of these things may influence the decision to spin off a business unit, and the valuation of the transaction.

Equity Carve-outs

Equity carve-out. The public sale of stock in a subsidiary in which the parent usually retains majority control.

An **equity carve-out** is similar in some ways to the two previous forms of divestiture. However, common stock in the business unit is sold to the public. The

[12] For an analysis of these various reasons, see Katherine Schipper and Abbie Smith, "Effects of Recontracting on Shareholder Wealth," *Journal of Financial Economics*, 12 (December 1983), 437–67.

initial public offering of the subsidiary's stock usually involves only some of it. Typically, the parent continues to have an equity stake in the subsidiary and does not relinquish control. Under these circumstances, a minority interest is sold and the carve-out represents a form of equity financing. The difference between it and the parent selling stock under its own name is that the claim is on the subsidiary's cash flows and assets. For the first time, the value of the subsidiary becomes observable in the marketplace.

One motivation for the equity carve-out is that with a separate stock price and public trading, managers may have more incentive to perform well. For one thing, the size of the operation is such that their efforts will not go unnoticed as they sometimes do in a large, multibusiness company. With separate stock options, it may be possible to attract and retain better managers and to motivate them. Also, information about the subsidiary is more readily available. In turn, this may reduce asymmetric information between managers and investors and cause the subsidiary's worth to be more accurately assessed by the marketplace.

Some suggest that the equity carve-out is a favorable means for financing growth. When the subsidiary is in leading-edge technology but not particularly profitable, the equity carve-out may be a more effective vehicle for financing than is financing through the parent. With a separate subsidiary, the market may become more complete because investors are able to obtain a "pure play" investment in the technology.

Empirical Evidence on Divestitures

As with mergers, the principal tests have involved event studies, where daily security return behavior, after isolating out market effects, is studied around the time of the announcement.[13] For liquidation of the entire company, the results indicate large gains to stockholders of the liquidating company, in the range of 12 to 20 percent. For partial sell-offs, stockholders of the selling company seem to realize a slight positive return (about 2 percent) around the time of the announcement. Stockholders of the buying company also experience small posi-

---

[13] Empirical evidence on divestitures includes E. Han Kim and John D. Schatzberg, "Voluntary Corporate Liquidations," research paper, University of Michigan (November 1986); Terrance R. Skantz and Roberto Marchesini, "The Effect of Voluntary Corporate Liquidation on Shareholder Wealth," *Journal of Financial Research*, 10 (Spring 1986), 65–76; Gordon J. Alexander, P. George Benson, and Joan M. Kampmeyer, "Investigating the Valuation Effects of Announcements of Voluntary Selloffs," *Journal of Finance*, 39 (June 1984), 503–17; Prem C. Jain, "The Effect of Voluntary Sell-off Announcements on Shareholder Wealth," *Journal of Finance*, 40 (March 1985), 209–24; James D. Rosenfeld, "Additional Evidence on the Relation Between Divestiture Announcements and Shareholder Wealth," *Journal of Finance*, 39 (December 1984), 1437–48; April Klein, "The Timing and Substance of Divestiture Announcements," *Journal of Finance*, 41 (July 1986), 685–96; Schipper and Smith, "Effects of Recontracting on Shareholder Wealth"; Gailen L. Hite and James E. Owens, "Security Price Reactions Around Corporate Spin-off Announcements," *Journal of Financial Economics*, 12 (December 1983), 409–36; James A. Miles and James D. Rosenfeld, "The Effect of Voluntary Spin-off Announcements on Shareholder Wealth," *Journal of Finance*, 38 (December 1983), 1597–1606; Thomas E. Copeland, Eduardo F. Lemgruber, and David Mayers, "Corporate Spinoffs: Multiple Announcement and Ex-Date Abnormal Performance," research paper, UCLA (June 1986); Katherine Schipper and Abbie Smith, "A Comparison of Equity Carve-outs and Seasoned Equity Offerings," *Journal of Financial Economics*, 15 (January–February 1986), 153–86; and Gailen L. Hite, James E. Owers, and Ronald C. Rogers, "The Market for Interfirm Asset Sales," *Journal of Financial Economics*, 18 (June 1987), 229–52.

tive gains on average, consistent with the subsidiary or division sold being more valuable to the buyer in terms of economic efficiency than it is to the seller.

For the spin-off, somewhat higher shareholder excess returns (5 percent or more) were recorded on average than for sell-offs. The findings here are consistent with a positive information effect of the spin-off announcement. The evidence is not consistent with a wealth transfer from debt holders to equity holders. Finally, for equity carve-outs a modest gain (around 2 percent) to shareholders was found around the time of the announcement. On balance, then, divestitures seem to have a positive informational effect, with voluntary liquidations having the largest.

OWNERSHIP RESTRUCTURING

Other corporate restructurings are designed to change the ownership structure of a company. Often this is accompanied by a dramatic change in the proportion of debt employed. In this section we explore going private and leveraged buyouts.

Going Private

Going private. Making a public company private by buying up the stock.

A number of well-known companies have "gone private," including Denny's Restaurants and Levi Strauss & Co. Going private simply means transforming a company whose stock is publicly held into a private one. The privately held stock is owned by a small group of investors, with incumbent management usually having a large equity stake. In this ownership reorganization, a variety of vehicles are used to buy out the public stockholders. Probably the most common involves cashing them out and merging the company into a shell corporation owned solely by the private investor/management group. Rather than a merger, the transaction may be treated as an asset sale to the private group. There are other ways, but the result is the same: The company ceases to exist as a publicly held entity and the stockholders receive a valuable consideration for their shares. While most transactions involve cash, noncash compensation, such as notes, sometimes is employed.

Motivations.   A number of factors may prompt management to take a company private.[14] There are costs to being a publicly held company. The stock must be registered, stockholders must be serviced, there are administrative expenses in paying dividends and sending out materials, and legal and administrative expenses are incurred in filing reports with the Securities and Exchange Commission and other regulators. In addition, there are annual meetings and meetings with security analysts leading to embarrassing questions that most

---

[14] The major paper dealing with going private is by Harry DeAngelo, Linda DeAngelo, and Edward M. Rice, "Going Private: Minority Freezeouts and Stockholder Wealth," *Journal of Law and Economics*, 27 (June 1984), 367–401, where most of these motivations are discussed.

chief executive officers would rather do without. All of these things can be avoided by being a private company.

With a publicly held company, some feel there is a fixation on quarterly accounting earnings as opposed to long-run economic earnings. To the extent decisions are directed more toward building economic value, going private may improve resource allocation decisions and, thereby, enhance value.

Another motivation is to realign and improve management incentives. With increased equity ownership by management, there may be an incentive to work more efficiently and longer. The money saved and the profits generated through more effective management largely benefit the company's management as opposed to a wide group of stockholders. As a result, they may be more willing to make the tough decisions, to cut costs, to reduce management "perks," and simply to work harder. The rewards are linked more closely to their decisions. The greater the performance and profitability, the greater the reward. In a publicly held company, the compensation level is not so directly linked, particularly for decisions that produce high profitability. When compensation is extremely high, there are always questions from security analysts, stockholders, and the press.

While there are a number of reasons for going private, there are some offsetting arguments. For one thing, there are transaction costs to investment bankers, lawyers, and others that can be quite substantial. A private company gives little liquidity to its owners with respect to their stock ownership. A large portion of their wealth may be tied up in the company. Management, for example, may create value for the company but be unable to realize this value unless the company goes public in the future. If the company later goes public, transaction costs are repeated—wonderful for investment bankers and lawyers, but a sizable cost nonetheless.

Empirical Evidence. There have been few studies of the effect of going private on security holder wealth.[15] The evidence we do have suggests that stockholders realize sizable gain (about 12 to 22 percent in the two studies) around the time of the announcement. In the case of a cash offer, the gain is much more, similar to the premiums realized in a merger. While stockholders clearly gain, whether or not they are treated fairly cannot be stated.

LEVERAGED BUYOUTS

Going private can be a straight transaction, where the investor group simply buys out the public stockholders, or it can be a **leveraged buyout,** where there are third and sometimes fourth party investors. As the name implies, a leveraged buyout represents an ownership transfer consummated primarily with debt. Sometimes called asset-based financing, the debt is secured by the assets of the enterprise involved. As a result, most leveraged buyouts involve capital-intensive as opposed to people-intensive businesses. While some leveraged buy-

Leveraged buyout (LBO). Buying all the stock of a public company by means of substantial debt financing of the company's assets.

[5] See ibid.; and Laurentius Marais, Katherine Schipper, and Abbie Smith, "Management Buyout Proposals and Corporate Claimholders: Explicit Recontracting and Differential Wealth Effects," research paper, University of Chicago (October 1986).

outs involve an entire company, most involve the purchase of a division of a company or some other subunit. Frequently, the sale is to the management of the division being sold, the company having decided that the division no longer fits its strategic objectives. Another distinctive feature is that leveraged buyouts are cash purchases, as opposed to stock purchases. Finally, the business unit involved invariably becomes a privately held as opposed to a publicly held company.

An Illustration in Detail

To illustrate a typical leveraged buyout, suppose that Alsim Corporation wishes to divest itself of its dairy products division. The assets of the division consist of plants, equipment, truck fleets, inventories, and receivables. These assets have a book value of $120 million. While their replacement value is $170 million, if the division were to be liquidated the assets would fetch only $95 million. Alsim has decided to sell the division if it can obtain $110 million in cash, and it has enlisted an investment banker to assist it in the sale. After surveying the market for such a sale, the investment banker concludes that the best prospect is to sell the division to existing management. The four top divisional officers are interested and eager to pursue the opportunity. However, they are able to come up with only $1.5 million in personal capital between them. More, obviously, is needed.

The investment banker agrees to try to arrange a leveraged buyout. Financial projections and cash budgets are prepared for the division to determine how much debt can be serviced. On the basis of these forecasts as well as the curtailment of certain capital expenditures, research and development expenses, and advertising expenses, it is felt that the likely cash throw-off is sufficient to service approximately $100 million in debt. The reduction in expenditures is regarded as temporary for the company to service debt during the next several years. The investment banker has lined up a wealthy individual to make an additional equity investment. The amount is $6 million, which together with management's investment brings total equity to $7\frac{1}{2}$ million. For this cash contribution, the individual is to receive one-half of the initial common stock, with management receiving the other half.

Arranging Debt Financing

With this equity capital commitment, the investment banker proceeds to arrange debt financing. In a leveraged buyout, two forms of debt typically are employed: senior debt and junior subordinated debt. For the senior debt, a large New York bank, through its asset-based lending subsidiary, has agreed to provide $85 million toward the cost plus an additional $8 million revolving credit for seasonal needs. The rate on both arrangements is 2 percent over the prime rate, and the loans are secured by liens on all of the assets—real estate, buildings, equipment, rolling stock, inventories, and receivables. The term of the $85 million loan is 6 years, payable in equal monthly installments of principal with interest for the month being added on. All major banking will be with the bank, and company receipts will be deposited into a special account at the bank for purposes of servicing the debt. In addition to the collateral, the usual protective covenants are imposed in a loan agreement.

Junior subordinated debt in the amount of $17½ million has been arranged with the merger-funding subsidiary of a large finance company. This debt sometimes is referred to as "mezzanine-layer" financing, as it falls between senior debt and the equity. The loan is for 7 years with an interest rate of 13 percent being fixed throughout. Only monthly interest payments are required during the 7 years, the full principal amount being due at the end. As the senior lender will have liens on all assets, the debt is unsecured and subordinated to the senior debt as well as to all trade creditors. For this subordinated financing, the lender receives warrants exercisable for 40 percent of the stock. These warrants may be exercised any time throughout the 7 years at a price of $1 per share, quite nominal. If exercised, management's stock and that of the equity investor will each go from 50 percent of the amount outstanding to 30 percent. To recapitulate, the financing is as follows:

Senior debt	$85.0 million
Junior subordinated debt	17.5
Equity	7.5
	$110.0 million

In addition, the company will have access to an $8 million revolving credit for seasonal needs.

Observations

We see that leveraged buyouts permit going private with very little equity involved. The assets of the acquired company or division are used to secure a large amount of debt. The equity holders, of course, are residual owners. If things go according to plan and the debt is serviced according to schedule, after 5 years they will own a healthy company with little debt. Of course, their position will be diluted as the junior subordinated lender exercises its warrants to purchase stock. In any leveraged buyout, the first several years are key. The company initially operates with a very thin equity base. If somehow it can make its payments, the interest burden declines over time as operating profits, it is hoped, improve.

There are two kinds of risk. The first is business risk. Operations may not go according to plan, and the cash-flow wherewithal to service debt may be lower than forecasted. The other risk involves changing interest rates. As the senior debt typically is floating rate and changes with the prime rate, a sharp rise in interest rates may very well carry the business under. By their very nature, leveraged buyouts have a modest safety cushion built into the calculations for the first several years. Even with good operations management, a sizable increase in interest costs will eliminate this cushion and cause the firm to default. If a large number of leveraged buyouts occur in an interest rate trough, there is the danger of large-scale defaults in the event that interest rates rise quickly.

Thus, the equity holders are playing a high-risk game, and the principle of leverage being a two-edged sword becomes abundantly clear. The reader can visualize their position in the option pricing model framework used earlier in the book. Another potential problem with the need to service debt is the focus on short-run profitability. This may work to the detriment of the long-run viability of the enterprise. If capital expenditures, research and development, and advertising are cut not only to, but through, the bone, the company may not be competitive once the debt is paid off. Once lost, the company may not be able to regain its competitive position despite reasonable expenditures later on. A rule of thumb is that the total value placed on an LBO (debt and equity) should be no more than six to eight times pretax operating cash flow. If higher than this, and if leverage is a large component of the total value, the probability of default is accentuated beyond what most would regard as reasonable.

An economic incentive for a leveraged buyout may be taxes. By selling a division or subsidiary, the new owners may be able to depreciate the assets more quickly than the old owners. Assets acquired prior to 1982 are subject to slower depreciation than now. By selling the business unit, the new owners are able to depreciate these assets using accelerated cost recovery tables, thereby enjoying a larger tax shield. Presumably part of this value will be realized by the selling company. Another incentive is behavioral. The managers of a business unit simply may work better and more productively for themselves than they do as a part of a large corporation. These potential advantages should be balanced against the out-of-pocket costs that go to investment bankers and lawyers who put the deal together. These costs typically range from 2 to 5 percent. With the "hype" involved with leveraged buyouts, one needs to evaluate carefully all dimensions before deciding if it is worthwhile. Whether leveraged buyouts continue to be popular or are just a fad depends at least in part on the behavior of future interest rates and the operating performance of the large number of leveraged buyouts that occurred in the 1980s to date.

SUMMARY

Corporate restructuring embraces many topics: mergers and the market for corporate control; divestitures, including liquidation, sell-offs, spin-offs, and equity carve-outs; and ownership restructuring, such as taking a publicly owned company private and leveraged buyouts. The motivation in all cases should be to enhance shareholder wealth. The sources of value creation include efficiency gains, management improvement, information effects, wealth transfers from debt holders, tax reasons, gains from leverage, too aggressive bidding (hubris hypothesis), and personal reasons by owners of a tightly held company.

A company may grow internally, or it may grow externally through acquisitions. The objective of the firm in either case is to maximize existing shareholder wealth. Both types of expansion can be regarded as capital budgeting decisions. The criterion for acceptance are essentially the same: Capital should be allocated to increase shareholder wealth. In this regard, a cash-flow method of analysis was presented. Whenever two companies exchange stock, certain financial relationships come into prominence. Many companies focus on the impact on earnings per share. When the price/earnings ratio of the company being acquired is lower than the price/earnings ratio of the acquiring company, there is an initial improvement in earnings per share of the latter company; a dilution occurs when the price/earnings ratio is higher. Instead of looking only at the effect on initial earnings per share, it is desirable to look at the effect on expected future earnings per share as well. Empirical evidence indicates substantial excess returns to the stockholders of the selling company, owing to the substantial premium paid, and no excess returns on average to those of the buying company.

Another company can be acquired through the purchase of either its assets or its stock. In turn, the means of payment can be cash or stock. Accounting considerations come into play in that the merger must be treated either as a purchase or as a pooling of interests. With a purchase, any goodwill arising from the merger must be amortized against future earnings. The accounting method used depends on the circumstances of the merger and the constraints imposed by rules of the accounting profession. Whether a combination is taxable or tax free is highly consequential to the selling company and its stockholders and, sometimes, to the buying company. The acquisition of another company can be negotiated with the management of the prospective acquisition, or the acquiring company can make its appeal directly to the stockholders through a tender offer to purchase their shares. These unfriendly takeovers usually are resisted by management. A number of antitakeover devices exist, and they were explored, as was their effect on shareholder wealth.

Voluntary liquidations, sell-offs, spin-offs, and equity carve-outs have both similar and dissimilar characteristics. A voluntary liquidation involves the sale of the overall company. A sell-off usually involves the sale of a business unit for cash or securities. In contrast, a spin-off involves distribution of common stock in the business unit to stockholders of the company spinning off the unit. In both the sell-off and spin-off, the company divests itself of all ownership and control. In an equity carve-out, common stock in a business unit is sold to the public, but the company usually keeps majority ownership and control. The various motives for these divestitures were taken up, as was the empirical evidence on valuation.

When a company goes private, it is transformed from public ownership to private ownership by a small group of investors, including management. There are a number of motivations for going private, and some reasons for expecting economic gain. The empirical evidence suggests sizable premiums being paid to the public stockholders, similar to those for mergers. One means for going private is the leveraged buyout. Here a large amount of debt is used to finance a cash purchase of a division of a company or a company as a whole. Both senior debt secured by assets and junior subordinated debt are employed. Given the small equity base, leveraged buyouts are risky. It does not take a very large adverse change in operations or interest rates for default to occur.

QUESTIONS

1. Explain the concept of *synergism*.
2. Illustrate and explain how the ratio of P/E multiples for two stocks affects the growth rate of reported earnings.
3. With a stock-for-stock acquisition, is it better to analyze the situation on a cash-flow basis or as to its effect on earnings per share?
4. It has been noted that the number of mergers tends to vary directly with the level of relative business activity. Why would this be?
5. Both Company X and Company Y have considerable variability in their earnings, but they are in unrelated industries. Could a merger of the two companies reduce the risk for stockholders of both companies? Could investors lower the risk on their own?
6. Many a corporate merger is made with the motive of increasing growth. What does this mean? Can you increase growth without increasing the overall risk of the surviving company?
7. Why is it that so many acquisition opportunities look good before the merger but later prove to be "dogs"?
8. Is an acquisition-minded company consistently able to find bargains? If so, why is it that other companies do not discover these bargains?
9. When evaluating a potential acquisition's future, why penalize the prospect by deducting the capital expenditures that will need to be made? Are not future earnings what really matter?
10. How does a pooling-of-interests accounting treatment differ from the purchase method?
11. Can a company pyramid its control through the holding company form? Are there any problems?
12. Why does it matter whether an acquisition is with cash or with stock?
13. As a stockholder in a company, would you like it to have antitakeover amendments? What are some of these devices?
14. In your opinion, does the threat of a tender offer lead to better management of corporations?
15. What is the purpose of a two-tier tender offer?
16. In corporate restructuring broadly defined, what are the principal sources of value creation?
17. How does a partial sell-off differ from a spin-off? How does an equity carve-out differ from a sell-off and a spin-off?
18. Under what circumstances does liquidation of an entire company make sense?
19. What are the motivations of going private? Do the stockholders bought out gain?
20. Much has been written about leveraged buyouts. Are they a good thing?
21. What is the incentive for senior lenders and junior subordinated lenders to finance a leveraged buyout? Are there risks to them?

SELF-CORRECTION PROBLEMS

1. Yablonski Cordage Company is considering the acquisition of Yawitz Wire and Mesh Corporation with stock. Relevant financial information is as follows·

	YABLONSKI	YAWITZ
Present earnings (in thousands)	$4,000	$1,000
Common shares (in thousands)	2,000	800
Earnings per share	$2.00	$1.25
Price/earnings ratio	12X	8X

Yablonski plans to offer a premium of 20 percent over the market price of Yawitz stock.

a. What is the ratio of exchange of stock? How many new shares will be issued?

b. What are earnings per share for the surviving company immediately following the merger?

c. If the price/earnings ratio stays at 12 times, what is the market price per share of the surviving company? What would happen if it went to 11 times?

2. Karoo Company has merged into Sandoz Pharmacies, Inc., where $1\frac{1}{2}$ shares of Sandoz were exchanged for each share of Karoo. The balance sheets of the two companies before the merger were as follows (in millions):

	KAROO	SANDOZ
Current assets	$ 5	$20
Fixed assets	7	30
Goodwill	0	2
Total	$12	$52
Current liabilities	3	9
Long-term debt	2	15
Net worth	7	28
Total	$12	$52
Number of shares (in millions)	.2	1.4
Market value per share	$35	$28

The fair market value of Karoo's fixed assets is $400,000 higher than their book value. Construct the balance sheets for the company after the merger using the purchase and pooling-of-interests methods of accounting.

3. Insell Corporation is considering the acquisition of Fourier-Fox, Inc., which

is in a related line of business. Fourier-Fox presently has a cash flow of $2 million per year. With a merger, synergism would be expected to result in a growth rate of this cash flow of 15 percent per year for 10 years, at the end of which level cash flows would be expected. To sustain the cash-flow stream, Insell will need to invest $1 million annually. For purposes of analysis and to be conservative, Insell limits its calculations of cash flows to 25 years.

   a. What expected annual cash flows would Insell realize from this acquisition?

   b. If its required rate of return is 18 percent, what is the maximum price that it could pay?

4. Aggressive Incorporated wishes to make a tender offer for the Passive Company. Passive has 100,000 shares of common stock outstanding and earns $5.50 per share. If it were combined with Aggressive, total economies of $1.5 million could be realized. Presently, the market price per share of Passive is $55. Aggressive makes a two-tier tender offer: $65 per share for the first 50,001 shares tendered and $50 per share for the remaining shares.

   a. If successful, what will Aggressive end up paying for Passive? How much incrementally will stockholders of Passive receive for the economies?

   b. Acting independently, what will each stockholder do to maximize his or her wealth? What might they do if they could respond collectively as a cartel?

   c. How can a company increase the probability of individual stockholders resisting too low a tender offer?

   d. What might happen if Aggressive offered $65 in the first tier and only $40 in the second tier?

5. Tokay Enterprises is considering going private through a leveraged buyout by management. Management presently owns 21 percent of the 5 million shares outstanding. Market price per share is $20, and it is felt that a 40 percent premium over the present price will be necessary to entice public stockholders to tender their shares in a cash offer. Management intends to keep their shares and to obtain senior debt equal to 80 percent of the funds necessary to consummate the buyout. The remaining 20 percent will come from junior subordinated debentures.

   Terms on the senior debt are 2 percent above the prime rate, with principal reductions of 20 percent of the initial loan at the end of each of the next 5 years. The junior subordinated debentures bear a 13 percent interest rate and must be retired at the end of 6 years with a single balloon payment. The debentures have warrants attached that enable the holders to purchase 30 percent of the stock at the end of year 6. Management estimates that earnings before interest and taxes will be $25 million per year. Because of tax loss carryforwards, the company expects to pay no taxes over the next 5 years. The company will make capital expenditures in amounts equal to its depreciation.

   a. If the prime rate is expected to average 10 percent over the next 5 years, is the leveraged buyout feasible?

b.   What if it averaged only 8 percent?

c.   What minimal EBIT is necessary to service the debt?

PROBLEMS

1.   The following data are pertinent for Companies A and B:

	COMPANY A	COMPANY B
Present earnings (in millions)	$20	$ 4
Shares (in millions)	10	1
Price/earnings ratio	18	10

a.   If the two companies were to merge and the exchange ratio were 1 share of Company A for each share of Company B, what would be the initial impact on earnings per share of the two companies? What is the market-value exchange ratio? Is a merger likely to take place?

b.   If the exchange ratio were 2 shares of Company A for each share of Company B, what would happen with respect to part a?

c.   If the exchange ratio were 1.5 shares of Company A for each share of Company B, what would happen?

d.   What exchange ratio would you suggest?

2.

	EXPECTED EARNINGS	NUMBER OF SHARES	MARKET PRICE PER SHARE	TAX RATE
Hargrave Company	$5,000,000	1,000,000	$100	50%
Hooper Company	3,000,000	500,000	60	50%

The Hargrave Company wishes to acquire the Hooper Company. If the merger were effected through an exchange of stock, Hargrave would be willing to pay a 25 percent premium for the Hooper shares. If done for cash, the terms would have to be as favorable to the Hooper shareholders; to obtain the cash, Hargrave would have to sell its own stock in the market.

a.   Compute the exchange ratio and the combined expected earnings per share for an exchange of stock.

b.   If we assume that all Hooper shareholders have held their stock for more than 1 year, have a 20 percent marginal capital gains tax rate, and paid an average of $14 for their shares, what cash price would have to be offered to be as attractive as the terms in part a?

3.   Assume the exchange of Hargrave shares for Hooper shares as outlined in Problem 2.

a.   What is the ratio of exchange?

b. Compare the earnings per Hooper share before and after the merger. Compare the earnings per Hargrave share. On this basis alone, which group fared better? Why?

c. Why do you imagine that Hargrave commanded a higher P/E ratio than Hooper? What should be the change in P/E ratio resulting from the merger? Does this conflict with your previous one? Why?

d. If the Hargrave Company were in a high-technology growth industry and Hooper made cement, would you revise your answers?

e. In determining the appropriate P/E ratio for Hargrave, should the increase in earnings resulting from this merger be added as a growth factor?

4. Copper Tube Company presently has annual earnings of $10 million with 4 million shares of common stock outstanding and a market price per share of $30. In the absence of any mergers, Copper Tube's annual earnings are expected to grow at a compound rate of 5 percent per annum. Brass Fitting Company, whom Copper Tube is seeking to acquire, has present annual earnings of $2 million, 1 million shares of common outstanding, and a market price per share of $36. Its annual earnings are expected to grow at a compound annual rate of 10 percent per annum. Copper Tube will offer 1.2 shares of its stock for each share of Brass Fitting Company.

a. What is the immediate effect on the surviving company's earnings per share?

b. Would you want to acquire Brass Fitting Company? If it is not attractive now, when will it be attractive from the standpoint of earnings per share?

5. The Resin Corporation, which has a 16 percent after-tax cost of capital, is considering the acquisition of the Smythe Company, which has about the same degree of systematic risk. If the merger were effected, the incremental cash flows would be as follows:

	AVERAGE FOR YEARS (IN MILLIONS)			
	1–5	6–10	11–15	16–20
Annual cash income attributable to Smythe	$10	$15	$20	$15
Required new investment	2	5	10	10
Net after-tax cash flow	$ 8	$10	$10	$ 5

What is the maximum price that Resin should pay for Smythe, assuming the business-risk complexion of the company remains unchanged?

6. Cougar Pipe and Brass Company is considering the cash acquisition of Red Wilson Rod, Inc., for $750,000. The acquisition is expected to result in incremental cash flows of $100,000 in the first year, and this amount is expected to grow at a 6 percent compound rate. In the absence of the acquisition, Cougar expects net cash flows (after capital expenditures) of $600,000 this year, and these are expected to grow at a 6 percent compound rate

forever. Presently, suppliers of capital require a 14 percent overall rate of return for Cougar Pipe and Brass Company. However, Red Wilson Rod is much more risky, and the acquisition of it will raise the company's overall required return to 15 percent.

   a. Should Cougar Pipe and Brass Company acquire Red Wilson Rod, Inc.?

   b. Would your answer be the same if the overall required rate of return stayed the same?

   c. Would your answer be the same if the acquisition increased the surviving company's growth rate to 8 percent forever?

7. Let it be assumed that a holding company can always be set up with 50 percent debt at 12 percent and 20 percent preferred stock at 10 percent. Further assume that all companies pay a tax rate of 50 percent, that the 85 percent intercorporate dividend exclusion applies in all cases, and that ownership of 40 percent of the stock of another company constitutes control. The shares of the Target Company can be obtained at their book value.

TARGET COMPANY			
Total assets	$25,000,000	Debt (12%)	$15,000,000
		Common	10,000,000
			$25,000,000

   a. A group of investors has set up Holding Company A to acquire control of the Target Company. If the group holds all the equity of Holding Company A, how much money must it put up? If Target has operating earnings equal to 20 percent of total assets and pays all earnings in dividends, what return on investment will the group earn?

   b. Suppose that the group sets up Holding Company B to acquire control of Holding Company A. If the group holds all the equity of B, how much money must it put up? If A pays all earnings in dividends, what return on investment will the group earn? How many dollars of operating assets does the group control per dollar of its own investment?

   c. How would your answers change if Target had operating earnings equal to 15 percent of total assets?

8. Biggo Stores, Inc. (BSI), has acquired the Nail It, Glue It and Screw It Hardware Company (NGS) for $4 million in stock and the assumption of $2 million in NGS liabilities. The balance sheets of the two companies before the merger were

	BSI	NGS
Tangible and total assets	$10.0 million	$5.0 million
Liabilities	4.0	2.0
Net worth	$ 6.0 million	3.0 million

Determine the balance sheet of the combined company after the merger under the purchase and pooling-of-interests methods of accounting.

9. R. Leonard Company has three divisions, and the total market value (debt and equity) of the firm is $71 million. Its debt-to-market value ratio is .40, and bond indentures provide the usual protective covenants. However, they do not preclude the sale of a division. Leonard has decided to divest itself of its Eltron division for a consideration of $20 million. In addition to this payment to Leonard, the buyer will assume $5 million of existing debt of the division. The full $20 million will be distributed to Leonard Company stockholders. In words, are the remaining debt holders of Leonard Company better or worse off? Why? In theory, are the equity holders better or worse off?

10. Lorzo-Perez International has a subsidiary, the DelRay Sorter Company. The company believes the subsidiary on average will generate $1 million per year in annual net cash flows after necessary capital expenditures. These annual net cash flows are projected into the far future (assume infinity). The required rate of return for the subsidiary is 12 percent. If the company were to invest an additional $10 million now, it is believed that annual net cash flows could be increased from $1 to $2 million. Exson Corporation has expressed an interest in DelRay, because it is in the sorter business and believes it can achieve some economies. Accordingly, it has made a cash offer of $10 million for the subsidiary.

    Should Lorzo-Perez

    a. Continue the business as is?

    b. Invest the additional $10 million?

    c. Sell the subsidiary to Exson? (Assume the subsidiary is entirely equity financed.)

11. Hogs Breath Inns, a chain of restaurants, is considering going private. The president, Clint Westwood, believes that with the elimination of stockholder servicing costs and other costs associated with public ownership, the company could save $800,000 per annum before taxes. In addition, the company believes management incentives and, hence, performance will be higher as a private company. As a result, annual profits are expected to be 10 percent greater than present after-tax profits of $9 million. The effective tax rate is 30 percent, the price/earnings ratio of the stock is 12, and there are 10 million shares outstanding. What is the present market price per share? What is the maximum dollar premium above this price that the company could pay in order to take the company private?

12. Bulaweyo Industries wishes to sell its valve division for $10 million. Management of the division wishes to buy it and has arranged a leveraged buyout. Management will put up $1 million in cash. A senior lender will advance $7 million secured by all the assets of the company. The rate on the loan is 2 percent above the prime rate, which is presently 12 percent. The loan is payable in equal annual principal installments over 5 years, with interest for the year payable at the end of each year. A junior subordinated loan of $2 million also has been arranged, and this loan is due at the end of 6 years. The interest rate is fixed at 15 percent, and interest payments only

are due at the end of each of the first 5 years. Interest and principal are due at the end of the sixth year. In addition, the lender has received warrants exercisable for 50 percent of the stock.

The valve division expects earnings before interest and taxes of $3.4 million in each of the first 3 years and $3.7 million in the last 3 years. The tax rate is $33\frac{1}{3}$ percent, and the company expects capital expenditures and investments in receivables and inventories to equal depreciation charges in each year. All debt servicing must come from profits. (Assume also that the warrants are not exercised and that there is no cash infusion as a result.)

If the prime rate stays at 12 percent on average throughout the 6 years, will the enterprise be able to service the debt properly? If the prime rate were to rise to 20 percent in the second year and average that for years 2 through 6, would the situation change?

SOLUTIONS TO SELF-CORRECTION PROBLEMS

1. a.

	YABLONSKI	YAWITZ
Earnings per share	$2.00	$1.25
Price/earnings ratio	12X	8X
Market price per share	$24	$10
Offer to Yawitz shareholders in Yablonski stock (including the premium) = $10 × 1.20 = $12 per share		

Exchange ratio = $12/$24 = .5, or one-half share of Yablonski stock for every share of Yawitz stock.
Number of new shares issued = 800,000 shares × .5 = 400,000 shares

b.

Surviving company earnings (in thousands)	$5,000
Common shares (in thousands)	2,400
Earnings per share	$2.0833

There is an increase in earnings per share by virtue of acquiring a company with a lower price/earnings ratio.

c. Market price per share $2.0833 × 12 = $25.00
Market price per share $2.0833 × 11 = $22.92
In the first instance, share price rises, from $24, due to the increase in earnings per share. In the second case, share price falls owing to the decline in the price/earnings ratio. In efficient markets, we might expect some decline in price/earnings ratio if there was not likely to be synergy and/or improved management.

2. With an exchange ratio of $1\frac{1}{2}$, Sandoz would issue 300,000 new shares of stock with a market value of $28 × 300,000 = $8.4 million for the stock of

Karoo. This exceeds the net worth of Karoo by $1.4 million. With the purchase method, Karoo's fixed assets will be written up by $400,000 and goodwill of Sandoz by $1 million. This does not happen, of course, with a pooling of interests. The balance sheets after the merger under the two methods of accounting are (in millions)

	PURCHASE	POOLING OF INTERESTS
Current assets	$25.0	$25.0
Fixed assets	37.4	37.0
Goodwill	3.0	2.0
Total	$65.4	$64.0
Current liabilities	$12.0	$12.0
Long-term debt	17.0	17.0
Net worth	36.4	35.0
Total	$65.4	$64.0

3. a, b.

YEAR	CASH FLOW	INVESTMENT	NET CASH FLOW	PRESENT VALUE OF NET CASH FLOW (18%)
1	$2,230,000	$1,000,000	$1,130,000	$ 957,630
2	2,645,000	"	1,645,000	1,181,406
3	3,041,750	"	2,041,750	1,242,670
4	3,498,013	"	2,498,013	1,288,450
5	4,022,714	"	3,022,714	1,321,259
6	4,626,122	"	3,626,122	1,343,224
7	5,320,040	"	4,320,040	1,356,147
8	6,118,046	"	5,118,046	1,361,605
9	7,035,753	"	6,035,753	1,360,821
10–25	8,091,116	"	7,091,116	8,253,350
			Total present value =	$19,666,562

The maximum price that is justified is approximately $19\frac{2}{3}$ million. It should be noted that these calculations use present-value tables. For cash flows going from year 10 to 25, we subtract the discount factor for 9 years of annuity payments, 4.3030, in Table B at the end of the book from that for 25 years, 5.4669. The difference, 5.4669 − 4.3030 = 1.1639, is the discount factor for cash flows for an annuity starting in year 10 and going through year 25. If a present-value function of a calculator is used, a slightly different total may be given due to rounding in the present-value tables.

4. a.

$$
\begin{aligned}
50{,}001 \text{ shares} \times \$65 &= \$3{,}250{,}065 \\
49{,}999 \text{ shares} \times \$50 &= \underline{2{,}499{,}950} \\
\text{Total purchase price} &= \$5{,}750{,}015 \\
\text{Total value of stock before} = 100{,}000 \text{ shares} \times \$55 &= \underline{5{,}500{,}000} \\
\text{Increment to Passive stockholders} &= \underline{\underline{\$\ 250{,}015}}
\end{aligned}
$$

The total value of the economies to be realized is $1,500,000. Therefore, Passive stockholders receive only a modest portion of the total value of the economies; in contrast, Aggressive stockholders obtain a large share.

b. With a two-tier offer, there is a great incentive for individual stockholders to tender early, thereby ensuring success for the acquiring firm. Collectively, Passive stockholders would be better off holding out for a larger fraction of the total value of the economies. They can do this only if they act as a cartel in their response to the offer.

c. By instigating antitakeover amendments and devices, some incentives may be created for individual stockholders to hold out for a higher offer. However, in practice it is impossible to achieve a complete cartel response.

d.

$$50{,}001 \text{ shares} \times \$65 = \$3{,}250{,}065$$
$$49{,}999 \text{ shares} \times \$40 = \underline{1{,}999{,}960}$$
$$\text{Total purchase price} = \$5{,}250{,}025$$

This value is lower than the previous total market value of $5,500,000. Clearly, stockholders would fare poorly if in the rush to tender shares the offer were successful. However, other potential acquirers would have an incentive to offer more than Aggressive, even with no economies to be realized. Competition among potential acquirers should ensure counterbids, so that Aggressive would be forced to bid no less than $5,500,000 in total, the present market value.

5. a. Shares owned by outsiders = 5 million × .79 = 3,950,000
Price to be offered = $20 × 1.40 = $28 per share
Total buyout amount = 3,950,000 shares × $28 = $110,600,000.
Senior debt = $110,600,000 × .80 = $88,480,000
Annual principal payment = $88,480,000/5 = $17,696,000
Junior debt = $110,600,000 × .20 = $22,120,000
Annual EBIT to service debt:

Senior debt interest $88,480,000 × .12 =	$10,617,600
Senior debt principal	17,696,000
Junior debt interest $22,120,000 × .13 =	2,875,600
Total EBIT necessary	$31,189,200

During the first 5 years, EBIT of $25 million will not be sufficient to service the debt.

b. $88,480,000 × .10 = $8,848,000, which, with the two other amounts above, comes to $29,419,600. Expected EBIT still will not be sufficient to service the debt.

c. $31,189,200.

SELECTED REFERENCES

ALEXANDER, GORDON J., P. GEORGE BENSON, and JOAN M. KAMPMEYER, "Investigating the Valuation Effects of Announcements of Voluntary Selloffs," *Journal of Finance*, 39 (June 1984), 503–17.

Asquith, Paul, "Merger Bids, Uncertainty, and Stockholder Returns," *Journal of Financial Economics*, 11 (April 1983), 51–84.

_____, and E. Han Kim, "The Impact of Merger Bids on the Participating Firms' Security Holders," *Journal of Finance*, 37 (December 1982), 1209–28.

Asquith, Paul, Robert F. Bruner, and David W. Mullins, Jr., "The Gains to Bidding Firms from Merger," *Journal of Financial Economics*, 11 (April 1983), 121–40.

Bradley, Michael, "Interfirm Tender Offers and the Market for Corporate Control," *Journal of Business*, 53 (October 1980), 345–76.

_____, Anand Desai, and E. Han Kim, "The Rationale Behind Interfirm Tender Offers: Information or Synergy," *Journal of Financial Economics*, 11 (April 1983), 183–206.

Dann, Larry Y., and Harry DeAngelo, "Standstill Agreements, Privately Negotiated Stock Repurchases, and the Market for Corporate Control," *Journal of Financial Economics*, 11 (April 1983), 275–300.

DeAngelo, Harry, and Edward M. Rice, "Antitakeover Charter Amendments and Stockholder Wealth," *Journal of Financial Economics*, 11 (April 1983), 329–60.

DeAngelo, Harry, Linda DeAngelo, and Edward M. Rice, "Going Private: Minority Freezeouts and Stockholder Wealth," *Journal of Law and Economics*, 27 (June 1984), 367–401.

Dennis, Debra K., and John J. McConnell, "Corporate Mergers and Security Returns," *Journal of Financial Economics*, 16 (June 1986), 143–88.

Dodd, Peter, "Merger Proposals, Management Discretion and Stockholder Wealth," *Journal of Financial Economics*, 8 (June 1980), 105–38.

_____, and Richard Ruback, "Tender Offers and Stockholder Returns," *Journal of Financial Economics*, 5 (November 1977), 351–73.

Elgers, Pieter T., and John J. Clark, "Merger Types and Shareholder Returns: Additional Evidence," *Financial Management*, 9 (Summer 1980), 66–72.

Halpern, Paul, "Corporate Acquisitions: A Theory of Special Cases? A Review of Event Studies Applied to Acquisitions," *Journal of Finance*, 38 (May 1983), 297–318.

Hite, Gailen L., and James E. Owens, "Security Price Reactions Around Corporate Spin-off Announcements," *Journal of Financial Economics*, 12 (December 1983), 409–36.

_____, and Ronald C. Rogers, "The Market for Interfirm Asset Sales," *Journal of Financial Economics*, 18 (June 1987), 229–52.

Hong, H., G. Mandelker, and R. S. Kaplan, "Pooling vs. Purchase: The Effects of Accounting for Mergers on Stock Prices," *Accounting Review*, 53 (January 1978), 31–47.

Jain, Prem C., "The Effect of Voluntary Sell-off Announcements on Shareholder Wealth," *Journal of Finance*, 40 (March 1985), 209–24.

Jensen, Michael C., "The Takeover Controversy: Analysis and Evidence," *Midland Corporate Finance Journal*, 4 (Summer 1986), 6–32.

_____, and Richard S. Ruback, "The Market for Corporate Control: The Scientific Evidence," *Journal of Financial Economics*, 11 (April 1983), 5–50.

Kim, E. Han, John J. McConnell, and Paul R. Greenwood, "Capital Structure Rearrangements and the Me-First Rules in an Efficient Capital Market," *Journal of Finance*, 32 (June 1977), 789–809.

Klein, April, "The Timing and Substance of Divestiture Announcements," *Journal of Finance*, 41 (July 1986), 685–96.

Langetieg, Terence C., Robert A. Haugen, and Dean W. Wichern, "Merger and Stockholder Wealth," *Journal of Financial and Quantitative Analysis*, 15 (September 1980), 689–717.

Larson, Kermit D., and Nicholas J. Gonedes, "Business Combinations: An Exchange-Ratio Determination Model," *Accounting Review*, 44 (October 1969), 720–28.

LEWELLEN, WILBUR G., and MICHAEL G. FERRI, "Strategies for the Merger Game: Management and the Market," *Financial Management*, 12 (Winter 1983), 25–35.

LINN, SCOTT C., and JOHN J. MCCONNELL, "An Empirical Investigation of the Impact of Anti-takeover Amendments on Common Stock Prices," *Journal of Financial Economics*, 11 (April 1983), 361–99.

MALATESTA, PAUL H., "The Wealth Effect of Merger Activity and the Objective Functions of Merging Firms," *Journal of Financial Economics*, 11 (April 1983), 155–82.

MEAD, WALTER J., "Instantaneous Merger Profit as a Conglomerate Merger Motive," *Western Economic Review*, 7 (December 1969), 295–306.

MILES, JAMES A., and JAMES D. ROSENFELD, "The Effect of Voluntary Spin-off Announcements on Shareholder Wealth," *Journal of Finance*, 38 (December 1983), 1597–1606.

ROLL, RICHARD, "The Hubris Hypothesis of Corporate Takeovers," *Journal of Business*, 59 (April 1986), 197–216.

ROSENFELD, JAMES D., "Additional Evidence on the Relation Between Divestiture Announcements and Shareholder Wealth," *Journal of Finance*, 39 (December 1984), 1437–48.

SALTER, MALCOLM S., and WOLF A. WEINHOLD, "Diversification via Acquisition: Creating Value," *Harvard Business Review* (July–August 1978), 166–76.

SCHIPPER, KATHERINE, and ABBIE SMITH, "A Comparison of Equity Carve-Outs and Seasoned Equity Offerings," *Journal of Financial Economics*, 15 (January–February 1986), 153–86.

————, "Effects of Recontracting on Shareholder Wealth," *Journal of Financial Economics*, 12 (December 1983), 437–67.

SKANTZ, TERRANCE R., and ROBERTO MARCHESINI, "The Effect of Voluntary Corporate Liquidation on Shareholder Wealth," *Journal of Financial Research*, 10 (Winter 1987), 65–76.

SMALTER, DONALD J., and RODERIC C. LANCEY, "P/E Analysis in Acquisition Strategy," *Harvard Business Review*, 44 (November–December 1966), 85–95.

CHAPTER 25

International Financial Management

During the last decade the financial markets of the world have become increasingly integrated. In many countries, deregulation has occurred. Across debt and equity markets the spectrum of financing opportunities has expanded enormously. Global competition in products and services has intensified. The **multinational company,** which has investment and sales in two or more countries, is increasingly common. As a result of the rapidly changing international scene, many a financial manager has had to keep abreast of fluctuating exchange rates, changing political and economic structures, international banking strains, changing financing methods and rates, and a host of other developments.

Multinational company. A company that does business and has assets in two or more countries.

How does financial management in a multinational enterprise differ from that in a domestic business firm? In principle, the concepts of efficient allocation of funds among assets and the raising of funds on as favorable terms as possible are the same for both types of companies. It is the environment in which these decisions are made that is different. In this chapter we shall see the institutional factors that make investing, financing, and dividend payout for a multinational company somewhat different from those for a domestic company. We shall take a look at the tax environment, accounting treatment, political risks, foreign exchange risk, investment constraints imposed by a government, financing instruments, and certain specialized documents used in foreign trade. Our purpose is not an in-depth understanding but rather an exposure to those factors that influence the basic decisions of the firm in an international setting.

INVESTING ABROAD

The decision to invest capital in a project abroad should be based on considerations of expected return and risk, the same as any investment proposal. Quantifying these parameters is complicated by disparities in currency exchange rates, differences in taxes, differences in accounting practices, and differences in factors affecting risk; but once expected return and risk are quantified, the evaluation of the project itself is largely the same, whether it be domestic or foreign in origin. Consequently, we shall concentrate on the various factors that make foreign investment unique rather than on the evaluation process itself. That process was taken up earlier in the book and has not changed.

Reasons for Foreign Investment

Risk Considerations.   International diversification is often more effective than domestic diversification in reducing a company's risk in relation to expected return. You will recall from our discussion of portfolio risk in Chapter 5 that the key element is the correlation among projects in the asset portfolio. By combining projects with low degrees of correlation with each other, a firm is able to reduce risk in relation to expected return. Since domestic investment projects tend to be correlated with each other, most being highly dependent on the state of the economy, foreign investments have an advantage. The economic cycles of different countries do not tend to be completely synchronized, so it is possible to reduce risk relative to expected return by investing across countries.

If a company in the machine tool business invested in another plant domestically, the return would likely be highly correlated with the return from existing assets. Consequently, there would be little reduction in relative risk. If it invested in a plant to market machine tools in a country whose economy was not highly correlated with the domestic economy, the project's return would not likely be highly correlated with the return from existing assets. Consequently, it may be possible to reduce risk relative to expected return by investing in the same industry internationally. The idea is simply that returns on investment projects tend to be less correlated among countries than they are in any one particular country.

Whether foreign diversification by a company benefits its stockholders depends on whether or not capital markets between countries are segmented. If they are not, there is little reason to believe that foreign diversification by a company will increase its value. This notion is the same as that for diversification of assets involving domestic projects, which was discussed earlier. If capital markets are perfect, investors can effectively replicate any asset diversification by the firm. Therefore, such diversification adds nothing at the margin to shareholder wealth. If currency restrictions, investment barriers, legal restrictions, lack of information, and other capital-market imperfections of this sort exist, capital markets between countries may be segmented. Under these circumstances, foreign diversification may enhance shareholder wealth.

Thus, whether stocks are better regarded as being traded in domestic markets, where the capital-asset pricing model would hold or in an international market is the question. The former implies a segmented capital market, whereas the latter suggests an integrated one with the relevant market portfolio being worldwide. The situation is illustrated in Fig. 25-1. With a domestic portfolio of stocks, one is able to reduce total risk through diversification in the manner shown by the top line. This illustration corresponds to Fig. 5-5 (Chapter 5), which dealt with the relationship among total, systematic, and unsystematic

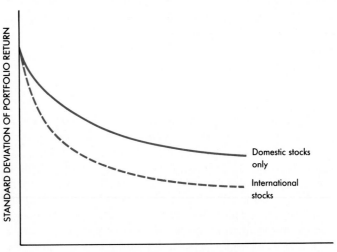

FIGURE 25-1
**Domestic versus internation
stock diversification**

risk. With an integrated market for securities, the investor is able to reduce risk more quickly and further by diversifying across international stocks as opposed to only domestic ones. Although there are problems in empirical testing, there is some evidence that markets for securities are at least partially integrated. We do know that an increasing number of institutional stock portfolios diversify internationally. This would suggest a movement toward integration, but does not rule out the presence of some segmentation effects. The degree of capital-market segmentation is what is at issue, and there is disagreement here.[1]

The concept of diversification is applicable also to the acquisition of foreign companies. To the extent again that market imperfections result in segmentation among international capital markets, the diversification properties associated with a foreign acquisition may be of value. We know from Chapters 8 and 24 that domestic acquisitions are a thing of value only if the acquiring company can do something for its investors that they cannot do for themselves. In the case of a company with a publicly traded stock, there is little reason to believe that stockholders cannot achieve the same diversification on their own by investing directly in the company involved. Making foreign acquisitions, however, the acquiring company may be able to do something for investors that they cannot do for themselves if specific international capital markets are partially segmented. As a result, the risk-reduction properties associated with the foreign acquisition may be a thing of value.

Return Considerations.   The other reason for investing abroad is the expectation of a higher return for a given level of risk. Within a firm's particular expertise, there may be gaps in markets abroad where excess returns can be earned. Domestically, competitive pressures may be such that only a normal rate of return can be earned. Although expansion into foreign markets is the reason for most investment abroad, there are other reasons. Some firms invest in order to produce more efficiently. In another country where labor or other costs are less, a company may seek foreign production facilities simply to operate at a lower cost. The electronics industry has moved toward foreign production facilities for this saving. Finally, some companies invest abroad to secure necessary raw materials. Oil companies and mining companies in particular invest abroad for this reason. All of these pursuits—markets, production facilities, and raw materials—are in keeping with an objective of securing a higher rate of return than is possible through domestic operations alone.

The relevant cash inflows for a foreign investment are those that can be repatriated to the parent. If the expected return on investment is based on non-remittable cash flows that build up in the foreign subsidiary, the investment is unlikely to be attractive. As we observed earlier, among the factors that make investment abroad different from investment at home are tax differences and political and foreign exchange risk. Before taking up each in turn, we should point out that there is more risk to a foreign investment than simply the political and foreign exchange risks and inability to repatriate earnings. Frequently, the predominant risk is business risk in the country itself. We discussed methods for analyzing this risk in Chapters 5, 14, and 15.

---

[1] For a review of international portfolio theory, see Michael Adler and Bernard Dumas, "International Portfolio Choice and Corporation Finance: A Synthesis," *Journal of Finance*, 38 (June 1983), 925–84.

Taxation

Owing to different tax laws and different treatments of foreign investment, the taxation of a multinational firm is extremely complex. Our purpose is to discuss some of the salient aspects of the problem, and we begin with the way in which the U.S. government taxes a company with foreign operations. Then we can move on to taxation by foreign countries.

Taxation by U.S. Government.   If a U.S. corporation carries on business abroad through a branch or division, the income from that operation is reported on the company's U.S. tax form and taxed in the same way as domestic income. If business is carried on through a foreign subsidiary, the income normally is not taxed in the United States until it is distributed to the parent in the form of dividends. The advantage here, of course, is that the tax is deferred until the parent receives a cash return. In the meantime, earnings are reinvested in the subsidiary to finance expansion. Unlike dividends from a domestic corporation (80 percent exempt), dividends received by a U.S. corporation from a foreign subsidiary are fully taxable.

Taxation by Foreign Governments.   Every country taxes income of foreign companies doing business in that country. The type of tax imposed varies. Some of these countries differentiate between income distributed to stockholders and undistributed income, with a lower tax on distributed income. Less developed countries frequently have lower taxes and provide certain other tax incentives to encourage foreign investment. One method of taxation that has been prominent in Europe is the value-added tax, in essence a sales tax on each stage of production, which is taxed on the value added. It works this way: An aluminum fabricator buys aluminum sheets for $1,000, cuts, shapes, and otherwise works them into doors, which are sold for $1,800. The value added is $800, and the fabricator is taxed on this amount. If the fabricator sold its doors to a wholesaler who, in turn, sold them to retailers for $2,000, the value added would be $200 and taxed accordingly.

The taxation policies of foreign governments are not only varied but also highly complex. The definition of what constitutes taxable income is different for different countries, and the tax rate varies among countries. Certain nations, such as Luxembourg, Panama, and the Bahamas, have low tax rates on corporate profits in order to encourage foreign investment, whereas the tax rates in most advanced industrial countries are high. The picture is complicated further by the numerous tax treaties that the United States has with other nations. Although the U.S. government restricts use of a low-tax country as a tax haven, enough latitude remains so that companies still devise complicated legal structures in order to take advantage of such havens.

In order to avoid double taxation, the United States gives a federal income tax credit for foreign taxes paid by a U.S. corporation. If a foreign country has a tax rate of less than that for the U.S. corporation, the company will pay combined taxes at the full U.S. tax rate. Part of the taxes are paid to the foreign government, the other part to the U.S. government. Suppose a foreign branch of a U.S. corporation operates in a country where the income tax rate is 27 percent.

The branch earns $2 million and pays $540,000 in foreign income taxes. The $2 million earnings are subject to a 34 percent tax rate in the United States, or $680,000 in taxes. The company receives a tax credit of $540,000; thus, it pays only $140,000 in U.S. taxes on earnings of its foreign branch. If the foreign tax rate were 50 percent, the company would pay $1 million in foreign taxes on those earnings and nothing in U.S. taxes. Here, total taxes paid are obviously higher.

Moreover, the size of foreign tax credit may be constrained. The United States taxes companies on their worldwide income and permits a foreign tax credit only to the extent that the foreign source income would have been taxed in the United States. Suppose 30 percent ot a multinational company's total income is attributable to foreign sources. If its precredit U.S. tax liability is $10 million, only $3 million in foreign tax credits may be used to offset the U.S. tax liability. If the company pays more in foreign taxes, it will be subject to double taxation on that portion. Relative sourcing of assets, income or value becomes important also in allocating certain corporate expenses, in particular, interest expenses. It is clear that tax planning for an international operation is complex and highly technical. The advice of tax experts and legal counsel, both foreign and domestic, should be sought at the time the foreign operation is organized.

Political Risk

A multinational company faces political risks ranging from mild interference to complete confiscation of all assets. Interference includes laws that specify a minimum percentage of nationals who must be employed in various positions, required investment in environmental and social projects, and restrictions on the convertibility of currencies. The ultimate political risk is expropriation, such as that which occurred in Chile in 1971, when the country took over the copper companies. Between mild interference and outright expropriation, there are discriminatory practices such as higher taxes, higher utility charges, and the requirement to pay higher wages than a national company. In essence, they place the foreign operation of the U.S. company at a competitive disadvantage.

Because political risk has a serious influence on the overall risk of an investment project, it must be assessed realistically. Essentially, the job is one of forecasting political instability. How stable is the government involved? What are the prevailing political winds? What is likely to be a new government's view of foreign investment? How efficient is the government in processing requests? How much inflation and economic stability is there? How strong and equitable are the courts? Answers to these questions should give considerable insight into the political risk involved in an investment. Some companies have categorized countries according to their political risk. If a country is classified in the undesirable category, probably no investment will be permitted, no matter how high its expected return.

Once a company decides to invest, it should take steps to protect itself. By cooperating with the host country in hiring nationals, making the "right" types of investment, and in other ways being desirable, political risk can be reduced. A joint venture with a company in the host country can improve the public image of the operation. Indeed, in some countries a joint venture may be the only way to do business, because direct ownership, particularly of manufacturing, is prohibited. The risk of expropriation also can be reduced by making the subsidiary dependent on the parent for technology, markets, and/or supplies. A foreign government is reluctant to expropriate when the enterprise is not self-sustaining. Though every effort should be made to protect an investment once it is made, often when sharp political changes occur nothing can be done. The time to look hardest at political risk is before the investment is made.

ACCOUNTING TREATMENT

Financial Accounting Standards Board (FASB). The rule-making body of the accounting profession that sets its standards.

Statement No. 52 of the **Financial Accounting Standards Board** deals with the translation of foreign currency changes on the balance sheet and income statement. Under these accounting rules, a U.S. company must determine a functional currency for each of its foreign subsidiaries. If the subsidiary is a stand-alone operation that is integrated within a particular country, the functional currency may be the local currency; otherwise, it is the dollar.[2] Where high inflation occurs (over 100 percent per annum), the functional currency must be the dollar regardless of the conditions given.

Translation gain or loss. An accounting gain or loss arising from the translation of the assets and liabilities of a foreign subsidiary into the parent company's currency.

The functional currency used is important because it determines the translation process. If the local currency is used, all assets and liabilities are translated at the *current rate of exchange*. Moreover, **translation gains or losses** are not reflected in the income statement, but rather are recognized in owners' equity as a translation adjustment. The fact that such adjustments do not affect accounting income is appealing to many companies. If the functional currency is the dollar, however, this is not the case. Gains or losses are reflected in the income statement of the parent company using what is known as the *temporal method*. In general, the use of the dollar as the functional currency results in greater fluctuations in accounting income, but in smaller fluctuations in balance sheet items than does the use of the local currency. Let us examine the differences in more detail.

Differences in Methods

With the dollar as the functional currency, balance sheet and income statement items are categorized as to historical exchange rates or as to current exchange rates. Cash, receivables, liabilities, sales, expenses, and taxes are translated using current exchange rates, whereas inventories, plant and equipment, equity, cost of goods sold, and depreciation are translated at the historical exchange rates existing at the time of the transactions. This differs from the situation where the local currency is used as the functional currency; here all items are translated at current exchange rates.

[2] Various criteria are used to determine if the foreign subsidiary is self-contained, including whether sales, labor, other costs, and debt are primarily dominated in the local currency. Also, the nature and magnitude of intercompany transactions are important. Under certain circumstances, it is possible for a foreign currency other than the local one to be used.

To illustrate, a company we shall call Richmond Precision Instruments has a subsidiary in the Kingdom of Spamany where the currency is the liso. At the first of the year, the exchange rate is 8 lisos to the dollar, and that rate has prevailed for many years. However, during 19x2, the liso declines steadily in value to 10 lisos to the dollar at year end. The average exchange rate during the year is 9 lisos to the dollar. Table 25-1 shows the balance sheet and income statement for the foreign subsidiary at the beginning and end of the year and the effect of the method of translation.

Taking the balance sheet first, the 12/31/x1 date serves as a base, and the dollar statement in column 3 is simply the liso amounts shown in column 1 divided by the exchange rate of 8 lisos to the dollar. For the two separate dollar statements at 12/31/x2, shown in the last two columns, we see that cash, receiv-

TABLE 25-1
Foreign Subsidiary
Richmond Precision Instruments

| | IN LISOS | | IN DOLLARS | | |
| | | | | Local Functional Currency | Dollar Functional Currency |
	12/31/x1	12/31/x2	12/31/x1	12/31/x2	12/13/x2
Balance Sheet (in thousands)					
Cash	L 600	L 1,000	$ 75	$ 100	$ 100
Receivables	2,000	2,600	250	260	260
Inventories (FIFO)	4,000	4,500	500	450	500
Current assets	6,600	8,100	825	810	860
Net fixed assets	5,000	4,400	625	440	550
Total	L11,600	L12,500	$1,450	$1,250	$1,410
Current liabilities	L 3,000	L 3,300	$ 375	$ 330	$ 330
Long-term debt	2,000	1,600	250	160	160
Common stock	600	600	75	75	75
Retained earnings	6,000	7,000	750	861	845
Accumulated translation adjustment				−176	
Total	L11,600	L12,500	$1,450	$1,250	$1,410
Income Statement (in thousands with rounding)					
Sales		L10,000		$1,111	$1,111
Cost of goods sold		4,000		444	500
Depreciation		600		67	75
Expenses		3,500		389	389
Taxes		900		100	100
Operating income		L 1,000		$ 111	$ 47
Translation gain					48
Net income		L 1,000		$ 111	$ 95
Translation adjustment				−176	

ables, current liabilities, and long-term debt are the same for both methods of accounting. These amounts are determined on a current exchange rate basis by dividing the amounts shown in column 2 by the exchange rate at year end of 10 lisos to the dollar. For the local functional currency statement, column 4, inventories and fixed assets are determined in the same manner, that is, by use of the current exchange rate. For the dollar functional currency statement, inventories and fixed assets are valued using historical exchange rates. Because cost of goods sold equals beginning inventory, the ending inventory is purchased throughout the year. Assuming steady purchases, we divide the ending liso amount by the average exchange rate (9 : 1) to obtain $500,000. Using historical exchange rates again, net fixed assets are determined by dividing the liso amount at year end by the earlier 8 lisos to the dollar exchange rate. The common stock account is carried at the base amount under both methods.

Finally, the change in retained earnings is a residual. (We defer until the discussion of the income statement the accumulated translation adjustment item.) Because of the upward adjustment in inventories and fixed assets, total assets are higher with the dollar functional currency (temporal method) than they are with the local functional currency (current method). The opposite would occur in our example if the liso increased in value relative to the dollar. We see that there is substantially more change in total assets when a local functional currency is used than when a dollar functional currency is employed.

The opposite occurs for the income statement. In our example, sales are adjusted by the average exchange rate that prevailed during the year (9 : 1) for both accounting methods. For column 4, local functional currency, all cost and expense items are adjusted by this exchange rate. For the last column, dollar functional currency, cost of goods sold, and depreciation are translated at historical exchange rates (8 : 1), whereas the other items are translated at the current average rate (9 : 1). We see that operating income and net income are larger when the local functional currency is used than when the functional currency is the dollar. For the latter method, the translation gain is factored in, so that net income agrees with the change in retained earnings from 12/31/x1 to 12/31/x2. We see that this change is $845 − $750 = $95. In contrast, when the functional currency is local, the translation adjustment occurs after the net income figure of $111. The adjustment is that amount, −$176, that, together with net income, brings the liability and net-worth part of the balance sheet into balance. This amount then is added to the sum of past translation adjustments to obtain the new accumulated translation adjustment figure that appears on the balance sheet. As we assume past adjustments total zero, this item becomes −$176.

Thus, the translation adjustments for the two methods are in opposite directions. Should the liso increase in value relative to the dollar, the effect would be the reverse of that illustrated; operating income would be higher if the functional currency were the dollar.

Implications

Because translation gains or losses are not reflected directly on the income statement, reported operating income tends to fluctuate less when the functional currency is local than when it is the dollar. However, the variability of balance sheet items is increased, owing to the translation of all items by the current **exchange rate.** Because many corporate executives are concerned with accounting income, FASB No. 52 is popular, as long as a subsidiary qualifies for a local functional currency. However, this accounting method also has its drawbacks. For one thing, it distorts the balance sheet and the historical cost numbers. Moreover, it may cause return on asset calculations and other measures of return to be meaningless. It is simply inconsistent with the nature of other accounting rules, which are based on historical costs. Most financial ratios are affected by the functional currency employed, so the financial analyst must be careful when foreign subsidiaries account for a sizable portion of a company's operations.[3] The method also has been criticized for not allowing proper assessment of the parent's likely future cash flows. In summary, there is not a universally satisfactory way to treat foreign currency translation, and the accounting profession continues to struggle with the issue.

> **Exchange rate.** The number of units of a foreign currency that may be purchased with one unit of another currency.

CURRENCY EXPOSURE MANAGEMENT

An exchange rate represents the number of units of the currency of one country that can be exchanged for another. The currencies of the major countries are traded in an active market, where rates are determined by the forces of supply and demand. The market itself is known as the *spot market,* as currencies are traded currently or on the spot.

Foreign exchange risk is the risk that the currency of a country in which a U.S. firm does business will decline in value relative to the dollar or that its convertibility into dollars will be restricted. (If the dollar declines in value relative to the currency in question, this works to the advantage of the company.) When a currency declines in value relative to the dollar, the U.S. company suffers a loss on the currency and on the assets payable in currency it holds. Say that the British pound is worth $1.60. If XYZ Multinational Company held currency and receivables amounting to 500,000 pounds, and the pound dropped in value by 10 percent, XYZ would suffer a loss in dollar terms of $80,000. Thus, a significant drop in price of a currency can be very costly to the multinational company. Another risk is that a country may block its currency so that it cannot be converted into other currencies.

Protecting Against Fluctuations

The exchange-risk exposure of a company is not confined to monetary assets. It encompasses all factors that give rise to the foreign operation's cash flows. When a devaluation or sharp drop in currency value occurs, it may affect future sales, costs, and remittances. This effect often influences total value to a greater extent than does the immediate effect on the operation's monetary position. The long-run effects of a currency value change on cash flows and value are difficult to quantify and certainly important, but beyond the scope of this book. We shall

---

[3] See Thomas I. Selling and George H. Sorter, "FASB Statement No. 52 and Its Implications for Financial Statement Analysis," *Financial Analysts Journal,* 39 (May–June 1983), 64–69.

concentrate on the way a change in currency value affects the monetary assets and liabilities of a company.

If a company believes that the currency of a country is going to drop sharply in value, it makes sense to reduce monetary assets in that currency to as low a figure as possible and to borrow extensively in that currency. As we have discussed, the drop in the value of a currency works to the advantage of a net debtor and to the disadvantage of a net creditor. To protect itself against adverse exchange rate fluctuations, a multinational company can hedge its monetary position. By hedging, we mean offsetting monetary assets—such as cash, marketable securities, and receivables—with monetary liabilities, such as payables and loans, of the same amount. If a change in currency value occurs, monetary assets and liabilities will be equally affected, and the company will suffer neither a gain nor a loss. Its net monetary position (assets less liabilities) is zero before and after the change in currency value.

If a company knew a currency were going to fall in value, it would want to do a number of things. First, it should reduce its cash to a minimum by purchasing inventories or other real assets. Moreover, the company should try to avoid extended trade credit. As quick a turnover as possible of receivables into cash is desirable. In contrast, it should try to obtain extended terms on its accounts payable. It may also want to borrow in the local currency to replace advances made by the U.S. parent. The last step will depend on relative interest rates. If the currency were going to appreciate in value, opposite steps should be undertaken. Without knowledge of the future direction of currency value movements, aggressive policies in either direction are inappropriate. Under most circumstances we are unable to predict the future, so the best policy may be one of balancing monetary assets against monetary liabilities in order to neutralize the effect of exchange rate fluctuations.

Forward Exchange Market

In addition to the foregoing, a company can protect itself against exchange rate fluctuations by use of the forward, or futures, market. In this market, one buys a forward contract for the exchange of one currency for another at a specific future date and at a specific **forward exchange rate.** A forward contract is assurance of being able to obtain conversion into the desired currency at a specific exchange ratio.

Forward exchange rate. The rate today for exchanging one foreign currency for another at a specific future date.

The Xicon Electronics Company is hedging through the futures market. It sold equipment to a French customer through its Paris branch for 1 million francs with terms of 90 days. Upon payment, Xicon intends to convert the francs into dollars. The **spot rate** and 90-day future rate of French francs in terms of dollars were the following:

Spot rate. The rate of exchange for the immediate delivery of a foreign currency.

Spot rate	$.168
90-day future	.166

The spot rate is simply the current market-determined exchange rate for French francs. In our example, 1 franc is worth 16.8 cents, and $1 will buy 1.00/.168 = 5.95 francs. A foreign currency sells at a *forward discount* if its forward price is less than its spot price. In our example, the French franc sells at a discount. If the forward price exceeds the spot price, it is said to sell at a *forward premium*. For example, the Swiss franc sells at a forward premium. In other words, Swiss francs buy more dollars for future delivery than they do for present delivery.

If Xicon wishes to avoid foreign exchange risk, it should sell 1 million francs forward 90 days. When it delivers the francs 90 days hence, it will receive $166,000 (1 million francs times the 90-day futures price of $.166). If the spot rate stays at $.168, of course, Xicon would be better off not having sold francs forward. It could sell 1 million francs in the spot market for $168,000. In this sense, Xicon pays $.002 per franc, or $2,000 in total, to ensure its ability to convert French francs to dollars. On an annualized basis, the cost of this protection is

$$\left(\frac{.002}{.168}\right)\left(\frac{360}{90}\right) = 4.76\%$$

For stable pairs of currencies, the discount or premium of the forward rate over the spot rate varies from zero to 3 percent on an annualized basis. For somewhat less stable currencies, the discount or premium will be higher. For an unstable currency, the discount may go as high as 20 percent. Much beyond this point of instability, the forward market for the currency ceases to exist. In summary, the forward exchange market allows a company to ensure against devaluation or market-determined declines in value.

Quotations on selected foreign exchanges at a moment in time are shown in Table 25-2. The spot rates reported in the first column indicate the conversion rate into dollars. What is quoted in the financial press is the interbank or wholesale rate. Retail transactions provide fewer units of the foreign currency per U.S. dollar. Near the top of the table the Austrian schilling is seen to be worth $.08, or $1/.08 = 12.5 schillings to the U.S. dollar. Future rates for 30, 90, and 180 days are shown for the British pound, the Canadian dollar, the French franc, the Japanese yen, the Swiss franc, and the German mark. Note that the first three currencies decline in U.S. dollar value with the length of time in the future, whereas the last three increase in U.S. dollar value. These relationships imply that at that time the market regarded British pounds, Canadian dollars, and French francs as slightly more risky currencies than the U.S. dollar. The yen, Swiss franc, and mark were regarded as less risky. Through the use of the forward market for these currencies, as well as for other currencies not shown here, transactions are undertaken to blunt the effect of foreign exchange fluctuations. However, a transaction cost is involved. If a company has enough transactions, it may not wish to hedge. Instead, it self-insures. By so doing, the law of large numbers ensures that no one loss will be large relatively.

Inflation, Interest Rates, and Exchange Rates

If product and financial markets are efficient internationally, we would expect certain consistent relationships to hold. Over the long run, markets for tradable

TABLE 25-2
Foreign exchange rates, May 18, 1987

	U.S. DOLLARS REQUIRED TO BUY ONE UNIT	UNITS REQUIRED TO BUY ONE U.S. DOLLAR
Australia (dollar)	$ .7225	1.384
Austria (schilling)	.0800	12.50
Brazil (cruzado)	.0321	31.15
Britain (pound)	1.6820	.594
30-day future	1.6804	.595
90-day future	1.6778	.596
180-day future	1.6746	.597
Canada (dollar)	.7455	1.341
30-day future	.7452	1.342
90-day future	.7439	1.344
180-day future	.7418	1.348
France (franc)	.1680	5.953
30-day future	.1678	5.959
90-day future	.1676	5.968
180-day future	.1673	5.977
Hong Kong (dollar)	.1282	7.798
Italy (lira)	.00078	1,282.1
Japan (yen)	.00714	140.15
30-day future	.00716	139.70
90-day future	.00720	138.81
180-day future	.00728	137.41
Mexico (peso)	.00082	1,220.0
Netherlands (guilder)	.4979	2.009
Saudi Arabia (rial)	.2666	3.751
Singapore (dollar)	.4724	2.117
Spain (peseta)	.0080	124.4
Sweden (krona)	.1606	6.223
Switzerland (franc)	.6838	1.463
30-day future	.6863	1.457
90-day future	.6899	1.449
180-day future	.6973	1.434
West Germany (mark)	.5611	1.782
30-day future	.5629	1.777
90-day future	.5664	1.766
180-day future	.5723	1.747

Purchasing power parity. A theorem that states that a basket of goods should sell for the same in two countries, after exchange rates are taken into account.

goods and foreign exchange should move toward **purchasing power parity.** The idea is that a basket of standardized goods should sell at the same price internationally. If it is cheaper to buy wheat from Argentina than it is from a U.S. producer, after transportation costs and after adjusting the Argentine price for the exchange rate, a rational U.S. buyer will purchase Argentine wheat. This action, together with commodity arbitrage, will cause the Argentine wheat price to rise relative to the U.S. price and, perhaps, for the Austral exchange rate to strengthen. The combination of rising Argentine wheat prices and a changing Austral value raises the dollar price of Argentine wheat to the U.S. buyer. Theory would have it that these transactions would continue until the dollar cost of wheat is the same. At that point, there would be purchasing power parity for the U.S. buyer; that is, he or she would be indifferent between U.S. and Argentine wheat. For that matter, an Argentine buyer of wheat also should be indifferent, for purchasing power parity works both ways. Because of frictions, trade barriers, government intervention in the exchange market, and other imperfections, purchasing power parities between various tradable goods generally do not hold in the short run. They are a long-run equilibration phenomenon and they help us to understand the likely direction of change.

As reflected, relative inflation rates have an important effect on exchange rates over the long run. If purchasing power parity were to hold, the change in exchange rates during a period of time would depend on relative changes in prices for that period. From Chapter 3, where we discussed inflation and interest rates, we know that inflation affects nominal interest rates as well. The *Fisher effect* implies that the nominal rate of interest is composed of the real rate plus the rate of inflation expected to prevail over the life of the instrument. While there is disagreement as to the precise relationship between nominal interest rates and inflation, most people feel that the expected inflation for a country has a powerful effect on interest rates in that country.

Interest Rate Parity Theorem.   The interest rate parity theorem states that there is an orderly relationship between forward and spot currency exchange rates and nominal interest rates for two countries. Expressing the relationship between the U.S. dollar ($) and the British pound (£) both now and 90 days in the future, the theorem suggests that

$$\frac{F_£}{S_£} = \frac{1 + r_£}{1 + r_\$}$$

where $F_£$ = current 90-day forward exchange rate in pounds per dollar
   $S_£$ = current spot exchange rate in pounds per dollar
   $r_£$ = nominal interest rate on risk-free 90-day British securities, expressed in terms of the 90-day return
   $r_\$$ = nominal interest rate on risk-free 90-day U.S. securities, expressed in terms of the 90-day return.

If the nominal interest rate in Britain were 10 percent and the nominal U.S. rate 8 percent, these annualized rates would translate into 90-day rates of 2.5 percent and 2 percent, respectively. If the current spot rate were .60 pound per dollar, we would have

$$\frac{F_£}{.60} = \frac{1.025}{1.02}$$

Solving for the implied forward rate, we get

$$1.02F_£ = .615$$

$$F_£ = .603$$

Thus, the implied forward rate is .603 British pound per U.S. dollar. The British pound forward rate is at a discount from the spot rate of .60 pounds to the dollar. That is, a pound is worth less in terms of dollars in the forward market, 1/.603 = $1.658, than it is in the spot market, 1/.60 = $1.667. The discount is (.603 − .60)/.60 = .005. With interest rate parity, the discount must equal the relative difference in interest rates and, indeed, this is the case, for (1.025 − 1.02)/1.02 = .005. If the interest rate in Britain were less than that in the United States, the implied forward rate in our example would be less than the spot rate. In this case, the British pound forward rate would be at a premium above the spot rate. For example, if the U.S. interest rate (annualized) were 10 percent and the British rate 8 percent, the implied 90-day forward rate for British pounds would be

$$\frac{F_£}{.60} = \frac{1.02}{1.025}$$

Solving for $F_£$, we have

$$1.025F_£ = .612$$

$$F_£ = .597$$

Therefore, the forward rate is at a premium in the sense that it is worth more in terms of dollars than in the spot market. If interest rate parity did not occur, presumably arbitragers would be alert to the opportunity for profit.

Does this mean that interest rate parity prevails between all sets of currencies at all times? For European and other currencies where there is largely an absence of imperfections, interest rate parity generally holds within the limits of transaction costs. Where government restrictions on exchange and tax imperfections occur, interest rate parity is not expected. With reasonable adherence to interest rate parity, one is able to determine the cost in dollars of a foreign sale or purchase where a future receipt or payment is involved.

In summary, the forward exchange market permits a multinational company to protect itself against foreign exchange risk. This risk embodies both devaluation, where a sharp decline in value occurs, and downside fluctuations in the spot rate. For this protection there is a cost, determined by the relationship between the forward rate and the future spot rate. Whether or not one wishes to use the forward market depends on one's view of the future and one's risk aversion. The greater the possibility of currency value changes and the greater the risk aversion, the greater the case that can be made for use of the forward market. If others feel the same way, unfortunately, the cost of this insurance will rise.

Foreign Currency Swap

Yet another means for hedging against foreign exchange risk is a swap arrangement, an agreement between two parties to exchange one currency for another at a specific future date and at a specified exchange ratio. In effect, the swap is a simultaneous spot and forward transaction, with the forward transaction reversing the original swap transaction. A U.S. parent company might wish to transfer funds temporarily abroad to a foreign subsidiary with the understanding that the funds would be returned in 120 days. To protect itself against exchange risk, it might enter into a swap arrangement with a private trader, another company, or a bank. This arrangement assures the company that it will be able to get dollars back 120 days hence. The cost of the arrangement is the difference in exchange ratios at the time of the initial swap and at reversion 120 days later. Because the latter exchange ratio is set in advance, the cost can be determined in the same way as the cost of a forward transaction.

Foreign exchange, or Forex, swaps are made available also by foreign governments and central banks in an effort to encourage international trade and investment. When economic conditions are volatile and the currency markets unsettled because of the possibility of devaluation, the government often is the only party that can effectively underwrite exchange risk. From time to time central banks are active in currency swaps as a means for stabilizing their own currencies. These swaps, of course, do not involve companies; they are directly between central banks. They do protect the firm against devaluation, particularly in transactions with countries whose currency is soft and where viable forward exchange markets are lacking.

Parallel Loans

Similar in concept to the swap are parallel loans between two companies. Suppose that a U.S. parent company wishes to lend $100,000 to its French subsidiary for 5 years. At the same time a French company wishes to lend money to its U.S. subsidiary. If the amount and maturity are roughly the same, an investment bank or some other party might bring the two companies together in a parallel loan arrangement. Instead of lending to its French subsidiary, the U.S. company extends a $100,000 5-year loan to the U.S. subsidiary of the French company. Likewise, the French company makes a franc loan of the same dollar equivalent to the French subsidiary of the U.S. company. Parallel loans often are used when there are capital and/or credit restrictions in one or both countries.

To the extent that there are differences in credit risk, the loans may bear different interest rates. Moreover, if one currency is likely to appreciate relative to the other, this too may be reflected in the relative interest rates. Obviously, the interest rate differential, if any, must be agreed to by both parties. If there is an interest rate differential, a forward exchange contract is effectively involved. However, a company may not be able to replicate the transaction in the forward exchange market owing to maturity being too long or to restrictions that preclude a viable forward exchange market. Therefore, parallel loans may serve a very useful role, despite their cost in terms of interest rate and investment banker fees.

The parallel loan, which originated in the 1960s, was the antecedent to much of the interest rate and currency swaps we observe today. While the mechanics of swapping currencies, fixed rate loans, and floating rate loans are involved, they permit flexibility in the shifting of risk that was unknown several decades ago.

Adjustment of Intercompany Accounts

Finally, a company with multiple foreign operations can protect itself against foreign exchange risks by adjusting transfer of funds commitments between countries. You may hold a high position in such a company at a time when you think the German mark will soon be revalued upward, but the French franc will hold steady. Your company has foreign subsidiaries in both countries. The French subsidiary purchases approximately $100,000 of goods each month from the German subsidiary. Normal billing calls for payment 3 months after delivery of the goods. Instead of this arrangement, you instruct the French subsidiary to pay for the goods on delivery, in view of the likely revaluation upward of the German mark.

In addition to these arrangements, the multinational company also can adjust intercompany dividends and royalty payments. Sometimes the currency in which a sale is billed is varied in keeping with anticipated foreign exchange movements. Transfer pricing of components or of finished goods, which are exchanged between the parent and various foreign affiliates, can be varied. (However, the tax authorities in most countries look very closely at transfer prices to ensure that taxes are not being avoided.)

In all of these cases as well as others, intercompany payments are arranged so that they fit into the company's overall management of its currency exposure.

Should Currency Risk Exposure Be Managed?

If international product and financial markets were perfect and complete, of course, it would not be optimal for a company to engage in any of the defensive tactics just considered. The transaction costs of such moves would be a net drain to suppliers of capital. Instantaneous price adjustments to change would occur in both markets, and suppliers of capital would not be concerned with the variability of cash flows and earnings of an individual firm. It is only when we admit to imperfections and incompleteness in such markets that a case can be made for the various hedging strategies discussed.[4] There is evidence that purchasing power parity and interest rate parity do not entirely hold in practice, although they are useful theories about what should occur. Moreover, there are imperfections in foreign debt and equity markets that limit the efficient flow of funds on the basis of overall risk (including exchange risk) and return.

While large companies may engage in self-insurance, based on the notion that changes in exchange rates average out over time with enough commercial transactions, costs of bankruptcy and agency costs make extensive exposure,

---

[4] For an excellent review of the arguments for and against exchange risk management, see Gunter Dufey and S. L. Srinivasulu, "The Case for Corporate Management of Foreign Exchange Risk," *Financial Management*, 12 (Winter 1983), 54–62.

particularly for the smaller firm, unwise. For reasons of imperfections and incompleteness in international product and financial markets, then, most companies manage their currency risk exposure. Certainly a degree of self-insurance occurs, but few companies are willing to risk everything on future exchange rates. Not only is currency exposure management consistent with managerial survival, but it can be defended on the basis of maximizing shareholder wealth. The real issue is not so much whether a company manages currency risk exposure or not, but the degree of management. It may well overemphasize such management in an attempt to ensure managerial survival when shareholders would be better off with a degree of self-insurance.

MULTINATIONAL FINANCING

Another major facet of financial management is raising funds on as favorable terms as possible. In a multinational company, this involves raising funds from either internal or external sources to finance a foreign affiliate. Internal funds are composed of equity investment and loans from the U.S. parent, retained earnings, and depreciation and depletion allowances. Recently, internal sources of funds have accounted for somewhat over 70 percent of the total financing of U.S.-owned foreign affiliates. Of the internal sources, approximately three quarters is composed of retained earnings and depreciation and depletion allowances.

External Financing

Although the major sources of funds for a foreign affiliate are internal, external sources are often used, particularly for temporary requirements. A wide variety of sources of external financing are available to the foreign affiliate. These range from commercial bank loans within the host country to loans from international lending agencies. In this section we consider the chief sources of external financing.

Commercial Bank Loans and Trade Bills.   One of the major sources of financing abroad, commercial banks perform essentially the same financing function as domestic banks—a topic discussed in Chapter 12. One subtle difference is that banking practices in Europe allow longer-term loans than are available in the United States. Another is that loans tend to be on an overdraft basis. That is, a company writes a check that overdraws its account and is charged interest on the overdraft. Many of these banks are known as merchant banks, which simply means that they offer a full menu of financial services to business firms. Corresponding to the growth in multinational companies, international banking operations of U.S. banks have increased. All the principal cities of the free world have branches or offices of a U.S. bank.

In addition to commercial bank loans, discounting trade bills is a common method of short-term financing. Although this method of financing is not used extensively in the United States, it is widely used in Europe to finance both domestic and international trade. More will be said about the instruments involved later in the chapter.

Eurodollar Financing.   A *Eurodollar* is defined as a dollar deposit held in a bank outside the United States. Since the late 1950s an active market has developed for these deposits. Foreign banks and foreign branches of U.S. banks, mostly in Europe, bid actively for Eurodollar deposits, paying interest rates that fluctuate in keeping with supply and demand. The deposits are in large denominations, frequently $100,000 or more, and the banks use them to make dollar loans to quality borrowers. The loans are made at a rate in excess of the deposit rate; the differential varies according to the relative risk of the borrower. All loans are unsecured. Essentially, borrowing and lending Eurodollars is a wholesale operation, with far fewer costs than are usually associated with banking. The market itself is unregulated, so supply and demand forces have free rein. The Eurodollar deposit rate usually is slightly above the rate paid by American banks on large, domestic certificates of deposit of the same maturity.

The Eurodollar market is a major source of short-term financing for the working capital requirements of the multinational company. Many American firms arrange for lines of credit and revolving credits from Eurodollar banks. For the revolving credit arrangement, the firm pays a commitment fee, the same as it does for a domestic revolving credit. In addition, there often is a front-end fee that is expressed as a percentage of the total loan. This one-time load charge might be 1 to 3 percent. The interest rate on loans is based on the Eurodollar deposit rate and bears only an indirect relationship to the prime rate. Typically, rates on loans are quoted in terms of the London interbank offering rate, commonly called LIBOR. The greater the risk, the greater the spread above LIBOR. A prime borrower will pay about one-half percent over LIBOR for an intermediate-term loan. One should realize that LIBOR usually is more volatile than the U.S. prime rate, owing to the sensitive nature of supply and demand for Eurodollar deposits. Consequently, it is more difficult to project the cost of a Eurodollar loan than that of a domestic loan. Nevertheless, no compensating balances are required, thus enhancing the attractiveness of this kind of financing.

We should point out that the Eurodollar market is part of a larger Eurocurrency market where deposit and lending rates are quoted on the stronger currencies of the world. The principles involved in these markets are the same as for the Eurodollar market, so we do not repeat them. The development of Eurocurrency markets has greatly facilitated international borrowing and financial intermediation. In addition to the Eurocurrency markets, the Asiadollar market has developed rapidly during the last decade what with the large trade surpluses of Japan and other Far Eastern countries.

International Bond Financing.   The Eurobond market developed in the late 1960s into a highly regarded source of long-term funds for the multinational company. A **Eurobond** is a long-term security issued by an internationally known borrower in several countries simultaneously. The currencies in which the bonds are denominated usually are actively traded and strong. Most bonds are straight, fixed-income bonds; some are convertible into common stock and

Eurobond. A bond issue that is sold in another country.

others are floating rate bonds. The market for Eurobonds is truly international; investment banking syndicates are composed of bankers from a number of countries, and the securities are placed all over the world. Like Eurocurrency markets, it is free of government regulation. Somewhat over half of its total volume of funds raised is in dollars. Still, its volume is only a fraction of that which occurs in the U.S. bond market.

A Eurobond issue is denominated in a single currency, though it usually is sold to investors in a number of countries. This type of issue should be distinguished from a bond issue floated entirely in a single foreign country. While both issues involve only one currency, the latter is restricted to investors in a single country. Also, Eurobonds are different from bond issues denominated in two or more currencies. For example, some issues allow the bondholder to choose the currency in which payment is to be received prior to each coupon or principal payment. This option typically is confined to two currencies, but it can be more. Finally, bond issues may be initially floated in multiple currencies. Known as a "currency cocktail," the market value of a bond is likely to be less volatile than is that of a bond denominated in a single currency. We see, then, that a variety of bond financing is possible.

FINANCING INTERNATIONAL TRADE

Foreign trade differs from domestic trade with respect to the instruments and documents employed. Most domestic sales are an open-account credit; the customer is billed and has so many days to pay. In international trade, sellers are seldom able to obtain as accurate or as thorough credit information on potential buyers as they are in domestic sales. Communication is more cumbersome and transportation of the goods slower and less certain. Moreover, the channels for legal settlement in cases of default are more complicated and more costly to pursue. For these reasons, procedures for international trade differ from those for domestic trade. There are three key documents: an order to pay, or draft; a bill of lading, which involves the physical movement of the goods; and a letter of credit, which guarantees the creditworthiness of the buyer. We examine each in turn.

The Trade Draft

The international draft, sometimes called a bill of exchange, is simply a written statement by the exporter ordering the importer to pay a specific amount of money at a specific time. Although the word "order" may seem harsh, it is the customary way of doing business internationally. The draft may be either a *sight draft* or a *time draft*. A sight draft is payable on presentation to the party to whom the draft is addressed. This party is known as the *drawee*. If the drawee, or importer, does not pay the amount specified upon presentation of the draft, he defaults, and redressment is achieved through the letter of credit arrangement (to be discussed later). A time draft is payable so many days after presentation to the drawee.[5] A 90-day time draft indicates that the draft is payable 90 days after sight. An example of a time draft is shown in Fig. 25-2.

Several features should be noted about the draft. First, it is an unconditional order in writing signed by the drawer, the exporter. It specifies an exact amount of money that the drawee, the importer, must pay. Finally, it specifies an exact interval after sight at which time this amount must be paid. Upon presentation of the time draft to the drawee, it is accepted. The *acceptance* can be by either the drawee or a bank. If the drawee accepts the draft, he or she acknowledges in writing on the back of the draft the obligation to pay the amount specified 90 days hence. The draft then is known as a trade acceptance. If a bank accepts the draft, it is known as a bankers' acceptance. The bank accepts responsibility for payment and thereby substitutes its creditworthiness for that of the drawee.

If the bank is large and well known—and most banks accepting drafts are—the instrument becomes highly marketable upon acceptance. As a result, the drawer, or exporter, does not have to hold the draft until the due date; he or she can sell it in the market. In fact, an active market exists for bankers' acceptances of well-known banks. A 90-day draft for $10,000 may be accepted by a well-known bank. Say that 90-day interest rates in the bankers' acceptance market are 8 percent. The drawer then could sell the draft to an investor for $9,800, or $10,000 − [$10,000 × .08(90/360)]. At the end of 90 days, the investor would present the acceptance to the accepting bank for payment and would receive $10,000. Thus, the existence of a strong secondary market for bankers' acceptances has facilitated international trade by providing liquidity to the exporter.

[5] The draft itself can be either "clean" or "documentary." A clean draft is one to which documents of title are not attached. They are attached to a documentary draft and are delivered to the importer at the time the draft is presented. Clean drafts are usually used when there is no trade as such and the drawer is simply collecting a bill. Most drafts are documentary.

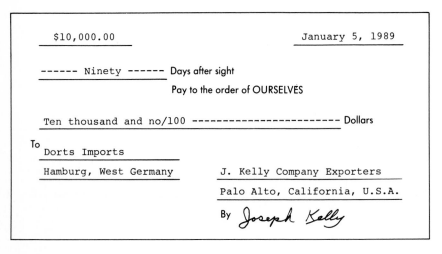

FIGURE 25-2
A time draft

Bills of Lading

A **bill of lading** is a shipping document used in the transportation of goods from the exporter to the importer. It has several functions. First, it serves as a receipt from the transportation company to the exporter, showing that specified goods have been received. Second, it serves as a contract between the transportation company and the exporter to ship the goods and deliver them to a specific party at a specific point of destination. Finally, the bill of lading can serve as a document of title. It gives the holder title to the goods. The importer cannot take title until he receives the bill of lading from the transportation company or its agent. This bill will not be released until the importer satisfies all the conditions of the draft.[6]

> **Bill of lading.** A shipping document indicating the details of the shipment and delivery of goods and their ownership.

The bill of lading accompanies the draft, and the procedures by which the two are handled are well established. Banks and other institutions able to handle these documents efficiently exist in virtually every country. Moreover, the procedures by which goods are transferred internationally are well grounded in international law. These procedures allow an exporter in one country to sell goods to an unknown importer in another and not release possession of the goods until paid, if there is a sight draft, or until the obligation is acknowledged, if there is a time draft.

Letters of Credit

A commercial **letter of credit** is issued by a bank on behalf of the importer. In the document, the bank agrees to honor a draft drawn on the importer, provided the bill of lading and other details are in order. In essence, the bank substitutes its credit for that of the importer. Obviously, the local bank will not issue a letter of credit unless it feels the importer is creditworthy and will pay the draft. The letter of credit arrangement almost eliminates the exporter's risk in selling goods to an unknown importer to another country. An example of a letter of credit form is shown in Fig. 25-3.

> **Letter of credit.** An obligation of a bank to honor drafts drawn on a customer. An extension of credit used mostly in foreign trade.

Illustration of a Confirmed Letter. The arrangement is strengthened further if a bank in the exporter's country *confirms* the letter of credit. A New York exporter wishes to ship goods to a Brazilian importer located in Rio de Janeiro. The importer's bank in Rio regards the importer as a sound credit risk and is willing to issue a letter of credit guaranteeing payment for the goods when they are received. Thus, the Rio bank substitutes its credit for that of the importer. The contract is now between the Rio bank and the beneficiary of the letter of credit, the New York exporter. The exporter may wish to work through her bank, because she has little knowledge of the Rio bank. She asks her New York bank to confirm the Rio bank's letter of credit. If the New York bank is satisfied with the creditworthiness of the Rio bank, it will agree to do so. When it does, it

---

[6] The bill of lading can be negotiable if specified at the time it is made out. It also can be used as collateral for a loan.

IRREVOCABLE
COMMERCIAL
LETTER OF
CREDIT

Since 1852

WELLS FARGO BANK, N.A.

☐ 475 SANSOME STREET, SAN FRANCISCO, CALIFORNIA 94111
☐ 770 WILSHIRE BLVD., LOS ANGELES, CALIFORNIA 90017

INTERNATIONAL DIVISION   COMMERCIAL L/C DEPARTMENT   CABLE ADDRESS: WELLS

OUR LETTER
OF CREDIT NO.   AMOUNT: DATE:
THIS NUMBER MUST BE MENTIONED
ON ALL DRAFTS AND CORRESPONDENCE

SPECIMEN

GENTLEMEN:

BY ORDER OF

AND FOR ACCOUNT OF   S P E C I M E N

WE HEREBY AUTHORIZE YOU TO DRAW ON

UP TO AN AGGREGATE AMOUNT OF

AVAILABLE BY YOUR DRAFTS AT
ACCOMPANIED BY

S P E C I M E N

DRAFTS MUST BE DRAWN AND NEGOTIATED NOT LATER THAN   SPECIMEN
ALL DRAFTS DRAWN UNDER THIS CREDIT MUST BEAR ITS DATE AND NUMBER AND THE AMOUNTS
MUST BE ENDORSED ON THE REVERSE SIDE OF THIS LETTER OF CREDIT BY THE NEGOTIATING BANK.
WE HEREBY AGREE WITH THE DRAWERS, ENDORSERS, AND BONA FIDE HOLDERS OF ALL DRAFTS
DRAWN UNDER AND IN COMPLIANCE WITH THE TERMS OF THIS CREDIT, THAT SUCH DRAFTS WILL
BE DULY HONORED UPON PRESENTATION TO THE DRAWEE.
THIS CREDIT IS SUBJECT TO THE UNIFORM CUSTOMS AND PRACTICE FOR DOCUMENTARY CREDITS
(1974 REVISION), INTERNATIONAL CHAMBER OF COMMERCE PUBLICATION NO. 290.

SPECIMEN
AUTHORIZED SIGNATURE

FIGURE 25-3
Letter of credit form
Source: *Wells Fargo Bank. Reprinted by permission.*

obligates itself to honor drafts drawn in keeping with the letter of credit arrangement.

Thus, when the exporter ships the goods, she draws a draft in accordance with the terms of the letter of credit arrangement. She presents the draft to her New York bank and the bank pays her the amount designated, assuming all the conditions of shipment are met. As a result of this arrangement, the exporter has her money, with no worries about payment. The New York bank then forwards the draft and other documents to the Rio bank. Upon affirming that the goods have been shipped in a proper manner, the Rio bank honors the draft and pays the New York bank. In turn, it goes to the Brazilian importer and collects from him once the goods have arrived in Rio and are delivered.

Facilitation of Trade.   From the description, it is easy to see why the letter of credit facilitates international trade. Rather than extending credit directly to an importer, the exporter relies on one or more banks, and their creditworthiness is substituted for that of the importer. The letter itself can be either *irrevocable* or *revocable,* but drafts drawn under an irrevocable letter must be honored by the issuing bank. This obligation can be neither canceled nor modified without the consent of all parties. On the other hand, a revocable letter of credit can be canceled or amended by the issuing bank. A revocable letter specifies an arrangement for payment but is no guarantee that the draft will be paid. Most letters of credit are irrevocable, and the process described assumes an irrevocable letter.

The three documents described—the draft, the bill of lading, and the letter of credit—are required in most international transactions. Established procedures exist for doing business on this basis. Together, they afford the exporter protection in selling goods to unknown importers in other countries. They also give the importer assurance that the goods will be shipped and delivered in a proper manner. The financial manager should be acquainted with the mechanics of these transactions if the firm is engaged in exporting or importing.

SUMMARY

The multinational corporation, doing business in two or more countries, has become prominent in recent years. As in domestic operations, its financial manager is concerned with allocation of capital to investment projects and raising funds. Foreign investments should be judged on the basis of expected returns and risk, the same as a domestic project. Owing to market segmentation, foreign projects sometimes afford risk-reduction properties that are not available in domestic projects. If capital markets are partially segmented, diversification of stocks internationally may reduce portfolio risk further than can be accomplished through domestic stock diversification.

Expansion abroad is undertaken to go into new markets, acquire less costly production facilities, and secure raw materials. A number of factors make foreign investment different from domestic investment. Taxation is different, risks are present in political conditions, and the accounting treatment of earnings and balance sheet items may differ. Forecasting potential political instability and its effect on expected returns is essential at the time an investment is being considered. FASB No. 52 governs the accounting treatment of a foreign subsidiary, and it allows currency translation losses and gains to be reflected outside the income statement. The result is less fluctuation in accounting income and more fluctuation in balance sheet items than occurs if the temporal method of accounting is used.

Foreign exchange risk is the danger that a foreign currency will decline in value relative to the dollar or its convertibility will be restricted. In its currency exposure management, a company can protect itself against exchange risk by balancing foreign monetary assets and liabilities, by use of the forward exchange market, by engaging in a foreign currency swap arrangement, by parallel loans between two companies in different countries, or by adjusting intercompany account arrangements. A good deal of attention was devoted to illustrating how to hedge in the currency futures market. The exchange rate equilibration process is influenced by two theorems. In the long run, there is a tendency to move toward purchasing power parity, where a standardized good sells at the same price internationally, after adjusting for exchange rates. In turn, relative changes in inflation will strongly influence changes in exchange rates. The interest rate parity theorem implies a consistent relationship between the forward and spot currency exchange rates and relative differences in nominal interest rates for two countries. Both political and foreign exchange risk must be integrated with business risk in judging the overall risk of a foreign investment.

Raising funds abroad is another major function of the financial manager. Although internal financing—composed of equity investments and loans from the parent, retained earnings, and depreciation and depletion allowances—is the chief source of funds, external financing is important as well. The major sources of external funds are commercial banks, discounted trade drafts, Eurodollar and Asiadollar loans, and Eurobonds. Financing international trade differs from financing domestic trade in the procedures employed. The differences in procedures are attributable to the lower quality of credit information, poorer communications, slower transportation, and different legal processes in foreign trade. Three principal documents are involved in international trade. The draft is an order by the exporter to the importer to pay a specified amount of money either upon presentation of the draft or a certain number of days after presentation. A bill of lading is a shipping document that can serve as a receipt, as a shipping contract, and as title to the goods involved. A letter of credit is an agreement by a bank to honor a draft drawn on the importer. It greatly reduces the risk to the exporter and may be confirmed by another bank. These three documents greatly facilitate international trade.

QUESTIONS

1. Is the risk-reward trade-off the same with an international investment as it is with a domestic investment?

2. Why would a company want to enter a joint venture when it loses partial control over its foreign operations?

3. Many countries require that nationals control more than 50 percent of the voting stock in any venture. Is this wise? Explain.

4. Do income taxes paid by a foreign branch work to the detriment of the U.S. parent company?

5. What difference does it make whether the dollar or the local currency is the functional currency when it comes to the accounting treatment of currency translation gains and losses?

6. How does a company protect against exchange rate fluctuations and manage its risk exposure? List the various ways.

7. What are monetary assets? monetary liabilities? With respect to a foreign subsidiary, what if they are mismatched?

8. What is a forward rate discount? a forward rate premium? Illustrate with an example. What is the purpose of forward exchange rate markets?

9. Should not purchasing power parity always hold in international markets?

10. What is meant by interest rate parity? Does it work?

11. Why should a company manage its currency risk exposure? Cannot it "self-insure" at less cost?

12. Explain the function performed by the Eurodollar market.

13. How does a Eurobond differ from a currency option bond and a "currency cocktail"?

14. What are the functions of the bill of lading?

15. In a letter of credit arrangement, who is the borrower? Who is the lender?

16. What is the creditworthiness of a bankers' acceptance? How does it differ from that of the trade draft? What determines the face value of the acceptance?

17. In general, how does financing foreign trade differ from financing domestic trade?

SELF-CORRECTION PROBLEMS

1. The following exchange rates prevail in the foreign currency market:

	U.S. DOLLARS REQUIRED TO BUY ONE UNIT
Spamany (liso)	.100
Britland (ounce)	1.500
Chilaquay (peso)	.015
Trance (franc)	.130
Shopan (ben)	.005

Determine the number of

a. Spamany lisos that can be acquired for $1,000
b. Number of dollars that 30 Britland ounces will buy
c. Chilaquay pesos that $900 will acquire
d. Number of dollars that 100 Trench francs will purchase
e. Shopan ben that $50 will acquire

2. Fog Industries, Inc., has a subsidiary in Lolland where the currency is the guildnote. The exchange rate at the beginning of the year is 3 guildnotes to the dollar; at the end of the year, it is 2.5 guildnotes, as the guildnote strengthens in value. The subsidiary's balance sheets at the two points in time and the income statement for the year are as follows (in thousands):

	IN GUILDNOTES	
	12/31/x1	12/31/x2
Balance Sheet		
Cash	300	400
Receivables	1,800	2,200
Inventories (FIFO)	1,500	2,000
Net fixed assets	2,100	1,800
Total	5,700	6,400
Current liabilities	2,000	1,900
Common stock	600	600
Retained earnings	3,100	3,900
Total	5,700	6,400
Income Statement		
Sales		10,400
Cost of goods sold		6,000
Depreciation		300
Expenses		2,400
Taxes		900
Operating income		800

The historical exchange rate for the fixed assets is 3 guildnotes to the dollar. The historical cost exchange rate for inventories and cost of goods sold, using the dollar as the functional currency, is 2.70. Using the guildnote, it is 2.60 for cost of goods sold purposes. The average exchange rate for the year is 2.75 guildnotes to the dollar, and sales, depreciation, expenses, and taxes paid are steady throughout the year. Also assume no previous translation adjustments. On the basis of this information, determine to the nearest thousand dollars the balance sheet and income statement for 12/31/x2, assuming the functional currency is the guildnote. Assuming that it is the dollar, what are the differences?

3. Four-Forty Athletic Shoe Company sells to a wholesaler in West Germany. The purchase price of the shipment is 50,000 marks with terms of 90 days.

Upon payment, Four-Forty will convert the marks to dollars. The present spot rate for marks in terms of dollars is $.55, whereas the 90-day forward price is $.56.

  a. If Four-Forty were to hedge its foreign exchange risk, what would it do? What are the transactions necessary?

  b. Is the mark at a premium or a discount?

  c. What is the implied interest rate? Will Four-Forty be better or worse off by hedging?

PROBLEMS

1. Table 25-2 shows foreign exchange rates. On the basis of this information, compute to the nearest second decimal the number of

  a. British pounds that can be acquired for $100

  b. Dollars that 50 Dutch guilders will buy

  c. Swedish krona that can be acquired for $40

  d. Dollars that 200 Swiss francs can buy

  e. Italian lira that can be acquired for $10 (to the nearest lira)

  f. Dollars that 1,000 Japanese yen will buy

2. The U.S. Imports Company purchased 100,000 marks' worth of machines from a firm in Dortmund, West Germany. The value of the dollar in terms of the mark has been decreasing. The firm in Dortmund offers 2/10, net 90 terms. The spot rate for the mark is $.55, the 90-day future rate is $.56.

  a. Compute the dollar cost of paying the account within the 10 days.

  b. Compute the dollar cost of buying a future contract to liquidate the account in 90 days.

  c. The differential between part a and part b is the result of the time value of money (the discount for prepayment) and protection from currency value fluctuation. Determine the magnitude of each of these components.

3. In 1977 the Vermont Maple Industries Company obtained a $100,000 loan in Canadian dollars from the Bank of Quebec to finance an exploratory maple sugar farm in Quebec. At the time of the loan the exchange rate was 1.00 U.S. dollars required to buy one Canadian dollar. Ten years later, when the loan was paid, the exchange rate had dropped to .75 U.S. dollars to the Canadian dollar. What gain or loss did the company sustain by virtue of the change in currency value?

4. Wheat sells for $3.50 a bushel in the United States. The price in Canada is Can. $4.45. The exchange rate is .76 Canadian dollars to 1 U.S. dollar. Does purchasing power parity exist? If not, what changes would need to occur for it to exist?

5. Presently, the dollar is worth 140 Japanese yen in the spot market. The interest rate in Japan on 90-day government securities is 4 percent; it is 8 per-

cent in the United States. If the interest rate parity theorem holds, what is the implied 90-day forward exchange rate in yen per dollar? What would be implied if the U.S. interest rate were 6 percent?

6. Cordova Leather Company is in a 38 percent U.S. tax bracket. It has sales branches in Algeria and in Spain, each of which generates earnings of $200,000 before taxes. If the effective income tax rate is 52 percent in Algeria and 35 percent in Spain, what total U.S. and foreign taxes will Cordova pay on the above earnings?

7. McDonnoughs Hamburger Company wishes to lend $500,000 to its Japanese subsidiary. At the same time, Yasufulu Heavy Industries is interested in making a medium-term loan of approximately the same amount to its U.S. subsidiary. The two parties are brought together by an investment bank for the purpose of making parallel loans. McDonnoughs will lend $500,000 to the U.S. subsidiary of Yasufulu for 4 years at 13 percent. Principal and interest are payable only at the end of the fourth year, with interest compounding annually. Yasufulu will lend the Japanese subsidiary of McDonnoughs 70 million yen for 4 years at 10 percent. Again the principal and interest (annual compounding) are payable at the end. The current exchange rate is 140 yen to the dollar. However, the dollar is expected to decline by 5 yen to the dollar per year over the next 4 years.

   a. If these expectations prove to be correct, what will be the dollar equivalent of principal and interest payments to Yasufulu at the end of 4 years?

   b. What total dollars will McDonnoughs receive at the end of 4 years from the payment of principal and interest on its loan by the U.S. subsidiary of Yasufulu?

   c. Which party is better off with the parallel loan arrangement? What would happen if the yen did not change in value?

8. The government of Zwill presently encourages investment in the country. Comstock International Mining Corporation, a U.S. company, is planning to open a new copper mine in Zwill. The front-end investment is expected to be $25 million, after which cash flows are expected to be more than sufficient to cover further capital needs. Preliminary exploration findings suggest that the project is likely to be very profitable, providing an expected internal rate of return of 34 percent, based on business considerations alone.

   The government of Zwill, like that of many countries, is unstable. The management of Comstock, trying to assess this instability and its consequences, forecasts a 10 percent probability that the government will be overthrown and a new government will expropriate the property, with no compensation. The full $25 million would be lost, and the internal rate of return would be −100 percent. There also is a 15 percent probability that the government will be overthrown but that the new government will make a partial payment for the properties; this would result in an internal rate of return of −40 percent. Finally, there is a 15 percent probability that the present government will stay in power, but that it will change its policy on repatriation of profits. More specifically, it will allow the corporation to repatriate its original investment, $25 million, but all other cash flows generated by the project would have to be reinvested in the host country forever. These probabilities still leave a 60 percent chance that a 34 percent internal rate of return will be achieved.

Given these political risks, approximate the likely return to Comstock. Should the mining venture be undertaken?

SOLUTIONS TO SELF-CORRECTION PROBLEMS

1. a. $1,000/.100 = 10,000 lisos
   b. 30 × $1.500 = $45
   c. $900/.015 = 60,000 pesos
   d. 100 × $.13 = $13
   e. $50/.005 = 10,000 ben

2.

	IN DOLLARS 12/31/x2	
	Functional Currency Guildnote	Functional Currency Dollar
Balance Sheet		
Cash	$ 160	$ 160
Receivables	880	880
Inventories	800	741
Net fixed assets	720	600
Total	$2,560	$2,381
Current liabilities	$ 760	$ 760
Common stock	200	200
Retained earnings	1,198	1,412
($1,033 at 12/31/x1)		
Accumulated translation adjustment	402	
Total	$2,560	$2,381
Income Statement		
Sales	$3,782	$3,782
Cost of goods sold	2,308	2,222
Depreciation	109	100
Expenses	873	873
Taxes	327	327
Operating income	$ 165	$ 260
Translation gain		128
Net income	$ 165	$ 388
Translation adjustment	$ 402	

When the guildnote is used as the functional currency, all balance sheet items except common stock and retained earnings are translated at the current exchange rate, 2.50. All income statement items are translated at the average exchange rate for the year, 2.75, except cost of goods sold, which is translated at 2.60. Net income is a residual, after deducting costs and expenses from sales. Retained earnings are net income, $165, plus retained earnings at the beginning of the year, $1,033, to give $1,198. The translation adjustment is that amount necessary to bring about an equality in the two totals on the balance sheet. It is $402. For the dollar as the functional currency, inventories and cost of goods sold are translated at the historical exchange rate of 2.70 and fixed assets and depreciation at the historical exchange rate of 3.00. Other items are translated in the same manner as with the other method. Retained earnings are a balancing factor to bring equality between the balance sheet totals. Operating income is a residual. The translation gain is that amount necessary to make net income equal to the change in retained earnings: $1,421 − $1,033 = $388 − $260 = $128. Depending on the accounting method, income is more variable with the dollar as the functional currency, whereas balance sheet totals are more variable with the guildnote as the functional currency.

3.   a. It would hedge by selling marks forward 90 days. Upon delivery of 50,000 marks in 90 days, it would receive 50,000 × .56 = $28,000. If it were to receive payment today, Four-Forty would receive 50,000 × .55 = $27,500.

    b. The mark is at a premium because its 90-day futures price exceeds the spot price. The implied expectation of the market is that the mark will rise in value relative to the dollar.

    c. $\left(\dfrac{.01}{.55}\right)\left(\dfrac{360}{90}\right) = 7.27$ percent

Due to the expectation of the mark strengthening in value, the implicit interest rate return to Four-Forty is 7.27 percent on an annualized basis. If the mark should fall in value, remain the same, or rise in value up to $.56, the company is better off by hedging. If the mark should rise in value by more than 1 cent, Four-Forty would have been better off by not hedging.

SELECTED REFERENCES

ADLER, MICHAEL, and BERNARD DUMAS, "International Portfolio Choice and Corporation Finance: A Synthesis," *Journal of Finance*, 38 (June 1983), 925–84.

———, "Exposure to Currency Risk: Definition and Measurement," *Financial Management*, 13 (Summer 1984), 41–50.

BALDWIN, CARLISS Y., "Competing for Capital in a Global Environment," *Midland Corporate Finance Journal*, 5 (Spring 1987), 43–64.

BANKER, PRAVIN, "You're the Best Judge of Foreign Risks," *Harvard Business Review*, 61 (March–April 1983), 157–65.

CORNELL, BRADFORD, "Inflation, Relative Price Changes, and Exchange Risk," *Financial Management*, 9 (Autumn 1980), 30–34.

DUFEY, GUNTER, and S. L. SRINIVASULU, "The Case for Corporate Management of Foreign Exchange Risk," *Financial Management*, 12 (Winter 1983), 54–62.

EITEMAN, DAVID K., and ARTHUR I. STONEHILL, *Multinational Business Finance*, 4th ed. Reading, Mass.: Addison-Wesley, 1986.

ERRUNZA, VIHANG R., and LEMMA W. SENBET, "The Effects of International Operations on the Market Value of the Firm: Theory and Evidence," *Journal of Finance*, 36 (May 1981), 401–18.

EUN, CHEOL S. and BRUCE RESNICK, "Estimating the Correlation Structure of International Share Prices," *Journal of Finance*, 39 (December 1984), 1311–24.

FATEMI, ALI M., "Shareholder Benefits from Corporate International Diversification," *Journal of Finance*, 39 (December 1984), 1325–44.

FEIGER, GEORGE, and BERTRAND JACQUILLAT, *International Finance*. Boston: Allyn & Bacon, 1982.

FLOOD, EUGENE, JR., and DONALD R. LESSARD, "On the Measurement of Operating Exposure to Exchange Rates," *Financial Management*, 15 (Spring 1986), 25–36.

GRAUER, ROBERT R., and NILS H. HAKANSSON, "Gains from International Diversification," *Journal of Finance*, 42 (July 1987), 721–39.

LESSARD, DONALD, "International Portfolio Diversification: A Multivariate Analysis for a Group of Latin American Countries," *Journal of Finance*, 28 (June 1973), 619–34.

————, EUGENE FLOOD JR., and JAMES PADDOCK, *International Corporate Finance*, forthcoming.

LEVY, HAIM, and MARSHALL SARNAT, "International Diversification of Investment Portfolios," *American Economic Review*, 60 (September 1970), 668–75.

LIETAER, BERNARD A., *Financial Management of Foreign Exchange: An Operational Technique to Reduce Risk*. Cambridge, Mass.: MIT Press, 1971.

RODRIQUEZ, RITA M., "Corporate Exchange Risk Management: Theme and Aberrations," *Journal of Finance*, 36 (May 1981), 427–38.

————, and E. EUGENE CARTER, *International Financial Management*, 3rd ed. Englewood Cliffs, N.J.: Prentice-Hall, 1984.

SELLING, THOMAS I., and GEORGE H. SORTER, "FASB Statement No. 52 and Its Implications for Financial Statement Analysis," *Financial Analysts Journal*, 39 (May–June 1983), 64–69.

SHAPIRO, ALAN C., "International Capital Budgeting," *Midland Corporate Finance Journal*, 1 (Spring 1983), 26–45.

————, *Multinational Financial Management*, 2nd ed. Boston: Allyn & Bacon, 1986.

SOLNIK, BRUNO, "The International Pricing of Risk: An Empirical Investigation of the World Capital Market Structure," *Journal of Finance*, 29 (May 1974), 365–78.

————, "The Relation Between Stock Prices and Inflationary Expectations: The International Evidence," *Journal of Finance*, 38 (March 1983), 25–48.

STONEHILL, ARTHUR I., and DAVID K. EITEMAN, *Finance: An International Perspective*. Homewood, Ill.: Richard D. Irwin, 1987.

STONEHILL, ARTHUR I., and DAVID K. EITEMAN, *Finance: An International Perspective*. Homewood, Ill.: Richard R. Irwin, 1987.

STULZ, RENE M., "A Model of International Asset Pricing," *Journal of Financial Economics*, 10 (December 1981), 923–34.

CHAPTER 26

Finance for the Smaller Company and Start-up

The small business, one of the cornerstones of a competitive economy, far out-numbers the large business and often provides more fertile ground for creativity and entrepreneurship. Because new entry into a market is possible, small businesses spring up all the time, keeping the competitive environment lively, a phenomenon that leads to productivity gains and real economic growth. Most of the principles taken up earlier in the book apply to firms of varying size. All companies allocate funds to assets, and they raise funds. The difference is in emphasis. The small firm faces different problems than the large one does, and it has more limited access to financial markets. But it also has connections with certain institutions, such as the Small Business Administration. The focus of this chapter is on the specific aspects that make financial management in the smaller company different from that in the large one.

CHARACTERISTICS OF THE SMALL FIRM

There is no generally accepted definition of what constitutes smallness in a firm. Usually one mentions sales, assets, or number of employees. Frequently, firms with less than $5 million in sales, less than $2 million in assets, and fewer than 200 employees are classified as small. The limits are arbitrary and may be adjusted up or, more likely, down, depending on the situation. Nonetheless, they give the reader some idea of what constitutes smallness.

The Growth-Oriented Smaller Firm

A new venture in a growth segment of the economy is a different genre from the more traditional small business that will always remain small. A high-technology company may start out small but grow into a larger company, particularly in the electronics, computer, and information systems industries.

For the smaller growth firm, the challenge is to manage growth in an efficient manner. Fast growth brings with it the need to hire large numbers of new employees—often to double the number each year or to even grow more rapidly. With the inevitable turnover of employees, this means an even larger number of new hires who must be assimilated into the organization, and new management must be developed. Frequently, entrepreneurs who start a business are technically oriented and not necessarily good managers of increasing numbers of people. Many a growth firm founders because its top people, who have been able to do things themselves when the firm was small, cannot manage others.

The growth-oriented smaller business faces a number of strategic decisions in marketing, new products, production, and a host of other areas. Financing is an ever-present problem. For most smaller, growth-oriented, high-technology companies, growth in assets outpaces growth in retained earnings. Although these companies typically pay no dividends, the percentage buildup in receivables, inventories, and fixed assets usually is much greater than the percentage buildup in retained earnings. Sometimes the problem is alleviated by leasing buildings and equipment and by being labor intensive, instead of capital intensive, in the production process. Even at that, receivables and inventories continue to grow.

Whenever growth in assets outstrips growth in retained earnings, debt increasingly must fill the gap. Debt may take the form of bank loans or increasing reliance on trade payables. Because the firm is small, even though growing, a straight bond issue to the public is out of the question. Consequently, the firm is restricted in its sources of debt funds. With the unbalanced growth mentioned, debt ratios increase, and these ratios ultimately are questioned by lenders. Eventually it becomes necessary either to raise equity capital or to curtail growth. Equity capital often comes from venture capitalists, a topic considered later in the chapter.

Thus, the small, high-technology company faces a number of problems: personnel, marketing, production, and financing. Resolution of the financing problem is instrumental in solving many of the former. Building a company on a proportionally smaller and smaller equity base is precarious. Often the problem is masked by growing profits, but, as long as assets are growing more rapidly, debt ratios deteriorate. The problem often is compounded by using short-term financing—bank loans and payables—to finance long-term funds requirements, that is, permanent buildups in receivables, inventories, and fixed assets. Eventually a day of reckoning must come. It is far better to face the issue of balanced financial growth earlier rather than later.

The risks of starting and nurturing a growth-oriented, high-technology company are many. Usually there is little margin for error. The equity base simply does not provide an adequate cushion. If things go wrong, the smaller company frequently is unable to weather the storm. Although one remedy might be to curtail growth, few entrepreneurs have the temperament to do so. Usually it is forced upon them by outside suppliers of capital, often too late. Thus, there is a higher mortality of small firms than of large ones.

The Traditional Smaller Firm

The traditional smaller company tends to be outside a high-technology industry. It may be a retail store, a franchise outlet, a service company, or a small manufacturing company. Even though the company may be quite successful, it probably always will remain small. This forecast does not denigrate the traditional small business, for such firms are essential to the economy. It simply recognizes the fact that high growth is not an appropriate objective. Usually the traditional small firm is heavily dependent on one or two individuals who own it and are involved in all areas of the enterprise. Indeed, specialization for them is not possible. They are on the firing line all the time, making most of their decisions without elaborate analysis. Their management style is loose and personal; control is informal. They take in stride their day-to-day operations but cannot extricate themselves from these operations for enough time to engage in strategic planning.

Financial management of the small, traditional firm is a good deal different from that of the large firm and even from that of the small, but growth-oriented, high-technology firm. For one thing, the small firm cannot sell common stock.

All equity capital must come from the owners and from earnings retained in the business. The lack of ability to engage in equity financing seriously limits any expansion plans that management might have. The chief sources of financing are trade payables and bank or finance company loans. Often trade credit serves as a cushion to offset unfavorable cash swings. When the small firm is in a temporary cash bind, it leans on the trade by slowing its payments. If it is desperate, it may use accrual financing as well. It may postpone wages and payments on withholding and income taxes. Of course, there frequently are costs to such actions, as discussed in Chapter 9. Moreover, such reliance may mask the fact that the funds requirements of the firm are permanent instead of temporary and should be financed by some other means. Bank and finance company loans usually must be secured, usually by receivables and inventories. Often the owners are required to guarantee the loan, to put all their personal wealth at stake and compound their risk.

Any intermediate- or long-term debt also must be secured. Equipment may be purchased on a conditional sales contract or through a secured loan, or it is often leased. If the firm owns its building, it may use a mortgage loan, but the small business usually enters into short-term debt.

Table 26-1 illustrates some financial differences between a small and a large firm. It compares the average balance sheet percentages and financial ratios for two sizes of a machine tool company. These data were compiled by Robert Morris Associates. The smaller firm has a greater need to hold cash than does the larger one, owing to economies of scale in liquidity management. Also, it has far lower inventories, which may be due to differences in the nature of the business. The inventory turnover ratio is much more than that for larger firms, which may support the idea of differences in the nature of the business. With respect to financing, the smaller business uses more debt and less equity than does the larger business. This relationship may reflect the difficulties of raising equity capital. Also, profitability on sales is less. The other numbers speak for themselves. Thus, the most noticeable differences between the two size categories is the much heavier reliance of the smaller firm on debt financing and the lower level of inventory and higher turnover.

The typical small business is greatly involved, perhaps overly involved, in managing working capital. Because many small businesses are thinly capitalized, management worries a lot about liquidity. Planning cash flows is critical. Receivables must be watched closely, and late payers hounded. So as not to tie up funds unnecessarily, inventories must be managed efficiently. When either receivables or inventories are mismanaged, financial problems typically arise. As mentioned before, current liability management also is important. Many a small business must delay payments to suppliers and sometimes even to employees in order to weather what is hoped to be only a temporary downturn. Some small businesses are franchises, such as fast-food outlets and muffler shops, and they usually lease their buildings. Their managements' principal concerns are sales, inventory management, expense control, and planning ahead to pay bills.

In summary, the small business has somewhat different characteristics from those of the large business. Typically, it must rely on internal financing. A great deal of attention should, and indeed must, be paid to working capital management. Continual effort must be devoted simply to remaining solvent. Deci-

TABLE 26-1
Comparison of balance sheet percentages and
financial ratios for small and larger manufacturers
of machine tools and metalworking equipment

	ASSET SIZE	
	Under $1 Million	$10 Million to $50 Million
Cash	8.1%	4.8%
Receivables	29.9	20.3
Inventories	19.0	36.8
Other current assets	1.9	4.1
Net fixed assets	34.1	28.0
Other noncurrent assets	7.0	6.0
Total assets	100.0%	100.0%
Notes payable	10.0%	13.0%
Accounts payable	14.9	11.1
Accruals	6.4	2.8
Other current liabilities	10.1	10.4
Long-term debt	21.8	17.5
Net worth	36.8	45.2
Total liabilities and net worth	100.0%	100.0%
Current ratio	1.5	2.0
Quick ratio	1.0	.7
Average collection period	47	54
Inventory turnover	9.0	2.4
Debt/net worth	1.6	1.0
Before-tax profit margin	2.3%	3.3%

sion making is concentrated in one or at most only a few individuals. Management is spread thin over all facets of the enterprise, so long-range planning receives little attention. The principles taken up in previous chapters apply to the small business as they do to any business, but the relative emphasis is different.

SPECIAL FINANCING OPPORTUNITIES

We have discussed the differences in financing the small versus the large firm. Previous chapters involving trade and accrual financing, secured short-term lending arrangements, equipment financing, and lease financing (Chapters 11, 12, and 20) are particularly germane; however, certain special financing arrangements are applicable to the small business. These include Small Business Administration loans, venture capital, and special Securities and Exchange Commission rulings involving small public offerings. The last two are more applicable to the growth-oriented, high-technology firm than they are to the more traditional small business. The purpose of this section is to explore these special arrangements.

Small Business Administration Loans

The Small Business Act gives the Small Business Administration, an agency of the federal government, the authority to make loans to small businesses when they are unable to obtain funds elsewhere. The definition of a small business depends on its sales in relation to those of the industry and on the number of employees. Any manufacturing firm with less than 250 employees is eligible for an SBA loan. (In some cases, 1,000 employees is the limit.) The SBA seeks to make sound business loans to creditworthy borrowers, as private lenders do. It thoroughly analyzes every application before it decides whether or not to make a loan. The maximum loan is $350,000.

When possible, the SBA prefers to participate with a private lending institution in extending credit. In fact, it can make direct loans only when borrowing from other sources is not available on reasonable terms. The participation by the SBA may be up to 90 percent of the loan, the balance being provided by the private lender. This participation does not necessarily have to consist of a loan from the SBA. The SBA may, instead, guarantee payment of up to 90 percent of a loan by a private investor. In recent years, participation loans have been stressed and have tended to dominate direct lending.

Venture Capital

Venture capital represents funds invested in a new enterprise. Debt funds sometimes are provided, but, for the most part, common stock is involved. Almost always this stock is not registered for a period of years. Known as **letter stock,** it cannot be sold until the issue is registered; therefore investors have no liquidity for a period of time. Their hope is that the company will thrive and that after 5 years or so it will be large and profitable enough to sell its stock in the public market. In turn, venture capitalists hope to sell their stock for many times what they paid for it. This is one scenario. Others, unfortunately, are possible. The risks associated with a new venture are many, and the frequency of failure is significant. With failure, the investor loses everything. The probability distribution of possible returns for most venture capital portfolio investments is highly skewed to the right. That is, there is a significant chance that the investors will lose all their investment, but there also is some probability that their investment will increase in value ten- or even fiftyfold. The overall portfolio return to the venture capitalist is very sensitive to those few investments that do very well, perhaps 1 or 2 in 10.[1]

In general, the relative availability of venture capital is tied to the tone of the stock market. When the market is buoyant and price/earnings ratios are high, venture capitalists are interested in making investments. The reason is that they can look to a viable and active stock market for ultimate payout. One could argue that it is not the present tone of the market but the expected tone several years hence that is decisive. However, expectations of future market conditions

> **Venture capital.** The financing of a new venture either with stock or with securities convertible into stock or having options.
>
> **Letter stock.** Privately placed common stock that cannot be immediately sold. May be sold only when registered with the Securities and Exchange Commission.

---

[1] This phenomenon is confirmed by an excellent survey: Blaine Huntsman and James P. Hoban, Jr., "Investment in New Enterprise: Some Empirical Observations on Risk, Return, and Market Structure," *Financial Management,* 9 (Summer 1980), 44–51.

are influenced by present market conditions. On the other hand, when the stock market is in the doldrums, venture capital funds tend to be less available. So far in the 1980s, the venture capital market has been robust, with considerable competition among venture capitalists to finance the "good idea."

New venture proposals in the high-technology area are more attractive to venture capitalists than new ventures in a mundane industry. The reason is simple. In high technology, there is the perceived possibility of substantial growth and ultimate capital gains. Thus there are a number of venture capital firms in the greater Boston and San Francisco areas, owing to the hotbed of electronic activities in these areas. In addition, there are a number of venture capitalists in New York, Chicago, and Dallas. Perhaps the most prominent venture capitalist in the post–World War II era was Laurence Rockefeller, who was actively involved in a number of young and ultimately successful companies. For the company engaged in operations not deemed to be "high-tech," it is very difficult to convince venture capitalists of the merits of its case. The potential for growth and payout are not sufficiently large.

The sources of venture capital are several. Wealthy individuals, the traditional source, are still important but no longer dominant. Individuals make venture capital investments directly or indirectly. In a direct investment, the individual or partnership of individuals screens applicants, investigates the investment, and reaches a decision. With an indirect approach, the first step is undertaken by a venture capitalist who presents situations and a certain amount of analysis to the investor. In another variation, the venture capitalist will form a partnership and seek capital in advance from investors. The venture capitalist then will develop venture situations in which to invest. As general partner, the venture capitalist receives 20 to 25 percent of the profits of the overall partnership, known as carried interest, together with a small annual fee to cover costs, say, 2 percent.

In addition to individuals, investors include institutional investors such as pension funds, trusts, university endowments, and life insurance companies. The intent is to invest a certain portion of the overall portfolio, usually less than 10 percent, in new ventures. Some of these investors have local offices in areas of the country where high-technology companies are prevalent. The interest of banks in venture capital increased with the advent of the bank holding company concept, whereby a number of nonbank financial services were placed under the holding company umbrella.

The Small Business Investment Company (SBIC) particularly in the past was an important source of venture capital. The Small Business Investment Act of 1958 enabled the Small Business Administration to license SBICs and to provide them with a degree of financing. The SBIC is privately owned and must have at least $150,000 in equity capital. Its investments consist mainly of convertible and debt instruments with warrants attached. In other words, they obtain an indirect equity position in the companies they finance. The SBIC may obtain financing from the Small Business Administration as well as from outside sources. In a number of instances, banks have established SBICs to engage in venture capital investing.

The enterprise seeking financing must convince any of the various sources that sizable returns will offset the substantial risks involved. That may be hard to do, so venture capital is not available to all new companies, but it gives some of them their start.

Public Offerings

For the smaller, private company having its first public stock offering, the change in atmosphere is pronounced. Quarterly financial statements are necessary, and information about the company must be released to outsiders on a timely basis. Management's perquisites must be monitored. Whereas the private owner may have felt a company plane was justified, such justification may erode when the firm becomes a public company. Even though the founders may still hold controlling interest in a company, they must consider how their actions affect outside stockholders. When a firm goes public, there is a great concern with quarterly earnings. This preoccupation with short-run profits may be to the detriment of profitability over the longer run. Certain long-term investments and research and development may be curtailed in the pursuit of short-term profits. Another factor is the board of directors. In a public company, it usually includes some outsiders, people not formally affiliated with the company. All of these aspects significantly change the atmosphere as a firm goes from a private company to a public one.

The procedures involved in a public offering of bonds or stock were described in Chapter 19; however, the Securities and Exchange Commission has special provisions that make it easier for a small company. Under Regulation A, which involves offerings of $1.5 million or less, a company is not required to conform to standard SEC registration procedures. The amount of paperwork is much less, and the preliminary circular may be used as a sales tool for the offering. In contrast, the large company must wait for final clearance of the circular by the SEC. For companies with less than $1 million in assets and fewer than 500 stockholders, the S-18 registration form is substantially easier than the standard form. These procedures and more to come are designed to eliminate some of the red tape for the smaller firm making a public security offering.

Most initial public offerings (IPOs) are through an underwriter. Having no previous public market, there is no stock price benchmark. Consequently, there is more uncertainty than there is when a public company sells additional stock. Empirical studies suggest that, on average, IPOs are sold at a significant discount (over 15 percent) from the prices that prevail in the after-market.[2] For the corporation, the implication is that the initial public stock offering will need to be significantly underpriced from what is believed to be its true value. This is the price of admission to the public market. Subsequent public offerings will not need to be underpriced as much, as a benchmark price will exist and thus less uncertainty.

---

[2] For a synthesis of these studies, see Clifford W. Smith, Jr., "Investment Banking and the Capital Acquisition Process," *Journal of Financial Economics*, 15 (January–February 1986), 19–22.

SUMMARY

A small business may be either a growth-oriented, high-technology company or the more traditional small business that will remain small. The key ingredient in the former is rapid growth, and this growth brings with it problems in personnel management, in strategic decision making, and in financial management. A typical problem is that of the assets of the firm growing at a faster rate than retained earnings, which results in debt ratios being stretched. For most of these firms, the risks are high because there is little liquidity to compensate for error. The owner of the traditional smaller firm, involved in all aspects of the enterprise, has little time for forward planning. In most cases, there is no ability to engage in equity financing and little ability to place long-term debt. Financing usually is confined to trade payables, accruals, and short-term secured financing. The balance sheet percentages for the small and for the large firm are not the same, and these differences were illustrated. The typical small business focuses heavily on working capital management.

Several special financing vehicles are available to the small business. The Small Business Administration makes loans when private lending is not forthcoming, or it will usually participate with a private lender. Venture capital is equity capital invested in a new enterprise. A network of venture capitalists usually invests in high-technology companies. Banks also are a source of venture capital, often through a Small Business Investment Company (SBIC). Public offerings of securities by small businesses have been made easier by the Securities and Exchange Commission's reducing the registration requirements for smaller offerings.

QUESTIONS

1. How would you define a small business? in terms of sales? assets? profits? employees? other?
2. What effect do small businesses have on the economy? Are they essential?
3. Identify some of the problems associated with a new enterprise in a high-technology, fast-growing area.
4. What are some of the repercussions of receivables, inventories, and fixed assets growing at a faster rate than do retained earnings? What are the remedies?
5. Are there dangers to using short-term debt for financing a small but growing company?
6. Identify the characteristics of the traditional smaller business.
7. In the traditional smaller business, with what aspects of finance is management primarily concerned?
8. Under what circumstances might you obtain a Small Business Administra-

tion loan if you run a small business and were unsuccessful in obtaining a bank loan?

9. What does a venture capitalist hope to gain from an investment in a new enterprise? How liquid is the investment?

10. Can any small, new business look to venture capital as a source of financing?

11. Why do the Securities and Exchange Commission and the Small Business Administration, as well as other departments of the government, try to assist small businesses?

12. If you decide to start a retail store or take on a new franchise, how will you finance it?

PROBLEM

Zeus Electronics Company is a new enterprise formed to exploit a technological innovation. It is to be capitalized with $6 million in equity, of which venture capitalists are being asked to provide $5.6 million. For this cash investment venture capitalists will receive 70 percent of the common stock, with the management/founders keeping 30 percent. At the end of 6 years, management believes that the equity portion of the company is likely to be worth $50 million. At that time, it envisions an initial public offering where venture capitalists and the management/founders can sell all their stock if they so choose.

For initial public offerings, a discount of 20 percent is believed to be required from the "true" worth of the company. While $50 million is the most likely "true" value of the company's stock 6 years hence, there is a 30 percent probability the company will fail and be worth nothing to stockholders, and a 20 percent probability that its true worth (equity portion) will be worth $80 million.

If the most likely value prevails, what will be the compound annual return on investment to a venture capitalist who decides to sell stock at the end of 6 years? What is the compound expected annual return based on all possibilities?

SELECTED REFERENCES

COOLEY, PHILLIP L., "Managerial Pay and Financial Performances of Small Business," *Journal of Business*, 52 (September 1979), 267–76.

DAY, THEODORE E., HANS R. STOLL, and RICHARD E. WHALEY, *Taxes, Financial Policy and Small Business*. Lexington, Mass.: Lexington Books, 1985.

HUNTSMAN, BLAINE, and JAMES P. HOBAN, JR., "Investment in New Enterprise: Some Empirical Observations on Risk, Return, and Market Structure," *Financial Management*, 9 (Summer 1980), 44–51.

MARTIN, JOHN D., and J. WILLIAM PETTY, "An Analysis of the Performance of Publicly Traded Venture Capital Companies," *Journal of Financial and Quantitative Analysis*, 18 (September 1983), 401–10.

PETTIT, R. RICHARDON, and RONALD F. SINGER, "Small Business Finance: A Research Agenda," *Financial Management*, 14 (Autumn 1985), 47–60.

WALKER, ERNEST E., and WILLIAM J. PETTY II, "Financial Differences Between Large and Small Firms," *Financial Management*, 7 (Winter 1978), 61–74.

CHAPTER 27

Failure and Reorganization

Our analysis throughout most of the book has assumed that the firm is a going concern; nevertheless, we must not lose sight of the fact that some firms fail. Internal management must keep this in mind, and so must a creditor who has large amounts due from a company in financial distress. The word "failure" is vague, partly because there are varying degrees of failure. A company is regarded as technically insolvent if it is unable to meet its current obligations; however, such insolvency may be only temporary and subject to remedy.[1] Technical insolvency, then, denotes only a lack of liquidity. Insolvency in bankruptcy, on the other hand, means that the liabilities of a company exceed its assets; in other words, the net worth of the company is negative. Financial failure includes the entire range of possibilities between these extremes.

The remedies for saving a failing company vary in harshness according to the degree of financial difficulty. If the outlook is sufficiently hopeless, liquidation may be the only feasible alternative. With some hope—and luck—many failing firms can be rehabilitated to the gain of creditors, stockholders, and society. Although the major purpose of a liquidation or rehabilitation is to protect creditors, the interests of the owners also are considered. Still, legal procedures favor creditors. Otherwise, they would hesitate to extend credit, and the allocation of funds in the economy would be less than efficient.

Although the causes of financial difficulty are numerous, many failures are attributable either directly or indirectly to management. Very seldom is one bad decision the cause of the difficulty; usually the cause is a series of errors, and the difficulty evolves gradually. Because the signs of potential distress usually are evident prior to actual failure, a creditor may be able to take corrective action before failure occurs. Many companies can be preserved as going concerns and can make an economic contribution to society. Sometimes the rehabilitation is severe, in keeping with the degree of financial difficulty. Nevertheless, these measures may be necessary if the firm is to obtain a new lease on life. In this chapter we take up the full spectrum of remedies available to a firm in financial distress.

VOLUNTARY SETTLEMENTS

Extensions

An extension involves nothing more than creditors' postponing the maturity of their obligations. In cases of temporary insolvency of a basically sound company, creditors may prefer to work the problem out with the company. By not forcing the issue with legal proceedings, creditors avoid considerable legal expense and the possible shrinkage of value in liquidation. Moreover, they maintain their full claim against the company involved; they do not agree to a partial settlement. The ability of creditors to realize the full value of their claims depends, of course, on the company's improving its operations and its liquidity. In

---

[1] See James E. Walter, "Determination of Technical Insolvency," *Journal of Business*, 30 (January 1957), 30–43.

an extension situation, existing creditors often are unwilling to grant further credit on new sales and insist that current purchases be paid for in cash. Obviously, no one creditor is going to extend an obligation unless others do likewise. Consequently, a creditors' committee is usually formed by the major creditors to negotiate with the company and to formulate a plan mutually satisfactory to all concerned.

No creditor is obligated to go along with the plan. If there are dissenting creditors and they have small amounts owing, they may be paid off in order to avoid legal proceedings. The number of dissenters cannot be too large, for the remaining creditors must, in essence, assume their obligations. Obviously, the remaining creditors do not want to be left holding the bag. If an extension is worked out, the creditors can institute controls over the company to ensure proper management and to increase the probability of speedy recovery. The creditors' ultimate threat is to initiate bankruptcy proceedings against the company and to force it into liquidation. By making an extension, they show an inclination to cooperate with the company.

Composition

A composition involves a pro rata settlement of creditors' claims in cash or in cash and promissory notes. The creditors must agree to accept a partial settlement in discharge of their entire claim. A debtor may propose a settlement of 60 cents on the dollar. If creditors feel that the settlement is more than they could obtain in liquidation after legal expenses, they will probably accept. Even if it is somewhat less, they may still accept, because no company likes to be responsible for forcing another into bankruptcy. The settlement is a friendly one in the sense that legal proceedings are avoided.

As in an extension, all creditors must agree to the settlement. Dissenting creditors must be paid in full, or they can force the company into bankruptcy. They can be considerable nuisances who may all but preclude a voluntary settlement. Overall, voluntary settlements can be advantageous to creditors as well as to the debtors, for they avoid legal expenses and complications.

Liquidation by Voluntary Agreement

In certain circumstances, creditors may feel that the company should not be preserved, because further financial deterioration seems inevitable. When liquidation is the only realistic solution, it can be accomplished either through a private settlement or through bankruptcy proceedings. An orderly private liquidation is likely to be more efficient and may result in a significantly higher settlement. Such a voluntary liquidation is known as an *assignment*. A private settlement can also be through a formal assignment of assets to an appointed trustee. The trustee liquidates the assets and distributes the proceeds to creditors on a pro rata basis. Because the voluntary settlement must be agreed to by all creditors, it usually is restricted to companies with a limited number of creditors and with securities that are not publicly held.

SETTLEMENTS INVOLVING LITIGATION

Legal procedures undertaken in connection with a failing company fall under bankruptcy law provided by the Bankruptcy Reform Act of 1978, as subsequently amended, and the Bankruptcy Act of 1898. The law itself is carried out through bankruptcy courts which exist in every federal judiciary district. Bankruptcy law has many facets, but we are concerned with only two, which pertain to business failure. Chapter 7 of the bankruptcy law deals with liquidation; Chapter 11 deals with the rehabilitation of an enterprise through its reorganization.

In both cases, proceedings begin with the debtor or creditors filing a petition in the bankruptcy court. When the debtor initiates the petition, it is called a voluntary proceeding, whereas if the initiative is taken by creditors, it is said to be involuntary. In voluntary proceedings, merely filing the petition gives the debtor immediate protection from creditors. A stay restrains creditors from collecting their claims or taking actions until the court decides on the merit of the petition. The court can either accept the petition and order relief or dismiss it.

For an involuntary bankruptcy, three or more unsecured creditors with claims totaling $5,000 or more are required. Here the petition must give evidence that the debtor has not paid debts on a timely basis or has assigned possession of most of its property to someone else. The bankruptcy court then must decide whether the involuntary petition has merit. If the decision is negative, the petition is dismissed. Moreover, petitioning creditors sometimes are required to pay the debtor's court costs. (This is designed to protect debtors from nuisance petitions being filed.) If the petition is accepted, the court issues an order of relief pending a more permanent solution. The idea behind this stay of creditor action is to give the debtor breathing space to propose a solution to the problem. In what follows, we observe the solutions of liquidation and the reorganization of an enterprise.

LIQUIDATION IN BANKRUPTCY

Trustee. Acts in behalf of the bondholders or in behalf of the creditors and claimholders in the case of a bankruptcy.

If there is no hope for the successful operation of a company, liquidation is the only feasible alternative. Upon petition of bankruptcy, the debtor obtains temporary relief from creditors until a decision is reached by the bankruptcy court. After issuing the order of relief, the court frequently appoints an interim **trustee** to take over the operation of the company and to call a meeting of creditors. The interim trustee is a "disinterested" private citizen who is appointed from an approved list and who serves until at least the first meeting of creditors. At the meeting, claims are proven and the creditors then may elect a new trustee to replace the interim trustee. Otherwise the interim trustee serves as the regular trustee, continuing to function in that capacity until the case is completed.

The trustee has responsibility for liquidating the property of the company and distributing liquidating dividends to creditors. Creditors with secured claims are entitled to the value of the property on which they hold a valid lien.

Holbrook Leather Company owes Fernandez Machine Company $10,000, and Fernandez has a lien on a machine it previously sold Holbrook. If Holbrook files a Chapter 7 petition, and the machine can be sold for only $6,000, Fernandez's secured claim is $6,000 and its unsecured claim is $4,000. With respect to the latter, Fernandez becomes a general creditor.

In distributing the proceeds of a liquidation to creditors with unsecured claims, the priority of claims must be observed. The order of distribution is as follows:

1. Administrative expenses associated with liquidating the property, including the trustee's fee and attorney fees.
2. Creditor claims that arise in the ordinary course of the debtor's business from the time the case starts to the time a trustee is appointed.
3. Wages of employees earned within 90 days of the bankruptcy petition. These are limited to $2,000 per employee.
4. Claims for contributions to employee benefit plans for services rendered within 120 days of the bankruptcy petition. These claims are limited to $2,000 per employee times the number of employees.
5. Claims of customers who make money deposits for goods or services not provided by the debtor.
6. Income tax claims for 3 tax years prior to the petition, property taxes for 1 year prior to the petition, and all taxes withheld from employees' paychecks.
7. Unsecured claims that are either filed on time or tardily filed if the creditor did not know of the bankruptcy.
8. Unsecured claims filed late by creditors who had knowledge of the bankruptcy.
9. Fines and punitive damages.
10. Interest that accrued to claims after the date of the petition.

Claims in each of these classes must be paid in full before any payment can be made to claims in the next class. If anything is left over after all of these claims are paid in full, liquidating dividends can then be paid to subordinated debt holders, to preferred stockholders, and finally, to common stockholders. It is unlikely, however, that common stockholders will receive any distribution from a liquidation. Special provision is made in the Bankruptcy Act for damage claims by lessors to the debtor. In general, lessors are limited to the greater of 1 year of payments or 15 percent of the total remaining payments, but not to exceed 3 years. (If a company is reorganized, the trustee may assume the lease and is then responsible for future payments on the leased property.)

Upon the payment of all liquidating dividends, the debtor is discharged and relieved of any further claim. The principal objective of bankruptcy proceedings is an orderly liquidation of assets and an equitable, formal distribution to creditors. The disadvantage of these proceedings is that they are slower and usually more expensive than a private liquidation. Some court-appointed officials are inefficient, being more concerned with their remuneration than with the proceeds available to creditors. As a result, a liquidation in bankruptcy may be less efficient than a private liquidation, providing creditors with a lower settlement. When creditors cannot come together in a voluntary manner, however, bankruptcy proceedings are the only recourse.

REORGANIZATION

It may be in the best interests of all concerned to reorganize a company rather than liquidate it. Conceptually, a firm should be reorganized if its economic worth as an operating entity is greater than its liquidation value. It should be liquidated if the converse is true, that is, if it is worth more dead than alive. **Reorganization** is an effort to keep a company alive by changing its capital structure. The rehabilitation involves the reduction of fixed charges by substituting equity and limited-income securities for fixed-income securities.

Reorganization. Recasting of the capital structure of a financially troubled company in order to reduce fixed charges. Claimholders may be given other securities. Occurs under Chapter 11 of the Bankruptcy Act.

Procedures

Reorganizations occur under Chapter 11 of the bankruptcy law and are initiated in the same general manner as liquidation in bankruptcy. Either the debtor or creditors file a petition, and the case begins. The idea in a reorganization is to keep the business going. In most cases, the debtor will continue to run the business, although a trustee can assume operating responsibility of the company. One of the great needs in rehabilitation is interim credit. To provide inducements, Chapter 11 gives postpetition creditors priority over prepetition creditors. If this inducement is not sufficient, the bankruptcy court is empowered to authorize new creditors to obtain a lien on the debtor's property.

If a trustee is not appointed, the debtor has the sole right to draw up a reorganization plan and to file it within 120 days. Otherwise, the trustee has the responsibility of seeing that a plan is filed. It may be drawn up by the trustee, the debtor, the creditors' committee, or individual creditors, and more than one plan can be filed. All reorganization plans must be submitted to creditors and stockholders for approval. The role of the court is to review the information in the plan, to make sure disclosure is full. If the securities of the debtor are publicly held, the Securities and Exchange Commission may want to review the question of disclosure.

In a reorganization, the plan should be *fair, equitable,* and *feasible.* This means that all parties must be treated fairly and equitably and that the plan must be workable with respect to the earning power and financial structure of the reorganized company as well as the ability of the company to obtain trade credit and, perhaps, short-term bank loans. For example, the reorganized company may not have too great an amount of fixed financial charges relative to its expected earning power. If the future earning power of the company is not estimated fairly or if the fixed financial charges are too great, the reorganized company may have little prospect for success. As a result, the plan would not be considered to be fair, equitable, and feasible.

Each class of claimholders must vote on a plan. More than one-half in number and two-thirds in amount of total claims in each class must vote in favor of the plan if it is to be accepted, and *claimholders may accept more than one plan.*

The next step is for the bankruptcy court to hold a confirmation hearing. If claimholders accept more than one plan, the court must choose the best plan. It may also confirm a plan that has been approved by one class but not by every class of claimholder. In all cases, the reorganization plan must meet certain standards if it is to be confirmed by the court. These standards have to do with its being fair, equitable, and feasible. Upon confirmation of a plan by the bankruptcy court, the debtor then must perform according to the terms of the plan. Moreover, all creditors and stockholders, including dissenters, are bound by the plan.

Reorganization Plan

The difficult aspect of a reorganization is the recasting of the company's capital structure to reduce the amount of fixed charges. In formulating a reorganization plan, there are three steps. First, the total valuation of the reorganized company must be determined. This step, perhaps, is the most difficult and the most important. The technique favored by trustees is a capitalization of prospective earnings. If future annual earnings of the reorganized company are expected to be $2 million, and the overall capitalization rate of similar companies averages 10 percent, a total valuation of $20 million would be set for the company. The valuation figure is subject to considerable variation, owing to the difficulty of estimating prospective earnings and determining an appropriate capitalization rate. Thus the valuation figure represents nothing more than a best estimate of potential value. Although the capitalization of prospective earnings is the generally accepted approach of valuing a company in reorganization, the valuation may be adjusted upward if the assets have substantial liquidating value. The common stockholders of the company, of course, would like to see as high a valuation figure as possible. If the valuation figure the trustee proposes is below the liquidating value of the company, common stockholders will argue for liquidation rather than reorganization.

Once a valuation figure has been determined, the next step is to formulate a new capital structure for the company to reduce fixed charges so that there will be an adequate coverage margin. To reduce these charges, the total debt of the firm is scaled down by being partly shifted to income bonds, preferred stock, and common stock. In addition to being scaled down, the terms of the debt may be changed. The maturity of the debt can be extended to reduce the amount of annual sinking-fund obligation. If it appears that the reorganized company will need new financing in the future, the trustee may feel that a more conservative ratio of debt to equity is in order to provide for future financial flexibility.

Once a new capital structure is established, the last step involves the valuation of the old securities and their exchange for new securities. In general, all senior claims on assets must be settled in full before a junior claim can be settled. In the exchange process, bondholders must receive the par value of their bonds in another security before there can be any distribution to preferred stockholders. The total valuation figure arrived at in step 1 sets an upper limit on the amount of securities that can be issued. The existing capital structure of a company undergoing reorganization may be as follows:

Debentures	$ 9 million
Subordinated debentures	3 million
Preferred stock	6 million
Common stock equity (at book value)	10 million
	$28 million

If the total valuation of the reorganized company is to be $20 million, the trustee might establish the following capital structure in step 2:

Debentures	$ 3 million
Income bonds	6 million
Preferred stock	3 million
Common stock	8 million
	$20 million

Having established the "appropriate" capital structure for the reorganized company, the trustee then must allocate the new securities. In this regard, the trustee may propose that the debenture holders exchange their $9 million in debentures for $3 million in new debentures and $6 million in income bonds; that the subordinated debenture holders exchange their $3 million in securities for preferred stock; and that preferred stockholders exchange their securities for $6 million of common stock in the reorganized company. The common stockholders would then be entitled to $2 million in stock in the reorganized company, or 25 percent of the total common stock of the reorganized company. Before, these stockholders held 100 percent of the stock. It is easy to see why common stockholders would like to see as high a valuation figure as possible. To encourage high valuation, they may attempt to discount the troubles of the company as temporary and argue that the earning potential of the company is favorable.

Thus each claim is settled in full before a junior claim is settled. The example above represents a relatively mild reorganization. In a harsh reorganization, debt instruments may be exchanged entirely for common stock in the reorganized company and the old common stock may be eliminated completely. Had the total valuation figure in the example been $12 million, the trustee might have proposed a new capital structure consisting of $3 million in preferred stock and $9 million in common stock. Only the straight and subordinated debenture holders would receive a settlement in this case. The preferred and the common stockholders of the old company would receive nothing.

Absolute priority. In bankruptcy or reorganiation, the rule that a set of claimholders must be paid, or settled, in full before the next, junior, set of claimholders may be paid anything.

These examples show that the common stockholders of a company undergoing reorganization suffer under an **absolute priority** rule, whereby claims must be settled in the order of their legal priority. From their standpoint, they would much prefer to see claims settled on a *relative priority basis*. Under this rule, new securities are allocated on the basis of the relative market prices of the securities. The common stockholders could never obtain senior securities in a reorganization, but they would be entitled to some common stock if their present stock had value. Because the company is not actually being liquidated, common stockholders argue that a rule of relative priority is really the fairest. The Supreme Court decided otherwise when it upheld the absolute priority rule (*Case v. Los Angeles Lumber Products Company*, 1939).

By and large, the principle of absolute priority is used in reorganization cases, although the Bankruptcy Reform Act of 1978 did provide a degree of flexibility shifting modestly in the direction of relative priority. For example, large creditors may want to allow stockholders to receive some stock in the reorganized company for incentive reasons, even though they are not entitled to it. The court may permit this allocation despite the protest of junior creditors. Another example of relative priority occurs when senior claimholders, in order to get junior claimholders to vote for a plan, allow these lesser claimholders partial payment, even though the senior claim is not satisfied in full. A key consideration is whether all classes of claimholders receive securities with a value equal to or greater than the value they would have received if the corporation were liquidated. When this can be demonstrated, strict adherence to the rule of absolute priority no longer is required. However, the deviation from this rule usually is modest.

Purposes Other Than Insolvency

In the 1980s, many people grew concerned with voluntary bankruptcies by corporations not on the verge of insolvency. Continental Airlines declared bankruptcy in 1983, allegedly for the purpose of reducing labor costs through deunionization. Its cash flow was sufficient to sustain operations for a while, although losses were heavy. Similarly, other airlines threatened bankruptcy and reorganization in order, it is alleged, to get labor unions to accept lower wages. Mansville Corporation, a very profitable company, declared bankruptcy for the express purpose of limiting potential asbestos production–related lawsuits. As these voluntary bankruptcy filings are for purposes different from the usual technical insolvency problem, considerable controversy surrounds such use of the bankruptcy laws.

BANKRUPTCY COSTS

In our economic system, the new entry and exit of companies is essential if the economy is to run efficiently. We have discussed the laws and procedures by which a company goes out of business or is reorganized. It would be desirable, of course, for the process to be costless and frictionless. Unfortunately, this is not the case; bankruptcy costs and delays exist, and they must be recognized by suppliers of capital. In previous chapters, the effects of these costs on the important decisions of the firm were examined in a valuation context. In this section, we define more precisely what is meant by bankruptcy costs and look at the limited evidence available on their magnitude.

Types of Costs

The cost of bankruptcy can be thought to be composed of two parts: (1) direct costs, represented by out-of-pocket fees that arise in the course of going through a bankruptcy, and (2) indirect costs, represented by the "shortfall" in value arising from delays and economic inefficiencies in operating a company when it is about to go bankrupt. Included in this part is the liquidation of assets at distress prices below their economic values.

The first facet to bankruptcy costs involves fees and other compensation to third parties. Bankruptcy courts have jurisdiction over both the allowance and magnitude of fees and costs paid in proceedings under the Bankruptcy Act. In general, there is a reluctance to allow fees that are not authorized under the act and that do not benefit the estate. While the idea is to minimize such expenses, there often is a gap between this goal and reality.

A number of different fees are involved in a bankruptcy: filing fees with the court, referee and trustee fees, attorney fees, appraiser fees, accountant fees, auctioneer and liquidator fees, reporting and transcribing fees, and probably others. All of these costs represent a direct cash drain from suppliers of capital.

We saw in Chapter 17 that impending bankruptcy frightens suppliers, customers, and employees, with the result that operations usually are less efficient. This inefficiency works to the detriment of suppliers of capital and, for that matter, of society. If the company is liquidated, it may be reasonable to expect receivables to be liquidated at a value close to their true market value; however, inventories and fixed assets may bring far less. The bankruptcy auction process does not lend itself to the realization of economic values. In a distress sale, a finished good frequently brings only 30 to 70 percent of the wholesale price. Depending on market conditions, a fixed asset may bring even less. While most bankruptcy auctions are honest, the very nature of the process coupled with some shady practices do not favor the seller. The shortfall in the value realized on an asset sold in bankruptcy clearly works to the disadvantage of suppliers of capital.

Empirical Evidence

Unfortunately, the empirical evidence on bankruptcy costs is limited, owing in no small part to the difficulty involved in extracting information from the chaotic records available in the bankruptcy courts. However, in recent years there have been a handful of studies.[2] While the results are rather far ranging in their estimates of bankruptcy costs, we still are able to get some idea as to their dimensions. For direct, out-of-pocket bankruptcy costs, the estimates range from

---

[2] See David T. Stanley and Marjorie Girth, *Bankruptcy: Problem, Process, Reform* (Washington, D.C.: The Brookings Institution, 1971); Jerold Warner, "Bankruptcy Costs: Some Evidence," *Journal of Finance*, 32 (May 1977), 337–47; James S. Ang, Jess H. Chua, and John J. McConnell, "The Administrative Costs of Bankruptcy: A Note," *Journal of Finance*, 37 (March 1982), 219–26; Michelle J. White, "Bankruptcy Costs and the New Bankruptcy Code," *Journal of Finance*, 38 (May 1983), 477–88; Edward I. Altman, "A Further Empirical Investigation of the Bankruptcy Cost Question," *Journal of Finance*, 39 (September 1984), 1067–89; and Robert E. Kalaba, Terence C. Lagetieg, Nima Rasakhoo, and Mark I. Weinstein, "Estimation of Implicit Bankruptcy Costs," *Journal of Finance*, 39 (July 1984), 629–42.

4 percent of value to over 20 percent, depending on the type of company analyzed and other sample characteristics. One would expect that sizable indirect costs would exist, as a result of inefficiencies involved when bankruptcy is pending. The one study of indirect costs suggests that they are larger than direct costs. While the evidence is fragmentary, it seems clear that total bankruptcy costs are not trivial. They may approach 20 percent of value immediately prior to bankruptcy. As taken up elsewhere in the book, these costs represent a dead weight loss to society in general and to suppliers of capital in particular.

SUMMARY

Business failure, encompassing a wide range of financial difficulty, occurs whenever a company is unable to meet its current obligations. The remedies applied to a failing company vary in severity with the degree of financial difficulty. Voluntary settlements are informal and must be agreed to by all creditors and the company itself. The difficulty with a voluntary settlement is in obtaining agreement of all parties concerned. Voluntary settlements include extensions, compositions, a creditors' committee controlling the operations of the company, and a private liquidation.

Legal settlements are effected under Chapters 7 and 11 of the Bankruptcy Reform Act of 1978. Liquidation of a company occurs under Chapter 7. A trustee has the responsibility of liquidating the property of the debtor in an orderly manner. The proceeds of the liquidation must be made to creditors according to a specified priority of claims. The bankruptcy court oversees the process and makes the final discharge of the debtor.

When a company is rehabilitated through a reorganization, it occurs under Chapter 11. In a reorganization, the capital structure of a company is changed to reduce the total amount of fixed charges. The reorganization plan should be fair, equitable, and feasible, as determined by claimholders and the court. For a plan to be accepted, it must be approved by one-half in number and two-thirds in amount of each class of claims. The court must confirm the plan; upon confirmation, it is binding on all creditors and stockholders.

Bankruptcy costs are both direct and indirect. Direct out-of-pocket costs include fees paid to lawyers, accountants, trustees, and others. Indirect costs have to do with economic inefficiencies arising in the course of approaching bankruptcy as well as any shortfall in value of assets that might occur in their liquidation. The empirical evidence on bankruptcy costs is limited. On the basis of available studies, direct and indirect costs of bankruptcy appear sizable. As a result, these costs should be factored into many of the financial decisions discussed earlier in the book.

QUESTIONS

1. Contrast a technically insolvent situation with an insolvency-in-bankruptcy situation.
2. Why are taxes and administrative costs involved in the bankruptcy paid prior to any creditor's claim?

3. It is argued that a small number of bankruptcies is a healthy sign of economic development. Explain.

4. As a creditor, why might you prefer a voluntary liquidation as opposed to a liquidation in bankruptcy? On what does a voluntary liquidation depend?

5. Can you explain why utilities, railroads, and banks are seldom liquidated? Are the risks in these industries less than those in industrial corporations?

6. Before a firm can be reorganized, a valuation must be placed on it. How should this valuation be arrived at? What conceptual problems would you encounter in the process?

7. Contrast an extension and composition with a reorganization of a firm in distress.

8. In an economic sense, when should a firm be reorganized and when should it be liquidated?

9. Contrast absolute and relative priority bases for settling claims.

10. When liquidation of a company is in litigation, do creditors whose claims originated before the trouble began have priority over recent employees and the federal government's claim for income taxes?

11. In a reorganization, what is meant by the plan being fair, equitable, and feasible?

12. What are the costs of bankruptcy? Are these costs of concern to suppliers of capital?

SELF-CORRECTION PROBLEMS

1. Are the following companies technically insolvent (illiquid), insolvent in bankruptcy, or likely to go into bankruptcy in the future? Classify each into the best category.

   a. Company A has current assets of $400,000, net fixed assets of $300,000, current liabilities of $500,000, and long-term debt of $400,000.

   b. Company B has current assets of $1.8 million, net fixed assets of $3.9 million, current liabilities of $1.6 million, and long-term debt of $3.3 million. The company lost money in each of the last 4 years, the last year the loss having risen to $500,000.

   c. Company C has current assets of $600,000, net fixed assets of $1,100,000, current liabilities of $500,000, and long-term debt of $400,000. The company has grown rapidly with most recent profits of $80,000. However, it is overdue in many of its accounts payable, has $50,000 in overdue tax payments, and is 1 week behind in its payroll.

2. Merry Land, an amusement park in Atlanta, has experienced increased difficulty in paying its bills. Although the park has been marginally profitable over the years, the current outlook is not encouraging, as profits during the last 2 years have been negative. The park is located on reasonably valuable real estate and has an overall liquidating value of $5 million.

After much discussion with creditors, management has agreed to a voluntary liquidation. A trustee, who is appointed by the various parties to liquidate the properties, will charge $200,000 for his services. The Merry Land Company owes $300,000 in back property taxes. It has a $2 million mortgage on certain amusement park equipment that can be sold for only $1 million. Creditor claims are as follows:

PARTY	BOOK-VALUE CLAIM
General creditors	$1,750,000
Mortgage bonds	2,000,000
Long-term subordinated debt	1,000,000
Common stock	5,000,000

What amount is each party likely to receive in liquidation?

3. Fascile Fastener Company had the following liabilities and equity position when it filed for bankruptcy under Chapter 11 (in thousands):

Accounts payable	$ 500
Accrued wages	200
Bank loan, 12% rate (secured by receivables)	600
Current liabilities	$1,300
13% first-mortgage bonds	500
15% subordinated debentures	1,700
Total debt	$3,500
Common stock and paid-in capital	500
Retained earnings	420
Total liabilities and equity	$4,420

After straightening out some operating problems, the company is expected to be able to earn $800,000 annually before interest and taxes. Based on other going-concern values, it is felt that the company as a whole is worth five times its EBIT. Court costs associated with the reorganization will total $200,000, and the expected tax rate is 40 percent for the reorganized company. As trustee, suppose that you have the following instruments to use for the long-term capitalization of the company: 13 percent first-mortgage bonds, 15 percent capital notes, 13 percent preferred stock, and common stock.

With the new capitalization, the capital notes should have an overall coverage ratio, after bank loan interest, of four times, and preferred stock should have a coverage ratio after interest and taxes of two times. Moreover, it is felt that common stock equity should equal at least 30 percent of the total assets of the company.

    a. What is the total valuation of the company after reorganization?

    b. If the maximum amounts of debt and preferred stock are employed, what will be the new capital structure and current liabilities of the company?

    c. How should these securities be allocated, assuming a rule of absolute priority?

PROBLEMS

1. The Vent Corporation has been liquidated under Chapter 7 proceedings. The book and liquidation values are as follows:

	BOOK	LIQUIDATION
Cash	$ 700,000	$ 700,000
Accounts receivable	2,000,000	1,600,000
Inventory	3,500,000	2,000,000
Office building	5,000,000	3,000,000
Plant	8,000,000	5,000,000
Equipment	7,000,000	3,000,000
Total	$26,200,000	$15,300,000

The liability and equity accounts at the time of liquidation were as follows:

Accounts payable	$ 2,000,000
Accrued federal taxes	500,000
Accrued local taxes	200,000
Notes payable	1,000,000
Accrued wages	500,000
Total current liabilities	$ 4,200,000
Mortgage on office building	3,000,000
First mortgage on plant	3,000,000
Second mortgage on plant	2,000,000
Subordinated debentures	5,000,000
Total long-term debt	$13,000,000
Preferred stock	5,000,000
Common stock	7,000,000
Retained earnings	(3,000,000)
Total net worth	$ 9,000,000
Total	$26,200,000

    Expenses of liquidation (lawyers' fees, trustee fees, etc.) came to 20 percent of the proceeds. The debentures are subordinated only to the two first-mortgage bonds. All of the accrued wages are less than 3 months old and less than $2,000 per employee. Determine the appropriate distribution of the proceeds of liquidation.

2. The Greenwood Corporation is in Chapter 11. The trustee has estimated that the company can earn $1.5 million before interest and taxes (50 percent) in the future. In the new capitalization, she feels that debentures should bear a coupon of 10 percent and have coverage of 5 times, income bonds (12 percent) should have overall coverage of two times, preferred stock (10 percent) should have after-tax coverage of 3 times, and common stock should be issued on a price/earnings ratio basis of 12 times. Determine the capital structure that conforms to the trustee's criteria.

3. Assume that the Greenwood Corporation (see Problem 3) originally had the following capital structure:

	BOOK VALUE	MARKET VALUE
Senior debentures	$ 6,000,000	$ 5,500,000
Subordinated debentures	7,500,000	6,000,000
Junior subordinated debentures	2,500,000	1,000,000
Preferred stock (par $100)	2,500,000	500,000
Common stock (1,000,000 shares)	−4,500,000	1,000,000
	$14,000,000	$14,000,000

Determine which of the new securities each class of holders of securities would get under an absolute priority rule.

4. Tara Plantation Company has run into financial difficulty and is facing possible reorganization. It currently has the following capital structure (in thousands):

	BOOK VALUE
Long-term bonds	$ 40,000
General unsecured debt	30,000
Preferred stock	10,000
Common stock	20,000
	$100,000

Unfortunately, the trustee under Chapter 11 estimates that Tara has a value of only $75 million as a going concern, not the $100 million shown on the books. The trustee has recommended the following capital structure for the reorganized company (in thousands):

Long-term bonds	$10,000
Unsecured debt	20,000
Preferred stock	5,000
Common stock	40,000
	$75,000

If this plan is accepted by the claimholders and confirmed by the bankruptcy court, what will be the distribution of the new securities to the holders of old claims?

SOLUTIONS TO SELF-CORRECTION PROBLEMS

1. a. Insolvent in bankruptcy. Total debt exceeds total assets.
    b. Approaching bankruptcy. If losses continue, the equity position of $1.8 + $3.9 − $1.6 − $3.3 = $.8 million will be wiped out.
    c. Technically insolvent. The company is unable to pay its bills in a timely fashion. Chances are that the situation can be worked out, perhaps by growing less rapidly.

2. Out of the $5 million, the trustee's fee of $200,000 and the back taxes of $300,000 must first be paid, leaving $4.5 million for distribution to creditors. The mortgage bondholders would receive $1 million from the sale of the mortgaged equipment and become general creditors for the balance owed them of $1 million. However, there are sufficient proceeds to pay all mortgage bondholders and general creditors, but this leaves only $750,000 to pay subordinated debt holders. Stockholders would receive nothing. In summary, the distribution is

	ORIGINAL CLAIM	DISTRIBUTION
Trustee	$ 200,000	$ 200,000
Property taxes	300,000	300,000
General creditors	1,750,000	1,750,000
Mortgage bonds	2,000,000	2,000,000
Long-term subordinated debt	1,000,000	750,000
Common stock	5,000,000	0
	$10,250,000	$5,000,000

3. a. Overall value of company = $800,000 × 5 = $4,000,000. From this amount, court costs of $200,000 must be subtracted to give a total valuation of $3,800,000.
    b. The bank loan and first-mortgage bonds are secured, so they simply will be continued as they are. Given bankruptcy rules, accrued wages must be paid as a priority item. Consequently, they will be carried forward in their entirety. Trade creditors (accounts payable) are general creditors. However, these claims come before the subordinated debentures, preferred stock, and common stock. To obtain future trade credit as an ongoing concern, it is important that these creditors be paid on a

timely basis and that they not receive a lower-priority security. There-fore, their claims will be carried forward in their entirety.

The maximum amount of capital notes that can be issued is

EBIT	$800,000
Less: Bank loan interest	72,000
Adjusted EBIT	$728,000
Divide by coverage ratio	÷ 4
Interest on long-term debt	$182,000
Less: Interest on 13%	
first-mortgage bonds	65,000
Capital note interest	$117,000
Divide by interest rate	÷ .15
Maximum capital notes	$780,000

The maximum amount of preferred stock that can be issued according to the coverage ratio is

EBIT	$ 800,000
Less: Bank loan interest	72,000
Less: Capital note interest	117,000
EBT	$ 611,000
Less: Taxes (40%)	244,400
EAT	$ 366,600
Divide by coverage ratio	÷ 2
Preferred stock dividend	$ 183,300
Divide by preferred rate	÷ .13
Maximum preferred stock	$1,410,000

If these maximum amounts were employed, we would have the following for the reorganized company (in thousands):

Current liabilities	$1,300
13% first-mortgage bonds	500
Capital notes	780
Preferred stock	1,410
	$3,990

As this amount exceeds the total valuation of $3.8 million, it obviously is not feasible. Something must give, and the most likely candidate is preferred stock, owing to preferred dividends coming after taxes. To provide a 30 percent equity base, .3 × $3.8 million = $1,140,000 in common stock is needed. Using preferred stock as the slack variable, we have

Current liabilities	$1,300,000
13% first-mortgage bonds	500,000
Capital notes	780,000
Preferred stock	80,000
Common stock	1,140,000
	$3,800,000

c. Allocation of these securities in keeping with the rules of absolute priority would result in the following:

	OLD CLAIM	NEW POSITION	
Accounts payable	$ 500,000	$ 500,000	same
Accrued wages	200,000	200,000	same
Bank loan	600,000	600,000	same
13% first-mortgage bonds	500,000	500,000	same
15% subordinated debentures	1,700,000	780,000	Capital notes
		80,000	Preferred stock
		840,000	Common stock
Common stock	920,000	300,000	Common stock
	$4,420,000	$3,800,000	

Only the subordinated debenture holders receive securities different from what they previously held. The common stockholders, as residual owners, receive less common stock ownership than they had before.

SELECTED REFERENCES

ALTMAN, EDWARD I., "Financial Ratios, Discriminant Analysis and the Prediction of Corporate Bankruptcy," *Journal of Finance*, 23 (September 1968), 589–609.

——, "Bankruptcy and Reorganization," in *Financial Handbook*, 5th ed., ed. Edward I. Altman. New York: Wiley, 1982.

——, "A Further Empirical Investigation of the Bankruptcy Cost Question," *Journal of Finance*, 39 (September 1984), 629–42.

——, ROBERT G. HALDEMAN, and P. NARAYANAN, "Zeta Analysis: A New Model to Identify Bankruptcy Risk of Corporations," *Journal of Banking and Finance*, 1 (June 1977), 29–54.

ANG, JAMES S., JESS H. CHUA, and JOHN J. MCCONNELL, "The Administrative Costs of Corporate Bankruptcy: A Note," *Journal of Finance*, 37 (March 1982), 219–26.

CHEN, KUNG H., and THOMAS A. SHIMERDA, "An Empirical Analysis of Useful Financial Ratios," *Financial Management*, 10 (Spring 1981), 51–60.

CLARK, TRUMAN A., and MARK I. WEINSTEIN, "The Behavior of the Common Stock of Bankrupt Firms," *Journal of Finance*, 38 (May 1983), 489–504.

COLLINS, ROBERT A., "An Empirical Comparison of Bankruptcy Prediction Models," *Financial Management*, 9 (Summer 1980), 52–57.

EPSTEIN, DAVID G., *Debtor-Creditor Law*, 2nd ed. St. Paul, Minn.: West, 1980.

GRIMMIG, ROBERT J., "Corporate Bankruptcy," *Journal of Commercial Bank Lending*, 63 (November 1981), 2–11.

KALABA, ROBERT E., TERENCE C. LANGETIEG, NIMA RASAKHOO, and MARK I. WEINSTEIN, "Estimation of Implicit Bankruptcy Costs," *Journal of Finance*, 39 (July 1984), 629–42.

SCOTT, JAMES, "The Probability of Bankruptcy," *Journal of Banking and Finance*, 5 (September 1981), 317–44.

VAN HORNE, JAMES C., "Optimal Initiation of Bankruptcy Proceedings by Debt Holders," *Journal of Finance*, 31 (June 1976), 897–910.

WALTER, JAMES E., "Determination of Technical Insolvency," *Journal of Business*, 30 (January 1957), 30–43.

WARNER, JEROLD, "Bankruptcy Costs: Some Evidence," *Journal of Finance*, 32 (May 1977), 337–47.

WHITE, MICHELLE J., "Bankruptcy Costs and the New Bankruptcy Code," *Journal of Finance*, 38 (May 1983), 477–88.

APPENDIX

Present-Value
Tables

TABLE A
Present value of one dollar due at the end of *n* years

N	1%	2%	3%	4%	5%	6%	7%	8%	9%	10%	N
01	.99010	.98039	.97007	.96154	.95238	.94340	.93458	.92593	.91743	.90909	01
02	.98030	.96117	.94260	.92456	.90703	.89000	.87344	.85734	.84168	.82645	02
03	.97059	.94232	.91514	.88900	.86384	.83962	.81630	.79383	.77218	.75131	03
04	.96098	.92385	.88849	.85480	.82270	.79209	.76290	.73503	.70843	.68301	04
05	.95147	.90573	.86261	.82193	.78353	.74726	.71299	.68058	.64993	.62092	05
06	.94204	.88797	.83748	.79031	.74622	.70496	.66634	.60317	.59627	.56447	06
07	.93272	.87056	.81309	.75992	.71068	.66506	.62275	.58349	.54703	.51316	07
08	.92348	.85349	.78941	.73069	.67684	.62741	.58201	.54027	.50187	.46651	08
09	.91434	.83675	.76642	.70259	.64461	.59190	.54393	.50025	.46043	.42410	09
10	.90529	.82035	.74409	.67556	.61391	.55839	.50835	.46319	.42241	.38554	10
11	.89632	.80426	.72242	.64958	.58468	.52679	.47509	.42888	.38753	.35049	11
12	.88745	.78849	.70138	.62460	.55684	.49697	.44401	.39711	.35553	.31863	12
13	.87866	.77303	.68095	.60057	.53032	.46884	.41496	.36770	.32618	.28966	13
14	.86996	.75787	.66112	.57747	.50507	.44230	.38782	.34046	.29925	.26333	14
15	.86135	.74301	.64186	.55526	.48102	.41726	.36245	.31524	.27454	.23939	15
16	.85282	.72845	.62317	.53391	.45811	.39365	.33873	.29189	.25187	.21763	16
17	.84438	.71416	.60502	.51337	.43630	.37136	.31657	.27027	.23107	.19784	17
18	.83602	.70016	.58739	.49363	.41552	.35034	.29586	.25025	.21199	.17986	18
19	.82774	.68643	.57029	.47464	.39573	.33051	.27651	.23171	.19449	.16351	19
20	.81954	.67297	.55367	.45639	.37689	.31180	.25842	.21455	.17843	.14864	20
21	.81143	.65978	.53755	.43883	.35894	.29415	.24151	.19866	.16370	.13513	21
22	.80340	.64684	.52189	.42195	.34185	.27750	.22571	.18394	.15018	.12285	22
23	.79544	.63416	.50669	.40573	.32557	.26180	.21095	.17031	.13778	.11168	23
24	.78757	.62172	.49193	.39012	.31007	.24698	.19715	.15770	.12640	.10153	24
25	.77977	.60953	.47760	.37512	.29530	.23300	.18425	.14602	.11597	.09230	25

TABLE A
Present value of one dollar due at the end of n years

N	11%	12%	13%	14%	15%	16%	17%	18%	19%	20%	N
01	.90090	.89286	.88496	.87719	.86957	.86207	.85470	.84746	.84034	.83333	01
02	.81162	.79719	.78315	.76947	.75614	.74316	.73051	.71818	.70616	.69444	02
03	.73119	.71178	.69305	.67497	.65752	.64066	.62437	.60863	.59342	.57870	03
04	.65873	.63552	.61332	.59208	.57175	.55229	.53365	.51579	.49867	.48225	04
05	.59345	.56743	.54276	.51937	.49718	.47611	.45611	.43711	.41905	.40188	05
06	.53464	.50663	.48032	.45559	.43233	.41044	.38984	.37043	.35214	.33490	06
07	.48166	.45235	.42506	.39964	.37594	.35383	.33320	.31392	.29592	.27908	07
08	.43393	.40388	.37616	.35056	.32690	.30503	.28478	.26604	.24867	.23257	08
09	.39092	.36061	.33288	.30751	.28426	.26295	.24340	.22546	.20897	.19381	09
10	.35218	.32197	.29459	.26974	.24718	.22668	.20804	.19106	.17560	.16151	10
11	.31728	.28748	.26070	.23662	.21494	.19542	.17781	.16192	.14756	.13459	11
12	.28584	.25667	.23071	.20756	.18691	.16846	.15197	.13722	.12400	.11216	12
13	.25751	.22917	.20416	.18207	.16253	.14523	.12989	.11629	.10420	.09346	13
14	.23199	.20462	.18068	.15971	.14133	.12520	.11102	.09855	.08757	.07789	14
15	.20900	.18270	.15989	.14010	.12289	.10793	.09489	.08352	.07359	.06491	15
16	.18829	.16312	.14150	.12289	.10686	.09304	.08110	.07078	.06184	.05409	16
17	.16963	.14564	.12522	.10780	.09293	.08021	.06932	.05998	.05196	.04507	17
18	.15282	.13004	.11081	.09456	.08080	.06914	.05925	.05083	.04367	.03756	18
19	.13768	.11611	.09806	.08295	.07026	.05961	.05064	.04308	.03669	.03130	19
20	.12403	.10367	.08678	.07276	.06110	.05139	.04328	.03651	.03084	.02608	20
21	.11174	.09256	.07680	.06383	.05313	.04430	.03699	.03094	.02591	.02174	21
22	.10067	.08264	.06796	.05599	.04620	.03819	.03162	.02622	.02178	.01811	22
23	.09069	.07379	.06014	.04911	.04017	.03292	.02702	.02222	.01830	.01509	23
24	.08170	.06588	.05322	.04308	.03493	.02838	.02310	.01883	.01538	.01258	24
25	.07361	.05882	.04710	.03779	.03038	.02447	.01974	.01596	.01292	.01048	25

TABLE A
Present value of one dollar due at the end of *n* years

N	21%	22%	23%	24%	25%	26%	27%	28%	29%	30%	N
01	.82645	.81967	.81301	.80645	.80000	.79365	.78740	.78125	.77519	.76923	01
02	.68301	.67186	.66098	.65036	.64000	.62988	.62000	.61035	.60093	.59172	02
03	.56447	.55071	.53738	.52449	.51200	.49991	.48819	.47684	.46583	.45517	03
04	.46651	.45140	.43690	.42297	.40906	.39675	.38440	.37253	.36111	.35013	04
05	.38554	.37000	.35520	.34411	.32768	.31488	.30268	.29104	.27993	.26933	05
06	.31863	.30328	.28878	.27509	.26214	.24991	.23833	.22737	.21700	.20718	06
07	.26333	.24859	.23478	.22184	.20972	.19834	.18766	.17764	.16822	.15937	07
08	.21763	.20376	.19088	.17891	.16777	.15741	.14776	.13878	.13040	.12259	08
09	.17986	.16702	.15519	.14428	.13422	.12493	.11635	.10842	.10109	.09430	09
10	.14864	.13690	.12617	.11635	.10737	.09915	.09161	.08470	.07836	.07254	10
11	.12285	.11221	.10258	.09383	.08590	.07869	.07214	.06617	.06075	.05580	11
12	.10153	.09198	.08339	.07567	.06872	.06245	.05680	.05170	.04709	.04292	12
13	.08391	.07539	.06780	.06103	.05498	.04957	.04472	.04039	.03650	.03302	13
14	.06934	.06180	.05512	.04921	.04398	.03934	.03522	.03155	.02830	.02540	14
15	.05731	.05065	.04481	.03969	.03518	.03122	.02773	.02465	.02194	.01954	15
16	.04736	.04152	.03643	.03201	.02815	.02478	.02183	.01926	.01700	.01503	16
17	.03914	.03403	.02962	.02581	.02252	.01967	.01719	.01505	.01318	.01156	17
18	.03235	.02789	.02408	.02082	.01801	.01561	.01354	.01175	.01022	.00889	18
19	.02673	.02286	.01958	.01679	.01441	.01239	.01066	.00918	.00792	.00684	19
20	.02209	.01874	.01592	.01354	.01153	.00983	.00839	.00717	.00614	.00526	20
21	.01826	.01536	.01294	.01092	.00922	.00780	.00661	.00561	.00476	.00405	21
22	.01509	.01259	.01052	.00880	.00738	.00619	.00520	.00438	.00369	.00311	22
23	.01247	.01032	.00855	.00710	.00590	.00491	.00410	.00342	.00286	.00239	23
24	.01031	.00846	.00695	.00573	.00472	.00390	.00323	.00267	.00222	.00184	24
25	.00852	.00693	.00565	.00462	.00378	.00310	.00254	.00209	.00172	.00142	25

TABLE A
Present value of one dollar due at the end of _n_ years

N	31%	32%	33%	34%	35%	36%	37%	38%	39%	40%	N
01	.76336	.75758	.75188	.74627	.74074	.73529	.72993	.72464	.71942	.71429	01
02	.58272	.57392	.56532	.55692	.54870	.45066	.53279	.52510	.51757	.51020	02
03	.44482	.43479	.42505	.41561	.40644	.39745	.38890	.38051	.37235	.36443	03
04	.33956	.32939	.31959	.31016	.30107	.29231	.28387	.27573	.26788	.26031	04
05	.25920	.24953	.24029	.23146	.22301	.21493	.20720	.19980	.19272	.18593	05
06	.19787	.18904	.18067	.17273	.16520	.15804	.15124	.14479	.13865	.13281	06
07	.15104	.14321	.13584	.12890	.12237	.11621	.11040	.10492	.09975	.09486	07
08	.11530	.10849	.10214	.09620	.09064	.08545	.08058	.07603	.07176	.06776	08
09	.08802	.08219	.07680	.07179	.06714	.06283	.05882	.05509	.05163	.04840	09
10	.06719	.06227	.05774	.05357	.04973	.04620	.04293	.03992	.03714	.03457	10
11	.05129	.04717	.04341	.03998	.03684	.03397	.03134	.02893	.02672	.02469	11
12	.03915	.03574	.03264	.02984	.02729	.02498	.02887	.02096	.01922	.01764	12
13	.02989	.02707	.02454	.02227	.02021	.01837	.01670	.01519	.01383	.01260	13
14	.02281	.02051	.01845	.01662	.01497	.01350	.01219	.01101	.00995	.00900	14
15	.01742	.01554	.01387	.01240	.01109	.00993	.00890	.00789	.00716	.00643	15
16	.01329	.01177	.01043	.00925	.00822	.00730	.00649	.00578	.00515	.00459	16
17	.01015	.00892	.00784	.00691	.00609	.00537	.00474	.00419	.00370	.00328	17
18	.00775	.00676	.00590	.00515	.00451	.00395	.00346	.00304	.00267	.00234	18
19	.00591	.00512	.00443	.00385	.00334	.00290	.00253	.00220	.00192	.00167	19
20	.00451	.00388	.00333	.00287	.00247	.00213	.00184	.00159	.00138	.00120	20
21	.00345	.00294	.00251	.00214	.00183	.00157	.00135	.00115	.00099	.00085	21
22	.00263	.00223	.00188	.00160	.00136	.00115	.00098	.00084	.00071	.00061	22
23	.00201	.00169	.00142	.00119	.00101	.00085	.00072	.00061	.00051	.00044	23
24	.00153	.00128	.00107	.00089	.00074	.00062	.00052	.00044	.00037	.00031	24
25	.00117	.00097	.00080	.00066	.00055	.00046	.00038	.00032	.00027	.00022	25

TABLE B
Present value of one dollar per year, n years at r%

YEAR	1%	2%	3%	4%	5%	6%	7%	8%	9%	10%	YEAR
1	.9901	.9804	.9709	.9615	.9524	.9434	.9346	.9259	.9174	.9091	1
2	1.9704	1.9416	1.9135	1.8861	1.8594	1.8334	1.8080	1.7833	1.7591	1.7355	2
3	2.9410	2.8839	2.8286	2.7751	2.7232	2.6730	2.6243	2.5771	2.5313	2.4868	3
4	3.9020	3.8077	3.7171	3.6299	3.5459	3.4651	3.3872	3.3121	3.2397	3.1699	4
5	4.8535	4.7134	4.5797	4.4518	4.3295	4.2123	4.1002	3.9927	3.8896	3.7908	5
6	5.7955	5.6014	5.4172	5.2421	5.0757	4.9173	4.7665	4.6229	4.4859	4.3553	6
7	6.7282	6.4720	6.2302	6.0020	5.7863	5.5824	5.3893	5.2064	5.0329	4.8684	7
8	7.6517	7.3254	7.0196	6.7327	6.4632	6.2098	5.9713	5.7466	5.5348	5.3349	8
9	8.5661	8.1622	7.7861	7.4353	7.1078	6.8017	6.5152	6.2469	5.9852	5.7590	9
10	9.4714	8.9825	8.5302	8.1109	7.7217	7.3601	7.0236	6.7101	6.4176	6.1446	10
11	10.3677	9.7868	9.2526	8.7604	8.3064	7.8868	7.4987	7.1389	6.8052	6.4951	11
12	11.2552	10.5753	9.9539	9.3850	8.8632	8.3838	7.9427	7.5361	7.1607	6.8137	12
13	12.1338	11.3483	10.6349	9.9856	9.3935	8.8527	8.3576	7.9038	7.4869	7.1034	13
14	13.0038	12.1062	11.2960	10.5631	9.8986	9.2950	8.7454	8.2442	7.7861	7.3667	14
15	13.8651	12.8492	11.9379	11.1183	10.3796	9.7122	9.1079	8.5595	8.0607	7.6061	15
16	14.7180	13.5777	12.5610	11.6522	10.8377	10.1059	9.4466	8.8514	8.3125	7.8237	16
17	15.5624	14.2918	13.1660	12.1656	11.2740	10.4772	9.7632	9.1216	8.5436	8.0215	17
18	16.3984	14.9920	13.7534	12.6592	11.6895	10.8276	10.0591	9.3719	8.7556	8.2014	18
19	17.2261	15.6784	14.3237	13.1339	12.0853	11.1581	10.3356	9.6036	8.9501	8.3649	19
20	18.0457	16.3514	14.8774	13.5903	12.4622	11.4699	10.5940	9.8181	9.1285	8.5136	20
21	18.8571	17.0111	15.4149	14.0291	12.8211	11.7640	10.8355	10.0168	9.2922	8.6487	21
22	19.6605	17.6580	15.9368	14.4511	13.1630	12.0416	11.0612	10.2007	9.4424	8.7715	22
23	20.4559	18.2921	16.4435	14.8568	13.4885	12.3033	11.2722	10.3710	9.5802	8.8832	23
24	21.2435	18.9139	16.9355	15.2469	13.7986	12.5503	11.4693	10.5287	9.7066	8.9847	24
25	22.0233	19.5234	17.4131	15.6220	14.0939	12.7833	11.6536	10.6748	8.8226	9.0770	25

TABLE B
Present value of one dollar per year, *n* years at *r*%

YEAR	11%	12%	13%	14%	15%	16%	17%	18%	19%	20%	YEAR
1	.9009	.8929	.8850	.8772	.8696	.8621	.8547	.8475	.8403	.8333	1
2	1.7125	1.6901	1.6681	1.6467	1.6257	1.6052	1.5852	1.5656	1.5465	1.5278	2
3	2.4437	2.4018	2.3612	2.3216	2.2832	2.2459	2.2096	2.1743	2.1399	2.1065	3
4	3.1024	3.0373	2.9745	2.9137	2.8550	2.7982	2.7432	2.6901	2.6386	2.5887	4
5	3.6959	3.6048	3.5172	3.4331	3.3522	3.2743	3.1993	3.1272	3.0576	2.9906	5
6	4.2305	4.1114	3.9976	3.8887	3.7845	3.6847	3.5892	3.4976	3.4098	3.3255	6
7	4.7122	4.5638	4.4226	4.2883	4.1604	4.0386	3.9224	3.8115	3.7057	3.6046	7
8	5.1461	4.9676	4.7988	4.6389	4.4873	4.3436	4.2072	4.0776	3.9544	3.8372	8
9	5.5370	5.3282	5.1317	4.9464	4.7716	4.6065	4.4506	4.3030	4.1633	4.0310	9
10	5.8892	5.6502	5.4262	5.2161	5.0188	4.8332	4.6586	4.4941	4.3389	4.1925	10
11	6.2065	5.9377	5.6869	5.4527	5.2337	5.0286	4.8364	4.6560	4.4865	4.3271	11
12	6.4924	6.1944	5.9176	5.6603	5.4206	5.1971	4.9884	4.7932	4.6105	4.4392	12
13	6.7499	6.4235	6.1218	5.8424	5.5831	5.3423	5.1183	4.9095	4.7147	4.5327	13
14	6.9819	6.6282	6.3025	6.0021	5.7245	5.4675	5.2293	5.0081	4.8023	4.6106	14
15	7.1909	6.8109	6.4624	6.1422	5.8474	5.5755	5.3242	5.0916	4.8759	4.6755	15
16	7.3792	6.9740	6.6039	6.2651	5.9542	5.6685	5.4053	5.1624	4.9377	4.7296	16
17	7.5488	7.1196	6.7291	6.3729	6.0472	5.7487	5.4746	5.2223	4.9897	4.7746	17
18	7.7016	7.2497	6.8399	6.4674	6.1280	5.8178	5.5339	5.2732	5.0333	4.8122	18
19	7.8393	7.3658	6.9380	6.5504	6.1982	5.8775	5.5845	5.3162	5.0700	4.8435	19
20	7.9633	7.4694	7.0248	6.6231	6.2593	5.9288	5.6278	5.3527	5.1009	4.8696	20
21	8.0751	7.5620	7.1016	6.6870	6.3125	5.9731	5.6648	5.3837	5.1268	4.8913	21
22	8.1757	7.6446	7.1695	6.7429	6.3587	6.0113	5.6964	5.4099	5.1486	4.9094	22
23	8.2664	7.7184	7.2297	6.7921	6.3988	6.0442	5.7234	5.4321	5.1668	4.9245	23
24	8.3481	7.7843	7.2829	6.8351	6.4338	6.0726	5.7465	5.4509	5.1822	4.9371	24
25	8.4217	7.8431	7.3300	6.8729	6.4641	6.0971	5.7662	5.4669	5.1951	4.9476	25

TABLE B
Present value of one dollar per year, *n* years at *r*%

YEAR	21%	22%	23%	24%	25%	26%	27%	28%	29%	30%	YEAR
1	.8264	.8197	.8130	.8065	.8000	.7937	.7874	.7813	.7752	.7692	1
2	1.5095	1.4915	1.4740	1.4568	1.4400	1.4235	1.4074	1.3916	1.3761	1.3609	2
3	2.0739	2.0422	2.0114	1.9813	1.9520	1.9234	1.8956	1.8684	1.8420	1.8161	3
4	2.5404	2.4936	2.4483	2.4043	2.3616	2.3202	2.2800	2.2410	2.2031	2.1662	4
5	2.9260	2.8636	2.8035	2.7454	2.6893	2.6351	2.5827	2.5320	2.4830	2.4356	5
6	3.2446	3.1669	3.0923	3.0205	2.9514	2.8850	2.8210	2.7594	2.7000	2.6427	6
7	3.5079	3.4155	3.3270	3.2423	3.1611	3.0833	3.0087	2.9370	2.8682	2.8021	7
8	3.7256	3.6193	3.5179	3.4212	3.3289	3.2407	3.1564	3.0758	2.9986	2.9247	8
9	3.9054	3.7863	3.6731	3.5655	3.4631	3.3657	3.2728	3.1842	3.0997	3.0190	9
10	4.0541	3.9232	3.7993	3.6819	3.5705	3.4648	3.3644	3.2689	3.1781	3.0915	10
11	4.1769	4.0354	3.9018	3.7757	3.6564	3.5435	3.4365	3.3351	3.2388	3.1473	11
12	4.2785	4.1274	3.9852	3.8514	3.7251	3.6060	3.4933	3.3868	3.2859	3.1903	12
13	4.3624	4.2028	4.0530	3.9124	3.7801	3.6555	3.5381	3.4272	3.3224	3.2233	13
14	4.4317	4.2646	4.1082	3.9616	3.8241	3.6949	3.5733	3.4587	3.3507	3.2487	14
15	4.4890	4.3152	4.1530	4.0013	3.8593	3.7261	3.6010	3.4834	3.3726	3.2682	15
16	4.5364	4.3567	4.1894	4.0333	3.8874	3.7509	3.6228	3.5026	3.3896	3.2832	16
17	4.5755	4.3908	4.2190	4.0591	3.9099	3.7705	3.6400	3.5177	3.4028	3.2948	17
18	4.6079	4.4187	4.2431	4.0799	3.9279	3.7861	3.6536	3.5294	3.4130	3.3037	18
19	4.6346	4.4415	4.2627	4.0967	3.9424	3.7985	3.6642	3.5386	3.4210	3.3105	19
20	4.6567	4.4603	4.2786	4.1103	3.9539	3.8083	3.6726	3.5458	3.4271	3.3158	20
21	4.6750	4.4756	4.2916	4.1212	3.9631	3.8161	3.6792	3.5514	3.4319	3.3198	21
22	4.6900	4.4882	4.3021	4.1300	3.9705	3.8223	3.6844	3.5558	3.4356	3.3230	22
23	4.7025	4.4985	4.3106	4.1371	3.9764	3.8273	3.6885	3.5592	3.4384	3.3254	23
24	4.7128	4.5070	4.3176	4.1428	3.9811	3.8312	3.6918	3.5619	3.4406	3.3272	24
25	4.7213	4.5139	4.3232	4.1474	3.9849	3.8342	3.6943	3.5640	3.4423	3.3286	25

TABLE B
Present value of one dollar per year, n years at r%

YEAR	31%	32%	33%	34%	35%	36%	37%	38%	39%	40%	YEAR
1	.7634	.7576	.7519	.7463	.7407	.7353	.7299	.7246	.7194	.7143	1
2	1.3461	1.3315	1.3172	1.3032	1.2894	1.2760	1.2627	1.2497	1.2370	1.2245	2
3	1.7909	1.7663	1.7423	1.7188	1.6959	1.6735	1.6516	1.6302	1.6093	1.5889	3
4	2.1305	2.0957	2.0618	2.0290	1.9969	1.9658	1.9355	1.9060	1.8772	1.8492	4
5	2.3897	2.3452	2.3021	2.2604	2.2200	2.1807	2.1427	2.1058	2.0699	2.0352	5
6	2.5875	2.5342	2.4828	2.4331	2.3852	2.3388	2.2939	2.2506	2.2086	2.1680	6
7	2.7386	2.6775	2.6187	2.5620	2.5075	2.4550	2.4043	2.3555	2.3083	2.2628	7
8	2.8539	2.7860	2.7208	2.6582	2.5982	2.5404	2.4849	2.4315	2.3801	2.3306	8
9	2.9419	2.8681	2.7976	2.7300	2.6653	2.6033	2.5437	2.4866	2.4317	2.3790	9
10	3.0091	2.9304	2.8553	2.7836	2.7150	2.6495	2.5867	2.5265	2.4689	2.4136	10
11	3.0604	2.9776	2.8987	2.8236	2.7519	2.6834	2.6180	2.5555	2.4956	2.4383	11
12	3.0995	3.0133	2.9314	2.8534	2.7792	2.7084	2.6409	2.5764	2.5148	2.4559	12
13	3.1294	3.0404	2.9559	2.8757	2.7994	2.7268	2.6576	2.5916	2.5286	2.4685	13
14	3.1522	3.0609	2.9744	2.8923	2.8144	2.7403	2.6698	2.6026	2.5386	2.4775	14
15	3.1696	3.0764	2.9883	2.9047	2.8255	2.7502	2.6787	2.6106	2.5457	2.4839	15
16	3.1829	3.0882	2.9987	2.9140	2.8337	2.7575	2.6852	2.6164	2.5509	2.4885	16
17	3.1931	3.9071	3.0065	2.9209	2.8398	2.7629	2.6899	2.6206	2.5546	2.4918	17
18	3.2008	3.1039	3.0124	2.9260	2.8443	2.7668	2.6934	2.6236	2.5573	2.4941	18
19	3.2067	3.1090	3.0169	2.9299	2.8476	2.7697	2.6959	2.6258	2.5592	2.4958	19
20	3.2112	3.1129	3.0202	2.9327	2.8501	2.7718	2.6977	2.6274	2.5606	2.4970	20
21	3.2147	3.1158	3.0227	2.9349	2.8519	2.7734	2.6991	2.6285	2.5616	2.4979	21
22	3.2173	3.1180	3.0246	2.9365	2.8533	2.7746	2.7000	2.6294	2.5623	2.4985	22
23	3.2193	3.1197	3.0260	2.9377	2.8543	2.7754	2.7008	2.6300	2.5628	2.4989	23
24	3.2209	3.1210	3.0271	2.9386	2.8550	2.7760	2.7013	2.6304	2.5632	2.4992	24
25	3.2220	3.1220	3.0279	2.9392	2.8556	2.7765	2.7017	2.6307	2.5634	2.4994	25

Glossary

Absolute priority. In bankruptcy or reorganization, the rule that a set of claimholders must be paid, or settled, in full before the next, junior, set of claimholders may be paid anything.

Accelerated cost recovery system. A system that specifies annual depreciation for various types of assets falling into 3-year, 5-year, 10-year, and 15-year categories. Introduced in the 1981 Tax Act.

Accruals. Amounts owed but not yet paid for wages, taxes, interest, and dividends. A short-term liability.

Accounts payable. Amounts owed to suppliers. A short-term liability.

Accounts receivable. Amounts owed the firm by customers. A current asset.

Acid-test ratio. Ratio of cash, marketable securities, and receivables to current liabilities. Known also as the quick ratio.

Agency costs. The cost of monitoring management so that it and the firm behave in ways consistent with contractual agreements with stockholders and lenders. Example: auditing fees.

Amortization. The installment repayment schedule on a loan necessary to pay it off eventually.

Annuity. A series of equal payments for a specified period of time.

Arbitrage. The sale of an overvalued asset in one market and the purchase of an undervalued like asset in another market to give a riskless profit.

Arbitrage pricing theory. A theory of market equilibrium where the price of an asset depends on multiple factors.

Arrearage. A late or overdue payment, which may be cumulative.

Average collection period. Accounts receivable times days in year divided by annual credit sales.

Balloon payment. When periodic payments on a loan do not retire it, and there is a large balloon payment at the end that retires it.

Bankers' acceptance. A promissory trade note between two parties that is accepted by a bank, thereby guaranteeing it. A money market instrument.

Best efforts offering. A security offering where the investment bank agrees to do its best to sell it. No guarantee of sale as occurs with an underwriting.

Beta. A coefficient measuring the average responsiveness of a stock's return with that of the market. Systematic risk.

Bill of lading. A shipping document indicating the details of the shipment and delivery of goods and their ownership.

Book value. The accounting value of an asset. In the case of common stock, net worth divided by the number of shares.

Bond. A long-term debt instrument.

Break-even analysis. Analysis of the relationship between fixed and variable costs and profits. The break-even point is the sales level where profits are zero.

Business risk. The operating risk of the company due to the business it is in, as distinct from its financial risk.

Call option. An option to buy an asset at a specified price, the exercise price, during a specified period of time.

Call premium. The excess of the call price of a security over its par value.

Call price. The price the company must pay for a security when it wishes to redeem it.

Capital-asset pricing model. A model of market equilibrium, where a security's expected return is the risk-free rate plus a premium based on the risk of the security in a portfolio context.

Capital budgeting. The allocation of capital to long-term capital investments used in the production of a good or service.

Capital rationing. A fixed ceiling on the annual amount of capital expenditures that forces the rationing of capital.

Capital gain. The sales price of an asset less its cost.

Capital structure. The proportion or mix of securities used to finance the firm.

Capitalization. The long-term financing of the firm: debt, preferred stock, and common stock equity.

Capitalization rate. The discount rate used to determine the value of a stream of expected future cash flows.

Cash budgeting. A forecast of the future cash flows of the firm arising from collections and disbursements, usually on a monthly basis.

Certificate of deposit. A time deposit at a bank that earns a stated interest. A money market instrument for large CDs.

Characteristic line. A line that describes the relationship between the variation of returns on a stock and the variation of returns on the market portfolio. The slope of this line is beta.

Chattel mortgage. A lien on property, usually equipment, backing a loan.

Commercial paper. The unsecured, short-term promissory notes of large companies. A money market instrument.

Commitment fee. The fee charged by a lender for making a contractual commitment to lend the company money.

Compound interest. Interest earned on reinvested interest payments.

Concentration banking. A system where customers make payments to regional centers and surplus funds are channeled to a concentration bank.

Conditional sales contract. A means of financing provided by the seller of equipment, who holds title to it until the financing is paid off.

Conglomerate merging. A merger between companies in unrelated lines of business.

Conversion price and ratio. The conversion ratio is the number of shares of stock into which a security may be converted. The conversion price is the face value of the security divided by the conversion ratio.

Convertible security. A bond or a preferred stock that is convertible into a specified number of shares of common stock at the option of the holder.

Correlation coefficient. A measure that describes how closely two variables move together over time.

Cost of capital. The explicit or implied return required on various types of financing. The overall cost of capital is a weighted average of the individual costs.

Coupon rate. The stated rate of interest on an instrument; the annual interest payment divided by the instrument's face value.

Covenant. A restriction on a borrower imposed by a lender, such as the former must maintain a minimum amount of working capital.

Credit period. The length of time over which trade credit is granted. A specified term.

Credit standard. The minimum quality of creditworthiness of a credit applicant that is acceptable to the firm.

Cumulative dividends. A feature that requires that all cumulative unpaid dividends on the preferred be paid before a dividend may be paid on the common stock.

Cumulative voting. A method for electing corporate directors, whereby a shareholder may cast up to the shares held times the number of directors to be elected for a single director.

Current ratio. Current assets divided by current liabilities.

Debenture. An unsecured, long-term debt instrument.

Debt ratio. The amount of debt divided by either the amount of equity or the amount of total assets.

Default. The failure to meet the terms of a contract, such as the failure to make a payment on a loan.

Depository transfer check. A means for transferring money from bank to bank by check.

Depreciation. The annual charge made to earnings to recover the cost of an asset. Deductible for tax purposes.

Dilution. Reduction in value or in proportion of income to a shareholder.

Discount bond. A bond whose market value is less than its face value.

Discount factor. The present value of $1 received so many periods in the future.

Discount rate. The rate of interest used to determine the present value of future cash flow(s).

Divestiture. The divestment of a portion of the enterprise or the firm as a whole.

Dividend. The amount of periodic cash distribution of a company to its stockholders.

Dividend payout. The amount of annual dividends divided by the amount of annual earnings of a company.

EBIT. The earnings before interest and taxes of a company.

Efficient market. A market where security prices instantaneously reflect all available information.

EPS. Earnings per share.

Equity. The net worth of a company consisting of common stock, paid-in capital, and retained earnings.

Equity carve-out. The public sale of stock in a subsidiary in which the parent usually retains majority control.

Eurobond. A bond issue that is sold in another country.

Eurodollar. A U.S. dollar deposit in a bank outside the United States.

Ex-dividend. The date at which a purchaser of a stock is no longer entitled to the declared dividend.

Ex-rights. The date at which a purchaser of a stock is no longer entitled to subscription rights to buy new shares.

Exchange rate. The number of units of a foreign currency that may be purchased with one unit of another currency.

Exercise price. The price that must be paid for a share of stock when either a call option or a warrant is exercised.

Expected value. The weighted average of possible outcomes, with the weights being the probabilities of occurrence.

Face value. The stated value of an asset, such as the face value of a bond being $1,000.

Factoring. The selling of receivables to a financial institution, the factor, usually without recourse. This is a method of financing.

Field warehousing. A means of secured financing where goods are segregated at the place of the borrower and the lender has a lien on them.

Financial Accounting Standards Board (FASB). The rule-making body of the accounting profession that sets its standards.

Financial ratio. The ratio of one accounting number to another.

Float. Funds tied up in checks that have been written, but have not yet been collected at the drawee bank.

Floating lien. A general, or blanket, lien against a group of assets, such as receivables and inventories, without the assets being specifically identified.

Flotation costs. The costs associated with issuing securities.

Forward exchange rate. The rate today for exchanging one foreign currency for another at a specific future date.

Funds. Either cash or working capital of the firm.

Future value. The value in the future of $1 invested today. Also known as terminal value.

Going private. Making a public company private by buying up the stock.

Goodwill. The intangible assets of the firm arising from paying more for them than their book value. Goodwill must be amortized.

Holding company. A corporation that owns a controlling interest (common stock) in other companies.

Horizontal merger. The merger of two companies in the same line of business.

Hurdle rate. The minimum required rate of return on investment in capital assets. The rate at which a project is acceptable.

Income bonds. A bond where the payment of interest is contingent upon the earnings of the firm.

Indenture. A formal agreement establishing the terms of a bond issue and the relationship among borrower, bondholders, and trustee.

Insolvency. The inability to meet contractual financial obligations.

Interest rate parity. A theory stating that the differential between forward and spot exchange rates equals the differential between foreign and domestic interest rates.

Internal rate of return. The rate of discount that equates the present value of cash inflows with the present value of cash outflows.

Investment banker. A financial institution that underwrites and distributes securities.

Junk bond. A bond with a rating of Ba or less.

Lease. The economic use of an asset for which the lessee agrees to pay the owner, the lessor, a series of periodic lease payments.

Letter of credit. An obligation of a bank to honor drafts drawn on a customer. An extension of credit used mostly in foreign trade.

Letter stock. Privately placed common stock that cannot be immediately sold. May be sold only when registered with the Securities and Exchange Commission.

Leverage. The use of debt having a fixed return to magnify the earnings available to common stockholders. Also known as gearing and in general simply describes borrowing.

Leveraged buyout (LBO). Buying all the stock of a public company by means of substantial debt financing of the company's assets.

Leveraged leasing. A lease arrangement where the lessor borrows a portion of the funds necessary.

Lien. A legal claim on certain assets. Used to secure a loan.

Line of credit. A moral obligation of a bank to extend loans up to some specified maximum (the line) when a company wishes to borrow.

Liquidation. The sale of assets of a firm, either voluntarily or in bankruptcy.

Liquidity. The assets of the firm that are readily marketable, such as cash and marketable securities. Assets that may be converted to cash quickly and with little price concession.

Listed security. A security that is traded on an organized exchange.

Loan agreement. A legal agreement specifying the terms of loan and obligations of the borrower.

Lock box. A method for accelerating the collection of checks. Customers send checks directly to a bank, which processes them immediately and sends a statement of record to the company.

Merger. The combination of two companies where one loses its corporate identity.

Money market. The market where short-term, safe instruments are traded. Money flows on the basis of small differences in return and risk.

Mortgage. The pledge of real property to secure a loan.

Mortgage bond. A bond issue secured by a mortgage.

Multinational company. A company that does business and has assets in two or more countries.

Mutually exclusive investments. Two investments where the acceptance of one project precludes the acceptance of the other.

Negative pledge clause. A protective covenant whereby the borrower agrees not to allow a lien on any of its assets.

Net lease. A lease where the lessee maintains and insures the asset.

Net present value. The present value of the cash inflows minus the present value of the cash outflows.

Net worth. The book value of a company's common stock, paid-in capital, and retained earnings.

Normal distribution. A symmetric bell-shaped distribution that allows probability statements to be made on the basis of its mean and standard deviation.

Operating lease. A short-term lease that is cancellable.

Operating leverage. The employment of fixed assets that magnify variations in profits.

Opportunity cost. The return available on the next best investment alternative.

Option. A contract that gives the option holder the right to buy or sell an asset at a stated price, known as the exercise price.

Paid-in capital. Funds received by a company in a sale of common stock that are in excess of the par value of the stock.

Participating preferred stock. Stock where the holder is allowed to participate in increasing dividends if the common stockholders receive increasing dividends.

Par value. The stated value of a security, such as bonds having a par value of $1,000. The same as face value.

Payback period. The length of time before the cumulative expected cash flows from an investment project equal its cost.

Perpetuity. An investment that promises a fixed cash payment forever.

Poison pill. A device used by a company to make it less attractive as a takeover candidate.

Pooling of interests. A method of accounting treatment for a merger where the balance sheets of the two companies are simply combined.

Portfolio. The combination of two or more securities or assets.

Preemptive right. The right given to common stockholders to purchase new issues of common stock, or securities convertible into common, in order to preserve their proportional ownership.

Preferred stock. Stock that promises a fixed dividend but at the discretion of the board of directors. Claim on assets after all debt holders, but before common stockholders.

Premium bond. A bond whose market value is greater than its face value.

Present value. The discounted value of future cash flow(s).

Price/earnings ratio. The market price per share divided by the most recent 12 months of earnings per share.

Prime rate. Interest rate charged by banks to large, creditworthy customers.

Principal. The amount of money that must be repaid on a loan, exclusive of interest payments. The par value of a bond at issuance.

Privileged subscription. The sale of security to existing stockholders. Also known as a rights offering.

Profitability index. The present value of future cash flows of a project divided by its cost.

Pro forma. Projected future financial statements.

Promissory note. A legal promise to pay a sum of money to a lender.

Proxy. A document giving one person the authority to act in behalf of another. Example: a proxy for management to vote the shares of a stockholder. Can also mean the substitution of one for another. Example: a proxy company.

Purchasing power parity. A theorem that states that a basket of goods should sell for the same in two countries, after exchange rates are taken into account.

Quick ratio. The ratio of cash, marketable securities, and receivables to current liabilities. Also known as the acid-test ratio.

Receivables. Accounts receivable. Amounts owned by customers.

Record date. The date set for determining whether a person who buys a stock is entitled to a dividend, a right, or something else.

Refunding. The replacement of one debt issue with another, usually to realize a lower interest cost.

Reorganization. Recasting of the capital structure of a financially troubled company in order to reduce fixed charges. Claimholders may be given other securities. Occurs under Chapter 11 of the Bankruptcy Act.

Residual risk. The risk of a stock unique to the company involved. This risk may be diversified away. Known also as unsystematic risk.

Residual value. The value of a leased asset at the end of the lease period.

Retained earnings. The cumulative earnings of the company after dividends.

Return on equity. Average annual earnings divided by equity, usually in book-value terms.

Return on investment Average annual earnings divided by the amount of the investment.

Revolving credit. A legal commitment to extend credit up to some maximum amount over a stated period of time.

Rights issue. A security issue to existing stockholders. Also known as a privileged subscription.

Rights on. Security traded with rights.

Reverse split. A stock split where the stockholder receives one share for a specified number held.

Safety stock. Inventories held as a cushion against uncertain demand or usage.

Sale and leaseback. The sale of an asset with the agreement to lease it back for an extended period of time with specified payments.

Salvage value. The value of a capital asset at the end of the planning period. Also known as scrap value.

Seasonal dating. The extension of credit with the period geared to the customer's selling season.

Securities and Exchange Commission. The U.S. government agency responsible for policing the sale of securities and the organized exchanges.

Security market line. The market equilibrium linear trade-off between expected return and systematic risk.

Sell-offs. The sale of a division of a company, known as a partial sell-off, or the company as a whole, known as a voluntary liquidation.

Shelf registration. Rule 415 of the Securities and Exchange Commission permitting a corporation to file one registration statement covering a number of successive security issues.

Sinking fund. Fund established to retire a bond issue before maturity. The corporation is required to make periodic sinking-fund payments to a trustee.

Spin-off. The distribution to shareholders of stock in a subsidiary, after which the subsidiary becomes an independent company.

Spot rate. The rate of exchange for the immediate delivery of a foreign currency.

Spread. The difference between the sell and the buy prices in a security offering or the difference between the bid and the ask prices in the secondary market.

Standard deviation. A statistical measure of the dispersion or wideness of a distribution.

Standby arrangement. Occurs in a rights issue where an underwriter agrees to purchase any unsold stock.

Stock dividend. A dividend paid in additional stock as opposed to cash.

Stock repurchase. The repurchase of stock by a company, either in the secondary market or by tender offer. A means for distributing excess funds.

Stock split. An increase in the number of shares outstanding by reducing the par value of the stock. Example: a 2-for-1 stock split where par value per share is reduced by one-half.

Subordination. A debt issue giving a lower claim on assets and income than other classes of debt. Known as junior debt.

Systematic risk. The risk of a stock that is associated with movements in the overall market that cannot be diversified away. This risk is measured by the security's beta.

Synergy. Economies realized in a merger where the whole is greater than the sum of the parts.

Takeover. The acquisition of another company where management of the target firm opposes the merger.

Tender offer. An offer to the stockholders of a company to purchase their shares at a specified price. Tender can be made by the company or by others.

Term loan. A loan from a bank or insurance company with a maturity of more than 1 year.

Terminal warehouse receipt loan. A loan secured by goods held in a public warehouse for which the lender holds the receipt.

Times interest earned. Annual earnings divided by annual interest on debt. A coverage ratio.

Trade credit. Credit extended to customers. Accounts receivable.

Trade debt. Monies owed to suppliers. Accounts payable.

Translation gain or loss. An accounting gain or loss arising from the translation of the assets and liabilities of a foreign subsidiary into the parent company's currency.

Treasury stock. Common stock that has been repurchased and is held by the company.

Trust receipt. Used in secured lending, where the goods are held in trust for the lender.

Trustee. Acts in behalf of the bondholders or in behalf of the creditors and claimholders in the case of a bankruptcy.

Underwriting. An investment bank bears the risk of a security sale by virtue of giving the issuer a check for the offering. It is up to the underwriter to distribute the securities.

Unsystematic risk. Risk that is unique to a particular company, being independent of the systematic risk of the security. This risk is diversifiable. Also known as residual or unique risk.

Venture capital. The financing of a new venture either with stock or with securities convertible into stock or having options.

Vesting. Employee being entitled to part or all of his or her pension upon departure prior to the official retirement age.

Warrant. An option to purchase stock of a company at a specified exercise price over a specified period of time.

Working capital. Current assets minus current liabilities.

Yield. Rate of discount that equates the present value of the stream of expected future interest and principal payments with the security's market price.

Zero coupon bond. A bond that pays no interest. The return to the investor arises in the appreciation of the bond from the initial discount to the par value realized at maturity.

Index